MARKET RESPONSE MODELS
Econometric and Time Series Analysis

Second Edition

INTERNATIONAL SERIES
IN QUANTITATIVE MARKETING

Series Editor:

Jehoshua Eliashberg
The Wharton School
University of Pennsylvania
Philadelphia, Pennsylvania USA

Other books in the series:

MARKET RESPONSE MODELS
Econometric and Time Series Analysis

Second Edition

by

Dominique M. Hanssens
University of California, Los Angeles

Leonard J. Parsons
Georgia Institute of Technology

Randall L. Schultz
University of Iowa

KLUWER ACADEMIC PUBLISHERS
Boston / Dordrecht / London

Distributors for North, Central and South America:
Kluwer Academic Publishers
101 Philip Drive
Assinippi Park
Norwell, Massachusetts 02061 USA
Telephone (781) 871-6600
Fax (781) 681-9045
E-Mail < kluwer@wkap.com >

Distributors for all other countries:
Kluwer Academic Publishers Group
Distribution Centre
Post Office Box 322
3300 AH Dordrecht, THE NETHERLANDS
Telephone 31 78 6392 392
Fax 31 78 6546 474
E-Mail < services@wkap.nl >

 Electronic Services < http://www.wkap.nl >

Library of Congress Cataloging-in-Publication Data

Hanssens, Dominique M.
 Market response models : econometric and time series analysis / by Dominique M. Hanssens, Leonard J. Parsons, Randall L. Schultz.--2nd ed.
  p.cm.
 Includes bibliographical references and index.
 ISBN 0-7923-7826-1 (alk. paper)
1.Market surveys--Econometric models. 2. Sales forecasting--Econometric models. 3. Time-series analysis. I.Parsons, Leonard J. II. Schultz, Randall L. III. Title.

HF5415.3 .H36 2001
658.8'.'015195--dc21   **00-054610**

To Benjamin, Elisabeth, Kate, Nicholas and Patrick, with love, DMH

To Piet Vanden Abeele, LJP

To my granddaughters, Delaney Schultz and Reilly Jackman, RLS

CONTENTS

PREFACE

From 1976 to the beginning of the millennium—covering the quarter-century life span of this book and its predecessor—something remarkable has happened to market response research: it has become *practice*. Academics who teach in professional fields, like we do, dream of such things. Imagine the satisfaction of knowing that your work has been incorporated into the decision-making routine of brand managers, that category management relies on techniques you developed, that marketing management *believes in* something you struggled to establish in their minds. It's not just us that we are talking about. This pride must be shared by all of the researchers who pioneered the simple concept that the determinants of sales could be found if someone just looked for them.

Of course, economists had always studied demand. But the project of extending demand analysis would fall to marketing researchers, now called marketing scientists for good reason, who saw that *in reality* the marketing mix was more than price; it was advertising, sales force effort, distribution, promotion, and every other decision variable that potentially affected sales. The bibliography of this book supports the notion that the academic research in marketing led the way. The journey was difficult, sometimes halting, but ultimately market response research advanced and then insinuated itself into the fabric of modern management.

The main reasons for this success are now obvious: information, software, and competition. In the late 1960s and early 1970s, academics scratched for data that companies barely collected. Some of the first studies were done on data sets so common that the enterprise was slightly scandalous. (How could it be that all of those different models fit the same data?) But those were, it turned out, precisely the studies that laid the foundation for further work on new, better, and *different* data. Marketing researchers had to learn a lot of things. They had to master econometrics, time series analysis, computers even. *Marketing Models and Econometric Research* was published in 1976 to report on the progress that had been made and to provide an agenda for future research. Much of that agenda had to do with data.

As data availability (and researcher competence) accelerated, things began to change, at least academic things. By 1990, when the first edition of this book appeared—as a sequel to the initial volume—there were literally hundreds of studies that had demonstrated that market response models were potentially the answer to a marketing manager's greatest tactical need: figuring out what determined sales and how to set the marketing mix variables to influence it. Since then, the tidal wave of marketing information from scanner data and corporate information systems has led to a situation where many companies are data rich. But the key to using this information was getting it out of the back room.

For years marketing information—particularly consumer information—was gathered and analyzed by the marketing research staff of organizations. The output of this research was typically the marketing research report. Sales reports too were made available to marketing managers. The actual data analysis, of course, was done by the analysts. They gathered the data in response to a request, analyzed it on mainframe computers, and then delivered the report, sometimes weeks after the request. Reports took on a life of their own. The rule seemed to be never make a marketing decision without a report.

What's wrong with this picture? The thing that's wrong is that the manager isn't close enough to the data query process. The process isn't interactive and it isn't quick. What changed all of this was desktop software. Managers can now do their own research, ask "what if" questions, compute in virtually real time, and make decisions *without* reports. And by doing all of these things, managers gained the potential to move beyond their tactical orientation to true strategic decision making. Market response models, designed with tactics in mind, literally force strategic thinking when managers use them themselves. So, did marketing managers then simply jump on the bandwagon of data and software? No—it took an even more powerful force to finally turn the tables: competition.

It is a commonplace to talk about increased competition or to point out how product life cycles have shortened. Perhaps these are exaggerations. But the perception of strong, smart, and product-stopping competition has made every company more aware of improving their decisions. And it did not take them long to see that market response models were the key to dealing with the dilemma of competition. After all, how smart can you be if you sit on all of that data and make marketing plans by guessing? So it was the combination of information and competition that guaranteed the success of market response research. As much as we may like to attribute the growth of this industry to champions or charisma, the fact is that *money* made it what it is. Market response helped companies compete better.

Today market response *is* an industry. Leading firms make brand and category decisions using it, market research vendors supply data and models for it, and academics such as us take the opportunity to report (again) on its achievements and limitations. We have taken quite seriously the responsibility to lead marketing research in this area. While the dream has come true, we cannot leave the project unfinished. There are many companies that can use market response to improve their decision making that have yet to do so. There are organizations struggling with how to assess their performance that could benefit from market response thinking. There are many research puzzles still to be solved.

This book is a history, a roadmap, a storehouse, and a challenge. Whatever can be said of market response research, the most important thing to us is this: it has made a difference.

Nature of Revision

The Second Edition is more applied in the sense of being more helpful to marketing scientists working in industry while at the same time keeping a sound scientific foundation. It is updated to include recent developments, such as store-level analysis, promotion evaluation, and the assessment of long-run marketing effects. The Second Edition contains new material on forecasting. It has *Industry Perspectives* written by practicing marketing scientists. Marketing scientists at GlaxoWellcome, Kraft, Polaroid, and elsewhere provide examples of how ETS is actually applied. All in all, the Second Edition should be much more appealing to MBA students and industry practitioners.

The Second Edition has retained the thrust of First Edition, that is, it still

1. integrates state-of-the-art technical material with discussions of its relevance to management.
2. provides continuity to a decades-long research stream.
3. illustrates how marketing generalizations are the basis of marketing theory and knowledge.
4. shows how research can be applied to marketing planning and forecasting.
5. presents original research in marketing.

What has been added? The Second Edition

1. places much more emphasis on the basic building blocks of market response modeling: markets, data, and sales drivers, through a separate chapter.
2. splits the design of response models into separate chapters on static and dynamic models.
3. discusses techniques and findings spawned by the marketing information revolution, e.g., scanner data.
4. emphasizes new insights available on marketing sales drivers, especially improved understanding of sales promotion.
5. demonstrates methodological developments to assess long-term impacts, where present, of current marketing efforts.
6. includes a new chapter on sales forecasting.
7. adds mini-case histories in the form of boxed inserts entitled *Industry Perspectives*, which are primarily written by industry executives.

To accommodate this new material, the Second Edition drops material on doing optimal control and differential games with response models. While this material can, and has, provided insight into the actions that a manager should take, the reality is that it has had little impact on a manager's daily activities.

The emergence of market response as an essential tool for world-class marketing has made the Second Edition even more relevant to practicing managers. The Second Edition of *Market Response Models* captures the vitality of this expanding enterprise and once again provides the blueprint for its future.

Acknowledgements

While we each contributed substantive content and editorial suggestions throughout this book, in the end, each author had primary responsibility for different sections. Professor Schultz focused on Part I and Part V, Professor Parsons on Part I, II and IV, and Professor Hanssens on Part III and IV. In addition, Professor Schultz wrote the preface. He also provided a site where we could share computer files. Professor Parsons formatted and produced the electronic version of the book using Microsoft Word along with MathType and Visio. He also had responsibility for the bibliography and entries in the indexes. Professor Hanssens compiled the page numbers for the indexes and produced the camera-ready copy of the book.

We would like to thank several people who have helped us with the Second Edition. The authors of the Industry Perspectives—acknowledged in the text—have shared their experiences with real-world applications of market response models. They are truly among the leading practitioners in the field. We gained additional about insight about industry practices from Dennis Bender of Management Science Associates, Ross Link from Marketing Analytics, John Totten of Spectra, and Mike Wolfe from Coca-Cola.

We thank Koen Pauwels and Andres Terech, PhD students at UCLA, Sangkil Moon, a Ph.D. student in Marketing at Iowa, Gregory Greaves, an MSM graduate from Georgia Tech, Christopher Drummond, an MSM student at Georgia Tech, and Jon Hainer, an MBA graduate from UCLA, for proofreading portions of the manuscript. Julian Villanueva, a PhD student at UCLA and Subramanian Viswanathan, an MBA graduate from Iowa, provided help with the indexes. James Hagar, a graduate from UCLA, worked on formatting, editing, and graphics. We are very grateful for their assistance.

As always, we are most appreciative of the support of the management and staff at Kluwer Academic Publishers, especially Zachary Rolnik. We also thank Suzanne St. Clair, Judith Pforr, Julie Kaczynski, and Rose Antonelli.

Dominique M. Hanssens, *Santa Monica, California*
Leonard J. Parsons, *Dunwoody, Georgia*
Randall L. Schultz, *Coralville, Iowa*
October 2000

I INTRODUCTION

1 RESPONSE MODELS FOR MARKETING MANAGEMENT

For every brand and product category there exists a process generating its sales. By incorporating the basic premise of marketing—that a company can take actions that affect its own sales—market response models can be built and used to aid in planning and forecasting.[1] For over 40 years, market response research has produced generalizations about the effects of marketing mix variables on sales. Sales response functions and market share models are now core ideas of marketing science. Together with discrete choice models that explain household behavior and market structure analysis that describes the pattern of competition, research on market response paints a rather complete picture of customer and market behavior.

Market response models have become accepted tools for marketing decision making in a wide variety of industries. Companies have relied on market response models to set prices, allocate advertising expenditures, forecast sales, and test the effectiveness of alternative marketing plans. Many examples of these applications are shown in the boxed *Industry Perspectives* that appear throughout this book. At the millenium, market response analysis was estimated to be a $125 million sector of the marketing research industry, proving its economic value to marketing management.[2]

The underlying methodology of market response is econometric and time series analysis (ETS). Each market response model is a realization of the technology of ETS. Thus, the purpose of this book is to explain how ETS models are created and used.

We begin this chapter with an example of how a simple marketing system can be modeled. We next define empirical response models and discuss various modeling approaches. The relation of marketing management tasks to measures of effectiveness is then discussed. Finally, we present an approach to planning and forecasting based on market response models and show how ETS is instrumental to it.

Modeling Marketing Systems

The principal focus of ETS analysis in marketing is on the relationship between marketing mix variables that are controlled and performance measures, such as sales or market share, that represent the outcomes of marketing plans. Consider a simple marketing system where there is little or no competition, so that the firm and industry are identical. Figure 1-1 illustrates such a simple marketing system. The system is made up of two primary elements: the marketing organization or firm and the market or customers. Linking these elements are three communication flows and two physical flows of exchange. The firm communicates to the market through various marketing actions, such as distributing its products or services, setting prices, and so forth. The customers in the market respond to the firm's actions through sales (or the lack of sales), and the firm seeks this information. In an internal flow of communication, the firm makes plans for future actions on the basis of current and past information. The physical flows are the movement of products or services to customers and the simultaneous movement of sales revenue to the firm. The process of physical exchange is characteristic of all commercial trade. The process of communication flows is the distinguishing characteristic of modern marketing systems.[3]

If a firm had only one marketing decision variable (or instrument) that was thought to influence demand, say advertising, a descriptive model of its market behavior might be the *sales response function*

$$Q_t = f(A_t, E_t), \qquad (1.1)$$

where

Q_t = firm's sales in units at time t,
A_t = firm's advertising expenditures at time t,[4] and
E_t = environmental factors at time t.

For a specific market, say a retail trade area, environmental factors might include such influences as population size and disposable personal income.

If this firm had, in addition, a *decision rule* for setting its advertising budget at time t equal to some percentage of the prior period's sales revenue, this policy could be represented as

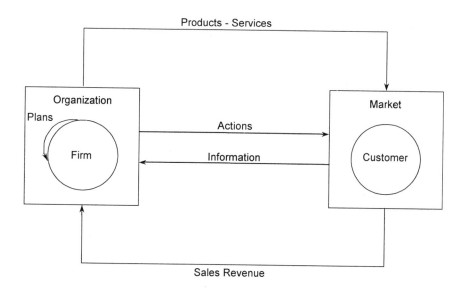

Figure 1-1. A Simple Marketing System. *Source*: Parsons and Schultz (1976, p. 4).

$$A_t = f(P_{t-1}, Q_{t-1}),$$ (1.2)

where

A_t = firm's advertising expenditures at time t,

P_{t-1} = price of the product at time $t-1$, and

Q_{t-1} = firm's sales in units at time $t-1$.

This type of decision rule, or some variation of it in terms of current or expected sales, is a descriptive statement of management behavior. Ultimately, we may be interested in some expression for A^*, the optimal advertising budget, which would be a normative decision rule for managers to follow.

Functions (1.1) and (1.2) completely specify the marketing system model in this case. The system works in the following manner. Some firm offers a product at a specific price. Its marketing *action* at time t is advertising. The *market* responds to this action in some manner. The *customers* may become aware of the product, develop preferences for it, purchase it, or react negatively to it. The firm obtains this information on buyer behavior, including sales, either directly or through marketing research. If purchases have been made, physical exchange has taken place. On the basis of its sales in period t, the firm makes marketing *plans* for period $t + 1$. In this case, the advertising budget is planned as a percentage of the prior period's sales.

This decision rule yields a new level of advertising expenditure, which is the marketing action of the firm for period $t + 1$. Thus, the process is continued for all t.

Despite the obvious simplifications involved, this model can be thought of as a representation of a marketing system. In ETS research, models of this kind (and more complex versions) can be formulated, estimated, and tested in order to discover the structure of marketing systems and explore the consequences of changes in them. For example, suppose an analyst wants to model the demand structure for a daily metropolitan newspaper. As a starting point, the preceding model is adopted, since it captures the essential characteristics of the marketing situation. The firm offers a product, a newspaper, to a well-defined geographic market at price that is fixed over the short run. Thus, advertising is seen as the only marketing instrument. Although there are competitive sources for news, many communities have only one daily newspaper; industry and firm demand are identical in this monopoly situation. The analyst completes the model by specifying environmental factors, say population and income, and a decision rule for advertising.

To simplify further, the analyst assumes that the relations in the model will be linear with stochastic errors.[5] The linearity assumption may be one of convenience but the stochastic representation is necessitated both by (possible) omitted variables and by truly random disturbances (even a percent-of-sales decision rule will be subject to managerial discretion). The analyst is now ready to write the model of the newspaper company as an *econometric model*, so that it can be calibrated with empirical data. In this way, the analyst seeks to test the model and to estimate its parameters. The model to be tested is

$$Q_t = \gamma_{12} A_t + \beta_{11} Y_t + \beta_{12} N_t + \beta_{13} + u_{1t} \tag{1.3}$$

$$A_t = \beta_{21} R_{t-1} + u_{2t}, \tag{1.4}$$

where, in addition to the variables defined above,

N_t = population at time t,

Y_t = disposable personal income at time t,

R_{t-1} = firm's sales revenue at time $t-1$, $R = PQ$,

γ = parameter of an endogenous variable,

β = parameter of a predetermined variable,

u_t = random disturbance.

This model includes two endogenous variables, Q_t and A_t, which means that they are determined within the system at time t. The predetermined variables include the purely exogenous variables Y_t and N_t and the variable R_{t-1}, which is a lagged

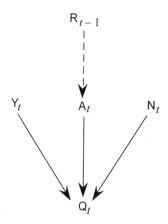

Figure 1-2. Causal Ordering of a Simple Econometric Model. Solid arrows represent causal links; dashed arrow, a decision rule. *Source*: Parsons and Schultz (1976, p. 8).

endogenous variable whose value is known at time t. The causal ordering of this econometric model is shown in Figure 1-2.

The theory of identification, estimation, and testing of econometric models is explained in Chapter 5, and so we can just hint at the analyst's next steps. If the analyst can assume that the structural disturbances, u_{1t} and u_{2t} are independent, the model is a special kind of econometric model called a *recursive model*. In such a model, the equations are identified and ordinary least-squares estimates are consistent and unbiased. This simplifies the statistical problem, and if a time series of sufficient length is available, these data can be used to test the model. With some luck, the analyst will end up with a model that describes the demand for newspapers and yields estimates of advertising effect, income effect, and so forth. The model may have value for forecasting future sales and for designing better decision rules.

Another form for a model involving sales and advertising, where the advertising decision rule is based on current or expected sales, would be a *simultaneous-equation system*. Besides being different in a substantive sense, such a model requires special estimation techniques if consistent parameter estimates are to be obtained. Our preoccupation with the quality of estimates, especially the consistency property, stems from the policy implications of the parameters, e.g., their use in finding an optimal advertising budget. These issues of model form, parameter estimation, and model use unfold in subsequent chapters.

Our example assumes quite a bit of knowledge about the market situation being modeled. Many times there is not this much a priori information about which variables should be in the model or how they should be related. In such instances, *time series analysis* can be employed to deal with questions of causal ordering and the structure of lags. This topic is discussed in Chapters 6 and 7.

Most marketing systems are not as simple as this illustration. The effects of competition, more than one marketing decision variable, multiple products, distribution channels, and so forth make the task of modeling complex marketing systems a difficult one.

Empirical Response Models

A *response model* shows how one variable depends on one or more other variables. The so-called dependent variable could be company sales, company market share, customer awareness, or any other variable of interest to marketing managers. The explanatory variables are those thought to produce changes in the dependent variable. Together, dependent and explanatory variables make up the systems of equations that are used to model market behavior. When such models include competitive reaction functions, vertical market structures, cost functions, or other behavioral relations, they are referred to as *models of market mechanisms* (Parsons 1981). A response model based on time series or cross-section data is called an *empirical response model* (Parsons and Schultz 1976). This is the category of response models that is the subject matter of this book. We do not deal with situations where no historical data are available; hence we do not deal with new products or established products with no data. However, a lack of historical data may be remedied through experimentation, including test marketing.[6]

Sales and Market Share Models

By far the largest category empirical response models are those dealing with sales and market share as dependent variables. Companies want to know what influences their sales—*the sales drivers*. They want to know how to set the marketing mix so that they can control their sales. And they also want to know how to forecast sales. Each of these requires knowledge of the process *generating* sales, the sales response function.

Sales is the most direct measure of the outcome of marketing actions and so market response models with sales as the dependent variable are very common. These sales models can be estimated for company sales as a whole, product line sales, or brand sales and for various definitions of markets. Consumer packaged goods companies, for example, focus almost exclusively on volume as the dependent variable for store and market data.[7]

Sometimes, however, market share is a more appropriate measure of company or brand performance. Models with market share as the dependent variable can often accommodate competition in an efficient way, but they also pose problems for estimation and testing in markets with many brands. For models that focus on household choice, market share is the only alternative.

In addition to sales and market share, response models can be built for any other dependent variable of interest and importance. One dependent variable of interest besides sales is awareness, an intermediate-level variable influenced by advertising weight and leading, in turn, to sales. The consulting firm Millward Brown International and some of its clients have pioneered the integration of continuous measures of awareness into market response models. (See *Millward Brown Industry Prespective* in Chapter 2.) In principle, any behavioral measure could be added to a response model to enrich its ability to capture the underlying process of customer choice.[8]

Reaction Functions and Other Relations

In addition to response functions, there may be competitive reaction functions, channel reaction functions, and cost functions, as will be discussed in Chapter 3. These relations can be integrated in structural models of the entire market mechanism. Sometimes the models merely include sales response functions and separate relations designed to capture the firms' decision rules for the marketing mix variables that affect sales. More ambitious are simultaneous-equation models that attempt to explain all competitors' decision rules endogenously.

This book is devoted to explaining how models of sales, competition, cost, and so on can be estimated for use in planning and forecasting. Although the models resemble each other in form and typically use the same estimation methods, their use by management varies by coverage and task. But they are all designed to utilize data and have an impact on the quality of decision making.

Response Models for Brand, Category, and Marketing Management

The first applications of market response were general attempts to model a company's sales or market share with little regard for the model's fit with the process of marketing decision making. We will see later (in Chapter 10) that this approach was not well suited to managing implementation. Many model building efforts were demonstrations of feasibility and, although they successfully produced models, they were less successful at producing change. Today market response models are being developed for specific business uses. By more closely matching the actual decisions made in an organization, market response models have become the decision-making tools that they were originally designed to be.

For brand management, market response models provide a basis for fine tuning marketing mix variables such as price, sales promotions, advertising copy, weight, media selection and timing, and other brand-specific marketing factors. Category management systems designed to support field sales need ways to relate retail actions to sales and thus offer perfect opportunities for market response modeling. Integrating brand and category management—from either the manufacturer's or retailer's point of view—only works if the relationships between brand and category sales are known. Market response models provide these relationships. The marketing mix elasticities identified in such models can be thought of as benchmarks for measuring brand, and consequently brand management, success. Higher advertising elasticities, for example, would be consistent with better brand decisions, e.g., better copy, timing, etc.

Marketing directors would find value in market response models used to set overall budgets and allocate them across brands. Higher-level decisions would benefit from market response models that were themselves aimed at higher levels of data aggregation. A vice president of marketing could use such results to set total advertising and promotion expenditures. Similarly, sales force size and allocation decisions would be the beneficiaries of market response models completed at an aggregate level, while details about number of sales calls, say, would require less aggregate account-specific data.

At even more senior levels, market response models could be designed to investigate the impact of economic cycles, new product introductions, and other environmental and technological changes on business unit or corporate sales. Different levels of decision making suggest different levels of data analysis. Market response models have emerged as the main alternative to budgeting and allocation decisions based on pure judgment or outmoded decision rules.[9]

Marketing Management Tasks

The principal reason that market response models have become attractive to many organizations, and indispensable to some, is that they can help with the tasks that marketing managers have to do.[10] Like any product, they must meet a need before they will be purchased and used. The need in this case is better decision making.

Planning

All companies want to know how to forecast performance and how performance is affected by factors under their control. They can define certain performance measures of relevance, such as earnings, sales, or market share, at certain levels of planning, such as company, division, or product. They can also identify certain factors that influence the performance measures, such as marketing mix, competition, channel members, and environmental variables. The performance measures, factors, and organizational level of planning define the planning task for the company.

Planning is the primary task of marketing management because it is what implements the basic premise of marketing. If a company can take actions that affect its own sales, then the first task of marketing managers must be to determine those actions. Perhaps it was once true that actions based on hunches and common sense served to generate satisfactory results in the marketplace, but the days when plans can be made in such a capricious way are long gone. Laser-sharp competition and smart, demanding customers conspire to produce high penalty costs for bad decisions. *Market response models infuse planning with discipline and logic.*

Nowhere is that logic more apparent than in the natural precedence relationship between planning and forecasting: *marketing plans should precede sales forecasts.* Meaningful forecasts can only be made on the basis of a firm's plans and expectations regarding environmental conditions or competitive reactions. For example, suppose a sales response equation shows a relation between market share and distribution share. To forecast market share, the firm's plans and competitors' plans with respect to distribution expenditures must be known or at least estimated. If total industry demand is known, the firm can forecast its sales from these data. Although this prescription may seem straightforward, many firms reverse the functions, first forecasting company sales and then determining distribution expenditures. Familiar percent-of-sales decision rules for marketing expenditures imply this reverse order. It is only when plans precede forecasts that the logical nature of the dependence is maintained.

Budgeting

The budgeting task follows directly from the planning task because plans can only be made operational through budgets. While most organizations can produce marketing plans as evidence of planning (usually on an annual basis), all business organizations *require* budgets for planning and control. The marketing budget often assumes a life of its own, either propelling the product forward or braking its momentum depending on the budget's adequacy and administration. Whether crafted through consensus or fiat, the budget usually reigns supreme. So it makes sense that anything that makes budgeting more efficient and effective holds great promise rewarding the companies that use it. *Market response models optimize budgets by linking actions to results.*

Forecasting

The third major task of marketing management is forecasting. As we have seen, forecasting should follow planning and the conversion of plans to budgets. Otherwise, the basic premise of marketing is violated, and a company would be presumed helpless to try to determine its own fate. Unlike planning and budgeting, however, the forecasting task many times is delegated (wrongly) to a staff that produces the forecasts on just shreds of plans. Worse, forecasts sometimes are simply restatements of goals that have morphed into estimates of sales (Parsons and Schultz 1994).

The use of market response models restores the precedence of planning over forecasting because, by definition, they show the results of planned actions on performance. It is difficult to hide from the illumination of a market response model. Basically it says: if you do this, that is what will happen to you.[11]

Controlling

Another, often neglected, marketing management task is *controlling: investigating the differences between actual and planned sales and profits*. As a management function, controlling lacks the charisma of planning, the power of budgeting, or the discipline of forecasting. It is easy to see how marketing managers can become excited about a new product launch or a new advertising campaign. Increased budgets are exhilarating too since budgets are in some ways measures of who has the most marketing clout. Even forecasting has an element of swagger in that most forecasts are optimistic in the extreme. But controlling, as the name implies, sounds like something accountants do, not marketers.

Yet managers—and companies—that fail to monitor the success of marketing plans or the efficiency of marketing budgets are not going to outperform their competitors. Indeed, they will be underperforming precisely because they will not be aware of how they can improve. However painful it may be, there is no substitute for taking stock.

Market response models can come to the rescue of such managers by providing a way to do this. An interesting framework for this purpose is presented by Albers (1998). Differences, or *variances* in accounting terminology, between planned and actual profits are decomposed as:

- *planning* variance, due to managers using incorrect response parameters;

- *execution* variance, due to actual pricing and marketing spending levels that are different from planned levels;

- *reaction* variance, due to competitors reacting differently from what was anticipated; and

- *unexplained* variance.

Response models for market size and market share are used in order to distinguish between variances caused by exogenous factors (assumed to influence market size) and variances caused by the firm's marketing effort (assumed to influence market share). Overall, this approach allows marketing managers to identify and quantify the actual causes of profit variance, rather than only the symptoms.

Managing Costs and Revenues

The final basic task of marketing management is the management of costs and revenues. Since profit equals revenue minus cost, marketing managers with profit and loss responsibility need a way to manage revenue and cost. For a product that meets a need and has meaning in the mind of customers—and thus good positioning—the settings of the marketing mix variables clearly affect sales revenue. Since they speak to this, market response models can have a direct effect on revenue. Furthermore, the process of using market response models instills order in decision making because it provides a reason for decisions. This order tends to reduce costs, particularly opportunity costs.

We will see in the final chapter of this book that the leading factor in the implementation of models and systems in organizations is "personal stake," or impact of the model or system on job performance. Market response models grab the attention of marketing managers because they are directly related to the way they are rewarded. If we know anything at all about human behavior, we know that rewards produce results. It is little wonder, then, that market response models are now becoming essential to organizations.

For the organization as a whole, market response *information* becomes an *asset* that can lead to competitive advantage. It is one method for implementing the idea that firms benefit from having greater knowledge about their customers and competitors (Glazer 1991). In this case the knowledge is not about needs and wants per se, but about how customers and competitors respond to the marketing actions taken to meet those needs and wants. Market response information thus contributes to both the efficiency and effectiveness of marketing decisions.

Marketing Information

The way better decision making is achieved through the use of market response models is by making marketing decisions data-based. The marketing information revolution, spawned by advances in data collection such as scanner and single-source data, has made *ignoring* marketing information foolhardy. Companies at the cutting edge of marketing are increasingly those at the cutting edge of data analysis. There are many success stories of companies improving their competitive position through the sophisticated use of marketing information (Blattberg, Glazer, and Little 1994; Parsons et al. 1994).

ETS is the modeling technology behind market response analysis. Empirical response models are obtained through ETS and a combination of market information, or data, and management information, or experience. By utilizing both market and management information, the ETS method seeks the best possible answer to the question of what determines a company's performance. The models to be discussed in this book are very much in the spirit of decision support systems: they provide marketing managers with the means to make quick, intelligent, and measurable decisions—three characteristics essential to success in highly-competitive markets.

Market Information

Two principal kinds of data are used in ETS research: time series data and cross-section data. A time series is a set of observations on a variable representing one entity over t periods of time. A cross-section is a set of observations on n entities at one point in time. Sales of a product for 104 weeks is an example of a time series. Prices for 25 goods during one month is an example of a cross-section. Since our interest focuses on market response models, showing relations among variables, we almost always deal with what can be called multiple time series or cross-sections.

Time series and cross-section data are empirical in that they are observed outcomes of an experiment or some natural process. This can be contrasted with data that are subjective in that they are obtained from managers as judgments based on experience.[12] As will be seen, ETS utilizes judgment in a peripheral way. Management experience shapes every aspect of response research and its application to planning and forecasting. But response itself is not parameterized through judgment; rather, it is data-based.

Another aspect of market information relevant to ETS research is the growth and variability of a performance measure such as sales over time. Figure 1-3 shows two sales curves: (1) a standard S-shaped growth curve, and (2) a growth curve showing increased sales variability over time, i.e., increased variability resulting from an economic rather than a growth process.[13] Planning and forecasting in stage A can only be accomplished with growth models because very few historical data are available. In stage B growth and ETS models should be used together to produce plans and forecasts. Finally, in stage C, the growth process is exhausted and ETS becomes the natural method for modeling response and producing plans, budgets, and forecasts.

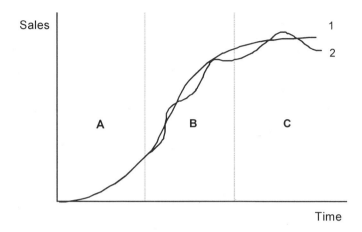

Figure 1-3. Sales Growth and Variability over Time

Management Information

ETS research relies on management information in five important ways. First, managers help to define the modeling task. In the case of market response analysis, managers can suggest the major variables of interest, including performance measures, factors, and the appropriate planning level. The fact that a study may be done on industry sales for a division of an industrial company with a focus on sales effort across territories may be due to management judgment.

Second, managers help to specify the models. Their experience is used to decide which variables are candidates as explanatory factors and what lags, if any, could occur in the process. This judgment ensures that the subsequent empirical analysis conforms to reality and is not a statistical artifact. At the same time, managers do not tell how the response takes place. They are not very good at this (cf. Naert and Weverbergh 1981b), and so the burden of proof falls on the empirical data.

Third, managers forecast the values of certain independent variables, such as competitive and environmental variables, if necessary. A model in which a firm's sales are a function of its price, its competitors' prices, and disposable personal income, for example, requires that its management forecast the price of competition and income. Together with the firm's planned price, then, a forecast of its sales can be made. Alternatively, time series analysis could be used to forecast competitive price and income, or, in some cases, the econometric model could account for these variables. In these instances, direct management judgment would not be needed.

Fourth, managers adjust model-based forecasts as required. Response and planning models serve managers, not the reverse, so managers are asked to evaluate model output as if the model was another expert.[14] Response modeling, model-based planning, and ETS do much to lay out the logic of analysis before managers. For this reason, as we have stated before, managers are more likely to face questions of bias and uncertainty directly.

The fifth way in which ETS research relies on management information is that managers evaluate alternatives for action. The managerial end product of a market response analysis is a plan. Response models give managers insight on what factors influence their sales and in addition provide an approach to planning and forecasting that integrates response with decision making. Much like the decision makers in van Bruggen, Smidts, and Wierenga's (1998) study using a simulated marketing environment—where managers were "better able to set the values of decision variables in the direction that increases performance" (p. 655)—we expect managers to rely more and more on models to help them set marketing budgets close to optimal levels. Still, the buck stops with managers. ETS can blend market and management information in a formidable mix of decision technology, but the *responsibility* for decision making falls on the managers, not the models.

Model-Based Planning and Forecasting

The planning, budgeting, and forecasting tasks of marketing management can be integrated with information-based decision making by following the approach shown in Figure 1-4. We call the approach model-based planning and forecasting.

The model-based approach begins with determining past sales performance. As we will see, the process can be expanded to include other performance measures, say profit, but even in these cases, increasing sales is a sub-goal or co-goal of considerable management, shareholder, or public interest. If increasing sales is the goal, a future sales goal will usually be set by top management. In addition to past performance, market opportunity will have a leading role in determining this figure. Some companies use a bottom-up procedure to arrive at this sales goal. But often, when this "planning" process is done, the outcome is just a company sales *forecast*; goal and forecast have become one and the same. This may account for top managers being so pleased at the beginning of each year.

The model-based approach maintains the strict logical relationship between planning and forecasting. It tries not to confuse goals—often presented as financial plans—and forecasts. Thus, the next step after goal setting is forecasting total market or industry sales using an industry response model. This is where factors typically beyond the control of the firm are related to total market sales, or if industry sales is not a focus of the research, to the environment determining company or brand sales. An industry response model does not give a rote forecast; rather, managers are presented with various scenarios of industry demand (cf. Naylor 1983). The industry sales forecast becomes the one associated with the most likely scenario. Since there is

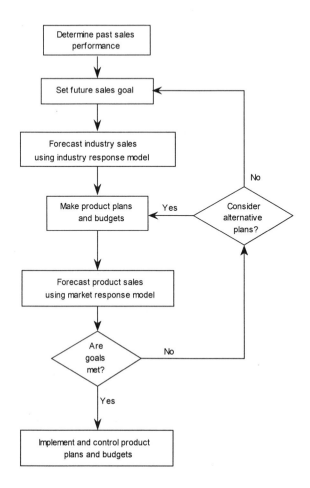

Figure 1-4. Model-based Planning and Forecasting

a model on which to base the forecasts, managers can see how the forecasts depend on their own assumptions about the leading factors determining industry sales.

Given an industry sales forecast, the company makes plans and converts the plans into budgets. These are not just general plans, but plans associated with specific marketing mix variables identified through a market response analysis for the product or brand being considered. If price and advertising are the factors driving sales, the company must have specific planned levels of price and advertising before it can use a market response model to forecast sales. Plans can be made directly from management judgment, through the use of decision rules based on previous management experience, through normative models or optimization (see Chapter 9), or as the result of "what if" simulations. Product plans, together with estimates of competitive response based on models or management experience, are then used in the market response model to forecast sales.

Given the model-based sales forecast, the company evaluates whether goals are met. If they are, product plans and budgets are implemented and then controlled. If they are not, the company would decide if it should consider alternative plans that might meet the sales goal or if it should change the sales goal. This would result in another run through the company planning and forecasting system to produce new company sales forecasts. If goals simply cannot be achieved, they should be revised to make them more realistic. Then the model-based planning process would start over again.

Performance Measures

The model-based approach to planning and forecasting is quite robust. It accommodates different performance measures and factors, different planning levels, and different organizational arrangements for planning and forecasting. The most commonly used performance measures in planning are sales revenue, market share, and earnings. Since most companies serve multiple markets, market share is typically used only as a measure of *product* performance. Division or company-wide planning typically requires the common denominator of sales revenue or earnings. For this same reason, sales measured in units must usually be restricted to product- and brand-level analyses.

Other aspects of the performance measures chosen for a study are the time, space, and entity dimensions. Typically we think of increasing the sales of a product over time; the performance measure in this case would be "product sales over time," and hence a time series analysis would be indicated. But sales can also be expanded across geographic territories or by increasing the sales of other products in the product line. In these cases, the performance measures would define a planning and forecasting task involving cross-section data. We see that by choosing a performance measure we also choose between time series, cross-section, or combined time series and cross-section analysis.

Planning Levels

Just as the model-based approach accommodates different performance measures, it also accommodates different planning levels. The process shown in Figure 1-4 can be used for product, brand, or category planning, division planning, or corporate planning. The highest level of product aggregation to be pursued in a response analysis usually defines the most logical performance measure. For example, if an analysis were to focus on both product sales *and* company sales, a problem with nonhomogeneous products would be overcome by using the common denominator of sales revenue. Similarly, an aggregation of divisional products would require a performance measure based on revenue.

The planning and forecasting task for any one company, then, is unique with respect to the particular variables being studied but general in the overall process of planning. In our experience, model-based planning and forecasting is usually more effective when it covers company-wide planning activity and begins with top management support. Still, there are many examples of response studies that have aided decision making at the brand or product level alone.

Organization of Planning and Forecasting

A final element of flexibility of model-based planning and forecasting is that it can be used with different organizational arrangements for planning and forecasting. A dedicated forecasting staff, for example, could easily develop and maintain the response models that underlie the model-based planning procedure. This staff would also be responsible for producing forecasts and doing whatever further analysis was needed. They would interact with planners as a true decision support system. Alternatively, product or category managers could be given the responsibility for maintaining response models developed by in-house analysts or outside consultants.

Although the model-based approach is essentially a top-down forecasting method, nothing precludes incorporating bottom-up forecasts or, as we have seen, bottom-up goals based on market opportunity. Indeed, nothing in the approach precludes management from overriding the model-produced forecasts. However, market response models now have become so sophisticated that managers ignore their predictions at their own peril. An example of model-based planning and forecasting is given in the *Mary Kay Industry Perspective.*

Plan of the Book

This book is organized into five sections. The first section establishes the case for market response models as a basis for marketing planning, budgeting, and forecasting. It describes the data and variables used as building blocks for such models. Section II presents the design, econometric estimation, and testing of static and dynamic response models in stationary markets. Section III addresses the use of time series analysis in understanding evolving markets. Section IV discusses how marketing problems can be solved with ETS. Finally, in Section V, the book concludes by examining the factors that lead to the successful implementation of model-based planning and forecasting.

Planning and Forecasting at Mary Kay Cosmetics

For Mary Kay, Inc. sales are a function of an ability to attract individuals to sell its products as well as an ability to offer quality cosmetics. Mary Kay's current system for planning and forecasting was enhanced and revised by Randall Schultz to broaden the focus of existing forecasting models to response models. This work later contributed to Mary Kay directly avoiding an error that would have resulted in approximately 10 percent slower growth.

In the mid-1980's a member of top management proposed increasing the minimum order quantity necessary for a salesperson to achieve the maximum discount. The straight numbers showed that such a change would result in sales force productivity increasing. If the sales force averaged larger orders, then the reasoning was that overall sales would increase accordingly. Similar strategies had been used previously in 1978, 1981, and 1984.

To understand how to integrate forecasting with plans (such as the minimum order strategy), Mary Kay modeled market response as a function of sales force size and sales force productivity. A system of equations shows how Mary Kay sales are generated. Sales force productivity is a function of the economic environment, product promotions, product pricing, order quantity pricing, and sales force compensation. Sales force size is a function of the beginning sales force size, the recruitment rate, and termination rate. In turn, the recruitment rate is a function of new product offerings, promotions, economic environment, and sales force compensation. Terminations are a function of current reorders, new orders, and past orders, etc. Sales force members who do not reorder within a certain time frame are automatically terminated although they will be reinstated if they reorder within a year.

The response model showed management that increasing the minimum order size for the maximum discount would increase productivity by increasing the order size. This was what management expected. However, fewer sales force members would order and would start terminating five months later. The net result was higher sales force productivity but fewer sales because of fewer orders and a smaller sales force size.

Mary Kay's forecasting group was able to convince top management to change the strategy by quantitatively showing the sales response to the proposed change and showing graphically what the model indicated had happened in the past. In this way, Mary Kay saved 10 percent of sales.

Prepared by Richard Wiser, Vice President, Information Center, Mary Kay Cosmetics, Inc.

Notes

[1] Throughout the book when we say plans, we will mean marketing plans. What managers often mean when they say plans are financial plans, that is, goals.

[2] Commenting on trends in the market response sector, John Totten of Spectra (in a personal communication) noted that there has been a diversion of marketing moneys out of traditional advertising, trade promotion, and couponing into frequent shopper programs and web-based advertising and promotional activites. In particular, the proliferation of frequent shopper programs has eroded the market for market response research based on time series regression of store sales. When a chain is heavy into loyalty marketing programs, the pricing and promotional causal information is incomplete, biasing the estimates of marketing response when analysis is done on store data. On the up side, there has been a push by big accounting firms into response analysis. Coopers/Lybrand, Price/Waterhouse, and McKinsey all have made pitches and presentations to major retailers such as Sears and Wal-Mart on analysis of market response based on the retailer's data.

[3] For a formal treatment of the value of marketing information relative to the flow of money and goods, see Glazer (1991).

[4] Checkoffs, which are mandatory assesments on regional or national agricultural producers, fund generic advertising and promotion programs to develop and expand commodity markets. When evaluating the effectiveness of such commodity marketing programs, expenditures on advertising and promotion are defined as CK, the checkoff expenditures, instead of A (Forker and Ward 1993, p. 163).

[5] It will be seen that most market response models are nonlinear to accommodate diminishing returns to scale.

[6] Although management input and prior knowledge have a role to play in the development and estimation of market response models, we specifically exclude models based on subjective estimates of model parameters.

[7] Of course there are other types of "sales" response models as well—such as the modeling of store assortments by retailers.

[8] An extension of this reasoning leads to discrete choice models built on household data.

[9] This does not rule out, of course, either the *appropriate* use of judgment in decision making or the identification of *optimal* decision rules.

[10] The traditional use of market response models has been to support tactical marketing decisions. Even in network organizations, "management science" is seen as most appropriate at the operating level (Webster 1992).

[11] Naturally it is a bit more complicated than this, but not much. Market response models that take competition into account (where it is necessary) are very complete.

[12] An example of the subjective approach is provided by Diamantopolous and Mathews (1993). Data were obtained from a large manufacturing company operating the UK medical supplies industry. The firm produced a wide variety of repeat-purchase industrial products—over 900 in all. The products were used in the operating theater and fall broadly into the single-use (disposable) hospital supplies product category. The main customers were institutional buyers, mainly hospitals. The products were organized in 21 product groups, each of which was managed by a product manager. Each relevant product manager was asked to estimate the likely percentage increase (decrease) in volume sold over a 12-month period that would result if current prices were decreased (increased) by 5 percent, 10 percent, and 50 percent, respectively.

[13] The best known growth model is the Bass model (Bass 1969a).

[14] Our position is much closer to Morwitz and Schmittlein (1998) rather than Blattberg and Hoch (1990) in that we would use management judgment where management judgment excels and models where models excel, and not average them, especially at 50 percent.

2

MARKETS, DATA, AND SALES DRIVERS

Market response models capture the factors that drive a market, showing how one variable depends on one or more other variables. The variables of interest are not mathematical abstractions, but measures meaningful to marketing managers. So we focus on measures of sales, measures of marketing effort, and any other factors that affect performance. The performance-influencing factors are called *sales drivers*. When management knows what these factors are and how they produce changes in sales, plans can be formulated to influence sales and profitability.

To construct a market response model, a manager or analyst needs to understand the makeup of a market. Who are the players: the channel members, the customers or end-users, and the competitors? What product forms compete against each other? When are sales recorded? How can marketing variables be measured? Where do these data come from in the first place? The answers to these questions require a great deal of information on data sources and measurement, not to say operational definitions of the variables themselves. Even the term "sales" has many meanings.

In this chapter we first briefly discuss the nature of markets. We then cover the aspects of data sources and measurement that will be typically encountered in market response research. We next deal at some length with operational definitions of the leading variables in market response studies, including some technical issues that affect all econometric studies. Finally, we have the first of many discussions on aggregation. The chapter concludes with appendices on scanner data collection, baseline methods, and the construction of stock variables.

Markets

The term market has several nuances. A market can be a region in which goods are bought, sold, or used. A market can be a location where buyers and sellers convene for the sale of goods; hence the term marketplace. A market can be a store. A market can be a group of existing or potential buyers for specific goods and services. Finally, a market can be the demand for a product. It is in this latter sense that we speak of market response models.[1] Nonetheless, the other definitions of market enter into how we model market response.

A distinction is made between business-to-business markets and (business-to-) consumer markets. Business goods and services are used to create products that are then sold to final users. These final buyers are usually individuals or households. The efficient movement of goods and services from point of production to points of consumption requires channels of distribution. These channels may include marketing intermediaries, such as wholesalers or retailers, who buy and then resell merchandise. A prototypical system of markets is shown in Figure 2-1.

For example, the national dairy industry consists of three markets: farm, wholesale, and retail. The farm market is solely for raw milk. However, the wholesale and retail markets can be further subdivided in the fluid and manufactured products (e.g., cheese) markets. The national dairy promotion program has made funds available to national and state organizations. This money comes from an assessment of 15 cents per hundredweight on all milk sold by diary farmers and has averaged over $200 million annually since its inception.[2] Evaluation of the effectiveness of the dairy promotion program requires building market response models. Initial research focused on each market in isolation and often on a regional basis. More recently, the importance of conducting analysis on both fluid and manufactured product sectors of the dairy market simultaneously has been emphasized because of the interaction and competition for raw milk between the two sectors (Kaiser et al. 1992).

As indicated in Figure 2-1, the market for one product may be dependent on the market for another product. Consumers or end-users do not demand the product directly. Instead, they demand final products that incorporate the product. This is called *derived demand*. Examples include fractional-horsepower direct-current motors, micro-motors for short, and acetic acid (Dubin 1998). Micro-motors have numerous applications in automobiles for power mirrors, door locks, and air-conditioning dampers. Other applications include those in children's toys and small appliances, hair dryers, and shavers. Thus the number of cars and number of appliances sold determine the number of micro-motors needed. Acetic acid is used in the production of cellulose acetate products including acetate fiber, cigarette filters, photographic film, and vinyl acetate monomer (VAM). In turn, VAM is used in the production of latex paints, adhesives, and emulsifiers. These products are mainly

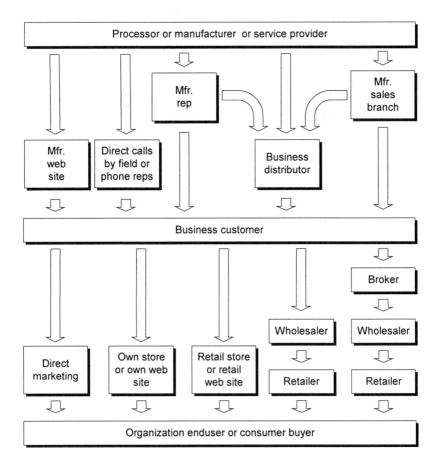

Figure 2-1. Markets, Channels, and Data Sources

used in construction.[3] The strength of the construction industry is determined by the state of the economy.

Data

Data may be of different types. Individual units at one point in time are observed in *cross-section data*. The data may be on different sales territories, on different channel members such as retail outlets, on different individual customers, or on different brands. The same units at different points in time are observed in *time series data*. While these observations may take place at any interval, the most common interval in marketing is weekly. Other intervals used include monthly, bi-monthly, quarterly, and annually. A database may well contain a combination of cross-section and time series data. For instance, information may be available on a number of brands over a number of weeks.

The choice among the three kinds of databases should depend on the purpose of the research. The dynamic character of marketing activities can only be investigated by a time series. The generality of market response models may require a cross-section of territories, brands, stores, or firms. Unfortunately, a choice may not exist because of lack of some data. Sometimes time series data may not be systematically recorded, or perhaps only recorded annually or quarterly when the appropriate data interval would be monthly or weekly. Cross-section studies are often limited by competitive considerations—many times data for all firms in an industry cannot be obtained.

Sources of Data

For many years, more detailed data have been available for consumer market response studies than industrial market response studies. The main reason for this disparity is the keen interest that consumer packaged goods marketers have shown in tracking their own sales and trying to figure out how to manage their marketing expenditures. Although the techniques described in this book have equal applicability to both types of markets, the fact is that much of extant research, beyond pricing research, is for consumer markets. This is why this section is weighted heavily toward consumer data sources.

Marketing sales performance for consumer goods might be measured in terms of factory shipments, warehouse withdrawals, or retail sales. Factory shipment information is usually available from company records. Retail sales can be measured by collecting data from retail stores or their customers.[4] Since much of the published research on market response uses scanner data (for consumer-packaged goods), our primary focus is data collected on a continuous basis, i.e., *tracking studies*.

Factory Shipments. A brand manager can usually find out how much product has been shipped. While this internal information contains no competitive data, sometimes factory shipment data are shared through an industry trade association. Unfortunately, shipments may not track consumer purchases very closely, especially if a high proportion of the product has been sold on deals. The trade will engage in forward buying, that is, it will stock up at lower prices and carry the product in inventory (Chevalier and Curhan 1976; Abraham and Lodish 1987, p. 108). Are there situations where intermediary inventories are low or nonexistent? If so, then shipments might make a good proxy for retail sales. This could happen when a product has a short shelf life, is expensive to store, or store-door delivered (Findley and Little 1980, p. 10). Ice cream, which is bulky and requires refrigeration, would be a good example.

Factory shipments are the main basis for industry demand studies of industrial goods. Trade associations, trade magazines, government agencies, and international organizations collect the data. The sources of such data are industry specific and we cannot provide details for all industries. An illustration for acetic acid (Dubin 1998, p. 64) will have to suffice. Here the best general source is the *Chemical Economics Handbook*, which contains data on production, prices, and capacity for several countries including the United States. The International Trade Commission (ITC) publishes an annual report on U.S. production and sales and a quarterly report on production. *Chemical Week* publishes a weekly report on U.S. and European spot and contract prices. *Chemical and Engineering News* publishes an annual statistical summary on the chemical industry which reports on production in major industrial countries. These data are based on a variety of sources including the ITC, the United States Bureau of Census, the British Plastics Federation, the Ministry of International Trade and Industry (MITI), and other government sources. The *Chemical Marketing Reporter* publishes price data on a weekly basis. For other industries the starting point is to do an Internet search.[5]

One problem that both industrial and consumer firms face is the lack of segment-level sales data. Financial data seldom require a breakdown by market segment, yet marketing managers need to know where their sales are coming from. Something as basic as sales by territory may be missing from the company database. Or information about demographic segments may be collected but not processed. Marketing managers need to make their case with senior management and with information systems professional: *proper decision making requires data by market segments.*

Warehouse Withdrawals. In the physical distribution process, most consumer products pass through a distribution warehouse on the way from the manufacturer to the retailer. Products from many manufacturers are combined for efficient delivery to a retailer. Information collected by the warehouse withdrawal method is virtually a census of all product movement. However, data on products in the intermediate stages of a channel are sparse. For many products sold in supermarkets, Selling Areas Marketing, Inc. (SAMI) used to provide sales and distribution information on a monthly basis for the national (U.S.) and approximately 50 individual markets.[6] SAMI also reported the average of distributors' suggested retail prices. This information was obtained from supermarket chains and food distributors. To maintain confidentiality, chain-by-chain breakdowns were not available. Sales response studies that have used SAMI data included Wittink (1977b), Pekelman and Tse (1980), and Eastlack and Rao (1986).

IMS Health collects information from every pharmaceutical channel.[7] Their data are sourced from wholesalers, pharmacies, physicians, and hospitals. The weekly orders and deliveries of wholesalers are analyzed to provide a census in many countries. Orders and sales are collected directly from internal systems in pharmacies. Physician information comes from representative panels and prescription analysis. Product orders and stock levels are tracked in hospitals. IMS marketing data was used in an evaluation of alternative estimators of a linear response model in the presence of multicollinearity (Rangaswamy and Krishnamurthi 1991).

The warehouse withdrawal method does not measure any product that is delivered directly to the store by the manufacturer. Examples of store-door delivered products in a food store include bakery items and soft drinks. In addition, inventory control policies at the warehouse level tend to disguise the full impact of short-term marketing activities.

It is also the case that modern, proprietary distribution systems that bring logistics in-house (such as the one pioneered by Wal-Mart) make warehouse withdrawal data less appropriate for studies of market response across all competitors in a market.

Retail Shelf Audits. Retail sales of many consumer products for an audit period can be estimated from a stratified sample of food, drug, and mass merchandise stores. An auditor takes an inventory of the amount of product available for sale (*front stocks*) and in any temporary storage area and collects records of any purchases by the store since the last audit. Retail sales can then be calculated as beginning inventory less ending inventory plus purchases less credits, returns, and transfers. Sales can be estimated by brand and package size. The leading supplier of syndicated retail shelf audits has been the ACNielsen. Its audit period historically was every two months. Sales response studies that used ACNielsen retail shelf audit data include Kuehn, McGuire, and Weiss (1966), Bass and Parsons (1969), and Clarke (1973). The lack of syndicated retail shelf audits in outlets other than food, drug, and mass merchandise stores and especially outside of developed countries has forced global marketers such as The Coca-Cola Company to pay suppliers to conduct audits specifically for them.

In addition to retail sales data, the store shelf audit provides estimates on average retail prices, wholesale prices, average store inventory, and promotional activity. Retail availability of a product can be calculated from the percentage of stores weighted by volume selling the product. *Out-of-stock* situations are also noted. Special promotional activities, such as premiums or bonus packs, may also be recorded.

Although store shelf audits capture trends very accurately, they do less well at detecting short-run effects. For example, looking at sales aggregated over an eight-week period would dampen the impact of a weeklong in-store display. Moreover, not every store can be audited on the first day of a reporting period. Consequently, some audits are conducted before or after the start of the period. The bias resulting from this was discussed in Shoemaker and Pringle (1980). In markets and channels where scanner penetration is high, store shelf audits have been phased out.

Retail Scanner Audits. Retail sales on a store-level daily or weekly basis can be tracked using automated checkout scanners. A computer-controlled reader identifies each product from its bar code. The bar code may represent an industry standard for the manufacturer, such as the universal product code (UPC), European Article Numbering (EAN), or Japan article number (JAN), or a retailer's stock keeping unit (SKU). The computer matches the product with its price, already stored in the database, and then records the purchase in the database. The scanner method yields more precise information than the store shelf audit method. Information is available on the characteristics of the product or brand, the exact price paid, the amount bought, and the purchase date and the time of day.

Scanners are present in the primary packaged-goods retail outlets, that is, supermarkets, drugstores, and mass-market merchandisers, in the United States. Each chain will have scanner data for its stores. For example, Dominick's Finer Foods, a major chain in the Chicago metropolitan area, has data from its more than 80 stores. This allows the retailer to build market response models. Sales response studies that have used own-store audit data include Hoch et al. (1995).

Manufacturers need data from more than one chain. They are particularly interested in their key accounts, i.e., their most important chain customers. Scanner data are collected from stores and resold by IRI (Information Resources, Inc.) and by ACNielsen.[8] ACNielsen's main service is ScanTrack, which provides weekly data on packaged goods sales, market shares, and retail prices from a sample of 3,000 UPC scanner-equipped supermarkets. Selection of this sample is discussed in Appendix 2-A. ScanTrack data have been used to study how income and prices influenced consumer juice beverage demand in the United States (Brown, Lee, and Seale 1994). ACNielsen's Procision service tracks health and beauty aid (HBA) product sales through 3,700 drug and mass merchandiser stores. Sales response studies that have used ACNielsen retail scanner audit data include Broadbent (1988) and Foekens, Leeflang, and Wittink (1997). Sales response studies that have used other retail scanner audit data include Kalyanam (1996) and Terui (2000).

One problem with scanner data has been that in most markets not all retail outlets in a category were scanned. First, not all chains shared their data with the IRI or ACNielsen. Second, even those chains that did participate traditionally only sent in information for a sampling of stores. This issue raised some questions of accuracy that subsequently caused IRI to start to collect data from all stores in participating chains and call it "census" data. Across the U.S., IRI gets weekly data from 29,000 supermarket, drug, and mass merchandiser outlets and daily data through Catalina Marketing for 4,100 stores. Its service is called InfoScan Tracking Service. In response, ACNielsen started collecting census-level data and gets weekly data from 15,000 stores and daily data from thousands of stores from its partner, Efficient Market Service.

The census approach provides *store-level data*, which can be used by not only the manufacturer but also the retailer. The retailer can now find optimal price points, shelf allocations, and merchandising combinations for each store. The manufacturer can now evaluate trade promotions. Both can more quickly assess how promotions are working. Access to common data fosters better relations between manufacturers and retailers and encourages implementation of efficient consumer response (ECR) and category management programs. However, the store-by-store data are driving up scanner costs, which already consume over half of a consumer goods manufacturer's marketing research budget (Heath 1996).

Scanner data cannot distinguish between no demand situations (no customer purchases even though product is on shelf) and out-of-stock situations (customer demand but no product on shelf). This can be critical if one wants to model at the SKU-level, especially for slow-moving items. No sales occurrences are often treated as outliers and omitted from analyses. However, this would be an appropriate action only if the out-of-stock situation was true. The obvious remedy would to do supplementary shelf audits but this would be too expensive in most cases. Another tack would be to adjust the data for possible out-of-stock situations (Abraham and Lodish 1993, p. 256). This approach will be discussed briefly in our upcoming discussion of baselining.

Another issue with scanner data is their accuracy in certain circumstances. Error rates in stores employing UPC scanner systems have been investigated by Welch and Massey (1988), Garland (1992), Goodstein (1994), and the Federal Trade Commission (see O'Donnell 1998). One study found errors averaging 1.57% of the shelf price (Goodstein 1994). While under-ring and over-ring rates were statistically equivalent across regular-priced purchases, they systematically favored the retailer for purchase of advertised specials and items on end-of-aisle displays. Advertised specials were not delivered to customers more than 7 percent of the time. The Federal Trade Commission (FTC) found similar results in a 1998 survey of more than 100,000 scanned items in food, mass merchandiser, department, hardware, and stores. One bright spot was that one in 30 items was priced incorrectly compared to one in 21 items in a 1996 FTC study.

Shipment data, warehouse withdrawal data, store audit data, and scanner data all share a common problem: the lack of any information about the consumer. This precludes conducting any analyses at the segment level. Consumer panels provide this level of information, as do direct-response marketing programs.

Consumer Mail Panels. In a consumer mail panel, consumers report their purchase behavior by returning by mail a purchase diary or recall questionnaire. The purchase diary is given to consumers before they buy, and they are asked to record each purchase as it is made. The recall questionnaire is given to consumers after they buy, and they are asked to recall purchases made during a specified period of time. The recall questionnaire method is currently the more popular method (Totten and Block 1994, p. 42). Members of panels are asked to record the prices of their purchases and whether purchases were on promotion. This major advantage of mail panels is that information can be collected on any product. National Family Opinion (NFO) and Market Facts maintain pre-recruited mail panels.[9] Sales response studies that used the Market Research Corporation of America (MRCA) consumer purchase diary panel include Urban (1969) and Nakanishi (1973).

There are problems with mail panels. They are subject to selection bias, attrition bias, response bias, and measurement bias. Not everyone agrees to participate in a mail panel when asked. Not everyone remembers past purchase behavior accurately. Not everyone records information completely, legibly, or accurately. Winer (1983, p. 185) notes: "For panels on which dropouts are replaced, ... replacement by household descriptors such as demographic/ socioeconomic variables ensures a representative panel only in terms of those variables, not in terms of behavior variables such as purchase quantity."

Store Scanner Panels. Store scanner panels combine the individual-level detail of the mail panel with the accuracy of the store scanner. Individuals are given special cards that can be read by the bar code reader in a store. Thus, information is available on all scannable purchases for a subset of households. Naturally store and cashier cooperation is necessary to ensure participation.

IRI's InfoScan Household Panel has 60,000 households who agree to allow their purchases to be scanned and provide demographic, lifestyle, and media information on themselves.

Home Scanner Panels. With home scanner panels, panelists use handheld scanners to scan at home UPC-coded purchases from each shopping trip. Price, promotions, and quantity purchased are recorded. Purchases from all retail outlet types—from athletic footwear, home improvement, music, office supply, software, and toy stores as well as from food stores and mass merchandise outlets—can be captured. However, display and store advertising must be monitored separately.

The shopping climate in some countries favors the use of home scanning panel. For example, Katahira and Yagi (1994, p. 312) observed that in Japan:

- The geographical density of the retail stores is very high and consumers patronize various kinds of stores.
- Supermarket chains are not cooperative in the installation of external scanner terminals.
- Shoppers are mobile and make a substantial proportion of their purchases at stores outside the "designated" panel area.

The store-scanning panel is not appropriate in such an environment.

ACNielsen's HOME*SCAN Panel has 52,000 demographically balanced and statistically reliable U.S. households. Data are collected on 16 local markets. ACNielsen also has 7,250 households in Canada and 10,500 in Great Britain and Northern Ireland. Information Resources' Shoppers' Hotline multi-outlet panel has 55.000 U.S. households.

Direct Response Data.   As companies become more adept at tracking prospect inquiries and customer transactions, they can turn these data into valuable intelligence that is proprietary in nature. For example, American Airlines pioneered the electronic reservation system and, with it, developed large databases on airline seat sales and prices, and on customers' flying patterns. The former served as a basis for developing demand-driven pricing strategies for *yield (revenue) management*, and the latter became the backbone of a successful and widely copied customer loyalty program. Similarly, companies in financial, insurance, medical, education, and other services can now tap into direct response databases to help shape effective strategies for customer acquisition, retention, and cross-selling (Blattberg and Deighton 1996). These data are mostly generated internally, i.e., individual-level records of prospect or customer response to marketing campaigns and time series of customer transactions. In many cases, the information is supplemented by commercially available data on individual or household demographics (for direct consumer marketing) and firmographics (for direct business marketing). Leading suppliers of such data include Acxiom, TRW, Dun & Bradstreet, and American Business Information. Transactional data can also be tied to actual names and addresses through frequent shopper programs.

The direct marketing paradigm lends itself well to market response modeling and, in fact, such models have become essential for implementing response based marketing strategy in the information age (see the *Acxiom Industry Perspective*). The marketing manager makes choices on customer target, offer, creative execution, and timing. Metrics are developed for each of these constructs, and either historical or experimental data are collected to parameterize market response. Depending on the nature of the dependent variables, multiple regression, probit, logit, hazard, or CHAID models are used to estimate the parameters. The economic impact of the results is often measured with gains charts, i.e., tables that show how marketing's effect on performance (e.g., probability of response) increases as the target market is better defined. Direct response data and models are among the most promising areas of research and practice in market response modeling.

Advertising Data. Price, promotion, and distribution data are often by-products of one or more of the sales-performance data collection methods just discussed; however, advertising data are not. A firm knows its own advertising expenditures but must purchase reasonable estimates of competitors' advertising from suppliers like

---

Acxiom's Database and Direct Marketing Perspective

Acxiom is the leading database marketing company in the world, providing global data warehousing, decision support, modeling and demographic enhancement services. Since the late-1970's, modeling techniques have experienced widespread acceptance by the direct marketing community. Our company has been using these regression-, CHAID- and time-series-based techniques for about 20 years with a wide spectrum of clients, including automotive concerns, banks and lending institutions, high tech concerns, insurance companies, and consumer packaged goods entities.

The rise of models mirrors the growth of the direct advertising medium over general advertising, where for the first time marketers started gathering vast amounts of response, acquisition, and conversion data from their lead generation and account acquisition processes. These internally generated data could then be enhanced with demography and firmographics, attributes resold by data compilers such as Dataquick, D & B, Equifax, Metromail, R.L. Polk, and TRW. For consumer marketers, they are able to secure reasonable approximations of family ages/children, income, auto ownership, real estate value, credit and financial instrument usage, and lifestyle interests at a household level. For business marketers, data enhancements include company size, estimated revenue, Standard Industrial Classification code, and decision-maker level.

Direct marketers know that it is five to ten times more costly to market to a new prospect than an existing customer. Modeling allows companies to quickly ascertain the financial attractiveness of their best customers and prospects. Modeling correlates response and purchase data to the firmo-graphics and demographics. A company is then free to adjust their marketing communication budgets to penetrate more deeply within a business location or household or to target non-performing segments for elimination and suppression.

Nielsen Media Research's Monitor Plus and Competitive Media Reporting's MediaWatch. These suppliers often use the so-called media-counting technique, which, as the name suggests, is a method of counting advertisements and adding up their (presumed) market value. NMR's Monitor Plus Service provides TV advertising exposure data and expenditure estimates in 75 markets across 11 monitored media.

A study by the American Association of Advertising Agencies found that at least 4 percent of all television commercials were not counted or improperly counted by the two leading commercial monitoring services (Mandese 1993). This error rate is

---

Here are some of the results of model-driven programs:

- A direct response program that acquired credit cardholders at a 12.8% response rate;
- A direct response automotive program that closed dealer prospects at a 20% conversion rate;
- A credit card model that predicted cardholder attrition 2 years out;
- A mortgage model that captured 75% of likely loan attritors, i.e., customers who defect, by mailing 40% of the client's portfolio;
- A business PC model that predicted inbound telemarketing calls to within 5% of actual.

Prepared by Richard Birt, Senior Marketing Consultant, Acxiom.

---

generally regarded as acceptable for market response modeling. However, the error rate is larger for certain types of commercials, for example, those whose length is different than the standard 30- and 15-second spot or those run on independently-owned television stations.

Consumer reading, listening, and viewing habits are also tracked by surveys and diary panels. For example, Arbitron measures the radio audiences in over 250 markets while tracking consumer, media, and retail activity in more than 100 markets.

European advertising-monitoring operations are summarized in Table 2-1. For example, in a market response study of a frequently purchased nonfood consumer good in the Netherlands, advertising data were obtained from the advertising audit firm BBC as well as weekly market-level scanner data from ACNielsen (Foekens, Leeflang, and Wittink 1997).

New media advertising is measured by companies such as Media Matrix and Nielsen eRatings.com. Media Metrix harvests data from more than 50,000 Web-surfing panelists at home, work, and college. It also captures non-Web digital media such as proprietary online services; for example, America Online. Data is collected on sites visited, exposure to ads and interactive marketing, and surfing frequency and patterns.

Millward Brown International (MBI) tracks various measures of television advertising awareness, the best known of which is their Awareness Index. People are asked if they have seen a brand advertised recently and a simple yes or no qualifies people as being aware or not. MBI notes that no content recall is required so that the Awareness Index should be thought of as an opportunity to communicate since no message assimilation is assumed.

Table 2-1. European Advertising Monitoring Services

Market	Monitoring Company	Ownership
Austria	Media Focus	Independent
Belgium	Sabermap Marketing SA (Media Mark)	Groupe Sofres
Denmark	Gallup A/S	The Gallup Organization
Finland	Suomen Gallup AdFacts	The Gallup Organization
France	Secodip Pige	Groupe Sofres
Germany	ACNielsen GmbH	ACNielsen
Italy	ACNielsen SpA	ACNielsen
Netherlands	BBC	Cebuco
	BRS	Independent
Norway	Nielsen Norge	ACNielsen
	Mediakontrol	Independent
Portugal	Sabatina	Independent
	Marktest	Independent
Spain	Infoadex	Joint between Duplo and ACNielsen
Sweden	IMU Testologen AB	Turator
	Sweden Barromenterm	Independent
UK	Media Monitoring Services (MMS)	ACNielsen (1999)
	Register Meal	ACNielsen
European media	Adtrack	The Register Group
	LNA Competitive Reporting	VNU

Source: Adapted from Jonas (1997, p. 10).

Rather than model with disparate multi-source data, one may be able, in certain circumstances, to model with more accurate and/or more detailed data obtained from a single source or from the fusion of two more disaggregated data sources. We now turn our attention to these integrated marketing/media information data sources.

Single-Source Data. Single-source data occur when sales and media data come from the same individual household on a continuous basis. For example, the opportunity for exposure to television commercials may be monitored electronically. A television set meter least intrusively does this. A TV meter records TV ad exposures by brand, minute of day, and five-second intervals. Because a TV meter sometimes breaks down, the days when a meter is not working is also tracked. Transactional data on individual households are then combined with television advertising data to produce single-source data. Such data have been used to measure the short-term effects of TV advertising (Tellis and Weiss 1995; Ogawa, Kido, and Yagi 1996).

A television set meter only monitors viewing at the household level. Individual viewing can be imputed by means of factors from a survey or can be obtained directly by means of peoplemeters. Whether the additional information gleaned by

Table 2-2. European Single-Source Data Services

Country	Service	Supplier	Comment
France	Marketing Scan	GfK/ Médiamétrie	Anger. 3,000 homes. Married female homemakers scan household purchases. Household viewing recorded by set meter. Split transmissions in fieldwork area allows controlled TV exposure testing in 2,000 homes.
Germany	BehaviorScan	GfK	Hassloch. 2,000 homes have buying behavior measured via ID cards and in-store scanning. Set meters record viewing in 1,000 households. Press survey conducted yearly. Can be used as a test region due to control of which households receive which ads.
	Nielsen Single Source	ACNielsen	Currently 4,800 but aim is 6,000 single-source homes. All purchasers in household scan their purchases. Individuals viewing recorded by peoplemeter. Press recorded by scanning as purchased. Yearly readership survey.
Italy	NSSI	ACNielsen	6,000 homes record their purchase via scanner. 1,500 of these have set meters installed to provide home ratings.
UK	TV Span	TSMS/ TN AGB	750 homes. Married female homemakers scan household purchases. Household viewing recorded by set meter. Can analyze sales and media data within region or, via TN AGB, compare it to sales data of other UK regions.

Source: Adapted from Elms (1997, p. 63).

peoplemeters is worth the additional trouble has been questioned. GfK in Germany has conducted an experiment showing that the respondent overload inherent in human-based single-source causes lost accuracy for both sales and media exposure data (Elms 1997, p. 65). One way around this is the use of fusion data, which will be discussed in the next section.

In the United States, IRI's BehaviorScan offers eight geographically dispersed test markets with panel data from over 3,000 households, complete coverage of food, drug, and mass merchandiser outlets and targeted TV capabilities to execute varying media plans at the household level. In Japan, Video Research Ltd.'s HomeScan System consists of 1,000 households living in a 1.3 mile radius in a typical Tokyo suburban residential area (Katahira and Yagi 1994). European single-source data suppliers are listed in Table 2-2. The commercial viability of single-source panels seemed to be marginal.[10]

Insights into the effectiveness of Internet marketing on consumer buying habits are provided by measurement services such as e-SCAN. e-SCAN combines the capabilities of Information Resources and Media Metrix. Media Metrix's metering software has been installed of the personal computers of several thousand existing IRI Shoppers' Hotline panel members. This service allows consumer products companies to assess the impact of online marketing investment on offline consumer purchase behavior.

Fusion Data. As more detail is added to a model, more exhaustive product and media information is required from respondents. Rather than collecting information in one large single study, with fusion data information is collected from two or more studies and then merged. This avoids overloading respondents. The merger algorithm involves a process of matching on variables common across studies. If correctly done, the claim is that the results obtained from such fused data will be as accurate as single-source data (Baker 1996). European suppliers of fusion data are shown in Table 2-3.

The keys to successful fusion are identifying the appropriate set of common variables and conducting surveys with future fusion in mind. Simply having a set of common variables, say demographics, is usually not enough. The common variables must be able to explain the true correlation between any two variables, one from one study and the other from another study.

Fast-moving consumer goods (FMCG) manufacturers are interested in the sales volume attributable to on-deal pricing. Aggregation loses this information. On the other hand, they find difficult to read advertising effects at the store level where these trade deals are best measured. Because the signal to noise ratio for ads is just too low, they assess advertising at the market level or higher (Garry 2000). John Totten of Spectra Marketing[11] has working with store level models where the differential effects of advertising are estimated at the store level:

> Using *data fusion methods*, we obtain a decomposition of each stores trading area population into various geodemographic groups. These results are further fused with information about marketing mix delivery (advertising, couponing, loyalty marketing programs, etc) to obtain measures of effective delivery levels. The models further assume different response functions as a function of geodemographics.
>
> The resulting models have found significant differential responses across geodemographic groups, and have been yielding some insights into some of the problems that plague market level models. For example, when we fit market level advertising response models, we generally obtain some distribution of effects across markets, and have no method for

Table 2-3. European Fusion Data Services

Country	Service	Provider	Comment
France	Aude	Mediametrie/ SECODIP	9,000 married female homemakers. Six-monthly or so fusion of Mediametrie TV meter data with SECODIP sales scanning panel. Done on demographic and TV viewing items.
	Symic	Mediametrie/ Nielsen	9,000 married female homemakers. Similar to Aude but uses Nielsen sales scanning panel.
Italy	NSSI	ACNielsen	1,500 homes. In order to attribute individual's viewing habits to the sales panel members, a fusion is conducted with Auditel TV meter panel aided by the single source set meters.
Spain	Aud	Dimpanel (sister company of SOFRES)	5,000 homes. Married female homemakers record purchases by diary. Audience data come from SOFRES and are fused to the sales panel.
UK	Mediaspan	TN AGB	10,000 married female homemakers. Attribution of viewing characteristics to the continuous sales panel. Based on a media habits questionnaire which allows continuous link to BARB panel members via demographic and viewing habit similarities.

Source: Elms (1997, p. 63).

further decomposing these differences. Using the store level data, we can exploit the fact that the geodemographic differences across stores within a market are generally nearly an order of magnitude greater that the average differences across markets (Totten 2000).

Managerial Judgment Data. Sometimes historical data are insufficient or not available at all, as in the case of new products. In such situations, knowledgeable managers are asked how they expect the market to respond to marketing actions. For example, they might be asked: "Given the reference levels of your and your competitors' marketing efforts (perhaps last period's values) and given that all marketing instruments except one (say price) remain at these levels during the next period, what sales do you expect if competitors do not change their levels (prices) and your company effort (price) increases (decreases) by specified percentages?" The question is repeated for each instrument in the firm's marketing mix. For example, subjective data was collected for some industrial products sold by a multinational multiproduct firm (Gijsbrechts and Naert 1984).

The use of judgment-based marketing decision models is controversial (Chakravarti, Mitchell, and Staelin 1979; Little and Lodish 1981). Chakravarti, Mitchell, and Staelin have pointed out the dangers of relying on management judgment to estimate parameters, especially when the sales response function is nonlinear. Fraser and Hite (1988) advocate an adaptive utility approach to integrating information from managerial experience with that provided by marketing models. In practice, the data-based approach to measuring market response is becoming increasingly dominant.

Experimental Data. The experimentation involves controlled field experiments and simulated shopping exercises. For example, the impact of advertising spending and weight variations in test markets may be compared to baseline results from controlled markets. With proper sampling, all other effects should wash out. The criterion variable, sales, can then be compared group to group. Today controlled market testing often involves split cable markets or electronic test markets and scanning data. Intervention analysis (to be discussed in Chapter 7) has been used in conjunction with data from a field experiment with test and control panels connected to a split-cable TV system (Krishnamurthi, Narayan, and Raj 1989). Also see the BehaviorScan boxed insert and *Frito-Lay Industry Perspective* in Chapter 8.

Simulated shopping exercises can generally work better than in-store tests because of greater control over factors such as stock-outs, facings, and marketing activities. The key is to properly control the control the competitive array and account for differences in availability (distribution) and awareness. The use of market surveys is illustrated in the *Kao Corporation Industry Perspective.*

Consumer Durables, Industrial Goods, and Services. The sources of data for consumer durables, industrial goods, and service industries are somewhat different from those for consumer nondurable goods. Some consumer durables like automobiles or personal computers are shipped from the factory directly to dealers; some are shipped directly to final customers. For industrial goods, such direct channels of distribution are commonplace, and industrial goods may also be shipped to distributors or to value-added resellers. Finally, both consumer and industrial services may involve direct sales to customers. Quick-service restaurants and security services, for example, record only one level of sales, which we would not call shipments.

The NPD Group's Syndicated Tracking Services business unit collects store movement and consumer purchasing data on a number of industries using a variety of data collection methods used in combination. Industries covered include toys, apparel, textiles, sporting goods, athletic footwear, petroleum/auto products, home electronics, cameras, large and small domestic appliances, housewares, prestige cosmetics and fragrances, and restaurants. Their SalesTrac service for restaurants uses actual cash register sales.

Kao Corporation's Pricing Research for Merries Disposable Diaper

Kao Corporation, a leading manufacturing company of toiletry and household products, grabbed a market share of more than 40 percent of the Japanese disposable diaper market with a newly invented polymer technology for its Merries brand. After Procter and Gamble introduced its New Pampers brand, Merries lost a sizable sales volume with a resultant share of under 30 percent. In response, Kao's marketing research department conducted pricing research involving a consumer price survey.

At the time of the survey, there were five major brands in the market: Pampers (P&G), Merries (Kao), Merries-E (Kao), Moony (Uni-Charm), and Mammy Poco (Uni-Charm). Merries-E and Mammy Poco brands were both positioned to be economy brands. The other three brands were marketed as premium brands. Total share of these five brands accounted for more than 80 percent of the entire market.

The questionnaire for mothers consisted of two blocks. The first block collected information on demographics of respondents, such as age of mother, age of baby (in terms of months), the number of children or babies for whom they care. It also included questions about which brands the respondents purchased most frequently, and what types of retailers (supermarket or drug store) they shopped in more often.

The other block in the questionnaire was for the price experiment using trade-off analysis based on a factorial design. For each treatment, photographs of the product packages were shown with the sales prices attached. The respondents were instructed to check one brand under each treatment. In designing the questionnaire sheet, price levels for each brand were selected based on the POS data. Scanner data was collected from three stores in the areas where this survey was conducted.

The resultant information was analyzed with a logit model and used simulate how market share changed as prices changed for any one of the existing brands. To validate the results since the brand choice environment was quite different than the actual sales conditions at the stores, actual sales were tracked for 16 weeks. While the weekly actual sales fluctuated markedly depending on promotional activity, the actual and predicted market shares were relatively close when averaged over the whole period.

Drawn from Kohsuke Ogawa, "Measuring Brand Power by Pricing Experiment," Chain Store Age (Japan), (February 15, 1996). English translation by Kyoko Aoki.

Although it is true that most market response studies focus on consumer nondurable goods, the techniques discussed in this book are perfectly generalizable to all types of products and services. Their use may require a little extra digging for appropriate data, but by combining company, industry association, business publication, and other sources, it should be possible to model any real-life marketing situation. A summary assessment of data sources is given in Table 2-4.

Whether the data come from objective or subjective sources, the number of observations should be greater than the number of parameters. Even assuming that the appropriate data can be obtained, a number of important issues regarding the use of those data remain. These include sample selection, adjustments to the data, and aggregation. We will defer our discussion of aggregation until later in the chapter.

Sample Selection

In evaluating performance, the units under review, such as stores or salespeople, should be comparable. Those units not capable of being compared are typically dropped from the analysis. For example, retailers are continually opening new stores and refurbishing old stores in order to improve performance. This by itself will cause an increase in sales. Existing stores are not comparable to "new" stores. Similarly, pharmaceutical detailers calling on institutions such as hospitals should not be compared with those sales reps calling on the practices of individual doctors.

Adjustments to the Data

Patterns may exist in data that confound the relation between marketing effort and marketing results. The most common patterns are trend, seasonality, price-level changes, and population changes. In addition, marketers often try to distinguish between base volume and incremental volume when assessing sales promotions.

Trend. If a variable, say sales, is highly correlated with time, it is said to exhibit trend. In trying to explain sales behavior, a linear trend variable (TREND = 1, 2, ..., T) could be introduced into the sales response function to capture the time-dependent nature of sales growth. Marketing applications using trend as a variable include Ball and Agarwala (1969), Rao and Bass (1985), Eastlack and Rao (1986), and Gius (1996). Be warned that conventional tests for trend are strongly biased toward finding trend even when none is present. The treatment of nonlinear trends and cycles involves classical time series analysis. The introduction of a trend variable (or variables) may serve forecasting quite well, but if the model also has explanatory purpose, it would be better to search further for the cause of the trend. [12]

Table 2-4. Assessment of Data Sources

Source	Advantages	Disadvantages
Factory shipments	May be very precise information about *manufacturer* sales [no respondent (consumer) errors] Most relevant for direct distribution	May be very different from *consumer* sales Neglects filling or depleting of distribution pipelines Difficult to model customer response to marketing efforts
Wholesale audit	Only source of information at the wholesale level [no respondent (consumer) errors] Product movement figures include those for all types of retailers	Still one step removed from consumer Coverage of wholesalers may be incomplete [nonresponse bias] May not cover your product
Retail shelf audit	Relatively precise information at the retail level [no respondent (consumer) errors] Information on out-of-stocks	Audit may not cover your product Entry and exit of stores make it difficult to keep sample intact [population definition error] There is often no up-to-date list of stores [sampling frame error] Classification of store type may be difficult [sampling frame error] Retail coverage may be incomplete [nonresponse bias] Stores are audited on different days; i.e., a rolling sample [measurement (instrument) error] Auditing staff introduces human error [recording error (reduced by training and handheld computers)] Matching data on competitive activity may be difficult
Retail scanner audit	Greater accuracy as human errors [interviewing, recording, memory, expert] in recording product movement are eliminated Relatively low costs of data collection Shorter data intervals (week)	Lack of representativeness Recording errors (MktIS as "interviewer") Misreading (e.g., high-cone problem for multi-packages; clerk misrings of heavy items; multi-flavors of same item)

Table 2-4 (*continued*). Assessment of Data Sources

Source	Advantages	Disadvantages
Retail scanner audit (*continued*)	Exact data intervals Speed of reporting (household: 1 week; store: 3 weeks) More data facts	Retailer mistakes updating price-lookup files Manufacturer temporarily use "old" bar codes for promoted items which may lead to errors by clearing houses or research agencies Misalignment of causal and performance data Missing data (human error) 　Retailer fails to report 　In-store observers miss causal data Out-of-stocks cannot be noted Do not provide information on underlying attitudes, preferences, and reasons for specific choices Dramatic growth of bar codes is an administrative burden for retailers Scanner databases are very large
Consumer mail (postal) diary panel	Changes, if any, in behavior can be observed Recorded purchase behavior can be linked to demographic or psychographic characteristics Covers wide range of products Does not use personal interviewers 　Cheaper than home audits 　Sample does not have to be closely clustered	Lack of representativeness Maturation bias Response bias 　Prone to exaggerate purchasing behavior 　Function of interpurchase interval Non-receipt of a diary for a week requires quick action
Store scanner panel	Allows prices to be recorded accurately The small selection of stores can be monitored for display and store advertising information	Limit panel members to specific geographic areas Purchases recorded only at participating stores (Ameliorated by having members keep receipts from non-participating stores)

Table 2-4 (*continued*). Assessment of Data Sources

Source	Advantages	Disadvantages
Home scanner panel	Not limited to households in specific geographic regions Provides means for recording purchases from all retail outlets	Data entry by the consumer rather than a trained cashier (less compliance, more nonresponse, more obtrusive) Difficult to monitor display and store advertising inexpensively since households are generally dispersed geographically Fails to identify competitive conditions of price and display at the store where the product is bought. Tracking pushes the boundary of privacy and confidentiality
Single-source data	Sales *and* media data come from the same individual household on a continuous basis	Information gathered, especially detailed media information, may be limited by respondent overload. Households with large disposable incomes, Hispanics, and dwellers in high rises may be under-represented.
Fused data	Possibility for improved media planning.	Common variables may not explain the true correlation between variables from different studies. Fusion algorithm may not match respondents in different studies perfectly on all common variables.
Direct-response data	One-to-one connection between marketing action and customer response.	Only partial marketing-mix information. One-to-one response may overstate marketing impact.

Seasonality. If a variable follows a systematic pattern within the year, it is said to exhibit seasonality. Seasonality arises from climatic changes, the timing of holidays and religious festivals, business practices, and business/consumer expectations. In some cases, seasonality makes successive time observations not comparable; for example, the sales in each month could vary around different means. There are several ways to deal with this problem. First, the data can be seasonally adjusted, i.e., the effects of the seasonality can be removed from the data, primarily by employing some type of moving average. For example, in the ratio-to-moving-average method, a moving average is first calculated, say a 12-month centered moving average. Then the ratio between an actual value and the corresponding moving average yields a preliminary estimate of the unobserved seasonal value. The medians of the seasonal values for each month are computed to minimize irregularities and adjusted to sum to one. Seasonally adjusted figures are found by dividing actual values by the seasonal indices. Many forecasting programs use the U.S. Bureau of Census (1969) X-11 method, a refinement of the ratio-to-moving-average method.

The argument against using seasonally-adjusted data has been made by Hylleberg (1986) and goes as follows:

> The problem with using deseasonalized data is that seasonal adjustment methods treat variables one at a time as if each was an isolated phenomenon. However, the seasonality in one variable may be related to the seasonality in other variables. Indeed, the seasonal components themselves may contain information about the relationship among series. Thus, the use of seasonally adjusted figures increases the danger of obtaining misspecified models with spurious dynamic relationships and poor forecasting performance.

His recommendation is to treat seasonality as an integrated part of the structural econometric modeling.

Second, variables can be expressed relative to the same period a year ago; that is, *seasonal ratios* (differences in logs). For example, this was done in a study of one international air travel market (Carpenter and Hanssens 1994). Here monthly data were used so that the dependent variable was defined as total passenger volume in the current period divided by total passenger volume lagged 12 months.

Third, *dummy variables* can be used to represent the seasons. Dummy variables, also known as indicator variables, are "off/on switches" describing which level of a qualitative variable is currently in effect:

$$D_i = \begin{cases} 1 & i^{th} \text{ characteristic present} \\ 0 & \text{otherwise} \end{cases}. \tag{2.1}$$

There will be one dummy variable for each level of a qualitative variable. In a study of the relation between alcoholic beverage advertising and consumption, one dummy variable was used to capture marked increases in beer consumption in the second and third quarters of each year and another dummy variable to represent a fourth-quarter peak in wine consumption (Franke and Wilcox 1987). In an investigation into whether price discounts by national brands influenced price-label sales, a seasonal indicator for the November-December holiday season was included for products such as flour and margarine (Sethuraman 1995, p. 277). A study of Dockers khaki pants used two dummy variables: one for the sharp increase in retail sales in December; the other for the drop in sales in January (Naik 1999, p. 358). In research on the salmon market in France, a dummy variable for August was included because demand was low due to this being the nationwide vacation holiday month (Bjørndal, Salvanes, and Andreassen 1992, p. 1030). Seasonal dummy variables work well if the seasonal component modeled exhibits a regular intrayear movement.

Fourth, harmonic (i.e., sine, cosine) variables can be used instead of dummy variables (Doran and Quilkey 1972). Dummy variables can consume a relatively large number of degrees of freedom and may be unnecessarily precise if seasonality, per se, is not of prime interest. A study of the effects of generic and brand advertising on cheese sales found that three harmonics (used in place of 11 monthly dummy variables) accounted for a major part of the seasonal variation in cheese sales (Kinnucan and Fearon 1986). Harmonic variables were also employed in assessing the effect of generic advertising created by the Ontario (Canada) Milk Marketing Board (rather than the American Dairy Association) on milk demand in Buffalo, New York (Kinnucan 1987) and in capturing seasonal variation in the goodwill effect of advertising on milk sales in New York City (Kinnucan and Forker 1986). See also Liu et al (1990).

Fifth, a time-varying parameter model could be used. These models are described in Chapter 4. Sixth, Box-Jenkins time-series analysis could be applied. This method is discussed in detail in Chapters 6 (especially note the coverage of the seasonal ARIMA model). Finally, a traditional econometric model and a time-series model could be combined and integrated, as in Chapter 7. This approach, which we call ETS, is a theme of this book.

Price-Level Change. Another pattern that may exist in the data is inflation (or deflation) and hence the changing real value of the unit of currency. Price changes must be accounted for by adjusting current dollar figures to real dollar figures using some deflator or price index. Consumer prices could be deflated by the Consumer Price Index (CPI) since this series is designed to reflect price changes in a "market basket" of goods and services. See, for example, a study of salmon demand in France (Bjørndal, Salvanes, and Andreassen 1992, p. 1030, fn. 2). Similarly, business prices might be deflated by Gross National Product (GNP), Disposable Personal Income (DPI), or the Producer Price Index (PPI). For example, in an investigation of first-class mail, the GNP deflator was used instead of CPI because first-class mail is driven in general by business rather than households (Taylor 1993, p. 531). Any other variables expressed in monetary terms should be deflated in a similar manner. All advertising series can be deflated using the McCann-Erickson or Bates Media Survey cost-per-thousand price index for the appropriate medium (see, for example, Franke and Wilcox 1987; Slade 1995, p. 456). The point of these adjustments is to ensure that the effect on sales of the variable being measured is due to true changes and not due to artificial ones like changes in the price level.

Population Change. The final adjustment to the data is straightforward. Just as price levels change, so does population, and thus sales in market response models covering longer periods of time may be more appropriately measured by per capita sales. In a study of alcoholic beverage consumption over a 21-year period, removal of the effect of population growth was necessary. Per capita consumption figures were obtained by dividing total consumption of the beverages in gallons by the number of adults age 21 and older (Franke and Wilcox 1987). In an assessment of the demand for first-class mail over 63 quarters, first-class letter and card volumes were divided by the total U.S. population, including military personnel overseas, to put the dependent variable on a per capita basis (Taylor 1993, p. 530).

Baselining. If a brand manager wants to see the impact of a brand's direct-to-consumer actions, the indirect store effects of trade promotions—temporary price reductions, displays, and features—must first be removed from total sales volume to get a (permanent) baseline volume measure:

$$\text{total volume} \equiv baseline \text{ volume} + \text{immediate } incremental \text{ volume.} \qquad (2.2)$$

IRI, ACNielsen, and Millward Brown use this general approach to removing immediate effects of retailer-to-consumer promotions with, albeit, slightly different techniques for identifying these effects. IRI and Nielsen smooth their raw weekly volume data. [See Chapter Appendix 2-B.] Millward Brown does not. Millward Brown believes that smoothing can hide actual volume response effects, especially with respect to advertising. Most practitioners seem to use the terms "baseline" and "base" interchangeably. We will do the same and add "smoothed" or "unsmoothed" as an adjective when we want to emphasize this distinction.

A measure of the short-run effect of merchandising is *lift*. Lift is defined as the fractional increase in sales volume attributable to merchandising activity during the week in which it takes place. Lift is often expressed as a percentage.

Immediate incremental volume can be related to retailer promotions:

$$\frac{\text{incremental}}{\text{volume}} = f(\text{temporary price reduction, displays, features,}\cdots); \qquad (2.3)$$

while base (or baseline) volume can be related to manufacturer marketing actions and other factors:

$$\frac{\text{base}}{\text{volume}} = f\left(\begin{array}{l}\text{regular shelf price, advertising stock, distribution,}\\ \text{coupon stock, competitive activity, seasonality,}\cdots\end{array}\right). \qquad (2.4)$$

A criticism of this two-stage approach is that it assumes that there are no synergies between manufacturer-to-consumer actions and retailer-to-consumer actions. Practical issues in applying this approach include the handling of seasonality and out-of-stock situations.

While there are a number of methods of handling seasonality in scanner data, which we have noted above, Ross Link of Marketing Analytics, Inc. (1996) has noted that most fall into one of three categories:

1. Use smoothed *category* base volume as a seasonality indicator. Some models additionally add holiday dummy variables, and/or apply a modeled coefficient to the category seasonality index.

2. Use some type of Fourier series to model a 52-week repeating pattern. Again, some models additionally add holiday dummy variables.

3. Use a dummy variable for every week. This approach may only be practical for store-level data because of the number of variables involved. Forecasting the dummy variables then becomes an issue.

Link added that Marketing Analytics had had its best success to date with a variant of approach #1. Michael Wolfe of Coca-Cola (1996) has commented that he liked to use a modified X-11 or decomposition approach to baseline volume and then to adjust for holidays, if necessary, using dummy variables. Moreover, Link warned that:

> All three approaches have the potential of confounding base price effects with seasonality effects. This is because base price can be correlated across all stores in a market because of the way manufacturers set list prices, can be correlated across products in a market, and can additionally even be seasonal. However, I would think that approach #2 would theoretically be the least susceptible to this sort of problem.

We have already pointed out that it may be difficult to distinguish between out-of-stock situations and no customer demand situations in the case of slow-moving items. Consider the following example (Abraham and Lodish 1993, p. 256). Suppose that the weekly sales series during non-promoted weeks was 1, 0, 2, 0, 1, and 2. If weeks with few sales were caused by out-of-stock, then the correct baseline would be $[(1 + 2 + 1 + 2)/4] = 1.5$. However, if zero sales were normal occurrences caused by a stochastic sales process, then the correct baseline would be $[(1 + 0 + 2 + 0 + 1 + 2)/6] = 1$. Estimating the mean of the process using the mean conditioned on positive sales has been proposed as a way to address this problem.

Response Measures and Drivers

Whether a commercial enterprise ultimately is interested in obtaining gross margin and profits or nonprofit organization interested in service to society, the first step is to get "customers." Customers are broadly defined. A volunteer military must get recruits and reenlistments. A community orchestra must sell seats. This section focuses on measures of market response and their drivers, covering first operational definitions and then some important technical issues.

Operation Definitions of Variables

Definitional issues arise whenever theory or observation suggests a concept for analysis. For example, in the study of sales response to advertising, what is included in the concept "sales" and what in the concept "advertising"? Sales might be factory shipments, distributor warehouse withdrawals, or retail sales (or equivalently, consumer purchases). While advertising could imply a broad spectrum of activities from public relations to point of purchase, the definition usually focuses on media expenditures. And yet "advertising impact" comes closer than other concepts to representing the factor that we seek to relate to sales. Does "impact" include advertising expenditures, impressions, or what?

Once advertising has been defined, problems of operationalization arise. Suppose we operationalize the concept-definition of advertising as mass media expenditures on advertising in a certain time and space frame. Of course, by varying time, space, or the selection of media, other operationalizations of the same concept-definition would be possible.

Before discussing individual variables, there are some operational-definition options that apply to more than one variable. These include dummy variables, relative variables, differenced variables, and stock variables.

Dummy Variables. We have already discussed that a qualitative variable, such as seasonality, may be represented by a dummy variable. Let's consider some other applications. In a study of the role of advertising quality in market response models, dummy variables were used to control for three product reformulations made over a nine-year period (Arnold et al. 1987). In a study of trade promotion, a dummy variable was used to represent the offering of a premium to a manufacturer's sales force every September (Blattberg and Levin 1987). In an evaluation of sales contests, one set of dummy variables was used to represent contest periods and another set to designate post-contest periods. There were no dummy variables for pre-contest periods because salespeople were not informed of the contests prior to their beginning (Wildt, Parker, and Harris 1987). In an investigation of first-class mail, dummy variables were used to represent changes in the structure of postal rates. Separate dummy variables represented the introduction of the 5-digit presort discount, the carrier-route presort discount, and the ZIP+4 presort discount (Taylor 1993, p. 530).

When two or more unique events occur in the same period, it is impossible to untangle their individual influences. Any dummy variable must capture their joint influence. In one bimonth, U.K. sales of Murphy's Irish Stout, owned by Heineken

Worldwide, showed an unusual uplift. Two events occurred simultaneously. There was a burst of TV advertising and an unprecedented "four for one" sales promotion. Thus, a dummy variable, which was one for this particular bimonth and zero otherwise, captured the joint effect of the advertising burst and the sales promotion (Duckworth 1997, p. 302.)

Relative Variables. Variables are typically represented in terms of their *absolute* levels. However, sometimes they may be expressed in *relative* terms: relative to the industry, relative to the competition, relative to usual values, or relative to past values. The use of relative variables reduces the number of explicit factors, i.e., explanatory variables, that need to be taken into account in a model. Seasonality and other macro influences drop out if a brand moves in line with its market.

In a *relative-to-industry* formulation, the variable for one competitor, X_i, is compared to all members of the market, including itself:

$$RIX_i \equiv \frac{us}{us + them} = \frac{X_i}{\sum_{j=1}^{N} \omega_j X_j} \equiv SX_i, \tag{2.5}$$

where ω_j is usually equal to 1, i.e., everyone is equally weighted. This formulation is known as *share*. Examples would be market share and *share of voice*. For instance, in building a market response model for Nestlé UK's Gold Blend, a freeze-dried coffee, advertising GRPs were weighted by share of voice. The premise was that those GRPs without competitive activity were assumed to be more effective than those with.[13] However, another weighting scheme may be more appropriate for some variables. In particular, if the variable in question is price, the weights are the competitors' volumetric market shares. When the weights are not all equal to 1, the resultant variable is simply called a relative variable. For example, in one research project, a brand's relative price was defined as relative to the category average (Broadbent and Fry 1995, p. 338).

In a *relative-to-competition* (RCX) formulation, the variable for one competitor is compared to all other competitors only:

$$RCX_i \equiv \frac{us}{them} = \frac{X_i}{\sum_{\substack{j=1 \\ j \neq i}}^{N} \omega_j X_j}, \tag{2.6}$$

where ω_j is as above. This would lead to a somewhat different definition of relative price (or any other variable) than above. For example, in developing a sales response function for Murphy's Irish Stout, the relative price of Murphy's to Guinness was used (Duckworth 1997, p. 301).

Moreover, there is a third definition of relative, *relative-to-base* (RBX), in which the actual level of a variable is compared to the "normal" level, B, of the variable

$$RBX_i \equiv \frac{X_i}{B_i}. \tag{2.7}$$

For example, in studies on sales promotions, relative (to base) price would be defined as actual over nonpromoted price. At least one study has defined relative price as one in which all prices within a product category are divided by the lowest price across all the brands and all the weeks in that product category (Klapper and Herwartz 2000, pp. 409-10). Thus, when looking at other's research, one must be careful to pay attention to how a variable is actually operationalized and not how the researchers may have labeled it.

Differenced Variables. Sometimes we are interested in the absolute change in a variable and it is expressed in terms of a first difference:

$$\Delta X_t \equiv X_t - X_{t-s}. \tag{2.8}$$

By setting $s = 1$, the focus is on recent change. Alternatively, by appropriate choice of s, one can remove seasonality by making a comparison to the same period in the previous year, for example, setting $s = 52$ in weekly data. Rather than absolute changes, the emphasis might be on relative change. Thus the fourth definition of relative, relative-to-past (RPX):

$$RPX_t \equiv \frac{X_t}{X_{t-s}}. \tag{2.9}$$

This expresses relative change. That this is a change variable can be shown by taking logs:

$$ln\left(\frac{X_t}{X_{t-s}}\right) = ln(X_t) - ln(X_{t-s}). \tag{2.10}$$

Differenced variables may be sensitive to the level of temporal aggregation.

Stock Variables. The impact of marketing effort, especially advertising spending but also coupon drops, may be spread over time. Various models have been proposed to capture this phenomenon. These models, especially the closely-related Koyck model, will be addressed in the Chapter 4. For now we want to consider the case where a new variable is constructed to represent the *stock* of present and past efforts. The use of stock variables, most particularly *adstock*, has been championed by Broadbent (1979). An early use of a stock variable for the advertising expenditures, which was called "effective advertising expenditure," appeared in Emshoff and Mercer's study of a semi-durable product (1970, p. 15). Generally the contribution of effort in each period is assumed to be a constant fraction λ of the amount in the previous period. In one study of a household-products group, prior research indicated that the weekly advertising retention rate was 0.8 (George, Mercer, and Wilson 1996).[14] The first period is handled differently depending on whether marketing effort has had a chance to have its full impact in the first period or whether it impact has been spread out over the period. If the $X_1, X_2, \ldots, X_t$ represent marketing effort in periods 1,2, …, t, then the stock of X in period t is

$$XSTOCK_t \equiv \frac{1-\lambda}{f(1-\lambda)+\lambda}\left(fX_t + \lambda X_{t-1} + \lambda^2 X_{t-2} + \cdots + \lambda^{t-2}X_2 + \lambda^{t-1}X_1\right), \quad (2.11)$$

where the first term is a constant that ensures that the effort spread over time will add up to the initial amount, that is, except for end effects, the average *XSTOCK* will be the same as the average X for a brand, and f is one, a half, or free depending on whether the first period counts in full (à la Koyck), counts as a half (preference of Broadbent), or is determined by the data. The derivation of the constant is shown in the Appendix 2-C. The relationship among adstock, awareness, and sales also has been studied by Colman and Brown (1983), Broadbent (1984), Broadbent and Colman (1986), Brown (1986), Broadbent (1990a,b), and Broadbent and Fry (1995).

The redemption of coupons from current and various past drops can also be captured by a stock variable, *couponstock*. Empirical evidence indicates that redemptions from a particular drop are highest immediately following the drop date and decline geometrically (Ward and Davis 1978b for orange juice, Bowman 1980, Neslin 1990 for instant coffee, and Inman and McAlister 1994 for spaghetti sauce). The coupon expiration date can cause a secondary mode as the coupon expires (Inman and McAlister 1994). The impact of a particular drop will depend on the number of coupons dropped, the medium used, and the coupon's face value.

Revenue, Volume, and Market Share. Revenue (also called monetary sales or turnover) is a composite variable. This may create problems when it is the performance measure in a market response function (see Farris, Parry, and Ailwadi 1992; Jacobson and Aaker 1993). Most obviously, when price is a driver of (monetary) sales, then price is on both sides of the equation although it only explicitly appears on the right-hand side:

$$R \equiv P \times Q = f(P).$$ (2.12)

This causes *spurious correlation*. The same effect occurs to a lesser degree when there is any monetary variable, say advertising expenditures, on the right-hand side of the equation. Then inflation, if not corrected for, can impact both sides of the equation. This means it is better to work in real rather than nominal terms when possible. Furthermore, if the analyst wants to imbed the sales response function in a profit function to assess the impact of changes in the marketing mix, this cannot be done when revenue is the dependent variable. Thus, sales are almost always measured in volume (or quantity) in sales response modeling and we will always mean sales volume when we say sales.

There are various measures of sales volume depending on the product category. In the ethical drug industry, it could be the total number of prescriptions (Shankar, Carpenter, and Krishnamurthi 1999).

There are exceptions to using sales volume instead of sales value. Revenue is used when aggregating across product categories, such as when the aim is to forecast store sales. Revenue is also used when marketing actions are specifically designed to affect sales value. For example, a mobile phone company might use promotions as a way of persuading would-be customers to subscribe to higher talk plans, i.e., getting them to trade up, rather than using money-off promotions to close sales. See, for example, the chapter on "Orange" in Duckworth (1997).

Many firms evaluate their relative success in terms of selective demand position or market share. Market share (*MS*) is traditionally based on sales volume (*Q*):

$$MS \equiv \frac{Q}{Q_T},$$ (2.13)

where Q_T is the total relevant industry sales. Three reasons for this are suggested. One is that the product category is simply mature and the primary demand has a zero growth rate, e.g., the frequently purchased, inexpensive, consumable good studied by Beckwith (1972) or the product category within the hypnotics and sedative segment of the British pharmaceutical market described by Leeflang, Mijatovich, and Saunders (1992). Another is that trends in primary demand are frequently not controllable by the firm and affect the industry as a whole (cf. Kleinbaum 1988). The third is that marketing instruments, in particular advertising, may have minimal impact on total industry sales. Instead, the setting of managerial decision variables serves to allocate this total amount among the competing firms. One practical problem with market share models is defining the relevant market, i.e., industry boundaries.

Other variations of market share are possible. In his work on Short-Term Advertising Strength (STAS), Jones (1995b) used Nielsen single-source data. He initially intended to compare the volume share of a brand in the households that had received television advertising for it during the previous seven days with the volume share in the households that had not received such advertising. However, Nielsen found it difficult to compile these figures. Rather than use the quantity of the brand that was bought, it was necessary to use purchase occasions, the number of times the brand was bought. Thus, the performance measure was share of purchase occasions.

Another variation is shown in the work of agricultural economists who study commodity promotion. In this case, they focus on commodity shares.

Other Measures of Performance. While our focus is on sales volume, we note that awareness, recall, and other intermediate measures that capture non-sales impacts of marketing efforts are sometimes used as performance measures. They are particularly useful in providing diagnostic information.

Inquiries or sales leads are often the goal of advertising efforts. This performance measure was used in econometric analyses of advertising done by the U.S. Naval Recruiting Command (Morey and McCann 1983) and by a British insurance company, whose main product was automobile insurance ("Frizzell Insurance" in Duckworth 1997).

In the case of trade shows, there could be five dependent variables for a particular product: (1) the number of attendees, Q, (2) the number of attendees who are potentially interested in the product—the target audience, Q_{TA}, (3) the number of attendees from the target audiences who visited the firm's booth, Q_B, (4) the number of attendees from the target audiences who visited the firm's booth with whom salesperson talked, i.e., established contact, Q_C, and (5) the number of sales leads generated, Q_L. These can be used to express efficiency ratios such as

$$\text{attraction efficiency} = \frac{Q_B}{Q_{TA}}, \tag{2.14}$$

$$\text{contact efficiency} = \frac{Q_C}{Q_B}, \text{ and} \tag{2.15}$$

$$\text{conversion efficiency} = \frac{Q_L}{Q_C}. \tag{2.16}$$

Leads can be adjusted for quality, i.e., the attractiveness of the prospect to the seller. See Gopalakrishna and Lilien (1995) and Dekimpe et al. (1997).

Advertising. Advertising was initially measured primarily in terms of expenditures, often called *adspend*. Sometimes a physical measure of advertising weight is used. For example, lines of advertising in local newspapers was used in a dynamic model of product rivalry among saltine cracker brands (Slade 1995, p. 456). While monetary measures are still widely used, many analysts desire to have a measure closer to potential buyers, that is, a measure of delivered advertising. Thus, the emphasis has shifted to measures of exposure.[15]

In many practical situations, being exposed to advertising simply means that a person has had an *opportunity to see* (OTS) an advertisement, not that the advertiser knows that the person did see it. An advertiser is particularly interested that a person in its particular target audience has had an opportunity to see. Such a measure of "net" OTS is called "impact" in the United Kingdom (for example, Broadbent 1999, p. 18). In this book we generally use impact in its common meaning, i.e., effect, rather than in this narrow technical definition.

Exposure involves reach and frequency. Unduplicated reach is the number of people exposed once to a commercial during a period while frequency is the average number of times a person is exposed during this same period. A measure of potential reach in the broadcast industry is the program rating, usually expressed as a percentage of the homes with a television (or radio) set. A measure of exposure that combines the program ratings and the average number of times a home is reached is called *gross rating points (GRPs)*.

$$GRPs \equiv reach \times frequency. \qquad (2.17)$$

If reach is expressed as a fraction instead of a percentage, this formula is multiplied by 100. A purchase of 100 GRPs could mean that 100 percent of the market is exposed once or 50 percent of the market is exposed twice or 25 percent of the market is exposed 4 times and so on. This phenomenon is illustrated in Figure 2-2. Most likely, of course, is some distribution such as 45 percent of the market exposed once, 20 percent exposed twice, and 5 percent exposed three times that adds up to 100.

GRPs were used in modeling response to advertising changes for "V-8" Cocktail Vegetable Juice (Eastlack and Rao 1986). Delivered GRPs were calculated for spot TV placements using quarterly sweeps conducted by the Nielson Station Index of areas of dominant influence (ADI's) aggregated to SAMI markets. Delivered GRPs for national TV placements were based on Nielsen Audimeter Data (NTI data). Spot radio delivered GRPs were based on Arbitron data and network radio delivered GRPs were from RADAR.

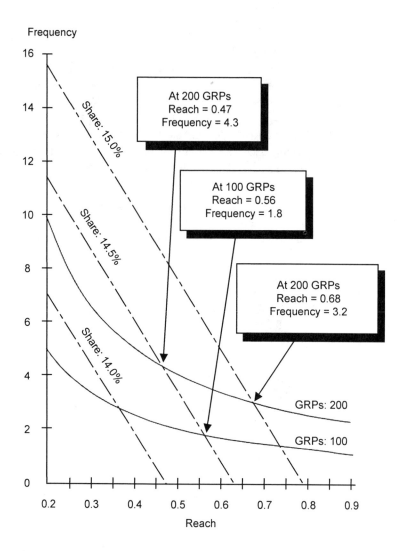

Figure 2-2. Media Reach and Frequency Tradeoff. *Source:* Pedrick and Zufryden (1993, p. 17). Reprinted from the *Journal of Advertising Research*, © 1993, by the Advertising Research Foundation.

Advertisers follow different allocations of their advertising budgets over time. Consider the allocation of an annual budget over weeks. One basic pattern is *burst* with advertising only appearing one, two, or three times a year. One year Unilever advertised its Persil Wash-up Liquid, a soapless detergent, on the main commercial channel in Central Scotland in three bursts: March, April/May, and September. The

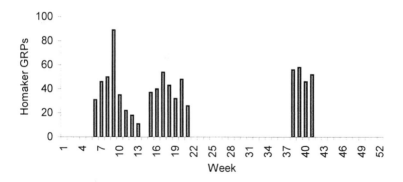

Figure 2-3. 1997 Schedule for Persil Wash-up Liquid on ITV in Central Scotland
Reproduced from Broadbent, S. (1999), *When to Advertise*, with permission from
Admap Publications.

schedule is shown Figure 2-3. Advertising done in conjunction with a sales
promotion would be an example of a one-time burst. The second basic pattern is
flighting with advertising being on for several weeks, followed by several weeks off.
The third basic pattern is *continuous* with advertising being shown, even at a low
weight nearly all the time. This pattern is also called "drip." One study by TSMS and
Taylor Nelson Sofres of scheduling in the United Kingdom found a propensity to
burst (reported by Broadbent 1999, p. 13; p. 185, note 3). The weekly rate when on
was 102 GRPs for bursts, 83 GPRs for flight, and 63 GRPs for continuous.

In the United Kingdom gross rating points for television spots are called TV
ratings (TVRs). One study illustrates some of the some of the practical steps in
constructing an operational measure of advertising (Broadbent 1979). TVRs were
taken over the same TV areas and periods. Commercials of different lengths were
standardized on 30 seconds—increasing the TVRs for longer advertisements and
decreasing them for shorter ones in proportion to their costs. Each period's actual
TVRs were then replaced by a measure of the amount of advertising that was
effective then. This measure, called *adstock*, will be discussed later in the chapter.

The effect of advertising spending is mediated by *advertising quality*. Market
share studies by Buzzell (1964b) and Buzzell, Kolin, and Murphy (1965) used data
from Schwerin Research Corporation theater test scores (pretest, posttest, and norm
values) to supplement advertising expenditures. They found that "the advertising
message quality is more important than the level of advertising expenditure"
(Buzzell, p. 31). The "V-8" study referred to earlier also used a creative approach to
advertising and concluded that

> the creative component of advertising has been found to be far more important than the
> actual spending rates or patterns (Eastlack and Rao 1986, p. 259).

An econometric consultancy, The Decision Shop, found that a particular campaign increased the advertising elasticity for Safeway stores in the United Kingdom. (Duckworth 1997, p. 200).[16]

Another way to handle the "quality" of advertising expenditures would be to use an index of quality. Parsons and Schultz (1976, p. 85) suggested that survey data on awareness or attitude might be used to define a qualitative adjustment factor, θ_t, such that

$$A_{Q',t} = \theta_t A_t, \tag{2.18}$$

where $A_{Q',t}$ is the unobservable quality-adjusted (Q') advertising spending at time t.

This intuitive notion of Parsons and Schultz was formally treated by (Arnold et al. 1987). They posited that the quality adjustment factor is a function of K quality attributes of the copy:

$$\theta_t = g(q_{1t}, \cdots, q_{kt}, \cdots, q_{Kt}), \tag{2.19}$$

where q_{kt} is the kth quality attribute.[17] Technically, this is an example of systematic parameter variation, which we discuss in Chapter 3. A questionnaire was developed to capture two broad dimensions of advertising quality. One dimension was the extent to which advertising strategies and production values were met by the commercial, and the other dimension was the performance of each commercial against the target audience. Their results (p. 111) indicated that "the sales effect of a 1% change in the advertising quality attribute 'creative device' rating is 20 times as large as that of a 1% increase in advertising spending." Another recommendation is that qualitative adjustment in advertising spending should take into account media efficiency as well as copy effectiveness (Little 1975a, p. 637).

Millward Brown has addressed the advertising efficiency issue by creating a new measure. They first construct a working variable by multiplying the GRPs weight by their Awareness Index. They then develop an adstock-type variable using the working variable. The new variable is called *adfactor*. They illustrate the impact of different operational definitions of advertising on sales response with the example shown in Table 2-5. For a general overview of Millward Brown International's services and approach to market response modeling, see the *MBI Industry Perspective*.

Millward Brown International's Approach to Market Response

As part of its consulting practice, Millward Brown International (MBI) has developed an integrated system for systematically analyzing sales response to advertising expenditures. This system is designed to identify advertising sales *effectiveness*. A sales response model is used to measure the sales response to each element of the marketing mix. The model produces estimates utilizing cross-sectional, time series, nonlinear, "mixed model" (with inequality sign constraints) and shrinkage-based estimators. The model estimates the sales contributions of coupons, relative distribution, relative shelf price, feature ads, displays, temporary price reductions, pantry-loading, and advertising. Competitive effects on sales are separated out.

Special emphasis is placed on measuring advertising effects. MBI does this by analyzing the contributions of advertising both to short-term incremental sales *and* over the longer term, as advertising sustains base volume sales and contributes to the underlying sales momentum of the brand.

The MBI approach to the analysis of advertising effects is different from traditional sales response models that utilize "adstock" formulations. "Adstocks" tend to capture only short-term advertising carryover effects, but MBI's approach captures *both* short-term *and* long-term advertising effects. This is accomplished by using a market-level ad awareness variable projected from a separate ad awareness model. In a recent side-by-side comparison with a traditional adstock-based model, MBI was able to show that the longer-term advertising effect accounted for *twice* the shorter-term effect (consistent with IRI's *BehaviorScan™* in-market test results reported in *How Advertising Works*). This approach has helped MBI to properly account for the sales contributions of advertising and therefore to properly value advertising expenditures.

A CD-ROM-based client-deliverable containing a marketing plan simulator, along with the fully calibrated model and its weekly market-level database, allows marketing managers to run retrospective marketing-mix and financial analyses and to forecast future volume and profits given "what if?" scenarios.

Prepared by J. Dennis Bender, V.P. Sales Response Modeling & Advanced Analytics, Millward Brown International. Editors' Note: Mr. Bender is now V.P. Business Analysis at Management Science Associates, Inc.

Price. Price would seem to be a simple measure to quantify but often it is not. For consumer goods, price is usually taken to be the retail cost to the customer. However,

Table 2-5. Short-Term Advertising Effects for One Brand

Advertising Variable	Correlation with Base Volume	Constant (Sales level in the absence of advertising response, expressed as percent of mean base volume)	Percent of Total Sales Due to Advertising Response
GRPs	0.19	98	2
Adstock*	0.38	89	9
Adfactor*	0.54	85	13

* Using MBI's average rate for the decay of weekly TV ad awareness.

Source: Millward Brown "Relationship," p. 3.

determination of optimal retailer and manufacturer pricing and promotional policies requires the separation of consumer price promotions from regular prices (Briesch 1997). In particular, the list price for many products is a fiction. No or few sales may be made at list price for an individual stock keeping unit (SKU) because of a sale or discounting.

Brand-level analysis means, moreover, that entity aggregation must be done. For example, one study of automatic dishwashing detergent data in one Canadian supermarket chain found that each brand had, on average, 3.5 SKUs (Chen, Kanetkar, and Weiss 1994, p. 266). Price was expressed as the average *unit price* of all SKUs for a brand that particular week.

Note that the notion of *regular price is a property of an SKU, not a brand*, which is an aggregation of SKUs. The problem with the aggregation of prices is that, unless all items have the same price per equivalent volume, simply adding up total dollars and dividing by total equivalized volume will introduce spurious variation in price. This spurious variation arises from random shifts in relative sales among SKUs and systematic changes in prices associated with activities such as promotion, where the promoted item will generally receive more weight in the pricing calculation than in a normal week (Totten 1999).[18]

When analyzing price of an individual product in a particular store over time, the regular shelf price is likely to have few changes. In this case, each of these changes might be represented by its own dummy variable. The dummy variable would be 0 before the price change and 1 after the change. This was the approach taken in the examination of a household-product group in which the overall market size did not change over the 52 weeks studied (George, Mercer, and Wilson 1996, p. 16).

Dummy variables may also be used to represent special price conditions. For example, there could be a dummy variable for prices ending in 9. This usage can be found in a chain/price-zone model that uses store-level scanner data (Blattberg and Wisniewski 1987, as described in Blattberg and Neslin 1990, pp. 368-69).

In making a purchase, a customer often compares the current observed price with the price he or she anticipated paying, a *reference price*. A marked difference between the two is sometimes called "sticker shock." Two processes for price formation have been proposed (Winer 1986). In the *extrapolative expectations hypothesis*, perception of the current price of a brand is formed by the most recently observed price and trend. In the *rational expectations hypothesis*, perception of the current price is determined by the customer's model of how management sets prices. Under either hypothesis, the unobservable reference prices are expressed in terms of observables. See Kalyanaram and Winer (1995) for a recent review.

In Nielsen's SCAN*PRO Monitor's baseline methodology, "regular" price is defined as the consumer's expectation of the current price based upon the consumer's previous observations of current price. Its expectation-generating algorithm involves (1) generating an initial value of regular price even though prior observations of current price are not available and then (2) generating values of regular price based upon preceding values of the current price. The resultant "regular" price would seem to be a reference price.

In the end, as in all marketing, what is relevant is often customer perceptions—not actual conditions. For example, in doing an econometric analysis of local and long-distance calls in the United Kingdom, the telecom giant BT found that while its actual individual call prices had been falling, perceptions of its call charges had not because total bills were rising.[19] Thus, BT chose to use price perceptions as the price variable (Duckworth 1997, p. 178).

Price-cut level may be used instead of price itself. Price cut can be represented in a variety of ways. See, for example, Kondo and Kitagawa (2000).

Manufacturer Consumer Promotions. Manufacturer promotions to consumers include couponing, sampling, refunds, bonus offers, price packs, premiums, contests, and tie-ins.[20] A *coupon* is a certificate allowing the buyer to get a reduced price at time of purchase. The means of distributing coupons include free-standing inserts (FSIs), newspaper run-of-press (ROP), direct mail, magazines, in-pack, on-pack, and specialty distributed. An FSI is booklet of coupons distributed with newspaper, usually on Sunday. It is the most prevalent type of coupon (80%). Couponing is often operationalized as the size of the coupon drop, that is, the number of coupons distributed. Because coupons are not redeemed instantaneously, couponing is often treated as a stock variable, *couponstock*. The amount of a coupon is known as its *face value*. One operational definition of face value is the circulation-weighted average of the face values of coupons dropped in a period. See, for example, Vilcassim, Kadiyali, and Chintagunta (1999, p. 509). Another operational definition is the average per-package (per-box) value of manufacturer coupons. See, for instance, Slade (1995, p. 456). The face value of a coupon dropped can also be expressed as a fraction of the regular price of the brand. This definition was used, for instance, in an

Table 2-6. FSI Data for Selected Products

Characteristics	Breakfast Cereal	Spaghetti Sauce	Hot Dogs
Mean Face Value ($)	0.69 (0.26)	0.47 (0.53)	0.49 (0.59)
Mean Price ($)	2.90 (0.57)	0.87 (0.16)	1.72 (0.29)
Mean Face Value (%)	24%	54%	28%
Mean Duration (Days)	68.6 (46.0)	63.7 (30.4)	106.8 (61.9)

Source: AC Nielsen as reported in Krishna and Zhang (1999, p. 1042).

attempt to explain *coupon duration*, the time from coupon drop to expiration (Krishna and Zhang 1999, p.1043). Some illustrative FSI data is given in Table 2-6. *Bonus packs* may be represented by dummy variables with value of 1 if offered and 0 otherwise. This was done in a study of the variations in price elasticities in stores of a large retailing chain (George, Mercer, and Wilson 1996, pp. 15-16).

Retailer Merchandising. Retailers determine the allocation of shelf space and the breadth of variety offered across categories. Retailer promotions to consumers include temporary price cuts, e.g., shelf-price reductions, displays, feature advertising, free goods, retailer (store) coupons, premiums, and contests.

One measure of *shelf space* is the number of linear feet or meters given to a brand or category. Another measure is the number of *facings* (e.g., Urban 1969, Frank and Massy 1970). The problem is that one facing for a big item will have more effect than one facing for a small item. Alternatively, the actual cross-sectional area occupied by the product could be used (e.g., Dreze, Hoch, and Purk 1994). For example, if there are two facings of a product whose dimensions are 3 inches by 4 inches, then it occupies a total space of 24 square inches.[21] *Category variety* is the number of SKUs stocked in a given category.

The *deal-discount* can be operationalized as either an absolute amount or as a percentage: [22]

$$\text{amount off} \equiv \text{regular price} - \text{discounted price} \qquad (2.20)$$

or

$$\text{deal discount percentage} \equiv \frac{\text{amount off}}{\text{regular price}} \times 100\%. \qquad (2.21)$$

One empirical study has reported that the percentage discount from regular price worked as well as or better than alternative deal specifications for most brands that were analyzed (Blattberg and Wisniewski 1989, p. 299). The prices used may be unit prices. Often the discounted price is not known but will be estimated as the lowest unit price available in a store for a brand (a proxy variable).

Two other numbers that adjust for competition are sometimes calculated (Kondo and Kitagawa 2000, p. 55). The first says that a deal discount will have an effect only it is when greater than any of its competitors. Let

$$\text{amount off}_{\text{them}} = \max_{\text{competitors}} \left(\text{amount off}\right),$$

then

$$\begin{array}{c} \text{maximum effective} \\ \text{deal discount} \end{array} \equiv \begin{cases} \text{amount off}_{\text{us}} & \text{if amount off}_{\text{us}} \geq \text{amount off}_{\text{them}} \\ 0 & \text{otherwise} \end{cases}. \qquad (2.22)$$

The second says that the difference of the deal from any of its competitors is what is important. Let

$$\text{amount off}_{\text{diff}} = \min_{\text{competitors}} \left(\text{amount off}_{\text{us}} - \text{amount off}_{\text{them}}\right),$$

then

$$\begin{array}{c} \text{minimum effective} \\ \text{deal discount} \end{array} \equiv \begin{cases} \text{amount off}_{\text{diff}} & \text{if amount off}_{\text{diff}} \geq 0 \\ 0 & \text{otherwise} \end{cases}. \qquad (2.23)$$

These two measures, and others, have been used with daily milk data (Kondo and Kitagawa 2000).

A brand may be *featured* in a store advertisement or have a point-of-purchase (POP) *display*. Features and displays are represented by their own dummy variables with value of 1 if featured (displayed) and 0 otherwise. Rather than simply using one dummy, there may be a dummy to represent different sizes of ads (or different types or store locations of displays). See Cooper et al. (1999, pp. 313-14) for a detailed description of measures of newspaper advertisements and store displays. Three ad sizes were used studying features for one grocery chain (Blattberg and Wisniewski 1987, as described in Blattberg and Neslin 1990, p. 368).

Sometimes relative indices are calculated for feature and display. If N_f of N_d denotes the number of brands featured (displayed) among N competing brands in a given period, then

$$\text{feature (display) index} = X_{f(\text{or } d)i} \equiv \begin{cases} \dfrac{N}{N_{f(\text{or } d)}} & \begin{array}{l} \text{if brand } i \text{ is featured} \\ \text{(displayed)} \end{array} \\[2ex] 1 - \dfrac{N_{f(\text{or } d)}}{N} & \text{otherwise} \end{cases} \qquad (2.24)$$

This type of index, called a *distinctiveness index*, was introduced by Nakanishi, Cooper, and Kassarjian (1974). The index is intended to show how distinctive one brand is from another. Such indexes have been used in studies of disposable diapers and toilet tissue (Kumar and Heath 1990, p. 166; Kumar 1994), of saltine crackers and baking chips (Kumar 1994), of automatic dishwashing detergent (Chen, Kanetkar, and Weiss 1994, p. 267) and coffee (Gruca and Klemz 1998, p. 54). If all brands or no brands are featured (displayed), then the index is 1.0. For example, five major brands comprised the toilet tissue market above. If only brand i is on display, its index is 5.0. If brand i is not on display but its four competitors are, its index is 0.2. The empirical averages for the display index of the five brands were 1.826, 0.884, 1.021, 1.117, and 1.016 (Kumar 1994, p. 305). Relative to competitors, Brand A emphasized display promotions while Brand B downplayed them.

The frequency of each of these promotions can be calculated:

$$\text{frequency of feature (display)} \equiv \\ \frac{\text{number of weeks with feature advertising (display) only}}{\text{total number of weeks}}. \qquad (2.25)$$

A product may be featured and displayed at the same time. This interaction is represented by dummy variables (value of 1 if displayed and featured and 0 otherwise). As before, the frequency can also be calculated:

$$\text{frequency of feature and display} \equiv \frac{\text{number of weeks with both}}{\text{total number of weeks}}. \qquad (2.26)$$

The presence of "N for" promotions can be represented by a dummy variable. This usage can be found in the chain/price-zone model mentioned earlier (Blattberg and Wisniewski 1987, as described in Blattberg and Neslin 1990, pp. 368-69).

Manufacturer Trade Promotions. Trade promotions include case allowances, advertising allowances, display allowances, and contests. Manufacturer trade promotions frequently fund retailers' temporary price reductions (TPRs), displays, and feature advertising.

Retail Distribution. Retail distribution coverage is typically operationalized in one of three ways (Reibstein and Farris 1995, p. G192). The simplest is the percentage of retail outlets carrying a brand. The problem with this operationalization is that it treats outlets having low sales the same as outlets having high sales. This problem is overcome by weighting the outlets appropriately. This is done in one of two ways. The usual weighting is the All Commodity Volume (ACV), the percentage of retail outlets, weighted by total outlet sales in "all commodity groups," selling a brand. Proxies for total sales, such as square area of selling space, are commonly used. The problem here is that category potential is assumed to be the same for all outlet types even though the product assortment in supermarkets is different from that in convenience stores. To address this problem, Product Category Volume (PCV), the percentage of retail outlets selling a brand, weighted by category sales, can be used. Retail audit services typically only report ACV, but they can usually calculate PCV as well. Otherwise, PCV can be approximated from ACV by weighting ACV for outlet types by their respective category shares. Each of these three measures may be gross or net of out-of-stocks.

A major problem with using these distribution measures in market response models is its lack of variability over time for established products. Market leaders have high levels of distribution that change little, if at all, from period to period. This is compounded by the fact that if a store carries only one variant of a product, it is viewed as carrying the product; see, for example, the Ocean Spray Cranberry Juice Cocktail data in Table 2-7. One way to get more variation is to use the number of items carried. This figure can be treated as a relative variable: number of UPCs vs. others. Relative share of shelf and freezer space is also better measure than the simple %-ACV distribution (Bender and Link 1994).

Personal Selling. Alternate measures of personal selling include expenditure, the number of salespeople, the number of sales calls completed, and the amount of customer contact time. Personal selling expenditure was related to sales of a mature industrial product (Gopalakrishna and Chatterjee 1992). The number of sales people was used to predict the sales volume of medical X-ray film (Lambert 1968) and to forecast the store sales for an apparel store in Canada (Lam, Vandenbosch, and Pearce 1998). The number of calls was the measure employed in a studies of the dollar sales of the lamp division of General Electric (Waid, Clark, and Ackoff 1956) and the sales of an established ethical drug from a Belgian pharmaceutical manufacturer (Parsons and Vanden Abeele 1981).

A major problem with using number of calls when assessing the performance of salespeople is its lack of variability across territories. If a sales manager demands N calls per period, each salesperson's call report will show N calls or so. The problem might be addressed by a more sensitive operational definition of calling effort, such

Table 2-7. Ocean Spray Cranberry Juice

(A) Cran-Cocktail by Packaging

Product	Distribution (%ACV)	Display (%ACV)
Liquid Concentrate	74	0.4
Aseptic 3-pack	69	2.1
32 oz. Bottle	97	3.2
48 oz. Bottle	99	5.8
64 oz. Bottle	95	0.3
128 oz. Bottle	88	0.3
Low Calorie 32 oz.	48	0.4
Low Calorie 48 oz.	79	2.9
Total US (week 2-22)	100a	12.9b

Source: IRI Infoscan as reported in Little (1996)

(B) 64 oz. Bottle by Flavor

Product	Distribution (%ACV)	Display (%ACV)
Cran-Cocktail	98.2	4.6
Cran-Apple	94.8	5.0
Cran-Cherry	44.8	1.2
Cran-Grape	93.6	3.5
Cran-Rasberry	91.0	2.4
Cran-Strawberry	80.6	3.7
Cran-Kiwi	8.8	1.7
Cran-Currant	71.1	1.7
Total US (week 7-13)	99.7a	14.0b

a The product line is considered to be *in distribution* in a store if *any* of its component items are in distribution.
b The product line is considered to be *on display* in a store if *any* of its component items are on display.

Source: IRI Infoscan as reported in Little (1998).

as one found by multiplying the number of calls by the number of people seen per call (see Turner 1971).

When sales call effort varies significantly across territories and over time, as is the case for the U.S. Navy recruitment sales force, opportunities exist to study its market response effects. The findings of six empirical studies of military recruiter productivity on a variety of performance measures are reported in Vandenbosch and Weinberg (1993).

Product. Product has occasionally appeared as a driver of sales. Measures that have been used include product mix indexes, package mix indexes, variety indexes, quality indexes, product content, new variety activity, and frequency of service. A product mix index might be defined as the number of brands, such as the number of filter cigarette brands (Lambin 1976). A packages mix index might be defined as the number of container sizes, such those for soft drinks or yogurt (Lambin 1976). A variety index might be defined as the number of variants, such as flavors of yogurt or destinations of an auto-train (Lambin 1976). New variety activity might be defined as the share of subcategories on the market less than one year, such as for a grocery item (Claycamp 1966). Quality index might be defined in terms of expert ratings of selected attributes, such as those for electric shavers (Lambin 1976) or for prescription drugs (Shankar, Carpenter, and Krishnamurthi 1999).[23] Alternatively, consumers' perceptions of quality can be used. For example, the EquiTrend survey by Total Research Corporation (TRC) asks participants to evaluate the quality of brands on an 11-point scale, with 0 for poor quality, 5 for acceptable, and 10 for outstanding quality. This data has been used to assess the effect of market share on consumers' perceptions of quality (Hellofs and Jacobson 1999). Product content might be represented by either the absolute amount or the percentage amount of a product component or ingredient, such as the chocolate weight in a confectionery (Lambin 1976). Frequency of service might be defined as the number of trips, such as the number of trains per week (Lambin 1976) or the number of flights per quarter (Schultz 1971). A more sophisticated quantification of product value in a marketing-mix model is to construct a time series of conjoint-derived product preferences. Such a scale was used to assess the impact of technology improvements on the sales of a computer peripheral product (Hanssens 1998).

Environmental Variables. Every market is affected by its own unique set of environmental variables. These variables can be classified as competitive or autonomous. For every decision variable a firm has control over, each of its competitors has a similar decision variable. There are also autonomous variables impacting markets over which the competing firms have no control. Typical of these are macroeconomic variables such as interest rates. For example, an investigation of automobile demand at the dealership level found that demand was interest sensitive and that compact cars were more interest sensitive than full size cars (Helmuth 1987, p. 42). We have already discussed factors such as trend, seasonality, price-level changes, and population changes. Related to seasonality can be factors such as weather and holidays. For example, temperature and rainfall as well as Christmas and Easter impacted the sales performance of Safeway stores in the United Kingdom (Duckworth 1997, p. 200).

In performance measurement, a key driver may be competitive intensity. This may require the construction of an *index of competition*. For trade shows this may simply be the share of square space among firms exhibiting similar products (Gopalakrishna and Lilien 1995, pp. 30-31).

Technical Issues Concerning Variables

Before going on to discuss aggregation, some technical issues involving variables, in particular, omitted variables, errors in variables, and unobservable variables, will be covered. In Chapter 4, we will introduce some nomenclature for classifying variables

Omitted Variables. Occasionally the importance of a variable goes unrecognized and is unintentionally omitted from an analysis. Other times a variable is recognized but data cannot be obtained. Perhaps there is no economical way to collect the information. In any case, an omitted variable will handicap our ability to estimate relations among variables. The consequences of an omitted variable are discussed in Chapter 5.

Sometimes another variable is used in place of the omitted variable. Such a measured variable is called a *proxy variable*. For example, to account for the impact of differences in taste on U.S. beer demand, immigrants were conjectured to be more prone to beer drinking than native drinkers (Hogarty and Elzinga 1972). The proxy variable used was the percentage of each state's population that was foreign-born. For another example, the attractiveness of booth location on the show floor is important in assessing a firm's performance at a trade show. A study of the Institute of Food Technologists' Annual Food Exposition found that show management offered preference in booth location to exhibiting firms who had more points. Points were awarded on the basis of the number of pages of advertising in the show bulletin and the annual amount booth space in each of the previous five years.[24] Thus, "points" was used as a proxy variable for attractiveness of booth location (Gopalakrishna and Lilien 1995, p. 30).[25] In yet another study, marketing expenditures in France on salmon were not available. The annual marketing budget of the Norwegian Fish Farmers' Sales Organization was used as a proxy. The budget share spent on salmon promotion in France was assumed to have remained constant during the period of study so that variations in the total budget represented variations in the French marketing budget (Bjørndal, Salvanes, and Andreassen 1992, p. 1029). In an assessment of the impact of the number of salespeople and the amount of store traffic on an apparel store's sales, a higher proportion of full-time workers in store traffic was believed increase store sales. This proportion was not available. Assuming that full-time workers can generally only find time for shopping during non-office hours, a dummy variable, which was one for non-office hours and zero otherwise, was used as a proxy (Lam, Vandenbosch, and Pearce 1998, pp. 65-66). A time series analysis of daily scanner sales of milk in Japan used maximum price during the entire period as a proxy for regular price (Kondo and Kitagawa 2000, p. 55).

A proxy variable is typically treated as the true variable with measurement error (Maddala 1992, pp. 464-66, Greene 1997, pp. 442-43, Kennedy 1998, pp. 148-49). Some technical aspects of proxy variables are discussed in the section on stochastic regressors in Chapter 5.

Errors in Variables. Errors in variables means that one or more variables have been measured or recorded inaccurately. As almost anyone who has worked with marketing data knows, variables are often measured with considerable uncertainty. We have already encountered three kinds of measurement problems: (1) problems of definition, (2) problems of operationalization, and (3) errors of measurement. To the list of measurement errors, we could add mere errors of transcription and other mechanical mistakes. In any event, it should be apparent that an assumption of error-free variables in marketing is likely to be unfounded.

In the case of market response models, a common problem is that a data series does not exist with the time interval desired. For example, many sales drivers, price and promotion, are now available on a weekly basis, but some, such as advertising, may only be available monthly or quarterly basis. The problem is addressed by *data stretching*. The simplest solution is to spread the longer time period equally over the shorter time period. Thus, if advertising spending is assumed to occur at a constant rate, quarterly advertising data is converted into weekly advertising data by dividing by 13. This was done in a market response study for a nonfood product in a mature category (Jedidi, Mela, and Gupta 1999, p. 8). A more complex solution involves using a weighted moving average (Slade 1995, p. 456). Consider the case of converting monthly data to weekly data. First, the monthly data is converted into weekly data as above, creating a new data series $\hat{X}_t$. Then this data series is smoothed using a linear filter:

$$\hat{\hat{X}}_t = 0.25\hat{X}_{t-1} + 0.50\hat{X}_t + 0.25\hat{X}_{t+1} \tag{2.27}$$

The value of the weekly variable $\hat{\hat{X}}_t$ in the first (last) week of each month is now a combination of the current and previous (following) month's values. This procedure was used in an analysis of price and advertising competition among four brands of saltine crackers (Slade 1995). Data stretching generally results in biased estimators of coefficients and error variances and its routine use is to be avoided (Greenberg, Pollard, and Alpert 1989).[26] While data stretching addresses one problem, it introduces another—measurement error.

Missing Observations. An extreme case of measurement error is missing observations on a variable. A data set may well have gaps. For example, in survey data, respondents may not answer all the questions asked.

Although various suggestions for filling in missing values of the dependent variable in a regression model have been proposed, the conclusion is the appropriate course is to omit the observation (Greene 1997, pp. 427-30). There is some prospect for filling in missing values of an independent variable, see Little (1992) and Greene (1997, pp. 430-31). Simply filling in missing values with the mean of the non-missing values of the variable, however, is simply equivalent to deleting the incomplete data but at the cost of lowering R-square. Two methods for imputing missing data in regression have been proposed by Cooper, de Leeuw, and Sogomonian (1991). The goal of these methods is to obtain "good" estimates of the regression coefficients, influenced as little as possible by the missing values in an observation.

Unobservable Variables. Marketing studies often contain observations on quantity of goods sold, expenditures on advertising, prices, and so on. These kinds of variables tend to have well-defined meanings and measurements. However, a number of other marketing variables, such as attitudes about products, intentions to purchase, and feelings of cognitive dissonance, are unobservable in any direct way. For such psychological variables, observable correlates of behavior can be sought.

Unobservable variables may play important roles in certain market response models. For example, advertising often affects future demand for a product as well as present demand. Advertising can be viewed as an investment in advertising capital. This advertising capital is called *goodwill*. Goodwill is an unobservable. Note that demand is also an unobservable variable—only sales are actually observed.

There are two fundamental solutions to the problem of unobservable variables. First, they can be omitted from the analysis. A study on the relation between advertising and sales, for example, could omit the intermediate and unobservable levels of the "hierarchy of effects" and focus simply on the observable variables, sales and advertising. The second solution would be to devise instruments to measure the unobservable variables, either directly or as a function of observable variables. Which solution is chosen depends on the purpose of the research.

Aggregation

Closely related to the questions of the data and variables to be used, which we have just discussed, and model form, which we will address in Chapter 3, is the issue of the level of aggregation at which the analysis should take place. In the past, model-building efforts appeared to exclude considerations about the level of aggregation, probably because of the constraints surrounding availability of data.

With the marketing information explosion, aggregation issues are an increasingly important consideration.

Aggregation Space

Marketing aggregation can take place over entities, time, space, or variables. The intersection of the various levels of aggregation for each of these dimensions defines the *aggregation space* of the response study. For example, the aggregation space of a study might be brand sales recorded as monthly data for metropolitan sales territories and advertising spend equal to television expenditures plus radio expenditures. It should be clear that the specification of the levels of aggregation has an important bearing on the nature of the relations that can be discovered. In Chapter 3, we address the aggregation of relations.

Entity Aggregation. Aggregation over entities can be of two types, corresponding to the two basic types of entities in a marketing system. The first is aggregation over buyers, and the second is aggregation over product levels. *Buyer aggregation* occurs when individual buying units are added to obtain market segment sales, total brand sales, or industry sales of the product. *Product aggregation* occurs when individual universal product codes (UPCs) are added to obtain brand totals, larger product category totals, firm totals, or industry totals.[27]

Temporal Aggregation. Temporal aggregation refers to the collection of shorter observation periods into longer ones. Research regarding the relation between sales and marketing and other economic variables can be carried out on daily, weekly, monthly, bimonthly, quarterly, or annual data. To some extent, aggregation over time is unavoidable. In fact, the length of the time period that forms the basis of the analysis is often not determined by the researcher. The researcher simply uses the data made available for analysis. However, even if constrained in this respect, the researcher is not absolved of responsibility for considering the effect of temporal aggregation on the outcome of the analysis. Using the smallest possible time period allows proper investigation of the reasons for changes in the market position of a brand. If the average time between purchases for a given product is approximately one month, it is important to have, as a minimum, monthly data. Each time period would then reflect, on average, one purchase per customer. Using annual data for such a product instead would smooth the data, thereby not allowing the researcher to determine the reasons for changes on a month-to-month basis.

Spatial Aggregation. Spatial aggregation means the gathering of smaller geographic areas into larger ones. Data describing the behavior of marketing variables over geographic areas are available in increasingly more detailed forms. This allows separate analyses to be carried out for each of the geographic areas or sales territories in which a firm is competing. Analysis at the national level will certainly not reveal information about marketing differences among such territories. Moreover, such an aggregate analysis is likely to be invalid if the relation between marketing variables is not the same for all areas. There are several reasons why this relation may differ across sales territories. At least in some industries, the structure of the market is not homogeneous across territories, that is, some brands are available in some areas and not in others. The market position of a selected brand may differ substantially across territories, partly as a result of differences in market structure. Furthermore, the characteristics of customers may vary substantially across territories. If the relation of interest depends on some of these characteristics or on the presence and extent of competition provided by competing brands, a certain amount of variation in the effectiveness of marketing decision variables can be expected.

Variable Aggregation. Sometimes variables are summed across their various components. For example, total advertising may be comprised of television advertising, radio advertising, magazine advertising, newspaper advertising, and outdoor advertising. Television advertising itself may be the sum of network, syndicated, spot, and cable.[28] Although each medium is measured on a common basis (monetary or GRPs), each may have a different effect on sales. A major problem that arises is that the "optimal" advertising budget derived from a sales response function based on total advertising is unlikely to be the same as the "optimal" advertising budget derived from a sales response function based on the individual advertising media.

Variable aggregation is one way to address the problem of variables whose values move so closely together—i.e., variables that are highly correlated—that their individual effects cannot be separated one from another. This problem, called collinearity, is discussed in Chapter 5. In developing an advertising evaluation system for a national seller of household electronic appliances, one metropolitan market was studied (Bhattacharya and Lodish 1994). Daily expenditure data were available for 20 newspapers. One of these newspapers, the leading daily for the metropolitan area, received about 80 percent of the total expenditures, with suburban newspapers accounting for the remaining spending. The same pattern of advertising was often followed across all newspapers; that is, the print advertising variables were highly collinear. To address this problem, expenditures were aggregated across all newspapers to create a composite print variable (p. 95).

Consistent Aggregation

To be useful to managers, measures of sales, distribution, and merchandising should have parallel and consistent meanings across different levels of aggregation. This is generally not much of a problem for sales. Equivalent units make different sizes comparable. However, the widely disseminated measures of distribution and merchandising produced by major tracking services are non-additive. Non-additive means that their values under aggregation are not simple sums or averages. This has already been illustrated by the Ocean Spray Cranberry Juice example (Table 2-7).

To address this problem, a class of integrated measures has been proposed. Starting from the decomposition of sales into base and incremental volume (as provided by data suppliers) at the underlying level of item-store-week, a deterministic, accounting-like model permits each of its variables to be aggregated analytically into store groups, product lines, and multi-week periods. The model retains its form at each level of aggregation. For details, see Little (1998).

Some integrated measures for display-only promotions of Ocean Spray products are given in Table 2-8. They can be compared with conventional ones. Overall, the comparison for 1 and 52 weeks shows that conventional measures can only increase with 52 week aggregation whereas the 52-week integrated measure can act as a norm for judging the performance of an individual week. For example, the conventional measure of distribution, %ACV, increased from 99.7 to 99.9 whereas the integrated measure, average number of items, actually decreased from 5.829 (out of 8) to 5.730. The table shows how integrated measures fit together, especially across rows. The same calculation would apply to other types of merchandising. The integrated measures fit together in the same fashion at all levels of aggregation across products, geographies, and time periods.

Choice of Aggregation Level

Scanners are now virtually everywhere in appliance, clothing, department, electronic, and hardware stores in the United States as well as in the grocery, convenience, and discount stores that first used them. The availability of detailed scanner data means that some analyses can be performed on the item—type, size, and/or flavor—as well as the brand. The model builder has more flexibility in modeling, the more data are disaggregated. However, some data are not simply available on a disaggregated basis. Manufacturers' advertising data are usually only available at the brand-market level. Moreover, some effects may be missed by store-level analysis. Strong and consistent "pantry-loading" effects is one example (Bender and Link 1994).

In building market-response models from scanner data, two decisions frequently need to be made (Cooper, Klapper, and Inoue 1996, p. 224). The first decision is whether to aggregate individual UPCs into the respective brands, as the brand is the most common unit of analysis. Nothing will be lost by aggregation if the UPCs within a brand are promoted using the same strategy and buyers respond similarly to the brand's marketing effort.[29] But does one know that this is the case?

Table 2-8. Ocean Spray Brands: Integrated Measures Due to Display-Only

Base Volume (64 oz. bottles)	Average Number of items	Base Volume per Item	Base Volume	Fraction Base Volume with Display Only	Lift Due to Display Only	Incre- mental Volume Due to Display
(A) 1 Week						
Cran-Cocktail	0.982	123,648a	121,422b	0.0600	0.73	5,351c
Cran-Apple	0.948	55,448	52,565	0.0582	0.69	2,106
Cran-Cherry	0.448	32,734	14,665	0.0321	0.95	447
Cran-Grape	0.936	58,201	54,476	0.0350	0.68	1,301
Cran-Raspberry	0.910	54,329	49,439	0.0467	0.97	2,229
Cran-Strawberry	0.806	32,931	26,542	0.0342	0.88	801
Cran-Kiwi	0.088	22,511	1,981	0.4478	1.60	1,417
Cran-Currant	0.711	20,444	14,536	0.0272	1.99	785
Total Cran Drink	5.829d	57,579	335,628	0.0513	0.84	14,437
(B) 52 Weeks (e)						
Cran-Cocktail	0.984f	7,079,248	6,965,980	0.0678g	1.10	517,921
Cran-Apple	0.956	3,328,598	3,182,140	0.0591	1.08	204,069
Cran-Cherry	0.428	1,865,729	789,532	0.0241	1.44	27,639
Cran-Grape	0.934	3,389,390	3,165,690	0.0405	0.99	126,856
Cran-Raspberry	0.922	3,156,963	2,910,720	0.0447	1.36	176,613
Cran-Strawberry	0.842	1,943,812	1,636,690	0.0292	1.15	55,087
Cran-Kiwi	0.189	1,231,652	109,617	0.2540	2.02	56,283
Cran-Currant	0.575	1,588,941	913,641	0.0350	1.30	41,729
Total Cran Drink	5.730	3,435,080	19,683,010	0.0531	1.15	1,206,197

a Volumes in equivalent volumes.

b Base volume = (base volume per item of distribution) × (average number of items in distribution).

c Incremental volume from display-only = (base volume) × (fraction of base volume having display only) × (lift for display-only).

d Provides summary of how widely available in store are the eight items in the product line.

e An item is considered to be (on display) in a store during the period if it was there (on display) during *any* of the 52 weeks. An approximation to this rule is actually used.

f Conventional %ACV: 98.9, 96.9, 46.1, 94.4, 93.8, 86.7, 24.7, 82.9, and 99.9.

g Conventional %ACV with display-only: 13.6, 12.5, 2.6, 7.8, 8.1, 4.9, 8.3, 5.2, and 30.7.

Source: Little (1998, pp. 482-83).

The second decision is whether to ignore some sales drivers that are infrequently used or are used only by a few UPCs. A number of sales drivers are tracked in syndicated data. Some are used much less frequently than others. This raises the issue of at what point can sales drivers safely be ignored. To help managers make these two decisions, a methodology based on three-mode (UPCs × sales drivers × weeks) factor analysis has been proposed. In an application to the ketchup category, empirical analysis revealed that aggregation of UPCs within a firm into brands would distort the relations between sales drivers and market responses. See Cooper, Klapper, and Inoue (1996) for details.

The level of data analyzed is dependent on the purpose of the analysis and the level at which budgeting decisions are made. Is the focus on long-term (strategic) analysis of the marketing mix or is it on short-term (tactical) promotional analysis at the individual event, retailer, and/or store-trade-area level? Is the focus on the item or the brand?

Consistent theme advertising analysis is typically done with market level data; whereas detailed trade promotion analysis is often done using key-account level data. Thus base-volume market level data or key-account level data or both may be used depending on the needs of the analysis.

It should be kept in mind that while total volume is measured, albeit with error, base volume and incremental volume are not. There must be a procedure for estimating base volume. Incremental volume is then calculated as the difference between the *measured* total volume and the *estimated* base volume. The estimated numbers obtained from a source such as IRI are likely to be different from the ones obtained from ACNielsen. Indeed, these numbers could be substantially different (Meade 1994). This warning applies to the use of Little's integrated measures, which are based on this decomposition.

Road Map of Market Response Modeling Techniques

Since for every product or brand there must be some unknown process generating sales, the objective of market response analysis is to discover this process. In a way, this is like solving a mystery: What are the factors that determine sales? Each "case" of sales response is different and yet all have common features. Market response analysts do this detective work by using the tools described in this book.

Market response models accommodate different objectives and are based on different data sources. Sections II and III of this book provide the methodological foundations of these models, which differ depending on whether the market environment is stationary or evolving. We now discuss the road map of these differences and summarize them in Table 2-9.

The chapters in Section II address modeling in stationary markets, i.e. where the data are either known or are assumed to have fixed means and variances. When cross-sectional data are available, stationarity is the norm, as there is no information available on possible changes over time. Chapter 3 focuses on the key challenges in building such static response models, including the choice of a functional form and the problem of heterogeneity in market response. Examples of questions that can be answered with such models are: how does sales force effectiveness compare to advertising effectiveness? Which regions of the global market are the most price-sensitive or, in a direct-response setting, what types of prospects are the most likely to respond to a direct-marketing campaign?

When time-series data or pooled cross-section time-series data are available, we can extend the insights of static models to include lagged effects of marketing variables. This is the subject matter of Chapter 4, on the design of dynamic response models, which still assume that the data are sampled from fixed-mean distributions. Sample questions are: how long do advertising effects on sales last, how much and how fast is competitive reaction to a price change? Most of the models reported in the literature and in practice—including the Industry Perspectives in this book—are based on either static response, or lagged-effects response.

The model design issues in Chapters 3 and 4 result in a number of important issues in parameter estimation and model testing. For example, different estimators may be used for single-equation vs. multiple-equation models, or for models on cross-sectional vs. pooled time-series cross-sectional data. This is the subject matter of Chapter 5.

Section III addresses the modeling of environments that are possibly evolving, i.e. observations collected over time may not have a fixed mean and/or variance. The chapters in this section are necessarily restricted to time-series databases with minimum 50 consecutive periods, and use some relatively new techniques developed in the time-series literature. We start with the analysis of single time series (Chapter 6), and learn the principles of time-series pattern recognition, leading to the diagnosing of evolution in a variable over time. These principles will also be useful in forecasting by extrapolating single time series, as discussed in Chapter 8. Sample questions are: what is the relative strength of seasonal fluctuations in sales, and, if sales suddenly increase by fifty percent, how much of that change can be considered permanent in nature?

Chapter 7 examines multiple time series and, again, provides a framework for dealing with possible evolution in marketing data. We first discuss the single-equation case known as the transfer function, and then examine multiple equations known as VAR models. We pay close attention to the way in which marketing actions are responsible for long-term movements in sales, i.e. sales evolution. These relatively new long-term time-series models can have far reaching implications for marketing management, even at the strategic level. Sample questions are: if a marketing campaign produces a short-term lift in sales of twenty percent, what is the expected long-term impact? By how much should the long-term sales and production forecast be adjusted? Another question is, if competition engages in an aggressive pricing campaign, will the damage to my business be of a temporary or a permanent nature?

Table 2-9. Key Characteristics of Market Response Models in Sections II and III

	Chapter 3	*Chapter 4*	*Chapter 6*	*Chapter 7*
Data needs	Cross-sectional or time series	Time series	Long time series	Long time series
Focus on functional form	Yes			
Customer or market heterogeneity?	Yes			Yes if cross-sectional data
Short-term forecasts and simulations?	Yes if time series data	Yes	Yes (unconditional)	Yes
Lagged marketing effects ?		Yes		Yes
Permanent marketing effects?				Yes
Response equilibrium?	Static			Dynamic
Long-term forecasts and simulations?			Yes (unconditional)	Yes (conditional)

These five methodological chapters are the foundation for our discussion of solutions to marketing problems in Section IV. We begin by reviewing the major quantitative insights on marketing effectiveness that market response models have produced. Next, we study the optimal allocation of scarce marketing resources and how various optimal rules relate to empirical market-response findings. We conclude with a discussion of the sales and market forecasting process with and without market-response models. Our final section and chapter address the implementation of market-response models, with specific reference to the opportunities offered by the information age.

Notes

[1] Economists speak of demand models.

[2] A hundredweight is a unit of avoirdupois weight commonly equivalent to 100 pounds (45.359 kilograms) in the U.S. and is abbreviated as cwt.

[3] Approximately 60 percent of all acetic acid goes into the production of VAM and about 80 percent of VAM production is used in construction (Dubin 1998, p. 62).

[4] The following discussion of data sources draws on Findley and Little (1980) and Totten and Block (1994).

[5] For the chemical industry, a good starting point is www.chemindustry.com.

[6] SAMI was bought by Control Data, which subsequently disbanded it.

[7] IMS was acquired by Dun & Bradstreet in 1988 and spun off as part of Cognizant Corp. in Dun & Bradstreet's 1996 restructuring. Cognizant combined IMS International and Nielsen Media Research. Thus, NMR was no longer part of ACNielsen. In July 1998, Cognizant was split into IMS Health and Nielsen Media Research. Subsequently, in August 1999, Nielsen Media Research was merged into VNU, the Netherlands-based international publishing and information company.

[8] ACNielsen was founded in 1923, acquired by Dun & Bradstreet in 1984, and became a separate public company in November 1996.

[9] Market Facts was acquired by Carat, the leading media specialist in Europe, in 1999.

[10] For example, Nielsen's 2,000 household people-meter panel in the United States ran only from 1991 to 1993.

[11] Market Metrics and Spectra merged in 1995. Spectra is a division of VNU.

[12] For more on the pitfalls in the use of time as an explanatory variable, see Nelson and Kang (1984).

[13] One study of laundry detergents found no substantive difference in results when advertising was measured independently as the level of a brand's advertising and when it was measured in relation to competition as share of voice (Tellis and Weiss 1995, p. 7). Consequently, levels were used to construct advertising stock for ease of computation and interpretation. Otherwise, share of voice was used because it was considered more managerially relevant.

[14] Fader, Lattin, and Little (1992, p. 381) reported that Abe developed an adstock-type advertising exposure variable for the individual household using single source scanner panel data. The retention rate for advertising was found to be about 0.9 for cranberry drinks when time was measured in days. This value would imply a half-life of 6.6 days for a single exposure. The authors discussed how to estimate such multinomial logit models when they contain explanatory variables that are nonlinear functions of the parameters to be estimated.

[15] Exposure could be operationalized as either incidence (number of exposures) or duration (time of exposure). However, number of exposures is managerially more meaningful. See Tellis and Weiss (1995, p. 7).

[16] During the campaign the advertising elasticity was 0.105; whereas, for the modeling period as a whole, the advertising elasticity was 0.081.

[17] Problems can arise when the independent variables in a regression analysis are interval scaled, as they would most likely be in the case of quality attributes. Yi (1988) has recommended mean centering of interval variables used in regression models with interaction effects.

[18] Totten (1999) has further noted that most proposed schemes for addressing this problem involve manipulations of SKU base volume and SKU base price but still fail to be completely satisfactory for forecasting purposes. A major complication is that, in time-series analysis, the addition of new SKUs to the aggregation or the deletion of some SKUs from the aggregation leads to discontinuities in the series. If these are handled by dummy variables (pre/post change), the forecasting side becomes very complicated. If not handled, however, there will be confounds of price with assortment.

[19] BT constructed eight models to describe calls-per-line and duration for four combinations of rates and destinations.

[20] See Schultz, Robinson, and Petrison (1998) for a discussion of basic sales promotion techniques.

[21] Just as retail product movement is related to shelf space, the number of visitors at a booth at a trade show is related to the size of the booth. Booth space might be expressed as the size of the booth in square feet, e.g., Gopalakrishna and Lilien (1995, p. 30).

[22] *Deal depth* has been defined as the average percentage discount for a brand conditional upon the brand being on promotion. See Bell, Chiang, and Padmanabhan (1999, p. 523).

[23] In the case of the ethical drug industry study, data on perceived product quality were obtained from 38 physicians on four dimensions: efficacy, dosage, side effects, and range of indicators. Each dimension

was measured on a five-point scale from "Very Good" to "Very Poor." An overall product quality measure was computed by averaging across dimensions.

[24] For example, 6 to 11 ad pages in one year was worth 4 points and a 10 feet by 10 feet booth in the past year was worth 1 point (Gopalakrishna and Lilien 1995, p. 30, fn. 1).

[25] To some degree points indicate the firm's visibility/familiarity among the target audience.

[26] When a related lower level of aggregation (weekly) series is available, an estimator has been proposed to expand the higher level of aggregation (monthly) series into a corresponding lower level of aggregation (weekly) series (Chow and Lin 1971).

[27] The aggregation of volumes is generally straightforward; however, as we have noted in our discussion of price, this may not be the case for other variables.

[28] For instance, Vilcassim, Kadiyali, and Chintagunta (1999, p. 508).

[29] In a similar vein, consider the relatively simple case of aggregating possibly correlated but non-competitive entities. For example, is it or is it not acceptable to aggregate stores within the same chain and city? Marketing Analytics, Inc.'s position is it generally is, as long as the aggregated stores were all doing the same thing (Link 1999).

Appendix 2

2-A Nielsen Survey of Supermarkets (circa 1995)

Harter and Cameron (1995) provided the following description of ACNielsen's primary marketing research survey of the supermarket trade:

> ScanTrack U.S. collects data from a selected sample of about 3,000 supermarkets. The target population for the ScanTrack sample consists of approximately 30,000 supermarkets in the continental United States. For the market research industry, a supermarket is a grocery store, as defined by the Standard Industrial Classification (SIC) Manual, with over two million dollars in annual sales. Supermarkets comprise 84 percent of all grocery volume. The ACNielsen Company maintains a listing of the supermarket population with input from a variety of proprietary and commercially available sources.
>
> The sample for this study is selected using implicit geographic stratification within explicit strata. Supermarkets are first divided into 75 geographically defined strata. Fifty of these strata are metropolitan markets, such as the Phoenix market, roughly corresponding to television viewing areas. The 50 market strata are further stratified into major retailer organization strata, such as Safeway in Phoenix, and two size strata for "all others." Two size strata are used within each of the remaining non-market strata, as well. This two-step stratification into explicit strata allows for efficient estimates by stratifying on both market differences and on retail chain differences.
>
> The implicit stratification arises from geographically sequencing the stores within each explicit stratum prior to systematic sample selection. Good geographical representation is a proxy for representation of various demographic and socio-economic variables that affect consumer buying. To sequence the stores geographically, each stores latitude and longitude are converted into a single number called a Peano key. The Peano keys are sorted to create a one-dimensional list frame from the stores in the two-dimensional geographic area. Nielsen has applied for a patent for this application of Peano keys. One advantage of the Peano key method is that it largely preserves geographic contiguity.
>
> Finally, the geographically sequenced list within organization and market is sampled systematically for efficiency gains from the resulting implicit stratification. Retailers review their sample stratum to ensure that the Nielsen sample represents their population. Nielsen reviews the sample regularly to ensure that changes in the population are properly reflected in the sample on a timely basis.
>
> The separate ratio estimator is used to estimate retail sales for both individual items and aggregates of items such as brands or categories. The auxiliary variable in the ratio estimator is total store sales. In most cases, total store sales for each sample store and total organization sales figures are available directly from retailers. The ratio estimator takes advantage of the high correlation between a store's total sales and individual brand sales, providing for a higher level of accuracy than other estimators.

This article appears in the *Amstat News*.

2-B Baseline Methods (circa 1993)

Baseline volume is defined as the expected sales volume in a store in the absence of store level promotion. Thus, initial baselines are formed from non-promoted volume. The Nielsen baseline methodology is taken from Totten (1993) and the IRI baseline methodology is described in Abraham and Lodish (1993). The basic approach is to do exponential smoothing.

1. Forward-backward method [Nielsen Monitor]

$$BLQF_t = \theta Q_{t-1} + (1-\theta)BLQF_{t-1}$$
$$BLQR_t = \theta Q_{t+1} + (1-\theta)BLQR_{t+1} \tag{2.28}$$
$$BLQ_t = \frac{BLQF_t + BLQR_t}{2}$$

where

θ = smoothing constant subject to $0 < \theta < 1$,
$BLQF_t$ = forward estimate of baseline volume at time t,
$BLQR_t$ = backward estimate of baseline volume at time t,
BLQ_t = final estimate of baseline volume at time t.

2. Forward-backward method with cross-sectional adjustment [Nielsen Monitor]

$$BLQF_t = \theta Q_{t-1} + (1-\theta)BLQF_{t-1}$$
$$BLQR_t = \theta Q_{t+1} + (1-\theta)BLQR_{t+1}$$
$$PBLQP_t = \frac{BLQF_t + BLQR_t}{2} \tag{2.29}$$
$$ADJ_t = \frac{\sum_{i=1}^{S} Q_{it}}{\sum_{i=1}^{S} PBLQ_{it}}$$
$$BLQP_t = ADJ_t \times PBLQ_t$$

where

$PBLQ_t$ = preliminary estimate of baseline volume at time t,

ADJ_t = cross-sectional adjustment at time t based on similar
category items in market for no promotion observations.

3. Forward-only method with cross-sectional adjustment [Nielsen Solution System (NSS)]

$$BLQF_t = \theta Q_{t-1} + (1 - \theta)BLQF_{t-1}$$

$$BLQR_t = \theta Q_{t+1} + (1 - \theta)BLQR_{t+1}$$

$$BLQP_t = \frac{BLQF_t + BLQR_t}{2}$$

$$ADJ_t = \frac{\sum_{i=1}^{N} Q_{it}}{\sum_{i=1}^{N} BLQP_{it}}$$

(2.30)

$$COR_t \equiv \frac{\sum_{i=1}^{S} Q_{it}}{\sum_{i=1}^{S} BLQP_{it}}$$

$$BLQ_t = G_t \times BLQP_t$$

where N = the number of stores in market with no promotion and

$$G_t = \begin{cases} ADJ_t & \text{if } N > 20 \\ N \times ADJ_t + (20 - N) \times COR_t & \text{otherwise.} \end{cases}$$

(2.31)

Frank Slavik enhanced the baseline methodology used for Nielsen's SCAN*PRO Monitor. In the process, more than 40,000 randomly chosen store/UPC equivalized unit volume time series of actual scanner data from 18 product categories were analyzed. The appropriate time series representation was found to be an ARIMA (0 1 1) model. ARIMA process will be discussed in Chapter 6.

4. Forward-only method with deseasonalization [IRI PROMOTIONSCAN]

$$DLQF_t = \theta \frac{Q_t}{I_t} + (1 - \theta)DBLQF_{t-1}$$

$$PBLQ_t = I_t \times DBLQF_t$$

$$ADJ_t = \frac{\sum\limits_{i=1}^{N} Q_{it}}{\sum\limits_{i=1}^{N} PBLQ_{it}} \qquad (2.32)$$

$$BLQ_t = ADJ_t \times BLQP_t$$

where

I_t = estimate of seasonality index at category level at time t

$DBLQF_t$ = deseasonalized forward estimate of baseline volume at time t.

2-C Construction of Stock Variables

In a stock formulation, the impact of effort over time is

$$f + \lambda + \lambda^2 + \lambda^3 + \cdots \tag{2.33}$$

where f is the impact in the first period and λ is the retention rate from period to period. [Please note that, in his writings on adstock, Broadbent has variously used d for decay and f for fade to represent our parameter λ.] To get the sum of this series, recognize that after f there is a geometric progression with common ratio λ. In a geometric progression with first term a and common ratio r, the sum, s, of n terms is

$$s = a\frac{1 - r^n}{1 - r}. \tag{2.34}$$

When a also happens to be equal to r, the sum of its first n terms including f is

$$f + \lambda\frac{1 - \lambda^{n-1}}{1 - \lambda} = \frac{f(1 - \lambda) + r(1 - \lambda^{n-1})}{1 - \lambda}. \tag{2.35}$$

And the total impact of effort over time is

$$f + \lambda\frac{1 - \lambda^{\infty}}{1 - \lambda} = \frac{f(1 - \lambda) + \lambda}{1 - \lambda}. \tag{2.36}$$

By weighting effort by the reciprocal of this ratio, the sum of the efforts in each period will add up to the initial effort.

The number of periods T to achieve a certain fraction θ of the long-term effect is

$$\frac{f(1 - \lambda) + \lambda(1 - \lambda^{T-1})}{f(1 - \lambda) + \lambda} \geq \theta. \tag{2.37}$$

Two common values for f are 1 and ½. When $f=1$, reduces to

$$1 - \lambda^T \geq \theta \quad \text{or} \quad T \geq \frac{\log(1 - \theta)}{\log(\lambda)}. \tag{2.38}$$

Table 2-10. Half-Life versus Retention Rate

Half life	1	2	3	4	5	6	7	8
$f = 1$	0.500	0.707	0.794	0.841	0.871	0.891	0.906	0.917
$f = \frac{1}{2}$	0.334	0.640	0.761	0.821	0.858	0.882	0.899	0.912
Half life	9	10	11	12	13	14	15	16
$f = 1$	0.926	0.933	0.939	0.944	0.948	0.952	0.955	0.958
$f = \frac{1}{2}$	0.922	0.930	0.936	0.942	0.948	0.950	0.953	0.956

With $f = \frac{1}{2}$, it becomes

$$\frac{1 + \lambda - 2\lambda^T}{1 + \lambda} \geq \theta \quad \text{or} \quad T \geq \frac{log\left(\frac{(1+\lambda)(1-\theta)}{2}\right)}{log(\lambda)}. \tag{2.39}$$

A common benchmark is the *half-life* (HL) of a marketing effort, the time by which a marketing action has had half of its total effect, i.e., T when $\theta = \frac{1}{2}$ (median).[1] The relation between half-life and retention rate is shown in Table 2-10. An analyst or manager can estimate the half-life for a product is based on experience. The manager could then use this table to estimate the retention rate (or vice versa). Thus, if the manager believed that the half-life was 4 weeks and that the "first week counts half" convention should be used, then the estimate for the retention rate would be 0.821. Most practitioners round off the retention rate to the nearest tenth, i.e., 0.8, when using this subjective judgment approach. We prefer to estimate the retention rate from data; for example, see Broadbent (1999, p. 47).

What do adstocks look like? Consider the last burst of advertising for Persil Wash-up Liquid shown in Figure 2-3. The associated adstocks for half-lives of two and six weeks are shown in Figure 2-4. For more on modeling with adstock, see Broadbent (1997, pp. 153-166).

---

[1] When Naik (1999) addressed the half-life of an advertisement, he was not talking about the duration of advertising effect once advertising pressure is removed. Rather, he was talking about the wear out of advertising effectiveness when advertising pressure is on. He examined Levi Strauss's "Nice Pants" ad campaign, which was designed to influence adult men to buy casual Dockers khaki pants. He found that the half-life of this copy was 3 months whereas the 90% duration of advertising approximately 36 months.

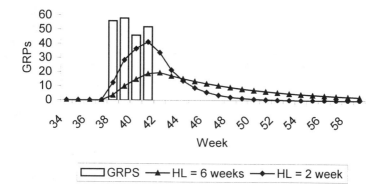

Figure 2-4. Adstocks from a Flight of 212 GRPs

Authors' Note: In *Admap* (May 1998, pp. 39-40), Paul Baker and Bryan Smith argued that adstock is out of date. They advocated using *effective frequency* instead of aggregate response models. The effective frequency is something like the X plus cover (level of exposures) in Y weeks (defined period of recency). For United Kingdom, one might have

OTC Distribution

Percent of Target Seeing Advertisements

TVRs	*1+*	*2+*	*3+*	*4+*	*6+*
100	56	26	11	4	1
200	71	47	31	19	8
300	77	58	43	32	18
400	81	65	52	42	26
600	86	73	62	55	39
200/400	14	38	68	120	225
300/600	12	26	44	72	117

Source: Baker (1999) in a personal communication.

By converting GRPs into levels of exposure, it is possible to test alternative scenarios. They find that it is nearly always necessary to have a recent exposure to generate a sales response; memory or decayed GRPs are not adequate. Where advertising generates sales, this also leads to changes in habit and repeat purchase. A debate between Simon Broadbent, who champions adstock and situation-specific marketing and Erwin Ephron, who favors a simple recency model, can be found in Ephron and Broadbent (1999). The focus is on media planning, not market response modeling.

II MARKET RESPONSE IN STATIONARY MARKETS

3 DESIGN OF STATIC RESPONSE MODELS

The design of response models involves variables, relations among variables, functional forms, and data. Variables represent the building blocks of a response study. An analysis of price elasticity, for example, would require at least two variables, price and unit sales. Relations are the connections among variables. To answer a question about the magnitude of price elasticity, it would be necessary to examine the special relation of price to unit sales. Functional form refers to the nature of a relation. One form of a relation between price and sales could be linear; a form like this would give both mathematical and substantive meaning to the relation. Finally, data are the actual realizations of variables. Taken together, these four elements provide the materials for building a response model.

In the last chapter we discussed variables and data. This chapter examines relations and functional forms. We first look at how relations among variables can be established and then at how each such relation can be made concrete by stating its functional form. At each step of the model building process, we report on research that establishes best practice procedures.

Relations Among Variables

Suppose a brand manager is interested in how the marketing mix variables affect sales for a product. A single relation—the sales response function—might be all that is necessary to model market response. Sales, the dependent variable, may be determined by a set of explanatory variables, say advertising and price, which represent the brand's marketing mix. The set of explanatory variables might be expanded to include environmental variables, which themselves might represent competitors' actions and relevant autonomous environmental variables such as interest rates. This situation is not very different from the simple sales response models discussed in Chapter 1. But what if the brand manager needed to understand the marketing system in more detail? The detail would help in managing all aspects of the brand's performance from marketing mix decisions to channel and customer relationships. In that case the multiple relations of a market mechanism would be the preferred modeling approach (Parsons 1981).

Models of Market Mechanisms

With a model of a market mechanism, not only will there be a sales response function, but there also may be supply curves, competitive reaction functions, vertical market structures, other behavioral relations, and cost functions. There also may be identities, for example, market shares adding to one. A market mechanism specifies the connections among these relations as well as among individual variables.

Supply Curves. The market mechanisms specified in marketing applications usually do not take into account *supply effects of demand*. This implies a horizontal supply curve; that is, increasing demand has no effect on *market-clearing price*, where supply and demand are equal. See Figure 3-1.[1] In particular, supplies for most agricultural products are predetermined for any fixed period less than a year (Forker and Ward 1993, p. 166). Thus, the price of a commodity is dependent on available market supplies. The assumption of a horizontal supply curve is a modeling convenience but may not be unrealistic, especially in the short run. For example, cheese sales in the New York City market were modeled using only a single equation because of the large dairy surpluses at the time (Kinnucan and Fearon 1986). In sum, a zero correlation between price and the error term in the sales response function is usually assumed. Moreover, advertising-induced shifts in the demand curve are often assumed not to influence price.

Competitive Behavior. In many situations, a firm must be able to forecast the levels for competitors' marketing instruments and other environmental variables. If competitors make their decisions without regard to the firm's actions, then time series

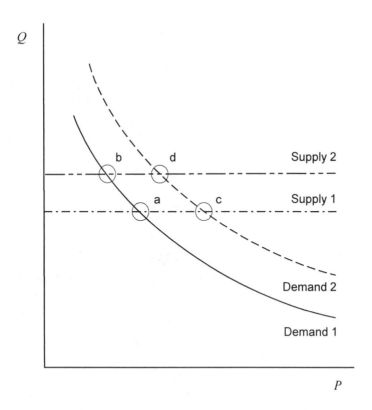

Figure 3-1. Supply Effects *Source*: Adapted from Forker and Ward 1993, p. 167.

analysis might be used to project future values for their marketing activities (see Chapter 6). If competitors react to the firm's actions, then reaction functions should be taken into account (see Chapter 4). If both the firm and its competitors are simultaneously trying to optimize their results in light of their opponents' likely behaviors, then game theory might be appropriate (see discussion on embedded competition in Chapter 9). This was the approach taken in an empirical analysis of competitive product line pricing (Kadiyali, Vilcassim, and Chintagunta 1996).

Vertical Market Structures. Most firms do not sell directly to their customers. Usually one or more intermediaries exist in a channel of distribution. Each channel member has its own sales response function. For example, the effectiveness and profitability of trade promotions was studied using a market mechanism containing two relations, one for shipments and another for consumer sales (Blattberg and Levin 1987). Factory shipments will respond to trade promotions by increasing sharply during the interval when an allowance is given on product purchases; shipments will fall markedly after the promotion is over. A similar pattern occurs just before a major price increase as the trade stocks up on a product at the existing price. Peaks and valleys in retail sales occur in response to the presence or absence of temporary sales promotions such as price features, special displays, and coupons. The dynamics of warehouse withdrawals tend to be smoother than factory shipments and retail sales according to Findley and Little (1980). They argued that this smoothing is mainly due to the buffer effect of retail inventories. We formally discuss lead and lag effects in Chapter 4.

Trade and retail promotions generate temporary sales gains. The decisions of channel members, especially retailers, more importantly affect a brand's base sales performance. A key retailer decision is how much space to allocate to a brand. In order for an established brand to earn a permanent increase in retail space, it must first increase its sales by other means, such as product reformulation and consistent theme advertising. Increased sales are often then rewarded by a greater share of retail space. In turn, the greater share of retail space can itself generate further sales gains. For example, by the mid-90s PepsiCo Foods International's Walkers Crisps (potato chips) had become the single largest food brand in the UK. Separate econometric models were constructed for each of its trade channels: grocery and impulse. The grocery channel covered large supermarket chains, minor multiples, and coops. The impulse channel covered a large variety of smaller outlets from independent grocers to garages to off-licenses. Each model contained two equations. In the grocery channel, share of volume and share of front stocks were jointly determined in a simultaneous system. In the impulse channel, the equations explained total volume and aggregate pack distribution ("Walkers Crisps" in Duckworth 1997).

Other Behavioral Relations. Managerial decision rules may govern marketing mix actions. Early on we noted the possible use of managerial decision rules, such as percent of sales, for setting advertising expenditures. Occasionally, the price-mark-up behavior of channel members is of interest. This is the case, for instance, in assessing the wholesale- and farm-level impacts of generic advertising. For example, the price-mark-up behavior of processors was modeled in a study of farm-raised catfish (Zidak, Kinnucan, and Hatch 1992, p. 962).

Comprehensive management-oriented models of the salesforce are used to determine the importance of personal selling in relation to other marketing instruments, to allocate selling effort across customers, geographic areas, or products, to set salesforce size, and to make other decisions required for managing the salesforce. A sales response function is a necessary building block for any decision model for salesforce resource management. A second relation should be specified describing the current managerial decision rule for resource allocation. Otherwise the direction of causality is unclear. By this we mean that empirical results may indicate that sales volume in a district is related to the number of salespeople employed by the company in the district, but we want to be sure that this relation is indeed the sales response function and not simply a replication of a decision rule that assigned the number of salespeople to a district based on sales in that district.

In a related example involving the evaluation of salesperson performance, a two-step model might be useful (Ryans and Weinberg 1979). The first relation would specify factors such as the ability to plan and organize time and work that influence the amount of effort a salesperson puts forth while the second relation would represent the impact of a salesperson's selling effort on sales.

Cost Functions. In many applications, a product's cost per unit, exclusive of marketing costs, is assumed to be constant. This is a satisfactory approximation in most circumstances. However, there are times when more attention should be given to the cost function. For instance, price promotions typically cause both consumer sales and factory shipments to be uneven. Irregular factory shipments often mean higher production or inventory costs. Another exception occurs in the case of technological innovations, including those for consumer durables. For these products, total unit costs usually decline, as experience with producing a product is gained (Hall and Howell 1985). Total unit costs also tend to decline in response to competitive entry. As new brands enter a market, the resultant growth of industry output forces prices downward, and consequently, costs must be reduced if profitability is to be maintained (Devinney 1987).

In this chapter, we simplify our discussion by emphasizing relations that describe actions that have effects only in the same period, that is, *static models*. In Chapters 4, 6, and 7, we will address the special features of relations that describe the impact of past actions on the present or current actions on the future, that is, *dynamic models*.

Structure of Competition

To this point, we have described markets in terms of channels of distribution. In addition, the structure of competition must be taken into account. Markets are usually made up of many brands and product forms offered by the same firms and by different competitors. To omit similar brands from a "brand group," say sliced and natural cheese, would be an *omission error*. The consulting firm Media Market Assessment (MMA) has found that advertising for the former increases sales of the latter.[2] On the other hand, not all seemingly-similar brands *should* be grouped. A *commission error* would occur if brands were grouped that differ on positioning, say low-fat and regular sliced cheese.

Most highly-competitive markets can be broken into brands and product forms and described as a hierarchy. A hierarchical tree can have any number of layers corresponding to customer choices, such as brand name, variety, package size, or price point. Customers might select a brand first, then a product form, in which case we have a product dominant hierarchy, or customers might pick a product form first, then pick a brand, in which case we have a product dominant hierarchy. The number of unique hierarchical trees in a market that can be differentiated on l layers is $l!$, assuming that there are no interactions among the levels. Our presumption is that there is more competition within branches of a hierarchical tree than between branches.

Moreover, the competition between brands/products may not be symmetric, that is, one company's actions may affect another's sales, but that company's actions may have little effect on its own sales. We will call this *market structure asymmetry*. Asymmetric competitive effects can arise for at least four reasons: (1) differences in marketing effectiveness, (2) differences in competitive vulnerability, i.e., relative positions in the market structure, (3) differences in marketing objectives, and (4) differences in timing of marketing efforts (Carpenter et al. 1988).

Separability

If there is a limited substitution between a product and other products, that product is assumed to represent a separable group for estimation purposes. For example, research has shown limited substitution between fish and meat products in general and, more specifically between catfish and other fish species, thus a response function can be constructed for catfish only (Zidack, Kinnucan, and Hatch 1992). Otherwise, the consumption system must be modeled. System-wide approaches are discussed briefly in Appendix 3-A.

Functional Forms

A relation is made concrete by specifying its functional form.[3] A functional form should exhibit the same properties as the relation is known to possess. Possible properties of a sales response function include what happens to sales when marketing effort is zero or very large; rate of change in sales as marketing activity increases, e.g., diminishing returns to scale; threshold effects like a minimum advertising investment; parameter variation, such as might occur over different market segments; and asymmetric response, such as a different magnitude of response to a decrease or increase in price. Reaction functions, since they usually represent decision rules, may be less complex. Response asymmetry and reaction functions as well as other dynamic issues will be discussed in Chapter 4.

Elasticity

One managerially useful attribute of sales response functions (and reaction functions) is the *elasticity* of effort. Elasticity expresses the relative change in one variable, in our case, sales volume Q, to relative change in another variable, for us, marketing effort X:

$$\varepsilon_X \equiv \frac{\partial Q}{Q} \Big/ \frac{\partial X}{X} = \frac{\partial Q}{\partial X} \times \frac{X}{Q}. \tag{3.1}$$

Because elasticity is dimensionless, a manager can compare an elasticity of a product in one country with that in another even though the countries use different weight and monetary systems.

Sometimes, especially when exploring changes in the effectiveness of sales drivers over the maturation of a market, the component parts of elasticities must be considered individually. In particular, focusing solely on elasticities may mask important offsetting movements in the *response sensitivity*[4] and *marketing-sales ratio*:

$$\frac{\partial Q}{\partial X} \text{ and } \frac{X}{Q}, \tag{3.2}$$

respectively. For example, a frequently purchased pharmaceutical in West Germany saw its sales volume increase more than six fold between the growth stage and the maturity stage while its price fell 12%. Yet its price response sensitivity increased by only slightly more than 2.5 times. The net effect was its price elasticity dropped by about a third (Simon 1979, p. 449). The message is that trends in relative and absolute measures of marketing effectiveness may be different. For a detailed discussion, see Andrews and Franke (1996).

Shape of a Sales Response Function

Marketing effort is represented by levels of the sales drivers. The shape of sales response to any of these drivers, holding the other factors affecting sales constant, is generally concave (downward). In a few instances, it may be convex or *S*-shaped. If the marketing driver has a relatively limited operating range, then a linear model often provides a satisfactory approximation to the true relation. Thus, empirical adequacy and analytic tractability may justify a linear specification. For example, see the investigation of competitive interactions among firms in a personal-care product category (Vilcassim, Kadiyali, and Chintagunta 1999). A linear model may suffice if the modeling goal is primarily to provide managers with directional guidance, for example, to advertise more heavily on Sunday (Bhattacharya and Lodish 1994).

Constant Returns to Scale. When sales always increase by a constant amount to equivalent constant increases in marketing effort, a sales response curve is said to exhibit constant returns to scale.[5]

Functional Forms. The simplest response model is the *linear* model:

$$Q = \beta_0 + \beta_1 X. \tag{3.3}$$

Changing effort by one unit changes sales volume by β_1 units. Its elasticity is

$$\varepsilon_X = \frac{\partial Q}{Q} \bigg/ \frac{\partial X}{X} = \frac{\partial Q}{\partial X} \times \frac{X}{Q} = \beta_1 \times \frac{X}{Q} = \frac{\beta_1 X}{\beta_0 + \beta_1 X} \tag{3.4}$$

Thus, in a linear model, the elasticity depends on the level of effort X. To get a single value for the elasticity, one uses the average value of X, its most recent value, or finds the elasticity for each observed X and then calculates the average elasticity. Linear functions have been used to study the impact of sales drivers on market share and volume (Banks 1961 and Lambert 1968, respectively); to examine promotional effects on intra- and inter-brand performance (Moriarty 1985c); to illustrate using regression analysis to investigate the effects on instant coffee sales of promotion, including features, displays, and temporary price cuts (Blattberg and Neslin 1990, pp. 197-204); and to investigate (dynamic) promotional effects on market share (Leeflang, Mijatovic, and Saunders 1992).

Comment. Before going further, a warning is necessary. The terms linear and nonlinear are used in two different ways in market response modeling. First, in the design of response models, linear refers to the functional form (3.3). Other functional forms are nonlinear. Second, in the estimation of unknown parameters, linear refers to all models that are *linear in the parameters*. This means that the derivatives of the functional form with respect to the parameters do not depend on the parameters. A linear functional form is obviously linear in its parameters and can be estimated by linear regression. The real distinction exists when a functional form, such as the quadratic (3.33), is nonlinear in shape but nonetheless linear in its parameters and thus able to be estimated by linear regression. Other nonlinear functional forms may be transformable into linear versions and again able to be estimated by linear regression. For example, the power model (3.11) can be made linear in its parameters by taking the logarithms (to the base e) of both sides of the equation. To distinguish between the two versions in such cases, the original model is designated the *structural model* and the second model the *estimation model*. Estimation is covered in Chapter 5. Some models are intrinsically nonlinear and must be estimated by nonlinear methods.

A linear model is frequently tried first not only because it is easy to estimate, but also because it provides a reasonable approximation to an underlying nonlinear sales function when observations are available only over a limited range. Thus, a linear model may not lead to *locally* different conclusions, a point made by Broadbent (1984) among others. While adequate for asking "what if" questions around the current operating range, the linear model may be very misleading if one strays very far from this range as might be the case in trying to find the optimal level of effort.

Before leaving linear models, let's look at how a qualitative variable might enter (3.3) operationalized as a dummy variable. For example, suppose that there is a news report that generates a lot of publicity about a key ingredient of your product and one wants to know its impact. Two dummy variables could be constructed. The pre-announcement dummy would take on the value 1 before the announcement and the value 0 afterward while the post-announcement dummy would take the value 0 before the announcement and the value 1 after the announcement. The announcement could have no effect, could shift the demand curve, could change the response to marketing actions, or both. Sales response to one market driver could be written as

$$Q_t = \beta_{0,pre}D_{pre} + \beta_{0,post}D_{post} + \beta_{1,pre}\left(D_{pre}X_t\right) + \beta_{1,post}\left(D_{post}X_t\right). \tag{3.5}$$

This formulation would require suppressing the intercept in the regression program. In addition, it would require additional calculations to determine whether there were statistically significant differences in the intercepts and slopes between the two conditions. Thus, an equivalent formulation is usually used:

$$Q_t = \beta_0(1) + \delta_0 D_{Post} + \beta_1 X_t + \delta_1\left(D_{Post}X_t\right). \tag{3.6}$$

Because this model includes an intercept, only one dummy variable is needed to represent the two conditions. Here we have chosen the post-period dummy because we want to know if the post period is different from the pre period but the other dummy variable could have been chosen instead. The coefficients of variables involving the dummy variable now represent changes (see Figure 3-2). Regression output shows whether the changes themselves are statistically significant or not. The changes may be positive or negative. For example, when original medical findings indicated that bran was good for you, the sales and effectiveness of advertising for ready-to-eat bran cereals went up. However, when these findings were later contradicted, sales and advertising effectiveness fell. A real-world application of dummy variables is given in the *Dell Industry Perspective*.

Dummy variables are often used to represent seasonality. For example, a linear quarterly sales response model might be expressed as

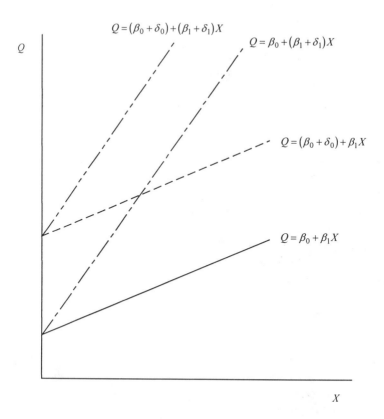

Figure 3-2. Dummy Variable Formulation in a Linear Model

$$Q_t = \beta_0(1) + \delta_{02}D_2 + \delta_{03}D_3 + \delta_{04}D_4 \\ + \beta_1 X_t + \delta_{12}(D_2 X_t) + \delta_{13}(D_3 X_t) + \delta_{14}(D_4 X_t). \tag{3.7}$$

Because this model includes an intercept, only three dummy variables are needed to represent the four quarters. The impact of one of the quarters, in this case the first, will be captured by this intercept. The other dummy variables will measure shifts from this (first-quarter) base. The coefficients δ_{02}, δ_{03}, δ_{04} capture shifts of the intercept β_0, and the coefficients δ_{12}, δ_{13}, δ_{14} capture shifts of the slope β_1. There is an inherently high degree of collinearity between seasonal intercept and seasonal slope variables for the same time period, which sometimes results in an inability to distinguish between the two forms of seasonal influence (Wildt 1977). Collinearity is discussed in Chapter 5.

**Measuring the Impact of Positive Public Relations and Awards
in Dell's Consumer Segment.**

Dell Computer Corp is the leading direct marketer of PC's in the world. As is customary in consumer direct marketing companies, the business model is generally pull based, relying on advertising-driven lead generation. Customers read ads placed in magazines, TV, newspapers and other media vehicles and call in on toll-free 800 telephone numbers to make a purchase. A common technique utilized in this industry is the assignment of unique 800 numbers on individual media sources to determine their call response and cost–effectiveness; a privilege enjoyed only by direct marketers to test advertising efficacy in real time.

Since call volumes are highly correlated to unit sales, substantial efforts in predictive modeling are conducted to analyze the business process and track the efficiency of the levers of lead generation. Stated formulaically,

$$\text{call volume} = f\left(\begin{array}{l}\text{quality of product offer, brand awareness, price,}\\ \text{advertising spend, reach of the marketing vehicles,}\\ \text{and disposable income of the target market}\end{array}\right).$$

Measurement of all these drivers, and their resultant elasticities, is imperative to help determine how these critical levers impact the business cycle. Nonetheless, certain seemingly intangible attributes, such as reputation of the vendor and quality of product, are often most significant factors in the consumer purchase decision. Yet they are more difficult to quantitatively define and thus measure. To this end, a PR/Awards (proxy) variable greatly helps to explain differing call volume levels among trade journals and magazines.

Since the marketplace is essentially a product-driven environment, awards and company-specific features in trade publications, computer and general media help drive in incremental leads and in many cases may be the determinant criterion in the consideration/trial process. For example, the December edition of *PC Magazine*, which featured a Dell product as an "EDITORS CHOICE AWARD" would be more effective as a lead generation vehicle than would the issue without the award owing to the positive messaging. To better understand and manage this phenomenon, we have attempted to quantify its dimensions and incorporate them in the following function in explaining lead lift generated from a particular magazine or trade journal (normalized for seasonality and circulation levels):

$$\text{leads generated by unique insertion} = f \begin{pmatrix} \text{the publication, awards, mentions, cover} \\ \text{presence, features, negative / positive} \\ \text{review versus competition, size of} \\ \text{the review, and the location where it} \\ \text{appeared in the publication} \end{pmatrix}.$$

By regressing leads generated against all the above binary-coded [dummy] variables in the linear regression model, we are able to measure significant levers that explain the variation in leads lift. The regressors are significant at the 95% level. Moreover, the results all make intuitive sense and have helped quantitatively prove many hypotheses, and at the same time provided us with direction as to the hierarchy of levers in the PR process.

Prepared by Jay Srinivasan, Senior Marketing Manager at Dell. He holds an MBA degree from the Wharton School.

Diminishing Returns to Scale. When sales always increase with increases in marketing effort, but each additional unit of marketing effort brings less in incremental sales than the previous unit did, a sales response curve is said to exhibit diminishing returns to scale. Several functional forms can be used to represent this phenomenon.

Functional Forms. One concave sales response function is the *semilogarithmic model:*

$$Q = \beta_0 + \beta_1 \ln X, \quad X > exp\left(\frac{-\beta_0}{\beta_1}\right). \tag{3.8}$$

The restriction on X ensures that sales will be nonnegative. Constant *absolute* increments in sales require constant *percentage* increases in marketing effort:

$$\partial Q = \beta_1 \frac{\partial X}{X}, \tag{3.9}$$

which also shows the diminishing returns to scale over the whole range of X, and

$$\varepsilon_X = \frac{\partial Q}{\partial X} \times \frac{X}{Q} = \frac{\beta_1}{X} \times \frac{X}{\beta_0 + \beta_1 \ln X} = \frac{\beta_1}{\beta_0 + \beta_1 \ln X}. \tag{3.10}$$

Semilog models have been used to model sales response to advertising for branded consumer products (Lambin 1969 and Wildt 1977), to automobile advertising by a General Motors dealership (Helmuth 1987), to multiproduct advertising for the merchandise lines of a leading European variety store (Doyle and Saunders 1990), and to retail prices for ground coffee (Kalyanam 1996). This model was elaborated upon in a (dynamic) study of wearout and pulsation (Simon 1982).

Another functional form that meets this requirement, provided that $0 < \beta_1 < 1$, is the *power model*:

$$Q = e^{\beta_0} X^{\beta_1}, \quad X > 0, \tag{3.11}$$

This model has the attractive property that the power coefficient of the marketing instrument can be directly interpreted as that instrument's elasticity.

$$\varepsilon_X = \frac{\partial Q}{\partial X} \times \frac{X}{Q} = \beta_1 e^{\beta_0} X^{\beta_1 - 1} \frac{X}{e^{\beta_0} X^{\beta_1}} = \beta_1. \tag{3.12}$$

Thus it is known as the *constant elasticity model*. This model can be transformed into a model that is linear in the parameters by taking the logarithms of both sides:

$$\ln[Q] = \beta_0 + \beta_1 \ln[X], \quad Q, X > 0.^6 \tag{3.13}$$

This is known as the *double-log model* or *linear-in-logs model*.[7] Thus, one sometimes sees (3.11) written as

$$Q = exp(\beta_0 + \beta_1 \ln[X]). \tag{3.14}$$

The power model can be extended to take into account all the *interactions* among marketing decision variables. The most general version of this model for three marketing instruments is

$$\begin{aligned} Q = {} & e^{\beta_0} + e^{\beta_{01}} X_1^{\beta_1} + e^{\beta_{02}} X_2^{\beta_2} + e^{\beta_{03}} X_3^{\beta_3} \\ & + e^{\beta_{12}} X_1^{\beta_3} X_2^{\beta_4} + e^{\beta_{13}} X_1^{\beta_5} X_3^{\beta_6} + e^{\beta_{23}} X_2^{\beta_1} X_3^{\beta_1} + e^{\beta_{123}} X_1^{\beta_9} X_2^{\beta_{10}} X_3^{\beta_{11}}. \end{aligned} \tag{3.15}$$

The full interaction model can quickly become unwieldy when all the possible interactions among marketing decision variables are taken into account. Because of small sample sizes or estimation problems, this model is usually simplified by having some of the parameters equal each other and often equal 0 or 1 as well. Prasad and Ring (1976), for example, looked at four main effects plus only the six pairwise interactions.

The most popular sales response function retains only the highest-order interaction, i.e.,

$$Q = e^{\beta_0} X_1^{\beta_1} X_2^{\beta_2} \cdots X_J^{\beta_J}. \tag{3.16}$$

This model is known as the *multiplicative model*. It maintains the property of (3.11) that the power parameters can be interpreted directly as elasticities. Thus, it is also known as the constant elasticity model (and its estimation form, the double log model). Multiplicative models have commonly been used to represent sales response to advertising of frequently purchased branded goods (Bass and Parsons 1969, Lambin 1976, and many others). These models have been used to estimate response to generic advertising as well, for instance, in the Australian meat industry (Piggott et al. 1996). Such models have also been used to find price elasticities for brands-package sizes; for example, of refrigerated orange juice (Montgomery and Rossi 1999), or of industry demand; for example, for wine types (Shapouri, Folwell, and Baritelle 1981). Multiplicative functional forms have also been specified for the relations in an econometric model of recruitment marketing in the U.S. Navy (Hanssens and Levien 1983), in a planning and performance assessment of industrial trade shows (Gopalakrishna and Williams 1992), and in an examination of how the stage of the product life cycle in which brands of ethical drugs enter the market affect their sales (Shankar, Carpenter, and Krishnamurthi 1999).

When there is only a single instrument, then (3.15) reduces to only its first two terms. If, in addition, β_1 lies between 0 and 1, the resultant model is called the *fractional-root model*. A special case of the fractional-root model is the *square-root model*, in which $\beta_1 = \frac{1}{2}$. Another special case is the *power model* (3.11), for which β_0 in (3.15) equals minus infinity and consequently the additive constant disappears.

Comment. The dummy variable approach may also be used in a multiplicative formulation but the dummy variables must appear as exponents; otherwise, sales would always be zero when any dummy variable's value was zero. For example, a quarterly multiplicative (double-log) sales response function could be written as

$$Q_t = e^{\beta_0 + \delta_{02} D_2 + \delta_{03} D_3 + \delta_{04} D_4} X_t^{\beta_1 + \delta_{12} D_2 + \beta_{13} D_3 + \beta_{14} D_4}, \tag{3.17}$$

where the model is semi-log with respect to the dummy indicator variables However, one is more likely to see it written as

$$Q_t = e^{\beta_0} \gamma_{02}^{D_2} \gamma_{03}^{D_3} \gamma_{04}^{D_4} X_t^{\beta_1 + \beta_{12} D_2 + \beta_{13} D_3 + \beta_{14} D_4}. \tag{3.18}$$

where the coefficients γ_1, γ_2, γ_3 are required to be positive and are called *multipliers*. Multipliers are used to represent the effects of other dummy variables as well, most notably features and displays. Applications of these dummy variable formulations can be found in Kalyanam (1996) and Shankar and Krishnamurthi (1996). The best known application is ACNiesen's SCAN*PRO model shown in the boxed insert.

Empirical Evidence. The preponderance of empirical evidence favors the strictly concave sales response to nonprice marketing decision variables. This is especially true for mass media advertising of frequently purchased goods. For instance, Lambin (1976, p. 95), after doing an analysis of 107 individual brands from 16 product classes and eight different countries of Western Europe, concluded that

> the shape of the advertising response curve is concave downward, i.e., that there is no *S*-curve and no increasing returns in advertising a given brand by a given firm.

Earlier, Simon (1970, pp. 8-22) had surveyed the evidence then available on the shape of the response function and found that

> both sales and psychological [non-sales measures of behavior] suggest that the shape of the advertising-response function is invariably concave downward, i.e., that there is no *S*-curve....

Other reviews also indicated diminishing returns to advertising (Simon and Arndt 1980 and Aaker and Carman 1982). There are several reasons to expect diminishing returns to increased advertising expenditures (Jagpal, Sudit, and Vinod 1979). For one, the fraction of unreached prospects is progressively reduced as advertising increases. Consequently, most of the impact of additional advertising messages at high levels of advertising takes place by means of increased frequency. Moreover, after a small number of exposures, perhaps as few as three, increased frequency has very limited marginal effectiveness. Grass and Wallace (1969), among others, have reported on the satiation effects of television commercials. Ottesen (1981) proposed a theory of the individual's purchase response function, and on the basis of this theory, he concluded,

> as advertising effort is being increased, returns in sales must generally be expected to diminish.

The ACNielsen SCAN*PRO Model

SCAN*PRO enables a marketing manager to understand a brand's responsiveness to promotions. ACNielsen databases hold weekly scanner information from key grocery chains, coupled with observational information of the in-store promotional environment. SCAN*PRO is widely used by industry—over one thousand commercial applications.

$$
Q_{ik[c]t} = \left[\prod_{j=1}^{\text{brands}} \left\{ \left(\frac{P_{jk[c]t}}{\tilde{P}_{jk[c]}} \right)^{\beta_{ijk[c]}} \prod_{l=1}^{3} \gamma_{ljk[c]}^{D_{ljk[c]t}} \right\} \right] \left[\prod_{\tau=1}^{51\text{weeks}} \delta_{ik[c]\tau}^{X_{k[c]\tau}} \right] \left[\prod_{s=1}^{\text{stores}} \lambda_{is[c]}^{Z_{is[c]t}} \right] e^{\nu_{ik[c]t}}
$$

where

$Q_{ik[c]t}$ = unit sales (e.g., kilograms) for brand i in store k [chain c], week t;

$P_{jk[c]t}$ = unit price for brand j in store k [chain c], week t

$\tilde{P}_{jk[c]t}$ = the (median) regular unit price (based on nonpromoted weeks) for brand j in store k [chain c];

$D_{1jk[c]t}$ = an indicator variable for feature advertising: 1 if brand j is featured (but *not* displayed) by store k [chain c], week t; 0 otherwise;

$D_{2jk[c]t}$ = an indicator variable for display: 1 if brand j is displayed (but *not* featured) by store k [chain c], week t; 0 otherwise;

$D_{3jk[c]t}$ = an indicator variable for simultaneous use of feature *and* display: 1 if brand j is featured *and* displayed by store k [chain c], week t; 0 otherwise;

$X_{k[c]\tau(t)}$ = a weekly indicator variable for store k [chain c]: 1 if observation is in week $\tau(t)$; 0 otherwise;

$Z_{k[c]t}$ = an indicator variable for store k: 1 if the observation is from store i; 0 otherwise;

$\beta_{ijk[c]}$ = the own price (deal) elasticity if $j=i$, or cross price elasticity if $j\neq i$, in store k, chain c;

γ_{1ict} = the own feature multiplier if $j=i$, or the cross-display multiplier if $j\neq i$, in store k, chain c;

$Z_{k[c]t}$ = the own display multiplier if $j=i$, or the cross-display multiplier if $j\neq i$ in store k, chain c;

γ_{3ict} = the own display and feature multiplier if $j=i$, or the cross-display and feature multiplier if $j\neq i$;

δ_{ict} = the (seasonal) multiplier for chain c, week t, when the criterion variable represents brand i;

$\lambda_{ik[c]}$ = the store intercept for store k [chain c];

$\upsilon_{ik[c]t}$ = a disturbance term for brand i in store k [chain c], week t

Academic research using the SCAN*PRO model includes Wittink et al. (1988), Foekens, Leeflang, and Wittink (1994, 1999), Christen et al. (1997), Kopalle, Mela, and Marsh (1999), and van Heerde, Leeflang, and Wittink (2001).

Increasing Returns to Scale. Although sales response to most marketing variables exhibits diminishing returns to scale, sales response to decreases in price may exhibit increasing returns to scale. One functional form that can be used is the *exponential model*:

$$Q = e^{\beta_0} e^{\beta_1 X}. \tag{3.19}$$

Price would typically be represented as $1/P$. For example, the effect of coupon face value on brand sales for the coupon-prone segment of a market can be written as (Leone and Srinivasan 1996, p. 280):

$$Q = exp\left(\beta_0 + \frac{\beta_1}{P - V\theta^\tau} \right) \quad \text{with } 0 \leq \theta \leq 1, \tag{3.20}$$

where P is actual shelf price, V is the value of the coupon for the brand, and τ is the number of weeks since the coupon was dropped. The parameter θ captures the decay effect of the coupon drop. Thus, the last term in the denominator is a measure of *couponstock* for a single drop.

Alternatively, in the special case of pricing models, this functional form is often expressed as

$$Q = e^{\beta_0} e^{-\beta_1 P} = Q^o e^{-\beta_1 P}, \quad \beta_1 > 0, \tag{3.21}$$

where Q^o is saturation sales. When price becomes large, sales tend to zero. This functional form has been used to explain the United Kingdom market for cars in terms of quality-adjusted price (Cowling and Cubbin 1971), to assess the effect of trade promotions on factory shipments (Blattberg and Levin 1987), to model household purchase quantity as a function of price (Krishnamurthi and Raj 1988), to explore asymmetric patterns of price competition (Blattberg and Wisniewski 1989), to estimate retail-level price elasticities and cross-elasticities for waffles, bleach, tissue, and ketchup (Bolton 1989b), and to represent the impact of air fares on the number of seats sold (Carpenter and Hanssens 1994).

A chain/price-zone level model developed on Jewel Food Stores, the leading grocery store chain in Chicago, is especially well known (Blattberg and Wisniewski 1989, p. 299):

$$Q_i = exp\left[\beta_0 - \beta_1 PR_i + \beta_2 \left(\frac{PR_i - PA_i}{PR_i} \right) - \sum_{j \neq i} \frac{\beta_{ij}}{PA_j} + \begin{array}{c} \text{other} \\ \text{factors} \end{array} \right], \tag{3.22}$$

where PR is the regular price, PA is the actual price, and the ratio in the parentheses is the deal discount percentage, D. It uses both of the price formulations mentioned above, one for the company's price and the other for competitors' prices. Many third-party models have been outgrowths of this model (Link 1995b, p. RC-8).

S-Shaped Response. Sometimes a response function might be S-shaped, more precisely "nicely convex-concave" functions (Ginsberg 1974). In such a formulation, sales initially may exhibit increasing returns to scale and then diminishing returns to higher levels of marketing effort.

Functional Forms. One functional form that meets this requirement is the *log-reciprocal (inverse) model:*

$$Q = exp\left(\beta_0 - \frac{\beta_1}{X} \right), \quad \beta_0, \beta_1 > 0, \tag{3.23}$$

or

$$ln Q = \beta_0 - \frac{\beta_1}{X}. \tag{3.24}$$

This model has been considered in a study of the advertising threshold effect (Bemmaor 1984) and in an investigation of the impact of the number of staff on apparel store sales (Lam, Vandenbosch, and Pearce 1998, p. 64). The inflection point, the point at which the change from increasing to decreasing marginal returns occurs, is $X = \beta_1/2$.[8] Even though the response function is S-shaped, the elasticity of the marketing instrument decreases as effort increases:

$$\varepsilon_X = \frac{\partial Q}{\partial X} \times \frac{X}{Q} = \frac{\beta_1 Q}{X^2} \times \frac{X}{Q} = \frac{\beta_1}{X}. \tag{3.25}$$

Another S-shaped functional form is the *Gompertz growth model*:

$$Q = \beta_0 \beta_1^{-\beta_2 \beta_1^{-\beta_3 X}}. \tag{3.26}$$

This model has been used to model the effect of shelf space on store sales (Drèze, Hoch, and Purk 1994, p. 313). Other S-shaped response functions are discussed next in the context of minimum and maximum sales potential.

Empirical Evidence. The shelf space study just mentioned examined eight product categories: analgesics, bottled juices, canned soup, canned seafood, cigarettes, dish detergents, frozen entrees, and refrigerated juices. The Gompertz function was statistically significant in all but one category. A typical profile was given by analgesics. Below 3 square inches, sales potential was virtually nonexistent, then increased sharply before leveling off at full potential at 15 square inches. At 10 square inches of display, a brand would reach 98 percent of its potential. The actual distribution of items across the size of displays was: below 10 square inches, 2.5 percent; between 10 and 20 square inches, 12 percent; and more than 20 square inches, 85.5 percent (with one percent more than 150 square inches!). Most items, therefore, had a number of facings in the flat portion of the S-curve, indicating that adding or removing a facing would not affect their sales. (Drèze, Hoch, and Purk 1994, p. 320).

An S-shaped sales response to advertising has long been conjectured (Zentler and Ryde 1956). However, this proposition has been rarely tested explicitly. Sales for two brands in the same product category were plotted separately against television gross rating points, which had been adjusted for adstock. These were important brands in a very large packaged-goods category. Data came from the 20 largest U.S. markets covering 1.5 years of weekly scanning and media data. One brand showed only diminishing returns to advertising. The other brand showed an S-shape, or possibly a threshold effect. At low levels of advertising there was virtually no response to advertising, after which, diminishing returns set in (Gold 1992). Some studies have

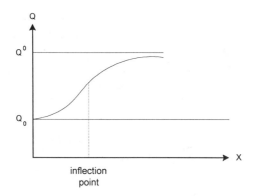

Figure 3-3. *S*-Shaped Response Function with Minimum and Maximum Sales

explored the proposition that the relation between *share* and advertising is *S*-shaped. The advertising effect for a women's hair spray was found to be concave rather than the proposed *S*-shape (Johansson 1973). An empirical test of a flexible communications response model for a mature industrial product yielded a concave rather than S-shaped function (Gopalakrishna and Chatterjee 1992, p. 191).

An ad hoc procedure was adopted to develop *S*-shaped response functions for five Lever brands (Rao and Miller 1975). This work seems suspect, however, since markets that were "out of line" were discarded. This meant that for the two brands discussed in detail, 27% and 20%, respectively, of the markets were omitted. Another study applied the same methodology (Eastlack and Rao 1986). Linear sales response to radio gross ratings points and television gross ratings points was estimated for each Selling Areas Marketing, Inc. (SAMI) market. Inspection of per capita estimates of marginal response to radio gross ratings points levels revealed no significant response below 180 GRPs (an indication of a threshold), a sharp increase in response as GRPs increased between 180 and 230 GRPs, a slight (almost flat) decline in response at GRPs increased from 230 to 340 (an indication of saturation), and low response to a few observations with GRPs above 400 (an indication of supersaturation?). These two works, unfortunately (because of their ad hoc nature), are the only published support for the existence of *S*-shaped response. Broadbent (1984, p. 310), in a discussion of the adstock model, reported that

> the uncertainty in the data makes it difficult, we would say from our experience impossible, to prove or disprove the reality of an *S*-shaped or step function.

The relation between market share and share of retail outlets might be *S*-shaped, but the evidence is mixed. For example, in a study on marketing of gasoline, incremental new outlets were substantially below average in gallonage until a certain share of market was achieved. Above this critical market share, performance improved markedly (Cardwell 1968). An S-shaped relation between share of market and share of outlets has also been postulated (Lilien and Rao 1976). Neither study provided empirical evidence supporting its claims. An analysis of the effect of market share on the distribution network of a major brand of gasoline in Italy supported the S-shaped hypothesis at the market share level (Naert and Bultez 1973). However, when the hypothesis was tested at the aggregate brand-switching level, it was rejected. In any event, the relation between market share and share of outlets may be simply an expression of the difference between demand and sales.

Implications. The lack of evidence for an S-shaped curve, perhaps caused by the early onset of diminishing returns, has important implications for shelf space management and the timing of advertising expenditures. In the first situation, the implication is that manufacturers, having achieved some shelf space, might receive a poor return on their investments in striving to gain additional shelf space and that retailers are likely to have been overgenerous in their shelf space allocations to individual brands.

In the second situation, an advertiser might want to choose between two alternative policies, a constant spending rate per period or a pulsed expenditure. A pulsing policy is defined as a pattern of advertising where periods with high advertising intensity alternate with very little or no advertising (Rao 1970, p. 55). A sufficient condition (Rao 1970, p. 5) for adopting a pulsing policy would be that the sales response function is S-shaped and the budget constraint be binding. The budget constraint has to require that the alternate constant rate policy be in the region of increasing returns to scale. But most empirical evidence says that a typical brand has a concave sales response function; consequently, the S-shape cannot be used to justify a pulsing policy.

Minimum Sales Potential. Even when marketing effort is zero, a firm might still have sales due to loyal buyers, captive buyers, or impulse buyers. Neither functional form (3.11) nor (3.23) allows for sales when marketing effort is zero. These functional forms can be modified by adding a positive constant, say K, to the functional form, as was done in (3.15), where $K = \exp(\beta_0)$. Metwally (1980) added a positive constant to (3.23). The resulting relation is intrinsically nonlinear. This relation is shown in Figure 3-3. Alternatively, a positive constant could be added to each marketing instrument. Predicted sales when marketing effort is zero, Q_o would be given by

$$Q_o = e^{\beta_0} K^{\beta_1} \text{ and } Q_o = e^{\beta_0 - \beta_1 / K}, \tag{3.27}$$

respectively, for (3.11) and (3.23). For convenience, K is often specified as 1.

Saturation. *Saturation* means that no matter how much marketing effort is expended, there is a finite achievable upper limit to the sales. Buyers become insensitive to the marketing stimulus or find themselves purchasing at their capacities or capabilities. The power model (3.11) does not have a finite upper limit, but the S-shaped model (3.23) does. As $X \to \infty, Q \to exp(\beta_0) \equiv Q^o$.

Functional Forms. The saturation level, Q^o, is explicitly represented in the *modified exponential model*:

$$Q = e^{\beta_0}\left(1 - e^{-\beta_1 X}\right) = Q^o\left(1 - e^{-\beta_1 X}\right). \tag{3.28}$$

This functional form has been used in an analysis of the optimal number of sales-people (Buzzell 1964a), for the study of advertising expenditures in coupled markets (Shakun 1965), in a probe of advertising budget allocation across territories (Holthausen and Assmus 1982), in an investigation of the effects of channel effort (Rangan 1987), in an assessment of resource allocation rules (Mantrala, Sinha, and Zoltners 1992), and in the examination of the impact of booth space, booth location, and number of personnel at the booth on industrial trade show performance (Gopalakrishna and Lilien 1995).

A *logistic model* can also depict an S-shaped function while taking into account market saturation. One version of the logistic function is

$$Q = \frac{Q^o}{1 + exp\left[-\left(\beta_0 + \sum_{j=1}^{J}\beta_j X_j\right)\right]}. \tag{3.29}$$

This relation can be rewritten as

$$ln\left(\frac{Q}{Q^o - Q}\right) = \beta_0 + \sum_{j=1}^{J}\beta_j X_j. \tag{3.30}$$

This S-shaped curve is symmetric around the inflection point, $Q = Q^o/2$.

A nonsymmetric S-shaped curve may be more appropriate in many marketing applications. One such logistic function would be

$$ln\left(\frac{Q - Q_o}{Q^o - Q}\right) = ln\,\beta_0 + \sum_{j=1}^{J}\beta_j\,ln\,X_j, \text{with } 0 \le Q_o \le Q^o, \tag{3.31}$$

where Q_o is the intercept. The independent variables are assumed to be positive. The dependent variable Q may vary between a lower limit Q_o and the saturation level Q^o.

The saturation level Q^o must be specified a priori in both the log-linear model (3.30) and the double-log model (3.31). In the latter model, the intercept must also be specified. When the dependent variable is a proportion such as market share, the most common assumption is that $Q^o = 1$ and $Q_o = 0$. Survey data were used to estimate the intercept and the saturation level for a new women's hair spray (Johansson 1973). The estimate of the intercept was the proportion of repeaters, and the estimate of the saturation level was the trial proportion.

When a priori information is not available, one must use a functional form that allows the intercept and saturation level to be estimated. One such functional form was used in the advertising budgeting model ADBUG (Little 1970):

$$Q = \beta_0 + (\beta_1 - \beta_0)\frac{X^{\beta_2}}{\beta_3^{\beta_2} + X^{\beta_2}},\tag{3.32}$$

where

$$\beta_0 = \text{intercept,}$$
$$\beta_1 = \text{saturation level,}$$
$$\beta_2, \beta_3 = \text{shape parameters.}$$

A dynamic version of this model was estimated for a mature industrial product (Gopalakrishna and Chatterjee 1992).

Empirical Evidence. The existence of a saturation level is universally accepted. Nonetheless, the saturation level is rarely explicitly modeled and measured. The usual procedure is to represent response by a function that allows any given level to be surpassed but requires increasing difficulty to exceed each higher level. Basic economics will dictate that a brand operate well away from saturation levels. This approach is probably adequate for use in decision models focusing on short-run marketing tactics; however, when interest is in long-term strategy, the saturation ceiling should be estimated.

One industry sales response function in which the saturation level was explicitly modeled was that for canned, single-strength grapefruit juice (Ward 1975). It used a reciprocal model (3.34). Saturation sales, Q^o, were estimated to be 69.82 million gallons. The highest sales that had been observed was 53.77 million gallons.

Supersaturation. Supersaturation results when too much marketing effort causes a negative response; for example, a buyer might feel that an excessive number of visits by a salesperson is intolerable.

Functional Forms. The simplest functional form that represents this effect is the *quadratic model*:

$$Q = \beta_0 + \beta_1 X - \beta_2 X^2. \tag{3.33}$$

The value of Q starts declining for values of $X > \beta_1/2\beta_2$.[1]

The notion of a supersaturation effect, excessive marketing effort causing negative sales, has been promulgated by Ackoff and his colleagues (Waid, Clark, and Ackoff 1956; Rao 1970; Ackoff and Emshoff 1975) and is being incorporated into marketing theory (Enis and Mokwa 1979). Still, the argument for advertising supersaturation is unconvincing. The only empirical evidence even tangentially bearing on the existence of such an effect comes from Ackoff's Budweiser study. While previous research, such as that of Parsons and Bass (1971), has shown that reducing advertising expenditures may increase profits even though sales are lost, the Budweiser study is the only research in which reducing advertising not only increases profits but also increases sales. In another beer test, those areas where advertising was stopped showed better results than the remaining areas (Haley 1978). However, subsequent investigation revealed that local distributors, upon finding their advertising support dropped, invested their own funds in advertising. Their efforts more than offset the cuts made by the manufacturer. Participants in the Budweiser study have asserted that adequate controls were maintained in their work; consequently, their results remain an anomaly. Even if supersaturation does exist, it is well outside the usual operating ranges for marketing instruments, since management has little incentive to operate, even at saturation. Of course, a firm could operate in this region by mistake.

A more plausible argument for supersaturation might be made for marketing decision variables other than advertising. For example, a reduction in sales force size might lead to more effort, and consequently sales, if territories and hence potential were realigned and salespeople were more highly motivated because of this. Also, it was reported in the business press that a major computer manufacturer increased its sales by decreasing the number of retail outlets carrying its personal computers. The explanation was that having fewer dealers resulted in less price competition, higher retail prices and hence increased margins, and thus more funds available to each retailer to support direct sales effort. Another example is Georgio perfume, whose sales decreased as the number of distribution outlets increased from department stores to discount department stores and off-price stores. After Procter & Gamble purchased the brand, sales came back up with reduced distribution. Still, there have been no empirical studies of supersaturation for sales force or distribution variables.

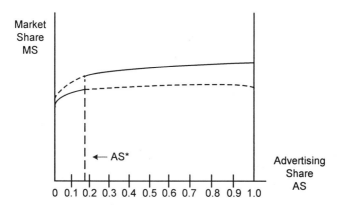

Figure 3-4. Switching Model. *Source:* Bemmaor (1984).

Threshold. A threshold occurs when some positive amount of marketing effort is necessary before any sales impact can be detected. For example, small expenditures in a highly competitive mass market is unlikely to show a sales effect.

Functional Forms. If the threshold marketing effort is X_o, any functional form can be used with X, marketing effort, replaced by $(X - X_o)$. For example, in advertising X_o might be 50 GRPs for reasons we shall discuss shortly.

The fact that the quantity sold must be non-negative (ignoring the possibility that returned product exceeds product sales) implies that some functional forms have thresholds built into them. Recall our discussion of the semilogarithmic model (3.8). The *saturation model with decreasing returns,*

$$Q = Q^o - \beta_1 X^{-\beta_2}, \tag{3.34}$$

is only valid if all the observations on X are greater than, or equal to, $\left(\beta_1/Q^o\right)^{1/\beta_2}$.

This restriction must be checked after the model is estimated. A special case of (3.34) is the *reciprocal (inverse) model,* in which $\beta_2 = 1$. A reciprocal model has been applied to the processed-grapefruit industry (Ward 1975).

Empirical Evidence. If support for S-shaped sales response is weak, even less support exists for the threshold effect. The two phenomena, however, may be empirically indistinguishable. In U.S. television, there appears to be a threshold of about 50

GRPs (35 target reach) to be able to read sales effects (Ephron and Broadbent 1999, drawing on Gold 1992 and von Goten and Donius 1997).

Even though the argument could be made at the individual level that a prospect might be unaware of a brand or unwilling to buy it until several advertising messages have been received, little evidence of this threshold phenomenon in aggregate sales response models has been found. One set of researchers has noted that

> little generalisable evidence of either phenomena [threshold and wearout levels of expenditure] seems to exist. This is mostly because managers and their agencies avoid operating at or near the supposed limits. [Corkindale and Newall 1978, p. 373]

Another researcher expressed his opinion that

> threshold effects ... constitute a monstrous myth. [Simon 1970, p. 22]

Many marketing managers, nonetheless, continue to believe that a threshold effect operates within their market (Corkindale and Newall 1978).

The most serious attempt to identify a threshold effect in an aggregate sales response was by Bemmaor (1984). A market share response function was partitioned into two regimes above and below the threshold (Figure 3-4). A multiplicative function (3.16) was used to describe each segment. A random shift between these two regimes was postulated. [See our discussion of random switching models, Equation (4.35).] For the product studied, the best fit occurred when the estimate of the proportion of observations above the threshold was 73%. The corresponding threshold advertising share was deduced to be about 18. Thus, these results indicate decreasing returns to scale but with a discontinuity.

Interaction. A distinction can be made between marketing mix *interaction effects* and marketing mix *interdependencies* (Longman and Pauwels 1998). Marketing mix interaction effects exist if the firm's decision level for one marketing mix instrument affects the sensitivity of sales to changes of the firm's decision level for another instrument. For example, consistent theme advertising expenditures can impact a market's sensitivity to price changes. Interaction effects may manifest themselves at the either the sales level or elasticity level or at both levels. A marketing mix interdependency exists if there is a relationship between a firm's decision levels for different marketing mix instruments. For example, the price charged by a firm can affect the advertising budget it sets. In this chapter we examine how to characterize marketing mix interaction effects in market response. In Chapter 9, we address how these interaction effects can affect the optimal marketing mix—in particular, how they induce interdependencies among a firm's optimal decision levels for different marketing mix instruments.

We have already discussed one way to model marketing mix interactions; i.e., (3.16). Perhaps a more general way is the *transcendental logarithmic* (*translog*) *model.* The translog model for three marketing instruments is

$$ln Q = \beta_0 + \beta_1 \ln X_1 + \beta_2 \ln X_2 + \beta_3 \ln X_3$$
$$+ \beta_{12} \ln X_1 \ln X_2 + \beta_{13} \ln X_1 \ln X_3 + \beta_{23} \ln X_2 \ln X_3 \qquad (3.35)$$
$$+ \beta_{11}(\ln X_1)^2 + \beta_{22}(\ln X_2)^2 + \beta_{33}(\ln X_3)^2.$$

The translog functional form is a quadratic approximation to any continuous function. The elasticities of the marketing instruments vary with changes in the entire marketing mix. For example, the elasticity of X_1 in (3.35) is

$$\varepsilon_{Q,X_1} = \beta_0 + \beta_{12} \ln X_2 + \beta_{13} \ln X_3 + 2\beta_{11} \ln X_1. \qquad (3.36)$$

A constant elasticity model is a special case in which $\beta_{12} = \beta_{13} = \beta_{23} = 0$. A translog model for Lydia Pinkham sales and advertising has been estimated using Palda's (1964) data (Jagpal, Sudit, and Vinod 1982).

Special cases of the translog model include the multiplicative nonhomogeneous model and the multiplicative model. The *multiplicative nonhomogeneous model* is defined by letting $\beta_{11} = \beta_{22} = \beta_{33} = 0$ in (3.35):

$$ln Q = \beta_0 + \beta_1 \ln X_1 + \beta_2 \ln X_2 + \beta_3 \ln X_3$$
$$+ \beta_{12} \ln X_1 \ln X_2 + \beta_{13} \ln X_1 \ln X_3 + \beta_{23} \ln X_2 \ln X_3. \qquad (3.37)$$

This model also has been illustrated with the Lydia Pinkham data set (Jagpal, Sudit, and Vinod 1979). Another application was the investigation of crossproduct media advertising effects for a commercial bank (Jagpal 1981). The *multiplicative model is* obtained by setting $\beta_{12} = \beta_{13} = \beta_{23} = 0$ in the multiplicative nonhomogeneous model:

$$ln Q = \beta_0 + \beta_1 \ln X_1 + \beta_2 \ln X_2 + \beta_3 \ln X_3. \qquad (3.38)$$

Economists are familiar with this functional form as the Cobb-Douglas production function (Zellner, Kmenta, and Dreze 1966).

Interaction is sometimes captured by making the response parameter with respect to one instrument in the market response function to be related to the decision levels for another instrument. Such a relationship is specified as a parameter function. We cover this next under the topic of coefficient variation.

Coefficient Variation. The effectiveness of each controllable marketing instrument is frequently treated as having the same value over time. However, market response to managerial decision variables might change because of the impact of marketing actions by either a company or its competitors or because of shifts in the environment.

If structural changes occur at known points in time, the changes in the coefficients of the relevant variables can be represented by dummy variables. Unfortunately the timing of structural changes is rarely known.

The parameters in a response function might vary between each time period rather than only between a few time periods. If the parameters follow some random process, the parameter variation is said to be *stochastic*. If the parameters themselves are functions of observable variables, the parameter variation is said to be *systematic*. Parameter variation, and especially temporal parameter variation, will be discussed in detail in Chapter 4.

Empirical Evidence. Systematic variation might occur over individuals or territories. For example, the price elasticities for a brand were found to vary from market to market and from segment to segment (Moran 1978). In another study, one brand was tested to evaluate whether demographic variables explained differences in the estimated parameters of the sales response functions for various territories (Wittink 1977b). They did not. Another study had only somewhat better luck relating household characteristics to the estimated parameters in purchasing response functions for different households (Elrod and Winer 1979). Finally, sales force effectiveness in military recruiting was reported to be related to environmental conditions, in particular, the civilian employment rate (Gatignon and Hanssens 1987).

One source of systematic parameter variation is the interaction of the marketing decision variables with each other. Advertising expenditures often influence the magnitude of price elasticity (Moran 1978; Sunoo and Lin 1979). Conventional wisdom is that advertising decreases price sensitivity. There is some empirical support for this proposition (Schultz and Vanhonacker 1978), yet some evidence shows that relative price becomes more elastic as advertising share increases (Wittink 1977a). The implication is that advertising tends to increase the price competitiveness of the brand investigated. This supports earlier findings (Eskin 1975; Eskin and Baron 1977) that a high advertising effort yields a higher price elasticity than a low advertising effort. A study using single source data for a Midwestern market found that increased advertising exposures were associated with increases in a household's brand choice sensitivity for two frequently purchased consumer products (Kanetkar, Weinberg, and Weiss 1992). The concept of vertical market structures might reconcile what appears to be conflicting evidence (Farris and Albion 1980). The relation between advertising and price was posited to depend on whether price is measured at the factory level or at the consumer level. One study found that, for a well-established brand, increased noninformational advertising of the mood type decreased price sensitivity (Krishnamurthi and Raj 1985).

The presence moderating effects (in the form of interactions) can be explored. In a study of the impact of market share on perceived product quality, the coefficient of market share was expressed as a linear function of an exclusivity ratio and a premium price ratio (Hellofs and Jacobson 1999). The exclusivity ratio was the percentage of respondents preferring that few people compared with the percentage of respondents preferring a large number of people use the product. The premium price ratio was the percentage of respondents who view the product as premium-priced compared with the percentage of the respondents who view it as regular-priced. The study found that increased market share had a negative effect on quality perceptions. As concerns for exclusivity became greater, the negative impact of market share on perceived quality became greater. The brand characteristic of premium pricing, however, lessened the negative effect of market share gains.

Finally, many secondary dimensions of marketing variables are only operative when the primary dimension of the variable is present. If no advertising expenditures are made, the advertising copy can have no impact on sales. Samples and handouts designed to be distributed in conjunction with a sales call can only have an impact *through* calls. For example, the effectiveness of the calls made by the sales force of a pharmaceutical manufacturer for an established ethical drug were demonstrated to vary systematically as a function of collateral material used, such as samples (Parsons and Vanden Abeele 1981). Similarly, personal selling effectiveness in U.S. Navy recruiting has been found to increase with local advertising support (Gatignon and Hanssens 1987).

Error Structure. Our discussion of functional forms has emphasized the specification of a functional relation between two or more variables. Such a functional relation does not explain everything. After all, it is only a model incorporating the salient features of some marketing phenomenon. Moreover, only the deterministic part of the underlying mechanism has been specified. There may be some inherent randomness in the marketplace, for instance, unpredictable variety seeking by customers. Consequently, any specification of a relation must be expanded to include a *random disturbance term* that captures *equation error,* i.e., the difference between actual observations of a dependent variable and those predicted by a particular functional relation.

The equation for a single relation can be written as

$$y = f(\mathbf{X}, \mathbf{u}; \boldsymbol{\beta}), \tag{3.39}$$

where

$\mathbf{y}$ = column vector of n observations on single endogenous variable,

$\mathbf{X} = n \times k$ matrix of n observations on k predetermined variables,

$\mathbf{u}$ = column vector of n observations on disturbances,

$\mathbf{\beta}$ = column vector of k (unknown population) parameters.

The random disturbances are realizations of a stationary probability distribution:[1]

$$\mathbf{u} \sim f(\mathbf{\theta}) \tag{3.40}$$

Many distribution functions can be characterized by their first two moments, that is, $\mathbf{\theta} = (\mu, \sigma^2)$.

When a single equation is the i th equation in a larger system, it is often written as

$$f(y_i, Y_i, X_i; \mathbf{\alpha}_i) = u_i \tag{3.41}$$

where $\mathbf{\alpha}_i$ is the coefficient vector and the covariance matrix among disturbances in *different* equations is Σ, the contemporaneous covariance matrix.

Design Decisions. As we have seen, the shape of response to a particular non-price sales driver, with the remainder of the marketing mix held constant, is generally concave. Sales generally increase with increases in marketing effort, but exhibit diminishing returns to scale. We also saw that—in theory—sales initially may exhibit increasing returns to scale, then diminishing returns to higher levels of marketing effort. But Jones (1984) has emphasized that

nowhere is it suggested that increasing returns are anything but limited and temporary.

The temporary increasing return phenomenon may be localized in the introductory stage of the product life cycle and related to increasing distribution coverage, i.e., an improvement in the conversion of demand into sales (cf. Steiner 1987).

Although the shape of the sales response function is almost surely concave, we should be alert to the possibility of other shapes (see, for example, Johansson 1979). The shape of the response function might be different depending on whether marketing effort is increasing or decreasing, that is, response may be asymmetric. The shape of the response function also might vary with changes in the environment. In general, because different combinations of phenomena such as threshold, asymmetry, and saturation effects might be present in a particular market, one should not think in terms of a single aggregate response function. *A specific response function should be constructed for each product or market situation.*

Most research on market response models assumes that each of the marketing mix instruments follows the same response function. In particular, each instrument is usually assumed to follow a power function, which, in turn, can be combined multiplicatively with other instruments to directly form the multiplicative sales response function. However, each instrument could follow a different functional form. In MARMIX, a computer-based model-building package designed to help managers in setting annual marketing budgets, separate response functions for the marketing mix elements are permitted to be estimated (de Kluyver and Pessimier 1986). These separate functions are then combined in an additive model if independence among the different elements in the marketing mix is assumed, or in a multiplicative model if interaction among these elements is expected. For example, in a sales response model for retail sales of an apparel store, the sales made by store personnel was constrained by the volume of store traffic. Consequently, a log-reciprocal function (3.23) was adopted for the number of sales people. This function was then combined multiplicatively with a power function for store traffic. The parameter associated with traffic is the *traffic elasticity* (Lam, Vandenbosch, and Pearce 1998, p. 64). Another example is given in a study of commodity advertising. The function for checkoff efforts,

$$\left(1 + e^{\frac{-\beta_1}{CK}} \right)^{\beta_2} , \tag{3.42}$$

with $\beta_1 \geq 0$ and $0 \leq \beta_2 \leq 1$, was multiplicatively related to a function of other demand factors (Forker and Ward 1993, p. 163). An application of this model to the beef checkoff program and to Washington State apple advertising are described in Forker and Ward (1993, pp. 206-12; 212-21). Refinements of MARMIX are discussed in Moore and Pessemier (1992).

Pooling

Combining time series and cross-section data raises some issues on how to specify a functional form. The simplest model, model I in Table 3-1, assumes a common intercept and a common set of slope coefficients for all units for all time periods. A more usual assumption (model II) is to allow for individual differences by introducing separate dummy variables for each cross-section entity. For example, in a study of the U.S. ethical drug industry, category-specific dummy variables were used (Shankar, Carpenter, and Krishnamurthi 1999). In a similar manner, differences over time could be represented. Individual differences and temporal differences could each be represented by dummy variables in the same equation (model III), although this results in a substantial loss of degrees of freedom. Moreover, interpretation of the dummy variables may be difficult. In addition, these dummy variables are likely to account for a large share of the explanatory power of the model. Consequently, an *error components model* is often used instead of the dummy variable technique.

Table 3-1. Taxonomy of Pooling Models

	Assumptions about	
Model	*Intercept*	*Vector of Slope Coefficients*
I	Common for all i,t *	Common for all i,t *
II	Varying over i (or t)	Common for all i, t
III	Varying over i, t	Common for all i, t
IV	Varying over i (or t)	Varying over i (or t)
V	Varying over i, t	Varying over i, t

* Disturbance term captures differences among individuals and over time.

In situations where the data represent observations from a combination of a cross-section and a time series, the disturbance term is sometimes partitioned into as many as three components:

$$u_{it} = \mu_i + \tau_t + v_{it} \tag{3.43}$$

The components are the individual or cross-section effect, μ_i, the temporal effect, τ_t, and the remaining effects, which vary over both individuals and time periods v_{it}. Thus, whereas the dummy variable model assumes the individual differences are fixed, the error components model assumes that these differences are random. Different versions of the error components formulation have been used to study the advertising, retail availability, and sales of new brands of ready-to-eat cereals (Parsons 1974) and regional fluctuations in the effectiveness of marketing decision variables for a single brand (Moriarty 1975).

The models that we have discussed assume that the individual and time effects manifest themselves in differences in the intercept. These effects also have an impact on the slope coefficients (models IV and V). One way they are captured is by means of random coefficients models. The *random coefficients model* assumes that the parameters are stochastic and can be expressed as

$$\boldsymbol{\beta}_i = \overline{\boldsymbol{\beta}} + \mathbf{v}_i \tag{3.44}$$

where

$\boldsymbol{\beta}_i$ = vector of random response coefficients for the i th individual unit,

$\overline{\boldsymbol{\beta}}$ = vector of mean response coefficients,

$\mathbf{v}_i$ = vector of random disturbances.

This model is very appealing when investigating cross-sectional data on a large number of microunits, for instance, a large consumer survey.

In sum, model builders must decide whether to pool times series and cross-sectional data, that is, treat coefficients as constant, or not. If not, should the intercept, slope, or both types of coefficients be allowed to vary, should this variation be over individuals, time, or both, and, furthermore, should any such variation be treated as fixed or random? For further discussion of the issues involved in combining time series and cross-sectional data, especially panel data, see Judge et al (1985, pp. 515-60) and Greene (1997, pp. 612-47).

Market Share Models

When the dependent variable in a response function is market share, an additional complication is introduced. A desirable property of any market share model is that it be *logically consistent* (McGuire et al. 1968; Naert and Bultez 1973; McGuire and Weiss 1976; Bultez 1978; Koehler and Wildt 1981). This means that the model produces an estimate of a brand's market share that lies between 0 and 1 when market share is expressed as a fraction. This is known as the *bound* (or *range*) *constraint*. Furthermore, the sum of these estimated market shares for all brands in any given period must equal 1. This is known as the *sum constraint*. Violations of the bound or sum constraints expose the internal inconsistencies of a model.

We want to be able to illustrate hierarchical market share models as well as nonhierarchical ones. Therefore, for illustrative purposes, we will assume a two-level hierarchy involving B brands and P product forms in a market that is brand primary. Market share, for example, could be partitioned as

$$MS_{bp} = MS_b \times MS_{p|b} = \frac{Q_b}{\sum_{i=1}^{B}\sum_{j=1}^{P} Q_{ij}} \times \frac{Q_{bp}}{Q_b} = \frac{Q_{bp}}{\sum_{i=1}^{B}\sum_{j=1}^{P} Q_{ij}}. \qquad (3.45)$$

In this example, product forms are said to be "nested" within brands ($p|b = p$ given b). In non-hierarchical models there will be no partitioning.

One approach has been to compare the "attractiveness," A, of each market alternative:

$$MS_{bp} = \frac{A_{bp}}{\sum_{i=1}^{B}\sum_{j=1}^{P} A_{ij}} \qquad (3.46)$$

This model has been called an *attraction model* (Bell, Keeney, and Little 1975). Alternative specifications of the attractiveness function have been compared (Cooper and Nakanishi 1988, Foekens 1995, Foekens, Leeflang, and Wittink 1997). For our own work, we simply recognize that a model must be logically consistent if it is based upon the definition of market share:

$$MS_{bp} \equiv \frac{Q_{bp}}{\displaystyle\sum_{i=1}^{B}\sum_{j=1}^{P} Q_{ij}} = \frac{f_{bp}\left(\mathbf{X}, \mathbf{u}_{bp}; \boldsymbol{\beta}_{bp}\right)}{\displaystyle\sum_{i=1}^{B}\sum_{j=1}^{P} f_{ij}\left(\mathbf{X}, \mathbf{u}_{ij}; \boldsymbol{\beta}_{ij}\right)}. \tag{3.47}$$

By including competitors' marketing instruments in the set of explanatory variables X for each sales response function, *cross-competitive* (market share) *effects* can be modeled, although this would typically result in a large number of parameters.

Alternatively, a different functional form could represent the sales response function for each brand-form combination. In practice, each combination would be assumed to have the same functional form. Furthermore, for ease of discussion, we cover only a few key market share models and their special cases: the Multiplicative Competitive Interaction Model, the Multinomial Model, the Cluster-Asymmetric Model, and the Nested Multinomial Model.

MCI Model. Not surprisingly, the most common approach is to use a nonhierarchical market share model with a multiplicative functional form (3.16), shown here in exponential form for ease of comparison with other models:

$$Q_{bp} = exp\left(\beta_{bp0} + \sum_{i}^{B}\sum_{j}^{P}\sum_{k=1}^{K1} \beta_{bpijk}\, ln\!\left[X_{ijk}\right] + \sum_{i}^{B}\sum_{j}^{P}\sum_{k=K1}^{K} \delta_{bpijk} D_{ijk} \right). \tag{3.48}$$

The corresponding market share model belongs to the class of models called *Multiplicative Competitive Interaction* (MCI) models, popularized by Cooper and Nakanishi (1988). In particular, it is known as the *Cross-Effects or Fully Extended MCI Model* because it allows each item to have its unique own effects $(i,j) = (b,p)$ while experiencing all possible cross effects $(i,j) \neq (b,p)$. Thus, it captures market structure asymmetry. More recently, this model has been called the Fully Extended Attraction (FEA) Model (Foekens 1995). Early work on the original formulation included Nakanishi and Cooper (1974) and McGuire, Weiss, and Houston (1977).

The full Cross-Effects MCI model places too many demands on the data. Let $M = B \times P$. Then the number of parameters to be estimated is $M + (M \times M \times K)$ (Cooper and Nakanishi 1988, p. 144). For example, if the number of items is 20 and the number of marketing instruments is 4, the number of parameters is 1620 (Foekens,

Leeflang, and Wittink 1997, p. 362). One approach is to set some of the parameters to zero. The problem then is to distinguish between fundamental asymmetries and those that are small enough to set equal to zero. One way to address this problem is to draw on managerial insight into the market. Another way is to conduct time series analysis, which we will discuss in Chapter 6. This was the tack taken in modeling the stable market of an Australian household product (Carpenter et al. 1988), which will be described in more detail in Chapter 9.

One could, of course, set all cross-effects parameters equal to zero a priori. The result would be

$$Q_{bp} = exp\left(\beta_{bp0} + \sum_{k=1}^{K1} \beta_{bpk} \, ln\left[X_{bpk} \right] + \sum_{k=K1}^{K} \delta_{bpk} D_{bpk} \right). \tag{3.49}$$

Unit sales of an item are now only determined by its own marketing mix and by those of its competitors. The effectiveness of a marketing instrument can still vary from one item to another. Thus, this market share model is known as the *Differential-Effects MCI Model*. It has also been called the Extended Attraction (EA) Model (Foekens 1995, Foekens, Leeflang, and Wittink 1997). The Differential-Effects MCI model has been used in studying interdependencies among brands in a firm's product line (Urban 1969), in investigating competitive marketing activities in the market for an inexpensive European consumer durable (Bultez and Naert 1975), and as part of a process for modeling asymmetric competition in an Australian household product market (Carpenter et al. 1988).

Finally, one could assume that the marketing effectiveness of any particular marketing instrument is equal across items. In effect, a prototype brand rather than a specific brand is being estimated. Usually items are allowed to have individual "intercepts" (Naert and Bultez 1973, p. 337):

$$Q_{bp} = exp\left(\beta_{bp0} + \sum_{k=1}^{K1} \beta_{k} \, ln\left[X_{bpk} \right] + \sum_{k=K1}^{K} \delta_{k} D_{bpk} \right). \tag{3.50}$$

This is called the *Simple-Effects MCI Model*, or simply the *MCI Model*. If all items also have the same constant, β_0, then this constant is unidentifiable because it appears in both the numerator and denominator of the market share expression and cancels out. This can occur when a prototypical relation must be estimated from cross-sectional data. In this situation, a market share model shouldn't be used, but rather the sales response function should be estimated. The sales response function will give exactly the same parameters estimates as the market share model but will also provide an estimate of the "unidentifiable" constant.

ECI (MNL) Model. Rather than using the multiplicative functional form in the market share model, one could use the exponential functional form (3.19):

$$Q_{bp} = exp\left(\beta_{bp0} + \sum_i^B \sum_j^P \sum_k^K \beta_{bpijk} X_{ijk} \right). \tag{3.51}$$

Here the distinction between continuous and dummy variables does not have to be made explicit. The corresponding market share model belongs to the class of models called Multinomial Logit (MNL) models (Cooper and Nakanishi 1988). The logit model, better known for its use in representing brand choice, falls in this class. We consider this nomenclature unfortunate and prefer to use the *Exponential Competitive Interaction* (ECI) for consistency with the usage of MCI. Thus, here we have the *Cross-Effects ECI (MNL) Model*.

The associated *Differential-Effects ECI (MNL) Model* and *Simple-Effects ECI (MNL) Model* use

$$Q_{bp} = exp\left(\beta_{bp0} + \sum_k^K \beta_{bpk} X_{bpk} \right) \tag{3.52}$$

and

$$Q_{bp} = exp\left(\beta_{bp0} + \sum_k^K \beta_k X_{bpk} \right), \tag{3.53}$$

respectively.

The MNL model is often used for modeling individual choice behavior. However, it is not appropriate for equilibrium analysis of marketing competition. This is because the exponential properties of the model do not allow for decreasing returns to scale for advertising or promotion for any brand with less than a 50 percent share of the market (Gruca and Sudharshan 1991). The MCI model is a superior choice for this type of application.

The own- and cross-elasticities for these various MCI and ECI (MNL) models are shown in Table 3-2. One desirable property of a market share model is that a brand's market share elasticity goes to zero as its share goes to one. This holds for MCI and ECI (MNL) models.

In using the Cross-Effects MCI or ECI models, the number of parameters to be estimated becomes unwieldy when the number of competitors and/or instruments is large. The question is how to capture market structure asymmetry more parsimoniously. Clusters could be based on similar product characteristics. The presumption is that competition between items within clusters is stronger than between items in different clusters. One could form clusters using a clustering algorithm or manage-

Table 3-2. Elasticities in Market-Share Models

Elasticities	
Own	*Cross*

MCI Cross-Effects

$$\varepsilon_{MS_b,M_{bk}} = \left(\beta_{bbk} - \sum_{h=1}^{B} MS_{ht}\beta_{hbk} \right) \qquad \eta_{MS_b,M_{jk}} = \left(\beta_{bjk} - \sum_{h=1}^{B} MS_{ht}\beta_{hjk} \right)$$

MCI Differential-Effects

$$\varepsilon_{MS_b,M_{bk}} = \beta_{bk}(1 - MS_{bt}) \qquad\qquad \eta_{MS_b,M_{kj}} = -\beta_{jk} MS_{jt}$$

MCI Simple-Effects

$$\varepsilon_{MS_b,M_{bk}} = \beta_{k}(1 - MS_{bt}) \qquad\qquad \text{NA}$$

ECI (MNL) Cross-Effects

$$\varepsilon_{MS_b,M_{bk}} = \left(\beta_{bbk} - \sum_{h=1}^{B} MS_{ht}\beta_{hbk} \right) M_{bkt} \qquad \eta_{MS_b,M_{jk}} = \left(\beta_{bjk} - \sum_{h=1}^{B} MS_{ht}\beta_{hjk} \right) M_{jkt}$$

ECI (MNL) Differential-Effects

$$\varepsilon_{MS_b,M_{bk}} = \beta_{bk} M_{bkt}(1 - MS_{bt}) \qquad\qquad \eta_{MS_b,M_{kj}} = -\beta_{jk} M_{jkt} MS_{jt}$$

ECI (MNL) Simple-Effects

$$\varepsilon_{MS_b,M_{bk}} = \beta_{k} M_{bkt}(1 - MS_{bt}) \qquad\qquad \text{NA}$$

Note: Product form p suppressed. M_{bk} is the kth sales driver for brand b. β_{bjk} is the parameter associated with the kth sales driver for brand j in brand b's sales response function.

Source: Cooper and Nakanishi (1988) and Cooper (1993).

ment judgment. One such model of market share is the *Cluster-Asymmetry Attraction* (CAA) *Model* (Vanden Abeele, Gijsbrechts, and Vanhuele 1990, 1992).

CAA Model. Suppose that brand name and product form are the clustering criteria so that there are B brand clusters and P product-form clusters. An item can be a member of more than one cluster and, in this example, must be a member of one brand cluster and one product-form cluster. Clusters are thus said to be "overlapping." The CAA model takes advantage of the attraction formulation to adjust one of the differential-effects models above, usually the multiplicative function (MCI model) for asymmetric competition. Each market structure criterion will have a correction factor. Each correction factor will be based on the attractiveness of the items within each competitive cluster. This includes the item (b,s) under consideration to ensure that the correction factor is always defined even if the item under consideration is the only member of its competitive cluster. Let C_k be the set of n_k items belonging to the kth competitive cluster. Then, the CAA model can be written (following Foekens 1995, pp. 81-82, and Foekens, Leeflang, and Wittink 1997, p. 366) as

$$MS_{bp} = \frac{A_{bp} \times AB^{\theta_B} \times AP^{\theta_P}}{\sum\limits_{i=1}^{B} \sum\limits_{j=1}^{P} A_{ij}}, \tag{3.54}$$

where

$$A_{bp} = exp\left(\beta_{bp0} + \sum_{k}^{K1} \beta_k \, ln\left[X_{bpk} \right] + \sum_{k=K1}^{K} \delta_k D_{bpk} \right),$$

$$AB_{bp} = \begin{cases} \dfrac{1}{n_{Pb}} \sum\limits_{\forall j' \in C_b} A_{bj'} & \text{if } p \in C_b \\ 1 & \text{otherwise} \end{cases}, \text{ and}$$

$$AP_{bp} = \begin{cases} \dfrac{1}{n_{Bb}} \sum\limits_{\forall i' \in C_p} A_{i'p} & \text{if } b \in C_p \\ 1 & \text{otherwise} \end{cases}.$$

The parameters θ_B and θ_P are asymmetry parameters, which measure the degree of competitive impact resulting from the corresponding cluster. When θ_K is zero, there is no cross-competitive effect emanating from the kth competitive cluster. For example, if θ_P is zero, competition is symmetric between package sizes of a given brand. A disadvantage of the CAA model is that the asymmetric correction factors are a function of the multiplicative attraction function and its unknown parameters. Thus, an iterative estimation procedure is required (Vanden Abeele, Gijsbrechts, and Vanhuele 1990, pp. 230-31). The CAA model has been applied to a branded appliance offered by a large number of competitors using Nielsen data on market share, retail price, and distribution coverage (Vanden Abeele, Gijsbrechts, and Vanhuele 1990).

Nested ECI Model. We indicated earlier that the market share of the pth product form of brand b can be written as the product of the market share for brand b and the conditional market share for product form p, given brand b. Let $Cp|b$ denote the set of product forms that have marketing instruments with a cross effect on the share of product form p (given brand b). Then conditional sales can be expressed in the exponential functional form as

$$Q_{p|b} = exp\left(\beta_{bp0} + \sum_{k}^{K} \beta_{bpk} X_{bpk} + \sum_{\substack{j \in C_{pb} \\ j \neq p}}^{P} \sum_{k}^{K} \beta_{bjk} X_{bjk} \right). \tag{3.55}$$

Variables in this expression are measured at the item level. This relation can be used to find $MS_{p|b}$. Now an expression to help one find MS_b is needed. The variables will have been aggregated over product form. An inclusive value (IV) variable will be introduced to extricate the effect of the total attractiveness of the set of product forms of brand b:

$$Q_b = exp\left(\beta_{b0} + \sum_{k=1}^{K} \beta_{bk} X_{bk} + \sum_{\substack{i \in C_b \\ i \neq p}}^{P} \sum_{k=1}^{K} \beta_{bjk} X_{bjk} + (1 - \theta) IV_{bi} \right). \tag{3.56}$$

where

$$IV_b = log\left[\sum_{p=1}^{P} exp\left(\beta_{bp0} + \sum_{k}^{K} \beta_{bpk} X_{bpk} + \sum_{\substack{j \in C_{p|b} \\ j \neq p}}^{P} \sum_{k}^{K} \beta_{bjk} X_{bjk} \right) \right]. \tag{3.57}$$

We would call the resultant market share model the Nested Cross-Effects ECI Model, but others have called it the Fully Extended Nested Multinomial (FENMNL) Model (Foekens 1995, Foekens, Leeflang, and Wittink 1997). As with other "extended" models, restrictions can be placed on parameters of this model to yield simpler special cases. When θ equals zero, the inclusive value variable has full effect. This version of the model has been called the Fully Extended Multinomial Logit (FEMNL) Model. When cross effects are eliminated in this model, the result is the Extended Multinomial Logit Model (EMNL). When θ equals one, the share models for different levels are independent of each other, resulting in what has been called the Fully Extended Squared Attraction (FESQA) Model. When cross effects are eliminated in this model, the result is the Extended Squared Attraction (ESQA) Model. The interrelations among various market share models are diagrammed in Foekens (1995, p. 78) and Foekens, Leeflang, and Wittink (1997, p. 361).

Empirical Evidence. A comparison of a number of market share models was conducted using weekly market-level scanner data for all existing combinations of seven brands and five package sizes (twenty items in total) of a frequently purchased nonfood consumer good in the Netherlands. The researchers found

> If we had to choose one particular model for the data at hand, the empirical results clearly favor ESQA. This model has by far the best predictive validity value and is second best on face validity. Thus a hierarchical model, based on (brand-size) structure s1, that excludes all unique cross-competitive effects and also excludes the inclusive variables is preferred for the product category studied. This model implies that (1) competition among package sizes within brands is symmetric, (2) competition between brands is symmetric, but (3) competition between package sizes of different brands is asymmetric. It also implies that the marketing activities for a given package size induce cannibalization from the other package sizes of the same brand (direct competition).   (Foekens 1995 and Foekens, Leeflang, and Wittink 1997, p. 375)

This, it must be noted, is only one study and more comparative studies need to be done on other databases.

Dirichlet Regression Model. Integrating micro (household panel) and macro (store tracking) data can generate further insights into the competitive structure of a product category. A two-stage procedure has been proposed (Russell and Kamakura 1994). The first stage uses latent class analysis of household purchase statistics taken from a household panel to identify preference segments and obtain information regarding brand preference within each of these segments. The second stage estimates a market share response model that takes into account the preference structure found at the household level. Store-level tracking data is analyzed. Modification of the Simple-Effects ECI (MNL) Model (3.53) yields

$$Q_{bs} = exp\left(\beta_{b0} + \hat{I}_{bs} + \sum_{k}^{K} \beta_k X_{bk} \right), \tag{3.58}$$

where $\hat{I}_{bs}$ is the intrinsic attraction of brand b within segment estimated from micro-level analysis. Even though the coefficients of the sales drivers are the same over segments, the elasticities of the sales drivers are segment specific because of the differences in intrinsic brand attractions across segments.

While aggregate market shares in panel data follow a multinomial distribution, market shares from retail-tracking data are a census of all households shopping at the store and consequently have no sampling error. The Dirichlet distribution is used as a parsimonious way of representing model misspecification in the macro model (Russell and Kamakura 1994, p. 294, fn. 5). The multivariate Beta distribution, referred to as the Dirichlet distribution, occurs in the statistical analysis of random variables defined as ratios.

Empirical Evidence. The Dirichlet Regression Model has been compared to MCI models using supermarket scanner data for powdered detergents (Russell and Kamakura 1994). Although the MCI models fit slightly better in the calibration period, differences in fit during the validation period were very small. The integrated approach has the advantage of providing the manager with a wide range of diagnostics.

Comment. We have argued that a desirable property of market share models is that they be logically consistent. Attraction formulations and market share formulations, such as Equations (3.47) and (3.47), meet this requirement. However, they do so at a cost. They are not very parsimonious and are often overparameterized, that is, they may contain a large number of parameters relative to the size of the sample and variability in the data. As a result, linear or multiplicative market share models are often used in practice despite not being logically consistent in most situations. This state of affairs has led to a series of studies on estimation and forecasting issues in market share models, which will be discussed in later chapters.

Aggregation of Relations

Many marketing theories are micro in nature because they are concerned with the behavior of individual family households or businesses. On the other hand, econometric estimation and hypothesis testing (Chapter 4) is based on data from groups of households at the store level, chain level, major metropolitan area-level, or, more likely, at the market level. We need to be concerned about what dangers exist when working with aggregated relations.

The appropriate level of entity aggregation would seem ultimately to be at the level of the marketing decision. When assessing store-level consumer sales promotions, such as temporary price reductions, then store-level data would seem most appropriate. When assessing manufacturer-to-retailer marketing activities, such as trade promotions, then chain-level (key account) data would seem most appropriate. When assessing manufacturer-to-consumer marketing activities, such as consistent theme advertising, then metro area-level data or market-level data would seem more appropriate. Indeed most brand management decisions, for better or worse, are based on market-level data.

Looking ahead to Chapter 5, one desirable property of estimators of parameters is that they be unbiased. What this means is that the expected value of estimated values

Table 3-3. Entity Aggregation Bias

| | Marketing Activities | |
Parameters	Homogeneous	Heterogeneous
Homogeneous	No bias	Linear relations: no bias Nonlinear relations: bias
Heterogeneous	Linear relations: no bias	Linear relations: bias if nonzero covariance between parameters and marketing activities
	Nonlinear relations: small bias for logit model	Nonlinear relations: bias plus additional bias if nonzero covariance

Source: Christen et al. (1997, p.323)

calculated from a large number of different samples equals the true value of the parameter. The problem of entity aggregation bias arises if one attempts to model store-level promotional decisions with market-level data. (See Appendix 3-B.) The degree of aggregation bias depends on three characteristics of what is happening at lower levels of aggregation: (1) whether the sales response model is linear or nonlinear; (2) whether its parameters are homogeneous or heterogeneous across entities; and (3) whether or not the entities face the same levels of market activities or not. These relationships are summarized in Table 3-3.

One analysis of the SCAN*PRO model revealed that the estimated effects from linearly aggregated market-level data differed substantially from comparable effects that were obtained from store-level data (Christen et al. 1997). For example, looking at the 18-ounce size in the peanut butter category, the estimated multiplier for display was 1.48 at the store-level and 2.05 at the market-level. Other differences were even larger. Two conjectures about the bias were made (p. 325):

1. An estimated own-brand multiplier is higher in a market model than in a store model.

2. The magnitude of the difference in corresponding own-brand multipliers between market and store models is
   (a) an increasing function of the store-model multiplier and
   (b) a decreasing function of the proportion of stores promoting.

No conjectures were possible about own-price elasticities.

Marketing Analytics has conducted numerous tests of various aggregate scanner-data models and their performance in comparison to store-level models, including aggregate versions of the Jewel model (3.22) that was originally intended for stores

Table 3-4. Marketing Mix Model Data Selection

Data	Aggregation Level	Feasible for Mix Analysis	Comments
Retail Scanner Audit	National	No	Unusable, not homogeneous
	Major metro market	Yes	Not usable for promotions
	Retailer/ City	Yes	Some imprecision as aggregates cross retailer price zones
	Store	Yes	Very voluminous data. Can be expensive to obtain, store, and process.
Scanner Panel	Household	Yes	Can directly measure diagnostics like loyalty, brand switching, and purchase quantity. Representativeness and projectibility an issue

Trade-Offs

	Major Metro Market Data and Aggregate Data in General	Retailer/City Data and Disaggregate Data in General
Pros	Data is readily available. Some cross-effects (cross-retailer, cross-UPC) cancel each other out and thus don't need to be modeled.	Can measure differences in retailers, items, copy, and coupons. Can explicitly model detailed cross-effects.
Cons	Aggregation distorts estimates if across heterogeneous groups (e.g., differing causal conditions or responses). For market models, promotions can not be modeled.	Estimates can be noisy and unstable.

Source: Link (1995, p. RC-12).

within the same chain and in the same price zone (Link 1995b). They found promotion multipliers as much as one thousand times too high!

The point is that managers who rely on market-level data will overestimate promotional effects. Thus, aggregation distorts estimates based on differing causal conditions and responses. Ross Link of Marketing Analytics provided the summary of the trade-off between aggregation level shown in Table 3-4.[2]

What can be done other than hiring a supplier, such as IRI or ACNielsen, to provide market response parameter estimates based on store-level data? One way to address the entity aggregation bias problem is to linearly aggregate only across stores that have the same promotional activities in a given week (Link 1995b). This would require data from a supplier that are grouped to maintain homogeneity on the activities of interest. Another approach is to apply a debiasing procedure to estimates obtained from market-level data (Christen et al. 1997). Equations for correcting some key promotion-related parameters factors were obtained from simulation data. While these correction factors should apply reasonably well to a number of frequently purchased consumer goods, their general applicability is unknown.

In summary, in order for a marketing decision model to be useful, it must embody some mechanism for relating the effects of marketing decisions to sales. This mechanism, usually called a sales response function, is the keystone of the model, and thus the quality of its measurement is an important determinant of the model's eventual success. We have described a sales response function as a model of the relation between sales and relevant marketing instruments. For example, the dependence of sales on advertising can be estimated from marketing data using econometric methods. The result is a sales response equation that shows the effect of advertising on sales. Of course, sales response equations can be quite complex and often include the effects of marketing mix interactions, lagged responses, competition, and simultaneous relations. The purpose of these more complex models is the same: to link marketing actions to market response.

Notes

[1] Note that market-clearing data, the coordinates points a-d in Figure 3-1, describe neither the supply nor the demand curves. Simultaneous-equation econometric techniques, described in Chapter 5, are required to identify these curves.

[2] MMA was acquired by Carat in 1997.

[3] Many of the functional forms of the market response function we will cover as well as other forms are discussed in Naert and Leeflang (1978: Chapter 5), Saunders (1987), and Lilien, Kotler, and Moorthy (1992: Appendix C).

[4] Response sensitivity should be used rather than elasticity when using logit models. Logit models are identified only up to a scale constant and so elasticities in logit models are scaled by brand choice probabilities. Scaling results in low-share brands tending to have high elastcities even the customer may not be more responsive to a small-share brand. Scaling can, moreover, introduce asymmetry into cross-elasticities even though ther might not be any underlying asymmetry in response. See Guadagni and Little (1983), Swait and Louviere (1993), Russell, Bucklin, and Srinivasan (1993), and Mela, Gupta, and Lehmann (1997, pp. 251-52). Category-adjusted response sensitivity is defined in Chapter 8.

[5] We talk about "scale economies of advertising" in the sense of the production function (sales response function) for an individual brand and do not address the purported advantages that large firms derive from advertising. With regard to the latter issue, Boyer and Lancaster (1986, p. 524) found no static relation between advertising costs per dollar of sales and the size of the advertiser.

[6] One cannot take the logarithm of a zero value. One can use a dummy variable to partition a response function on the basis of whether or not an explanatory variable has a zero (in which case the variable is suppressed) or a positive value. The dummy variable approach also allows the intercept to shift. See Battesse (1997). Other fixes are discussed in Chapter 5.

[7] Some refer to this model as the log-linear model. However, this terminology might create confusion as to whether one was discussing a semilog model or a double log model. The term log-linear should be reserved for the estimation model associated with an exponential structural model.

[8] See Leeflang et al. (2000, p. 73) for proof.

[1] The quadratic function form is often used as a second-order approximation to a general function. For example, Vilcassim, Kadiyala, and Chintagunta (1999, p. 502) use it to map advertising GRPs into dollar expenditures in a profit function. They note that as GRPs are the product of reach and frequency, the shape of the function if reach dominates is likely to be convex given frequency whereas if frequency dominates, it is likely to be concave given reach.

[1] Stationarity is discussed in Chapter 6.

[2] Note, however, data aggregation to market level does not always lead to biased response parameters. Allenby and Rossi (1991) proved that applying logit models on scanner data aggregated across heterogeneous consumers is not subject to aggregation bias when three conditions are met: all consumers are exposed to the same marketing-mix variables, the brands are close substitutes, and the price distribution is not concentrated at an extreme value. These conditions are relatively easily testable on any given dataset, so that the market response modeler can be informed a priori about the risk of aggregation bias.

Appendix 3

3-A. System-Wide Approaches to Demand Analysis

Economists describe the way in which the quantity demand for a bundle of N market goods, $\mathbf{Q} = [Q_1, Q_2, \dots, Q_N]'$, depends on the prices faced in the marketplace, $\mathbf{P} = [P_1, P_2, \dots, P_N]'$, and the consumer's budget constraint, B. They proceed by assuming utility maximizing behavior on the part of each consumer:

$$\begin{aligned} \text{maximize} \quad & u = u(\mathbf{Q}, B) \\ \text{subject to} \quad & \mathbf{P}'\mathbf{Q} \leq B \end{aligned} \tag{3.59}$$

The budget constraint is usually expressed as income or total expenditures.

As a practical matter, the concept of *separability* is used in empirical demand analysis. Consumers are assumed to have a particular structure of preferences that imparts a hierarchical form to optimal consumer behavior. The consumer first makes a global decision on the resources to be devoted to each set of natural groups of goods, and then determines expenditure on individual goods by only the prices of other goods in the group together with total group expenditure. When N goods can be divided into G groups such that (1) each good belongs to exactly one group and (2) every marginal rate of substitution involving two goods from the same group depends only on the goods in that group, the groups are said to show *weak separability*. Suppose that Swiss cheese belongs to the food group. Weak separability says that by working with expenditure on food rather than total expenditure on all goods, the prices of goods outside the food category can be ignored. The prices of goods outside the food sector and expenditures on these goods enter the demand functions for food only through their effect on total expenditure on food.

When N commodities can be divided into B blocks such that (1) each good belongs to exactly one block and (2) the utility function can be written as the sum of B functions, each involving quantities of only one block, the specification is called block-independent preferences. There is said to be *strong separability* of the B blocks of goods. Unlike groups, blocks can be combined into superblocks. For details, see Pollak and Wales (1992).

The product group of interest is usually assumed weakly separable from all other product groups. For example, in a study of the demand for meat in Australia, the meat group, which included beef and veal, lamb, pork, and chicken, was assumed to be weakly separable from other food groups as well as from all other commodity groups (Cashin 1991). This assumption made it possible to limit the number prices appearing in relations to those of items in the meat group. The budget constraint was the total expenditure on all meat.

The utility approach allows economists to study how income and prices influence product demand. The resultant optimal quantities have the general form

$$Q_i = Q_i(\mathbf{P}, B). \tag{3.60}$$

Economists call these demand functions.

Economists, in empirical analyses of consumer demand, have often used the double logarithmic function. This function is, however, inconsistent with standard utility theory assumptions (discussed below). Nonetheless, economists chose to use for it for the same reason market response analysts have: superior fit, ease of estimation, and ready interpretation of the estimated parameters. A further argument is that since demand equations are frequently estimated from market data, the double logarithmic function in some sense approximates aggregated individual maximizing behavior (Lee 1984, p. 135).

Rather than focus on demand equations directly, economists often examine on how they change—differential demand equations. The differential can be expressed as

$$W_i d(log\, Q_i) = \theta_i d(log\, Q) + \sum_{j=1}^{N} \pi_{ij} d(log\, P_j), \tag{3.61}$$

where $W_i = P_i Q_i / B$ is the budget share for product i, $\theta_i = \partial(P_i Q_i)/\partial B$ is the marginal budget share for product i, and $d(log\, Q) = \sum_{i=1}^{n} W_i d(log\, Q_i)$ is the Divisia volume index number for the change in the consumer's real income. π_{ij} is the compensated price effect and is given by

$$\pi_{ij} = \left(\frac{P_i P_j}{B}\right) s_{ij}, \tag{3.62}$$

where s_{ij} is the (i,j)th element of the Slutsky substitution matrix:

$$s_{ij} = \partial Q_i / \partial P_j + Q_j \partial Q_i / \partial B. \tag{3.63}$$

Demand theory imposes constraints on system parameters:

adding-up* $\displaystyle\sum_{i=1}^{N} \theta_i = 1, \ \sum_{i=1}^{N} \pi_{ij} = 0$

homogeneity $\displaystyle\sum_{j=1}^{N} \pi_{ij} = 0$ (3.64)

Slutsky symmetry $\pi_{ij} = \pi_{ji}.$

Adding-up constraints occur because the budget shares must sum to one. The adding-up restrictions require that the marginal propensities to consume sum to unity and that the net effect of a price change on the budget be zero. Demand homogeneity implies that an equiproportionate change in all prices has no effect on consumption. Slutsky symmetry implies the substitution effects of price changes are symmetric.

The Rotterdam Model. The Rotterdam model is simply a finite-change version of the demand equations (3.61) in which the demand parameters are assumed to be constant (Barten 1964, Theil 1965).

$$\overline{W}_i\left(\log Q_{i,t} - \log Q_{i,t-1}\right) = \theta_i\left(\log Q_t - \log Q_{t-1}\right) + \sum_{j=1}^{N} \pi_{ij}\left(\log P_{j,t} - \log P_{j,t-1}\right), \tag{3.65}$$

---

* The adding-up conditions imply a singular variance-covariance matrix for the disturbances. The conventional manner for handling this is to delete the Nth equation. The parameter estimates of the deleted equation are recovered from those of the included $N-1$ equations and the adding-up restriction.

where the budget share W_i is replaced with the arithmetic average of budget share in t -1 and t. The Rotterdam model obviously requires time-series data. An extension of the Rotterdam model to include advertising, which is assumed to impact the marginal utility of each good, is given in Duffy (1987).

Generalized Addilog Demand System (GADS). The GADS is one "levels version" of the Rotterdam model that can used for analyzing cross-section data or modeling dynamics that may be difficult to capture using first differences (Bewley 1986):

$$\overline{W}_i log\left(\frac{Q_i}{\overline{\overline{W}}}\right) = \alpha_i + \overline{\theta}_i log\left(\frac{B}{\overline{P}}\right) + \sum_{j=1}^{N} \overline{\pi}_{ij} log P_j \tag{3.66}$$

Extension of the GADS model to include advertising and promotion is described in Brown (1994).

Almost Ideal Demand System (AIDS). The AIDS gives an arbitrary first-order approximation to any demand system (Deaton and Muellbauer 1980). In AIDS, budget shares of various goods are linearly related to the logarithm of real total expenditure and the logarithm of relative prices:

$$W_i = \alpha_i + \sum_{j=1}^{N} \gamma_{ij} log P_j + \beta_i log\left(\frac{B}{P}\right) \tag{3.67}$$

where $\theta_i = \partial(P_iQ_i)/\partial B$, $\theta_i = \partial(P_iQ_i)/\partial B$, and P is a price index defined by

$$log P = \alpha_0 + \sum_{i=1}^{N} \alpha_i log P_i + \frac{1}{2} \sum_{i=1}^{N} \sum_{j=1}^{N} \gamma_{ij} log P_i log P_j. \tag{3.68}$$

Rather than use this inherently nonlinear price index, many demand studies use Stone's geometric price index to approximate P:

$$log P = \sum_{i=1}^{N} W_i log P_i \tag{3.69}$$

This Linear Approximate (LA) version of AIDS is called *LAIDS*. Unfortunately the Stone index is not invariant to changes in units of measurement, which may seriously affect the approximation properties of the model. Alternative indexes are discussed in

Moschini (1995). The following restrictions, which are derived from the theory of demand, are often imposed on L/AIDS models:

adding-up $\qquad \sum_{i=1}^{N} \alpha_i = 1, \; \sum_{i=1}^{N} \beta_i = \sum_{i=1}^{N} \gamma_{ij} = 0$

homogeneity $\qquad\qquad\qquad \sum_{j=1}^{N} \gamma_{ij} = 0$ $\qquad\qquad\qquad$ (3.70)

Slutsky symmetry $\qquad\qquad\qquad \gamma_{ij} = \gamma_{ji}.$

The LAIDS model can also be expressed in differential form. The predicted budget shares may not always lie in the zero-one interval. This is one reason AIDS is only almost ideal. Generalizations of AIDS and LAIDS to include advertising are given in Baye, Jansen, and Lee (1992) and Piggott et al (1996) among others.

3-B. Entity Aggregation of Relations

If every cross-sectional micro unit (customer, store) has the identical linear response function, i.e.,

$$Q_i = \beta_0 + \beta_1 X_i,$$ (3.71)

then the cross-sectional parameters are said to be homogeneous. In such a case it is easy to see that one can do entity aggregation (to store, market):

$$\sum_{i=1}^{N} Q_i = \sum_{i=1}^{N} (\beta_0 + \beta_1 X_i) = N\beta_0 + \beta_1 \sum_{i=1}^{N} X_i.$$ (3.72)

Suppose we keep the linear assumption, but relax the condition that all the parameters are homogeneous.

$$\sum_{i=1}^{N} Q_i = \sum_{i=1}^{N} (\beta_{0i} + \beta_{1i} X_i) = \sum_{i=1}^{N} \beta_{0i} + \sum_{i=1}^{N} \beta_{1i} X_i.$$ (3.73)

Then one can aggregate if each micro unit faces the same marketing pressure, that is, marketing activities are homogeneous. This could be true in a store environment wherein all shoppers face the same regular prices, temporary price reductions, and displays. However, it would not be true across stores.

$$\sum_{i=1}^{N} Q_i = \sum_{i=1}^{N} (\beta_{0i} + \beta_{1i}X) = \sum_{i=1}^{N} \beta_{0i} + \left[\sum_{i=1}^{N} \beta_{1i}\right] X. \tag{3.74}$$

Otherwise, even in the linear case, the expected value of the aggregate parameter of an explanatory variable will not equal the sum of its micro parameters except in a special case. This special case of no aggregation bias occurs when the covariance between marketing effort and the corresponding micro parameter is zero. We believe this is unlikely to occur. Marketers typically allocate more marketing effort to the more responsive customers of segments. Technical details can be found in Krishnamurthy, Raj, and Selvam (1988).

When one considers a simple multiplicative model, one can see the problem with entity aggregation in nonlinear models:

$$Q_i = \beta_{0i} X_i^{\beta_{1i}} \gamma_i^{D_i}. \tag{3.75}$$

Working with aggregate-level (market) data does not yield the same results as aggregating from micro-level (store) data (shown here in terms of the arithmetic average):

$$\frac{1}{N} \sum_{i=1}^{N} \beta_{0i} X_i^{\beta_{1i}} \gamma_i^{D_i} \neq \beta_{0i} \left(\frac{1}{N} \sum_{i=1}^{N} X_i\right)^{\beta_{1i}} \gamma_i^{\frac{1}{N} \sum_i^N D_i}. \tag{3.76}$$

Note, however, there would be no problem if aggregated sales and price data were available as geometric means:

$$\left(\prod_i \beta_{0i} X_i^{\beta_{1i}} \gamma_i^{D_i}\right)^{\frac{1}{N}} \neq \left(\prod_i \beta_{0i}\right)^{\frac{1}{N}} \left(\prod_i X_i\right)^{\frac{\beta_{1i}}{N}} \gamma_i^{\frac{1}{N} \sum_i^N D_i}. \tag{3.77}$$

Unfortunately, data are not available in this format. Thus, one must recognize that micro (store) heterogeneity introduces bias in a macro (market) level model. The empirical equations necessary to produce debiased key promotional parameters and associated technical details are found in Christen et al. (1997).

4 DESIGN OF DYNAMIC RESPONSE MODELS

Naturally things change. Yet the fact that marketing for a firm does not take place in a static environment sometimes escapes modeling since static models are so much easier to work with than their dynamic counterparts. Customers, channel members, and competitors anticipate or react to a firm's actions, so their adjustment processes are one basis for believing market mechanisms should be dynamic. Another reason to consider dynamic models is that they help to overcome a major limitation of traditional static econometric models, namely their assumption of a constant environment.

Consider a model that shows the relationship between sales and advertising for a product. What would a static model miss? For one thing, it would omit the potentially important lagged effects of advertising on customer behavior. For another, it would ignore the possibility of structural change involving new competitors or new ways of competing. There is something to be gained by looking at dynamics.

In this chapter, we first discuss briefly some specification issues in dynamic models, then examine in some detail discrete models of carryover. We go on to look at other dynamic effects, such as temporal parameter variation. We finish with an examination of temporal aggregation bias. Note that our focus in this chapter is still on stationary markets, in which marketing and other effects on sales eventually dissipate. The more complex case of modeling evolution (long-term change) in sales and marketing efforts is discussed in Chapters 6 and 7.

Specification Issues in Dynamic Models

The specification of a dynamic model begins with the choice of the appropriate time measure, discrete or continuous. Then any anticipation (lead) or carryover (lag) effects must be identified. Sometimes past marketing efforts are represented by a stock variable rather than a number of individual lag variables.

Continuous-Time versus Discrete-Time Models

The main issue in the specification of a dynamic model is whether to formulate a continuous-time model using differential equations, a discrete-time model using difference equations, or a mixed model using differential-difference equations. Before discussing this issue, it is necessary to make a distinction between instantaneous variables and flow variables.

An instantaneous variable is a variable that is measurable at a point in time. Prices, distribution coverage, and interest rates are examples of instantaneous variables in marketing. A flow variable is a variable that is not measurable at a point in time. Unit sales and advertising expenditures are examples of flow variables in marketing. The rate of change in an instantaneous variable is also treated as a flow variable. If τ is the length of an observation period, an observation on a flow variable at time t corresponds to the integral

$$X_i = \frac{1}{\tau} \int_{t-\tau}^{t} X(\theta) d\theta. \tag{4.1}$$

If X were an instantaneous variable, this integral would not be observable.

The primary advantage of a continuous-time model is that *its estimated parameters are independent of the observation period.* This does not hold for a discrete-time model. A discrete-time model that was estimated on weekly data would be different from one that was estimated on annual data. We revisit this issue of temporal aggregation bias in discrete models later in this chapter.

The two primary advantages of a discrete-time model are that it can capture discontinuous phenomena and that most econometric techniques, such as those to be discussed in Chapter 5, were developed for estimating it. Since most models to date have been discrete-time models, we focus on them.

Leads and Lags

Current expenditures on marketing instruments usually do not have their full impact on sales in the same accounting period. Moreover, their impact on sales may extend well into the future. The influence of current marketing expenditures on sales in future periods is called the *carryover effect.* It is possible to extend marketing dynamics to include *anticipations* as well as carryover. *Leads* occur when customers or competitors anticipate a marketing action and adjust their behavior even before the action takes place. Therefore, sales may react to marketing efforts in the future.

Two forms of carryover effects have been identified (Kotler 1971). The *delayed response effect* arises when there is an interval between making the marketing expenditure and realizing the associated sale. For instance, a salesperson may wait some time between making an initial call and consummating the deal. The *customer holdover effect* arises because the marketing expenditure may create a new customer who not only will make an initial purchase but also will repurchase in future periods. Thus, the current marketing effort must receive some credit for these subsequent sales. Some credit should also be given to *purchase experience reinforcement* (Givon and Horsky 1990).

Total sales may not react fully and immediately to changes in marketing inputs but may do so in a more gradual manner. Advertising, for example, can create new customers; however, the timing of the first purchases by these new customers will vary according to each buyer's shopping and usage behavior. Moreover, repeat purchases will also depend on usage rates. Therefore, in order to assess properly the effectiveness of marketing instruments, the fraction of total sales in the current period and each succeeding period that are attributable to the current marketing effort must be measured. The duration of the carryover effect induced by this effort must also be determined.

Creation of Stock Variables

Another specification issue is whether to explicitly model carryover or to do so implicitly through the creation of stock variables. The common formulation of the stock variable [recall our discussion surrounding Equation (2.11)] is closely related to the most common formulation of a distributed lag model [see upcoming discussion of Equation (4.9)]. Some practitioners prefer the use of stock variables because they can subjectively specify retention rate for marketing effort, which then simplifies estimating the sales response function. Other practitioners use stock variables but estimate the unknown retention rate econometrically. To the extent that they use the same model of carryover, their work is no different than that of those who estimate the model explicitly. The key advantage to the stock approach is the ease of communicating results to management.

Discrete-Time Models of Carryover

Sales, Q_t, may respond to marketing expenditures with lag k. A linear model of this relation might be

$$Q_t = \beta_0 + \beta_{k+1} X_{t-k}. \tag{4.2}$$

We will identify this as the *Simple Lag (SL[k]) Model*. When $k = 0$, this is called the *Current Effects (CE) Model*, i.e., the static model (3.2). The effect of a marketing expenditure in period $t - k$ occurs only, and completely, within period t. Sometimes variables are defined as the ratio of the current period to the same period a year ago as a way to control for seasonality. For example, see the *Star Enterprise Industry Perspective* in this chapter and the *UTA Industry Perspective* in Chapter 9.

Often the effect of a marketing variable is *distributed* over several time periods. Consequently, sales in any period are a function of the current and previous marketing expenditures:

$$Q_t = \beta_0 + \sum_{k=0}^{\infty} \beta_{k+1} X_{t-k}, \tag{4.3}$$

where

$$\sum_{k=0}^{\infty} \beta_{k+1} = \text{constant} = \beta < \infty. \tag{4.4}$$

This restriction (4.4) ensures that even if a finite change in the level of marketing expenditures persists indefinitely, it will cause only a finite change in sales.

The *Infinite Distributed Lag (IDL) Model* (4.3) cannot be estimated, because it contains an infinite number of parameters. Even if the maximum lag is known a priori to be finite, so that we have the *Finite Distributed Lag* (FDL[K]) *Model*:

$$Q_t = \beta_0 + \sum_{k=0}^{K} \beta_{k+1} X_{t-k}, \tag{4.5}$$

the exact value of the maximum lag K is rarely known. In any case, the number of parameters to be estimated still may be large and the exogenous variables highly collinear. Additional assumptions usually must be imposed to obtain estimates. When $K = 0$, this model reduces to the Current Effects Model (Equation 3.3).

Assessing a Sponsorship at Star Enterprise

Star Enterprise manufactures, distributes, and sells petroleum products under the Texaco brand name in 26 Eastern and Gulf Coast states, plus the District of Columbia. It is a joint venture of Texaco and Saudi Arabian Oil Company. If it were a publicly held company, it would be among the top 100 Fortune 500 companies.

In early 1994, Texaco introduced CleanSystem[3] gasoline, which provided customers with a whole new system of engine cleaning as well as high performance, reduced emissions, and improved mileage. To introduce drivers to this newly-improved product line, Star planned their most innovative advertising and sales promotions to date. One such promotion involved becoming Major League Baseball's exclusive petroleum sponsor. Boasting the longest season and generating the largest attendance of any professional team sport, Major League Baseball (MLB) seemed to provide a good opportunity to create brand awareness and generate sales. The sponsorship gained Texaco a presence on every national broadcast game and the right to use the MLB logo on promotional items and at all stations.

During the baseball season, Star ran two promotions to increase sales at the pump. Working with MLB, Star gas stations became the only locations outside the 28 Major League ballparks where baseball fans could vote for American League and National League All-Star players. In conjunction with the balloting, a sweepstakes was run. For the second promotion, Star offered self-liquidating baseball glassware to wholesalers and retailers. The 20 ounce glasses featured logos of Major League teams that were popular in Star markets. While the All Star Balloting promotion was valid for all three grades of gasoline: Regular Unleaded, Power Plus and Power Premium, the MLB glasses promotion was valid only for the latter two gasoline grades.

Did the promotions influence gasoline sales volume? To answer this question, monthly data at the retail store level were used. The variables were defined as 1994 values relative to 1993 values using the same stations in both years. Thus, extraneous variations, such as increases (decreases) in sales due to opening (closing) of a new (old) station and seasonal gasoline demands, were controlled. The data were pooled (months × stations). In addition, three dummy variables were constructed. One dummy, SRBallot, was equal to one for the month of June and zero otherwise. Another, LRBallot, was equal to one for the months of June through August and zero otherwise. For the Major League Baseball All-Star balloting promotion, SRBallot represented the immediate effect of the promotion when it ran and LRBallot represented the residual effects of the promotion in the two following two months as well as the immediate effects. A third dummy variable, Glasses, represented participation in the MLB glasses promotion and was one for the months of June and July and zero otherwise.

A linear functional form was used. A double-log model was also examined. There was one equation for each grade of gasoline:

$$\frac{Q\,Reg_t}{Q\,Reg_{t-12}} = \beta_{Reg0} + \beta_{Reg1}\frac{Price\,Reg_t}{Price\,Reg_{t-12}}$$
$$+ \delta_{RegSR}SRBallot + \delta_{RegLR}LRBallotD_3$$

$$\frac{QPlus_t}{QPlus_{t-12}} = \beta_{Plus0} + \beta_{Plus1}\frac{PricePlus_t}{PricePlus_{t-12}}$$
$$+ \delta_{PlusSR}SRBallot + \delta_{PlusLR}LRBallot + \delta_{PlusGlass}Glasses$$

$$\frac{Q\,Prem_t}{Q\,Prem_{t-12}} = \beta_{Prem0} + \beta_{Prem1}\frac{Price\,Prem_t}{Price\,Prem_{t-12}}$$
$$+ \delta_{PremSR}SRBallot + \delta_{PremLR}LRBallot + \delta_{PremGlass}Glasses$$

Statistical results showed that the volume of gasoline sold increased over the time frame of the MLB promotion efforts. However, what the results also indicated was that the promotion had very little impact on this increase; rather price seemed to have been the cause for the increase. Since many believe that a sponsorship needs to be run for at least three years before its full potential is reached, it was premature to say that this first year effort was not successful. Nonetheless, various business factors led Texaco to drop its MLB All-Star Balloting sponsorship within a few years. (*Editors' Note*: Pepsi-Cola became the sponsor. The 1997 All-Star balloting campaign tied Pepsi with Foot Locker, CompUSA, and 7-Eleven in an effort to distribute 65 million ballots.)

Prepared by Richard S. Arold, Manager, Research, at Star Enterprise.

The Lag Structure as a Set of Probabilities

A very useful assumption, and one that is usually plausible in marketing situations, is that the coefficients of the lagged terms of a marketing decision variable all have the same sign. The general distributed lag can now be written as

$$Q_t = \beta_0 + \beta \sum_{k=0}^{\infty} \omega_k X_{t-k}, \qquad (4.6)$$

where

$$\omega \geq 0 \text{ and } \sum_{k=0}^{\infty} \omega_k = 1. \qquad (4.7)$$

The sequence of omegas (ω's) describes the shape of the lag over time. More importantly, the omegas can be regarded as probabilities of a discrete-time distribution.

This probability formulation permits easy interpretation of some of the properties of the empirical response function. Properties like the average lag between making a marketing expenditure and obtaining a sales response, or the degree to which the impact is concentrated in an interval of short duration or diffused over an extended period, can be calculated using the moments of the probability distribution.

Geometric Distribution. The *Geometric Distributed Lag* (GL) *Model* is the most commonly used distributed-lag model in marketing. The maximum impact of marketing expenditures on sales is registered instantaneously. Then the influence declines geometrically to zero, that is, if a past expenditure has an impact in a particular period, its impact in subsequent periods will only be a constant fraction of that impact. This constant fraction is called the *retention rate*. This approach was introduced to marketing by Palda (1964) in his attempt to measure the cumulative effects of advertising. The average retention rate of advertising for frequently purchased consumer goods is about 0.5 for monthly data (Assmus, Farley, and Lehmann 1984, p. 73). A similar value (0.439) was found for generating leads for Navy recruiters (Morey and McCann 1983, p. 198).

If the retention rate is λ, the geometric distribution gives

$$\omega_t = (1-\lambda)\lambda^k, \quad k = 0,1,2, \ldots, \qquad (4.8)$$

where $0 < \lambda < 1$. Thus, the specification of the sales response function becomes

$$Q_t = \beta_0 + \beta(1-\lambda) \sum_{k=0}^{\infty} \lambda^k X_{t-k}. \qquad (4.9)$$

This is a special case of the stock-variable approach discussed in Chapter 2. Here we assume that that the first period has a full effect. Recall that in the very closely related adstock model, the first period is weighted one-half.

This relation (4.9) is nonlinear in the parameter λ. In the case of more than one independent variable, the same rate of decline could apply to different variables. This assumption was made in studies by Frank and Massy (1967) and Montgomery and Silk (1972). However, it is more probable that different rates of decline apply to different variables. For example, advertising expenditures by a firm and advertising expenditures by its competitors exhibited different carryover effects on the firm's sales of beer (Peles 1971a). Thus, rather than assuming equal retention rates, different retention rates should be specified and then empirically tested to see whether they are equal. In the case of a brand in the hypnotics and sedatives segment of the British pharmaceutical market, personal communications (detailing spending) and impersonal communications (magazine advertising and direct mail spending) were found to have the same retention rate (Leeflang, Mijatovic, and Saunders 1992).

Estimation. The parameters of the nonlinear model (4.9) can be estimated by applying the Koyck transformation (Koyck 1954):

$$Q_t = \beta_0 + \beta(1-\lambda)X_t + \beta(1-\lambda)\sum_{k=1}^{\infty}\lambda^k X_{t-k} + w_t$$

$$\frac{-\lambda Q_{t-1} = -\lambda\beta_0 \qquad\qquad - \beta(1-\lambda)\sum_{k=1}^{\infty}\lambda^k X_{t-k} - \lambda w_{t-1}}{Q_t = (1-\lambda)\beta_0 + \beta(1-\lambda)X_t + \lambda Q_{t-1} + (w_t - \lambda w_{t-1}).} \qquad (4.10)$$

Thus, by simply taking the structural equation, lagging it by one period, multiplying this lagged equation by λ, and subtracting the result from the structural equation, a linear estimating equation is obtained. [Using lag operators facilitates working with lagged variables; see Appendix 4.] This is sometimes written as

$$Q_t = (1-\lambda)\beta_0 + \beta_1 X_t + \lambda Q_{t-1} + u_t. \qquad (4.11)$$

where $u_t = w_t - \lambda w_{t-1}$. The short-term effect of marketing effort is $\beta(1-\lambda) = \beta_1$. The implied long-term effect is β. As we showed earlier in Chapter 2 (equation 2.38), a fraction θ of the long-run impact occurs in $\log[1-\theta]/\log[\lambda]$ periods (e.g., Russell 1985).

Testing. The Koyck estimating equation is very similar to two other models, which arise from different processes. The first is the *Autoregressive Current Effects* (ACE) *Model.* This model argues that marketing effort only has contemporaneous effects on sales:

$$Q_t = \beta_0 + \beta_1 X_t + u_t. \tag{4.12}$$

However, other factors such as consumer inertia and habit formation cause sales to fluctuate smoothly over time. These omitted variables are often captured by an autoregressive process of the error term:

$$u_t = \rho u_{t-1} + w_t, \tag{4.13}$$

where w_t is white noise. This approach was followed in a study of an apparel store's sales (Lam, Vandenbosch, and Pearce 1998, p. 65). The implied carryover effect in the ACE model is zero, so that the short- and long-run impact is the same, i.e., β_1. To get a regression form of the ACE process, (4.13) can be used to replace u in (4.12):

$$Q_t - \beta_0 - \beta_1 X_t = \rho(Q_{t-1} - \beta_0 - \beta_1 X_{t-1}) + w_t \tag{4.14}$$

or

$$Q_t = (1 - \rho)\beta_0 + \beta_1 X_t + \rho Q_{t-1} - \beta_1 \rho X_{t-1} + w_t. \tag{4.15}$$

If an ACE model does in fact underlie the data, it will be difficult to detect it with anything other than careful time series techniques. For example, the regression form of the model includes, among other things, a spurious lagged effect of marketing on sales. Thus, in general, transfer function specification techniques outlined in Chapter 7 are needed to discover an ACE process in the data.

The second model resembling the Koyck estimating equation is the *Partial Adjustment Model* (PAM). This response pattern occurs when consumers can only partially adjust to advertising or other marketing stimuli. However, they do gradually adjust to the desired consumption level, which causes the marketing effects to be distributed over time:

$$Q_t = (1 - \varphi)[\beta_0 + \beta_1 X_t] + \varphi Q_{t-1} + w_t, \tag{4.16}$$

where $1 - \varphi$ is the adjustment rate and $0 < \varphi < 0$. The partial adjustment model is very similar to the Koyck scheme, except for the structure of the error term. The implied long-term advertising effect is also β. If, in addition, the errors in (4.16) are not white noise but autoregressive as in (4.13), the *Autoregressive Partial Adjustment Model* (APAM) results. This model reduces to Autoregressive Current Effects if φ is zero, the Partial Adjustment Model if ρ is zero, or the Current Effects Model (Equation 3.3) if both are zero, and thus provides a way of identifying lag structure.

Selection among alternative dynamic specifications is done by *nesting*, a process in which the parameters of lower-order equations are contained within the parameters of higher-order ones.[1] A more common nesting is based on the *Autoregressive*

Geometric Lag (AGL) *Model*. This model yields: for $\rho = 0$, the Geometric Lag (Koyck) Model; for $\lambda = 0$, the Autoregressive Current Effects Model; and for $\rho = 0$ and $\lambda = 0$, the Current Effects Model. The special case where $\rho = \lambda \ (\equiv \varphi)$ gives the Partial Adjustment Model. The Autoregressive Partial Adjustment Model and the Autoregressive Geometric Lag Model themselves can be imbedded in a Second-Order Autoregressive Geometric Lag Model. Now the Autoregressive Geometric Lag Model holds when $\alpha_1 = \rho$ and $\alpha_2 = 0$; and the Autoregressive Partial Effects Model holds when $\alpha_1 = \rho + \varphi$ and $\alpha_2 = -\rho\varphi$. For details on the nesting process, see Bass and Clarke (1972), Weiss and Windal (1980), and Leeflang, Mijatovic, and Saunders (1992). The latter researchers present a complex nesting diagram that incorporates direct distributed lags and geometric distributed lags with different retention rates for different market drivers.

Negative Binomial Distribution. The monotonically decreasing pattern of coefficients in the geometric lag structure may be inappropriate in some marketing situations. The effect of marketing expenditures may be small initially, increase to a peak, and then decline. The geometric lag can be modified so that the geometric decline does not start immediately in the first period but rather starts at the *j*th period. The modification can be represented by

$$Q_t = \beta_0 + (1 - \lambda) \sum_{k=0}^{j-2} \beta_{k+1} X_{t-k} + \beta_j (1 - \lambda) \sum_{k=j}^{\infty} \lambda^{k-j} X_{t-k+1} + u_t . \tag{4.17}$$

This extension has been incorporated into models by Bass and Clarke (1972), Lambin (1972b), and Montgomery and Silk (1972). Alternatively, the *negative binomial distribution* (or Pascal distribution), which is a flexible two-parameter distribution, can represent such an effect:

$$\omega = \frac{(r + k - 1)!}{(r - 1)! \, k!} (1 - \lambda)^r \lambda^k, \quad k = 0, 1, 2, \dots , \tag{4.18}$$

where $0 < \lambda < 1$, and r *is* a positive integer. The mean lag is $\lambda r/(1 - \lambda)$ and the variability is $\lambda r/(1 - \lambda)^2$. For $r = 1$, the negative binomial reduces to the geometric distribution. An examination of the household-cleaning product category in a European country using a market share (attraction) model found the best r to be 1, indicating that the geometric distribution was sufficient (Bultez 1978, p. 255).

Promotional Modeling at Glaxo Wellcome

Glaxo Wellcome Inc., the nation's leading research-based pharmaceutical company and a subsidiary of the London-based Glaxo Wellcome PLC, is committed to fighting disease by bringing innovative medicines and services to patients and to healthcare providers. Most of its promotion is targeted to physicians who write prescriptions (Rxs) for their patients. A Glaxo decision support group measures the effect of these promotions with models to help management answer questions about promotion levels, targets, sales force size and structure.

Glaxo has retail Rx counts by product (its own and competitors), payer (e.g., cash, Medicaid/Medicare, and third party), month, and most individual physicians; these Rx counts are projected from a "convenience" sample of about 80% of the prescriptions filled in the United States. It has quantity purchases by product, month, and virtually all dispensers (e.g., hospitals or drug stores). It also has national "audits" of most types of promotions by product (its own and competitors) and month (or quarter). It has its own promotion by product, day, type, quantity, and targeted individual but does not have its competitors' promotions by individual.

Glaxo prefers to model "new" Rxs of individual physicians because new Rxes measure physicians' decisions, although it sometimes models product purchases. A "new" Rx is the first filling of an Rx; whereas, a "refill" Rx is a refilling of the original Rx. Glaxo eventually uses the refills in its economic analysis. Glaxo uses five different models.

The impact of a single promotional event is modeled with a "Test Minus Control, After Minus Before" Model:

$$MS_{m,p} = \beta_0(1 + \beta_1 m) MS_{m,c,p}, \text{ all months before the event, and}$$

$$R_{m,p} = MS_{m,p} - \left[\beta_0(1 + \beta_1 m) MS_{m,c,p}\right], \text{ all months,}$$

where MS is the share (but it could be the count) of new Rxs; R is the residual between selected "test" and "control" physicians; and m is month. Each physician who got a promotion is carefully matched to control physicians who did not get the promotion. Thus, p is a test physician and c is that physician's control physician. The response parameters are estimated from the data before the promotional event. Residuals after the promotional event are compared to those from before the event for changes and significance.

The following models are for repeated promotional events. In the next three, Glaxo first assigns physicians to similar groups. The two most important assignment criteria are the physicians' prior year's count of market new Rxs and the Glaxo brand's prior year's share of new Rxs. A "Lagged New Rx Model" provides monthly changes and an estimate of promotions' carryover:

$$MS_{m,p,g} = \beta_{g,0} + \lambda_g MS_{m-1,p,g} + \beta_{g,1} Promo_{m,p,g} + \beta_{g,2} Promo_{m-1,p,g}$$
$$+ \text{ other promotional terms of either more lags or types}$$

where *Promo* is a promotion type and level; and *g* indicates a physician's group membership. Glaxo may deseasonalize and de-trend the variables. Glaxo may normalize the promotion by dividing it by the physicians' market new Rxs. The carryover effect is captured by λ.

An "Exponentially-Smoothed Lagged New Rx Model" also provides monthly changes from promotion and an estimate of promotions' "carryover," but, in addition, allows a more rapid return toward the pre-promotion share:

$$L_{m,p,g} = \theta_g L_{m-1,p,g} + (1 - \theta_g) MS_{m-1,p,g}$$

$$MS_{m,p,g} = \beta_{g,0} + \lambda_g L_{m,p,g} + \beta_{g,1} Promo_{m,p,g} + \beta_{g,2} Promo_{m-1,p,g}$$
$$+ \text{ other promotional terms of either more lags or types}$$

where *L* is the exponentially smoothed share or "brand loyalty," *MS* is the new prescription share, and θ is an estimated smoothing weight; we choose $L_{0,p,g}$ as the physician's average share from prior and non-modeled observations. This model can be modified to use new Rx counts instead of share.

An "Annual New Rx Model by Promotion Level" provides the quickest analysis and easily produces graphical output. Share change between promotion levels, $MS_{y,Promo,g} - MS_{y,Promo-1,g}$, are used to measure the incremental prescriptions per promotion at each level of promotion, *Promo* = 0, 1, 2, ..., for each year *y*.

Finally, an "Annual Promotional 'Pressure' Model" incorporates competitive promotion. This model says that the change in share is proportional to the promotional pressure or that a brand's share moves toward its promotional share:

$$MS_{y,b} - MS_{y-1,b} = \beta_1 (PromoS_{y,b} - MS_{y-1,b}),$$

where *MS* is new Rx share and *PromoS* is promotional share for each brand *b* in the market. The rate of change β_1 can be found to depend on the level of market promotion.

Because Glaxo management has stressed the importance of "proving" that promotional efforts pay their way, market response modeling such as this has received considerable support.

Prepared by David R. Bamberger, Advisor to Decision Support Services and to Promotion Analysis, Glaxo Wellcome Inc.

Studies of monthly Lydia Pinkham patent medicine data tried different values of *r*. The best fit was either *r* = 4 (Mann 1975) or 6 (Bultez and Naert 1979, p. 460) depending on the number of observations used and whether or not the data was seasonally adjusted. Interestingly, the Bultez and Naert study found that the values of λ and the sales-goodwill elasticity were conditioned by the values chosen for *r*. In particular as *r* increases, λ diminishes in such a way that the mean lag and its standard deviation stabilize as soon as *r* equals 2. This finding indicates that different lag structures may not lead to very different implications for decision making. Research on the effects of advertising on cheese sales in New York City used the negative binomial distribution with different λs for generic advertising and brand advertising. In both cases, drawing on the findings of Bultez and Naert, the value of *r* was set equal to 2. The λ for generic advertising was estimated to be 0.80 while that for brand advertising 0.95 (Kinnucan and Fearon 1986, p. 97).

Polynomial Lag Structures

A more flexible approach to estimating the Finite Distributed Lag Model (4.5) involves expressing the coefficients, β_{k+1}, in terms of some function $f(k)$. The function $f(k)$ is not known. However, the Weierstrass theorem states that all continuous functions can be approximated by polynomials on any finite interval with arbitrary small error. Thus, the function $f(k)$ can be approximated by a polynomial in *k*. These two successive approximations can be written

$$\beta_{k+1} \cong f(k) \cong \sum_{p=0}^{P} \alpha_p k^p, \quad k = 0, 1, 2, \dots, K. \tag{4.19}$$

This *Polynomial Distributed Lag* (PDL[*K*, *P*]) *Model* (or *Almon lag model*) has a length of lag *K* and a polynomial of degree *P*. Presumably *P* is less than *K* so that there are fewer parameters to estimate in the restricted version. The order of the polynomial P is usually taken to be quite low, rarely exceeding three or four (Greene 1997, p. 790). The problem of choosing the lag length and the degree of the polynomial is addressed in Maddala (1992, pp. 426-29). See also Pindyck and Rubinfeld (1998, pp. 238-42). In assessing the demand for fractional horsepower direct-current motors as a distributed lag in historical automobile sales, a lag length of 12 was used to allow for seasonality and other lag effects in monthly data. A polynomial of degree 3 was used so that the lag coefficients achieved a smooth cubic shape (Dubin 1998, p. 32). The same values for lag length (12) and degree (3) provided the best empirical fit for television and radio advertising variables in a sales response model assessing the effect of generic advertising on monthly sales of fluid milk (Capps and Schmitz 1991, pp. 135-36).[2] In the case of yogurt, degree 2 and lag lengths 7 and 5 were used for brand advertising and generic advertising respectively (Hall and Foik 1982, pp. 21-22). Interestingly, while brand advertising exerted its highest impact on yogurt sales with a delay of two to three months after the expenditure occurred, the effectiveness of generic advertising declined almost geometrically. Capturing long-tailed lag distributions are difficult with a PDL Model. One way to handle this problem is to have a polynomial for the early β_{k+1} and a geometric lag for the latter portion.

One advantage of a polynomial lag structure is that the set of predetermined variables does not contain any lagged values of the dependent variable. Consequently, some of the estimation problems inherent in geometric lag models and other such similar models do not occur and ordinary least-squares regression can be used.

Untangling Purchase Reinforcement and Advertising Carryover

We have already noted that at least some of the impact of advertising in one time period may be carried over into future periods. The argument is that past advertising is remembered by those who see it and, as a result, a brand builds "goodwill." This goodwill influences brand choice. This approach may be too simplistic in that it ignores purchase experience. Yes, advertising may create the initial purchase, but customers will buy a brand again only if they find it acceptable in use. Thus, an alternative to an advertising carryover approach is a *current advertising effects with purchase feedback* approach. In reality we would expect both to be operating. Thus, a term is added to Geometric Distributed Lag Model (4.9) to capture simultaneously the relative magnitudes of the two influences (Givon and Horsky 1990):

$$Q_t = \beta_0 + \beta_1 \sum_{k=0}^{\infty} \lambda^k X_{t-k} + \beta_2 Q_{t-1} + w_t. \qquad (4.20)$$

This is known as the *Geometric Distributed Lag with Purchase Feedback* (*GLPF*) *Model*. Most work in this area has been done with market share, instead of unit sales, as well as with advertising as the marketing driver affecting goodwill.[3] A Koyck-type transformation gives:

$$MS_t = (1-\lambda)\beta_0 + \beta_1 A_t + (\beta_2 + \lambda) MS_{t-1} - \lambda \beta_2 MS_{t-2} + w_t - \lambda w_{t-1}. \tag{4.21}$$

Empirical work with several product categories indicated that purchase reinforcement dominated over advertising carryover in affecting the evolution of market share. Indeed, while significant purchase feedback effects were found, no advertising carryover was found (Givon and Horsky 1990, p. 184).

Possibly some consumers rely only on their experience with a product while others are also affected by past advertising (Givon 1993). If θ is the proportion of those who are not affected by the carryover effect of advertising out of all those who bought the product, the *Partial Geometric Distributed Lag with Purchase Feedback* (*PGLPF*) *Model* is specified as

$$MS_t = \beta_0 + \beta_1 A_{t-k} + \sum_{k=1}^{\infty} \lambda^k \left[\prod_{j=1}^{k} (1 - \theta MS_{t-j}) \right] A_{t-k} + \beta_2 MS_{t-1} + w_t, \tag{4.22}$$

with estimating equation

$$MS_t = (1 - \lambda[1 - \theta MS_{t-1}])\beta_0 + \beta_1 A_t + (\beta_2 + \lambda[1 - \theta MS_{t-1}]) MS_{t-1}$$
$$- \lambda[1 - \theta MS_{t-1}]\beta_2 MS_{t-2} + w_t - \lambda[1 - \theta MS_{t-1}]w_{t-1}. \tag{4.23}$$

Unfortunately this model is difficult to estimate. It has been recommended that one use only the first K terms for advertising in (4.22), i.e., truncate, and then do nonlinear regression (Givon 1993, p. 168). Using data from the Givon and Horsky study, λ was found to be zero as before and therefore θ was unidentifiable.

The Autoregressive Distributed Lag Model

The most general distributed lag model for market response, the *Autoregressive Distributed Lag (ADL) Model*, contains both an *autoregressive* (AR) process for sales along with a *moving average* (MA) distributed lag process for the sales driver (Tellis, Chandy, and Thaivanich 2000, p. 34):

$$Q_t = \alpha + \sum_{i=1}^{p} \gamma_i Q_{t-i} + \sum_{k=0}^{q} \beta_k X_{t-k} + w_t. \qquad (4.24)$$

The values of γ influence the rate at which the carryover effect peaks and decays whereas the values of β influence the number and heights of the peaks. The relative values of γ and β differentiate between purchase and reinforcement effects of various orders. The formulation (4.24) is practical because, in certain circumstances, an infinite-order MA can be captured by a first-order AR term and an infinite-order AR process can be captured by a first-order MA term. This will be discussed in Chapter 7.

Capturing Leads as well as Lags

An interesting catalog of lead/lag effects (Figure 4-1) has been provided by Doyle and Saunders (1985). By distinguishing between a steady state and a transient component of the effect of marketing on sales, they propose the following reduced forms for marketing dynamics.

Case 1. Steady State.

$$Q_t = \alpha_0 + \beta_0 X_t, \qquad (4.25)$$

a pure static model of sales versus marketing effort.

Case 2. Positive Lag.

$$Q_t = \alpha_0 + \beta_0 X_t + \sum_{k=1}^{K} \beta_{-k} X_{t-k}, \quad \beta_{-k} > 0, \qquad (4.26)$$

the typical distributed lag model.

Case 3. Negative Lag.

$$Q_t = \alpha_0 + \beta_0 X_t - \sum_{k=1}^{K} \beta_{-k} X_{t-k}, \quad \beta_{-k} > 0, \qquad (4.27)$$

in which smart and opportunistic customers stockpile when the brand is on deal. After the promotional campaign, sales temporarily sink below the steady-state level.

FUNCTION	EXPLANATION	BEHAVIOR
1 STEADY STATE	Simple effect	
2 POSITIVE LAG	Distributed lag	
3 NEGATIVE LAG	Stocking	
4 POSITIVE LEAD	Anticipation	
5 NEGATIVE LEAD	Regret reduction	
6 NEGATIVE LEAD & LAG	Opportunistic	

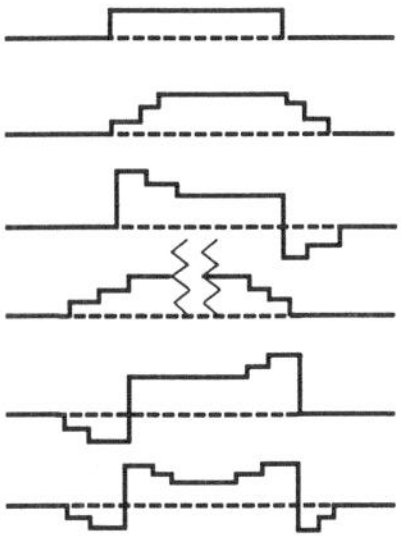

Figure 4-1. A Taxonomy of Dynamic Models. *Source:* Doyle and Saunders (1985, p. 57).

Case 4. Positive Lead.

$$Q_t = \alpha_0 + \beta_0 X_t + \sum_{k=1}^{L} \beta_{+k} X_{t+k}, \quad \beta_{+k} > 0, \tag{4.28}$$

in which customer anticipation causes a gradual buildup of sales before the marketing event takes place. For example, sales of child restraint seats for automobiles increased before laws making them mandatory went into effect.

Case 5. Negative Lead.

$$Q_t = \alpha_0 + \beta_0 X_t - \sum_{k=1}^{L} \beta_{+k} X_{t+k}, \quad \beta_{+k} > 0, \tag{4.29}$$

in which even smarter and more opportunistic customers than in Case 3 anticipate the promotion period and reduce current consumption before the event.

Case 6. Negative Lag and Lead.

$$Q_t = \alpha_0 + \beta_0 X_t - \sum_{\substack{k=-K \\ k \neq 0}}^{L} \beta_k X_{t+k}, \quad \beta_{+k} > 0, \quad \beta_{-k} > 0, \quad (4.30)$$

which is a combination of Cases 3 and 5.

These models can be embedded in the general model:

$$Q_t = \alpha_0 + \beta_0 X_t + \sum_{k=1}^{K} \beta_{-k} X_{t-k} + \sum_{l=1}^{L} \beta_{+l} X_{t+l}, \quad (4.31)$$

where β_{+k} and β_{-k} are now unrestricted in sign. In an empirical investigation of pre- and post-promotional dips using scanner data, this flexible model and a lead-lag version of the Almon model, in which the degree of the lagged effect polynomial could be different from the degree of the lead effect polynomial, were found to give similar results—and both were found to be superior to a finite lag version of the geometric model, in which the lagged effect decay parameter could be different from the lead effect parameter (van Heerde, Leeflang, and Wittink 2000).

In sum, market response models that do not include carryover effects are likely to be misspecified and consequently should fit less well. In the case of advertising carryover, the observation has been by Assmus, Farley, and Lehmann (1984, p. 67) that

> When omission of a carryover effect constitutes misspecification, upward bias of the coefficient for current advertising will result if current and past advertising are correlated positively and if past advertising has a positive impact on current sales.

In fact, their meta-analysis (p. 71) found short-term elasticities were substantially higher in models without a carryover coefficient than in models with one. Moreover, models with and without a carryover term fit equally well suggesting that the larger short-term elasticity captures both effects when carryover is not specified.

Shape of the Response Function Revisited

The coefficients of the controllable marketing instruments and the uncontrollable environmental variables in market response models are almost invariably assumed to be constant for the analysis period. However, the longer the time interval, the more tenuous this assumption is likely to be. Our focus in this section is consequently on the time effectiveness of marketing decision variables. We have already noted in Chapter 3 that coefficients can vary over cross-section units.

Coefficient variation may be either nonstochastic or stochastic. Nonstochastic variation occurs when the coefficients change as a function of observable variables. This variation is often called systematic. Stochastic variation occurs when coefficients are random parameters from either a stationary or nonstationary process. Any model of stochastic parameter variation that assumes an autoregressive process is called a *sequentially varying parameter model*. The modeling of changing market environments has been critically reviewed by Wildt and Winer (1983).

Systematic Coefficient Variation

Systematic variation can be expressed by a general model or by specific models for special cases. Specific models have been developed for situations where sample observations are generated by two or more distinct regimes. The seasonality model discussed in Chapter 3 was an example of these "switching" models.

General Systematically Varying Coefficient Model. The parameter vector β in some models, such as $q = f(\beta, X_1)$, may exhibit variation, and this variation may be systematic. The primary cause of systematic temporal coefficient variation in marketing is the product life cycle. Marketing theory states that the demand elasticities of managerial decision variables change over the product life cycle. The theory has been interpreted to say that the advertising elasticity is highest at the growth stage of a product's life because at that time advertising is increasing product awareness, and lowest during maturity, with elasticities increasing slightly through saturation and decline stages of the product life cycle (Mahajan, Bretschneider, and Bradford 1980). The theory supposedly conjectures that the price elasticity increases over the first three stages introduction, growth, and maturity and decreases during the decline stage (Mickwitz 1959).

Relations. Systematic variation implies that the parameter vector can be written as

$$\beta = f(\alpha, X_2). \tag{4.32}$$

The parameters β are expressed as a function of other parameters α and observable variables X_2. This set of variables may include some of the variables in X_1. Systematic variations in advertising, price, sales call, and perceived product quality elasticities were found in studies by Parsons (1975a), Arora (1979), Simon (1979), Shoemaker (1986), Parsons and Vanden Abeele (1981), and Shankar, Carpenter, and Krishnamurthi (1999). For example, in the last study, the marketing spending and perceived product quality elasticities for ethical drugs depended on whether the brand was a pioneer or entered in the growth or mature stage of the product life cycle. The innovation or imitation coefficients in the Bass market growth model may vary systematically with advertising (Simon and Sebastian 1987).

The deterministic relation (4.32) can be made stochastic by adding a disturbance term, v, or

$$\beta = f(\alpha, X_2, v), \tag{4.33}$$

When this relation is linear and it is imbedded in a linear response function, the resultant model

$$q_t = X'_{1t} X_{2t} \alpha + X'_{1t} v_t + u_t, \tag{4.34}$$

has a heteroscedastic disturbance term. Such a model was used to investigate the influence of advertising on a market's price sensitivity (Gatignon 1984) and to examine factors influencing sales force effectiveness (Gatignon and Hanssens 1987). A kindred model has incorporated store trading area heterogeneity in assessing the impact of everyday store prices on store sales (Montgomery 1997).

The static SCAN*PRO model described in Chapter 3 has been made dynamic by relating store intercepts and the brand's own price elasticity to a measure of cumulative price promotions for that brand as well as for its competitors and to the time since the most recent promotion for that brand and for its competitors. The brand's own non-price promotional response parameters are related to the time since any promotion for the brand and its competitors (Foekens, Leeflang, and Wittink 1999).

Empirical Evidence. Empirical evidence on changes in the efficiency of various marketing instruments at different stages of the product life cycle is sparse. Indications are that advertising elasticities generally fall as products pass through their life cycles (Arora 1979; Parsons 1975b). Price elasticities seem to decrease markedly during the introduction and growth stages, reaching a minimum in the maturity stage, after which they may experience an increase during the decline stage (Simon 1979). For industrial chemicals, Lilien and Yoon (1988, p. 273) concluded:

> The level of price elasticity tends to be lower during the later stages of the product life cycle (maturity and decline) than during the earlier stages (introduction and growth). There is no clear tendency of shift in the level of the price elasticity between the introduction and growth stages. Over the latter two stages of the product life cycle (maturity and decline), price elasticity shows a tendency to be stable.

Although these results may be tentative because of methodological problems, [e.g., Shoemaker's (1986) comment on Simon (1979)], nonetheless, the empirical findings do seem inconsistent with current marketing theory.

Switching Models. If structural changes occur at *known* points in time, the changes in the coefficients of the relevant variables can be represented by dummy variables. In the case of a patent medicine, restrictions placed upon Lydia Pinkham's advertising copy by the Food and Drug Administration in 1914 and again in 1925 and by the Federal Trade Commission in 1940 were assumed to be captured by dummy variables (Palda 1964). These dummy variables affect only the intercept of the sales response function. A somewhat more appropriate approach might have been to use the dummy variables to model changes in the slope coefficient, i.e., the effectiveness of advertising.

The switch from one regime to another may depend on time, but alternatively, it might depend on a threshold value for some variable or occur stochastically. Recall Figure 3-3. In the two-regime case, the model can be written as

$$\begin{array}{lll} \text{Regime 1:} & Q = f(\mathbf{X}_1;\boldsymbol{\beta}) & \text{if condition holds,} \\ \text{Regime 2:} & Q = f(\mathbf{X}_2;\boldsymbol{\alpha}) & \text{if condition does not hold.} \end{array} \tag{4.35}$$

In a study of the impact of market share on perceived product quality, brands were grouped into those that were premium priced and operating in categories dominated by concerns of widespread acceptance and those that weren't (see Hellof and Jacobson 1999, p. 22 for details). In another study, the existence of an advertising threshold effect was tested using the stochastic version of (4.35). Here, the first regime condition was "with probability θ" while the second regime condition was "with probability $1 - \theta$" (Bemmaor 1984). Yet another study looked at the impact of Florida Department of Citrus coupon promotional programs on the demand for frozen concentrated orange juice. Separate sales response functions were estimated for coupon users and nonusers. The probability of a household redeeming a coupon was itself a function of household characteristics, market conditions, and properties of various promotional programs (Lee and Brown 1985).

Coefficients in a response function might vary between each time period rather than only between a few time periods. If cross-section observations were also available, a random coefficients model (equation 3.44) could be used. Otherwise, some a priori constraint must be imposed to obtain unique estimates of the coefficients.

Stochastic Parameter Variation

The primary model involving random parameters from a stationary process is the random coefficients model discussed in Chapter 3, while that for random parameters from a nonstationary process is the Cooley-Prescott model. A generalization of the random coefficients model to time series data is the return-to-normality model. Parameters in this model are dynamic.

Return-to-Normality Model. Little (1966), whose work antedated econometric developments in this area, was the first to propose such a sales response function. The coefficient of promotion rate was assumed to be generated by a stochastic process:

$$\beta_i = (1 - \varphi)\overline{\beta} + \phi\beta_{t-1} + v_t,$$ (4.36)

where $0 \leq \phi \leq 1$. In this model, the value of the parameter β in any time period is a weighted average of its value in the previous period and its long-run average value plus a random disturbance. The term $1 - \phi$ represents a tendency to converge toward the mean value $\overline{\beta}$. As $\phi \rightarrow 1$, β_t becomes more dependent on β_{t-1} and wanders more freely from its mean value. On the other hand, as $\phi \rightarrow 0$, β becomes equal to the mean value plus a random coefficient, as in a random coefficients model. This model can be generalized by letting the process generating the parameters be an Autoregressive Regressive Moving Average (ARMA) process. ARMA processes are discussed in Chapter 6.

Cooley-Prescott Model. A model in which the parameters follow a nonstationary stochastic process is the random walk model. In this model, the parameters are assumed to adapt to permanent and transitory changes (Cooley and Prescott 1973). The transitory change of the parameter vector can be represented as

$$\boldsymbol{\beta}_t = \boldsymbol{\beta}_t^* + \boldsymbol{\tau}_t,$$ (4.37)

where $\boldsymbol{\beta}_t^*$ is the permanent component of $\boldsymbol{\beta}_t$, and $\boldsymbol{\tau}_t$ is the vector of transient change in period t. In addition to transient changes, which are in effect for only one period, there are permanent changes, which persist into the future:

$$\boldsymbol{\beta}_t^* = \boldsymbol{\beta}_{t-1}^* + \boldsymbol{\xi}_t,$$ (4.38)

where $\boldsymbol{\xi}_t$ is the permanent change vector.

The vectors $\boldsymbol{\tau}$ and $\boldsymbol{\xi}$ are assumed to be identically and independently distributed normal variables with mean vectors zero and known covariance structures. These covariance structures are written as

$$E(\boldsymbol{\tau}\boldsymbol{\tau}') = (1 - \phi)\sigma^2\boldsymbol{\Sigma}_\tau$$ (4.39)

and

$$E(\xi\xi') = \phi\sigma^2\Sigma_\xi, \tag{4.40}$$

where Σ_τ and Σ_ξ are known up to scale factors. The parameter ϕ indicates how fast the parameters are adapting to structural change. It is restricted to fall within the range $0 \le \phi \le 1$. In this formulation, if $\phi = 0$, once again the model is a random coefficients model.

Certain simplifying assumptions are often made for estimation purposes. In the absence of information to the contrary, first, the relative importance of permanent and transitory changes is assumed to be the same for all random parameters; thus, $\Sigma_\tau = \Sigma_\xi$. Second, these changes are assumed to be uncorrelated among parameters. Consequently, the covariance matrices will be diagonal. The variances of the estimated parameters under the assumption of no temporal changes provide an estimate of the variances in these matrices.

Winer (1979) applied this approach to Palda's Lydia Pinkham data. While Palda maintained that the regulatory actions should produce discrete changes in the constant of the sales response function and should leave the effectiveness of advertising otherwise unchanged, Winer argued that the shock is likely to induce some continuous change in the constant, and in any event, the assumption of parameter constancy for the other coefficients is not valid. Winer estimated the sales response function

$$Q_t = \beta_{0t} + \beta_{1t}A_t + \beta_{2t}Q_{t-1} + u_t \tag{4.41}$$

subject to (4.37)-(4.40) and the simplifications covered in the last paragraph. His empirical results indicated that the intercept β_{0t} showed a strong nondiscrete tendency to change over time, that the advertising coefficient β_{1t} showed an upward trend, and that the coefficient of sales in the previous period β_{2t} declined over time. The proportion of permanent parameter change, ϕ, was about 0.75 for these data.

An equation similar to (4.41) can be derived from a geometric advertising lag model provided that the coefficients are constant. In such a model, the coefficient of lagged sales will be equal to the advertising carryover parameter. It is not clear that the same correspondence holds if the coefficients are time-varying. Since we consider the measurement of advertising carryover difficult in even favorable circumstances, we think that superimposing time-varying parameters on top of distributed lag models may well create insurmountable problems.

The notion of sequentially-varying parameters can be incorporated into a cross-section-time series model. This combination is known as a *convergent parameter model* (Rosenberg 1973). The individual coefficient vectors follow first-order

Markov processes subordinated to a tendency to converge to the population mean
vector. The population mean vector will also evolve over time.

The individual parameter vector may contain both cross-varying parameters,
which vary across the population, and cross-fixed parameters, which are the same for
all individuals in any time period. The F cross-fixed parameters obey the relation

$$\beta_t = \beta_{t-1} + \tau_{t-1}. \tag{4.42}$$

The number of cross-fixed parameters, F, may be zero. The V cross-varying
parameters are assumed to obey the relation

$$\beta_\alpha = \overline{\beta}_{\alpha-1} + \Delta_\phi\left(\beta_{\alpha-1,i} - \overline{\beta}_{\alpha-1}\right) + v_{\alpha-1,i}. \tag{4.43}$$

The convergence matrix Δ_ϕ is diagonal with entries ϕ_v. Each ϕ, $0 \le \phi_v < 1$, is the
proportion of the individual divergence from the population mean that persists into
the next period. If there are no cross-fixed parameters and the divergence rates are set
equal to zero, the model reduces to a version of a random coefficients model.

The margarine market has been represented by a convergent parameter model
(Johansson 1974). The individual, or cross-sectional, units were the 15 largest brands
in the margarine market. The time units were 52 weeks. The focus was on the relation
between the price of the product and the quantity purchased:

$$Q_{ti} - Q_{t-1,i} = \beta_{1ti}\left(P_{ti} - P_{t-1,i}\right) + \beta_{1ti}\left(\frac{P_{ti}}{\overline{P}_t} - \frac{P_{t-1,i}}{\overline{P}_{t-1}}\right) + u_{ti}, \tag{4.44}$$

where

Q_{ti} = per-capita quantity (in pounds) of brand i at time t,

P_{ti} = price (in dollars) of brand i at time t,

$\overline{P}_t$ = mean price in the market at time t, and

u_{ti} = random component.

Both coefficients in this model were postulated to be cross-varying parameters and to
obey (4.43). The empirical results indicated that this model should be rejected. The
coefficients were rarely significantly different from zero and, contrary to theory,
often were positive in sign. One cause of these results might be misspecification—the
omission of a deal promotion variable.

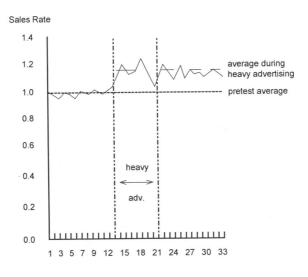

Figure 4-2. Fast Learning, Slow Forgetting. *Source*: Little (1979a, p. 633).

Asymmetry in Response

The magnitude of sales response to a change in a marketing instrument might be different depending on whether the change is upward or downward. This is different from asymmetry in competitive effects, that is, a change in a brand's marketing effort affecting each competitive brand differentially. The effect is also beyond any that might be explained by the nonlinearity of the sales response function. Sales might rise quickly under increased advertising but stay the same or decline slowly when the advertising is removed. This phenomenon, termed *hysteresis* (Little 1979a), is shown in Figure 4-2. See Simon (1997) for a discussion of how strategically important this concept is.

One explanation of the phenomenon is that higher advertising expenditures create more customers through greater reach as well as greater frequency (Parsons 1976). Under the customer holdover paradigm, these new customers subsequently repurchase the product. Thus, if advertising is cut back, sales will fall by less than would be the case in the absence of this carryover effect.

Sales response to price may also be asymmetric because of habit formation. The sales response function will be kinked. A price rise would be less elastic than a price fall. This has been called *addiction asymmetry* (Scitovsky 1978).

Functional Forms. Ratchet models capture asymmetry in response. There are two types of ratchet models. The first is saw-toothed in appearance, as shown in Figure

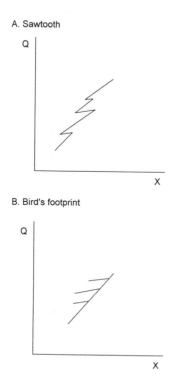

A. Sawtooth

B. Bird's footprint

Figure 4-3. Alternative Forms of a Ratchet Model.

4-3A. The sales response function is kinked at the prevailing level of a marketing instrument, irrespective of past changes in the instrument. Segments of the adjustment path for increases in level are parallel; segments for decreases are also parallel to each other. The second resembles a bird's footprint in appearance, as shown in Figure 4-3B. An example of this would be purchasing habits that were formed using a product under a condition of record-breaking marketing activity. Since these habits would presumably not be broken easily if marketing effort receded, the bird's footprint pattern would hold.

There are various formulations of a ratchet model. We consider only linear models. Sales could be a function of cumulative increases and cumulative decreases in marketing activity:

$$Q_t = \beta_0 + \beta_1 XI_t + \beta_2 XD_t, \quad \beta_1 > \beta_2, \tag{4.45}$$

where XI_t (XD_t) represents the sum of all period-to-period increases (decreases) in a marketing instrument. Using the decomposition $X_t = X_0 + XI_t + XD_t$, as suggested by Wolffram (1971), yields

$$Q_t = (\beta_0 - \beta_2 X_0) + (\beta_1 - \beta_2) XI_t + \beta_2 X_t. \tag{4.46}$$

This relation could be expressed in terms of XD_t instead of XI_t. This model was used in a study of the response of cigarette sales to price changes (Young 1983).

Formulation of the second type of ratchet model involves creating a record of marketing effort variable equal to $\max(X_i)$, $i = 1,\dots, t$ (or $\min(X_i)$ in the case of price):

$$Q_t = \beta_0 + \beta_1 X_t + \beta_2 \left[max(X_i) \right]. \tag{4.47}$$

This approach was used in a ratchet model of advertising carryover effects (Parsons 1976) and as an alternative model in a cigarette sales-price investigation (Young 1983).

A related model displaying asymmetry is

$$Q_t = \beta_0 + \beta_1 X_t + \beta_2 \left[max(0, \Delta X) \right], \tag{4.48}$$

where $\Delta X = X_t - X_{t-1}$. (Again, for price, the min operator would replace the max operator.) Simon's (1982) ADPULS model is in the spirit of this formulation. Just considering increases in marketing effort, the same magnitude of the marketing instrument X_t can have different responses depending on its previous value, X_{t-1}. Simon (p. 355) argued that this property is necessary when trying to reproduce the advertising wearout phenomenon correctly. Asymmetric models may be considered a special case of coefficient variation discussed in the last section.

Empirical Evidence. Some experiments have shown an immediate sales response to increased advertising. In addition, these experiments indicated that even though the advertising was maintained at the new and higher levels, the magnitude of response gradually became less and less (Haley 1978). Two explanations have been offered for this (Little 1979a). One is that advertising causes prospects to try a product. Only a portion of these new customers become regular purchasers. Consequently, sales taper off from their initial gain to a lower level. The second explanation is that the advertising copy is wearing out. We believe another possible explanation would be competitive reaction.

Reaction Functions

Construction of the sales response function is just one step in developing models of marketing systems. If competitors react to a firm's actions, competitive reaction functions must be developed. For some perspective on this, we briefly review the major relevant thrust in economics, then discuss reaction functions in marketing.

Reaction Functions and Oligopoly

Economists have used the concept of the reaction function to describe how oligopolists make their decisions. Major critiques of this approach can be found in Fellner (1949), who explicitly mentioned reaction functions and focused on cooperative equilibria, and in Friedman (1977a; 1977b), who focused on noncooperative equilibria. Friedman defined a reaction function as

> a function which determines for a firm in a given time period its action (price and/or quantity) as a function of the actions of (all) other firms during the preceding time period.

Cournot (1838) postulated a quantity market model whose key assumptions are that each firm produces the identical product as every other firm in the industry and does not set price but rather how much of the product it will produce. The market price will then be determined by the total production of the industry. The firms maximize single-period profits and know each others' profit functions. Additional assumptions specify the general shape of the demand and total cost curves. If the firms act simultaneously with single-period time horizons, the market will converge to the Cournot equilibrium, in which no firm, without colluding, can obtain a higher profit by changing its production level. Our interest is in the dynamic version of this model, which was ambiguously specified by Cournot. In this version, the firms remain single-period profit maximizers, but it is unclear whether the firms make their decisions sequentially or simultaneously. In a simultaneous-decision model, each firm determines its current production level in order to maximize its current-period profits, assuming its competitors will produce the same amount of product this period as they did last period. This relation between current production and the past production of competitors can be labeled a Cournot reaction function. If these reaction functions are stable, the market will converge to the Cournot equilibrium production levels.

Bertrand (1883) argued that firms set price, not output. In his view, each firm fixes its price on the assumption that its competitors will not change their prices. The assumption that a firm's decisions will have no impact on its rivals' actions seems unrealistic in general, but especially so for pricing decisions. Schmalensee (1976) maintained that Cournot/Bertrand reaction also might apply to non-price promotion.

Bowley (1924) posited a conjectural variation model to relax Cournot's restrictive assumption that a competitor will produce the same amount this period as last. A firm

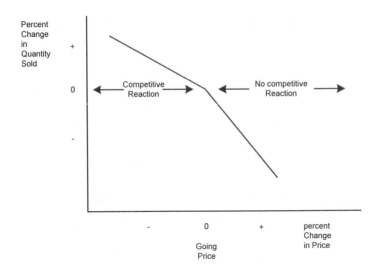

Figure 4-4. Kinked Demand Curve.

in a duopoly attempts to take into account two reaction functions. The first function describes how a firm believes its competitor will change output in reaction to its output last period. The second describes how the firm should react to the competitor's output last period if its beliefs about its competitor's behavior are correct.

Stackelberg (1934) introduced the notion that firms were either leaders or followers. A follower is a company that behaves as if its competitors are going to maintain their production at last period's level. A leader is a company that acts on the assumption that its competitors are followers. This can result in the Stackelberg leader-follower equilibrium.

Sweezy (1939), noting that the traditional demand curve did not apply to oligopolies, investigated the imagined demand curve. In particular, competitors may react differently to a price increase than to a price decrease. If a firm raises its price and its competitors do not, then it is likely to lose market share. Conversely, competitors must meet the firm's price cut to avoid loss of share. As a consequence, the imagined demand curve has a "corner" at the current price, as shown in Figure 4-4. The demand curve tends to be elastic when the firm raises price and inelastic when it cuts price. The imagined demand curve has been renamed the kinked, or kinkey, demand curve.

Stigler (1947) has elaborated on the theory of kinked demand curves. The difference in the slopes of the demand curve on the two sides of the kink was conjectured to be affected by the number of competitors, the relative size of these competitors, the differences among the competitors' products, and the extent of collusion among the competitors. Stigler presented some ad hoc empirical evidence that generally failed to show the existence of a kinked demand curve. One example supporting the possibility of its existence occurred in the cigarette industry. Lucky Strike increased its price by 25%, and its competitors continued to charge the lower price, with the result that Lucky Strike sales fell 31%. Aykac, Corstjens, and Gautschi (1984) proposed a way to investigate the presence of kinks using dummy variables. But Simon (1969b) has expressed doubts about our ability to observe kinked demand curves.

Economists have used the reaction function as a hypothetical construct to allow them to determine equilibrium conditions in an oligopoly. Yet their empirical work has ignored the reaction function and focused on the demand curve in an attempt to see whether it might be kinked. Marketing scientists have examined sales response functions together with decision rules as a system of relations encompassing the market mechanism, but they have been more interested in the sales response function than in the decision rules.

Our interest is in a typical decision rule for a firm. The level of a particular decision variable for a specific competitor may be affected by the firm's own managerial decision variables, by each of its competitors managerial decision variables, by its own and its competitors' past sales, and by autonomous environmental conditions, including seasonality. What is important to recognize is that the reaction function of the economist can be, and often is, embedded in the more general construct of the decision rule. One of the first studies to focus on a firm's own decision rules was Schultz (1971a).

Shape of a Reaction Function

In doing "what if" simulations, managers can manipulate the values of the sales drivers under their control. The managers also need to know what the competitors might do in response. One way is to estimate the reaction function for each relevant sales driver of each competitor. Fortunately, the shape of a reaction function is usually fairly simple. In most cases, a competitor will respond either to an absolute change or to a relative change in a firm's marketing instrument. For example, a firm might price its brand at $100 and a competitor its brand at $120. For simplicity, suppose that the firm matches competitive action. If a firm cuts its price to $90, the competitor would reduce its price to $110 ($120 + [$90 − $100]) if it reacts to absolute changes in competitive price levels, or to $108 ($120 + {[$90 − $100]/$100} × $120) if it reacts to relative changes.

Functional Forms. A simple *absolute change* reaction of a competitor (them) to an action taken by the firm (us) involving a marketing instrument X is

$$dX_{them} = \beta_1 dX_{us}. \tag{4.49}$$

which yields the linear reaction function

$$X_{them} = \beta_0 + \beta_1 X_{us}. \tag{4.50}$$

Sometimes (4.49) is estimated directly using first differences:

$$\left(X_{them,t} - X_{them,t-1}\right) = \beta_1\left(X_{us,t} - X_{us,t-1}\right). \tag{4.51}$$

This was the approach taken by Leeflang and Wittink (1992, pp. 43, 47) for promotion and Jedidi, Mela, and Gupta (1999, p. 11) for price, promotion, and advertising. The absolute change representation is used especially when zero values may occur as with promotional activities.

A simple *relative change* reaction is

$$\frac{dX_{them}}{X_{them}} = \beta_1\left(\frac{dX_{us}}{X_{us}}\right), \tag{4.52}$$

which yields a reaction function that is linear in logarithms

$$ln\left(X_{them}\right) = \beta_0 + \beta_1\, ln\left(X_{us}\right). \tag{4.53}$$

This model (4.53) is, in turn, equivalent to

$$X_{them} = e^{\beta_0} X_{us}^{\beta_1}, \tag{4.54}$$

which is a nonlinear functional form. Sometimes relative change is expressed as the logarithm of the ratio of the sales driver in two successive periods:

$$ln\left(\frac{X_{them,t}}{X_{them,t-1}}\right) = \beta_1\, ln\left(\frac{X_{us,t}}{X_{us,t-1}}\right). \tag{4.55}$$

This was the approach taken by Leeflang and Wittink (1992, pp. 43, 47), Leeflang and Wittink (1996, p. 112), and Kopelle, Mela, and Marsh (1999, p. 321) for price. These studies also incorporated lag structures to capture that the phenomenon that a reacting brand may change its price several periods or more after a competitor changes its price.

The phenomenon of the level of one marketing instrument affecting, or being affected by, levels of other marketing instruments within the same firm can be incorporated into a generalized reaction matrix [here shown for price and advertising only] (Hanssens 1980b):

$$
R = \begin{bmatrix}
1 & \rho_{P_c,P} & \vline & \rho_{A,P} & \rho_{A_c,P} \\
\rho_{P,P_c} & 1 & \vline & \rho_{A,P_c} & \rho_{A_c,P_c} \\
\hline
\rho_{P,A} & \rho_{P_c,A} & \vline & 1 & \rho_{A_c,A} \\
\rho_{P,A_c} & \rho_{P_c,A_c} & \vline & \rho_{A,A_c} & 1
\end{bmatrix}.
\tag{4.56}
$$

This matrix is partitioned so that the main diagonal blocks represent simple competitive reaction. The off-diagonal blocks represent multiple reaction. The diagonal elements within these blocks represent *intra*firm effects, and the off-diagonal ones represent *inter*firm effects. In an oligopoly the interfirm reaction elasticities should be zero if the firm is a follower (Cournot-Bertrand reaction function) and nonzero if the firm is a leader (Stackelberg reaction function).

Other phenomena might be present in reaction functions. A firm might react differently to positive or negative changes in a competitor's marketing instrument; that is, the reaction function might have a kink in it. A firm might be nonresponsive to "small" changes in a competitor's marketing instrument, as shown in Figure 4-5. Just as the parameters in the sales response function can change over time (e.g., Parsons 1975b and Simon 1979), so might those in a reaction function. Indeed, changes in the parameters in the reaction function are more likely as firms adjust their strategies and learn about competitive reactions. The modeling and estimation of this type of model have been reviewed in Wildt and Winer (1983).

If a competitor does not respond to a firm's actions when it is likely to gain market share, a large number of observations will cluster at zero. The observed value for a managerial decision variable is the actual value for adverse competitive actions and is zero for other competitive actions, that is, values for the dependent variable outside the bound are set equal to the bound itself and the dependent variable is said to be *censored*. This requires that such a reaction function be estimated by Tobit analysis (Tobin 1958).

If competitors are not sensitive to small changes in a firm's marketing mix, the dependent variables in the reaction functions are not related to the independent variables over some finite range. The presence of a mass point anywhere in the distribution of the dependent variable, not just at some upper or lower limiting value of it, can be addressed by a generalization of Tobit analysis due to Rosett (1959), which he called a statistical model of *friction*. A friction model has been used for describing and forecasting price changes (DeSarbo et al. 1987).

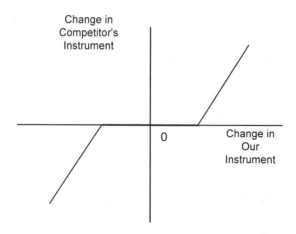

Figure 4-5. Friction.

There has been some indication in the business press that some managers operate under company guidelines that permit them to change the levels of the company's marketing instruments only up to some prescribed limit. In this case, two-limit Tobit analysis is required (Rosett and Nelson 1975).

To this point, we have been concentrating on the reaction function in isolation. From a managerial point of view, one also should be concerned about the impact of better specification of reaction functions on the estimation of the sales response function. Therefore, attention should be given to simultaneous Tobit models. The literature discusses different solutions, depending on the exact structure of the model (Amemiya 1974; 1979; Nelson and Olson 1977; Sickles and Schmidt 1978; Sickles, Schmidt, and White 1979).

More research is needed to improve the specification and estimation of reaction functions. The functional forms of reaction functions examined empirically have largely been restricted to either linear or multiplicative ones. That firms react to either an absolute change or a relative change in competitive behavior seems reasonable; however, no attempt has been made to show which of these is true. In order to test for the existence of the kinked demand curve, decision rules must be reduced to the corresponding reaction functions by factoring out the effects of the variables not directly related to competition using experimental or nonexperimental means.

Empirical Evidence. In a path-breaking article, a model of a market mechanism for cigarettes was presented that contained sales response functions and the corresponding advertising decision rules for the filter and nonfilter segments (Bass 1969b). The advertising decision rule equations indicated how one segment's sales influenced the other segment's advertising expenditure decision in the same year. This study was followed by a major investigation of the ready-to-eat cereal market (Bass and Parsons 1969). Again there was a four-equation model of the market mechanism. This time a pair of relations described the behavior of a particular brand and another pair that of all other brands combined. A major empirical result was that competitive advertising activities seem to stimulate primary demand in this market. The advertising decision rules were based on marketing actions and results in the previous bimonthly period. A very similar model was tested with data from three markets: scouring powders, toilet soaps, and household cleansers (Samuels 1970/1971). Another study examined retail price advertising as well as network advertising as a managerial decision rule. Since three firms accounted for the majority of sales in the industry, this market mechanism contained nine equations (Wildt 1974).

A small electrical appliance market was investigated from the Stackelberg leader-follower perspective (Lambin 1970a and Lambin, Naert, and Bultez 1975). The followers' reaction functions for advertising, price, and quality were constructed. What was found was that while competitors did react to a change in one marketing instrument by the leader with a change in the same instrument, they also changed other elements in their marketing mix. For instance, the competitors might only partly match a price cut and instead increase their advertising outlays. Kinked demand curves could also result if competitors did not react when this would result in increased market share. However, this possibility was not addressed in the ordinary least squares estimation of the reaction functions.

Weekly market-level scanner data have been used to calibrate competitive reactions involving price, sampling, refund, bonus, and features for a frequently purchased, nondurable, nonfood, consumer product sold in the Netherlands. The number of significant causal relations in the associated reaction matrix are shown in Leeflang and Wittink (1992, p. 51). The researchers conclude (p. 55):

> Our findings show that simple competitive reaction functions would fail to capture systematic effects due to other marketing variables. At the same time, simple reactions do account for a disproportionate number of reaction effects. Importantly, the estimated competitive reactions appear to be very complex.

Price-only reaction functions for store-level, weekly liquid dishwashing detergent data are shown in Kopalle, Meal, and Marsh (1999, p. 326). The brands included Crystal White Octagon, Dove, Dawn, Ivory, Palmolive, and Sunlight. Interpretation of reactions at the store level involves a new wrinkle.

Understanding the Nature of Reactions

For a more complete understanding of competitive reactions, the behavior of possibly competing store managers must be overlaid on the behavior of competing brand managers. Three types of reactions are possible (Leeflang and Wittink 1992, p. 44). *Manufacturer-dominated reactions* are in the spirit of the classical reactions that we have been discussing. Here, however, the reactions can occur only if the retailers cooperate with the manufacturers. The sign for simple competitive reaction should be positive. *Retailer-dominated reactions* arise when retailers alternate promotions among brands from one promotional period to another. Consequently, the sign for short-run (simultaneous or one week lag) simple competitive reaction should be negative. The sign for long-run (two to four weeks) simple competitive reaction is likely to be positive as promotional activities are likely to be driven by manufacturers trade promotions. Furthermore, when reactions occur largely within four weeks, they are likely to be retailer dominated whereas longer-duration responses tend to be manufacturer dominated. *Parallel price movements* arise because of planned price movements or expectations about competitors' brands. These may arise because of the need of the retailer to coordinate promotions within the store with the managers of various brands as part of the annual planning process. The retailer is also competing with other retailers and may want to offer a promotion for one brand at the same time other retailers are promoting another brand. Furthermore, a manufacturer with more than one brand will want to coordinate a portion of these brands' marketing programs as part of category management (Nielsen Marketing Research 1992). A decision support system for planning a manufacturer's sales promotion calendar is described in Silva-Risso, Bucklin and Morrison (1999). The sign for simple parallel reaction should be positive. Extension to multiple competitive reaction is discussed in Leeflang and Wittink (1992). Also see Leeflang and Wittink (1996). The price reaction functions for liquid dishwashing detergents revealed only a relatively modest lag effect, that is, four weeks or less, indicating retailer-dominated pricing reactions (Kopalle, Meal, and Marsh 1999, p. 327).

Temporal Aggregation Revisited

ETS models are built on real-world data, so the model builder seldom has the chance to select a time interval for analysis. Data or time intervals are typically set by accounting or business practice, reflecting the relevant decision interval but not necessarily the best market response interval. Therefore, extreme caution must be taken in making inferences about marketing dynamics from such data.

What constitutes a reasonable data interval? There seems to be an agreement that shorter intervals are better than longer ones. On the other hand, few would attempt to build a marketing model on the minute-by-minute sales transactions offered by scanner equipment. One popular rule is that the data interval should match the purchase cycle of the product, although that could not apply to consumer and industrial durables. In most cases, though, the model builder simply must accept the data interval as given and make the best possible use of it.

Data Interval Bias

A well-known survey of the advertising response literature introduced the concept of data interval bias, i.e., that some statistically sound results may be conceptually false because of a wrong (often too long) time interval (Clarke 1976). For example, many advertising response models estimated on annual data reveal advertising carryover effects on sales that are 20 to 50 times as long as those estimated on monthly series. This has spawned the marketing generalization for advertising (Leone 1995, p. G142):

> In estimating sales response models, when higher levels of aggregation are used in the analysis (e.g., week, month, bimonth, quarter, year), the estimate on the lag coefficient for sales decreases, and both the estimated (computed) duration interval of advertising and the estimated current-period advertising effect increase purely due to "aggregation bias."

Thus, findings from econometric studies based on highly aggregated data, which find very long carryover effects, are inaccurate.

Data interval bias occurs because making the assumption that an aggregate model has the same functional form as the underlying disaggregated model is usually wrong. The aggregate model will be misspecified. This problem has led to some econometric attempts at recovering micro-parameters when only macro-data are available. These efforts are summarized in Table 4-1. Micro-parameter recovery procedures start by assuming an underlying micro-response model (e.g., Koyck). Next, the shape of the implied macro-response model is derived, which typically requires an approximation in order to make the function estimable. Finally, the macro-function's ability to recover micro-parameters is investigated, usually with simulation methods.

The literature reviewed in Table 4-1 presents some inconsistent results. For example, Bass and Leone (1983) showed that with increasing aggregation, the short-term response parameter increases and the carryover parameter decreases for Koyck or partial adjustment models. On the other hand, simulation efforts by Weiss, Weinberg, and Windal (1983) failed to uncover a relation between aggregation level m and the carryover parameter λ. The simulation work of Vanhonacker (1983, 1984) suggested that empirical problems in parameter recovery occur for either the ACE or the partial adjustment model. More recent efforts, for example, by Kanetkar, Weinberg, and Weiss (1986a, 1986b), have improved the recovery procedures, but the performance of these methods on actual marketing data rather than simulated data remains largely unexplored.

Table 4-1. Discrete-Time Temporal Aggregation Research

Researchers	Micromodel	Contribution	Test
Clarke (1976)	Koyck	λ depends on data interval	Review
Windal and Weiss (1980)	ACE	Macro estimation of microparameters	Empirical
Sasieni (1982)	Koyck or partial adjustment	Derives macroresponse model when advertising is white noise	N/A
Weinberg and Weiss (1982)	Koyck	Estimate of λ appears independent of data interval	Review
Bass and Leone (1983)	Koyck or partial adjustment	Recovers bimonthly parameters from annual data	Empirical
Vanhonacker (1983)	Partial adjustment	Shows specification problems with aggregation	Simulation
Weiss, Weinberg, and Windal (1983)	Partial adjustment	Shows λ independent of m, improves on Bass-Leone method	Simulation
Vanhonacker (1984)	ACE	Shows empirical problems with aggregation methods	Simulation
Kanetkar, Weinberg, and Weiss (1986a)	Koyck or partial adjustment	Extends Weiss-Weinberg-Windal	Simulation
Kanetkar, Weinberg, and Weiss (1986b)	ACE	Improvement of Windal- Weiss method	Simulation
Bass and Leone (1986)	Koyck or partial adjustment	Finds Bass-Leone better than Weiss-Weinberg-Windal	Simulation
Srinivasan and Weir (1988)	Koyck	Direct aggregation better than either Bass-Leone or Weiss-Weinberg-Windal	Simulation
Russell (1988)	Koyck	Marketing decision behavior affects shape of distributed lag function	Simulation
Givon and Horsky (1990)	Koyck	Adds purchase reinforcement	Empirical

Recovery Procedures

Consider the micromodel with advertising as the only marketing driver:

$$Q_{m,t} = \beta_0 + \beta_1 A_{m,t} + \lambda Q_{m-1,t} + u_{m,t}, \qquad (4.57)$$

where m,t indicates the microperiod m (say a week) in aggregate period t (say a year). This is a "brand loyalty" partial adjustment type model. Summing over M micro periods yields the annual model:

$$Q_t = M\beta_0 + \beta_1 A_t + \lambda(Q_t - Q_{m,t} + Q_{m,t-1}) + u_t. \qquad (4.58)$$

The problem is that $Q_{m,t-1} - Q_{m,t}$ is unobservable when you have only aggregate data. Bass and Leone (1983) proposed the approximation

$$Q_{m,t} = cQ_t + v_t, \qquad (4.59)$$

where v_t is the approximation error. Substituting (4.59) into (4.58) and then rearranging terms yields

$$Q_t = \frac{M\beta_0}{1 - \lambda(1-c)} + \frac{\beta_1}{1 - \lambda(1-c)} A_t + \frac{\lambda c}{1 - \lambda(1-c)} Q_{t-1}$$
$$+ \frac{1}{1 - \lambda(1-c)}\left[u_t - \lambda(v_{t-1} - v_t)\right]. \qquad (4.60)$$

Identification of β_1 and λ from estimates of the coefficients requires that c be chosen in advance by judgment. Bass and Leone, following Mundlak (1961), choose c to equal $1/M$:

$$Q_t = \frac{M^2\beta_0}{M - \lambda(M-1)} + \frac{\beta_1}{1 - \lambda\left(1 - \frac{1}{M}\right)} A_t + \frac{\lambda}{M - \lambda(M-1)} Q_{t-1}$$
$$+ \frac{M}{M - \lambda(M-1)}\left[v_t - \lambda(u_{t-1} - u_t)\right]. \qquad (4.61)$$

This equation shows that, as the length of the data interval increases, the estimate of the lag coefficient declines monotonically and the estimate of the current advertising coefficient increase monotonically.

A second method by Weiss, Weinberg, and Windal (1983) follows from Moriguchi (1970). Their approach also ends up with an expression containing unobservable terms. Again an approximation must be used (corrected version from Kanetkar, Weinberg, and Weiss (1986), p. 299):

$$Q_t = \frac{M\beta_0\left(1-\lambda^M\right)}{1-\lambda} + \frac{\beta_1\left(1-\lambda^{k_1}\right)}{1-\lambda}A_t + \frac{\beta_1\lambda^{k_1}\left(1-\lambda^{k_2}\right)}{1-\lambda}A_{t-1} + \lambda^M Q_{t-1} + v_t, \qquad (4.62)$$

where

$k_1 = k_2 = M/2$ for even M,

$k_1 = (M+1)/2$, $k_2 = (M-1)/2$ for odd M, and

v_t = the error term arising from the sum of corresponding error terms from the micro-level relations and the error from approximating the micro-level advertising data.

These two methods, Bass-Leone and Weiss-Weinberg-Windal, can be extended to the Koyck model (Kanetkar, Weinberg, and Weiss 1986; Srinivasan and Weir 1988). They have been compared in simulations. While the results of the simulations are not clear-cut, the first approximation tended to do better in recovering the microparameters than the second. Furthermore, Srinivasan and Weir (1988, p. 147) have noted that both methods are more accurate in situations where the true value of λ is large and where the level of aggregation is low. When λ is small with high levels of aggregation, the estimates of λ often turn out to be negative or greater than one (first approximation) or not recoverable (second approximation).

A third approach based on the work of Zellner and Geisel (1970) has been proposed. It is known as *direct aggregation*. Starting with a geometric distributed lag micromodel, Srinivasan and Weir (1988) aggregated over the tth set of M micro periods $\{(t-1)M+1, (t-1)M+2, \ldots, tM\}$ to get

$$Q_t = M\beta_0 + \beta_1\tilde{A}_t + \lambda^{(t-1)M}\Delta + v_t, \qquad (4.63)$$

where

$$\tilde{A}_t = \sum_{m=1}^{M}A_{(t-1)M+m,t} + \lambda\sum_{m=1}^{M}A_{(t-1)M+m-1,t} + \cdots + \lambda^{(t-1)M}\sum_{m=1}^{M}A_{m,t},$$

$$\Delta = \beta_1\lambda\left(\sum_{m=0}^{M-1}A_{m,t} + \lambda\sum_{i=-1}^{M-2}A_{m,t} + \cdots\right), \text{ and}$$

$$v_t = \sum_{m=1}^{M} u_{(t-1)M+m,t} \cdot$$

While it is not possible to estimate this model directly because some of the terms in advertising are unknown, it is possible to do so if you approximate advertising in microperiods in the manner used in the Bass-Leone approximation for micro-sales. This third method seems to recover parameters more accurately than the other two. Givon and Horsky (1990) adapted the direct aggregation approach for their own work on purchase feedback.

The measurement interval in an econometric model involving advertising can have a significant impact on the estimated coefficients. A major assumption of the work on data aggregation bias is that the microprocess is known. In practice, however, it is difficult to state with confidence that an ACE or a Koyck advertising response pattern occurs at any level of aggregation. This is a good example of what we will discuss next as Level 1 a priori knowledge. There is little disagreement about the existence of an advertising-to-sales effect, but its duration is essentially unknown.

Marketing Models and Prior Knowledge

We have described the elements that constitute a market response model. In any given situation, the model builder may or may not have advance knowledge of these factors. For example, the analyst may be able to identify the elements of the marketing mix but know very little about the functional form of the model. It is the task of careful empirical analysis, using econometric and time series methods, to advance the model builder to a higher state of knowledge.

ETS models are useful for scientific as well as managerial inference. The marketing manager uses ETS to build planning and forecasting models. The marketing scientist uses ETS to build theory from empirical generalizations. However, in both cases, the analysts may face different modeling tasks that are primarily a function of their prior knowledge and the ultimate objectives of the model. Consider the following two marketing planning scenarios:

1. Company A markets a variety of products through different channels. It has, over the years, developed some simple decision rules for marketing mix allocations. Now, in the face of declining market shares and a squeeze on profit margins, the company needs hard facts on what is driving sales and profit performance.

2. Company B, a retailer, sells several hundred products via aggressive local advertising campaigns coupled with temporary price cuts. Management is well aware of the sales impact of advertising and lower prices but struggles with the question of the timing of promotional campaigns and the optimal combination of advertising budgets and profit margins.

Similarly, consider the following two marketing research scenarios:

1. Several authorities in industry and academia have advanced the notion that larger market share leads to higher profitability. Although several appealing arguments exist for this theory, it is also possible to describe conditions leading to the reverse relation i.e., profitability leads to larger market share. More research is needed in this area.

2. The issue of distributed lag effects of advertising on sales is in more disarray than ever before. Major research papers have argued that the effects last for months, not years; that the results are a function of the chosen data interval; that "current effects" models are as good as lag models; and even that lag structures do not matter. Here, too, more research is needed.

As different as these scenarios are, they are similar in the amount of prior knowledge available to the manager or the scientist and in the objective of the model building. In the first two scenarios, an information set (i.e., a collection of relevant variables) is given and the task is to sort out the causal ordering among the variables. In the second two scenarios, the causal ordering is given, but there is a lack of knowledge about functional forms and lag structures in the response structures. This implies that different ETS methods are needed to develop and test response models in marketing.

Our knowledge about the modeling environment can be organized in the following way:

- Level 0: only the information set is known.
- Level 1: the causal ordering among variables is known.
- Level 2: the functional form, causal ordering, and lag structure are known.

ETS techniques are not appropriate to situations with less than level 0 knowledge. We must start with an information set developed from subject matter theory or directly from managers. For example, the concept of the marketing mix leads to a commonly used information set in market response modeling consisting of product sales, price, distribution, sales force, and communication efforts. Once a level 0 prior knowledge is obtained, ETS methods can make substantial contributions in moving the marketing scientist up the knowledge hierarchy.

Each of the following three chapters addresses model building at a different level of prior knowledge, starting with the highest level. At level 2, the model builder estimates the parameters of a fully specified model using econometric techniques. The model may then be used for forecasting or marketing planning. Alternatively, the analyst may verify the adequacy of the model via testing procedures. This is the content of Chapter 5.

At level 1, the model builder is not ready to estimate parameters or predict sales. The functional form and dynamic structure of the model must first be specified. The latter may require a different set of techniques involving time series analysis. Chapter 6 starts with univariate techniques for lag structure specification and then discusses multiple time series methods. These techniques will also allow us to diagnose evolution vs. stationarity in sales and marketing variables, which forms the basis for modeling long-term marketing effects on sales.

At level 0, empirical methods should be used to establish the direction of causality among marketing variables. This can only be accomplished with time series data, because it requires the temporal ordering of events. Techniques for assessing the direction of causality are discussed in Chapter 7.

Notes

[1]   To facilitate nesting, variables in models are often expressed in deviation form, i.e., each variable is centered around its mean.

[2]   An earlier study of generic advertising for milk in California found the polynomial lag model superior to a geometric lag model. A third-degree polynomial was determined to be unsatisfactory in preliminary analysis and a second-degree polynomial with a lag length of five was used (Thompson 1974, p. 81). Another study in the New York standard metropolitan statistical area (SMSA) found a third-degree polynomial of lag length five to be the best representation of lagged response (Thompson and Eiler 1977, p. 332). An analysis of the U.S. dairy advertising program used a second-degree polynomial of lag length four for quarterly advertising data (Liu et al. 1990, pp. 41-42).

[3]   In principle, other marketing decision variables could result in goodwill such as when sales force effort produces relationships between a company and their customers.

APPENDIX 4 *The Lag Operator*

Specification of dynamic models is simplified by using the lag operator,

$$LX_t \equiv X_{t-1}, \tag{4.64}$$

to represent lagged variables (Greene 1997, pp. 785-86). The lag operator can be applied repeatedly to get more distant lags:

$$L(LX_t) = L^2 X_t = X_{t-2} \text{ and } L^p X_t = X_{t-p}. \tag{4.65}$$

When the lag operator is applied to a constant, the result is simply the constant. For example, the Infinite Distributed Lag Model (4.3) can be written as

$$Q_t = \beta_0 + \sum_{k=0}^{\infty} \beta_{k+1} L^k X_t + w_t. \tag{4.66}$$

This can be further simplified by use of a general polynomial in the lag operator

$$B(L) = \beta_0 + \beta_1 L + \beta_2 L^2 + \beta_3 L^3 + \cdots. \tag{4.67}$$

to get

$$Q_t = \beta_0 + B(L)X_t + w_t. \tag{4.68}$$

A geometric progression with common ratio r can be expressed in terms of a polynomial in L:

$$A(L) = 1 + rL + (rL)^2 + (rL)^3 + \cdots = \frac{1}{1 - rL}. \tag{4.69}$$

Now the Geometric Distributed Lag Model (4.9) can be written as

$$Q_t = \beta_0 + \beta(1 - \lambda)A(L)X_t + w_t = \beta_0 + \beta(1 - \lambda)\frac{X_t}{1 - \lambda L} + w_t. \tag{4.70}$$

This is the distributed lag form, or *moving average form*, of the model. Multiplying by $(1 - \lambda L)$ and collecting terms yields the *autoregressive form*:

$$Q_t = (1 - \lambda)\beta_0 + \beta(1 - \lambda)X_t + \lambda Q_{t-1} + (w_t - \lambda w_{t-1}). \tag{4.71}$$

This process is simply the Koyck transformation (4.10).

Other model can be expressed in terms of lag operators. The very general Autoregressive Lag Model would be

$$Q_t = \beta_0 + \frac{B(L)}{C(L)} X_t + w_t,$$
(4.72)

where $B(L)$ and $C(L)$ are polynomials in the lag operator. With relatively few parameters, the ratio of these two polynomials can produce any shape in the lag distribution desired. The autoregressive form is

$$C(L)Q_t = \beta_0 + B(L)X_t + C(L)w_t,$$
(4.73)

where both the dependent and explanatory variables are lagged and the disturbance is moving average (MA).

Recent advances in time series analysis have made the rational lag structure model much easier to use. We will argue in Chapter 7 that the statistical version of this model, the *transfer function,* is a sufficiently general model to accommodate the dynamic aspects of markets and marketing efforts. Working with transfer functions offers the distinct advantage that the data can be used to specify the dynamic structure of a market. Since different markets can have very different dynamic patterns, this approach offers considerable opportunity for marketing planning, forecasting, and theory testing.

5 PARAMETER ESTIMATION AND MODEL TESTING

When the functional form is believed known, the next step is to estimate the parameters of the model and to test hypotheses about them. Any assumptions, known as maintained hypotheses, underlying the estimation method used also should be examined. In what follows, our primary purpose is to link the marketing response literature to the econometric literature. Technical details can be found in most leading econometric texts: Judge et al. (1985), Davidson and MacKinnon (1993), Greene (1997), Johnston and DiNardo (1997), Kennedy (1998), Pindyck and Rubinfeld (1998), and Mittelhammer, Judge, and Miller (2000).

Steps in building market response models include specification, estimation, hypotheses testing, verification, and forecasting. While sound theory should always form the foundation of response models, marketing theory, at best, provides rough guidance to the specification of functional form. Moreover, rival theories may exist. Verification is consequently very important and may provide feedback to the specification step. Thus we begin this chapter with a discussion of model estimation. We next turn to model testing, including specification error analysis. Then we introduce flexible functional forms. Finally we cover model selection. Conventional tests for autocorrelation, heteroscedasticity, parameter constancy, and the like are model selection criteria inasmuch as models that fail such tests will be discarded.

Classification of Variables

Within a dynamic simultaneous equation model, it is possible to make several distinctions among the variables. As an illustration, consider a simple three-equation system involving a brand's unit sales, Q_t; retail availability, a measure of distribution, D_t; and advertising expenditures, A_t. This system can be represented as

$$Q_t = f(D_t, Q_{t-1}, P_t, u_{1t}) \tag{5.1}$$
$$D_t = f(A_t, Q_{t-1}, u_{2t}) \tag{5.2}$$
$$A_t = f(Q_t, A_{t-k}, P_t, u_{3t}) \tag{5.3}$$

where

Q_{t-1} = unit sales in the previous period,
A_{t-k} = advertising k periods ago (usually $k = 1$; i.e., the previous period),
P_t = price per unit,
u_t = random disturbance.

At least four distinctions can be made among the variables. The first is whether the variables pertain to the present time period (Q_t, D_t, A_t, P_t) or to previous time periods (Q_{t-1}, A_{t-k}). The presence of lagged variables makes a system dynamic. The second distinction is whether the values of the variables are independent of the operation of the model (P_t) or determined by the model ($Q_t, Q_{t-1}, D_t, A_t, A_{t-k}$). The former are called *exogenous variables;* the latter, *endogenous variables.* Third, is the variable stochastically independent of all current and future disturbances in the model? If yes, they are called *predetermined variables* (Q_{t-1}, A_{t-k}, P_t), if no, *current endogenous variables* (Q_t, D_t, A_t). The predetermined variables include lagged endogenous variables as well as both current and lagged exogenous variables. This partitioning is diagrammed in Figure 5-1.

The fourth distinction is whether within a given equation, say (5.1), the variable is to be explained. If it is, it is a *dependent variable;* if not, it is an *explanatory variable.* When an equation contains only one current endogenous variable, it is the dependent variable. When an equation like (5.1) contains more than one current endogenous variable, one must be the dependent variable (Q_t) while the others are classified as explanatory variables (D_t, A_t) along with the predetermined variables (Q_{t-1}, P_t).

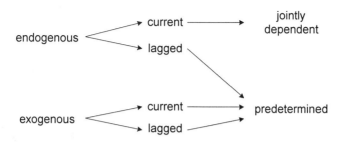

Figure 5-1. Distinguishing Predetermined Variables. *Source*: Naert and Leeflang (1978, p. 62); Leeflang et al. (2000, p. 60).

Estimation

Our focus is on finding estimates of the *unstandardized* parameters in a sales response function, or, more generally, in the relations in a market mechanism. This information will allow a marketing manager to evaluate the possible consequences of a marketing action. In this setting, the use of standardized parameter estimates, sometimes called beta weights, is not appropriate. Wittink (1983a) has demonstrated that "beta weights are meaningless for applications involving managerial decision making" by showing that "although beta weights allow for comparisons between predictor variables when the variables are measured in different units, they have no actionable interpretation to managers."

To make estimation as easy as possible and to ensure that any resultant parameter estimates have desirable statistical properties, simplifying assumptions are made about the error structure. A set of generally accepted assumptions is the starting point. If one or more of these assumptions is not reasonable, estimation is usually still possible but may be more difficult. Throughout we assume that there are more observations than there are parameters to be estimated. Indeed we would like at least five observations per parameter to be estimated.

Generally Accepted Assumptions

There are eight assumptions underlying classical estimation of a single equation linear model. These are shown in Table 5-1. When a response system or market mechanism involves more than one equation, additional assumptions are required. The first assumption, linearity, is now expressed as a linear simultaneous equation system:

Table 5-1. Classical Ordinary Least Squares (OLS) Assumptions

Assumption	*Violation*
1. Linearity $Q = \beta_0 + \beta_1 X_1 + \beta_2 X_2 + \cdots + \beta_k X_k + u$ or $\mathbf{q = X\beta + u}$	Nonlinearity (see Table 5-3)
2. Constant coefficients $\boldsymbol{\beta}$	Varying or random coefficients (see Table 5-4)
3. Nonstochastic regressor matrix $\mathbf{X}$	Contemporaneous correlations of regressor and disturbance (see Table 5-5)
4. Zero mean for disturbances $E[\mathbf{u}] = 0$	Nonzero mean for disturbances (see Table 5-6)
5. Constant variance σ^2 for disturbances	Heteroscedasticity (see Table 5-7)
6. Pairwise uncorrelated disturbances $E[\mathbf{uu'}] = \sigma^2 \mathbf{I}$	Autocorrelation (see Table 5-8)
7. Influence of each regressor distinguishable rank $\mathbf{X} = k+1$	Collinearity (see Table 5-9)
8. Disturbances distributed multivariate normal $u \sim N\left(0, \sigma^2 \mathbf{I}\right)$	Non-normality (see Table 5-10)

$$\mathbf{Y\Gamma + XB = U}. \tag{5.4}$$

When a model contains as many equations as current endogenous variables, the system is said to be complete. The generally accepted assumption is that an equation system is complete. Consequently, the matrix $\boldsymbol{\Gamma}$, which contains the coefficients of the current endogenous variables in each equation, is square. The matrix $\boldsymbol{\Gamma}$ is assumed to be nonsingular. Each equation in the model is assumed to be identifiable; that is, the a priori information necessary to distinguish the model from other models capable of generating the observed data exists.

Estimation Methods

General methods for obtaining point estimators for the unknown parameters of a model include (1) the least squares (LS) method, (2) the maximum likelihood (ML) method, the method of moments (MOM), and (4) the Bayesian method among others. The method of least squares involves finding the values of the parameters that make the sum of squares of the deviations of the predictions of the estimated function from the actual observations as small as possible. The estimated OLS coefficients are

$$\hat{\beta} = (\mathbf{X'X})^{-1}\mathbf{X'q} \qquad (5.5)$$

with variance-covariance matrix

$$\operatorname{var}(\hat{\beta}) = \sigma^2 (\mathbf{X'X})^{-1}. \qquad (5.6)$$

The maximum likelihood method involves finding the values of parameters that make the probability of obtaining the observed sample outcome as high as possible. A moment is an expectation of a given power of a random variable. The method of moments uses the corresponding sample moment to estimate a population moment.[1] The Bayesian method uses sample information to update any knowledge that may exist about the probability distribution on a parameter before sample information is observed. The maximum likelihood method, method of moments, and Bayesian method (under certain conditions) yield the same estimator of β as the OLS estimator above in the case of the standard linear model. This book focuses on least squares but draws on other estimation methods as well. For example, our hypothesis testing is based on maximum likelihood approach and is supplemented by Bayesian approach.

Choosing an Estimation Method

Identification is logically prior to estimation. Econometrics texts discuss the requirements for identification. A marketing illustration on evaluation of the identifiability of a model is given in Parsons and Schultz (1976, pp. 58-64). If the identifiability condition is met, the parameters of a model can then be estimated. There are many alternative techniques for estimation. Most techniques have been developed for the case where only sample information is available; occasionally, prior information is also available.

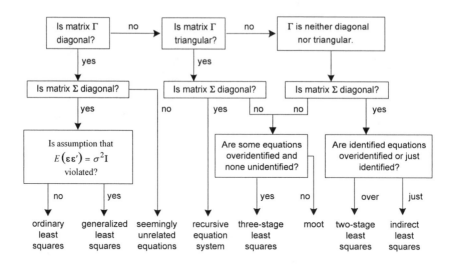

Figure 5-2. Selection of an LS Estimation Method. *Source*: Parsons and Schultz (1976, p. 65).

Sample Information Only. The choice among alternatives will be made primarily on the basis of the nature of the matrix of coefficients of the current endogenous variables Γ and the contemporaneous matrix Σ. Figure 5-2 diagrams this process. An introduction to the estimation procedures covered in Figure 5-2 can be found in Parsons and Schultz (1976, pp. 67-78). They briefly discussed the model, the estimation procedure, and properties of estimators for each technique. Lack of knowledge of the exact finite sample properties of estimators means that we cannot be sure we have made the correct choice in situations involving small samples.

The first step is to examine the matrix Γ. If the matrix Γ is diagonal, the matrix Σ is examined. If the matrix Σ is diagonal, determine for each equation whether $E(\varepsilon\varepsilon') = V = \sigma^2 I$ or not. If it does, use *ordinary least squares* (OLS) to estimate that equation; if not, use *generalized least squares* (GLS) if V is known. See Greene (1997, 507-9) or Johnston and DiNardo (1997, pp. 152-3). If V is not known, use a consistent estimate of V instead, in which case the technique is known variously as *estimated, approximate, or feasible generalized least squares* (FGLS). See Greene (1997, pp. 511-13) or Johnston and DiNardo (1997, pp. 319). A special case of the GLS procedure is *weighted least squares* (WLS), in which the dependent and explanatory variables are simply multiplied by weights that vary across observations (Davidson and MacKinnon 1993, p. 292). If lagged dependent variables or autocorrelated residuals are present, use *iterative generalized least squares* (IGLS). If the matrix Σ is not diagonal, use *disturbance related equations regression*, also called *seemingly unrelated equations regression* (SUR). When Σ is not known, an iterative procedure is again required.

If the matrix Γ is triangular and the matrix Σ diagonal, apply ordinary least squares directly to each equation in the recursive model. For the remaining categories involving the matrix Γ, if the matrix Σ is not diagonal and some equations are overidentified while none is not identified, use *three-stage least squares* (3SLS). When Σ is not known, an iterative procedure is once again required (I3SLS). See Greene (1997, pp. 752-54). If these conditions are not met, use *indirect least squares* if an equation is just identified or *two-stage least squares* (2SLS) if an equation is overidentified.

There are numerous applications of econometrics to a single linear estimating equation in marketing. Some examples of ordinary least squares estimation include relating the number of visitors in a recreational park to advertising effort (Wierenga 1981); analyzing sales contests (Wildt, Parker, and Harris 1987); and estimating elasticities with PIMS (Profit Impact of Market Strategies) data (Hagerty, Carman, and Russell 1988). Generalized least squares has been used to take into account autocorrelation across time—in studies of industrywide advertising and consumption of alcoholic beverages (Franke and Wilcox 1987) and of fluid milk (Capps and Schmitz 1991) and in an analysis of competitive reaction (Leelang and Wittink 1996)—and heterogeneity across brands—in a meta-analysis explaining price elasticities (Bell, Chiang, and Padmanabhan 1999).

Utilization of econometrics for multiple-equation systems is somewhat less common. OLS estimation of a recursive model has been employed to study the communication process (Aaker and Day 1971) and to integrate information from joint space maps into market response models (Moore and Winer 1987).

The sales response functions for different brands may be connected solely because their error terms are related. In such situations, a shock affecting the sales of one brand may spill over and affect the sales of other brands (Kennedy 1998, p. 181). One reason for contemporaneous correlation among the disturbances of different equations is a common omitted variable. Econometricians have shown that SUR will produce more efficient estimates of the parameters of the sales response functions (i.e., unbiased estimates with smaller sampling variances) than OLS in the general case of unrestricted correlations of the disturbances and different sales drivers in the response functions. The gains in efficiency by using SUR will be larger the greater the correlation of the disturbances across equations and the smaller the correlations among the explanatory variables (Greene 1997, p. 676). The question is whether the efficiency gains of SUR are substantial enough to be worth the effort. The answer seems to be yes. In a study of three brands in each four product categories—frozen waffles, liquid bleach, bathroom tissue, and ketchup—at 12 stores belonging to six different chains, the standard errors of the SUR estimates were found to be 25%

smaller than those of the OLS estimates of the same response functions (Bolton 1989c).

Disturbance related equations regression has been applied in the analysis of the response of competing brands to advertising expenditures (Beckwith 1972, Wildt 1974, Houston and Weiss 1974, Picconi and Olson 1978, Nguyen 1985, and Takada 1986); in the study of the response of competing brands to prices (Reibstein and Gatignon 1984; Allenby 1989); and in an exploration of retail strategy using cross-section rather than time series data (Parker and Dolich 1986). SUR has also been employed to assess the demand for automobiles of different sizes: subcompact, compact, intermediate, full size, and luxury (Carlson 1978). An extension of the disturbance related equations regression procedure that takes into account autocorrelated disturbances has been used in the investigation of sales-advertising cross-elasticities (Clarke 1973). Expenditure share equations for Canadian fats and oils (butter, margarine, shortening, and vegetable oils) were estimated by an iterative SUR with autocorrelated disturbances (Goddard and Amuah 1989). Similarly, a linear approximate, almost ideal demand system for meat (beef and veal, lamb, pork, and chicken) in Australia was estimated by an iterative, nonlinear SUR with autocorrelated disturbances (Cashin 1991).[2]

One place where generalized least squares is used is in market share models. Naert and Weverbergh (1981a, p. 149) concisely explained the reason:

> When one of the market shares is overestimated, the error must be compensated for by an underestimation of one or more of the other brands. It follows that the error terms ... will be contemporaneously correlated, that is, error terms in different equations but with respect to the same time period will not be independent. Estimation efficiency therefore can be improved by explicitly accounting for this correlation in the estimation process.

Building upon a foundation of work by McGuire et al. (1968), Beckwith (1972; 1973), Nakanishi and Cooper (1974), Bultez and Naert (1975), and McGuire and Weiss (1976), there have been a series of such studies comparing various estimation methods (ordinary least squares, generalized least squares, and iterative generalized least squares). See Naert and Weverbergh (1981a, 1985), Brodie and de Kluyver (1983), Ghosh, Neslin, and Shoemaker (1984), Leeflang and Reuyl (1984), and Kumer (1994). Key studies and their results are summarized in Appendix 5-A.

Any complete market share system is sum-constrained (by definition), and consequently its contemporaneous covariance matrix will be singular. In such a situation, one equation is deleted and disturbance related regression applied to the remaining equations. If the contemporaneous covariance matrix is known, the resulting parameter estimates are invariant as to which equation was deleted (McGuire et al. 1968). However, when the contemporaneous covariance matrix is unknown, the parameter estimates may indeed depend on the equation deleted. See Gaver, Horsky, and Narasimhan (1988) for recommendations on the estimation of market share systems that vary depending upon the balance of the error covariance structure and the correlation it exhibits.

The method of two-stage least squares is the most popular of the simultaneous equation estimating procedures. This method has been applied to a model of the distribution of branded personal products in Jamaica (Farley and Leavitt 1968); to models of the sales advertising relation of cigarettes (Bass 1969b and Rao 1972); to the analysis of sales and advertising of ready-to-eat cereals (Bass and Parsons 1969); to an investigation of market period demand-supply relations for a firm selling fashion products (Dalrymple and Haines 1970); to advertising and sales of household cleansers (Samuels 1970-1971); to advertising and sales of various products (Cowling 1972); and to pricing and sales of prescription drugs (Albach 1979).

Three-stage least squares has been used in an study of the airline industry (Schultz 1971a); in an econometric analysis of positioning (Houston (1977b); in two studies based on business-level (PIMS) data: one an investigation of competitive marketing strategies (Carpenter 1987) and the other an examination of the relation of advertising and product quality over the product life cycle (Tellis and Fornell 1988); in an assessment of the effectiveness of generic and brand advertising on fresh and processed potato products (Jones and Ward 1989); and in a game-theoretic model of dynamic price and advertising competition among firms (Vilcassim, Kadiyala, and Chintagunta 1999). *Iterative three-stage least squares* was employed to explore the relation of competitive brand advertising to industry, brand, and rival retail sales and market share in seven mature nondurable product categories (Lancaster 1984).

Whether a recursive or nonrecursive model is necessary to represent the system containing both sales response functions and reaction functions depends largely on the data interval. With a relatively short data interval, at least price movements would be simultaneous. Temporal interrelations might be identified using time series analysis (see Chapter 7).

Incorporating Other Information. Benefits may accrue from integrating marketing information from diverse sources (Parsons 1975a):

1. A source might provide information that is unique.

2. Even where alternative sources could provide the identical information, their costs may be quite different.

3. Different sources might provide complementary perspective of the same situation.

4. Different kinds of data are amenable to different types of analytical procedures.

5. Similar information from different sources is a basis for validation.

6. Together, different sources might improve the precision with which a structural relation can be measured.

7. Finally, but perhaps most importantly, there might be a theoretical connection among various information inputs.

These benefits justify developing methods for integrating various sources of marketing information. Our immediate concern is with methods for combining sample and non-sample information. This can be done either by traditional econometric approaches or by a Bayesian econometric approach.

The Traditional Approach. The basic econometric approach to incorporating extraneous information about some of the parameters in a linear relation is straightforward. The parameter vector is partitioned into two subvectors:

$$\mathbf{q} = \begin{bmatrix} \mathbf{X}_1 & \mathbf{X}_2 \end{bmatrix} \begin{bmatrix} \boldsymbol{\beta}_1 \\ \boldsymbol{\beta}_2 \end{bmatrix} + \mathbf{u}. \tag{5.7}$$

If an outside unbiased estimate $\widetilde{\boldsymbol{\beta}}_1$ of $\boldsymbol{\beta}_1$ is available, then the equation can be rearranged:

$$\mathbf{q} - \mathbf{X}_1 \widetilde{\boldsymbol{\beta}}_1 = \mathbf{X}_2 \boldsymbol{\beta}_2 + \left(\mathbf{u} - \mathbf{X}_1 \widetilde{\mathbf{u}} \right), \tag{5.8}$$

where $\widetilde{\mathbf{u}} = \widetilde{\boldsymbol{\beta}}_1 - \boldsymbol{\beta}_1$. Now the regression of $\mathbf{q} - \mathbf{X}_1 \widetilde{\boldsymbol{\beta}}_1$ on the smaller set of explanatory variables $\mathbf{X}_2$ can be run.

Exact nonsample information not only may be about a particular parameter but could also be about a linear combination of parameters. For instance, the sum of certain parameters may equal a known value, or two coefficients may be known to equal each other. All these various pieces of information can be expressed in the relation

$$\mathbf{R}\boldsymbol{\beta} = \mathbf{r}, \tag{5.9}$$

where $\mathbf{R}$ is a prespecified matrix of order $s \times k$ with $s \leq k$, and r is a prespecified s-element vector. The matrix $\mathbf{R}$ is often called the information design matrix. The least-squares method can be extended to take into account the linear equality restriction (5.9) by using classical Lagrangian procedures, in which case the method is known as *restricted least squares.*[3]

For example, application of a random utility model for consumer choice in the presence of submarkets within a broader market imposes restrictions on cross-elasticities (Allenby 1989). The proportional draw property says that a one percent change in the price of a brand produces an equal percent change in each of the brands within its submarket and equal but smaller percent changes for brands within each other submarket. The price cross-elasticities saying what the equal proportional change will be. The proportional draw property imposes an across market share equation equality restriction. For members of the same submarket, the proportional influence property says that a one percent change in the price of a larger-share competitor will have more impact on a brand than a one percent change in the price of a smaller brand. The proportional influence property imposes a within equation ratio restriction where the ratio of the price cross-elasticities of any two brands in a submaket will equal the ratio of their respective market shares. An empirical example involving bathroom tissue is given in Allenby (1989).

The estimates $\tilde{\beta}_1$ of the parameters β_1 often come from one sample, say, a cross-section sales response function, and are introduced into the subsequent equation, say, a time series sales response function, as if they were known with certainty. Thus, the parameter estimates obtained from the time series data are *conditional* upon the estimates obtained from the cross-section data. Consequently, sensitivity analysis, in which the values of $\tilde{\beta}_1$ are systematically varied, is often necessary. However, a better procedure would involve explicitly taking into account the random nature of $\tilde{\beta}_1$.

A more efficient procedure would also attempt to improve the estimate of β by taking into account the regression data. Thus, the two pieces of information can be combined, i.e.,

$$\begin{bmatrix} q \\ \tilde{\beta}_1 \end{bmatrix} = \begin{bmatrix} X_1 & X_2 \\ I & 0 \end{bmatrix} \begin{bmatrix} \beta_1 \\ \beta_2 \end{bmatrix} + \begin{bmatrix} u \\ \tilde{u} \end{bmatrix} \tag{5.10}$$

and then generalized least squares can be applied to this equation system as a whole.

The stochastic nonsample information can come from management judgment as well as from research findings. Suppose a manager believes that 0.5 is the most plausible value of a promotion elasticity and that the odds that this elasticity is in the interval (0.3,0.7) are 20 to 1. Since the range is approximately equal to 4 standard deviations, the manager's judgment can be considered a point estimate of the elasticity equal to 0.5 with a standard error of 0.1.

Whatever the source, stochastic nonsample information can be expressed in a more general form by modifying (5.10) to take into account v, an *s*-element normally distributed random vector

$$\mathbf{R\beta} + \mathbf{v} = \mathbf{r} \tag{5.11}$$

The generalized least squares estimation procedure that incorporates this restriction is called *stochastic restricted least squares.*

The estimation procedures discussed have involved two steps. First, estimate parameters from the first sample. Second, use these estimates as additional information for efficient estimation in the second sample. A logical extension is to combine the two samples. The relation would now be expressed as

$$\begin{bmatrix} \mathbf{q}_A \\ \mathbf{q}_B \end{bmatrix} = \begin{bmatrix} \mathbf{X}_{1A} & \mathbf{X}_{2A} & \mathbf{0} \\ \mathbf{X}_{1B} & \mathbf{0} & \mathbf{X}_{3B} \end{bmatrix} \begin{bmatrix} \mathbf{\beta}_1 \\ \mathbf{\beta}_2 \\ \mathbf{\beta}_3 \end{bmatrix} + \begin{bmatrix} \mathbf{u}_A \\ \mathbf{u}_B \end{bmatrix} \tag{5.12}$$

where A and B denote observations from samples 1 and 2, respectively. There is one subset of variables and corresponding parameters that the two samples have in common, and there are two other subsets each of which is specific to a particular sample. The parameters are estimated by generalized least squares. The procedure is said to be balanced in that the a priori information from one sample is not assumed to be error-free.

Up to this point, a one-to-one correspondence between parameters from different samples has been assumed. Unfortunately, these parameters may not be directly comparable. The problem occurs when there is temporal interdependence in the time series relation or when there is contemporaneous interdependence in the cross-section relation. This necessitates formulating a more general model that incorporates these phenomena in order to establish the relation between parameters from different sources.

The Bayesian Approach. A substantial amount of literature exists on Bayesian inference in regression and econometrics, e.g., Zellner (1971; 1988a), Pilz (1991). Although this approach is not without its critics, Bayesian methodology does focus on integration of different data.

Bayesian inference might be used to combine initial information with new data (Greene 1997, pp. 311-22; Kennedy 1998, pp. 205-20). The initial information could result from previous studies, theoretical considerations, or casual observation. Initial information about unknown parameters is expressed as a *prior* probability density function. The new sample information is represented by its *likelihood* function. Bayes' theorem is then used to obtain a *posterior* probability density function, which incorporates both the initial information and sample information:

$$p(\text{parameters}|\text{data}) = \frac{p(\text{parameters})\,p(\text{data}|\text{parameters})}{p(\text{data})}. \tag{5.13}$$

The data is treated as only a fixed set of information to be used for updating beliefs about the parameters. Once the data is known, all relevant sample information concerning the unknown parameters is contained in the likelihood function. This means that (5.13) can be simply written as

$$p(\text{parameters}|\text{data}) \propto p(\text{parameters})\,l(\text{parameters}|\text{data}), \tag{5.14}$$

where $\propto$ denotes the proportionality sign. This approach can be used in the context of regression models to find $\boldsymbol{\beta}$ and σ^2.

Given the appropriate expression for diffuseness, that is, priors for the situation where our knowledge about model parameters is vague or diffuse, the Bayesian approach often yields similar results to that of the traditional approach. For example, when the initial information is vague, $\boldsymbol{\beta}$ and log σ are assumed to be independently and uniformly distributed. The *noninformative* prior distribution is

$$p(\boldsymbol{\beta}, \sigma) \propto \frac{1}{\sigma}, \tag{5.15}$$

where $-\infty < \beta_i < \infty$, and $0 < \sigma < \infty$. The disturbances in regression usually are assumed to be normally distributed, in which case the likelihood function for the sample values is also a normal distribution. Application of Bayes theorem will yield a normal posterior distribution.

When prior information about the likely or unlikely values in $\boldsymbol{\beta}$ is the available from theory or previous research, informative priors are used. The most common informative prior is the natural conjugate prior, which leads to a posterior density with the same functional form.

A Bayesian analysis of the general linear model, which includes regression as a special case, has been given by Lindley and Smith (1972, pp. 4-5). Let the first-stage model be

$$[\mathbf{Q}|\boldsymbol{\theta}_1] \sim N(\mathbf{A}_1\boldsymbol{\theta}_1, \mathbf{C}_1), \tag{5.16}$$

where $\mathbf{Q}$ is an $n \times 1$ data vector, $\boldsymbol{\theta}_1$ is a $p_1 \times 1$ parameter vector, $\mathbf{A}_1$ is an $n \times p_1$ *known* design matrix, and $\mathbf{C}_1$ is an $n \times n$ *known* covariance matrix [using the notation given in Carlin and Lewis (1996, p 41)]. The distribution of the first-stage priors,

$$\theta_1 \sim N(A_2\theta_2, C_2), \tag{5.17}$$

is a function of θ_2, a $p_2 \times 1$ *known* second-stage hyperparameter vector, A_2, an $p_1 \times p_2$ *known* design matrix, and C_2, an $p_2 \times p_2$ *known* covariance matrix. The posterior distribution of θ_1 is

$$[\theta_1|q] \sim N(Dd, D), \tag{5.18}$$

where

$$D^{-1} = A_1'C_1^{-1}A_1 + C_2^{-1}, \text{ and} \tag{5.19}$$

$$d = A_1'C_1^{-1}q + C_2^{-1}A_2\theta_2. \tag{5.20}$$

The point estimate for θ_1 is given by

$$E(\theta_1|q) = Dd = \hat{\theta}_1, \tag{5.21}$$

with its variability captured by the posterior covariance matrix

$$Var(\theta_1|q) = D. \tag{5.22}$$

The second-stage hyperparameters θ_2 can themselves be expressed in terms of third-stage hyperparameters θ_3. Indeed, the results can be extended to as many stages as desired as long as the mean and dispersion are known for the final stage (Lindley and Smith 1972, p. 6).

In the special case of a linear regression, the values

$$A_1 = X, \quad \theta_1 = \beta, \text{ and } C_1 = \sigma^2 I \tag{5.23}$$

are substituted into the equations above. A noninformative prior is given by $C_2^{-1} = 0$ and

$$D^{-1} = X'(\sigma^2 I_n)^{-1} X = \frac{1}{\sigma^2}(X'X) \text{ and} \tag{5.24}$$

$$d = \mathbf{X}'\left(\sigma^2 \mathbf{I}_n\right)^{-1} \mathbf{q} = \frac{1}{\sigma^2}(\mathbf{X}'\mathbf{q}).$$ (5.25)

Therefore the posterior mean is

$$\hat{\boldsymbol{\beta}}_{\text{Bayes}} = \mathbf{D}\mathbf{d} = \left[\frac{1}{\sigma^2}(\mathbf{X}'\mathbf{X})\right]^{-1} \frac{1}{\sigma^2}(\mathbf{X}'\mathbf{q}) = (\mathbf{X}'\mathbf{X})^{-1}\mathbf{X}'\mathbf{q} = \hat{\boldsymbol{\beta}}_{\text{OLS}},$$ (5.26)

cf., Equation (5.5). The posterior distribution of $\boldsymbol{\beta}$ is

$$[\boldsymbol{\beta}|\mathbf{q}] \sim N\left(\hat{\boldsymbol{\beta}}_{\text{OLS}}, \sigma^2(\mathbf{X}'\mathbf{X})^{-1}\right),$$ (5.27)

which corresponds to the sampling distribution of the least-squares estimator. Using the mean of the posterior distribution as the estimator for $\boldsymbol{\beta}$, the same value is found as that given for the classical estimator. This is not surprising since a noninformative prior was used. The interpretation will, however, differ from classical sampling theory inasmuch as the Bayesian approach considers the parameters as random variables whereas the traditional approach views them as fixed numbers.

Bayesian analysts note that the traditional methods of introducing additional information about some coefficients in a regression model have only an asymptotic justification. In contrast, they argue, their approach yields "exact finite sample" results. However, these "exact finite results" are possible only through the introduction of a tractable continuous prior distribution. The arbitrariness in eliciting prior distributions remains a central problem of Bayesian analysis. Moreover, tractability requires that a priori opinion be represented by one of several special distributions. Nonetheless, the argument between Bayesians and traditionalists focuses on how prior information should be used and not on whether it should be used.

Skrinkage Approaches. Detailed scanner data permits the systematic analysis of brand competition patterns, estimation of price elasticities, and the development of pricing policies, including micropricing. One problem is that some unrestricted least-squares estimates of price own- and cross-elasticities produced may not have the correct signs and magnitudes.[4] This problem becomes more severe the lower the level of aggregation of the data. "Solving" the problem through spatial or product aggregation may introduce potentially large biases in the estimates of the price elasticities. Even the better approach of pooling may lose detail of interest to the marketing manager. Thus, various approaches have been put forth to help estimate store level price and promotion parameters.

Consider the construction of market response models for brands (or skus) within a product category by stores (or chains). Rather than treat each of the brand-store models as separate and unrelated, one large hierarchical model linking all of the parameters across store-brand can be specified. Estimators based on such a model use ensemble information to *shrink* brand-store estimators toward each other to dampen some of the undesirable variation of the separate OLS estimators.

A Bayesian approach would be to treat the parameters of the individual market response models, assuming a common functional form, as samples from a *common* prior distribution.[5] The market response model is an equation system. If each equation is estimated separately, the information about the least-squares estimator of each brand-store i is characterized by

$$\left[\hat{\beta}^i | \beta^i, \sigma_i^2\right] \sim N\left[\beta^i, \sigma_i^2\left(\mathbf{X}^{i\prime}\mathbf{X}^i\right)^{-1}\right]. \tag{5.28}$$

Suppose, however, that each of the equations is embedded in a hierarchical model and the individual parameter vectors treated as independent draws from a latent prior hyperdistribution:

$$\left[\beta^i | \theta^i, \Sigma\right] \sim N\left(\theta^i, \Sigma\right). \tag{5.29}$$

Then the posterior mean will be

$$E\left[\beta^i | \hat{\beta}^i, \sigma^2, \theta^i, \Sigma\right] = \mathbf{D}_i^{-1}\left(\sigma^{-2}\mathbf{X}^{i\prime}\mathbf{X}^i\hat{\beta}^i + \Sigma^{-1}\theta^i\right), \tag{5.30}$$

where

$$\mathbf{D}_i = \sigma^{-2}\mathbf{X}^{i\prime}\mathbf{X}^i + \Sigma^{-1}, \tag{5.31}$$

cf., Lindley and Smith 1972 (p. 10, Equation 24). This estimator shrinks each least-squares estimate $\hat{\beta}^i$ toward the hyperparameter θ^i by a shrinkage factor of $\mathbf{D}_i^{-1}\sigma^{-2}\mathbf{X}^{i\prime}\mathbf{X}^i$. As the prior covariance Σ decreases, $\hat{\beta}^i$ is shrunk more toward θ^i.

The Bayes rule is not available, however, as an estimator because the parameter σ^2 and the hyperparameters θ^i and Σ are not fully specified. Approaches to addressing this problem include hierarchical Bayes and empirical Bayes.

Hierarchical Bayes (HB). The hierarchical Bayesian framework improves individual OLS estimates by borrowing information across stores and shrinking the estimates toward a central tendency to avoid nonsensical estimates (Blattberg and George

1991) or by borrowing information across stores and shrinking the estimates toward one another (Montgomery 1997). Depending on the prior the assumptions about the prior, the second approach will produce estimates identical to the pooled or individual store-level models or somewhere in between.

A hierarchical Bayes estimator for (5.30) can be obtained by integrating out σ^2, θ^i, and Σ assuming that they are independent and follow an inverse gamma-normal-Wishart prior (natural conjugate priors). See Blattberg and George (1991, p. 309) for details. Exact calculation of the estimator is not feasible. An approximation is obtained using the Gibbs sampling approach (Blattberg and George 1991, p. 310; Cassella and George 1992; Carlin and Louis 1996, pp. 163-73).

Early forecasts for sales of new durable products, hospital equipment, and educational programs have been obtained using methods based on hierarchical Bayes procedures (Lenk and Rao 1990). The Bass model has been implemented within this framework using a nonlinear regression approach. Two stages of prior distributions use sales data from a variety of dissimilar new products. The first stage describes the variation among the parameters of the products and the second prior stage expresses uncertainty about the hyperparameters of the first prior. Before sales data become available, forecasts are the expectation of the first-stage prior. As sales data become available, forecasters adapt to the unique features of the product.

The HB methodology can be extended to situations where the population means are functions of explanatory variables. The market response model for products within particular stores of a chain can be written is an equation system. The parameters can then be stacked into a single vector. This parameter vector is treated as a draw from a latent distribution, known as a hyperdistribution. Each element of the parameter vector can be expressed in terms of a mean value across stores, one or more explanatory variables, and random error. The explanatory variables are the demographic and competitive variables for the trading area of a store. For example, in modeling store-level demand for refrigerated orange juice in a major regional supermarket chain in the Chicago area, Dominick's Finer Foods (DFF), the demographic variables included measures of age (over 60), education (college degree), ethnicity (black or Hispanic), income (median), family size (5 or more members), working women (percent), and house value (greater than $150,000). The competitive variables included distance to nearest warehouse and average distance to nearest five supermarkets (miles) as well as the ratio of DFF store sales to nearest warehouse and to average of nearest five supermarkets (Montgomery 1997, p. 319). Thus, cross-store estimates are shrunk toward a regression line.

Last but not least, theory can be incorporated into the HB framework. For example, a demand model derived from the hypothesis of utility maximization will have restrictions imposed upon it. Rather than imposing the exact restrictions of economic theory (e.g., Allenby 1989), a stochastic prior framework that does not require these restrictions to hold exactly may be more practical. Differential shrinkage, in which the prior is tighter on some set of parameters than on others, can also be beneficial. The standard normal-Wishart linear model cannot be used because the Wishart prior has only one tightness parameter for all elements of the covariance matrix. A nonstandard hierarchical method for addressing these issues has been proposed by Montgomery and Rossi (1999).

A stochastic spline approach in a HB framework can be employed to get the flexibility necessary to accommodate irregular response functions. An example is sales response to nonmonotic prices, such as odd prices (see Kalyanam and Shively 1998).

Empirical Bayes (EB). The Bayesian approach to inference depends on a prior distribution of model parameters. This prior can depend on unknown parameters, which in turn can follow another prior distribution. This sequence of parameters and priors constitute a hierarchical model. The hierarchy must stop at some point, with all remaining parameters assumed known. Rather than make this assumption, the *empirical Bayes* (EB) approach estimates these final-stage prior distribution parameters using the observed data before proceeding as in a standard Bayesian analysis. Thus, the EB method may be regarded as a compromise between the Bayes and classical approaches.

An empirical Bayes estimator for (5.30) can be obtained by using frequentist justifications to estimate the unknown σ^2, θ^i, and Σ. See Blattberg and George (1991, pp. 308-9) for details.

Stein-like rules. By imposing restrictions, out-of-sample information is being used to sharpen parameter estimates. Unless the restrictions are correct in the population, the restricted least squares estimator will be biased. Nonetheless, biased estimators may produce more precise estimators, in an expected square error sense, than unbiased estimators. There is an opportunity to find a compromise estimator that accepts some failure to satisfy the restrictions. Stein-like rules specify how to combine unrestricted and restricted least squares least squares estimators. Basically the least squares estimator is adjusted (shrunk) toward the restricted (hypothesis) estimator.

This approach has been applied to store level price-promotion models (Hill, Cartwright, and Arbaugh 1990). Here unrestricted and restricted seemingly unrelated regression estimators were combined. Four alternative restrictions were considered: (1) all parameters except the intercepts for each store are zero; (2) the parameters of each store are equal (pooling); (3) the parameters at the store level within chains are equal (chain homogeneity); and (4) a judgmental prior specified for the chain and market level and obtained by averaging the micro-level parameters across stores within the chain and within the market. For a particular product category, canned tuna, the best estimation rule was found to be the seemingly unrelated regressions estimator with the parameters restricted to be equal across regressions. The explanation was that the product category was very well behaved with the explanatory variables exhibited little variation. The resulting collinearity produced OLS estimates that were often of the wrong sign. The design variability introduced when the data was pooled virtually eliminated incorrect signs. Furthermore the store level parameters are roughly the same order of magnitude, which meant the pooling prior did not represent significant specification error. Consequently the mean squared error improvement was dramatic. The pooling prior may not serve as well for product categories exhibiting greater demand variation across stores.

Testing

A broad set of tests can and should be applied to a model during its development and implementation. The evaluation of a model begins with the testing of its statistical assumptions. The model must be examined for problems such as nonlinearity, contemporaneous correlation of regressor and disturbance, omitted variables, heteroscedasticity, autocorrelation, collinearity, and non-normality. This portion of the evaluation is called specification error analysis. If no violations of the assumptions are found, the regression results can be tested. This involves tests of significance concerning each individual model and subsequently discrimination among alternative models. First, however, we consider some tests of significance that assume there is no specification error.

Tests of Significance

When the disturbances in the standard linear model are assumed to be normally distributed

$$\mathbf{u} \sim N\left(\mathbf{0}, \sigma^2 \mathbf{I}\right),$$
(5.32)

then

$$\hat{\boldsymbol{\beta}} \sim N\left[\boldsymbol{\beta}, \sigma^2 (\mathbf{X}'\mathbf{X})^{-1}\right],$$
(5.33)

as linear combinations of normal variables are also normally distributed, and

$$\frac{\hat{\mathbf{u}}'\hat{\mathbf{u}}}{\sigma^2} \sim \chi^2(n-k-1)$$
(5.34)

(Johnston and DiNardo 1997, pp. 90-95, 493-95). Note that our k does not count the intercept to be consistent with our notation but the k in most textbooks does count the intercept for notational simplicity. Various linear hypotheses about the elements of $\boldsymbol{\beta}$

can be tested using the relation (5.9). For instance, the hypothesis that $\mathbf{R} = \begin{bmatrix} \mathbf{0} \ \mathbf{I}_k \end{bmatrix}$ and $\mathbf{r} = \mathbf{0}$ provides a test of the overall relation that assesses whether the explanatory variables have any influence upon the dependent variable. If $\hat{\boldsymbol{\beta}}$ and $\hat{\mathbf{u}}$ are the OLS parameter and residual vectors, then the test statistic

$$F = \frac{\left(\mathbf{R}\hat{\boldsymbol{\beta}} - \mathbf{r}\right)'\left[\mathbf{R}(\mathbf{X}'\mathbf{X})^{-1}\mathbf{R}'\right]^{-1}\left(\mathbf{R}\hat{\boldsymbol{\beta}} - \mathbf{r}\right)/\sigma}{\hat{\mathbf{u}}'\hat{\mathbf{u}}/(n-k-1)} \tag{5.35}$$

is distributed as $F(s, n-k-1)$ where s is the number of restrictions. Separate tests of hypotheses about each of the parameters of the model as well as a joint test on the significance of the entire linear relation can be conducted.

The manager first wants to know if a model explains anything. To test the null hypothesis that none of the independent variables has any influence upon the dependent variable, i.e., their true coefficients is zero,

$$\begin{aligned} &H_0: \beta_1 = \beta_2 = \cdots = \beta_k = 0 \text{ versus} \\ &H_A: \text{at least one } \beta_i \neq 0, \end{aligned} \tag{5.36}$$

the test statistic is $F(k, n-k-1)$. If the model does not explain anything, stop. If the model explains something, how much does it explain? Here one looks at a descriptive statistic, R^2 (the coefficient of determination). This statistic gives the fraction of variation in the dependent variable explained by the model and thus lies between zero and one. Reasonable values will depend on the aggregation space: on the order of 0.1 for a cross section of individual consumers, 0.5 for a cross section of sales territories, and 0.9 for an aggregate national time series. Except in the case of one independent variable, rejection of the null hypothesis of no fit does not tell which independent variables are contributing to the fit. One has to examine each independent variable separately. To test the null hypothesis that an individual independent variable explains nothing, i.e., its true coefficient is zero,

$$\begin{aligned} &H_{0i}: \beta_i = 0 \text{ versus} \\ &H_{Ai}: \beta_i \neq 0, \end{aligned} \tag{5.37}$$

the test statistic is $F(1, n-k-1)$, or, taking the square root, $t(n-k-1)$. A two-tail test is the default in most computer packages, but one may have a priori knowledge that would make a one-tail test, $\beta_i < 0$ or $\beta_i > 0$, more appropriate. Independent variables that are not statistically significant are trimmed from the model and the model reestimated. There is a subtle point of interpretation about what happens to the trimmed variables. Regression is a technique based on variation. If a variable varies little or not at all (recall our discussion of distribution and sales calls in Chapter 2), regression cannot assess its impact. The manager must be agnostic and consider such a variable as being represented by the intercept. On the other hand if a variable has varied markedly and has had no significant impact, then it usually can be safely ignored. For statistically significant variables, the question is now whether their estimated parameters conform to theory. For example, one would expect the estimated advertising parameter to be positive whereas the estimated price parameter should be negative. Finally, the regression results, and in particular the regression residuals, should be explored to see if any modifications to the model are suggested. A summary of the steps for evaluating a regression model is given in Table 5-2.

These tests of significance apply only to single-equation models. Except in a few special cases, the small-sample properties of various simultaneous equation estimators are unknown. We next turn to an examination of the maintained hypothesis that underlies the single-equation tests of significance.

Specification Error Analysis

A true model describes the distributional characteristics of a population. Specification error occurs when a model other than the true model is used. We view the distribution of the disturbance terms as an integral part of the model. Consequently, when an assumption about the error structure of a model is violated, the result is not merely being unable to obtain optimal properties for the estimators of the model parameters. Rather, the violation poses a fundamental challenge to the model. This section focuses on specification error tests constructed primarily for the single-equation standard linear model.

The common types of specification error are (1) omitted variables, (2) incorrect functional form, (3) simultaneous equation problems, (4) heteroscedasticity, (5) non-normality of the disturbance term, (6) autocorrelation, and (7) errors in variables. Tests for these errors can be either general or specific. A general test is one against a broad group of alternatives; a specific test is one against a limited alternative. For instance, we could use a general test against nonlinearity, or we might test against a specific alternative such as a quadratic relation:

$$Q = \beta_0 + \beta_1 X + \beta_2 X^2 + u. \tag{5.38}$$

The specific test would be the F-test for the null hypothesis $\mathbf{R} = [0\ 0\ 1]$ and $\mathbf{r} = \mathbf{0}$. In subsequent sections, we discuss general tests for specification error.

Table 5-2. Steps in Evaluating a Regression Model

Step	Task	Action
0. How important is model precision to the managerial decision?	Set level of significance.	Choose a smaller level of significance the more critical model precision is.
1. Does the model explain anything?	Compare overall F-test probabilities with level of significance.	No: Stop Yes: Continue.
2. How much does it explain?	Check R^2, the fraction of the variation in the dependent variable explained by the model.	Compare to what one would expect for the level of data aggregation.
3. Does an individual variable explain anything?	Compare individual t-test probability with level of significance.	No: Go to Step 4. Yes: Go to Step 5.
4. If an individual variable does not explain anything, can it safely be ignored?	Check coefficient of variation.	No: Collapse variable into intercept. Yes: Discard variable. In either case, trim insignificant variables and reestimate model.
5. Do the statistically significant estimated parameters conform to theory?	Check signs and magnitudes.	No: Revise model. Yes: Continue.
6. Do regression results suggest possible modifications in the model?	Check information in residuals.	No: Use model if results in the earlier steps were satisfactory; otherwise, try a very different model. Yes: Revise model accordingly.

Residual Vectors. Specification error tests involve examination of the regression residuals. The least-squares residual vector

$$\hat{\mathbf{u}} = \mathbf{q} - \mathbf{X}\hat{\boldsymbol{\beta}} = \left[\mathbf{I} - \mathbf{X}'(\mathbf{X}'\mathbf{X})^{-1}\mathbf{X}\right]\mathbf{q} = \mathbf{M}\mathbf{q} \qquad (5.39)$$

provides one approximation to the disturbance vector. Unfortunately, even though the disturbances are stochastically independent and homoscedastic, the least-squares residuals are usually not. This causes problems in testing the distribution of the disturbance vector. Consequently, a residual vector is required that has a scalar covariance matrix when the disturbance vector does. The BLUS residual vector is such a vector. BLUS stands for Best Linear Unbiased Scalar covariance matrix. Theil (1971, pp. 202-10) defined the BLUS residual vector and describes its properties. One property of the BLUS residual vector is that the maximum number of independent residuals that can be obtained is $n - k$. Thus, we must choose which subset of residuals to use. Theil (1971, pp. 217-18) discussed this selection procedure.

The Impact of Specification Error. One approach to specification error analysis, the Regression Specification Error Test (RESET) by Ramsey (1969; 1974) for example, is to consider broadly the impact of the various types of error (Davidson and MacKinnon 1993, pp. 195-96). The null hypothesis is that a particular single-equation linear model is the true model. Under the usual assumptions, the BLUS residuals are normally distributed with mean zero and covariance matrix $\sigma^2 I_{n-k}$. If an alternative model is true, use of this given model will result in specification error. This is a misspecification test in that no specific alternative hypothesis is involved (Kennedy 1998, p. 79). Alternative models that would give rise to omitted variables, incorrect functional forms, or simultaneous equation problems lead to the BLUS residuals being normally distributed with a nonzero mean and covariance matrix **V**. Thus, if the estimator were unbiased, the error creates bias, or if the estimator were biased but consistent, this error brings about a different bias and inconsistency.

The recognition of the presence of at least one of these errors is accomplished by regressing the BLUS residuals against a polynomial (usually of degree 2 or 3) in transformed least-squares estimates of the dependent variable:

$$\hat{\mathbf{u}} = \alpha_1 + \alpha_2 (\mathbf{C}\hat{\mathbf{q}}) + \alpha_3 (\mathbf{C}\hat{\mathbf{q}}^2) + \cdots. \tag{5.40}$$

Under the null hypothesis of no specification error, the alphas should all be zero. Unfortunately, if the null hypothesis is rejected, we do not know which of the three types of errors caused this shift in the central tendency of the estimator. For example, in assessing the impact of generic advertising on the meat group in Australia, double-log models for beef, lamb, and chicken passed the RESET test but pork did not. This suggested that the double-log model may not be an appropriate specification for pork, but no particular alternative is implied (Piggott 1996, pp. 271-72).

Specific tests exist for most of the individual specification errors we might encounter. We now turn to a discussion of these tests. Each test is for one specification error in the absence of other specification errors.

Customer Response Modeling at Wells Fargo Bank: A Financial Services Industry Perspective

Wells Fargo is a major California based bank with rapidly evolving presence nationwide in most major segments of financial services. The Business Banking Group, which has made more small business loans than any other bank in the U.S., has been aggressively pursuing growth opportunities in and outside California using a direct marketing paradigm. In so doing, we recognize the strategic importance of modern customer and prospect databases. Such databases allow for the effective and efficient targeting, retaining and cross-selling of customers and prospects. They also require us to develop quantitative marketing modeling skills, an expertise that is fairly new to the financial services industry.

The first applications of statistical modeling in BBG focused on assessing the risk of credit applicants and the likelihood of future loss from existing customers. Over the last 10 years or so we have become quite sophisticated in the development and use of statistical risk evaluation models. Soon after the development of credit modeling we began to turn our quantitative analysts to the challenge of improving marketing effectiveness. In what follows we describe an example of the use of market-response models to enhance our marketing effectiveness.

The general response equation for the task of predicting customer response to direct-marketing campaigns is of the following nature:

$$\frac{\text{probability}}{\text{of response}} = f\left(\frac{\text{business}}{\text{firmographics}}, \frac{\text{product}}{\text{offer}}, \frac{\text{creative}}{\text{execution}}, \text{timing}\right).$$

Business firmographics are characteristics such as industry, time in business, and location. This probability is typically estimated using a series of logistic regressions.

We use a sequence of experimental designs to understand and quantify the relative importance of each driver and its sub-components. For example, product offer may include line-of-credit offer amount, interest rate and opening fee. Each factor can have a differential effect on customer responsiveness, so that relatively large databases need to be developed representing millions of businesses solicited multiple times before we are comfortable estimating the individual response effects.

Prepared by Marc Bernstein, Senior Vice President at Wells Fargo Bank in San Francisco.

Table 5-3. Nonlinearity

When It Occurs	How to Detect	Possible Remedies
Incorrect functional form	Plot residuals; look for systematic patterns.	Improve specification. Transform nonlinear model into linear model; otherwise use nonlinear least squares (NLS) or maximum likelihood (ML).

Nonlinearity. Linear models are computationally easy to estimate. Unfortunately, most market response phenomena are nonlinear, including the phenomenon described in the *Wells Fargo Industry Perspective*. For example, a sales response function is believed to exhibit diminishing returns to scale over most, if not all, of its range.

Fortunately, many nonlinear functional forms can be transformed into linear ones for estimation purposes. Those that cannot be transformed must be estimated by nonlinear methods. The treatment of nonlinearity is summarized to Table 5-3.

Transformations. Transformations are often used to convert linearizable nonlinear structural models into linear estimating equation. Recall our use of logarithms to make the common sales response function with a multiplicative disturbance linear, for example, the conversion of the constant elasticity model (3.11) into the double-log model (3.14):

$$ ln[Q] = ln\left[e^{\beta_0} X^{\beta_1} e^u \right] = \beta_0 + \beta_1 \ln X + u . \tag{5.41} $$

For instance, this transformation was applied to a multiplicative dynamic adjustment model of sales response to marketing mix variables (di Benedetto 1985). A problem arises when using this transformation if an observation on a variable is zero ($\ln[0] = -\infty$). This often occurs with raw weekly advertising data. To get around this problem in explanatory variables, many researchers add a small positive number to all entries.[6] See, for example, Rao, Wind, and DeSarbo (1988, p. 132). In practice, rather than finding the optimal small constant that would minimize bias, the value of one is added to each observation of an explanatory variable (so now $\ln[1] = 0$). See, for example, Capps and Moen (1992, p. 30). When an observation on the dependent variable is zero, the recommendation is to drop this observation (Young and Young 1975; Cooper and Nakanishi 1988, pp. 153-55). For example, zero share values were dropped in a competitive pricing behavior study (Besanko, Gupta, and Jain 1998, p. 1539).

Most market share models are nonlinear. They can be converted into linear models for estimation purposes. Approaches to estimating market share models are addressed in the Appendices 5-*B* and 5-*C*.

Another common transformation is the Koyck transformation for finding an estimating equation for geometric distributed lag models. This transformation was discussed in Chapter 4 (equation 4.10).

Nonlinear Estimation. Some functional forms are intrinsically nonlinear. For example, if the constant elasticity sales response function (3.11) has an additive error instead of the multiplicative error assumed in (5.41),

$$Q = e^{\beta_0} X^{\beta_1} + u. \tag{5.42}$$

then the relation cannot be transformed and its parameters must be found by nonlinear estimation techniques.

The least-squares principle can be applied to nonlinear models, although the computations will be more complex. *Nonlinear least squares* (NLS) in general provides biased estimates of the parameter vector β. A more serious problem is that the distribution of β is usually unknown even if the distribution of the disturbance term is known. Again, we must rely on asymptotic results. Under suitable conditions, the NLS estimator is consistent and asymptotically normally distributed. When the error term follows the standard normal distribution, the maximum likelihood estimator is the same as the least-squares estimator, as was the case for linear models. Nonlinear regression has been used to estimate market share response to advertising in the cigarette industry (Horsky 1977a), to estimate sales response to advertising of eight Australian products (Metwally 1980), and to assess the impact of coupon face value on sales (Leone and Srinivasan 1996). Nonlinear least squares is recommended for the estimation of the Bass diffusion model (Srinivasan and Mason 1986). In this context, NLS has been used to estimate the effect of price on the demand for consumer durables (Jain and Rao 1990).

Direct search can be used to fit parameters to complex models (Van Wormer and Weiss 1970). For example, a constrained search was conducted by Srinivasan and Weir (1988) in the estimation of a version of the geometric distributed-lag advertising-sales model (see Equation 4.16). The relation of interest was nonlinear in the advertising carryover rate, which itself was constrained to lie between 0 and 1. Not surprisingly, direct search is done frequently with the closely related adstock model as well. Here the parameter being varied is often half-life, which is directly related to the retention rate. For a brand of chocolate cookies (biscuits), an adstock model was estimated with integer weekly half-lives between 0 and 8. The highest R-square was achieved for a half-life of 5, which corresponds to $\lambda = 0.858$ in Table 2-9 (Broadbent 1999, pp. 46-47). Assessment of the impact of checkoff expenditures (see

Table 5-4. Nonconstant Coefficients

When It Occurs	How to Detect	Possible Remedies
Microunits in cross-section data respond differently. Environment changes over time.	Suspect systematic change: Split data into separate regimes, estimate, and compare results. Farley-Hinich-McGuire. Brown-Durbin-Evans. Suspect randomness: Breusch-Pagan.	Improve specification. If coefficients are systematic and deterministic, use OLS; if systematic plus a disturbance, use FGLS; if random, use FGLS; if return-to-normality, use ML; if Cooley-Prescott, use ML at point in time.

Equation 3.42) also requires search procedures (Forker and Ward 1993, p. 164; p. 215).

Nonconstant Coefficients. The coefficients in the standard linear model are assumed to be constant. This may well not be true if microunits in a crosssection study respond differently or if the environment changes over time. The treatment of nonconstant coefficients is summarized in Table 5-4. These tests are designed to detect structural breaks within the data set. The use of ETS models for forecasting means that one must be concerned about out-of-sample stability as well.

Detection within Historical Data. If the changes are systematic and deterministic (see Equation 4.32), OLS regression can be used. However, if the systematic changes also incorporate a random disturbance (see Equation 4.33), then FGLS must be used because the error term will be heteroscedastic (see Equation 4.34). Gatignon (1984) extends this approach to take into account constraints on some of the parameters in his model.

When the timing of a structural change is known, the data can be partitioned into separate regimes. Segments of a sales response function can fit separately by linear regression. This method is called *piecewise regression.* A more elegant counterpart of this methodology can be found in the theory of *splines* (Poirier 1973).

A major difficulty is defining the segments, since the timing of structural changes is rarely known. A procedure has been developed for determining if structural change has occurred (Farley and Hinich 1970 and Farley, Hinich, and McGuire 1975). A set of interaction variables is created by multiplying each suspect explanatory variable by a time index. Then the coefficients of these interaction variables are examined to see if they are zero or nonzero. Another test has been proposed which uses a *moving regression* (Brown, Dubbing, and Evans 1975).

The random coefficients model (see Equation 3.44) can be shown to belong to the class of heteroscedastic error models in which the variance of the dependent variable is a linear function of a set of exogenous variables. An appropriate test for randomness is the Breusch-Pagan test. The estimation technique will be FGLS (Greene 1997, 669-74).

The return-to-normality model (see Equation 4.36) leads to serially correlated and heteroscedastic errors. In this case, the appropriate estimation method is maximum likelihood, conditional on ϕ and $\mathbf{V}$.

The Cooley-Prescott model (see Equations 4.37-4.40) creates special problems because the process generating the parameters is not stationary. A maximum likelihood function can be constructed by focusing at a particular point in time, say one period past the sample.

Monitoring Newly Arrived Data. New data arrives steadily. Structural change can occur at any time. If the data generating process (DGP) changes in ways not anticipated by an ETS model, then forecasts lose their accuracy. The question is does the estimated model continue to explain this new data. Given the costs of failing to detect a break in the DGP, as rapid detection of breaks as possible is desirable. Detection timing will depend on the magnitude of parameter change, the signal-to-noise ratio, and the location of the out-of-sample break point. Monitoring for structural change requires sequential testing. Proposed real-time monitoring procedures include those by Chu, Stinchcombe, and White (1996).

Stochastic Regressors. The regressor matrix $\mathbf{X}$ has been assumed to be nonstochastic. This should be no problem in marketing experiments where the values of the explanatory variables can be set. However, most marketing information is nonexperimental and thus the assumption may be violated.

Violations vary in their degree of complexity. In the simplest case, the regressor matrix $\mathbf{X}$ is stochastic but completely independent of the disturbance vector $\mathbf{u}$. The usual test statistics will not hold in finite samples, except in the unlikely case that we would want to limit any inferences made to the particular sample values of $\mathbf{X}$. Under certain conditions, the usual test statistics are asymptotically valid. The least-squares estimator does provide a consistent estimate. The least-squares estimator will be the maximum likelihood estimator if the other standard assumptions hold.

A more complex case occurs when the stochastic regressors are only partly independent of the disturbance vector. This can occur in time series data when the explanatory variables include lagged values of the dependent variable. The tth observation on the regressor vector is independent of the tth and subsequent values of the disturbance term but not of past values of the disturbance term, so the least-squares estimator will be biased. The estimator is still consistent, however, and the usual test statistics are asymptotically valid.

The most complicated case (summarized in Table 5-5) arises in situations where observations on some stochastic regressors are not even independent of the current disturbance. This can happen when lagged values of the dependent variable are cou-

Table 5-5. Contemporaneous Correlations of Regressor and Disturbance

When It Occurs	How to Detect	Possible Remedies
Lagged values of dependent variable coupled with serially correlated errors. Errors in measurement. Simultaneity.	Plot regressors against disturbances. Conduct Hausman specification tests (Wald statistics)	Improve specification. Use method of instrumental variables to get consistent but inefficient estimates.

pled with serially correlated errors, when there are errors in variables, and when an equation is in actuality part of a larger simultaneous equations system. The least-squares estimator will be biased and inconsistent in such cases. One solution is to replace the stochastic regressors with a new set of regressors, known as *instrumental variables* (IV), which are correlated with the stochastic regressors but uncorrelated with the disturbance (Greene 1997, pp. 440-42; Pindyck and Rubinfeld 1998, pp. 182-84). The new estimates will then be consistent. In assessing the effect of advertising on brand-level sales of distilled spirits, price was endogenous and IV etimation was employed (Guis 1996, p. 74).

A test for the presence of errors of measurement involves comparing the least squares estimator to the instrumental variables estimator using the Wald statistic as defined by Hausman (Greene 1997, pp. 443-45; Pindyck and Rubinfeld 1998, pp. 195-98). Under the hypothesis of no measurement error, both the least-squares estimator and the IV-estimator are consistent estimators of the parameter vector although only the least-squares estimator will be efficient. If the hypothesis is false, only the IV-estimator is consistent.

The test for the presence of simultaneity—called an *exogeneity* (endogeneity) *test*—is naturally similar to that for measurement error (Greene 1997, pp. 763-64; Pindyck and Rubinfeld 1998, pp. 353-55). Under the hypothesis of no simultaneity, both the least-squares estimator and an IV-estimator (including 2SLS) are consistent estimators of the parameter vector although only the least-squares estimator will be efficient. If there is simultaneity, the IV-estimator is both consistent and efficient. The appropriate Hausman test is based on 2SLS and 3SLS estimators. Testing is complex because of an equation system being involved. A single-equation version of the test has been proposed (Spencer and Berk 1981). A market response equation containing a suspect variable is estimated by 2SLS twice: once treating the variable as exogenous and once treating the variable as exogenous. The test statistic again based on the difference between two estimators and is a Wald statistic. In an empirical investigation of channel pricing for refrigerated juice and canned tuna, the null hypothesis of exogeneity of a measure of retail competition—category sales across all stores in the market not including the chain—could not be rejected. Retail

Table 5-6. Nonzero Mean Disturbances

When It Occurs	How to Detect	Possible Remedies
Omitted variable	Can only detect if not constant and repeated measures are available.	Improve specification. Use dummy variables.

competition thus served as a demand shifter (Kadiyali, Chinagunta, and Vilcassim 2000, pp. 138-39).

The Hausman test has been adapted for market share equations. Here SUR provides consistent estimates when under the null hypothesis that sales drivers are exogenous but not under the alternative hypothesis that sales drivers are endogenous. In contrast, 2SLS estimates are consistent both under the null and alternative hypotheses. Thus, a comparison of SUR with 2SLS estimates provides a test for endogeneity. In a study of competitive pricing behavior, the null hypothesis that prices were exogenous was rejected for both product categories studied: yogurt and ketchup (Besanko, Gupta, and Jain 1998, p. 1540). In an investigation dynamic multifirm market interactions in a distinct subcategory of brands within a personal-care product category, the null hypothesis that weekly advertising was exogenous was rejected (Vilcasim, Kadiyali, and Chintagunta 1999, p. 510).

Sometimes a variable in a market mechanism is unobservable. A choice may arise between using a proxy variable in place of the unobserved variable and simply omitting the unobserved variable. Generally, the use of a poor proxy is better than omission of the unobserved variable (Greene 1997, pp. 442-43). Qualifications to this conclusion are noted in Judge et al. (1985, pp. 710-11).

Nonzero Mean Disturbances. The mean of the disturbances is expected to be zero. This will not be true if there is an omitted variable. However, as long as the mean is constant, say θ, and the equation contains a separate intercept, β_0, no major problem arises. The constant simply becomes part of the intercept, $\beta_0 + \theta$. If the mean is not constant, then repeated measures become necessary. If the mean differs across microunits, then individual dummy variables can be used; i.e., we are now pooling time series and cross-section data. The treatment of nonzero mean disturbances is summarized in Table 5-6.

Heteroscedasticity. The variance of the disturbance term has been assumed to be constant. An alternative hypothesis is that this variance increases (decreases) with increases in an explanatory variable in a cross-section study or over time in a time series study. If the disturbances are heteroscedastic, OLS estimates of the coefficients of the model will be unbiased but not efficient. The solution is to use estimated generalized least squares—including weighted least squares—or maximum likelihood

Table 5-7. Heteroscedasticity

When It Occurs	How to Detect	Possible Remedies
Cross-section data Structural change in environment Change in accuracy in measurement Random coefficients model	Plot squared residuals against time (time series) or one or more explanatory variables (cross section) Breusch-Pagan/Godfrey Gleisjer Goldfeld-Quandt Szroeter White	Improve specification. Use EGLS or ML.

Alternative Error Model	Formula
No restriction on variance of Q	$\mathbf{V} = \text{diag}\left(\sigma_1^2, \sigma_2^2, \cdots, \sigma_T^2\right)$
Variances constant within subgroups of observations	$\mathbf{V} = \text{blk diag}\left(\sigma_1^2\mathbf{I}, \sigma_2^2\mathbf{I}, \cdots, \sigma_m^2\mathbf{I}\right)$
Standard deviation of Q is a linear function of exogenous variables	$\sigma_t^2 = \left(\mathbf{z}_t'\boldsymbol{\alpha}\right)^2$
Variance of Q is a linear function of exogenous variables	$\sigma_t^2 = \mathbf{z}_t'\boldsymbol{\alpha}$
Variance of Q is proportional to a power of its expectation	$\sigma_t^2 = \sigma^2\left(\mathbf{x}_t'\boldsymbol{\beta}\right)^p$
The logarithm of the variance of Q is a linear function of exogenous variables (multiplicative heterogeneity)	$\sigma_t^2 = exp\left(\mathbf{z}_t'\boldsymbol{\alpha}\right)$
Autoregressive conditional heteroscedasticity (ARCH)	$\sigma_t^2 = \alpha_0 + \alpha_1 u_{t-1}^2$

(Davidson and MacKinnon 1993, pp. 291-92, 303-5). The exact details of the estimation will depend on the alternative heteroscedastic error model posited. See Table 5-7 for a summary of the treatment of heteroscedasticity.

Weighted least squares is appropriate whenever the error terms are heteroscedastic with variances known up to a multiplicative constant and are not correlated with one another (Davidson and MacKinnon 1993, p. 292). In Chapter 8, we will discuss the determinants of model parameters by reporting on meta-analysis of parameter estimates. For example, one study estimated the price elasticity of demand (and calculated the asymptotic standard error of the elasticity estimate) for a sample of U.S. food and tobacco manufacturing industries, then examined explanations for differences in interindustry price elasticity (Pagoulatos and Sorensen 1986).[7] The second step related estimates of price elasticity to advertising expenditures, industry concentration, the stage of production, the existence of protection from domestic and foreign entry, and the extent of new product introduction. WLS was used. For each observation, all variables were weighted by the inverse of the corresponding estimated standard error of the dependent variable. Other meta-analyses using WLS, or, more generally, iterative generalized least squares (IGLS) include Sethuraman, Srinivasan, and Kim (1999, p. 31) and Bell, Chiang, and Padmanabhan (1999, p. 514).

General tests for heteroscedasticity have been proposed by Breusch-Pagan/ Godfrey, Goldfeld-Quandt, and White among others (Davidson and MacKinnon 1993, pp. 560-64; Greene 1997, pp. 549-55; Johnston and DiNardo 1997, pp. 166-70; Kennedy 1998, pp. 119-21; Pindyck and Rubenfeld 1998, pp. 152-56). Goldfeld-Quandt is a simple, finite-sample test if there is a single variable thought to be an indicator of the heteroscedasticity. Breusch-Pagan/Godfrey is a Lagrange multiplier (LM) test. It requires that the variables causing heteroscedasticity be known, but not the functional form of the heteroscedasticity. Unfortunately, information about the variables causing heteroscedasticity is rarely known. White is an asymptotic test that does not require that the variables thought to cause heteroscedasticity be specified. While White's test is consistent against a very wide range of heteroscedastic alternatives, it may not be very powerful in finite samples (Davidson and MacKinnon 1993, p. 561; Johnston and DiNardo 1997, p. 165). Moreover, it is nonconstructive; that is, if the null hypothesis of homoscedasticity is rejected, the test result does not indicate what to do next (Greene 1997, p. 551; Johnston and DiNardo 1997, p. 167). The Breusch-Pagan/Godfrey test has been used in analyzing price/quantity relations (Kristensen 1984) and in assessing asymmetric and neighborhood price cross-effects (Sethuraman, Srinivasan, and Kim 1999, p. 31). Both studies found some heteroscedasticity. In the first study, however, re-estimation using GLS did not alter the original estimates and the ultimate conclusion was that heterogeneity was not a problem. The White test has been used in assessing the relations between promotional elasticities and category characteristics (Narasimhan, Neslin, and Sen 1996, p. 23). The null hypothesis of no heterogeneity could not be rejected in this study.

Heteroscedasticity is usually associated with cross-sectional data. However, empirical researchers have found that in many time series, large and small residuals tend to come in clusters. This suggests that the variance of the error may depend on the size of the preceding error. A common form to represent this phenomenon is *autoregressive conditional heteroscedasticity* (ARCH) (Davidson and MacKinnon 1993, pp. 556-60; Greene 1997, pp. 569-73; Kennedy 1998, pp. 128-29; Pindyck and Rubinfeld 1998, pp. 285-92). The ARCH(1) process is

$$\sigma_t^2 = \alpha_0 + \alpha_1 u_{t-1}^2 . \tag{5.43}$$

A test for ARCH is a Lagrange multiplier test where the square of the OLS residual is regressed on its lagged values (with an intercept). This test was applied in the Murphy's Irish Stout analysis. All tests were below critical values, indicating the absence of ARCH errors (Duckworth 1997, p. 303). Even if heteroscedasticity is found, the underlying model will obey the classical assumptions—provided that the process generating the disturbances is variance stationary. The OLS estimator will be BLUE; however, there will be a nonlinear estimator that is more efficient. A four-step FGLS estimator is described in Greene (1997, p. 571). ARCH can be generalized to make the conditional variance a function of past conditional variances, in which case the model is called GARCH:

$$\sigma_t^2 = \alpha_0 + \alpha_1 u_{t-1}^2 + \lambda_1 \sigma_{t-1}^2 . \tag{5.44}$$

Here the GARCH(1,1) process is shown. As long as λ_1 is less than 1, the current variance depends on all past volatilities but with geometrically declining weights.

Autocorrelation. The standard linear model assumes that disturbances are independent, that is,

$$E(u_t u_{t-s}) = 0, \quad s \neq 0. \tag{5.45}$$

The alternative hypothesis may be that two disturbances s periods apart are correlated. The correlation between these disturbances is called the *autocorrelation coefficient, ρ.*

The most common cause of autocorrelation in marketing is misspecification, in particular, the omission of a relevant explanatory variable. This omitted variable becomes part of the error term. Because the omitted variable is autocorrelated, the error term will be autocorrelated. A review autocorrelation and related issues in applications of regression analysis showed that residuals can be autocorrelated as a result of having a misspecified model (Wittink 1983b). If autocorrelation is due to misspecification, the best course of action is to correct the specification.

Autocorrelation occurs most frequently with temporal data; it can, however, occur in cross-section data if spatially close units are similar to one another (Dubin 1988). For example, adjacent sales territories may be more similar to one another than to more distant territories.[8] Nonindependence of observations is a common problem in meta-analysis. Experience suggests that the bias due to this nonindependence may not be serious provided the number of nonindependent observations is small relative to the total number of observations (Farley and Lehmann 1986, p. 106). This criterion is not met in meta-analyses of cross-effects. The same brand will appear in multiple observations. This will require that equation error be modeled as random error *plus* brand-specific error components and estimated by generalized least squares. This was done in a study of price cross-effects (Sethuraman, Srinivasan, and Kim 1999, p. 33).

Estimation of the completely general covariance matrix $E(\boldsymbol{\varepsilon}\boldsymbol{\varepsilon}') = \mathbf{V}$ from any finite sample is not possible, as the number of parameters to be estimated will always exceed the number of observations available (Johnston and DiNardo 1997, p. 175). One alternative hypothesis is that the successive disturbances are positively (negatively) autocorrelated. In particular, the time-series process is often assumed to be first-order autoregressive AR(1), as in a sales response model of generic advertising of fluid milk (Thompson 1974):

$$u_t = u_{t-1} + w_t . \tag{5.46}$$

Although under this alternative hypothesis, the estimates of the regression coefficients are unbiased, the usual least-squares formula underestimates their sampling variance. Correspondingly, the usual F-statistic will be overestimated, and thus the model will seem to fit the data better than it actually does.

The test against autocorrelation is the modified von Neumann ratio. This test uses BLUS residuals. See Table 5-8 for a summary of this and other tests of autocorrelation. A somewhat less powerful test, but one that is computationally simpler, is the *Durbin-Watson* (DW) test, which uses least-squares residuals instead of BLUS residuals (Greene 1997, pp. 591-94; Johnston and DiNardo 1997, pp. 179-82; Pindyck and Rubinfeld 1998, pp. 164-69). The DW statistic approximately equals $2(1 - \hat{\rho})$. When there is no serial correlation, the DW statistic will be near 2. Values of the DW test below (above) 2 are associated with positive (negative) autocorrelation.[9] The Durbin-Watson statistic has been used in numerous marketing studies.

The Durbin-Watson test assumes that the independent variables are fixed. Thus, the test cannot be used when lagged values of the dependent variable are present among the predetermined variables. An alternative statistic, known as Durbin h, can be used in this situation (Greene 1997, pp. 596-97; Pindyck and Rubinfeld 1998, pp. 169-70). This test statistic was used by Montgomery and Silk (1972), for example.

When one of these tests indicates the presence of first-order autocorrelation, a two-step estimation procedure is required. The first step involves obtaining an estimate of ρ by means of ordinary least squares (OLS) estimation. The second step requires that this estimate of ρ be used in an estimated generalized least squares (FGLS) regression. Marketing applications include Simon (1982) and Vanhonacker (1984).

Although AR(1) error models are the most common alternative specifications, the error structure could be a higher-order autoregressive process AR(p),

Table 5-8. Autocorrelation

When It Occurs	Alternative Error Model	How to Detect	Possible Remedies
Misspecification: omitted variable(s), incorrect functional form, or misspecification of an equation's dynamics.	First-order autoregressive errors AR(1)	Periodogram of residuals von Neumann ratio Durbin-Watson Durbin h-statistic	GLS EGLS NLS ML B
	Second- and higher-order autoregressive errors AR(p)	Periodogram of residuals Breusch-Godfrey Box-Pierce-Ljung	GLS EGLS NLS ML
Inherently smooth behavior of time series data (inertia).	First-order moving average errors MA(1)	Periodogram of residuals	GLS NLS ML B
Data manipulation: interpolation or smoothing. Persistent effects of a random shock.	Higher-order moving-average errors MA(q)	Periodogram of residuals Breusch-Godfrey	NLS ML
Spatial relationship.	Autoregressive moving-average errors ARMA(p, q)	Periodogram of residuals Box-Pierce-Ljung	NLS ML

$$u_t = \rho_1 u_{t-1} + \rho_2 u_{t-2} + \cdots + \rho_p u_{t-p} + w_t , \qquad (5.47)$$

a moving-average process MA(q),

$$u_t = w_t + \theta_1 w_{t-1} + \theta_2 w_{t-2} + \cdots + \theta_q w_{t-q} , \qquad (5.48)$$

or an autoregressive moving-average process ARMA(p, q),

$$u_t = \rho_1 u_{t-1} + \rho_2 u_{t-2} + \cdots + \rho_p u_{t-p}$$
$$+ w_t + \partial_1 w_{t-1} + \partial_2 w_{t-2} + \cdots + \theta_q w_{t-q}. \qquad (5.49)$$

The Breusch-Godfrey test is a Lagrange multipler test of the null hypothesis of no autocorrelation against either AR(p) or MA(q) (Johnston and DiNardo 1997, pp. 185-87). This test essentially involves regressing the current residual on the explanatory variables and p lags of the residual (filling in missing values of the residuals with zeros). The Box-Pierce-Ljung test is a similar test (Greene 1997, p.

595, p. 838; Johnston and DiNardo 1997, p. 187; Pindyck and Rubinfeld 1998, p. 496, pp. 555-56).[10] The Breusch-Godfrey test uses partial correlations whereas the Box-Pierce-Ljung test uses simple correlations. Both tests have been criticized for the difficulty of determining the depth of lag to consider (Greene 1997, pp. 595-96). In practice, one examines different values of the lag. For example, in doing diagnostic tests on the fitted sales response function of Murphy's Irish Stout, lags between 1 and 6 were each tested. The tests indicated the absence of residual autocorrelation (Duckworth 1997, p. 303). If residual autocorrelation is found, nonlinear least squares or maximum likelihood methods can estimate the higher-order processes. A second-order serial correlation correction was employed in place of the traditional first-order correction in a market response study of the effects of generic advertising on fluid milk Capps and Schmitz (1991, p. 135). See also Liu and Forker (1988). ARMA processes are discussed in detail in Chapter 6.

Collinearity. Collinearity (sometimes called multicollinearity but the prefix is redundant) occurs when the predetermined variables are strongly related to each other; in this case, the influence of one is difficult to separate from that of another (Greene 1997, pp. 418-427; Pindyck and Rubinfeld 1997, pp. 95-98; Kennedy 1998, pp. 183-93). One reason that this occurs in marketing is because the strategy of a brand will impose correlations among the brand's sales drivers—else why have a strategy? For example, a brand's total promotion budget may change over time but the proportion of this budget allocated to sales promotion versus media advertising may remain relatively fixed. Thus, while the impact of total promotion on sales can be determined, the impact of sales promotion cannot be distinguished from that of media advertising. Temporary price cuts for leading brands are almost always announced in major newspaper announcements (Cooper, Klapper, and Inoue 1996, p. 225). Disentangling the effects of the correlated-components of marketing strategy, such as those of TPRs from newspaper advertising, is difficult. Near collinearities often arise when models are overspecified; e.g., all possible explanatory variables are included in a model without consideration for their relevance. Dummy variables have the potential to create multicollinearity. Dummy variables representing different aspects of a common phenomenon will have many zeros in common. These common zeros will artificially inflate the correlation coefficients among the dummy variables. Certain functional forms, such high degree polynomials, also risk collinearity.

The forecasting power of a regression is unaffected by collinearity, but the estimates of its coefficients may not be precise—indeed, some regression estimates may potentially not even have the correct sign. What happens is that the determinant of the cross-products matrix $\mathbf{X'X}$ becomes smaller as collinearity increases. This ultimately leads to "division by (near) zero" in estimation formulas (which involve the reciprocal of the determinant)—and consequently the estimates of coefficients (5.5) and their standard errors (5.6) become implausibly large. In extreme situations, small changes in the data could produce wide swings in the parameter estimates. Theoretically important variables may be statistically insignificant. For a marketing-research-based discussion of this, see Grapetine (1997).

As the degree of collinearity falls between no collinearity and perfect collinearity, one issue is when does collinearity become a concern in practice? This not a simple matter because the potential effects of collinearity are moderated by other factors such as sample size and the overall fit of the regression model. This is discussed in the context of cross-sectional data by Mason and Perreault (1991).

What is needed is a collinearity diagnostic that can determine the number of the strength and number of near dependencies and can identify which variables are involved.[11] A critique of various historical diagnostic measures can be found in Belsley 1991, pp. 26-37. The key to developing a diagnostic is recognizing that determinant can be expressed as the product of its eigenvalues (characteristic roots):

$$|\mathbf{X'X}| = \lambda_1\lambda_1 \cdots \lambda_k. \qquad (5.50)$$

This eventually led to two statistics being proposed: the *condition number* for detecting collinearity and regression coefficient variance-decomposition proportions for determining variate involvement, which were based on these eigenvalues (characteristic roots) and associated eigenvectors (for details, see Greene 1997, pp. 422-423). In practice, Belsley (1991) recommends using the singular-value decomposition of $\mathbf{X}$, which is closely to the eigenvalue system of $\mathbf{X'X}$, for constructing the statistics. The condition number of a matrix is the ratio of its largest eigenvalue to its smallest eigenvalue. To prevent rescaling of variables, such as changing from dollars to euros, from affecting the results, the data matrix should first be normalized so that each column has equal length—usually unit length. A condition index greater than 30 is considered to indicate a strong degree of collinearity (Kennedy 1998, p. 190).[12] Condition numbers were checked in an assessment of price cross-effects (Sethuraman, Srinivasan, and Kim 1999, p. 31) and in a study of pre- and promotion dips (van Heerde, Leeflang, and Wittink 2000). The first study did not find that multicollinearity was a problem but the second study did. Note that traditional diagnostics do not accommodate differences between negative and positive correlations nor do they consider moderating relationships with the dependent variable (Mela and Kopalle 1998).

The modeling question is what to do if do if one finds collinearity. One solution for collinearity is to combine variables. For example, in a study of sales response to price level and promotion for ground coffee (Kalyanam 1996, p. 212, *fn.* 9), the issue of how to treat the grind of the coffee arose. The grind is the grade of particle fineness into which coffee is ground, e.g., regular percolator, drip, or espresso.

> Since grinds of an UPC are priced and promoted together, treating each grind as a separate brand would result in perfect collinearity of own price and promotion and price and

promotion of other grinds of the same brand. Hence demand specifications cannot be estimated at the grind level and different grinds of a given brand-size are aggregated together.

While coffee manufacturers now sell an "all method grind for all coffee makers" instead of individual grinds, the issue of common promotion and pricing of product variants remains a common one and variable aggregation its practical solution.[13]

Rather than combine variables a priori, empirical information could be used to combine them. This could be done by constructing composite indexes with principal components analysis (Greene 1997, pp. 424-27; Kennedy 1998, p. 189). The resultant principal components are orthogonal to each other, eliminating collinearity. An econometric model for the demand and supply of potatoes—fresh, chips, frozen, and dehydrated—contained 15 relations (one an identity) with 14 endogenous variables and 20 predetermined variables. Considerable collinearity was present among many of the variables and was addressed by principal components analysis. The first few principal components served as instruments for second and third stage estimation (Jones and Ward 1989, p. 527). One problem with this approach is that interpretation of the subsequent regression results may be difficult. For syndicated marketing data, the use of three-mode factor analysis has been proposed (Cooper, Klapper, and Inoue 1996). Because marketing efforts are likely to be correlated, an oblique rotation, rather than an orthogonal rotation, of factor scores is recommended (p. 230). Where the collinearity arises because of a distributed lag on a variable in a dynamic model, a procedure involving filtering the underlying autoregressive pattern can be used to find the appropriate dynamic weights (Liu and Hanssens 1982). See, for example, Carpenter et al. (1988, p. 400).

The usual response to collinearity is to drop one or more of the offending variables from the equation. For example, in analyzing the market share response to price within a household-product group sold by one retailer in the UK, the product being modeled competed with 29 other products. The researchers (George, Mercer, and Wilson 1996, p. 15) found that

Perfect correlation between prices of some products prevented all being included.

Researchers trying to specify the sales response function for cheese encountered a similar problem (Kinnucan and Fearon 1987, p. 104).

Dropping variables doesn't really help us much if the variables in question are marketing control variables. It may not be too troublesome if the variables are autonomous environmental ones. Competitive environmental variables fall some-where in between. Dropping variables may cause the model to be misspecified and cause the estimates of some coefficients to be biased. The real danger in dropping variables, however, is that the relation between included and excluded variables might change over time. A better approach is to obtain new data or information that would resolve the collinearity issue.

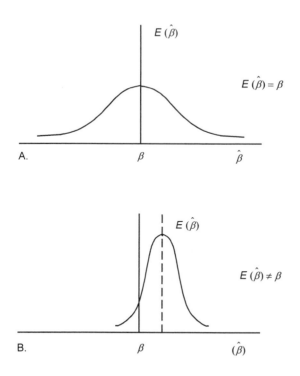

Figure 5-3. Bias and Variance in an Estimator. (A) Least-Squares Estimator: Zero Bias and a Large Variance. (B) Ridge Estimator: Nonzero Bias and a Small Variance. *Source*: Parsons and Schultz (1976, p. 108).

The collection of new data is often infeasible. For one thing, you have no experimental control over environmental variables. Thus you may have to look at ways of improving your estimates of model parameters with the data at hand. One way might involve estimating some of the parameters in a time series model by a cross-section study. Then these estimates would replace the corresponding unknown parameters in the time series model. Finally, the remaining unknown parameters could be estimated using the time series data.

Or it might require the use of *ridge regression*.[14] The mean-square error of an estimator is equal to its variance plus its bias squared. The least-squares estimator has zero bias but has a large variance in the presence of multicollinearity. In ridge regression, some bias is accepted in order to reduce the variance. This trade-off is shown in Figure 5-3. Applications of ridge regression include Mahajan, Jain, and Bergier (1977), Erickson (1981b), Hall and Foik (1983), Ofir and Khuri (1986), and Capps and Moen (1992). Sharma and James (1981) and Krishnamurthi and Rangaswamy (1987; 1991) have recommended that *latent root regression* and *equity estimator*, respectively, be used for biased estimation instead of ridge regression.

Table 5-9. Collinearity

When It Occurs	How to Detect	Possible Remedies
Poor sample design, e.g., highly correlated explanatory variables.	Coefficients have wrong signs or unlikely magnitudes. Overall regression is statistically significant with high R-square yet individual coefficients have high standard errors and low significance levels. Belsley	Collect better data. Introduce non-sample information. Use ridge-like/Stein-like estimators. Combine variables. Drop one or more variables.

Shipchandler and Moore (1988), on the other hand, found ridge regression to be better than latent root regression. Wildt (1993) concluded that there doesn't seem to be sufficient evidence to recommend the use of the equity procedure for market response estimation. One finding was that, under conditions of very high collinearity, both equity and OLS procedures were problem filled and consequently ridge might be a reasonable compromise. The treatment of collinearity is summarized in Table 5-9.

Non-Normality. The previous specification error tests assume that the distribution of the disturbance terms is normal. The failure of the normality assumption to hold means that the standard statistical tests cannot be performed although the least-squares estimates of the parameters remain unbiased as well as consistent. Fortunately, the standard tests are approximately correct for reasonably large sample sizes (i.e., are asymptotically valid). Table 5-10 summarizes the treatment of non-normality.

Tests for non-normality, Jarque-Bera for example, are really tests for either skewness or excess kurtosis (Davidson and MacKinnon 1993, pp. 567-71; Greene 1997, pp. 308-9).[15] For the normal distribution with variance σ^2, the next two higher central moments are

$$E\left[u^3\right] = 0 \text{ and } E\left[u^4\right] = 3\sigma^2.$$

If the third central moment is not zero, the distribution is skewed. If the fourth central moment is larger than $3\sigma^2$, the distribution is said to be leptokurtic, while if smaller, platykurtic. The leptokurtic case is the one likely to be encountered in practice. This means that the distribution of the residuals will display fat tails. The Jarque-Bera test was used in the study of Murphy's Irish Stout. The conclusion there was that the errors could be considered normally distributed (Duckworth 1997, p. 302).

Table 5-10. Non-Normality

When It Occurs	How to Detect	Possible Remedies
Error distribution has fat tails. Distribution of dependent variable skewed.	Shapiro-Wilk Jarque-Bera Keifer-Salmon	If a priori information about form of non-normal distribution is known, is use ML. Otherwise, if outliers in the error distribution are not likely, use OLS; if they are likely, use a robust estimator. When dependent variable has a skewed distribution, the Box-Cox transformation might be a solution.

Tests for non-normality can be considered a prelude to looking for outliers and influential observations (Kennedy 1998, p. 304). One diagnostic is Cook's $D(istance)$-statistic (Cook and Weisberg 1999, pp. 357-61). This descriptive statistic assesses whether there is a marked change in the regression coefficients if an observation is deleted from the sample; i.e., one is not simply looking for outliers but *influential observations* (Davidson and MacKinnon 1993, pp. 32-39). There is no significance test associated with D. The rule thumb is that cases where $D > 0.5$, and especially where $D > 1.0$, should be examined. One is looking at the impact on OLS estimates of not only observations with unusually large errors (*outliers*) but also any observation with an unusual value of an explanatory variable (high leverage or *leverage points*). The D-statistic has been used in salesforce and retail store performance studies to determine if relatively large territories have an undue influence on the results.

When the disturbances are not normally distributed but do possess a finite variance, the least-squares estimators will be unbiased and consistent but not efficient or asymptotically efficient. Given that appropriate regularity conditions are met, the maximum likelihood estimators will be asymptotically efficient, but the usual tests on the estimated coefficients not be valid. If the distribution of the disturbances has an infinite variance, it will have fat tails and outliers will be common. Least-squares estimation is very sensitive to outliers, and all results will be very unreliable.

If a priori information about the form of the non-normal distribution is known, maximum likelihood estimation can be used. Otherwise, if outliers in the error distribution are not likely, ordinary least-squares regression can be used. But if they are likely, it is necessary to use a robust estimator.

Robust Estimation. What can be done about the sensitivity of least squares to outliers? The simplest solution is to remove the outliers and re-estimate the model

(Pindyck and Rubinfeld 1998, p. 7). For example, in a study of asymmetric and neighborhood price cross-effects, approximately two to three percent of the observations for which the magnitude of the residuals was more than three times its standard error were identified as outliers and excluded from the analysis (Sethuraman, Srinivasan, and Kim 1999, p. 31). Outliers, in any event, should not be thrown away until they have been carefully examined. Such an examination may lead to refinements in the specification of the theoretical model (Kennedy 1998, p. 88).

Because the decision about what makes an outlier is arbitrary, estimators have been developed that place less weight on outliers than the ordinary least squares method does (Kennedy 1998, pp. 300-302). There are three classes of these so-called *robust estimators:* *M*-estimators, *L*-estimators, and *R*-estimators. *M*-estimators are maximum-likelihood-like estimators. *L*-estimators are based on linear combinations of the order statistics on the dependent variable. *R*-estimators are based on a ranking of the residuals in a linear model. Details and some marketing applications can be found in Mahajan, Sharma, and Wind (1984).

The Box-Cox Transformation. Sometimes a model may be specified in which the dependent variable is not normally distributed but for which a transformation may exist that will result in the transformed observations being normally distributed. The Box-Cox transformation discussed in Appendix 5-*D* is one possibility.

Systems of Equations. The analysis of specification error in simultaneous equations models involves two additional problems. First, when an estimation technique that incorporates more information than is contained in an isolated single equation is employed, the effects of specification error can be transferred across equations. Second, the inclusion of irrelevant variables or the omission of a relevant variable is a specification error that may affect the identifiability of one or more of the equations in the system. In general, the discussion of these problems is beyond the scope of this book. We discuss just one test.

An *identifiability test statistic* should be used whenever the order and rank conditions for identifiability indicate an equation is overidentified. The purpose of the test is to determine if the a priori restrictions that caused the overidentifying conditions are correct. Usually the overidentifying condition arises from variables in the system as a whole being excluded from a particular equation. Thus, a statistical test is required to judge if these extra exclusions are correctly specified in view of the evidence provided by the sample data. Basmann (1965) discusses the construction of identifiability tests, and Parsons (1968) gives a marketing application of such tests.

Flexible Functional Forms

The marketing information explosion and rapid advances in computation technology have led to the development of *data mining techniques* (Berry and Linoff 1997). Rather than determining the shape of the market response function with the guidance of theory, the data alone could be used determine a functional form—or even a specification using no functional form at all.

Specification tests become moot if specifications are unconstrained by a parametric structure. Such situations involve the use of special estimation techniques that have no meaningful parameters (Kennedy 1998, p. 302). These techniques will be robust to violations of the traditional regression assumptions.

Artificial Neural Networks

Artificial neural networks (ANN) allow the data to dictate the specification by means of an extremely flexible functional form, which has no economic meaning (Kennedy 1998, p. 302).[16] The danger is that ANN might too flexible—perhaps fitting noise in the data—and thus could be misleading in its specification of the underlying functional form.

The most common neural network model is the multilayer perceptron. The model is characterized by three types of layers—input, hidden layer(s) and output—and the number of nodes in each layer. The number of nodes in the input and output layers typically correspond to the number of predetermined variables and the number of endogenous variables respectively. Exploratory data analysis (EDA) may be used to reduce the number of input variables. Most marketing studies contain only one intermediate layer. Two layers may be desirable if severe nonlinearities, especially discontinuities, are present in the data. The number of nodes in the hidden layer is often empirically determined. An evolutionary model building approach is often taken, that is, starting simple and then making more complex as necessary. Thus, a marketing researcher may start with zero hidden units and successively increase the node of hidden nodes until generalization to a validation sample peaks. Too few nodes in the hidden layer and the network may not calibrate; too many and the network may not generalize.

The network may be fully connected (with all nodes of neighboring layers) or partially connected. Most published ANN marketing studies have been formulated initially as fully connected. Some end up as partially connected as a result of subsequent pruning. The network may be feed forward with feedback, or laterally connected. All published marketing studies have been feed forward. Processing takes place at each node in each layer other than the input layer. This processing involves two functions: a combination (aggregation) function and a transfer function, which when taken together are called the activation function. The combination function unites all "inputs" from the prior layer into a single value. This most common method for doing this is the weighted sum. Then a transfer function "squashes" the result from the combination function (usually plus a weighted constant called bias) into an "output" value, which is restricted to a small range. The transfer function may be linear or nonlinear, say hyperbolic tangent or logistic. The marketing studies mainly use a logistic activation function

Whereas market response modelers talk about estimating a model, ANN analysts talk about learning or training. Whereas market response modelers talk about parameters, ANN analysts talk about weights of the interconnections. The learning in the network may be unsupervised or supervised. Most published ANN marketing studies have employed supervised learning. In unsupervised learning, only values for the input nodes are used. The goal is to discover patterns in the data. In supervised learning, associated with each set of values for the input nodes (pattern) there is a set of known values for the output nodes. The goal of supervised training get the learned (estimated) output values to match the known output values. The most common supervised training algorithm is back propagation, which strives to adjust repeatedly the weights in a network so that the known input/output pair mappings can be correctly reproduced. If the training set (estimation data) spans input/output pattern space, then the learned functional mapping should also generate the correct output for an input pattern not present in the training set. In reality, training data will not span the input/output pattern space. By focusing on fitting a particular training data set, overfit may well occur and out-of-sample performance would decrease. One check on this is to split available data into training and validation samples. If the validation sample is used to determine the number of nodes in the hidden layer, a third sample called a testing sample may be necessary. The more weights there are in the network, the more likely overfit is to occur. Thus, other things being equal, the most parsimonious network model should be chosen. The process for doing this is called weight elimination. Parsimony is an argument for using only one hidden layer. Lets now look at some case histories of the use of ANN in the context of market-level response models.

In the case of an Austrian consumer brand, an econometric approach was compared to the neural network approach. Sales was the dependent variable and retail price, current advertising budget, advertising budget lagged one period, and average monthly temperature were the sales drivers (Hruschka 1993). The brand dominated its market and thus competitive influences could be ignored. A linear monthly model with first-order autoregressive residuals was estimated by general least squares estimated using the Cochrane-Orcutt procedure. Other functional forms were tried as well. The results indicated strong influences by price (negative) and temperature (positive). The advertising also had an effect (positive). The corresponding neural network consisted of four input variables plus bias, four hidden units, and one output unit with connections between variables of neighboring layers. Simplifications of this model were considered as well. All comparisons were on the basis of fit using mean square error and mean absolute deviations. The full ANN model fit best, but even the simplest version of the ANN model fit better than the econometric model. The weights in the ANN model had plausible economic interpretations. This research simply attempted to identify and estimate the market response function. No comparison of the forecasting ability of the econometric and ANN models was made.

In the case of a fast moving consumer good in continental European market, the competition among five brands could not be ignored (van Wezel and Baets 1995). Bimonthly observations were available on each brand's market share and marketing variables. The sales drivers included price, numerical distribution, weighted distribution, numerical out-of-stock, weighted out-of-stock, and advertising. In addition to a linear model (without autocorrelated errors), a multiplicative model was estimated. Note that market share rather than unit sales is the dependent variable in this study. The market response functions for the brands were estimated separately and together. Variants of the linear and multiplicative model, which used relative (to the market) rather than absolute variables, were also examined. The emphasis of this study was on forecasting so the sample was split into an estimation or training sample and a validation sample. Root mean squared errors were calculated. ANN performed better than traditional models.

In the case of the retail coffee market in one city, ANN was compared to Differential-Effects MCI model (Gruca and Klemz 1998). The Cross-Effects MCI model could not be estimated because of lack of data. ANN does not give the elasticities of marketing mix variables directly. They have to be calculated. For example, to calculate the price elasticity, each observed price is inputted to the ANN model having first set the non-price variables to their mean values and a predicted market share is generated. Using the resultant to data series, in this case price and market share, the definition of elasticity can be used to estimate the price elasticity. The elasticities of other sales drivers can be found in a similar manner. More than 95% of the elasticities in the Differential-Effects MCI model had the theoretically correct sign but in the ANN model this percentage was less than 75%. While the magnitudes of the elasticities of both models were generally comparable, there were exceptions. The ANN model was found to identify substantial cross-elasticities not detected by the MCI model, which couldn't by assumption (the cross-effects parameters having been set to zero). Furthermore, ANN surpassed the MCI model in forecasting ability. Here a hold-out sample was used and mean absolute percentage error (MAPE) was the criterion. One would have liked to have seen the ANN information about substantial cross-elasticities used to facilitate estimation of the Cross-Effects MCI model. Inconsequential cross-effect parameters could be set to zero reducing the data needed and perhaps making it possible to estimate the model.

A promising application of neural nets in market response modeling is a combined approach where response parameters are estimated econometrically, and a neural net is used on model residuals (Cooper and Giuffrida 2000). This approach preserves the interpretability of the models, while unleaching the power of the neural net on data with level-0 prior knowledge (i.e. residuals). Cooper and Giuffrida's combined approach on retail promotion data significantly improved the forecasting accuracy of traditional market-share models.

Non-Parametric Models

A general way of looking at the regression problem is

$$Q = E(Q|\mathbf{x}) + u. \tag{5.51}$$

As has been discussed, the conditional expectation of Q in the standard regression model is assumed to be a linear function of the parameters and explanatory variables and the density of the error u is assumed to be normal. In the non-parametric model, there is no parametric form of the conditional expectation of Q and the density of the error u is completely unspecified.

The conditional distribution is the ratio of the joint distribution of Q and $\mathbf{x}$ to the marginal distribution of $\mathbf{x}$. The keystone to nonparametric estimation is the joint distribution. The joint density at a particular point is estimated from the data by finding what proportions of the observations are close that point.[17] Nearby observations are weighted by a formula, called a kernel, to smooth the histogram. The procedure is thus known as *kernel estimation* (Kennedy 1998, pp. 303, 309-11). The next step is to find the marginal distribution of $\mathbf{x}$ by integrating over Q. Now the height of the conditional density can be estimated for a given value of $\mathbf{x}$. From this information, the conditional expectation of Q given $\mathbf{x}$ can be estimated and the corresponding "regression coefficients" found (see Rust 1988, pp. 12-13). These coefficients are not constant but will be different for every point on the regression surface. The approach can be extended to discrete dependent variables (Greene 1997, pp. 904-6). Nonparametric density estimation has been used to model consumer brand choice for three national brands of aseptic fruit drinks, Hi-C, KoolAid, and Ssips, using scanner data (Abe 1995).

Nonparametric models are superior in their robustness to underlying assumptions and predictive ability (based on better fit) within an operating range.[18] Parametric models are superior in their ability to describe an underlying process so that one can understand it, and to do so in a parsimonious manner. Parametric models can make response predictions outside the operating range (extrapolation) whereas nonparametric models can not. There should be little difference in terms of response prediction (interpolation) and tracking between a nonparametric model and a parametric model if the latter is correctly specified. Thus, the real strength of nonparametric models is as a diagnostic aid in improving parametric models (Abe 1995, pp. 321-23).

Semi-Parametric Models

Sometimes part of the specification is parameterized while the rest is not, yielding a semi-parametric model. This combined the efficiency of parametric analysis with the flexibility of nonparametric analysis. An example would be the partial linear model:

$$Q = \mathbf{x}'\boldsymbol{\beta} + \underbrace{E(Q - \mathbf{x}'\boldsymbol{\beta}|\mathbf{z})}_{\text{nonparametric}} + u . \tag{5.52}$$

The parameteric part is estimated first. The trick in doing this is to take $E(\cdot|\mathbf{z})$ of (5.52) and then to subtract the result from it. The resultant residualized y is regressed on residualized $\mathbf{x}$ to get the OLS estimator $\hat{\boldsymbol{\beta}}$:

$$Q - E(Q|\mathbf{z}) = (\mathbf{x} - E(\mathbf{x}|\mathbf{z}))'\boldsymbol{\beta} + u . \tag{5.53}$$

This requires first fitting Q and $\mathbf{x}$ nonparametrically as a function of $\mathbf{z}$ to get estimates of $E(Q|\mathbf{z})$ and $E(\mathbf{x}|\mathbf{z})$. Finally $E(Q - \mathbf{x}'\boldsymbol{\beta}|\mathbf{z})$ is found by fitting $Q - \mathbf{x}'\hat{\boldsymbol{\beta}}$ nonparametrically with $\mathbf{z}$ (Kennedy 1998, p. 312; van Heerde, Leeflang, and Wittink 2001, Appendix).

Model Selection

The specification problem in econometric models has been described as one of choosing the correct variables and the correct form of the relation between them (Theil 1971). It is thus a problem of choice, and a research strategy should be designed to aid in this decision process. We are, of course, seeking the true model of some marketing phenomenon out of all possible models, and so we are appropriately concerned with how the correct specification (if it were known) differs from any number of incorrect specifications. For econometric research, this issue becomes one of investigating alternative regression models according to some criterion. The criterion can either be informal decision rule such as maximizing $\overline{R}^2$ or a formal decision rule involving hypothesis testing.

Informal Decision Rule

A frequently used measure of the adequacy of a single estimated linear regression model is R^2, the coefficient of determination. This R^2 measure varies between 0 and 1 and can be interpreted as the fraction of the variation in the dependent variable (typically unit sales in a market response study) explained by the model (usually a linear combination of controllable marketing instruments and uncontrollable environmental factors).

Not surprisingly, the most common decision rule for choosing among alternative linear models with nonstochastic exogenous variables is to select the model with the largest $\overline{R}^2$, an adjustment of R^2 that approximately corrects for the bias caused by the fact that R^2 can be increased simply by adding more variables:

$$\overline{R}^2 = R^2 - \frac{k-1}{n-k}\left(1 - R^2\right), \tag{5.54}$$

where k *is* the number of exogenous variables including the constant term and n is the number of observations. An equivalent rule is to select the model with the smallest residual variance. The probability that the decision rule will choose a particular model when it is the correctly specified model can be calculated. Ideally, this probability should be large. See Schmidt (1973) and Ebbeler (1974). This approach was utilized by Parsons (1976) in a market response study.

There are several valid uses for goodness of fit, especially as measured by $\overline{R}^2$. Comparing the fit of the same response model over several territories would be one example. It is a particularly appropriate measure of the extent to which a (true) model accounts for total variation or, in a sense, approximates the real phenomenon under study. In this case, $\overline{R}^2$ is a measure of the degree of approximation by which a generalization holds. For testing theories, however, a more powerful criterion is necessary (cf. Bass 1969a).

The major weakness of this criterion is fundamental: it does not work when none of the alternative specifications are correct. Moreover, since it only holds "on the average," there is no small chance that the wrong specification prevails. Since the objective of response modeling is to identify true response models and market mechanisms, a criterion that relies on the fortuitous inclusion of the correct model as one of the set under evaluation seems to be an inefficient way of conducting research. It is inefficient because the process does not encourage the development of models that are otherwise readily falsifiable, and therefore incorrect models are more easily accepted.

Moreover, this criterion assumes that the dependent variables of the models are identical. Sometimes, for instance, a marketing researcher may want to explore regressions with Q and $\ln[Q]$ as alternative forms of the sales dependent variable. In this case, the $\overline{R}^2$ criterion does not obtain directly; however, it can be determined by drawing on an alternative interpretation of R^2 as the square of the correlation between the actual and predicted values of the dependent variable. Thus, in comparing a set of linear market share models with a set of log-linear ones, Weiss (1969) used antilog conversions for the log-linear models and then calculated correlation of Q with $\hat{Q}$, instead of $\ln[Q]$ with $\ln[\hat{Q}]$, to evaluate relative goodness of fit. Now the goodness of fit numbers for different models were measuring the fit of the same thing.

Hypothesis Testing

The maximum $\overline{R}^2$ selection rule discussed in the last section is a methodological convention. It involves an implicit assumption that disagreement between the theoretical model and observations is a monotone decreasing function of R^2. However, this convention can be in conflict with classical statistical inference. In classical statistical inference, the disagreement between the theoretical model and observations is a monotone decreasing function of the probability with which the observed event is supposed to occur.

The two conventions necessarily yield similar conclusions only if the *population* coefficient of determination, P^2, is equal to 1.0. The probability density function of the *sample* coefficient of determination is noncentral F. with $k-1$, $n-k$ degrees of freedom and noncentrality parameter n P^2. This reduces to the familiar central F (see Equation 3.28) when the null hypothesis is $P^2 = 0$.

The following illustrates this distinction (Basmann 1964). Suppose we are able to derive, from a conjunction of the underlying behavioral marketing postulates and the given sample observations of size 20 on three exogenous variables, a statement that R^2 just lies between 0.3 and 0.4. Furthermore, suppose we obtain $R^2 = 0.75$ in the regression run. Under the first convention, we may well judge that this test statistic does not disagree with our model. However,
since

$$\int_{0.75}^{1.0} f\left(R^2; 20P^2; 2\right) d\left(R^2\right) \leq 0.05, \qquad (5.55)$$

under the second convention, we would decide that the observed sample coefficient of determination is *too large* to be in good agreement with our marketing postulates.

Embedded Alternatives. Classical statistical inference can be used to compare two models when one model is a constrained version of the other. We consider the application of this approach to discriminating among nested models and to deciding whether to pool cross-section and time series data.

Nested Models. One way to discriminate among linear models is to nest the specific alternative models within one general model. Hypotheses about the values of certain parameters of the general model can be deduced from the specific alternative models. For instance, suppose we want to choose between these two alternative specific models:

$$Q_t = \beta_{01} + \beta_{11} X_t + \beta_{21} X_{t-1} + u_{1t} \tag{5.56}$$

and

$$Q_t = \beta_{02} + \beta_{12} X_t + \beta_{32} Q_{t-1} + u_{2t} \tag{5.57}$$

Then we can embed these two models in this general model:

$$Q_t = \beta_0 + \beta_1 X_t + \beta_2 X_{t-1} + \beta_3 Q_{t-1} + u_t \tag{5.58}$$

If at least one, but not both, of the last two parameters (β_2, β_3) in the general model is zero, then we can discriminate between the two models. If $\beta_2 = 0$, we will reject the model of (5.57). If $\beta_3 = 0$, we will reject the model of (5.58). Bass and Clarke (1972), Weiss and Windal (1980), and de Kluyver and Brodie (1987) applied this test to various nested models of advertising carryover.

A robust procedure for testing a regression model against a nested alternative model can be derived using the likelihood ratio method. A nested model implies that s of the variables in a full regression model with k variables will have zero regression coefficients. Kendall and Stuart (1973, pp. 257-61) show that the appropriate test statistic is

$$\hat{F} = \frac{n-k}{s} \frac{\left(SSE_r - SSE_f \right)}{SSE_f} \tag{5.59}$$

where SSE_r and SSE_f are the least-squares residual sum of squares for the nested and full regression models, respectively. The nested model will be rejected if $\hat{F} > F(\alpha, s, n-k)$.

The nested approach to model discrimination has some limitations. It is difficult to use if the number of alternative models becomes too large. A large number of alternative models would likely require a general model with a large number of variables. This, in turn, would necessitate a large sample size as well as increase the potential for collinearity problems. Moreover, if one of the specific alternative models is the correct model, then the general model will involve specification error because of the presence of irrelevant variables. However, the specification error involved in inclusion of irrelevant variables is minor. The parameters and the mean-squared error are estimated correctly; only the precision of the estimates is affected. The standard errors of the parameter estimates will be larger than they should be. This will become a problem if the collinearity between the relevant included variables and the irrelevant included variables is large.

Pooling. The F-statistic (5.59) can be used to test whether or not to pool T time periods and N cross-sections of data. The problem is one of testing the conditions under which pooling is appropriate, since we know that the microparameter vectors (say, of the different sales territories) have to be equal to prevent aggregation or "pooling" bias. The basic procedure is described briefly.

Perform *unconstrained* regression, viz.,

$$
\begin{bmatrix} Q_1 \\ Q_2 \\ \vdots \\ Q_N \end{bmatrix} = \begin{bmatrix} \mathbf{X}_1 & 0 & \cdots & 0 \\ 0 & \mathbf{X}_2 & & \vdots \\ \vdots & & \ddots & 0 \\ 0 & \cdots & 0 & \mathbf{X_N} \end{bmatrix} \begin{bmatrix} \beta_1 \\ \beta_2 \\ \beta_N \end{bmatrix} + \begin{bmatrix} u_1 \\ u_2 \\ u_N \end{bmatrix}, \tag{5.60}
$$

estimating $N \times k'$ parameters using $N \times T$ observations, and *constrained* regression, viz.,

$$
\begin{bmatrix} Q_1 \\ Q_2 \\ \vdots \\ Q_N \end{bmatrix} = \begin{bmatrix} \mathbf{X}_1 \\ \mathbf{X}_2 \\ \vdots \\ \mathbf{X_N} \end{bmatrix} [\beta] + \begin{bmatrix} u_1 \\ u_2 \\ u_N \end{bmatrix}, \tag{5.61}
$$

estimating k' parameters with $N \times T$ observations. The constrained regression amounts to pooling the observations from all sales territories, thereby constraining the coefficient vectors β_i, β_j for all i, j to be equal. This would imply that the sales territories exhibit equivalent sales responsiveness. Unconstrained regression, on the other hand, allows each sales territory to behave differently in this regard. The null hypothesis is

$$
H_o: \beta_1 = \beta_2 = \cdots = \beta_N = \beta. \tag{5.62}
$$

To test the null hypothesis of equal response coefficients, covariance analysis may be used. The general framework in which this testing can take place will be discussed briefly. In general, let the model under investigation be

$$Q_i = \mathbf{X}_i \boldsymbol{\beta}_i + u_i, \quad i = 1, 2, \ldots, N \text{(territories)} \qquad (5.63)$$

Making the usual assumptions, the ordinary least squares (OLS) estimator of $\boldsymbol{\beta}_i$ is unbiased and efficient.

To determine whether the response coefficient vectors, $\boldsymbol{\beta}_i, \boldsymbol{\beta}_j$ for all i, j differ significantly, we can proceed as follows. Assuming that

$$\sigma_{\varepsilon_i}^2 = \sigma_{\varepsilon_j}^2, \quad \text{for all } i, j, \qquad (5.64)$$

this hypothesis of overall homogeneity can be tested using the F-statistic (5.59) where $n = N \times T$, $k = N \times k'$, and $r = k' \times (n-1)$. This test was used in examining entity aggregation in market share response models of the West German cigarette market (Leeflang and Reuyl 1986, pp. 20-21). Aggregation from brand market shares to firm market shares was not appropriate for four out of the five companies tested. In researching the relations between promotional elasticities and category characteristics, the hypothesis of one model with different intercepts was rejected in favor of three separate models—one each for feature, display, and temporary price reduction (price cut) elasticities—with three different sets of regression coefficients. The decision was not to pool the data (Narasimhan, Neslin, and Sen 1996, p. 23). A study of market response in the U.S. ethical drug industry found heterogeneity in the intercepts across categories but not in the slope parameters (Shankar, Carpenter, and Krishnamurthi 1999, p. 273). Tests of equality of coefficients between models explaining price cross-effects using market share data versus sales data failed to reject the null hypothesis and observations were pooled (Sethuraman, Srinivasan, and Kim 1999, p. 31).

A number of issues relevant to this procedure for investigating the homogeneity in the overall relation should be considered, however. A lack of overall homogeneity may be the result of differences in only one or two of the parameters across sales territories. It is possible to use mixed models in the sense that all but one or a few of the parameters are constrained to be equal while the other parameters are allowed to be different. Similarly, it may be argued that some of the cross-sections have the same relation while others behave differently. Although it would be possible to segment sales territories according to similarity in the relation using some heuristic (Wittink 1973), it is not possible, in a strict sense, to test the appropriateness of such a procedure.

The F-statistic suggested to test the existence of homogeneity in the relation is based on several assumptions. First, the model is assumed to be correctly specified. If it is argued that it is never possible to include all relevant variables in a model, then the null hypothesis of homogeneity can always be rejected as long as the sample size is large enough. Wallace (1972, p. 690) has argued for constrained estimation (pooling) even when the null hypothesis is rejected, because "even if the restriction is strictly invalid, the constrained estimators have smaller variances and one might be willing to make a trade-off, accepting some bias in order to reduce variances." A study of fluid milk deliberately pooled data in order to exploit regional variation in the explanatory variables, which increased the precision of the estimates of their impact (Ward and Dixon 1989, p. 734).

A second assumption involves the homogeneity of disturbance variances. When comparing the relation across sales territories using covariance analysis, it is assumed that the variances are homogeneous. A likelihood test for cross-sectional hetero-scedasticity is given in Greene (1997, pp. 653-58).[19] This assumption can be relaxed, but only asymptotic tests (using the estimated disturbance variances) can be used to investigate the homogeneity of relations under conditions of heterogeneous variances (Swamy 1971, pp. 124-26). Furthermore, the appropriateness of the F-test for the purpose of comparing response coefficient vectors for each of the sales territories is also conditional upon the existence of homogeneity in the relation over time. The validity of each of these assumptions should be established. In addition, different pooling methods should be considered and compared from both theoretical and empirical viewpoints (Bass and Wittink 1975).

Disparate Alternatives. A variety of methods have been proposed for comparing non-nested models; that is, models in which there is no relation between the models' parameter spaces. These methods include artificial nesting, split-half cross-validation, Akaike's Information Criterion (AIC), and Bayesian.[20]

Two competing regression models purporting to explain the same dependent variable are embedded in a more general model, known as an artificial compound model or supermodel:

$$q = \theta(\text{model specification } 1) + (1 - \theta)(\text{model specification } 2) + u, \qquad (5.65)$$

where $0 \le \theta \le 1$. When $\theta = 1$, the supermodel reduces to the first model specification, and when $\theta = 0$, to the second. The problem is that, in most cases, the supermodel will not be estimable because its parameters will not all be separately identifiable. One solution is to use artificial regressions. Here one of the two underlying models is estimated assuming that it is true and the resultant predicted values used in (5.65), which is then estimated. This yields the J test, as it jointly estimates θ and the parameters of the remaining model specification. Because of the difficulty in joint estimation for the J test when the model being tested is nonlinear, the P test involves linearization using the derivatives of the model evaluated at the estimated values of the parameter estimates. Alternatively, one could first estimate both models separately and use these values in (5.65). This yields the C test, as it estimates θ conditional on the underlying model parameters. Note that, in the context of regression models, non-nested hypothesis tests are tests of model specification rather than of model selection criteria. While it may be that one of two rival models will be rejected and the other not, it could also be that both models, or neither model, will be rejected. Thus the warning that the results of non-nested hypothesis tests should be interpreted with caution when the sample size is small and that these tests should be used only when both models have similar numbers of parameters. The tests above can be used to test an hypothesis against several models at once. Details are given in Davidson and MacKinnon (1993, pp. 381-88). For example, the application of the RESET test to double-log models for in assessing the impact of generic advertising on the meat group in Australia has already been discussed. The double-log models were also tested against a specific alternative, the single-equation, share version of the LAIDS model (recall Appendix 3-A). Using C- and P-tests, tests against the share model indicated rejection of the double-log model for beef and chicken as well as for pork but not for lamb (Piggott 1996, pp. 272-73). The J test was used in examining the order of entry as a moderator of the effect the marketing mix on the market shares of minivans and sports utility vehicles (SUVs) (Bowman and Gatignon 1996, p. 237). A linear process function specification was found to be statistically superior to a logarithmic specification.

Split-half cross-validation involves estimating the models on one sample and then calculating error statistics on the holdout sample. Although a 50/50 split is suboptimal, it is performs well in a variety of circumstances (Steckel and Vanhonacker 1993).[21] This method should be used for time series data only with extreme caution, as we shall discuss shortly.

One form of Akaike's Information Criterion, AIC is

$$\text{AIC} = log(\text{maximum likelihood}) - (\text{number of estimated parameters}). \quad (5.66)$$

The decision rule is to choose the model with the largest AIC. There is a tendency for AIC to select over-specified models, even with a large sample. AIC and improved variants are discussed in Mittelhammer, Judge, and Miller (2000, pp. 511-14).

Bayesian methods generate posterior probabilities that might be interpreted as probabilities of model correctness.

Predictive Testing. The notion of predictive testing, in which the predictions of a theory are tested against empirical data, falls within long-established traditions of scientific inquiry. For this reason, the fact that predictive tests are not used more widely in marketing is somewhat surprising. The primary development of the ideas of predictive testing in econometric research was due to Basmann (1964; 1965; 1968). Initial studies involving predictive testing in marketing were made by Bass (1969a) and Bass and Parsons (1969). The concept was further discussed by Bass (1969b; 1971).

Horsky (1977a) provides an example of predictive testing. He derived a model of market share response to advertising:

$$Y_1 = K_1 X_1 + K_2 X_2 + \lambda_1 X_3 + \lambda_1^2 X_4 + K_1 \lambda_1 X_5 + K_2 \lambda_1 X_6, \tag{5.67}$$

where the definition of variables is not important to our discussion. He then estimated the model:

$$Y_1 = \beta_1 X_1 + \beta_2 X_2 + \beta_3 X_3 + \beta_4 X_4 + \beta_5 X_5 + \beta_6 X_6. \tag{5.68}$$

The theoretical model predicts relations among the parameters. In particular, the hypotheses $\beta_4 = \beta_3^2$, $\beta_5 = \beta_1 \beta_3$ and $\beta_6 = \beta_2 \beta_3$ must be tested.

An explanatory marketing model, such as a sales response function, is comprised of theoretical marketing premises and justifiable factual statements of initial conditions. From the model, a set of prediction statements that attribute definite probabilities to specified observable marketing events can be deduced. Deductive analysis of an explanatory marketing model should result in a statement of the exact finite sample joint distribution function of parameter estimates and test statistics.

Discourses on the scientific method usually consider a predictive test to be conducted under experimental conditions. Often it is implied that initial conditions appropriate for a particular theory are thoroughly known. Then an effective technology for controlling these initial conditions is assumed to exist and to have been used.

It is true, nevertheless, that careful consideration of initial conditions cannot be omitted when developing a marketing model. Since the model can be falsified by unsuccessful predictions, close attention must be given to substantiating statements that claim that external influences are negligible during the historical period analyzed.

A statement of initial conditions is really a combination of three statements. One statement specifies the observed values of the exogenous variables explicitly included in the structural relations of the model. Another statement specifies the statistical distribution of the random disturbances explicitly included in the structural relations. In addition, one statement asserts that relevant external conditions stay approximately constant during the historical period under consideration.

What we are saying is that in the marketing environment uncontrollable changes can be anticipated to cause the structure of a relation to change. Thus, we need to know how a theory can be tested in a situation where its structural form is not invariant to time. The necessary additional information is clearly a precise statement of the environmental conditions under which the theory is assumed to hold. In effect, we must guard against sampling from the wrong temporal population when testing a particular model; otherwise, we may falsely reject a theory.

The predictive test of an explanatory marketing model is implemented by specifying an observable event (the critical region for the test) with a very small probability of occurring if the conjunction of initial conditions and substantive premises is discredited. If factual investigation justifies the statement of initial conditions, then at least one, and maybe only one, of the marketing premises is discredited.

Note that forecast and prediction are not synonymous. Important and pragmatic statements about future occurrences can be made without deducing these statements from initial conditions with the aid of a model. A forecast is an extrapolation from statistical parameter estimates obtained in one historical period to observations generated in another historical period. Therefore, while forecasts *seem* to provide information concerning a hypothesis, neither "good" nor "bad" forecasts supply any relevant evidence in themselves (Brunner 1973). Forecasts do not satisfy the logical requirements of a test statement. Similar arguments would seem to hold for the application of split-half crossvalidation methods to time series data.

Managerial Usefulness

Market response models are usually formulated, estimated, and tested in terms of aggregated data. One exception is the work of Blattberg and Jeuland (1981 b). They built an advertising response model starting with microrelations and then derived a macromodel for estimation and testing purposes.[22] The problem is that the macrovariables do not relate to each other in the same way macrovariables do. The macromodel is likely to be quite complex unless very restrictive assumptions are made. Even worse, there may not even be an exact relation based only on macrovariables. Thus, when a macromodel is thought of as an aggregation of microrelations, it should be considered an approximation rather than an exact specification (cf. Clements and Selvanathan 1988). In this sense, a model may be more appropriately assessed in terms of its usefulness.

Perhaps too much emphasis is placed on significance tests. The model builder should always keep in mind the purpose for fitting the model in the first place. Consideration should be given to the consequences of erroneously choosing one model specification when a competing specification might be the true one. Thus, a broader concept of model adequacy is perhaps required. Fortunately, as we shall see in chapter 8, the consequences in terms of deviation from the optimal level of discounted profits that arise from misspecifying market response is usually not great.

Observational Equivalence

Discrimination among alternative models is impossible if they are *observationally equivalent*. This occurs when two or more theories yield exactly the same implications about observable phenomena in all situations. Under such conditions no sample, no matter how large, can resolve the issue.

We use the term *observational equivalence* loosely to cover any observed space in which the models under consideration are not observationally distinguishable. Saunders (1987, pp. 27-29) applied different functional forms to the same data sets and all fit quite well. He concluded:

> It is evident that good fit does not mean that an expression [functional form] gives the right shape. This is particularly true if an expression is used to fit data that only covers a small portion of the curve. In such cases it is not safe to draw conclusions about the shape that an expression gives beyond the limits of the data.

This warning should be kept in mind when implementing marketing policies based upon an estimated sales response function.[23]

Observational equivalence is an inherent problem with the hypotheticodeductive method of science. We can conclusively reject theories but cannot have the same confidence about their acceptance. The fact that a model cannot be rejected does not imply that every other model describing a sales response function is incorrect.

Even when we are able to set the values of variables for best discrimination among models, we should be aware that these values will not in general be those that give the best parameter estimation for the correct model. The impact, or the lack thereof, of sample size should also be noted. A model's total error can be partitioned into modeling error and estimation (sampling) error. Model error refers to the discrepancy between the particular parametric specification being estimated and the true model. Estimation error is sampling error arising from the fact that estimation is being done on one of many possible data sets. Rust and Schmittlein (1985, p. 23) have stated:

> As the sample size is increased the estimation error for a model may be decreased to any desired level, but modelling error cannot be reduced in this way. Using an incorrect parametric form . . . means that there is always a discrepancy between the estimated model and the true process, regardless of sample size. When compared with parsimonious models, complex models which include more effects (and more parameters) will generally have a smaller modelling error and a larger estimation error.... Akaike's information criterion is a Bayes solution for trading off these modelling and estimation errors in choosing models.

Confirmatory vs. Exploratory Data Analysis

At level 2 of prior knowledge, econometric methods can be applied to data to confirm or reformulate market response models. The focus of level 2 analysis is on estimation and testing.

Specification is a general problem of research strategy. It should be apparent that both scientific and creative talents are necessary to specify response models. Whether the level 2 knowledge involves market or management information, or both, the model builder's task is to specify a set of premises that imply that the model belongs to a small subset of all possible models, assuming that the model represents the true response phenomenon. The specification problem involves the procedures required to identify marketing variables and relations. Specification analysis is also concerned with the consequences of incorrect specifications on the interpretation of research results.

This chapter has emphasized *confirmatory* methods of data analysis; the next two chapters will stress *exploratory* methods of data analysis. Suppose sales of a brand are conjectured to be related to some explanatory variables, such as marketing instruments and socioeconomic variables, but there is no information about the shape of the relation. In such cases, exploratory data analysis can be used to probe the data for patterns that might justify testing in future studies.

Notes

[1] There may be more moment conditions than unknown parameters. Rather than throw away the extra information, an approach called generalized method of moments (GMM) attempts to choose the parameter values so as to minimize the extent to which the moments conditions are violated even to the extent that none of the conditions is exactly satisfied (Kennedy 1998, p. 132). GMM nests many common estimators and provides a useful framework for comparing and evaluating these estimators. GMM can be used when it is difficult to specify the ML estimator. These desirable GMM properties, however, are only availble if one has very large samples (Johnston and DiNardo 1997, pp. 327-44).

[2] Buse (1994) showed that the SUR estimator for the LAIDS model is inconsistent. He recommended full ML estimation of the complete AIDS model.

[3] Sometimes nonsample information will involve an inequality restriction rather than an equality restriction. In this case, the Kuhn-Tucker conditions can be used to construct an inequality-restricted least-squares estimator.

[4] IRI and ACNielsen say that they have virtually no problems with incorrectly signed estimates of own and cross-price elasticities (Bucklin and Gupta 1999, p. 251).

[5] The following discussion is from Blattberg and George (1991).

[6] In an investigation dynamic multifirm market interactions in price and advertising, there were zero values of advertising (Vilacassim, Kadiyala, and Chintagunta 1999, p. 510). Model estimates proved sensitive to the small number assigned. Consequently a decision was made to use a linear model rather than a log-log model.

[7] Asymptotic standard errors of the elasticity estimates were calculated following Miller, Capps, and Wells (1984).

[8] A major problem is the arbitrary nature of units of area. Openshaw and Taylor (1979) emphasize that "since the area over which data is collected is continuous, it follows that there will be numerous alternative ways in which it can be partitioned to form areal units for reporting the data."

[9] Exact interpretation of the DW statistic is difficult because its critical values depend on the data matrix. Tables are given in Greene (1997, pp. 1010-17), Johnston and DiNardo (1997, pp. 508-15), and Pindyck and Rubinfeld (1998, p. 610).

[10] The Box-Pierce and Ljung-Box tests are valid when testing ARIMA models for residual autocorrelation but are not generally valid when used with residuals from linear or nonlinear models that include both exogenous and lagged dependent variables in the regression functions (Davidson and MacKinnon 1993, p. 364; Kennedy 1998, p. 273).

[11] The correlation matrix can be examined to detect collinearity between any two specific explanatory variables. A high correlation coefficient would be about 0.8 or 0.9 in absolute value (Kennedy 1998, p. 187). The problem is that the correlation matrix does not reveal collinearity among three of more variables.

[12] A condition index greater than 20 is considered to indicate a strong degree of collinearity by some (Greene 1997, p. 422; Pindyck and Rubinfeld 1997, p. 98).

[13] The British telecommunication company BT found that its "Value for Money" rating (VfM = price + quality of service) was a key driver of brand share. It also wanted to take into account the rise in competition. However, there was no tracking figure for availability of competition. Time was used as a crude proxy for the missing variable. Unfortunately, the R-square between VfM and time was 0.96. BT's solution was used a weighted sum of these two variables as a new variable ("BT Business" in Duckworth 1997, pp. 270-71).

[14] The ridge estimator is $\hat{\beta}_{ridge} = \left(\mathbf{X'X} + k\mathbf{I}\right)^{-1}\mathbf{X'q}$. In a market response study of generic advertising for fluid milk products, the k-value chosen for the whole milk relation was 0.15 while that for the lowfat milk relation was 0.75 (Capps and Moen 1992).

[15] Urzua (1996) suggests a small-sample adjustment to the Jarque-Bera test and Deb and Sefton (1996) provide small sample critical values.

[16] This section on ANN reflects collaborative work with Ashotosh Dixit of the University of Georgia.

[17] "Close to" is defined by the choice of interval width. Correspondingly, results will be sensitive in kernel estimation to the choice of window width (smoothing parameter) in the kernel formula. Kennedy (1998, p. 311) notes that this choice will depend, in part, on the purpose of the analysis: oversmooth for presentation purposes and for help in selecting an appropriate parametric model or undersmooth to examine more carefully local structure.

[18] This discussion of which is better is based on Abe (1995, pp. 320-21).

[19] This test was used in the study of the U.S. ethical drug industry by Shankar, Carpenter, and Krishnamurthi (1999). The null hypothesis of equal error variance was rejected; thus estimation had to be done by groupwise weighted least squares.

[20] See Rust and Schmittlein (1985) for an overview of these methods. They proposed another method, a Bayesian cross-validated likelihood method and illustrated how it could be applied.

[21] Generally speaking, more observations should be used for estimation than for validation. Steckel and Vanhonacker (1993) found that, for very large samples, almost any reasonable split provides high power; for moderate samples (20 to 100), a 75-25 to 67-33 split provides high power; and for small samples, the validation sample proportion should be somewhat smaller (pp. 425-26).

[22] Weinberg and Weiss (1986) proposed an alternative estimation approach to the Blattberg and Jeuland model.

[23] Kinnucan (1987) reported in a study of generic advertising for fluid milk that the double-log model was empirically indistinguishable from four other functional forms tested: linear, semi-log, log-reciprocal, and reciprocal. The double-log was chosen for ease of comparison with the many other studies using it.

APPENDIX 5

5-A Comparative Studies of Functional Forms for Market Share Models

Study	*Comparison*	*Conclusion*
Naert and Weverbergh (1981a)	Linear, multiplicative, and attraction models	Attraction model is superior. Better predictions are derived from GLS, but IGLS affords no additional gain. There is a danger of overparameterization.
Brodie and de Kluyver (1984)	Linear, multiplicative, and attraction models	Linear and multiplicative models with brand-specific parameters perform as well as, or better than, the attraction model. OLS and GLS produce similar results.
Ghosh, Neslin, and Shoemaker (1984)	Linear, multiplicative, and attraction models	Linear and multiplicative models with brand-multiplicative, specific parameters perform as well as, or better than, the attraction model. OLS and GLS models produce similar results.
Leeflang and Reuyl (1984)	Linear, multiplicative, and attraction models	Neither attraction models nor models with parameter restrictions produce substantially better results than the other model specifications. GLS considerably increases the efficiency of parameter estimates.
Naert and Weverbergh (1985)	The above studies	No cookbook answer as to what functional form with what level of parameterization and what estimation procedure is appropriate when. The attraction model has a number of merits on theoretical grounds. Estimating heterogeneous parameters is difficult if only a few observations are available or if the coefficients of variation for some variables are small. GLS is unlikely to produce better results if the number of brands is large.
Kumar and Heath (1990)	Linear, multiplicative, and attraction models	GLS estimation of attraction models performed best when models were fully specified, whereas OLS estimation of linear models performed best when variables were omitted.
Kumar (1994)	Linear, multiplicative, and attraction models	It is better to use GLS estimation techniques for scanner data because of the presence of serial and contemporaneous correlation.

5-B Estimation of the MCI Model Using Log-Centering

Based on multiplicative sales response functions for each brand, the Cross-Effects MCI Model is

$$MS_{bt} = \frac{\left(e^{\beta_{b0}} \prod_{i=1}^{B} \prod_{k=1}^{K} X_{ikt}^{\beta_{bik}}\right) e^{u_{bt}}}{\sum_{h=1}^{B} \left[\left(e^{\beta_{h0}} \prod_{i=1}^{B} \prod_{k=1}^{K} X_{ikt}^{\beta_{hik}}\right) e^{u_{ht}}\right]}. \tag{5.69}$$

To transform this nonlinear model into a linear model for estimation, first take the natural logarithms of both sides to get:

$$\ln MS_{bt} = \beta_{b0} + \sum_{i=1}^{B} \sum_{k=1}^{K} \beta_{bik} \ln X_{ikt} + u_{bt}$$
$$- \ln \left[\sum_{h=1}^{B}\left[\left(e^{\beta_{h0}} \prod_{i=1}^{B} \prod_{k=1}^{K} X_{ikt}^{\beta_{hik}}\right) e^{u_{ht}}\right]\right]. \tag{5.70}$$

Sum over the brands and divide by the number of brands B:

$$\frac{1}{B}\sum_{h=1}^{B} \ln MS_{ht} = \frac{1}{B}\sum_{h=1}^{B} \beta_{h0} + \frac{1}{B}\sum_{h=1}^{B}\left(\sum_{i=1}^{B}\sum_{k=1}^{K}\beta_{hik} \ln X_{ikt}\right) + \frac{1}{B}\sum_{h=1}^{B} u_{ht}$$
$$- \ln\left[\sum_{h=1}^{B}\left[\left(e^{\beta_{h0}} \prod_{i=1}^{B}\prod_{k=1}^{K} X_{ikt}^{\beta_{hik}}\right) e^{u_{ht}}\right]\right]. \tag{5.71}$$

The term on the right-hand side is simply the natural logarithm of the variable's geometric mean:

$$\frac{1}{B}\sum_{h=1}^{B} \ln MS_h = \ln\left[\left(\prod_{h=1}^{B} MS_h\right)^{1/B}\right] \equiv \ln \widetilde{MS}, \tag{5.72}$$

where a $\sim$ over a variable indicates a geometric mean. Subtracting (5.71) from (5.70) and rearrange terms yields:

$$\left(\ln MS_{bt} - \ln \tilde{MS}_t\right) = \left(\beta_{b0} - \overline{\beta}_0\right) + \sum_{i=1}^{B}\sum_{k=1}^{K}\beta_{bik}\ln X_{ikt}$$

$$-\frac{1}{B}\sum_{h=1}^{B}\sum_{i=1}^{B}\sum_{k=1}^{K}\beta_{hik}\ln X_{ikt} + \left(u_{bt} - \overline{u}_t\right). \tag{5.73}$$

This equation is linear in its parameters. The equation can be written as

$$MS_{bt}^* = \beta_{b0}^* + \sum_{i=1}^{B}\sum_{k=1}^{K}\left[\sum_{h=1}^{B}\beta_{hik}\left(D_{Bht} - \frac{1}{B}\right)\right]\ln X_{ikt} + u_{bt}^*, \tag{5.74}$$

where D_{Bht} equals one if $h=b$ and zero otherwise [cf., Cooper and Nakanishi 1988, p. 144, Equation (5.28)]. The problem of estimating $(B \times B \times K) + B$ parameters seems insurmountable (Cooper and Nakanishi 1988, p. 144). Logical consistency requires that one equation in this system of B market share equations be dropped. This causes an identification problem (Houston, Kanetkar, and Weiss 1992). There are more parameters in the structural model than found by the estimating equations. The only solution is to fix (usually at zero) some of the parameters in the structural model. Empirical exploration or theoretical considerations can provide guidance in doing this.

The estimating equations for the Differential-Effects MCI Model and Simple-Effects MCI Model are special cases of the Cross-Effects MCI Model. The Differential-Effects Model is estimated by

$$\left(\ln MS_{bt} - \ln \tilde{MS}_t\right) = \left(\beta_{b0} - \overline{\beta}_0\right) + \sum_{k=1}^{K}\beta_{bk}\ln X_{bkt}$$

$$-\frac{1}{B}\sum_{h=1}^{B}\sum_{k=1}^{K}\beta_{hk}\ln X_{hkt} + \left(u_{bt} - \overline{u}_t\right) \tag{5.75}$$

or

$$MS_{bt}^* = \beta_{b0}^* + \sum_{k=1}^{K}\left[\sum_{h=1}^{B}\beta_{hk}\left(D_{Bht} - \frac{1}{B}\right)\right]\ln X_{bkt} + u_{bt}^* \tag{5.76}$$

[cf., Cooper and Nakanishi 1988, p. 128, Equation (5.15)]. Similarly, the Simple-Effects Model is estimated by

$$\left(\ln MS_{bt} - \ln \widetilde{MS}_t \right) = \beta_{b0}^* + \sum_{k=1}^{K} \beta_k \left(\ln X_{bkt} - \ln \widetilde{X}_{kt} \right) + u_{bt}^* \tag{5.77}$$

or

$$\ln \frac{MS_{it}}{\widetilde{MS}_t} = \beta_{b0}^* + \sum_{k=1}^{K} \beta_{ki} \ln \frac{X_{kit}}{\widetilde{X}_{kt}} + u_{bt}^* \tag{5.78}$$

[cf., Cooper and Nakanishi 1988, p. 109, Equation (5.7)]. Computation of geometric means is cumbersome, fortunately a transformation involving dummy variables can simplify the estimation process (Nakanishi and Cooper 1982). Consider the estimating equation (5.75) for the Cross-Effects Model, in which the brand-specific intercepts are captured using dummy variables:

$$\ln MS_{bt} = \alpha_1 + \sum_{h=2}^{B} \alpha_h D_{Bht} + \ln \widetilde{MS}_t - \frac{1}{B} \sum_{h=1}^{B} \sum_{k=1}^{K} \beta_{hk} \ln X_{hkt}$$
$$+ \sum_{k=1}^{K} \beta_{bk} \ln X_{bkt} + u_{bt}^*, \tag{5.79}$$

where D_{Bht} equals one if $h=b$ and zero otherwise. The insight that allows further simplification is that

$$\ln \widetilde{MS}_t - \frac{1}{B} \sum_{h=1}^{B} \sum_{k=1}^{K} \beta_{hk} \ln X_{hkt} \equiv \delta_t \tag{5.80}$$

is a constant (say δ) in a particular time period t and can be captured by a dummy variable, and so

$$\ln MS_{bt} = \alpha_1 + \sum_{h=2}^{B} \alpha_h D_{Bht} + \sum_{n=2}^{T} \delta_n D_{Tnt} + \sum_{k=1}^{K} \beta_{bk} \ln X_{bkt} + u_{bt}^*, \tag{5.81}$$

where D_{Tnt} equals one if $n=t$ and zero otherwise [cf., Cooper and Nakanishi 1988, p. 110, Equation (5.17)]. While simpler to compute, there is a danger of model-induced collinearity due to the presence of so many dummy variables (Bultez and Naert 1975; Cooper and Nakanishi 1988, pp. 134-37). The advice is to use Equation (5.81) for estimation when T is reasonably small; otherwise, use Equation (5.76).

5-C Estimation of the MCI Model Using Log Ratio

An alternative estimation approach is to compare the market share of one brand (b) relative to another brand (j):

$$\frac{MS_{bt}}{MS_{jt}} = \frac{\left(e^{\beta_{b0}} \prod_{i=1}^{B} \prod_{k=1}^{K} X_{ikt}^{\beta_{bik}} \right) e^{u_{bt}}}{\left(e^{\beta_{j0}} \prod_{i=1}^{B} \prod_{k=1}^{K} X_{ikt}^{\beta_{jik}} \right) e^{u_{jt}}}. \tag{5.82}$$

This approach was first proposed in the context of the ECI (MNL) Models (McGuire and Weiss 1976, p. 301; McGuire, Weiss, and Houston 1977, p. 130). Taking the logarithm of both sides yields

$$\ln MS_{bt} - \ln MS_{jt} = \left(\beta_{b0} - \beta_{j0} \right) + \sum_{i=1}^{B} \sum_{k=1}^{K} \left(\beta_{bik} - \beta_{jik} \right) \ln X_{ikt} \tag{5.83}$$
$$+ \left(u_{bt} - u_{jt} \right),$$

[cf., Houston, Kanetkar, and Weiss 1992, Equation (14)]. As with the log-centering transformation, the parameters are not identified. However, imposing the constraints

$$\sum_{b=1}^{B} \beta_{bik} = 0 \quad \forall\, i, k \quad \text{and} \quad \sum_{i=1}^{B} \beta_{bik} = 0 \quad \forall\, b, k, \tag{5.84}$$

the estimating equations can be written as

$$\ln MS_{bt} - \ln MS_{jt} = \left(\beta_{b0} - \beta_{j0} \right) + \sum_{i=1}^{B} \sum_{k=1}^{K} \left(\beta_{bik} - \beta_{jik} \right) \left(\ln X_{ikt} - \ln X_{jkt} \right) \tag{5.85}$$
$$+ \left(u_{bt} - u_{jt} \right).$$

[cf., Houston, Kanetkar, and Weiss 1992, Equation (15)].
    The log-ratio transformation for the Differential-Effects Model is

$$\ln MS_{bt} - \ln MS_{jt} = \left(\beta_{b0} - \beta_{j0} \right) + \sum_{k=1}^{K} \left(\beta_{bk} \ln X_{bkt} - \beta_{jk} \ln X_{jkt} \right) \tag{5.86}$$
$$+ \left(u_{bt} - u_{jt} \right),$$

[cf., Houston, Kanetkar, and Weiss 1992, Equation (11)], while that for the Simple-Effects Model is

$$
\ln MS_{bt} - \ln MS_{jt} = \left(\beta_{b0} - \beta_{j0}\right) + \sum_{k=1}^{K} \beta_k \left(\ln X_{bkt} - \ln X_{jkt}\right)
$$
$$
+ \left(u_{bt} - u_{jt}\right),
$$
(5.87)

[cf., Houston, Kanetkar, and Weiss 1992, Equation (9)]. The log-ratio and log-centering transformations yield the same parameter estimates for the Simple-Effects and Cross-Effects Models.

If the market share model contains first-order autoregressive error, i.e., is an Autoregressive Current Effects (ACE) Model, *and* the autocorrelation coefficient ρ is the same for all brands,

$$
u_{bt} = \rho u_{b,t-1} + w_{b,t}
$$
(5.88)

[recall Equation (4.13)], then the estimating equation (5.83) can be written as

$$
\ln MS_{bt} - \ln MS_{jt} = \left(1 - \rho\right)\left(\beta_{b0} - \beta_{j0}\right) + \rho\left(\ln MS_{b,t-1} - \ln MS_{j,t-1}\right)
$$
$$
+ \sum_{i=1}^{B} \sum_{k=1}^{K} \left(\beta_{bik} - \beta_{jik}\right)\left(\ln X_{ikt} - \rho \ln X_{ik,t-1}\right)
$$
$$
+ \left(w_{bt} - w_{jt}\right),
$$
(5.89)

[cf., Chen et al. 1994, Equation (7)].

5-D The Box-Cox Flexible Functional Form

The Box-Cox flexible functional form includes both the linear and double-logarithmic forms as special cases (Box and Cox 1964, Spitzer 1982). It may be expressed in the two-variable case as

$$Q^* = \beta_0 + \beta_1 X_1^*$$
(5.90)

where variables with asterisks are defined as

$$X^* = \frac{X^\lambda - 1}{\lambda}$$
(5.91)

in which λ is the transformation parameter to be estimated. Different values of λ lead to different specifications of the model. If $\lambda = 1$, equation (5.90) is linear. When λ approaches 0, equation (5.90) approaches the double-log form, that is,

$$\lim_{\lambda \to 0} \left(\frac{X^\lambda - 1}{\lambda} \right) = \ln X$$
(5.92)

Since the linear and double-log functional forms are restricted versions of the general Box-Cox flexible functional form, the (log of the) likelihood ratio test or Lagrange multiplier test can be performed to compare the performance of different functional forms (Greene 1997, pp. 490-92; Kennedy 1998, p. 106; Pindyck and Rubinfeld 1998, pp. 275-80).

An econometric analysis of a hedonic price function concluded that the empirical result, $\hat{\lambda} = 0.59$, supported the null hypothesis of a square-root model, i.e., $\lambda = 0.5$, and ruled out traditional specifications such as the linear and semilog models (Kristensen 1984).

III MARKET RESPONSE IN EVOLVING MARKETS

6 SINGLE MARKETING TIME SERIES

Variables of interest to marketing managers and researchers, such as sales, market share, price, and marketing spending, fluctuate over time. This simple fact has important ramifications for market response modeling that go beyond estimating the static relation between marketing effort and market response. By *marketing dynamics* we refer to the study of such marketing fluctuations, either by themselves—e.g., how current prices relate to previously observed prices—or in function of one another— e.g., how current prices influence current and future sales levels.

There are many reasons why marketing dynamics are important to marketing models. They are at the foundation of various buyer behavior theories, such as the linear learning model and the zero-order choice model. They separate short-term from long-term effects of marketing actions and thus help the manager decide what the optimal timing of marketing strategies should be. They even make it possible to empirically sort out the causal ordering of variables in a marketing system.

Our discussion of the time series approach to marketing dynamics is organized in two chapters. Chapter 6 starts with the basic components of univariate time series, where the behavior of a time series is studied strictly as a function of its own past. Then, we use these principles to examine the important difference between *stationary* and *evolving* markets, and introduce a new metric, *persistence*, to measure the strength of evolution. We conclude the chapter with some empirical estimates of marketing persistence. Chapter 7 focuses on modeling multiple time series, with particular reference to the testing for long-term equilibrium relationships among marketing variables.

Many of the methodological advances of time-series analysis have been made in the last two decades, especially in the area of long-term models. Since a detailed technical discussion of these methods is beyond the scope of the book, we refer the interested reader to Enders (1995) for an in-depth coverage of dynamic econometric modeling.

Why Analyze Single Marketing Time Series?

There are a number of scenarios in model-based planning and forecasting that make it desirable to analyze a marketing time series strictly as a function of its own past. These scenarios can be organized in three categories:

1. We have developed a planning model relating, say, product prices to product sales. However, price may be determined partly from market factors outside the control of the firm, so it is necessary to forecast prices separately. These predictions are then used to obtain sales estimates. We refer to such situations as forecasting exogenous variables.

2. The product line is so large that building individual planning models for each product is prohibitive. Nevertheless, separate forecasts for each are needed. Perhaps the company will invest in a comprehensive marketing mix model for the four or five leading products and use extrapolative methods to handle the remaining 200 or so items. This would be an example of forecasting performance variables.

3. Sometimes it is useful to decompose a marketing time series, say, price, into a systematic, predictable part and a random, unpredictable part. For example, product sales may react differently to predictable price changes, say, those due to inflation adjustments, and to unpredictable price shocks, say, surprise deals offered by the manufacturer. This decomposition of the price variable produces a smooth, predictable price series and a residual price series, which is uncorrelated over time (white noise). This is an example of prewhitening a marketing time series.

The three scenarios apply only when marketing data over time are available. Furthermore, we assume that the data are collected in regular intervals (e.g., weekly or quarterly) and that they are sufficiently long for statistical modeling (i.e., a minimum of 50 uninterrupted observations).[1] Under these assumptions we can apply principles of univariate time series analysis in order to obtain extrapolative forecasts.

The Components of a Time Series

The time series analyst examines the behavior of data over time as a function of deterministic and stochastic elements:

1. Deterministic elements, whose outcome is perfectly predictable at any point of time. For example, the linear trend model on some variable Z is

$$Z_t = \beta_0 + \beta_1 t, \tag{6.1}$$

   where t is a time counter. For every new period, a fixed value β_1 is added to the base level β_0.

2. Random or stochastic components, whose effects cannot be predicted with certainty. If the random component is correlated over time, it may contribute to forecasting, although imperfectly. It is referred to as a systematic time series component. If it is uncorrelated, however, it is strictly an error term and is of no use for forecasting. These terms are known as white noise, shocks, or innovations. For example,

$$Z_t = \beta_2 Z_{t-1} + w_t, \tag{6.2}$$

   where $E(w_t) = 0$, $E(w_t^2) = \sigma_w^2$, and $E(w_t w_{t-k}) = 0$ for all $k \neq 0$. The first right-hand term is a systematic effect of the last period on the current period and is useful for forecasting. The second term is white noise; while it may affect the current Z significantly, it cannot be used for estimating future Z.

A time series model combining the deterministic and random elements might be

$$Z_t = \beta_0 + \beta_1 t + \beta_2 Z_{t-1} + w_t. \tag{6.3}$$

Although model (6.3) is cast in a regression form, it does not have the straight-forward interpretation of the more common marketing regression models, relating, for example, unit sales to prices. The focus of model (6.3) is on the fluctuations over time of the marketing variable, Z, rather than on the underlying causes of these movements. In many cases, though, the time series patterns have a plausible marketing explanation. For example, if Z is product sales, then market growth may explain a positive trend parameter. Also, brand loyalty may result in a constant fraction of buyers at time $t-1$ who purchase the same brand at time t, which would explain a value for β_2 in the $(0,1)$ interval. Other examples of deterministic, system-

Table 6-1. Time Series Components in Marketing Data

Time Series Component	Market Performance	Marketing Decisions	Environment
Deterministic	Agreement to buy a fixed amount over an extended period	Ad agency does not serve competing accounts	Obligation to close stores on Sundays
Systematic	Repeat purchase rates, diffusion of innovation	Percent-of-last year decision rule in advertising	Fashion effects in clothing
White noise	Zero-order random market share fluctuations	Marketing director resigns	Earthquake destroys distribution center

atic, and pure random elements in market performance, marketing decisions, and market environment data are given in Table 6-1.

In conclusion, situations exist in model-based planning and forecasting where strictly extrapolative predictions of marketing variables are needed. Such models are developed using principles of modern time series analysis, which pay particular attention to the deterministic, systematic, and pure random elements in marketing data. We now discuss the most important aspects of time series modeling: the philosophy of linear filters, the specification method due to Box and Jenkins, the estimation of parameters, and the use of the model for forecasting.

The Linear Time Series Filter

Suppose a time series of weekly sales volumes of a brand is observed over a certain period. The series contains an upward trend and deviations from the trend, which may be systematic or random. If we are able to extract the deterministic and the systematic patterns from the series, the remaining fluctuations would be strictly random. The objective of the time series modeler is to find the mechanism that converts an observed time series of data to a series of serially uncorrelated values called white noise. This mechanism, or *filter,* does not change over time, and thus it can be used to predict future values of the time series strictly from its own past. The filter should be chosen so that all deterministic and systematic parts of the time series are captured, leaving only the white noise component unaccounted for. Schematically,

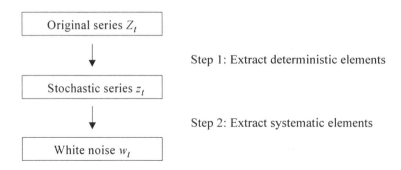

The challenge, of course, lies in finding the filter that makes these transformations (steps 1 and 2) possible. Once specified and estimated, these filters are the basis for forecasting, because they contain the maximum amount of information about the future based on the past. Although the choice of filters is theoretically unlimited, a general class of linear filters introduced by Yule in the 1920s has become the standard.[2] Yule proposed that time series observations are generated by an underlying stochastic process:

$$P(z_1, z_2, \cdots, z_{t-1}, z_t, \cdots, z_T)$$

in such a way that each observation z_t is a linear combination of all previous shocks:

$$z_t = w_t + \psi_1 w_{t-1} + \psi_2 w_{t-2} + \cdots + \psi_t w_0. \tag{6.4}$$

This underlying stochastic process is assumed to be stationary, i.e., it remains the same over time. In practice, we check the stationarity assumption by verifying that the first two moments of the distribution, i.e., the mean and the variance, are constant:

$$E(Z_t) = \mu \tag{6.5}$$

and

$$E(Z_t - \mu)^2 = \sigma^2. \tag{6.6}$$

We explain how this is done later in this chapter.

The stationarity condition makes it possible to sample the time series between any two dates and draw a statistical inference. But it also rules out the presence of deterministic elements, since they typically change the moments of the distribution. Specifically, there are four types of deterministic influences:

1. *Trend* is defined as any smooth function of time. It shifts the mean of a time
    series upward or downward. For example, nominal prices may go up because of
    inflation.

2. *Seasonality* creates within-year patterns that are the same across years. In the
    extreme, every month of the year may have its own mean, for example, the sales
    levels of toys or suntan lotion.

3. *Cyclical patterns* may emerge over many years, for example, owing to cycles of
    economic activity. Unless very long time series of 30 years or more are
    available, cyclical patterns not easily detected in marketing databases.

4. The variance may change over time, a condition called *heteroscedasticity.* For
    example, as retail promotion activities, such as couponing, expand in an
    industry, the volatility of the market shares of the competing brands may
    increase over time.

Yule's filter theory does not accommodate these phenomena, so they must be
removed prior to analyzing the data. Techniques for removing nonstationarity are
discussed later; we focus now on the analysis of stationary data z_t. These data can be
transformed to white noise by means of two distinctive linear filters, the
autoregressive (AR) *filter* and the *moving-average* (MA) *filter.*

Suppose a marketing manager allocates a yearly advertising budget as a fixed
amount 100, plus 90% of the previous year's expenditure. The actual advertising,
however, is also affected by random factors due to current market conditions and
execution errors. Then, part of the resulting advertising time series would be
predictable from its own past as follows:

$$\text{advertising}_t = 100 + 0.9 * \text{advertising}_{t-1} + \text{random amount}_t. \qquad (6.7)$$

To turn the scenario around, the analyst would have to discover the decision rule in
order to transform the time series "advertising" to the white noise series "random
amount":

$$\text{random amount}_t = -100 + \text{advertising}_t - 0.9 * \text{advertising}_{t-1}. \qquad (6.8)$$

The decision rule is linear and relates current values to previous values of the time
series. All these previous observations will be correlated with the current value. This
is an example of an autoregressive (AR) filter.

A moving-average filter may appear as follows: Suppose the advertising manager
sets this year's advertising budget as 100 plus an adjustment for the allocation error
that was made last year. Indeed, many errors in execution are possible because of

personnel changes, bankruptcies, limited ad space availability, unexpected competitive entry, and so on. As a result, last year's advertising target or budget was either exceeded or not met, and the manager may wish to build an adjustment factor to last year's budget error into this year's budget. Since execution errors will again occur this year, the resulting time series model on advertising may be

$$\text{advertising}_t = 100 + 0.5 * (\text{advertising}_{t-1} - \text{target}_{t-1})$$
$$+ \text{random amount}_t.$$

(6.9)

Unlike the AR case, current values of the time series are not directly related to previous values but to previous unexpected values, or shocks. In the example, this rule results in current advertising. being correlated with last year's advertising but not with previous years' expenditures. This is an example of a moving-average (MA) filter.

We are now in a position to introduce a formal notation for AR and MA filters. Yule's linear filter theory is represented as:

$$\text{White noise} \longrightarrow \boxed{\begin{array}{c}\text{Linear filter}\\ \Psi(L)\end{array}} \longrightarrow \text{Observed data}$$
$$w_0 w_1 \ldots w_t \qquad\qquad\qquad\qquad z_t$$

Thus, the observed stationary series $z_t (t = 1,2,\ldots,T)$ is generated by an unobservable white noise series $(w_0, w_1, \ldots, w_t)$, filtered by the linear filter $\Psi(L)$:

$$\begin{aligned} z_t &= w_t + \psi_1 w_{t-1} + \psi_2 w_{t-2} + \cdots \\ &= w_t + \psi_1 L w_t + \psi_2 L^2 w_t + \cdots \\ &= \left(1 + \psi_1 L + \psi_2 L^2 + \cdots\right) w_t \\ &= \Psi(L) w_t, \end{aligned}$$

(6.10)

where L is the lag operator, e.g., $L^k z_t = z_{t-k}$.

As explained earlier, an autoregressive filter relates current observations to previous observations, and a moving-average filter relates current observations to previous shocks. The AR filter is generally denoted by $\Phi(L)$ and operates on the left-hand side of the time series equation (z_t); the MA filter $\Theta(L)$ operates on the right-hand side (w_t). Thus, the basic univariate time series model is

$$\Phi(L) z_t = \Theta(L) w_t.$$

(6.11)

Rearranging terms shows that the linear filter $\Psi(L)$ has been decomposed in an AR and MA component:

$$z_t = \frac{\Theta(L)}{\Phi(L)} w_t = \Psi(L)w_t. \tag{6.12}$$

In the example, if the manager uses both the AR and the MA decision rule, the resulting advertising time series model would be (omitting the constant for ease of presentation):

$$z_t = 0.9z_{t-1} + 0.5(z_{t-1} - \hat{z}_{t-1}) + w_t, \tag{6.13}$$

where w_t is white noise, and $\hat{z}_{t-1}$ is the forecast value of z obtained in period $(t-1)$.

Although the equation is easy to understand, its form is not very efficient for time series analysis. A more common and much shorter notation is obtained by using the lag operator L, so the budgeting equation is rewritten as

$$z_t - 0.9z_{t-1} = 0.5(z_{t-1} - \hat{z}_{t-1}) + w_t, \tag{6.14}$$

and since the forecast error in $(t-1)$ is the shock in that period,

$$z_t - 0.9z_{t-1} = 0.5w_{t-1} + w_t. \tag{6.15}$$

By introducing lag operators,

$$z_t - 0.9Lz_t = w_t + 0.5Lw_t, \tag{6.16}$$

we obtain:

$$(1 - 0.9L)z_t = (1 + 0.5L)w_t. \tag{6.17}$$

This is a simple example of a linear filter with an AR and an MA component. Now, since we have carefully chosen the two parameters, we can also write:

$$\begin{aligned}
z_t &= (1 - 0.9L)^{-1}(1 + 0.5L)w_t \\
&= (1 + 0.9L + 0.81L^2 + 0.729L^3 + \cdots)(1 + 0.5L)w_t,
\end{aligned} \tag{6.18}$$

by arithmetic expansion, and ultimately:

$$z_t = (1 + 1.4L + 1.26L^2 + 1.13L^3 + 1.02L^4 + \cdots)w_t, \tag{6.19}$$

which is an expression in line with Yule's linear stochastic time series model. In this case, the linear filter $\Psi(L)$ is infinite. However, since w_t has a finite, constant mean and variance, the observed series will not "explode," because the influence of any shock w_t gradually declines. In other words, as long as the parameters of the model are within certain bounds, the resulting time series process will be stationary.

The example teaches some important properties of AR and MA filters. The AR filter is infinite, so its weights must converge in order to preserve stationarity. In the advertising case, this implies that the parameter ϕ must be less than 1 in absolute value:

$$(1 - \phi L)^{-1} = 1 + \phi L + \phi^2 L^2 + \phi^3 L^3 + \cdots \tag{6.20}$$

as long as $-1 < \phi < 1$. The MA filter is finite, so stationarity is always implied, although later we will argue that similar parameter restrictions may be applied to an MA filter as well. Most important, however, the example demonstrates that two conceptually different linear filters, one relating current data to previous data, the other relating current data to previous shocks, are compatible with Yule's general stochastic time series model.

We are now in the position to generalize the model to an autoregressive process of order p (AR(p)) and a moving-average process of order q (MA(q)). Let:

$$\Psi(L) = \frac{\Theta(L)}{\Phi(L)}, \tag{6.21}$$

where

$$\Phi(L) = 1 - \phi_1 L - \phi_2 L^2 - \cdots - \phi_p L^p,$$

$$\Theta(L) = 1 - \theta_1 L - \theta_2 L^2 - \cdots - \theta_q L^q.$$

The autoregressive filter $\Phi(L)$ models the dependence of the series on its p previous observations. The moving-average filter $\Theta(L)$ relates current observations to q previous shocks in the system. The combination produces an ARMA (p, q) model, which can be written as

$$\Phi(L)z_t = \Theta(L)w_t, \tag{6.22}$$

or

$$(1 - \phi_1 L - \phi_2 L^2 - \cdots - \phi_p L^p)z_t = (1 - \theta_1 L - \theta_2 L^2 - \cdots - \theta_q L^q)w_t. \tag{6.23}$$

The Autocorrelation and Partial Autocorrelation Function

The ARMA model relates current time series observations to previous observations and previous shocks. The order of the ARMA parameters, p and q, determines the *memory* of the series: the longer the memory, the longer the usable forecasting horizon of a series. AR models have an infinite memory, i.e., an observation contributes to the forecast of every future observation, although the strength of the contribution varies with p. Moving-average models have a finite memory of order q. The critical question, of course, is how to identify the order of the ARMA model for a given series.

Two useful tools for the identification of ARMA models have been proposed (Box and Jenkins 1976). The *autocorrelation* at lag k is simply the correlation of two data points that are k periods apart. The *partial autocorrelation* at lag k is a similar correlation, but it holds constant all $k-1$ observations between the two data points. Box and Jenkins use these tools because every ARMA(p,q) model comes with a unique set of predefined autocorrelations and partial autocorrelations. Thus, the idea is to infer (p,q) from the behavior of the autocorrelation and partial autocorrelation functions (ACF and PACF) at various lags k. To do this, we must first explain the ACF and PACF analytically and then examine their behavior for AR, MA, and general ARMA models.

Formally, the autocovariance γ_k and the autocorrelation ρ_k of a *stationary* series at lag k are defined as

$$\begin{aligned}
\gamma_k &= E\{(z_t - Ez_t)(z_{t-k} - Ez_t)\} \\
&= E\{(z_t - Ez_t)(z_{t+k} - Ez_t)\},
\end{aligned} \tag{6.24}$$

and

$$\rho_k = \frac{E(z_t - Ez_t)(z_{t-k} - Ez_t)}{E(z_t - Ez_t)^2} = \frac{E(z_t - Ez_t)(z_{t+k} - Ez_t)}{E(z_t - Ez_t)^2}, \tag{6.25}$$

$$\rho_k = \frac{\gamma_k}{\gamma_0}. \tag{6.26}$$

When viewed as a function of the lag index k, these definitions lead to the autocorrelation function (ACF) of a series. In practice, it is estimated as

$$r_k = \frac{\sum_{t=1}^{T-k}(z_t - \bar{z})(z_{t+k} - \bar{z})}{\sum_{t=1}^{T}(z_t - \bar{z})^2}, \qquad \forall k > 0, \tag{6.27}$$

where $\bar{z}$ is the sample mean:

$$\frac{\sum_{t=1}^{T} z_t}{T}.$$

Notice that the sample estimator is not unbiased, i.e., $E(r_k) \neq \rho_k$; however, it does produce a positive semidefinite matrix of autocorrelations, which will be useful later.

The ACF plays a predominant role in the identification of a time series filter $\Psi(L)$ via a *pattern recognition* of significant (nonzero) and zero elements for various lags k. Therefore, an expression for its variance is needed. Bartlett (1946) has provided the following approximation for a time series whose autocorrelations are zero beyond lag q:

$$\text{var}(r_k) \cong \frac{1}{T}\left\{1 + 2\sum_{v=1}^{q} \rho_v^2\right\} \quad (k > q). \tag{6.28}$$

This expression is quite useful, even though it is only an approximation. First, it shows that $\text{var}(r_k)$ is of the order T^{-1}, which is a simple yardstick. Second, under the assumption that higher-order autocorrelations are zero, we can always compute $\text{var}(r_k)$ from lower-order correlations. Furthermore, the expression reveals that $\text{var}(r_k)$ increases with k.

In interpreting an ACF, it is assumed that $r_k \sim N(\rho_k, \text{var}(r_k))$, so that a classical t- or z-test of significance is possible. We must, however, be careful, because r_k and $r_{k+s}(s \neq 0)$ are correlated, so spurious autocorrelations may occur. This is one of the reasons why the identification of a time series process is supplemented with the *partial autocorrelation function* Φ_{kk}, or the PACF.

The partial autocorrelation of kth order is the correlation between two observations k lags apart, holding constant all $(k-1)$ *intermediate* observations. As a simple example, consider the following sequence of observations and correlations:

The partial correlation between z_1 and z_3, holding z_2 constant, is

$$\rho_{13.2} = \frac{\rho_{13} - \rho_{12}\rho_{23}}{\sqrt{(1-\rho_{12}^2)(1-\rho_{23}^2)}}, \tag{6.29}$$

following the general definition of partial correlation. Now, if the series z_t is stationary, $\rho_{12} = \rho_{23}$, and we can simplify as

$$\rho_{13.2} = \frac{\rho_2 - \rho_1^2}{1-\rho_1^2} = \phi_{22}. \tag{6.30}$$

The example also shows that stationarity imposes restrictions on the permissible values of ρ_1 and ρ_2. For example, since $-1 < \phi_{22} < 1$, it follows that $2\rho_1^2 - 1 < \rho_2 < 1$.

Univariate Time Series Models

The ACF and the PACF are the major statistical tools for identifying a time series model. How they should be used will become clear from a discussion of autoregressive (AR), moving-average (MA), and mixed (ARMA) models. In each case, we derive the *theoretical* behavior of the ACF and PACF so that their diagnostic value can be determined.

Autoregressive Models

There are many reasons for the autoregressive behavior of marketing time series, and indeed AR patterns are often found. An earlier example was the memory decay hypothesis as applied to advertising effects: If each period's retention level z_t is a constant function of the previous period's level, a smooth first-order autoregressive pattern may appear:

$$z_t = \alpha_0 + \phi z_{t-1} + w_t, \tag{6.31}$$

or, in time series notation,

$$(1-\phi L)z_t = \alpha_0 + w_t, \tag{6.32}$$

The first-order autoregressive model is stationary only within a range of ϕ, $-1 < \phi < 1$. Under these conditions we can derive the first- and second-order moments. The AR(1) model may be written as:

$$z_t = \frac{\alpha_0}{1-\phi L} + \frac{1}{1-\phi L} w_t, \tag{6.33}$$

or

$$z_t = \frac{\alpha_0}{1-\phi} + \frac{1}{1-\phi L} w_t, \tag{6.34}$$

since the lag operator L does not affect a constant. Therefore,

$$E(z_t) = \frac{\alpha_0}{1-\phi}, \tag{6.35}$$

$$V(z_t) = \frac{1}{1-\phi^2} \sigma_w^2. \tag{6.36}$$

The autocorrelation function of an AR(1) process is particularly simple. Let $\tilde{z}_t = z_t - E(z_t)$. Then the autocovariance at lag k is

$$\begin{aligned} \gamma_k = E(\tilde{z}_t \tilde{z}_{t-k}) &= \phi E(\tilde{z}_{t-1} \tilde{z}_{t-k}) + E(w_t \tilde{z}_{t-k}) \\ &= \phi \gamma_{k-1}. \end{aligned} \tag{6.37}$$

Therefore,

$$\rho_1 = \frac{\gamma_1}{\gamma_0} = \phi, \tag{6.38}$$

$$\rho_2 = \frac{\gamma_2}{\gamma_0} = \frac{\phi \gamma_1}{\gamma_0} = \phi^2, \tag{6.39}$$

$$\rho_k = \phi^k = \rho_1^k. \tag{6.40}$$

The ACF pattern is intuitively clear: The AR(1) process is completely determined by $\phi = \rho_1$; for $0 < \phi < 1$, the ACF dies out monotonically; and for $-1 < \phi < 0$, it oscillates toward zero. This behavior is illustrated in Figure 6-1.

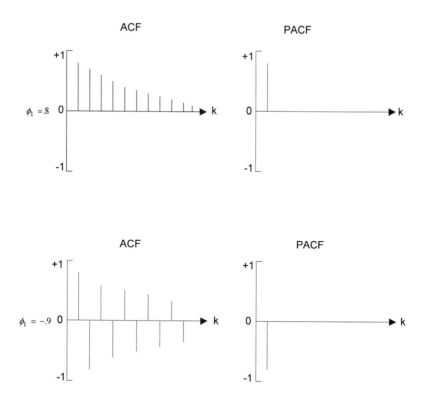

Figure 6-1. Autocorrelation Function and Partial Autocorrelation Function for an AR(1) Process.

The behavior of the PACF is easily derived from its definition, i.e.,

$$\rho_{13.2} = \frac{\rho_2 - \rho_1^2}{1 - \rho_1^2}.$$ (6.41)

Since $\rho_2 = \rho_1^2$, it follows that $\rho_{13.2} = 0$. Also, higher-order PACs can be shown to be zero, so that the general rule is

$$\phi_{kk} = \phi = \rho_1, \quad k = 1,$$
$$\phi_{kk} = 0, \quad k > 1.$$ (6.42)

The PACF pattern is intuitively clear: The AR(1) process is fully explained by ϕ; therefore, if we hold constant all autocorrelations up to lag k, the $(k+1)$th autocorrelation has no explanatory power to add and is therefore zero. A graph of the PACF is also shown in Figure 6-1.

The extension to higher-order autoregressive processes AR(p), where $p > 1$, is straightforward. For example, the AR(2) model,

$$z_t = \delta + \phi_1 z_{t-1} + \phi_2 z_{t-2} + w_t, \tag{6.43}$$

or

$$\left(1 - \phi_1 L - \phi_2 L^2\right) z_t = \delta + w_t, \tag{6.44}$$

has the following stationarity conditions:

$$\phi_1 + \phi_2 < 1, \tag{6.45}$$

$$\phi_2 - \phi_1 < 1, \tag{6.46}$$

$$|\phi_2| < 1. \tag{6.47}$$

When these are met, the critical moments of the process are

$$E(z_t) = \frac{\delta}{1 - \phi_1 - \phi_2}, \tag{6.48}$$

$$V(z_t) = \gamma_0 = \frac{1 - \phi_2}{1 + \phi_2} \frac{1}{\left(1 - \phi_2\right)^2 - \phi_1^2} \sigma_w^2, \tag{6.49}$$

$$\gamma_k = \phi_1 \gamma_{k-1} + \phi_2 \gamma_{k-2}. \tag{6.50}$$

The ACF is more complex than in the AR(1) case, but it will die out in a pattern dictated by ϕ_1 and ϕ_2. In particular, it can be shown that

$$\rho_1 = \phi_1 + \phi_2 \rho_1, \tag{6.51}$$

$$\rho_2 = \phi_1 \rho_2 + \phi_2, \tag{6.52}$$

$$\rho_k = \phi_1 \rho_{k-1} + \phi_2 \rho_{k-2}, \quad k = 2. \tag{6.53}$$

From $k=2$ on, the autocorrelations are fully determined by their lower-order values and ϕ_1 and ϕ_2, so the partial autocorrelations are zero. Therefore, the AR(2) process is characterized by a dying-out ACF and a PACF with nonzero values at $k=1$ and $k=2$ only.

The extension to the AR(p) model follows logically:

$$\left(1 - \phi_1 L - \phi_2 L^2 - \cdots - \phi_p L^p\right) z_t = \delta + w_t \tag{6.54}$$

is stationary when the roots of $\left(1 - \phi_1 L - \phi_2 L^2 - \cdots - \phi_p L^p\right) = 0$ are greater than 1 in absolute value. The ACF will die out in a pattern dictated by the ϕ parameters, and the PACF will have p distinctive values, followed by zeros.

Moving-Average Models

The term *moving average* is generally accepted, although ill chosen, for the class of models where current z_t depends on w_{t-k} $(k > 0)$. The simplest case is the first-order model MA(1):

$$z_t = \mu + w_t - \theta w_{t-1}, \tag{6.55}$$

or

$$z_t - \mu = (1 - \theta L) w_t. \tag{6.56}$$

This model is always stationary because the linear filter relating z_t to w_t is finite. However, we must impose restrictions on the parameter θ if the model is to be *invertible*, that is, it can be written as

$$(1 - \theta L)^{-1}(z_t - \mu) = w_t, \tag{6.57}$$

or

$$\left(1 + \theta L + \theta^2 L^2 + \theta^3 L^3 + \cdots\right)(z_t - \mu) = w_t. \tag{6.58}$$

The invertibility condition is useful for parameter estimation. In the MA(1) model, invertibility requires that $-1 < \theta < 1$, which is similar to the stationarity condition on ϕ in an AR(1) process. By analogy with linear programming, invertibility is the "dual" of stationarity.

The important moments of an MA(1) process are

$$E(z_t) = \mu, \tag{6.59}$$

$$V(z_t) = \gamma_0 = (1 + \theta^2)\sigma_w^2, \tag{6.60}$$

$$\gamma_k = E(\tilde{z}_t \tilde{z}_{t-k}) = E\big[(w_t - \theta w_{t-1})(w_{t-k} - \theta w_{t-k-1})\big] = \begin{cases} -\theta\sigma_w^2 & \forall k = 1 \\ 0 & \forall k > 1 \end{cases}. \tag{6.61}$$

and, therefore,

$$\rho_k = \begin{cases} \dfrac{-\theta}{1+\theta^2} & k = 1 \\ 0 & k > 1 \end{cases}. \tag{6.62}$$

So, the ACF of an MA(1) model has one *spike* at lag 1, uniquely determined by θ and zeros elsewhere. By contrast, the PACF *dies out* because an MA(1) model is equivalent to an AR(∞) process; therefore, each autocorrelation at lag k offers additional explanatory power beyond that explained by the $(k-1)$ lower-order autocorrelations. Examples of MA(1) correlograms are shown in Figure 6-2.

The MA(1) model is readily extended to the MA(q) process:

$$z_t = \mu + w_t - \theta_1 w_{t-1} - \cdots - \theta_q w_{t-q}, \tag{6.63}$$

or

$$z_t = \mu + \big(1 - \theta_1 L^2 - \cdots - \theta_q L^q\big)w_t, \tag{6.64}$$

which is invertible if the roots of $\Theta(L) = 0$ are outside the unit circle. Its autocorrelations will show q spikes as determined by

$$\rho_j = -\frac{\theta_j + \theta_1\theta_{j+1} + \cdots + \theta_{q-1}\theta_q}{1 + \theta_1^2 + \cdots + \theta_q^2}, \quad j \le q, \tag{6.65}$$

followed by $(j > q)$. In other words, the *memory* of an MA(q) process is exactly q periods long. The PACF dies out according to the θ parameter values.

Mixed Autoregressive-Moving-Average Models

The well-known autoregressive-moving-average, or ARMA, process combines AR(p) and MA(q) parameters:

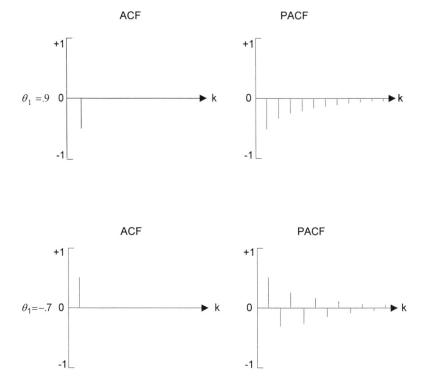

Figure 6-2. Autocorrelation Function and Partial Autocorrelation Function for an MA(1) Process.

$$z_t = \delta + \phi_1 z_{t-1} + \cdots + \phi_p z_{t-p} + w_t - \theta_1 w_{t-1} - \cdots - \theta_q w_{t-q}, \qquad (6.66)$$

or

$$\left(1 - \phi_1 L - \cdots - \phi_p L^p\right) z_t = \delta + \left(1 - \theta_1 L - \cdots - \theta_q L^q\right) w_t. \qquad (6.67)$$

Stationarity requires that the roots of $\Phi(L)$ be outside the unit circle, and invertibility occurs when the roots of $\Theta(L)$ are outside the unit circle. In practice, the ARMA (1, 1) is by far the most common of the mixed models, so we shall use it to illustrate the basic properties of mixed models. The ARMA (1, 1) is

$$(1 - \phi_1 L) z_t = \delta + (1 - \theta_1 L) w_t, \qquad (6.68)$$

with

$$E(z_t) = \mu = \frac{\delta}{1 - \phi_1}, \tag{6.69}$$

$$V(z_t) = \gamma_0 = \frac{1 + \theta_1^2 - 2\phi_1\theta_1}{1 - \theta_1^2}\sigma_w^2. \tag{6.70}$$

The ACF at lag 1 is complex because it is affected by both autoregressive and moving-average components:

$$\rho_1 = \frac{(1 - \phi_1\theta_1)(\phi_1 - \theta_1)}{1 + \theta_1^2 - 2\phi_1\theta_1}. \tag{6.71}$$

On the other hand, for $k > 1$, the only memory factors are contributed by the autoregressive side of the equation. Formally, it can be shown that

$$\rho_k = \phi_1\rho_{k-1}, \quad k > 1. \tag{6.72}$$

Therefore, the ACF has a spike at lag 1, followed by a typical autoregressive decay pattern for $k > 1$. The PACF pattern is more difficult to predict, except for the fact that it dies out as k increases. Examples of ARMA $(1,1)$ correlograms are shown in Figure 6-3.

Extending these findings to the ARMA (p,q) process, we conclude that the ACF shows spikes for the first q lags, followed by a decay pattern. The PACF dies out in function of the $(p+q)$ model parameters.

Model Identification and Estimation

Now that we have derived the theoretical ACF and PACF behavior of any linear time series process, we are in a position to apply the well-known search heuristic due to Box and Jenkins (1976) for the identification of a model. First, let us summarize the key findings from the previous section:

- Autoregressive processes have a dying-out ACF pattern, which also implies that their memory is infinite. To determine the order of the process, we can simply count the number of spikes in the PACF, which has a cutoff pattern.

- The situation for a moving-average process, which has a finite memory, is the reverse: The ACF cuts off at a point equal to the order of the MA process. The PACF is less informative, except that it must die out, since an MA(q) is equivalent to an AR(∞). The mixed ARMA model is more difficult to identify,

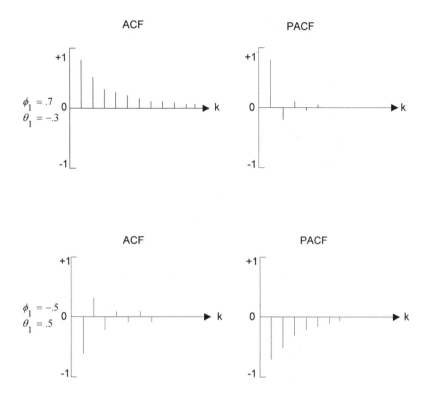

Figure 6-3. Autocorrelation Function and Partial Autocorrelation Function for an ARMA (1, 1) Process.

because both the ACF and the PACF die out. It will usually take more than one attempt to find the right model for such a process.

These findings are shown in Table 6-2.

The Method of Box and Jenkins

Box and Jenkins proposed a three-step modeling procedure, consisting of identification, estimation, and diagnostic checking (Figure 6-4). First, the modeler selects a candidate ARMA process by inspecting the ACF-PACF of the original series. Next, the model's parameters are estimated and the residuals are stored. If the candidate model is adequate, i.e., if the proposed filter does whiten the data, then the ACF-PACF of the residuals should be flat. If not, then some spikes will remain and their pattern will suggest ways of improving the original model. Thus, the modeler uses the diagnostic checking phase to return to model identification if necessary.

Table 6-2. The Behavior of the Autocorrelation Function (ACF) and the Partial Autocorrelation Function (PACF)

	Autoregressive Process	Moving-Average Process	Mixed Process
ACF	Dies out	Cuts off	Dies out
PACF	Cuts off	Dies out	Dies out

The method of Box and Jenkins is tremendously popular. If used properly, it virtually guarantees success, i.e., a filter that whitens the data will be found. Furthermore, the method promotes parsimonious models-those that whiten the data with a minimum of parameters. Therefore, it is highly recommended to build time series models bottom-up by starting with simple candidates such as AR(1) and only adding parameters if certain patterns in the residual ACF- PACF call for it.

Some other tools for univariate time series modeling have been proposed, but an extensive discussion is beyond the scope of this book. Methods include the inverse autocorrelation function (Cleveland 1972), the S-array (Gray, Kelly, and McIntire 1978), and the extended sample autocorrelation function (Tsay and Tiao 1984). Thus, the state-of-the-art in univariate time series analysis is such that virtually any time series can be transformed to white noise with a reasonable amount of effort.

One important assumption of the ARMA (p,q) that the order (p,q) and the parameters are constant. However, in many marketing modeling situations, we may suspect that different ARMA processes hold for different regions or brands or that the ARMA parameters change over time. This general problem has been addressed in a territory sales forecasting context by Moriarty and Adams (1979). For example, should a manager use one ARMA model for each region in the market or use separate models for separate regions? They proposed an interesting sequence of formal tests (Table 6-3), which can be applied in a practical situation. The procedure is very useful in deciding how many different forecasting models are needed for optimal performance.

Dealing with Nonstationarity

As crucial as the stationarity assumption is to the theoretical analysis of time series, it is often violated in real-world data, notably marketing data. First, many marketing series exhibit *trend*, i.e., the mean changes smoothly over time. Examples include sales growth due to market expansion and price increases due to inflation. Second, the use of short-interval data in marketing makes many analyses subject to *seasonality*, e.g., different means may be applicable to different periods. Third, a number of marketing series are *heteroscedastic* (variance changes over time), for

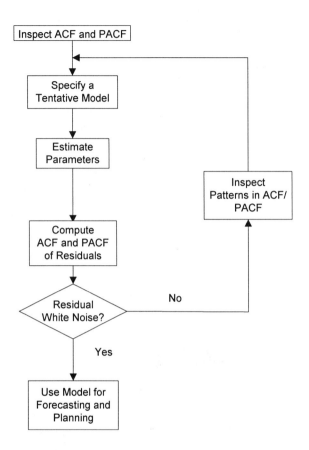

Figure 6-4. The Method of Box and Jenkins.

example, market shares may become more volatile over time as a result of aggressive marketing strategies. The last source of nonstationarity, *cyclicality*, is less influential in marketing: even though sales or price cycles may exist, they are typically not constant in length and thus pose less of a threat to stationarity.

Nonstationarity in Means and Variances. Nonstationarity in means (i.e., trend, seasonality, and cyclicality) is more serious than nonstationarity in variance (heteroscedasticity). The former may result in spurious correlations among the observations in a time series, because of a deterministic time factor common to all. Typically, the ACF of a series affected by trend or cycles will *fail to die out*, so that the usual identification techniques may not work. While the ACF of a heteroscedastic

Table 6-3. Moriarty-Adams ARMA Model Tests

Task	Test	Verdict
1. Are (p, q) the same?	t-test on model form	No: Build separate models. Yes: Continue.
2. Are the parameters the same?	F-test on coefficient equality	No: Estimate separately. Yes: Continue.
3. Is the error variance the same?	F-test on white noise variance equality	No: Estimate separately. Yes: Continue.
4. Is the forecasting accuracy affected?	Wilcoxon signed-ranks test on forecast errors	No: Use parsimonious model. Yes: Use separate parameters.

series will generally be well-behaved, parameter estimation may be inefficient, comparable to the case of heteroscedastic disturbances in a regression model.

To start with the latter, Box and Jenkins have suggested taking the logarithm of a heteroscedastic series in order to obtain variance homogeneity:

$$Z_t' = ln(Z_t + c), \qquad (6.73)$$

where c is an additive constant that removes nonpositive data values. This approach, while widely used, has been criticized for its arbitrariness (Chatfield and Prothero 1973). A more general class of transformations was formulated by Box and Cox (1964) as was discussed in the Appendix of our last chapter:

$$Z_t' = \frac{(Z_t + c)^\lambda - 1}{\lambda}, \qquad \lambda \neq 0, \qquad (6.74)$$

$$Z_t' = ln(Z_t + c), \qquad \lambda = 0. \qquad (6.75)$$

The advantage of this method is that the transformation parameter λ is obtained empirically, usually by maximum likelihood. Nevertheless, Box-Cox transformations seem to be used infrequently in time series applications, perhaps because the transformed series is difficult to interpret intuitively.

Nonstationarity in means is generally treated by differencing the data by order d, which leads to the specification of the "integrated" ARMA or ARIMA(p,d,q) model. Regular differencing removes a trend polynomial of order d:

$$z_t = (1 - L)^d Z_t. \qquad (6.76)$$

Trends in marketing data are mostly linear, sometimes quadratic, so that d is seldom greater than 2. The two most common transformations are linear differencing $(d = 1)$,

$$z_t = Z_t - Z_{t-1} = (1 - L)Z_t,$$ (6.77)

and quadratic differencing $(d = 2)$,

$$z_t = (Z_t - Z_{t-1}) - (Z_{t-1} - Z_{t-2}) = (1 - L)^2 Z_t.$$ (6.78)

Seasonal differencing of order d_s is a natural extension of regular differencing to deal with seasonal nonstationarity:

$$z_t = (1 - L^s)^{d_s} Z_t,$$ (6.79)

where s is the season length (e.g., $s = 12$ for monthly data). This is the equivalent of "same time last year" comparisons often made by marketing practitioners. Again, d_s is seldom greater than 2 in practice.

Regular and seasonal differencing are simple, widely used transformations to remove nonstationarity in means. Sometimes they are used excessively, creating a condition known as *overdifferencing*. Suppose the stationary AR(1) series z_t is "accidentally" differenced with $d = 1$:

$$(1 - \phi_1 L)z_t = \alpha_0 + w_t,$$ (6.80)

$$z_t' = (1 - L)z_t$$ (6.81)

Substitution then reveals

$$(1 - \phi_1 L)z_t' = \alpha_0' + (1 - L)w_t,$$ (6.82)

where α_0' is a different constant. Although the original AR(1) process is maintained, a spurious MA(1) process with parameter 1 is added. Therefore, overdifferencing may adversely affect the parsimony of the time series model (Plosser and Schwert 1977).

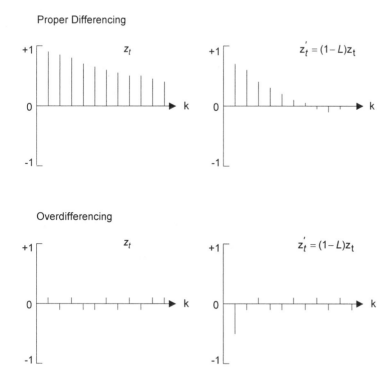

Figure 6-5. Autocorrelation Functions Before and After Differencing.

The most practical rule for detecting and thus avoiding overdifferencing is to inspect the ACF of the differenced series. Figure 6-5 compares the ACF of a properly differenced series to the ACF of an overdifferenced series. The negative spike at lag 1 has a value around -0.5, which corresponds to a moving-average parameter of 1.0. Formal tests on overdifferencing can be found in the growing literature on unit-root testing (e.g., Dickey, Bell, and Miller 1986), which will be discussed in the context of assessing stationarity vs. evolution in longitudinal data.

The Seasonal ARIMA Model. Seasonal time series are not necessarily nonstationary and can exhibit seasonal patterns even after differencing. The Box-Jenkins model takes such patterns into account by adding seasonal autoregressive and moving-average parameters to the base equation:

$$\Phi(L)\Phi_s(L)(1-L)^d\left(1-L^s\right)^{d_s} Z_t = \alpha_0 + \Theta(L)\Theta_s(L)w_t , \qquad (6.83)$$

where $\Phi_s(L)$ denotes the seasonal autoregressive process and $\Theta_s(L)$ the seasonal moving-average parameters. The model is multiplicative and is generally represented as ARIMA $(p,d,q)(p_s,d_s,q_s)_s$, where s is the length of the season.

It is convenient to think of seasonal AR and MA processes as regular processes on a different time interval. For example, on quarterly data ($s = 4$), the ACF may die out over the interval $k = 4,8,12,\cdots$ indicating a seasonal AR process, or it may display a single spike at lag $k = 4$, indicating a seasonal moving-average model. Of course, if the ACF fails to die out, we must transform the data to obtain stationarity. Figure 6-6 illustrates these different seasonal behaviors.

One of the best-known Box-Jenkins applications, the so-called airline model, illustrates these points. Many monthly airline passenger series have been found to follow an ARIMA $(0,1,1)(0,1,1)_{12}$ process, i.e.,

$$(1-L)(1-L^{12})Z_t = (1-\theta_1 L)(1-\theta_{12} L^{12})w_t \tag{6.84}$$

The forecasting equation derived from this model is insightful:

$$\hat{Z}_t = Z_{t-1} + Z_{t-12} - Z_{t-13} - \hat{\theta}_1\left(Z_{t-1} - \hat{Z}_{t-1}\right)$$
$$- \hat{\theta}_{12}\left(Z_{t-12} - \hat{Z}_{t-12}\right) - \theta_{13}\left(Z_{t-13} - \hat{Z}_{t-13}\right) \tag{6.85}$$

where $\hat{\theta}_1, \hat{\theta}_{12}$, and $\hat{\theta}_{13}$ are parameter estimates, and $\hat{Z}_t$ denotes the one-step forecast value at time t. The model suggests that passenger levels can be optimally predicted from "last month," "same month last year," and "previous month last year" levels, as well as shocks (i.e., deviations from previous forecasts) in these periods. The airline model is a complex combination of regular and seasonal time series patterns that seemingly predicts air travel very well (see, for example, Box and Jenkins 1976).

Parameter Estimation

The parameters of an adequately specified ARIMA model can be estimated in a variety of ways. The simplest case involves the AR(p) process, which can be expressed in regression form as

$$z_t = \alpha_0 + \phi_1 z_{t-1} + \cdots + \phi_p z_{t-p} + w_t. \tag{6.86}$$

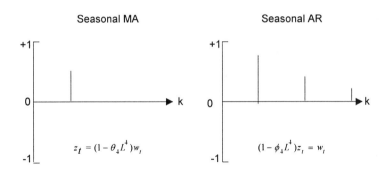

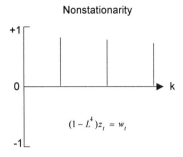

Figure 6-6. Autocorrelation Functions for Seasonal Processes (Quarterly Data).

Since w_t is white noise, the model can be parameterized with ordinary least squares, which provides consistent estimates.

The situation is more complex when MA parameters are included. Even the simplest MA(1) model,

$$z_t = w_t - \theta w_{t-1},\qquad (6.87)$$

is difficult to estimate because w_{t-1} is unobservable. Typically a maximum likelihood (ML) procedure, which involves a parameter search, is used. For example, ML estimation of the MA(1) model involves the minimization of the following sums-of-squares function:

$$s(\theta) = \sum \left[z_t + \theta\,\hat{w}(\theta)_{t-1}\right]^2 = \sum \hat{w}_t^2 .\qquad (6.88)$$

In order to execute a search, we need a starting value for $\hat{w}_0$ so that we can subsequently compute $\hat{w}_1 = z_1 + \theta \hat{w}_0$, and so forth. The most obvious choice is to set $\hat{w}_0 = 0$, i.e., to assume that there is no shock in the time series at its beginning. To the extent the assumption is wrong, the impact of the error will die out as long as the model is invertible, i.e., $|\theta| < 1$ in the MA(1) case. Indeed, we can write at time t:

$$\begin{aligned}
\hat{w}_t &= z_t + \theta \hat{w}_{t-1} \\
&= z_t + \theta z_{t-1} + \cdots + \theta^{t-1} z_1 + \theta^t \hat{w}_0.
\end{aligned} \tag{6.89}$$

Thus, for sufficiently long time series the effects of the initial observation die out exponentially as $\theta^t \to 0$. This example illustrates the importance of having invertible time series models.

Several variations of the likelihood method exist. A conditional likelihood approach for the ARMA (p,q) model assumes that $w_t = 0$ for $p \le t \le (p+q-1)$. An exact likelihood method estimates values for these w_t based on the exact likelihood derived by Newbold (1974). Furthermore, various nonlinear least-squares algorithms have been used, most notably the Gauss-Marquardt method. Issues in parameter estimation of ARMA models continue to receive attention in the statistical literature (e.g., Bustos and Yohai 1986).

Forecasting

It can be proved that the minimum squared-error forecast for a time series is obtained by a model that filters the data to white noise. Intuitively, whitening the data removes all systematic patterns so that only random error, which by definition cannot be forecast, remains. A poor time series model leaves autocorrelation in the data, which could have been used to improve the accuracy of the forecasts.

The quality of a forecast depends on σ_w^2, the residual variance of the ARIMA model, and on the forecasting horizon. Consider the MA (∞) expression of an ARMA model

$$z_t = \sum_{j=0}^{m} \alpha_j w_{t-j}, \tag{6.90}$$

where m is infinite when AR parameters are present. An observation at time $(t+k)$ can be decomposed into a predictable part (i.e., known at time t) and a forecast error:

$$z_{t+k} = \sum_{j=k}^{m} \alpha_j w_{t+k-j} + \sum_{j=0}^{k-1} \alpha_j w_{t+k-j} \tag{6.91}$$

or, more compactly,

$$z_{t+k} = f_{t,k} + e_{t,k}, \tag{6.92}$$

where $f_{t,k}$ is a forecast made at time t. It follows that the forecast error is

$$e_{t,k} = z_{t+k} - f_{t,k} = \sum_{j=0}^{k-1} \alpha_j w_{t+k-j} \tag{6.93}$$

with

$$var(e_{t,k}) = \sigma_j^2 \left[\sum_{j=0}^{k-1} \alpha_j^2 \right]. \tag{6.94}$$

Therefore, $var(e_{t,k}) \geq var(e_{t,k-1})$, or, the longer the forecasting horizon, the lower our confidence in the forecast.

The implication of this result is that frequent forecast updating will improve accuracy, at least theoretically. The options to the forecaster are to update the forecasts only, to update the parameter estimates and the forecasts, or to rebuild the model altogether.

Evolution vs. Stationarity

Principles of univariate time-series analysis can be used to assess which of two important conditions holds in a marketing system: stationary (mean-reverting) behavior vs. evolving (ever-changing) behavior. So, for example, if a brand enjoys a sudden surge in sales performance, the question arises whether that surge is of a temporary (short-run) or permanent (long-run) nature. *Unit-root tests* identify the presence of a long-run or stochastic-trend component in a series' data generating process. In the absence of a unit root, all observed fluctuations in a brand's performance or marketing support are temporary deviations from a deterministic component (such as a fixed mean or a deterministic trend). With a unit root, no such mean reversion occurs, i.e. the time series may wander widely apart from any previously held position.

Unit-Root Tests

Consider for simplicity the case where a brand's sales over time (Q_t) are described by a first-order autoregressive process:

$$(1 - \phi L)Q_t = \alpha_0 + w_t, \tag{6.95}$$

where ϕ is an autoregressive parameter, L the lag operator, i.e., $L^k Q_t = Q_{t-k}$, w_t a series of zero-mean, constant-variance s_w^2 and uncorrelated random shocks, and c a constant. Applying successive backward substitutions allows us to write equation (6.95) as

$$Q_t = \left[\alpha_0 / (1 - \phi)\right] + w_t + \phi w_{t-1} + \phi^2 w_{t-2} + \cdots, \tag{6.96}$$

in which the present value of Q_t is explained as a weighted sum of random shocks. Depending on the value of ϕ, two scenarios can be distinguished. When $0 < \phi < 1$, the impact of past shocks diminishes and eventually becomes negligible. Hence each shock has only a temporary impact. In this case, the series has a fixed mean $\alpha_0/(1 - \phi)$ and a finite variance $s_w^2/(1 - \phi^2)$. Such a series is called *stationary*. When $\phi = 1$, however, (6.96) becomes:

$$Q_t = (\alpha_0 + \alpha_0 + \cdots) + w_t + w_{t-1} + \cdots, \tag{6.97}$$

implying that each random shock has a permanent effect on the brand's sales. In this case, no fixed mean is observed, and the variance increases with time. Sales do not revert to a historical level, but instead wander freely in one direction or another, i.e. they *evolve*. Distinguishing between both situations involves checking whether the autoregressive polynomial $(1 - \phi L)$ in equation (6.95) has a root on the unit circle. [3]

The previous discussion used the first-order autoregressive model to introduce the concepts of stationarity, evolution and unit roots. The findings can easily be generalized to the more complex autoregressive moving-average process $\Phi(L)Q_t = \theta(L)w_t$. Indeed, the stationary/evolving character of a series is completely determined by whether some of the roots of the autoregressive polynomial $\Phi(L) = (1 - \phi_1 L - \cdots - \phi_p L^p)$ are lying on the unit circle.

Numerous tests have been developed to distinguish stationary from evolving patterns. One popular test, due to Dickey and Fuller (1979), is based on the following test equation:

$$(1 - L)Q_t = \Delta Q_t = \alpha_0 + \beta Q_{t-1} + \alpha_1 \Delta Q_{t-1} + \cdots + \alpha_m \Delta Q_{t-m} + u_t. \qquad (6.98)$$

The t-statistic of β is compared with the critical values in Fuller (1976), and the unit-root null hypothesis is rejected if the obtained value is smaller than the critical value. Indeed, substituting $\beta = 0$ in (6.98) introduces a random-walk component in the model, whereas $-1 < \beta < 0$ implies a mean-reverting process. The lag length m is chosen empirically to control for other temporary movements in sales changes.[4]

Within a marketing context, the presence of a unit root in performance has been shown to be a necessary condition for long-run marketing effectiveness (see e.g. Baghestani 1991; Dekimpe and Hanssens 1995a). Indeed, if brand sales are evolving, we would want to know whether or not that evolution is related to either temporary or permanent changes in the marketing mix. Chapter 7 will examine this important strategic question in more detail.

Unit-root testing also deserves more attention in marketing research for statistical reasons. Indeed, it has long been recognized in econometrics that traditional hypothesis tests may be misleading when applied to non-stationary variables (see e.g. Granger and Newbold 1986). Within the marketing literature, however, one seldom tests for non-stationarity, even though this could result in spurious relationships between the variables of interest. Moroeover, if based on a visual inspection of the data, a prolonged up-or downward movement is found in the data, one tends to automatically include a deterministic trend (see e.g. Eastlack and Rao 1986; Rao and Bass 1985). The inappropriate use of deterministic trends may again create statistical problems, however, a finding which has been largely ignored in marketing.

Other unit-root testing procedures have been advocated to test for seasonal unit roots (see e.g. Dickey, Hasza and Fuller 1984; Hasza and Fuller 1982), to correct for outliers (Franses and Haldrup 1994), for heteroskedasticity in the error terms (Phillips 1987), and for structural breaks (e.g. Perron 1989, 1990). These extensions may be highly relevant in several marketing settings. For example, many product categories are subject to seasonal fluctuations in demand. Structural breaks may occur for a variety of reasons, such as new-product introductions, changes in distribution channels or patent expiration for pharmaceutical products. Outliers may be caused by strikes or unexpected supply shortages, and the growing turbulence in many competitive environments is expected to contribute to an increasing variability in performance and spending.

How much evolution and stationarity are we observing in real marketing data? Consider forty-four studies reporting over 400 univariate time series models on market performance and marketing mix data (Dekimpe and Hanssens 1995b). Evolutionary behavior was found in 54 percent of the reported models and stationarity in 46 percent. Furthermore, sales measures were predominantly evolving (68 percent) whereas market-share measures were predominantly stationary (78 percent). Therefore, if marketing is to have a long-run impact on performance, it would be more likely to occur at the sales level than at the market-share level.

Univariate Persistence

Unit-root tests were introduced to distinguish stationary from evolving markets. We now focus on the *quantitative importance* of the long-run components, which will provide further indication on how effective marketing can be in the long run. Indeed, if the observed long-run sales fluctuations are small compared to total fluctuations, most marketing effects will still be temporary. The presence of a unit root implies that a portion of a shock in sales will persist through time and affect its long-run behavior. The magnitude of this portion determines how much our long-run sales forecast should be changed when the current performance is different than expected. Let us examine the two extreme scenarios first.

In the absence of a unit root, sales return to their pre-shock mean level, and the long-run forecast is not affected by the unexpected component in performance (zero long-run effect). On the other hand, for a pure random walk, the best forecast at any point in time is its current value. Hence, a one-unit sales decrease today translates into a one-unit reduction of the long-run forecast (100 percent long-run effect). This is also shown in equation (6.97), which gave the infinite-shock representation of a random-walk process. It is clear that a unit shock in $(t - k)$ has a unit impact on all future values of Q_t.

In between mean reversion and random walk, we may observe, for example, an ARIMA(0,1,1) model with $q_1 = 0.6$, so that equation (6.96) becomes

$$Q_t = Q_{t-1} + \left(u_t - 0.6u_{t-1}\right) = u_t + 0.4u_{t-1} + 0.4u_{t-2} + 0.4u_{t-3} + \cdots . \qquad (6.99)$$

In this case, only 40% of an initial shock keeps influencing the brand's future sales levels, and an unexpected 100,000 unit sales decrease in the current period would lead to a 40,000 unit reduction in the long-run forecast. For still other values of the autoregressive and/or moving-average parameters, the magnitude of the retained portion may be even smaller.

Campbell and Mankiw (1987) developed a simple procedure to derive a series' univariate persistence as the sum of the moving-average coefficients of the *first-differenced* series. Consider the following univariate ARIMA specification

$$\Phi(L)\Delta Q_t = \Theta(L)w_t. \tag{6.100}$$

The infinite-shock representation of ΔQ_t is given by

$$\Delta Q_t = \left[\Phi(L)\right]^{-1}\Theta(L)w_t = A(L)w_t = \left(1 + \alpha_1 L + \alpha_2 L^2 + \cdots\right)w_t. \tag{6.101}$$

The impact of a unit shock in period $t - k$ on the sales *growth* in t is α_k (i.e. the partial derivative of ΔQ_t with respect to w_{t-k}). Its impact on the sales *level* in t is $1 + \alpha_1 + \cdots + \alpha_k$ as is obtained by taking the partial derivative of Q_t with respect to w_{t-k} in equation (6.102):

$$Q_t = (1-L)^{-1}(w_t + \alpha_1 w_{t-1} + \cdots) = \sum_{i=-\infty}^{t} w_i + \alpha_1 \sum_{i=-\infty}^{t-1} w_i + \cdots + \alpha_k \sum_{i=-\infty}^{t-k} w_i + \cdots. \tag{6.102}$$

Thus, the long-run impact on Q_t is given by the sum of the moving-average coefficients in (6.102), often denoted as $A(1)$. Since $A(1)$ equals $\Theta(1)/\Phi(1)$, estimates of $A(1)$ can be obtained by fitting ARMA models to ΔQ_t, and taking the ratio of the sum of the moving-average coefficients $\left(1 - \theta_1 - \cdots - \theta_q\right)$ to the sum of the autoregressive coefficients $\left(1 - \phi_1 - \cdots - \phi_q\right)$.

Estimates of sales and marketing persistence are beginning to appear in the marketing literature. For example, the monthly order patterns for a computer peripheral product were found to be evolving, but with low persistence (12 percent). On the other hand, the retail sales patterns for the same product had much higher persistence (68 percent). Thus external signals coming from end-users have longer-lasting effects on demand than those coming from the channels (Hanssens 1998).

Notes

[1] Many important sample statistics have desirable large-sample properties for 30 observations or more. When complex models are needed to describe the data, this minimum may be higher, for example, in the case of seasonal models.

[2] As the section title implies, the discussion is restricted to linear time series models. Nonlinearities are typically incorporated by transforming the data. Formal nonlinear time series models exist, but they have not been used in marketing to date. See, for example, Mohler (1988).

[3] Evolving patterns may also arise because of seasonal factors. Consider, for example, the seasonal equivalent of (6.95): $\left(1 - \phi_d L^d\right)Q_t = \alpha_0 + w_t$, where d equals 12 for monthly data. Sales are seasonally evolving when $\left|\phi_d\right| = 1$. Tests for seasonal unit roots are similar in spirit to regular unit-root tests, but require different critical values (Dekimpe 1992).

[4] Because of these additional terms, this test is known as the "augmented" Dickey-Fuller (ADF) test. An important issue in applying the ADF test is the choice of m. Setting m too high results in a less powerful test, while a value that is too small may fail to make the u_t series white noise and bias the test statistics. Conventional significance tests on the α_t or an overall significance test can be used to determine the cut-off point.

7

MULTIPLE MARKETING
TIME SERIES

The major limitation of univariate time series analysis for the marketing model builder is that it does not handle cause-and-effect situations, which are at the heart of marketing planning. Thus, if we are using time series analysis to specify the lag structure in a response model, we must extend the techniques of univariate extrapolation to the case of multiple time series. As it turns out, empirical lag specification in marketing models is important because prior theory alone is insufficient to build models. In particular, there is a lack of understanding of the dynamic effects of marketing variables that are easy to control, such as price, sales calls and advertising.

There are two conditions for specifying lag structures on multiple time series:

1. Good time series data, i.e., sufficiently long time series (usually $T > 50$), collected at an appropriate data interval.

2. Statistical techniques that can effectively separate the lags between variables (the interstructure) from the lags within variables (the intrastructure).

Many of the advances in time series analysis in the last decades pertain to lag specification. We start with the single-equation marketing model, for example a sales response model, to illustrate transfer function analysis and intervention analysis. Next, we discuss the more difficult case of multiple-equation models, focusing on dynamic regression models and vector autoregressive techniques. We make specific reference to the inclusion of long-term equilibrium conditions in dynamic market response models. Last, but not least, we discuss methods for empirically assessing the causal ordering of a system of marketing time series.

The Transfer Function Model

Transfer function (TF) analysis is undoubtedly the most popular technique for analyzing multiple time series. It was first proposed by Box and Jenkins as a "dynamic" version of univariate analysis and has had numerous applications in the social and management sciences and in engineering. Helmer and Johansson (1977) introduced transfer functions in marketing for the purpose of modeling the sales-advertising relation. The basic model distinguishes an output series (Y) and one or more input series (X) in the following scheme:

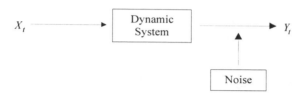

where the noise follows an ARIMA process independent of the input series. Thus, the model is (possibly after differencing X and Y):

$$y_t = \alpha_0 + \frac{\omega(L)}{\delta(L)} L^b x_t + \frac{\Theta L}{\Phi(L)} w_t, \tag{7.1}$$

where

$$\omega(L) = \omega_0 + \omega_1 L + \omega_2 L^2 + \cdots + \omega_s L^s,$$

$$\delta(L) = 1 - \delta_1 L - \delta_2 L^2 - \cdots - \delta_r L^r,$$

$$\Theta(L) = 1 - \theta_1 L - \theta_2 L^2 - \cdots - \theta_q L^q,$$

$$\Phi(L) = 1 - \phi_1 L - \phi_2 L^2 - \cdots - \phi_p L^p,$$

$$b = \text{delay operator.}$$

The *order* of the transfer function is said to be (r,s,b) and the added noise model is of order (p, q).

The transfer function is a straightforward extension of the ARMA model; for $\omega(L) = 0$, the model is equivalent to a univariate time series process. The transfer function parameters are interpreted as follows:

- The numerator parameters in $\omega(L)$ model the direct effects of changes in x on y over time. In the absence of denominator parameters [i.e., $\delta(L) \equiv 1$], the cumulative effect of x on y is simply the sum of these parameters:

$$\omega_0 + \omega_1 + \omega_2 + \cdots + \omega_s.$$

- The denominator parameters model the gradual adjustment of y to a change in x over time. Gradual adjustment occurs when a fraction of the direct effect carries over in subsequent periods. For example, an advertising campaign may introduce purchases from new buyers in the same period. In every subsequent period, a fraction of these new buyers may repeat their purchase. The cumulative effect of advertising is then computed as

$$\frac{\omega_0 + \omega_1 + \cdots + \omega_s}{1 - \delta_1 - \delta_2 - \cdots - \delta_r}.$$

The success of the transfer function in applied time series analysis is due in part to the fact that the traditional regression model is a special case of it. Indeed, if $\omega(L) = \omega_0$, and $\delta(L) = \Theta(L) = \Phi(L) \equiv 1$, we obtain:

$$y_t = \alpha_0 + \omega_0 x_t + w_t. \tag{7.2}$$

However, the philosophy of transfer function modeling differs from traditional regression modeling in two important ways: (1) specific attention is paid to the dynamic relation between input and output, i.e., the response parameter is polynomial in time, and (2) the error term is allowed to exhibit systematic behavior, as represented by the added noise term. For example, marketing efforts are known to have instantaneous and delayed effects on product performance; also, product sales often exhibit autoregressive patterns due to customer loyalty, slowly changing distribution, and the like. The transfer function is a highly realistic model for incorporating these phenomena.

Transfer function analysis is a set of techniques for specifying the dynamic relation between an output variable Y_t and one or more input variables X_t, plus an added noise ARMA process. The approach is similar to the iterative Box-Jenkins method for univariate time series: identification, tentative model specification, parameter estimation, and diagnostic checking. However, since multiple time series are involved, we need to introduce a new statistical tool, the cross-correlation function (CCF). Then, we explain the Box-Jenkins identification approach and the Liu-Hanssens (1982) method, which is more appropriate for multiple-input models.

Finally, we cover some principles of intervention analysis, i.e., transfer functions where the input variable is binary.

The Cross-Correlation Function

Without loss of generality, the bivariate stochastic process (X_t, Y_t), which generates successive observations over time, is

$$(X_1, Y_1), (X_2, Y_2), ..., (X_T, Y_T).$$

Assume that a transformation such as differencing exists so that each series (x_t, y_t) is stationary. Then we may define the sample autocovariance at lag k of x or y as

$$c_{yy}(k) = E(y_t - \bar{y})(y_{t-k} - \bar{y}) = \frac{1}{T} \sum_{t=k+1}^{T} (y_t - \bar{y})(y_{t-k} - \bar{y}), \tag{7.3}$$

$$c_{xx}(k) = E(x_t - \bar{x})(x_{t-k} - \bar{x}) = \frac{1}{T} \sum_{t=k+1}^{T} (x_t - \bar{x})(x_{t-k} - \bar{x}), \tag{7.4}$$

the sample cross-covariance between x and y at lag k as

$$c_{xy}(k) = E(y_t - \bar{y})(x_{t-k} - \bar{x}) = \frac{1}{T} \sum_{t=k+1}^{T} (y_t - \bar{y})(x_{t-k} - \bar{x}), \tag{7.5}$$

and the sample cross-correlation coefficient between x and y at lag k as

$$\gamma_{xy}(k) = \frac{E(y_t - \bar{y})(x_{t-k} - \bar{x})}{\sqrt{E(y_t - \bar{y})^2 \times E(x_t - \bar{x})^2}} = \frac{c_{xy}(k)}{\sqrt{c_{xx}(0) \times c_{yy}(0)}}. \tag{7.6}$$

Notice that while the autocovariance is symmetric around lag $k=0$, the cross-covariance and cross-correlation coefficients are not, i.e., $\gamma_{xy}(k) \neq \gamma_{yx}(k)$, but $\gamma_{xy}(k) = \gamma_{yx}(-k)$.

The cross-correlation function is the natural extension of the autocorrelation function when more than one time series is considered. Its interpretation is also parallel with univariate time series analysis: spikes in the CCF denote moving-average or numerator parameters, and dying-out patterns suggest autoregressive or denominator parameters. The CCF is used in virtually all applications of multiple time series analysis as a diagnostic tool for statistical relations among series, sometimes referred to as *interstructure*. However, such inferences are often hampered by the existence of within-series patterns, known as *intrastructure*, i.e., the sign and magnitude of a cross-correlation may be affected by the autocorrelation in both series. Formally, this implies that the standard errors of the CCF are a function of the ACFs of the series, so that we may obtain nonsensical correlations among time series. This problem was discovered long ago (Yule 1926) but it remains one of the main challenges in the statistical analysis of time series. We discuss its implications in conjunction with the various multiple time series models that are of interest to marketing modelers.

Transfer Function Identification: Single-Input Models

A transfer function is identified when appropriate order values of the transfer function (r, s, b) and the added noise (p, q) have been set. This is a sufficiently complex task so that we prefer to work with a simplified version of the model, called the *impulse response form:*

$$y_t = \alpha_0 + \left(v_0 + v_1 L + v_2 L^2 + \cdots \right) x_t + n_t \tag{7.7}$$

or

$$y_t = \alpha_0 + V(L) x_t + n_t, \tag{7.8}$$

where n_t is a short notation for the added noise process and $V(L)$ is finite when $r = 0$ and infinite when $r > 0$. Box and Jenkins (1976) suggest using the CCF to obtain preliminary estimates of the impulse response weights v_i as follows:

- *Step 1.* Find the ARMA model for the input x and store the residuals of that model. This step is known as *prewhitening* the input:

$$\hat{\Phi}(L) x_t = \hat{\Theta}(L) \hat{w}_t, \tag{7.9}$$

$$\hat{w}_t = \hat{\Theta}(L)^{-1} \hat{\Phi}(L) x_t. \tag{7.10}$$

- *Step 2.* Apply the *same* prewhitening filter to the output y and store the residuals:

$$\hat{\beta}_t = \hat{\Theta}(L)^{-1} \hat{\Phi}(L) y_t. \tag{7.11}$$

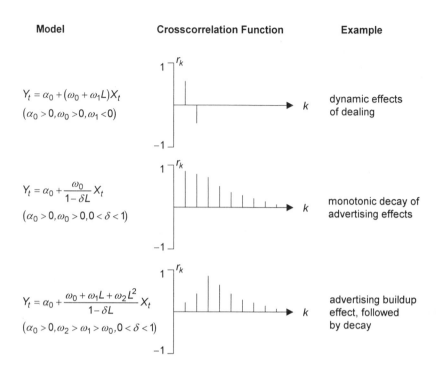

Figure 7-1. Transfer Functions and Cross-Correlation Patterns.

- *Step 3*. Compute the CCF between $\hat{w}_t$ and $\hat{\beta}_t$. It can be shown that

$$\hat{v}_j = \frac{s_{\hat{\beta}}}{s_{\hat{w}}} r_{\hat{w}\hat{\beta}}(j),\tag{7.12}$$

implying that the CCF is directly proportional to the impulse response weights.

The variance of a cross-correlation coefficient when at least one of the series is white noise is of the order $1/T$. Thus, hypothesis testing becomes relatively easy. Furthermore, a CCF pattern analysis similar to ACF analysis can be used to identify the values r, s, and b. Figure 7-1 shows some common transfer functions and the shapes of the CCFs that would lead to their identification. Once the values (r, s, b) are specified, the transfer function parameters can be estimated, usually by nonlinear least squares, and preliminary estimates of the noise series can be obtained:

$$\hat{n}_t = y_t - \hat{V}(L)x_t.\tag{7.13}$$

The ACF of the series $\hat{n}_t$ is now used to identify an appropriate added noise model. Finally, the complete transfer function-added noise model is estimated. As in univariate analysis, the method includes built-in diagnostic checking. In this case, two checks are necessary:

1. The ACF of the residuals should be flat. Any remaining patterns are modeled via the added noise parameters $\Phi(L)$ and $\Theta(L)$.

2. The CCF of the residuals and the (prewhitened) input should be flat. A spike at, say, $k=2$ would indicate that a response effect at lag 2 was omitted from the transfer function, which can be corrected by adding a parameter.

The prewhitening method for TF analysis has stood the test of time, as witnessed by its numerous applications. Nevertheless, there are a few weaknesses in this approach, which are due to the bivariate (pairwise) nature of the identification strategy. In multiple-input situations we must specify each transfer function separately, under the implicit assumption that the inputs are independent of one another. The method quickly becomes time-consuming and may produce conflicting results when the final model combining all inputs is estimated. Finally, some applications report that the results may be sensitive to the choice of a prewhitening model for x.

Transfer Function Identification: Multiple-Input Models

Multiple-input models are common in market response analysis. Indeed, most marketing decisions involve resource allocations among various activities, for example, media planning. The multiple-input transfer function allows for differences in the dynamic response of, say, sales to various marketing efforts.

Using the CCF method makes it necessary to individually prewhiten each explanatory variable in the model. If management uses one decision rule for advertising planning, another for price setting, and so on, substantially different ARMA models for these time series may be obtained. Furthermore, the sum of all these pairwise transfer functions may be different from the overall market response model. Regression analysis has long resolved the problems associated with pairwise correlations. The multiple regression model can be used in transfer function identification as long as we are particularly careful about the time series properties of the data. A least-squares regression method due to Liu and Hanssens (1982) offers the robustness and ease of use of multiple regression while avoiding the pitfalls of making inferences from autocorrelated data.

Suppose the following two-input transfer function model on stationary data is to be identified:

$$y_t = \alpha_0 + \frac{\omega_1(L)}{\delta_1(L)} L^{b_1} x_{1t} + \frac{\omega_2(L)}{\delta_2(L)} L^{b_2} x_{2t} + \frac{\Theta(L)}{\Phi(L)} w_t \,. \tag{7.14}$$

The impulse response form of the transfer function is

$$y_t = \alpha_0 + V_1(L)x_{1t} + V_2(L)x_{2t} + n_t \,. \tag{7.15}$$

If the transfer function contains rational (denominator) parameters, the impulse response polynomials are infinite. However, since these parameters die out under the stationarity assumption, they can be approximated in practice with a finite number of terms, say k_1 and k_2. Thus, the identification model is a *direct-lag regression equation*:

$$\begin{aligned}
y_t = \alpha_0 &+ \left(v_{10} + v_{11}L + \cdots + v_{1k_1} L^{k_1} \right) x_{1t} \\
&+ \left(v_{20} + v_{21}L + \cdots + v_{2k_2} L^{k_2} \right) x_{2t} + u_t,
\end{aligned} \tag{7.16}$$

where k_1 and k_2 are chosen sufficiently large to avoid truncation bias. The direct-lag regression model can be estimated by ordinary least squares, and the pattern of the OLS coefficients is used to identify cutoff versus dying-out patterns.

Two problems may arise in the least-squares procedure: (1) the lagged input variables may be highly collinear, and (2) the residuals of the model may not be white noise. It is well known that the first condition leads to unstable parameter estimates and the second condition makes OLS inefficient. Liu and Hanssens (1982) observe that collinearity results from highly autoregressive input series; for example, if x_{1t} is AR(1) with parameter 0.9, then each input variable is 0.9 correlated with the next variable. In contrast, if x_{1t} follows an MA(1) process with parameter 0.9, then the successive correlations in the data matrix would only be 0.45. Therefore, they propose to filter the data prior to OLS estimation, using a common filter that eliminates the AR factors close to 1. For example, if the ARMA processes for the inputs are

$$(1 - 0.8L)x_{1t} = \left(1 - 0.62L^2 \right) w_{1t}, \tag{7.17}$$

$$(1 - 0.5L)\left(1 - 0.85L^4 \right) x_{2t} = w_{2t} \tag{7.18}$$

a common filter $(1 - 0.8L)\left(1 - 0.85L^4 \right)$ would be recommended. The second problem, nonwhite residuals, can be handled by applying generalized least squares (GLS) estimates in lieu of OLS. The practical GLS application consists of two steps: (1) find the ARMA process underlying the residuals from OLS estimation, and (2) transform the data by these ARMA filters and reestimate. It is seldom necessary to engage in such an iterative procedure, though, as the OLS identification results alone are typically satisfactory.

There are several variations on least-squares identification of transfer functions. For example, a study on distributed lag modeling proposes the use of ridge regression estimators to circumvent the problem of collinearity in direct-lag estimation (Erickson 1981b). A transfer function identification method combining common filters and ridge regression has been developed (Edlund 1984).

Intervention Analysis

Although many marketing variables like price, distribution, and communication expenditures are quantifiable, some are not, and yet their impact on market performance may be substantial. A qualitative change in advertising copy, the advent of a new government regulation, or the sudden presence of a foreign competitor in a market are but a few examples of nonquantifiable inputs in a marketing model. To the extent that the effects of such inputs are spread over time, multiple time series methods are needed to identify their impact and measure their magnitude. Intervention analysis is a dynamic version of dummy variable regression analysis that was specifically designed to handle such modeling tasks (Box and Tiao 1975). Qualitative events or interventions exist in two forms:

1. A pulse dummy variable, where the intervention occurs and disappears sometime in the future:

$$D_{pulse,t} = \begin{cases} 0 & \text{for all } t < k, \text{ the intervention period} \\ 1 & \text{for } k \leq t \leq k+l \\ 0 & \text{for all } t > k+l \end{cases}.$$

Marketing examples include airline strikes, discount periods, "happy hours," and advertising campaigns.

2. A step dummy variable, where the intervention is permanent once it has occurred:

$$D_{step,t} = \begin{cases} 0 & \text{for all } t < k \\ 1 & \text{for all } t \geq k \end{cases}.$$

Examples are a major product reformulation, the exit of a competitor, and the deregulation of an industry.

The general form of a pulse intervention model is

$$Y_t = \alpha_0 + \frac{\omega(L)}{\delta(L)} L^b D_{pulse,t} + \frac{\Theta(L)}{\Phi(L)} w_t \,, \tag{7.19}$$

where all parameters are as previously defined.

The difference between pulse and step interventions is important because it affects the shape of the intervention response function. Following Vandaele (1983), we can classify intervention effects as having an abrupt or a gradual start and a permanent or a temporary duration. Price promotion effects on sales are typically abrupt, while some image advertising campaigns affect sales in a gradual way. Permanent effects in marketing are expected to be related mainly to step interventions, such as product modification or new distribution channels. However, even step interventions may have only temporary effects; for example, consumers may initially react negatively to a price hike but eventually adjust to previous purchase levels. Several intervention scenarios are shown graphically in Figure 7-2. In interpreting these graphs it is important to realize that the first difference of a step is a pulse, i.e.,

$$(1-L)D_{step,t} = D_{pulse,t} \,. \tag{7.20}$$

Thus, when a step intervention makes a time series nonstationary, we may model the change in the data (first differences) as a function of a pulse intervention. The identification of intervention models usually requires some a priori notion of the shape of the effect (i.e., abrupt or gradual start, temporary or permanent duration), which is not difficult to obtain in a marketing context. However, the intervention may interfere with the univariate ARMA model underlying the data, so that we must be careful to separate the two. Three situations may arise:

1. There is a sufficiently long pre-intervention time series so that the ARMA model can be identified from ACF-PACF analysis of the preintervention data. Then the ARMA and intervention components are estimated jointly on the entire time series.

2. A separate time series exists that has not been affected by the intervention. For example, in a study of the effects of a communication campaign on city bus ridership, Tybout and Hauser (1981) used the time series of an adjacent city to establish a univariate model, which was then applied to the campaign city. The method is commonly known as *interrupted time series analysis* and is most popular in experimental research (e.g., Cook and Campbell 1979). Krishnamurthi,

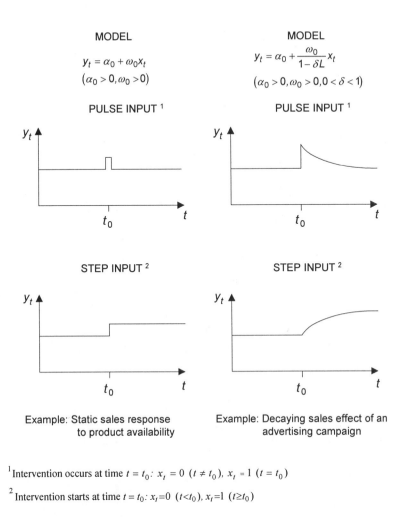

MODEL

$$y_t = \alpha_0 + \omega_0 x_t$$
$$(\alpha_0 > 0, \omega_0 > 0)$$

PULSE INPUT [1]

MODEL

$$y_t = \alpha_0 + \frac{\omega_0}{1 - \delta L} x_t$$
$$(\alpha_0 > 0, \omega_0 > 0, 0 < \delta < 1)$$

PULSE INPUT [1]

STEP INPUT [2]

STEP INPUT [2]

Example: Static sales response to product availability

Example: Decaying sales effect of an advertising campaign

[1] Intervention occurs at time $t = t_0$: $x_t = 0$ $(t \neq t_0)$, $x_t = 1$ $(t = t_0)$

[2] Intervention starts at time $t = t_0$: $x_t = 0$ $(t < t_0)$, $x_t = 1$ $(t \geq t_0)$

Figure 7-2. Intervention Scenarios.

Narayan, and Raj (1986) discuss intervention modeling techniques for measuring the buildup effect of advertising by experimental design.

3. Neither a long pre-intervention period nor an uninterrupted time series exist. Here the modeler is forced to specify one of the components first and to identify the other component from the residuals in the first step. We recommend starting the analysis with the dominant component; for example, an abrupt and permanent shift in the level of the data should be modeled first. Either way, careful judgment and prior knowledge must be used to specify the model, and the usual diagnostic checks should be applied to the residuals of the model.

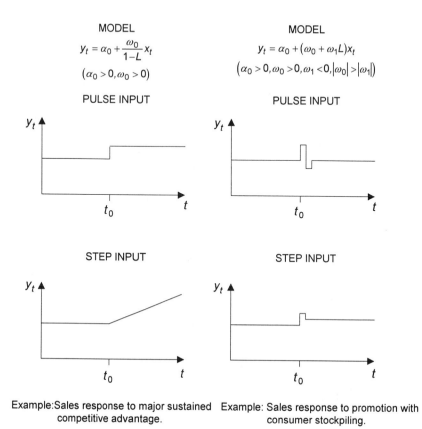

MODEL

$$y_t = \alpha_0 + \frac{\omega_0}{1-L} x_t$$

$$(\alpha_0 > 0, \omega_0 > 0)$$

PULSE INPUT

MODEL

$$y_t = \alpha_0 + (\omega_0 + \omega_1 L) x_t$$

$$(\alpha_0 > 0, \omega_0 > 0, \omega_1 < 0, |\omega_0| > |\omega_1|)$$

PULSE INPUT

STEP INPUT

STEP INPUT

Example: Sales response to major sustained competitive advantage.

Example: Sales response to promotion with consumer stockpiling.

Figure 7-2 (continued)

Lag Specification in Multiple-Equation Models

Whether an a priori theoretical or an empirical method for model specification is used, it is possible that the ultimate marketing model contains multiple equations. Then the identification of lag structures and the estimation of parameters pose some special challenges. First, some marketing variables may be jointly endogenous, i.e., they are both caused by and cause other elements in the system. Second, the shocks in the system may not be white noise, in which case we must be careful not to confuse lagged-variable effects and lagged-error effects in estimation.

The vector ARMA (VARMA) model is a general representation of a system of time-series processes. While empirical specification methods for the VARMA model exist, they have not found much application in the literature. Instead, the vector autoregressive (VAR) model, which is related to the VARMA specification, is more widely used to study the dynamics of market-response processes, and especially their long-term effects.

Vector ARMA (VARMA) Model. The multivariate ARMA model for a $k \times 1$ vector of stationary observations $\mathbf{z}_t$ is

$$\Phi(L)\mathbf{z}_t = \alpha_0 + \Theta(L)\mathbf{w}_t, \tag{7.21}$$

where $\alpha_0 = k \times 1$ vector of constants;

$\Phi(L) = \mathbf{I} - \phi_1 L - \cdots - \phi_p L^p$; each matrix ϕ contains autoregressive

parameters and is of order $k \times k$;

$\Theta(L) = \mathbf{I} - \theta_1 L - \cdots - \theta_q L^q$; each matrix θ contains moving average

parameters and is of order $k \times k$;

$\mathbf{w}_t = k \times 1$ vector of white noise error terms generally assumed to be i.i.d.

multivariate normal with $E(\mathbf{w}_t) = 0$ and $E(\mathbf{w}_t \mathbf{w}_t') = \Sigma$.

The vector ARMA model is a logical extension of univariate Box-Jenkins analysis to multiple time series. The diagonal elements of the matrices $\Phi(L)$ and $\Theta(L)$ contain within-series lagged effects. That makes it a very comprehensive model from a statistical perspective. Furthermore, the model does not require a priori distinction between endogenous and exogenous variables.

The original specification method is due to Tiao and Box (1981), and subsequent improvements and variations were proposed by Tiao and Tsay (1983) and Tsay (1985). The two basic identification tools are as follows:

1. The sample cross-correlation matrix that contains the simple correlations among the series at various lags k. Tiao and Box (1981) use indicator symbols +,−, and 0 for positive, negative, and insignificant correlations instead of the actual values in order to identify patterns that are cutting off or dying out with increasing k. As in univariate modeling, the cutoffs indicate moving-average parameters [matrix $\Theta(L)$], and the dying-out patterns suggest an autoregressive process [matrix $\Phi(L)$].

2. Partial autocorrelation matrices $\mathbf{P}(l)$, which are obtained by fitting successively higher AR(l) models to the data. They are interpreted in the same spirit as the PACF: as soon as the "true" AR order p is reached, the elements of $\mathbf{P}(l)$ for $l > p$ will be zero.

Once the model is identified, the parameters are estimated using conditional or exact likelihood procedures. Diagnostic checking of the residual cross- correlation matrices may reveal model inadequacies that can be correlated, as in the univariate diagnostic checking stage.

Vector ARMA modeling is a promising tool for forecasting multiple time series without regard to causal ordering in the system. For example, Moriarty (1985b) used it to illustrate the relative value of objective versus judgment forecasts in a marketing setting. VARMA models have some limitations, though. First, the technique is based on a "reduced form" model, where contemporaneous endogenous effects are represented through the residual covariance matrix. Furthermore, the use of correlational techniques on raw data carries the danger of modeling spurious effects and, in general, may cause overparameterized models.

Vector Autoregressive (VAR) Model. Recent attention in dynamic econometrics has focused on the VAR model, which is a VARMA model in which the moving-average terms are inverted and included on the autoregressive side. The VAR specification allows relatively straightforward least-squares estimation since there are no non-linear moving-average terms with which to deal. The general representation of a VAR model is:

$$\Phi(L)\mathbf{z}_t = \alpha_0 + \mathbf{w}_t, \tag{7.22}$$

where the parameters are defined as in (7.21).

Since VAR models are easier to estimate and interpret than VARMA models, they have been used more frequently in market response models, notably by Dekimpe and Hanssens (1995a, 1999) and by Dekimpe, Hanssens and Silva-Risso (1999). In particular, VAR modeling offers a unique opportunity to study the long-run dynamic structure among marketing variables, using the concept of multivariate persistence.

Multivariate Persistence

Multivariate persistence derives the long-run impact of an unexpected change in a control variable. Following Dekimpe and Hanssens (1995a), we first discuss the quantification of a marketing decision's *total* impact and then the *unexpected* nature of the effort. Next, we discuss the mechanics involved in the derivation of multivariate persistence estimates.

The Total Effect

There are six channels through which a marketing action can influence a brand's performance: 1) contemporaneous, 2) carryover, 3) purchase-reinforcement, and 4) feedback effects, 5) firm-specific decision rules and 6) competitive reactions (Dekimpe and Hanssens 1995a). In quantifying the total long-run impact of a marketing action, all channels of influence should be accounted for. The authors use the advertising-sales relationship as a case in point to illustrate the six channels.

Contemporaneous effects. Advertising often has a considerable immediate impact on sales. For example, Leone and Schultz (1980) call the positive elasticity of selective advertising one of marketing's first empirical generalizations.

Carryover effects. The effect of advertising in one period may be carried over, at least partially, into future periods (see e.g. Givon and Horsky 1990). Consumers are supposed to remember past advertising messages and create "goodwill" towards the brand. However, because of a gradual forgetting, only part of an initial effect may remain effective in subsequent periods.

Purchase reinforcement. A given ad effort may create a new customer who will not only make an initial purchase, but also repurchase in future periods (Givon and Horsky 1990). Likewise, advertising can provide an incentive for innovators to try a new product after which an imitation effect takes over, creating a larger customer base and higher future sales (Horksy and Simon 1983). According to Bass and Clarke (1972) and Hanssens, Parsons, and Schultz (1990, p. 49), current advertising spending should receive credit for these subsequent sales, *since, without the effort, no incremental sales would have occurred.*

Feedback effects. Bass (1969) warned that advertising spending may be influenced by current and past sales, and should not be treated as exogenous. This is certainly the case when percentage-of-sales budgeting rules are applied. As a result, an initial ad spending increase may cause a chain reaction via higher sales and profits, leading to further ad budget increases.

Firm-specific decision rules. Advertising spending levels are generally correlated with previous expenditures or levels of other marketing variables. For example, time-series models often find significant autoregressive components in a firm's spending pattern (see e.g. Hanssens 1980). In other words, spending this January tends to be related to last December's advertising, or to current levels of sales support to the product line. Here again, a chain reaction may occur which affects the total long-run impact.

Competitive reactions. Competitive activities may change advertising's effectiveness. For example, even though the instantaneous sales response may be positive, its long-run effect could be near zero because of competitive reactions. Leeflang and Wittink (1992) and Metwally (1978) offer some discussion on this self-canceling effect.

Modeling Unexpected or Shock Movements

Persistence calculations not only incorporate total effects, they also focus on tracing the over-time impact of *unexpected* movements (shocks), as opposed to more traditional market-response models which consider *absolute* spending or price levels.

When deciding on marketing spending, managers start with the formulation of a baseline sales forecast against which marketing mix changes can be evaluated. A logical choice is *a no-change scenario* in which all historically observed spending and reaction patterns are assumed to persist in the future (Litterman 1984). Within this framework, one-step-ahead sales and advertising forecasts (i.e., $\hat{Q}_{t+1}$ and $\hat{A}_{t+1}$) can be interpreted as the performance and expenditure levels that are expected on the basis of the available information up to that time. Deviations from the one-step ahead forecasts reflect unexpected shocks, whose *differential* impact can be traced over time. Multivariate persistence provides empirical estimates of these differential impacts.

Multivariate Persistence Estimates

We use a vector-autoregressive (VAR) model to derive multivariate persistence estimates, because it easily captures Dekimpe and Hanssens' six channels of influence and is free of a priori structural restrictions. Consider the following bivariate model between stationary advertising and sales:

$$\begin{bmatrix} Q_t \\ ADV_t \end{bmatrix} = \begin{bmatrix} \pi_{11}^1 & \pi_{12}^1 \\ \pi_{21}^1 & \pi_{22}^1 \end{bmatrix} \begin{bmatrix} Q_{t-1} \\ ADV_{t-1} \end{bmatrix} + \cdots + \begin{bmatrix} \pi_{11}^I & \pi_{12}^I \\ \pi_{21}^I & \pi_{22}^I \end{bmatrix} \begin{bmatrix} Q_{t-I} \\ ADV_{t-I} \end{bmatrix} + \begin{bmatrix} w_{Q,t} \\ w_{ADV,t} \end{bmatrix}, \quad (7.23)$$

where I is the order of the model, which may be determined using Akaike's Information Criterion, and where $\mathbf{w}_t = \begin{bmatrix} w_{Q,t}, w_{ADV,t} \end{bmatrix}'$ is a white-noise vector. All elements in $\bar{\mathbf{X}}_t = \begin{bmatrix} Q_t, ADV_t \end{bmatrix}'$ are related to all elements in $\bar{\mathbf{X}}_{t-1}$ ($i=1, ..., I$), making VAR models very useful for describing the lagged structure in the data.

Contemporaneous effects are captured indirectly in the covariance matrix of the residuals **S**. This matrix can detect significant effects, but cannot establish their direction.

To analyze the impact of marketing shocks over time, we can write the VAR model as an infinite-order vector-moving-average (VMA) representation:

$$\begin{bmatrix} Q_t \\ ADV_t \end{bmatrix} = \begin{bmatrix} 1 & 0 \\ 0 & 1 \end{bmatrix} \begin{bmatrix} w_{Q,t} \\ w_{ADV,t} \end{bmatrix} + \begin{bmatrix} \alpha_{11}^1 & \alpha_{12}^1 \\ \alpha_{21}^1 & \alpha_{22}^1 \end{bmatrix} \begin{bmatrix} w_{Q,t-1} \\ w_{ADV,t-1} \end{bmatrix}$$
$$+ \begin{bmatrix} \alpha_{11}^2 & \alpha_{12}^2 \\ \alpha_{21}^2 & \alpha_{22}^2 \end{bmatrix} \begin{bmatrix} w_{Q,t-2} \\ w_{ADV,t-2} \end{bmatrix} + \cdots,$$

(7.24)

where α_{12}^k gives the impact on Q_t of a one-unit advertising shock that happened k periods ago. A sequence of successive α_{ij}s is called an impulse-response function, and it reflects the complex interactions of all included channels of influence. Impulse response functions are often depicted graphically for effective communication of dynamic marketing effects.

When the marketing time series are stationary, the impulse response function eventually wears out and the brand's performance returns to its pre-shock mean level, as shown in Figure 7-3. In that case, the persistence is zero. When dealing with evolving variables, $\bar{\mathbf{X}}_t$ is replaced by $D\bar{\mathbf{X}}_t = [\Delta Q, \Delta ADV]'$ in equation system (7.24), in which case α_{ij}^k gives the impact of a unit shock on the sales growth k periods later. The response function tracing the impact on an evolving variable can converge to a non-zero level, and this level corresponds to the multivariate extension of Campbell and Mankiw's $A(1)$ measure discussed in the previous chapter. Figure 7-3 also shows a scenario of non-zero multivariate persistence: an unexpected change in advertising spending leads to a permanent change, both in advertising spending and in sales response.

On a technical note, estimates of multivariate persistence are sensitive to the specification of a causal ordering among the contemporaneous effects [see Dekimpe and Hanssens (1999) for details]. In the reality of high-quality, short-time interval marketing databases, instant marketing effects are usually of the market response variety because customers can react more quickly to marketing mix changes than competitors. This makes it easier to hypothesize a causal ordering and estimate persistence. Good practice suggests checking the robustness of the results with several causal orderings, or using methods that simulate correlated shocks without the need for causal ordering (e.g. Evans and Wells 1983).

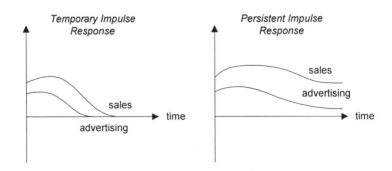

Figure 7-3. Examples of impulse response functions

Multivariate persistence of advertising media effects have been estimated for a chain of home-improvement stores (Dekimpe and Hanssens 1995a). The authors found that price-oriented print advertising had high short-term impact on sales with low persistence. On the other hand, image-oriented radio/TV advertising had lower short-term sales effect, but higher persistence. When netting out the persistent spending effects of changes in print or electronic advertising, both media turned out to have negative long-run profit consequences for the firm.

Another use of multivariate persistence is in consumer sales and dealer order forecasting for manufacturers of high-technology products (Hanssens 1998). The author's key finding is that unexpected changes in dealer orders have very low persistence, i.e., most of the short-term change dissipates in the long run. On the other hand, sudden changes in consumer demand carry a strong long-term signal, as their persistence level is high. Whether the context is marketing mix planning or sales forecasting, estimating multivariate persistence is a powerful approach for assessing the long-term consequences of observed changes in market or marketing mix conditions.

In some cases, marketing variables can be hypothesized to be in a long-run equilibrium condition with one another. For example, gradual increases in product distribution may be associated with steady sales increases, but if the distribution trend is reversed, sales may move downward. We will use a somewhat different approach for incorporating such equilibrium conditions in market response.

Incorporating Long-term Equilibrium Conditions

Suppose two marketing variables each have a unit root, i.e., they are individually evolving over time. Then an important question arises to what extent these underlying stochastic trends are related to each other, i.e. whether a systematic or long-run equilibrium relationship exists between the variables that prevents them from wandering apart. For example, we may ask whether a product's sales and advertising are moving together (co-evolving) over time as a result of market response and advertising budgeting behaviors (see e.g., Baghestani 1991; Zanias 1994). Managers also wonder whether a product category's long-run evolution is related to the evolution in some macro-economic variables (Franses 1994) and, if so, which ones.

Cointegration

Formally, the existence of such long-run equilibria is quantified through the cointegration concept (Engle and Granger 1987). In the case of two evolving marketing variables sales and advertising, cointegration means that a systematic relationship exists between the two variables that prevents them from moving too far apart in the long run. If ad spending is increased, market response pressure eventually increases sales to restore the equilibrium. Conversely, when sales are higher, budgeting pressures eventually increase ad spending to again restore the equilibrium.

If an exact relationship existed between the two series, they would be tied together under a linear constraint of the form (e.g., Powers et al. 1991):

$$Y_t = \beta_0 + \beta_1 X_t. \qquad (7.25)$$

In practice, however, it is unlikely for any equilibrium relationship to hold exactly in every single time period. Rather, we expect to see in every period some finite deviation from the perfect equilibrium. The actual relationship is then given by

$$Y_t = \beta_0 + \beta_1 X_t + e_t, \qquad (7.26)$$

where e_t is called the *equilibrium* error. The existence of a long-run equilibrium relation between X_t and Y_t (each of which has a unit root), requires e_t to be mean-reverting. Indeed, if e_t still had a unit root, X_t and Y_t could drift widely apart from one another, and they would not be tied together in the long run. In conclusion, cointegration exists when the individual variables are each evolving, but the error series of the regression between them is stationary. This intuitively appealing setup is empirically testable and therefore implementable in long-run market response modeling.

A simple test for cointegration was proposed by Engle and Granger (1987): first estimate equation (7.26) with OLS, and subsequently test the residuals for the presence of a unit root, albeit with somewhat different critical values (Engle and Yoo 1987). This simple OLS estimator has been shown to be super-consistent, which implies that simultaneous-equation biases disappear asymptotically, and that the rate of convergence to the true underlying value is fast. On the other hand, there could be small-sample bias, and with more than two variables, there could be more than one cointegrating vector that cannot be estimated with OLS.

Johansen's (1988) full-information maximum-likelihood testing and estimation method addresses these limitations and has become the most widely used procedure. It starts from the following vector-autoregressive representation:

$$\bar{\mathbf{X}}_t = \mathbf{c} + \mathbf{\Pi}_1 \bar{\mathbf{X}}_{t-1} + \cdots + \mathbf{\Pi}_k \bar{\mathbf{X}}_{t-k} + \mathbf{w}_t . \tag{7.27}$$

Let $\mathbf{\Gamma}_i = -\mathbf{I}_N + \mathbf{\Pi}_1 + \cdots + \mathbf{\Pi}_i$ ($i = 1, 2,...,k$). Then the number of cointegrating vectors is determined by the rank of $\mathbf{\Gamma}_i$, which can be written as the product of two full-rank matrices:

$$\mathbf{\Gamma}_k = -\mathbf{w}\boldsymbol{\beta}', \tag{7.28}$$

where the rows of $\boldsymbol{\beta}'$ provide the base vectors for the r-dimensional cointegration space. We refer the reader to Johansen (1988) or Johansen and Uselius (1990) for a more detailed discussion of this FIML approach.

Error-Correction Models

If cointegration exists between two or more variables, these long-run linkages should be accounted for when modeling the short-run relationships between them. Engle and Granger (1987) showed that this can be achieved through a special error-correction mechanism, which is a response model in differences augmented by the lagged equilibrium error:

$$\Delta Y_t = \alpha_0 + \alpha_1 \Delta Y_{t-1} + \alpha_2 \Delta X_{t-1} + \alpha_3 e_{t-1} + u_t \tag{7.29}$$

The lagged equilibrium error parameter is a measure of the speed of adjustment towards the long-run equilibrium. For example, if sales are unusually high given the current level of advertising spending, the resulting disequilibrium in budgeting may push the company to increase its advertising spending. Engle and Granger's OLS approach to error-correction modeling saves the residuals of the equilibrium regression (7.26), and subsequently adds the lagged-residuals term e_{t-1} as an additional explanatory variable. In Johansen's FIML approach, equation (7.28) is already written in error-correction form, so the speed of adjustment parameters are estimated as part of the procedure.

Powers et.al. (1991) used the Engle and Granger method to estimate the adjustment of narcotics abuse to changes in methadone administration. More recently, Dekimpe and Hanssens (1995a) used Johansen's estimator to model differences in long-term effectiveness between print and electronic media advertising. From a forecasting perspective, the addition of error-correction terms in a transfer function model on differences ensures that information on the system's long-run equilibrium is taken into account. Because of this additional piece of long-run information, a higher forecasting accuracy is obtained, especially for longer forecasting horizons (Engle and Yoo 1987; Powers et al. 1991). For example, Hanssens (1998) found that incorporating equilibrium adjustment between factory orders and retail sales in a model of orders improved the accuracy of forecasts by 63 percent over a benchmark univariate model. The *Hewlett-Packard Industry Perspective* in this chapter elaborates on the application of time-series techniques for order forecasting.

Diagnosing Long-Term Marketing Strategic Scenarios

The methods of unit-root testing and measuring persistence and cointegration can be combined to diagnose four strategic marketing scenarios (Dekimpe and Hanssens 1999). When market performance and the marketing mix are all stationary, i.e. they follow I(0) patterns, we conclude that the strategic scenario is *business as usual*. Sales and/or market share have reached an equilibrium, i.e. their fluctuations are only temporary in nature, and the same can be said for marketing spending and prices. In this case, market-response models pick up temporary marketing effects, even though these can be distributed over several time periods. Many stationary market-share models fall in this category (see, for example, Srinivasan et al. 1999).

When market performance evolves, but marketing is stationary, we diagnose a condition called *hysteresis*: temporary movements in price or marketing can permanently impact future sales (Little 1979). Positive hysteresis can be highly beneficial to a marketer because permanent economic returns are generated from temporary actions. Some cases of hysteresis have been described by Simon (1997), and empirical support is provided in Dekimpe, Hanssens, and Silva-Risso (1999) and in Hanssens and Ouyang (2000). Hanssens and Ouyang also develop long-term profit maximizing allocation rules when marketing has hysteretic effects on sales.

Forecasting Inkjet Printers at Hewlett-Packard Company

At the Vancouver Division of Hewlett-Packard, where several models of DeskJet printers are produced, factory orders are forecast for printers by product number, by option, and by region. The division is responsible for the worldwide consolidation of numbers from all the different regions and creating the overall forecast. The regions (represented by marketing centers) provide input to the division in the form of a first-pass forecast. To develop their forecasts, the marketing centers receive input from the sales people in the different countries that make up their regions. In some cases the marketing centers also receive input from major customers.

In a search for a more consistent and accurate forecast process, HP investigated a variety of tools and techniques, while continuing to collect data. The conclusion was that the existing forecast process was sound for HP's business environment, but that there was a need to restrict the degrees of freedom in the process by making it more quantitatively and less judgmentally based.

HP re-evaluated regression techniques on time-series data, the equivalent of transfer functions. Six years of data on some printer families turned out to be sufficient to construct some multiple regression models that have reasonable predictive ability for the short term. Management likes the idea of time-series regression models because they provide a "causal" structure similar to their current judgmental models and allow for "what if" scenario based forecasting. The models are designed around the components of the "marketing mix" since management knows in advance of the changes that are likely to be made in HP's marketing plans. The models can also be used to determine what changes would be most successful. The basic model is as follows:

$$
\begin{array}{c}
\text{customer} \\
\text{sales}\,(t)
\end{array}
= f \left(
\begin{array}{c}
\text{customer} \\
\text{sales}\,(t-1)
\end{array},
\begin{array}{c}
\text{advertising} \\
\text{spend}
\end{array},
\begin{array}{c}
\text{new} \\
\text{distribution}
\end{array},
\text{price},
\begin{array}{c}
\text{product} \\
\text{feature} \\
\text{index}
\end{array}
\right)
$$

With this basic model, HP is able to explain up to 90% of the variance of historical sales on the key products with ex post forecasts.

For new products, HP will continue to use a combination of historical analogy, time-series regression, conjoint modeling, and judgment. An updated conjoint model, which is a primary research model of end user preferences of product attributes, will be the foundation of HP's future products.

Using modern multiple-time series techniques can help companies such as Hewlett Packard incorporate long-terms movements in end-user demand into their order forecasts. For example, the persistence of shocks in end-user demand is much greater than the persistence in order shocks. When manufacturers' orders suddenly increase, much of that change should be discounted, i.e. it has little effect on the long-term order outlook of the product, unless the shock is accompanied by a shock in end-user demand. In the long run, factory orders and end-user demand are cointegrated, so it is important to monitor the development in both for the purpose of sales forecasting and marketing-mix intervention.

Drawn from Joel Bryant and Kim Jensen, "Forecasting Inkjet Printers at Hewlett-Packard Company," Journal of Business Forecasting, 13:2 (Summer 1994), 27-28, and from Dominique M. Hanssens, "Order Forecasts, Retail Sales and the Marketing Mix for Consumer Durables," Journal of Forecasting, 17:3 /4 (June-July 1998), 327-46.

In conclusion, research on long-term marketing effects has benefited from recent developments in dynamic econometrics and multivariate time-series analysis. While the accumulated knowledge base is far from complete, a number of interesting findings have been published to date. Table 7-1 provides a summary of these findings, based on a recent review by Dekimpe and Hanssens (2000).

The reverse scenario is when market performance is stationary, yet marketing spending continues to evolve, a condition called *escalation*. Companies are some-times engages in fierce marketing spending battles, yet industry demand does not increase and, consequently, profit pressures develop. A more favorable scenario for the marketer is when prices escalate, but relative prices and overall demand remain stable. A case of price escalation with stable sales for a frequently purchased product has been diagnosed (Dekimpe and Hanssens 1999).

Finally, a *co-evolution* condition may be observed, where both sales and the marketing mix evolve over time. This implies that a long-term dynamic equilibrium exists between them, and that vector-error correction is needed to represent both the short-run and the long-run movements in the market. illustrate The long-term profit implications of pharmaceutical marketing actions that co-evolve with sales is illustrated in Dekimpe and Hanssens (1999).

Table 7-1. Findings from Long-Run Time Series Models in Marketing

Study	Years	Period	Variable	Finding
Bronnenberg et al. (2000)	5	Weekly	Market share	Distribution coverage drives long-run market shares, especially the coverage evolution early in the life cycle.
Dekimpe and Hanssens (1995a)	6.3	Monthly	Industry sales (chain level); sales	Persistence measures quantify marketing's long-run effectiveness. Image-oriented and price-oriented advertising messages have a differential short- and long-run effect.
Dekimpe and Hanssens (1995b)	—	—	—	Sales series are mostly evolving, while a majority of market-share series is stationary.
Dekimpe and Hanssens (1999)	5; 4.4	Monthly	Sales	Different strategic scenarios (business as usual, escalation, hysteresis and evolving business practice) have different long-run profitability implications.
Dekimpe et al. (1999)	2.2	Weekly	Industry sales; sales	Little evidence of long-run promotional effects is found in FPCG markets.
Dekimpe et al. (1997)	1 or 2	Monthly and bi-monthly	Estimated brand loyalty (sales)	New product introductions may cause structural breaks in otherwise stationary loyalty patterns
Hanssens (1998)	3.7	Monthly	Sales	Factory orders and sales are in a long-run equilibrium, but shocks to either have different long-run consequences
Hanssens and Ouyang (2000)	5	Monthly	Sales	Derivation of advertising allocation rules (in terms of triggering versus maintenance spending) under hysteresis conditions

Source: Adapted from Dekimpe and Hanssens (2000).

Study	Years	Period	Variable	Finding
Nijs et al. (2001)	4	Weekly	Industry sales	Limited long-run category expansion effects of price promotions. The impact differs in terms of the marketing intensity, competitive structure, and competitive conduct in the industry.
Pauwels et al. (2000)	2.2	Weekly	Sales; industry sales	The decomposition of the promotional sales spike in category-incidence, brand-switching and purchase-quantity effects differs depending on the time frame considered (short versus long run).
Srinivasan and Bass (2000)	2	Weekly	Market share; sales; industry sales	Stable market shares are consistent with evolving sales if brand and category sales are cointegrated
Srinivasan et al. (2000)	7	Weekly	Market share	Temporary, gradual and structural price changes have a different impact on market shares.
Zanias (1994)	27	Annual	Sales	Feedback effects occur between sales and advertising. The importance of cointegration analysis is demonstrated with respect to Granger causality testing and multi-step forecasting.

Empirical Causal Ordering

Although logically the first task in market response modeling, the empirical causal ordering of variables is a relatively new ETS technique and, in fact, can be performed only with time series data. Traditionally, marketing models have been estimated under the assumption of a simple market response mechanism: market performance = f(marketing effort).

There are, however, two major marketing phenomena that may invalidate models based on unidirectional causality. First, it has been shown empirically and theoretically that marketing decisions may depend on past, present, or future marketing outcomes. And, second, competitive actions and reactions may occur as a result of marketing outcomes. In both cases, the resulting marketing model may exhibit multidirectional causality:

$$\text{market performance} = f \text{(own and competitive marketing effort)}$$

$$\text{own marketing effort} = g \text{(market performance, competitive marketing effort)}$$

$$\text{competitive marketing effort} = h \text{(market performance, own marketing effort).}$$

Econometric estimation solutions for these more complex models have existed for some time (see chapter 5). These techniques require the a priori specification of a simultaneous-equation model, including endogenous, exoge-nous, and lagged endogenous variables. More often than not, however, such a priori specification is difficult in a marketing context, and until recently the model builder was confronted with the following dilemma: one needs a correctly specified structural model in order to make statistical inferences about the parameters, but the parameters must be known in order to validate the structural model. In other words, one cannot test the model without estimating its parameters but cannot use the parameters until the structural model is known to be valid.

Time series analysis has produced an elegant solution to this dilemma: the key contribution is that *the model builder does not need to know the exact structural model in order to make causal inferences.* Every structural model on longitudinal data implies a set of time series processes on the variables, which can be used to establish causal ordering, functional form, and lag structures. When prior knowledge is sparse, some preliminary time series analyses on the data can be performed that advance the researcher to level 1 or level 2 prior knowledge. At that point, the structural model can be estimated and evaluated.

The Concept of Granger Causality

It is difficult to establish a workable definition of causality in non-experimental research. As far as statistical analysis is concerned, we often hear the remark that "correlation does not imply causation." But when we adopt a stochastic view of time series behavior, temporal ordering of events can be used to make an empirical distinction between leading and lagging variables. That distinction is at the basis of a well-known definition of causality due to Granger (1969).

Suppose a marketing system is defined by a two-variable information set (X, Y). In an attempt to forecast Y, we could build a univariate model, considering the past of Y alone, or we could combine the past of Y and the past of X in a bivariate model. Now, X is said to *Granger cause* Y if the mean squared forecast error (MSFE) of Y using the bivariate model is smaller than the MSFE of the univariate model. Formally:

For the information set containing X and Y, X is said to Granger cause Y if

$$\text{MSFE}(Y_t | Y_{t-1}, \dots, Y_{t-k}, X_{t-1}, \dots, X_{t-m}) < \text{MSFE}(Y_t | Y_{t-1}, \dots, Y_{t-k}) \qquad (7.30)$$

where k and m are positive integers indicating the maximum memory length in Y and X.

There are three distinctive components to Granger's definition:

1. It stresses the importance of an adequately formulated information set.

2. The empirical detection of causality between X and Y is valid only insofar as no major factors Z are missing from the information set. The null model, against which forecasting performance is evaluated, is a powerful rival. For example, univariate time series models have been shown to outperform complex econometric models of the U.S. economy (Nelson 1972).

3. The ultimate test is done out-of-sample. Thus, statistical significance of transfer function parameters alone is not sufficient to establish Granger causality.

Granger causality applies well in marketing contexts. For example, monthly time series of the number of airline passengers on a route have often been found to follow an ARIMA (0,1,1) process—known as the airline model—which predicts future passenger levels remarkably well. The marketing question, "Does manipulating the air fares affect demand?" might be poorly answered by merely correlating or regressing passenger and air fare series. Granger's definition would assess whether or not air fare information improves the prediction of passenger levels beyond what is achieved by extrapolation. If the airline pricing managers act rationally and forecast demand accurately, the air fares may follow a rigid seasonal pattern with little extra variation. In that case, we may well find that they do not Granger cause passenger demand but instead are caused by (perfectly anticipated) passenger movements. One extension of the definition includes present as well as past values of X in the prediction of Y. This is known as *Granger instantaneous causality* and is more difficult to measure empirically (Layton 1984).

Test Procedures

Although the concept of Granger causality was developed in economics, it did not achieve recognition until time series methods for its execution became available. Several procedures have been proposed, of which we discuss the three most popular: the double prewhitening technique and two regression based methods due to Granger(1969) and Sims (1972).

The *double prewhitening* method, first proposed by Haugh (1976) and later extended by Haugh and Box (1977), Pierce (1977), and Pierce and Haugh (1977), establishes the direction of causality between two series by crosscorrelating the residuals of univariate models fitted to each. Formally, let:

$$\phi_1(L)x_{1t} = \theta_1(L)w_{1t},\tag{7.31}$$

$$\phi_2(L)x_{2t} = \theta_2(L)w_{2t}.\tag{7.32}$$

Then $r_{w_1 w_2}(k) \sim N(0, \sigma_r^2)$ under the assumption of independence between the series. Haugh (1976) has shown that this property also holds asymptotically for the estimated ARMA residuals $\hat{w}_1$ and $\hat{w}_2$. Thus, we can construct a chi-square test on the ARMA residuals to test an hypothesis of overall independence of the series:

$$Q = T \sum_{k=-M}^{M} r_{\hat{w}_1 \hat{w}_2}(k) \sim \chi^2(2M+1),\tag{7.33}$$

where M is the maximum cross-correlation lag under consideration and is set separately by the analyst.

The extension of Haugh's test to the direction of causality is as follows:

X causes Y is tested by the statistic

$$Q_1 = T \sum_{k=1}^{M} r_{\hat{w}_1 \hat{w}_2}(k) \sim \chi^2(M).\tag{7.34}$$

Y causes X:

$$Q_2 = T \sum_{k=-1}^{-M} r_{\hat{w}_1 \hat{w}_2}(k) \sim \chi^2(M).\tag{7.35}$$

X causes Y instantaneously:

$$Q'_1 = T \sum_{k=0}^{M} r_{\hat{w}_1 \hat{w}_2}(k) \sim \chi^2(M+1).\tag{7.36}$$

Y causes X instantaneously:

$$Q'_2 = T \sum_{k=0}^{-M} r_{\hat{w}_1 \hat{w}_2}(k) \sim \chi^2(M+1).\tag{7.37}$$

How does the double prewhitening method relate to the definition of Granger causality? In a first stage, the predictive power of each series' past is removed via the prewhitening operation. Then, by cross-correlating the residuals at various lags, the method scans the data for any additional sources of covariation. If a significant cross-correlation exists at lag $k \neq 0$, it contributes to Granger causality in one direction. If the spike occurs at $k = 0$, it contributes to Granger instantaneous causality, but the direction of the effect cannot be established by itself. The main restriction of double prewhitening, though, lies in the fact that both stages are typically carried out on the same sample, so there is no true forecasting test. That limitation prompted Ashley, Granger, and Schmalensee (1980) to develop a supplementary test for the out-of-sample performance of univariate versus bivariate time series models.

The double prewhitening method has been instrumental in stirring controversial debates of cause and effect in the macroeconomic and financial economics literature. For example, Pierce (1977) reported a lack of relations among several key interest and money indicators previously thought of as highly interrelated. In marketing it was first used to establish primary demand versus market share effects of airline flight scheduling and advertising and to sort out various patterns of competitive reactions among airlines (Hanssens 1977; 1980b). A more comprehensive overview of causality tests in marketing can be found in Table 7-2.

The double prewhitening method has been criticized for rejecting the null hypothesis of independence too infrequently, i.e., it may produce spurious independence. It is indeed true that the statistical power of a cross-correlation test is low (e.g., Schwert 1979), but that reflects the fact that the research hypothesis is rather vague, which is consistent with having level 0 prior knowledge. For example, by increasing M in the test (which implies reducing the precision of the research hypothesis), we can sometimes change the outcome with the same Type I error. In conclusion, the test should be carried out with care and its results supplemented by other analyses.

Regression methods have been used as well, in particular one technique attributed to Granger (1969) and a second one due to Sims (1972). The Granger method is based on the following model:

$$Y_t = \alpha_0 + \sum_{i=1}^{\infty} \gamma_i Y_{t-i} + \sum_{j=1}^{\infty} \beta_j X_{t-j} + u_t, \qquad (7.38)$$

which establishes Granger causality if $\{\beta_j\} \neq 0$. The Sims method regresses Y against all possible past and future X:

Table 7-2. Tests for the Direction of Causality in Marketing

Source	Industry	Method	Findings
Asker, Carman, and Jacobson (1982)	Ready-to-eat cereals	Double prewhitening and Sims test	Weak or no causality between advertising and sales.
Bass and Pilon (1980)	Catsup	Double prewhitening	Relative price causes market share.
Batra and Vanhonacker (1988)	Liquor	Sims test with forecasting test	High brand awareness, advertising frequency attitudes predict purchase intentions. Low brand awareness, advertising frequency: ad and brand awareness influence attitudes and purchase intentions.
Doyle and Saunders (1985)	Natural gas	Double prewhitening	Sales lead commission rates, advertising leads sales.
Hanssens (1980a)	Lydia Pinkham (monthly series)	Double prewhitening with forecasting test	Causality in both directions between sales and advertising.
Hanssens (1980b)	Domestic air travel	Double prewhitening	Flights cause primary demand or market share, advertising does not; various competitive reactions.
Jacobson and Nicosia (1981)	N/A	Double prewhitening and Sims test	Causality in both directions between advertising and aggregate consumption.
Leone (1983)	Frequently purchased grocery product	Double prewhitening	Advertising has primary and selective demand effects.

N/A = not applicable

$$Y_t = \alpha_0 + \sum_{i=1}^{\infty} \gamma_i X_{t-i} + \sum_{j=1}^{\infty} \beta_j X_{t+j} + u_t, \qquad (7.39)$$

which establishes Granger causality from Y to X if $\{\beta_j\} \neq 0$, and from X to Y if $\{\gamma_i\} \neq 0$. In both cases, we must truncate the parameter polynomials $\{\gamma_i\}$ and $\{\beta_j\}$ in order to carry out the test. If Y_t is an autoregressive series, there is little problem as long as the lags are long enough. To the extent that Y_t contains moving-average elements ($q>0$ in the ARMA model for Y_t), the autoregressive approximation may not capture all of the predictive power of the series' own past.

It has been shown that these three methods of causality testing are asymptotically identical (Geweke, Meese, and Dent 1983). As far as finite sample performance is concerned, some Monte Carlo simulations suggest that the double prewhitening method has less power than the regression methods and that Sims's method is about as powerful as Granger's when a correction is made for autocorrelated disturbances (Nelson and Schwert 1979). In addition, the Granger method is the easiest to implement on statistical software packages, as it requires neither prewhitening nor regression against future variables. Indeed, the Granger method is readily implemented by estimating VAR models discussed earlier in the chapter.

Regression-based causality tests were first used in marketing to determine the causal ordering of advertising and aggregate consumption. Using the Sims method, Jacobson and Nicosia (1981) established a contemporaneous relation between annual advertising and personal consumption in the U.K., plus one-year lagged effects in both directions. Interestingly, these results were confirmed by a double prewhitening test on the same data.

On Using Time Series Analysis

We have discussed techniques for specifying the dynamics of a model from a combined time series and structural perspective. First, in a number of cases, univariate time series extrapolation of marketing data is sufficient, in particular when the objective of marketing model building is strictly forecasting. The autoregressive-moving-average, or ARMA, filter first proposed by Yule was made practical for model builders by the pioneering work of Box and Jenkins. The method converts a time series to white noise, i.e., a series of uncorrelated random shocks, and in so doing, extracts the maximum amount of systematic behavior from the data for forecasting.

Most marketing models, however, are structural, i.e., they are built on cause-and-effect mechanisms. The transfer function extends the ARMA model by allowing input variables other than white noise to affect a performance variable such as sales. We have discussed the prewhitening method due to Box and Jenkins as a technique for specifying single-input transfer functions. When there is more than one input variable, as is very common in marketing, this method becomes cumbersome, even unreliable. We follow the proposition of Liu and Hanssens to use least-squares techniques and common filters to specify such models. This method is an example of the combined use of time series and structural (econometric) analysis.

In some cases, marketing models contain several equations, a situation that poses special challenges to lag specification. The vector ARMA model can be used in this case as a direct extension of univariate Box-Jenkins analysis. However, that model is less useful when structural equations are needed. A more relevant approach for marketing modelers is to work with a dynamic econometric model and to specify its dynamic structure by an instrumental-variables least-squares technique.

When used in conjunction with the unit-root tests discussed in Chapter 6, multiple time-series models, and especially the vector-autoregressive (VAR) model, can detect and model long-run effects of marketing. The presence or absence of such effects largely determines what strategic scenario the marketer faces, and what types of response models are needed to model short-term and long-term market response.

With the exception of the vector ARMA model, all the methods discussed in this chapter assume that the model builder knows the causal ordering of the marketing variables (level 1 prior knowledge). When this is not the case, the model builder may use time series techniques for empirically determining the direction of causality in the marketing system.

IV

SOLVING MARKETING PROBLEMS WITH ETS

8 EMPIRICAL FINDINGS AND MANAGERIAL INSIGHTS

Marketing's main claim to be a science, apart from using the scientific method, is that it now has a body of scientific generalizations. If not quite the neat laws of natural science, the generalizations are reasonably precise and robust. They serve the same purpose as laws in that they provide the foundation of marketing knowledge that allows explanation. This is relevant to market response modeling in that many of the generalizations came from empirical market response research.

Many studies have produced findings that have themselves converged as marketing generalizations. This means that, although a market response model is built for a particular brand or category, the *class* of behavior for that brand or category may be sufficiently general that it is predictable by laws. Individual market response situations are still mysteries to be solved, but now we have some very big clues—the biggest are the regularities of behavior among certain marketing mix variables. Rather than starting a market response study from (a null hypothesis of) zero effect, we can start from real knowledge (Farley, Lehmann, and Sawyer 1995).

All of this is relevant to marketing management because, once there are empirical generalizations, principles based on them can be used as guides to action. If we know that advertising causes a certain increase in sales under certain conditions (an empirical generalization), then we can conclude that under those conditions a company can use advertising to increase its sales by a certain amount.

This chapter begins with a discussion of measuring marketing effects. After addressing the nature of empirical generalizations, the bulk of the chapter reports on empirical findings and generalizations. Managerial implications are noted.

Measuring Marketing Effects

Marketing managers are interested in identifying and measuring the effects of marketing decision variables on brand and industry (or market) demand.[1] When the effect of a brand's marketing activities is to increase its own sales without affecting competitors' sales, it is called a *primary sales effect*. When the effect is to increase its own sales and those of its competitors, it is a *primary demand effect*. And when the effect is to increase its own sales and to decrease those of its competitors, it is a *competitive effect*. To understand the consequences of marketing actions, we must be able to separate these effects in a model.

Estimated Response and Reaction Functions

Empirical studies have tended to examine marketing elasticities with respect to market share rather than absolute sales. A summary of the algebra of brand sales models, which forms the basis of our discussion, can be found in Naert and Leeflang (1978). Market share, *MS*, is defined to equal brand sales, Q, divided by product class sales, Q_T. This relation can be rewritten as

$$Q = Q_T \times MS . \tag{8.1}$$

Then the impact of a change in marketing effort, X, is

$$\frac{\partial Q}{\partial X} = MS \frac{\partial Q_T}{\partial X} + Q_T \frac{\partial MS}{\partial X} , \tag{8.2}$$

and the corresponding relation between elasticities is

$$\varepsilon_{Q,X} = \varepsilon_{Q_T,X} + \varepsilon_{MS,X} . \tag{8.3}$$

The sales elasticity is equal to the *product class elasticity*, also know as the *category expansion elasticity*, plus the market share elasticity. The sales elasticity is equal to the market share elasticity only if the product class elasticity is zero. This assumption was made in order to obtain "conservative" bounds for sales elasticities in a study of ready-to-eat cereals (Clarke 1973) and to construct a measure for assessing asymmetric and neighborhood price cross-effects (Sethuraman, Srinivasan, and Kim 1999, p. 31). The sales elasticity will, in general, be larger in absolute magnitude than the market share elasticity.

The impact of a change in marketing effort, say advertising expenditures, can be partitioned into direct and indirect effects. Direct effects are denoted by *:

$$\frac{\partial Q}{\partial A} = \frac{\partial Q^*}{\partial A} + \frac{\partial Q^*}{\partial P_c}\frac{\partial P_c}{\partial A} + \frac{\partial Q^*}{\partial A_c}\frac{\partial A_c}{\partial A} + \frac{\partial Q^*}{\partial X_c}\frac{\partial X_c}{\partial A}. \tag{8.4}$$

Indirect effects arise from competitive reaction to a firm's actions. The brand elasticity can be written in terms of an own-elasticity, ε, cross-elasticities, η, and reaction elasticities, ρ. For example, the advertising elasticity can be written

$$\varepsilon_{Q,A} = \varepsilon_{Q^*,A} + \eta_{Q^*,P_c}\rho_{P_c,A} + \eta_{Q^*,A_c}\rho_{A_c,A} + \eta_{Q^*,X_c}\rho_{X_c,A}. \tag{8.5}$$

The various brand elasticities and cross-elasticities can be partitioned into their product class and market share elasticities, as shown earlier.[2]

The empirical information we possess on cross-elasticities is increasing but still centers on advertising and price. Because much of the literature has focused on improving estimation techniques for market-share models, the marketing decision variables in these market-share models are often expressed in some "share" form. As a result, independent estimates of the cross-elasticities are not obtained. Early estimates of advertising cross-elasticities were primarily provided by Lambin (1976). His work suggested that elasticity and cross-elasticity typically are not equal in magnitude. Product cross-elasticities as well as advertising cross-elasticities were estimated by Wildt (1974). Price cross-elasticities have become increasingly available at the store level as well as the market level due to the explosion of scanner data (Blattberg and Wisniewski 1989).

One issue is whether a cross-elasticity is equal in magnitude, although opposite in sign, to the corresponding own elasticity under any set of conditions. This issue is important because it is either an implicit or explicit assumption in many sales response functions reported in the literature. For instance, the most common functional form is the multiplicative model:

$$Q = \beta_0 X^\varepsilon X_c^\eta. \tag{8.6}$$

In models in which the marketing decision variable is expressed in relative share form, this equation becomes

$$Q = \beta_0\left(\frac{X}{X_c}\right)^{\beta_1} = \beta_0 X^{\beta_1} X_c^{-\beta_1}. \tag{8.7}$$

The implicit assumption, then, is that

$$\varepsilon = -\eta \quad \text{or} \quad \varepsilon + \eta = 0. \tag{8.8}$$

This last restriction was explicitly imposed in a model of the market mechanism for cigarettes (Bass 1969b). This property of relative share models has been recognized by other researchers, e.g., Lambin (1976). In a similar vein, sales response to relative price differential, (them-us)/them, was expressed as a hyperbolic (sine) function in a study of pharmaceuticals or detergents in West Germany (Simon 1979).[3] The model had a separate linear term for absolute price effects. The absolute price levels were found to have had no significant impact on sales during the period analyzed. As a consequence of the functional form, the direct price elasticity and cross-price elasticity had to have the identical magnitude.

Consider the situation in which firms compete solely to maintain market share equilibrium through advertising. This relation can be written as

$$\varepsilon_{MS^*,A} + \eta_{MS^*,A_c} \rho_{A_c,A} = 0,$$

or

$$\frac{-\varepsilon_{MS^*,A}}{\eta_{MS^*,A_c}} = \rho_{A_c,A}. \tag{8.10}$$

A major research project on Australian industries found this relation to hold in most studies: beer, cigarettes, detergents, instant coffee, toilet soap, and toothpaste (Metwally 1978). In these industries advertising is market-defensive, i.e., done to protect share. In the preceding relation, the own-elasticity and cross-elasticity will equal each other in magnitude only if the reaction elasticity equals one. A number of the estimated values of Australian reaction coefficients were about one. More recent work on reaction elasticities includes that by Leeflang and Wittink (1992) and Jedidi, Mela, and Gupta (1999).[4]

A Taxonomy of Marketing Effects

In any empirical situation, the three pure cases of marketing effects can be confounded, resulting in a number of mixed cases. A taxonomy due to Schultz and Wittink (1976) is shown in Table 8-1. In their taxonomy, cases I, II, and III represent the pure cases of primary demand effect only, primary sales effect only, and competitive effect only. Cases IV, V, and VI represent the combinations of primary demand effect and primary sales effect, primary demand effect and competitive effect, and primary sales effect and competitive effect. Case IV would seem more likely than case I. If a firm's selective marketing effort stimulates primary demand, it should benefit more from this new market demand than its competitors. (Recall the discussion of differential-effects models in Chapter 3.) If it accrues all the benefits of the new market demand as well as taking sales from competitors, we have case VI.

Table 8-1. A Taxonomy of Marketing Effects

		Response to an Increase in a Firm's Marketing Effort				
Case	*Effect*	*Industry Sales*	*Brand Sales*	*Rival Sales*	*Brand Share*	*Rival Share*
I	Primary demand only	Increase	Increase	Increase	No change	No change
II	Primary sales only	Increase	Increase	No change	Increase	Decrease
III	Competitive only	No change	Increase	Decrease	Increase	Decrease
IV	Primary demand/ primary sales	Increase	Increase	Increase	Increase	Decrease
V	Primary demand/ competitive	Increase	Increase	?	Increase	Decrease
VI	Primary sales/ competitive	Increase	Increase	Decrease	Increase	Decrease

The existence of case V, in which the way competitors' sales are affected depends on the strength of the primary demand effect relative to that of the competitive effect, creates a discrimination problem. Depending on the net effect, case V cannot be distinguished from case II, case IV, or case VI. Schultz and Wittink argue that the existence of case V is implausible, but consider a new brand of a consumer product. Its marketing activities may stimulate primary demand by drawing less knowledge-able consumers into the market. Some of these might purchase competitive brands. At the same time, more knowledgeable existing consumers might recognize the advantages of the new product and switch to it. We accept Schultz and Wittink's argument only when it is restricted to competition among established brands.

The empirical conditions necessary to identify the remaining five cases are de-scribed by Schultz and Wittink. Our restatement of these conditions is shown in Table 8-2. Three pieces of information are needed: (1) the signs of the brand's mar-ket share elasticity, (2) its primary demand elasticity, and (3) its rival sales cross-elasticity. In addition, we note that the firm's sales elasticity can be calculated, since it is equal to the firm's primary demand elasticity plus its market share elasticity as shown earlier in Equation (8.3). The sales elasticity is always assumed positive.

The needed information requires that a market share response function be estimated for the brand and that sales response functions be estimated for the industry and for competitors. Thus, a complete understanding of the effects of a

Table 8-2. Discriminating Among a Brand's Marketing Effects

Case	Effect	Market Share Elasticity	Primary Demand Elasticity	Rival Sales Cross-Elasticity
I	Primary demand only	Zero	Positive	Positive
II	Primary sales only	Positive	Positive	Zero
III	Competitive only	Positive	Zero	Negative
IV	Primary demand/ primary sales	Positive	Positive	Positive
VI	Primary demand/ competitive	Positive	Positive	Negative

marketing activity requires decomposing a brand's sales response function into an industry sales response function and its market share response function.

The Schultz and Wittink framework has been used to assess the effects of advertising in several product categories (Lancaster 1984). Annual data within product categories were pooled so that the results represented a prototypical brand. A primary demand only effect was found for shaving cream and ready-to-eat cereal, a competitive effect only for bath and toilet soap and cigars, a combined primary demand and primary sales effect for deodorants and antiperspirants, a combined primary sales and competitive effect for heavy-duty laundry detergents, and no measurable effect for light-duty liquid detergents.[5] These results are shown in Table 8-3.

We have just seen that we must be able to decompose the market response function in order to identify certain effects of marketing decision variables. But we know that for planning purposes (cf. Chapter 1), we may choose only to estimate a sales response function directly. Thus, if we care where sales are coming from, we decompose; if we don't, we don't.

Empirical Marketing Generalizations

A marketing manager's central concern is how selective marketing activities of a brand affect its sales. One way is through changes in selective demand. The other is through changes in primary demand, and, as a consequence, the manager might want to couple a model of industry demand with a market share model. Whether interested in the brand level or the industry level, the manager would like to know what empirical marketing generalizations have been discovered. This is especially helpful when confronting a new market or product situation.

Table 8-3. Empirical Evidence on Advertising Effects

Product Category	Market Share Elasticity	Primary Demand Elasticity	Rival Sales Cross-Elasticity	Conclusion about Effects
Cereals, ready-to-eat	N/S	0.029 (0.006)	0.038 (0.006)	Primary demand only
Cigars	0.076 (0.007)	N/S	−0.079 (0.012)	Competitive only
Deodorants, antiperspirants	0.177 (0.028)	0.015 (0.005)	0.043 (0.004)	Primary demand/primary sales
Detergents, heavy-duty laundry	0.191 (0.044)	0.079 (0.026)	−0.078 (0.006)	Primary sales/competitive
Detergents, light-duty liquid	N/S	N/S	N/S	None measurable
Shaving cream	N/S	0.025 (0.010)	0.053 (0.014)	Primary demand only
Soap, bath and toilet	0.258 (0.069)	N/S	−0.046 (0.024)	Competitive only

Note: Lancaster (1984) used advertising share as the independent variable in his market share equation. To get the correct market share elasticity, we calculated it from the sales elasticity and the primary demand elasticity. Significance is based on a one-sided (positive) test for the market share elasticity and the primary demand elasticity and a two-sided test for the rival sales cross-elasticity. Asymptotic standard errors are in parentheses.

N/S = not significant

What is a Good Marketing Generalization?

A marketing generalization is an approximate summary of the data describing some marketing phenomena—in our case, market response. What is summarized is the regularity of the relationships found in the data. For example, when we find that price has a regular relationship to sales over limiting conditions made clear by repeated empirical observations, we have an empirical generalization.

As well as being based on repeated empirical evidence, good generalizations are likely to possess five other characteristics: scope, precision, parsimony, usefulness, and a link with theory (Barwise 1995). While an empirical generalization is not universal, it should have sufficient scope so that it holds under a wide variety of conditions so as to be meaningful.[6] In any event, we should try to understand the domain within which an empirical generalization holds. The more precisely we can state an empirical generalization the better. At the same time, we want parsimony—to cut through to the heart of a phenomenon. When all is said and done we believe practitioners should find an empirical generalization useful. We are, moreover, mindful as marketing scientists that a good empirical generalization should be connected in some way with a theory—the explanation of the described phenomena.

This insight also reconciles why theories tend to change over time while empirical generalizations do not. New theories replace older theories as new generalizations are discovered or new testing procedures are developed. Many times the new theories have the original explanations as special cases. The upshot is that for both theory building and for practical application, empirical generalizations about market response are crucial to the research enterprise.

How Are Empirical Generalizations Found?

Empirical generalizations are found by analyzing the results from multiple empirical studies. Three broad approaches can be taken to accumulate knowledge across market response studies: (1) informal observation, (2) literature review, and (3) meta-analysis (Hunter and Schmidt 1990, pp. 468-89; Bass and Wind 1995 p. G2).

Informal Observation. Informal observation typically entails an experienced researcher recognizing a pattern that has recurred in studies with which the researcher is familiar. The resultant qualitative insights are often labeled "from experience." Articles in trade magazines, such as *Admap*, often report such insights. See, for example, von Gonten (1998).

Literature Review. A literature review may involve either narrative-discursive methods or voting methods. In a narrative review, studies are taken at face value. The reviewer mentally attempts to integrate findings from all studies in an attempt to find an overarching theory that reconciles the findings. This approach has been shown to break down with as few studies as seven. To ease the information-processing burden on the reviewer, a voting method can be used to tabulate findings. The reviewer counts nonsignificant, positive significant, and negative significant results. Although a systematic voting method approach may be an improvement over less formal methods, its focus is still on significance levels while the purpose of research integration is more descriptive than inferential. Studies of the nature of advertising effect on sales were surveyed by Clarke (1976) and by Aaker and Carman (1982). The nature of price was studied by Gijsbrechts (1993).

Meta-Analysis. Meta-analysis focuses on the effect sizes rather than significance levels. The researcher conducts a statistical analysis of a large collection of analysis results from individual studies. *The dependent variable must be dimensionless.* In the market response studies, elasticities meet this requirement.

The logic behind using meta-analysis is given by Farley, Lehmann, and Sawyer (1995, p. G37):

> Meta-analysis begins with the assumption that different brands and different markets are comparable on a general level and that model *structures* generalize to new research settings but that model *parameters* to some extent vary systematically over settings in an identifiable manner.

Thus meta-analysis can deliver generalized quantitative estimates of response parameters such as the elasticities of marketing instruments. Advertising has been looked at by Aaker and Carman (1982), and Assmus et al. (1984), personal selling by Churchill et al. (1985), price by Tellis (1988) and Sethuraman, Srinivasan, and Kim (1999), and price elasticity variations by Bell, Chiang, and Padmanabhan (1999). The ratio of the price elasticity to the advertising elasticity when both were estimated in the same model was examined by Sethuraman and Tellis (1991). For a discussion of how to conduct meta-analysis in marketing, see Farley and Lehmann (1986).

The methods above emphasize the need to move away from collecting a single set of data (SSoD) toward explicitly collecting many differentiated sets of data (MSoD) as advocated by Ehrenberg (1995, p. G27). One wants to know if the same basic result is observed under different circumstances.

A Cautionary Note on Empirical Generalizations

Since all empirical data and resulting parameters are subject to error, Morrison and Silva-Risso (1995) argued that the search for empirical generalizations should begin with the relation

$$\text{Observed Value} \; = \; \text{True Score} \; + \; \text{Error} \tag{8.11}$$

and then warned that the generalization in question should be based on the latent true scores rather than the observed values as commonly done. In the case of market response models, the $O = T + E$ approach yields

$$\text{Measured Elasticity} \; = \; \text{True Elasticity} \; + \; \text{Error.} \tag{8.12}$$

Morrison and Silva-Risso (1995, p. G68) realized that we must work with observed data but recommended that the $O = T + E$ framework be explicitly considered when deriving empirical generalizations from such observed data. They warned that marketing managers who ignore the fact the data they observe are generated by a true component and a random error are likely to base their decisions on overreaction to random events.

Guidance for marketing action comes from regularities in aggregate response behavior across markets. Of course, marketing is very product-market specific and these generalizations are not too precise. Most brand-level generalizations relate to short-term effects. Remember that an argument has been made that a necessary condition for the existence of long-run (persistent) marketing effectiveness is the presence of evolution in performance (Dekimpe and Hanssens 1995, p. G111). However, until recently, marketing data were not tested for evolution, so little inference could be made about long-run marketing effectiveness. We begin with brand-level findings and generalizations, then turn to industry-level ones.

Brand-Level Findings and Generalizations

Many, but not all, brand-level findings and generalizations are based on elasticities. Sometimes they are based on sensitivities. Although enormous progress has been made in discovering market response relationships, it is still difficult to classify them as either generalizations (by definition, well-supported across multiple studies or data sets) or findings from isolated studies that may become generalizations. Most of what follows can be regarded as generalizations, but some findings are also reported for completeness of coverage across the marketing decision variables. Wherever possible, we will report market response estimates (elasticities) to augment the qualitative generalization. On a few occasions we are able to separate short-run from long-run effects, though the vast majority of the generalizations are still restricted to the short term.

Advertising Effects

One of the first marketing generalizations (Leone and Schultz 1980, hereafter LS) is

The short-term elasticity of selective advertising on own brand sales of frequently purchased consumer goods is positive but low. [LS]

Support. This generalization is supported by the literature survey of Aaker and Carman (1982) and by the meta-analysis of Assmus, Farley, and Lehmann (1984).[7] The second study reports an average short-term elasticity of 0.22 (p. 66). This study went on to recommend using 0.30 as the null hypothesis for short-run advertising elasticities in future models (p. 73). Other studies have found the average advertising elasticity to be closer to 0.10 (Lambin 1976, pp. 95, 98 and Sethuraman and Tellis 1991, p. 168). Advertising weight tests conducted using split-cable consumer panels (see BehaviorScan boxed insert and *Frito-Lay Industry Perspective*) found an average elasticity of 0.13 (Lodish et al. 1995, p. 129). We are comfortable with the value of 0.10.

This value for the advertising elasticity is a prototypical one and an individual brand could have a quite different value. Elasticities differ among products and settings, for example they are higher for advertised food products and higher in Europe than in the United States (Assmus, Farley, and Lehmann 1984, p. 72). In one study, the overall advertising elasticity for a GM dealership was 0.635, with advertising elasticities of 0.785 for compact cars and 0.113 for full size cars (Helmuth 1987, p. 42).

Most empirical results on advertising are based on television advertising. The advertising elasticity will, however, vary by media. For example, a study of U.S. Navy advertising found an advertising elasticity of 0.192 for nonprint media and one of 0.489 for print media (Morey and McCann 1983, p. 199).

The average long-term effect of successful advertising spending is approximately double its initial effect.

Support. An early literature review of the duration of advertising effect on sales found that the average retention rate of advertising for monthly studies was $\lambda = 0.430$ (Clarke 1976, p. 355). A formal meta-analysis found it to be 0.468 (Assmus, Farley, and Lehmann 1984, p. 66). The recommendation was to use 0.5 as the null hypothesis for the advertising retention rate in future models (p. 73). A similar value has been found for lead generation (Morey and McCann 1983, p. 198).

These studies fail to take into account the data interval bias effect on the estimated coefficients in market response models and the related bias on the computation of the duration interval of advertising. Using the recovery methods discussed in Chapter 4, aggregation-adjusted (weighted monthly) values for the retention rate of advertising are 0.775 and 0.69 for the literature survey and meta-analysis respectively (Leone 1995, p. G148).

The 90% duration interval for advertising of mature, frequently purchased, low-priced packaged goods is brief, averaging between six and nine months. [C]

Support. The literature review mentioned above calculated that 90% of the cumulative effect of advertising occurred within 3 to 9 months of the advertisement (Clarke 1976, p. 355). The aggregation-adjusted values suggest a narrower range of six to nine months (Leone 1995, p. G148). For example, plugging an advertising retention rate of $\lambda = 0.7$ into Equation (2.37) yields

---

BehaviorScan Advertising Weight Tests

The BehaviorScan system, a service of IRI, is a real life laboratory in which manufacturers test marketing variables within a controlled environment for both new and established brands. For tests of alternative television advertising plans, the BehaviorScan household panels are split into two or more subgroups that are balanced on past purchasing, demographics, and stores shopped over a one-year base period. This matching procedure makes it easier to attribute differences in the test period to the effect of the treatment rather than to pre-existing differences between groups or to an interaction between the test variable and pre-existing differences.

Using split-cable technology, commercials can be substituted at the individual household level, allowing one subgroup to view a test commercial, while the other views a control ad—usually a public service announcement, or enabling one subgroup to receive heavier advertising weight than the other.

The data are treated as a post-test/pre-test with control group design. The scanner panel purchases are aggregated to the store week level for both the treatment and control groups. A key source of sales variation unrelated to the treatments is a temporary promotion, which varies across stores in the same week. In order to accommodate this source of variation, the market share for the brand in question for the total store for that week is used as a covariate. This covariate can be used because panelists are only a small fraction of a store's volume. Other covariates are those used originally to balance the experimental groups.

Source: Lodish et al. (1995, p. G139).

$$T \geq \frac{log(1-0.9)}{log(0.7)} = \frac{-1}{-0.155} = 6.5 \text{ months.} \tag{8.13}$$

A brand's elasticity to advertising depends on a number of factors. Millward Brown International, hereafter MBI, for instance, identified five such factors: category development, brand development, competitive context, strategy effectiveness, and execution effectiveness (Millward Brown International 1995, p. 3). The first two of these factors relate to the stage of the life cycle in which a brand or market is operating.

How T.V. Advertising Works at Frito-Lay

Frito-Lay, the market leader in the U.S. snack chip category, conducted 23 split-panel experiments over a four-year period in order to identify the unique contribution of television advertising to the sales volume and market share of its brands.

These experiments were designed to be a robust yet realistic test of the effectiveness of television advertising across Frito-Lay brands. The basic design was an advertising/no-advertising split-panel BehaviorScan test in which each brand's advertising was tested in at least two markets over a full year. Media plans for each brand were those previously approved by management during the annual planning cycle and were not modified during a given year. Each brand's media plan was composed of at least 1500 GRPs but was otherwise unconstrained in make-up. Brand managers and advertising agencies were responsible for devising the media plans, and no constraints other than those mentioned previously were applied to those plans. At the end of each year, markets were reassigned to brands such that no brand was tested in a given market for more than one consecutive year.

Cable, radio, and outdoor advertising were not manipulated as a part of this experiment. These forms of advertising, however, represented only a small portion of the marketing mix. Promotional activities also were not manipulated, but because of random assignment of consumers to conditions, it was presumed that this factor was counterbalanced across treatment conditions.

In addition to the advertising versus no-advertising conditions, the BehaviorScan tests were categorized further along two other dimensions. First, the tests were categorized as "news" versus "base brand" depending on the content of the commercial. Commercials introducing a significant innovation such as a meaningful line extension (e.g., Doritos Thins, Fritos Scoops) or a new brand (e.g., SunChips Multigrain Snacks) were designated as "news" advertisements. Commercials focusing an existing brand attributes of an established brand (eg., Ruffles "Get Your Own Bag"; Lay's "Betcha Can't Eat Just One") were designated as "base brand" advertisements. Second, tests were categorized on the basis of brand sales (large brands such as Doritos versus small brands such as Rold Gold).

About 60% of television commercials demonstrated sizable volume increases—producing an average gain of 15%—among advertised households compared with a matched no-advertising control group. Commercials for larger brands had a much lower likelihood of generating meaningful volume gains. Among advertisements for the larger brands, only 27% showed sizable volume increases associated with television advertising. In contrast, smaller brands represented in the study had a higher likelihood of showing sizable volume increases from advertising. Nearly 88% showed sizable volume gains due to advertising. Commercials for innovations (i.e., line extensions) on smaller brands or entirely new brands (e.g., SunChips Multigrain Snacks) showed significant gains 100% of the time (Riskey 1997).

Dwight R. Riskey is Senior Vice President of Marketing, PepsiCo Restaurants International, and formerly Vice President of Marketing Research and New Business, Frito-Lay, Inc. This write-up is based on Riskey (1997). Editors' Note: Empirical evidence shows that brand advertising is effective in stimulating the demand for potato chips. The estimated elasticity for current advertising is 0.1189 and that one-year lagged advertising is 0.0262, giving a total elasticity of 0.145 (Jones and Ward 1989, p. 530).

Advertising elasticities decline as a brand or market matures.

This generalization has two corollaries:

The advertising elasticity of a brand within a small growing category is likely to be larger than that of one in a large, static or declining category. [MBI]

The advertising elasticity of a new brand is likely to be temporarily larger than for a large established brand in the same category. [MBI]

Support. The marketing (advertising and sales force) elasticity for pioneering ethical drug brands was estimated to be 0.625, for growth-stage entrants: 0.496, and for mature-stage entrants: 0.274. This suggests that response to total marketing spending declines monotonically with stage of life cycle entry (Shankar, Carpenter, and Krishnamurthi 1999, pp. 274-75). An examination of thirty years of data on Sapolio, a quality household cleanser in cake form, indicated that its advertising elasticity did decline over time (Parsons 1975). While the average elasticity in the advertising weight tests was 0.13, the average advertising elasticity for new products was 0.26 and that for established products was 0.05. (Lodish et al. 1995, p. 129)

Even within a maturing industry, new products come out and new segments may emerge. In the ready-to-eat cereal market, Kellogg's Sugar Frosted Flakes was found to have a substantially higher advertising elasticity than the existing Corn Flakes. This study involved 16 years of bimonthly data (Parsons 1968).

Implications. Time-varying advertising elasticities imply that marketing effort in the early years of the product life cycle should be greater than would be suggested by constant elasticities. This shift in resource allocation also serves to raise the barrier to imitative new brands. The Bass diffusion of innovation model has been extended for the optimal allocation of advertising over the product life cycle (Horsky and Simon 1983).

Price Effects

There is an extensive body of information on price elasticities.

The elasticity of price on own brand sales is negative and elastic.

Support. One meta-analysis found, after taking into account predictable method-induced biases, a mean own-price elasticity of about –2.5 (Tellis 1988, p. 337). An econometric study using weekly IRI scanner data supplemented by field survey data revealed a simple average value of –2.5 over four products: frozen waffles, –1.74; liquid bleach, –2.41; bathroom tissue, –3.12; and ketchup, –2.55 (Bolton 1989a, p. 162). A field experiment involving five product categories (ready-to-eat breakfast cereals, confectionery, soup, tea, and biscuits) yielded a mean elasticity, weighted by brand size, of –2.6 (Ehrenberg and England 1990, pp. 48-49, 53). A regression analysis based on data from 216 public houses of Whitbread Inns Limited concluded that the estimated price elasticity for Murphy's Irish Stout was approximately –2.0. This value was claimed to be what one would expect for a canned beer (Duckworth 1997, p. 301). A regression study of AGB Superpanel data on the top five brands in each of 100 United Kingdom markets also found a value of –2.5 (Hamilton, East, and Kalafatis 1997, p. 291). This value was based on using relative price, correcting for trend in category but not brand, and excluding weak estimates (with low R^2 coefficients, i.e. less than 0.2). Thus, the magnitude of own-price elasticities is about –2.5.[8] The large discrepancy in the magnitudes between the advertising and price own-elasticities has led to a debate about whether or not price change is a superior tactic to advertising (Broadbent 1989, Tellis 1989, Sethuraman and Tellis 1991).

   While we focus on the mean elasticities, a particular brand's elasticity varies from the mean of the product category because of systematic differences across brands as well as random error. For example, the mean price elasticity for liquid dishwasher detergent was found to be –1.6 using weekly store-level data from ACNielsen. The price elasticities for individual brands were –1.7 for Crystal White Octagon, –1.8 for Dove, –1.5 for Dawn, –2.2 for Ivory, –1.5 for Palmolive, and –1.0 for Sunlight (Kopalle, Mela, and Marsh 1999, p. 325). Yogurt provides another example. The market share weighted average price elasticity for yogurt in a single chain in Springfield, Missouri was –3.4. Meanwhile, the price own-elasticities for individual

Table 8-4. Own-Price Elasticities for Tuna Fish in Chicago

Star Kist	−3.30
Chicken of the Sea	−3.62
Bumble Bee	−4.19
Mean	−3.70
Variance	0.20
Standard Deviation	0.45

Note: Compare results with Kadiyali, Chintagunta, and Vilcassim (2000, p. 144)

Source: Wittink et al. (1988) reported in Morrison and Silva-Risso (1995, p. G66).

brands were −4.5 for Dannon, −0.9 for Yoplait, −3.3 for Weight Watchers, and −4.9 for Hiland, a regional brand (Besanko, Gupta, and Jain 1998, pp. 1540-41). The same study also examined ketchup.

The ketchup results show how the price elasticity varies across package sizes. Here the market share weighted average price elasticity was −2.7. The price elasticities for Heinz were −0.7. −3.5, and −2.6 for 28, 32, and 44 ounces, respectively. Hunts 32-ounce price elasticity was −4.3.[9] Another example is shown in Table 8-4, which gives the own elasticities for tuna fish in Chicago. Even for a given brand, elasticities will differ across the country based on market differences. This is shown in Table 8-5, which gives the elasticities for Star Kist tuna fish in different cities.

A brand's upside and downside own-price elasticity can differ.

Support. Asymmetry in response to price has been discussed by Moran (1978). He provided a summary of price research that had been conducted in a variety of consumer product categories. He argued that the only way to analyze price elasticity is in terms of relative price.[10] Relative price expresses a brand's price relative to the average price for the product category in which it competes. One of his major findings was that a brand's upside demand elasticity and downside elasticity could differ. He conjectured that one reason for the difference is that consumer segments are not equally informed about what is going on. For instance, an unadvertised price change is more likely to be noticed by current customers.[11]

The cross-elasticity of price on rival brand sales is nonnegative.

Support. A price cut by a brand should, if it has any effect at all, cause a decrease in the sales of a competing brand. The magnitude of price cross-elasticities is roughly 0.5 (e.g., Bolton 1989b). One literature search uncovered more than one thousand price cross-elasticity estimates. About 70 percent of the estimated elasticities were

Table 8-5. Price Elasticity for Star Kist

Boston	-2.53
Chicago	-3.30
Houston	-1.51
Indianapolis	-1.42
Jacksonville/Orlando	-1.30
Kansas City	-1.93
Los Angeles	-3.19
New York	-2.67
San Francisco	-1.90
Seattle	-2.52
Mean	-2.22
Variance	0.52
Standard Deviation	0.72

Source: Wittink et al. (1988) reported in Morrison and Silva-Risso (1995, p. G67).

between 0 and 1, with another 15% between 1 and 2. The mean cross-elasticity was 0.52 (Sethuraman, Srinivasan, and Kim 1999, p. 30). The mean price cross-elasticity for liquid dishwasher detergent was found to be 0.6 using weekly store-level data from ACNielsen (Kopalle, Mela, and Marsh 1999, p. 325).

Price cross-effects are asymmetric.

Support. The effect of Brand A's price on Brand B's sales is not the same as the effect of Brand B's price on Brand A's sales. Consider, for example, the refrigerated juice cross-elasticities shown in Table 8-6. MinuteMaid sales are not affected by private label price but MinuteMaid price impacts private label sales. Conversely, while Tropicana sales are affected by private label price, the reverse is not true (Kadiyali, Chintagunta, and Vilcassim 2000).

This has lead to the development of summary measures of brand competition based on cross elasticities (e.g., Cooper 1988, p. 711). *Competitive clout* is the ability of a brand to take share away from competitors and has been operationally defined as

$$\text{competitive clout}_i = \sum_{\substack{j \\ j \neq i}} \eta_{ji}^2 ; \tag{8.14}$$

whereas *vulnerability* is the ability of competitors to take share away from the brand and has been given by

Table 8-6. Price Competition among Refrigerated Juice in Chicago

Brand	MinuteMaid	Tropicana	Private Label
Volume Share	0.2964	0.3986	0.3051
Mean Retail Price	$2.78	$3.35	$1.43
		Sales Elasticities	
MinuteMaid	−2.16	0.90a	NSb
Tropicana	0.64	−2.26	0.5
Private Label	1.46	NS	−2.64

a The percentage change in the sales of MinuteMaid with respect to a one percent change in the price of Tropicana.
b NS = not significant.

Source: Kadiyali, Chintagunta, and Vicassim (2000, p. 144).

$$\text{vulnerability}_i = \sum_{\substack{j \\ j \neq i}} \eta_{ij}^2 \qquad (8.15)$$

(Kamakura and Russell 1989, p. 386). A generalization of much of the work on brand price competition has been provided by Russell (1992). The *Latent Symmetric Elasticity Structure* (LSES) *Model* assumes that the market-share cross-price elasticity η_{ij} is equal to the product of the (asymmetric) clout factor of brand j and a symmetric index of the substitutability of the brand pair (i,j). His empirical work showed that clout factors depend upon both market share and average price while the pattern of substitution indices is influenced by the brand's average price level. Assuming that price is correlated with quality, this work suggests that both the pattern of asymmetry (explained by the clout factors) and the draw pattern from price promotions (explained by substitution indices) depend on quality levels. This work was further extended by Russell and Kamakura (1994). In their research, the general impact of brand j over its competitors is defined as *momentum*. The relative impact of one brand's price promotions on another is given by the ratio of their momentum statistics. Momentum thus determines the pattern of asymmetry in competition whereas substitution provides a measure of the draw pattern expected during a price promotion. A brand will most vulnerable to price changes by a highly substitutable competitor that also hold high momentum. Price competition among powdered detergents is described in Table 8-7.[12]

Table 8-7. Price Competition among Powdered Detergents

Brand	Tide	Surf	Oxy	Cheer	Bold	All	Purex	Dash	Ntl(a)	PL(a)
Volume Share	0.330	0.123	0.116	0.105	0.057	0.056	0.041	0.025	0.117	0.032
Mean Price (¢/oz)	4.56	4.55	5.30	4.80	5.32	3.76	2.97	4.42	4.54	2.43

Market Share Cross Elasticities

	Tide	Surf	Oxy	Cheer	Bold	All	Purex	Dash	Ntl(a)	PL(a)
Tide	−1.55	0.39b	0.13	0.30	0.05	0.05	0.04	0.05	0.16	0.04
Surf	0.79	−3.37	0.21	0.58	0.07	0.07	0.19	0.30	0.36	0.04
Oxydol	0.56	0.43	−1.25	0.52	0.08	0.06	0.18	0.07	0.17	0.03
Cheer	0.42	0.40	0.17	−3.82	0.07	0.03	0.03	0.03	0.28	0.02
Bold	0.90	0.61	0.33	0.78	−0.75	0.10	0.16	0.08	0.25	0.06
All	0.41	0.30	0.12	0.20	0.05	−1.38	0.12	0.06	0.22	0.63
Purex	0.22	0.49	0.22	0.13	0.05	0.08	−2.37	0.06	0.45	0.05
Dash	0.59	1.61	0.19	0.25	0.05	0.08	0.13	−2.20	0.38	0.05
National	0.38	0.42	0.10	0.48	0.03	0.06	0.20	0.08	−1.49	0.07
PL	0.43	0.22	0.06	0.16	0.04	0.76	0.09	0.05	.30	−1.72

Substitution Indices (c)

	Tide	Surf	Oxy	Cheer	Bold	All	Purex	Dash	Ntl(a)	PL(a)
Tide	—	2.7	1.9	1.4	3.1	1.4	0.7	2.0	1.3	1.5
Surf	2.7	—	3.0	2.8	4.3	2.1	3.4	11.2	2.9	1.5
Oxydol	1.9	3.0	—	2.5	4.8	1.8	3.2	2.7	1.4	0.9
Cheer	1.4	2.8	2.5	—	3.8	1.0	0.6	1.2	2.3	0.8
Bold	3.1	4.3	4.8	3.8	—	2.9	3.0	3.0	2.0	2.2
All	1.4	2.1	1.8	1.0	2.9	—	2.2	2.4	1.8	21.9
Purex	0.7	3.4	3.2	0.6	3.0	2.2	—	2.3	3.7	1.7
Dash	2.0	11.2	2.7	1.2	3.0	2.4	2.3	—	3.1	1.8
National	1.3	2.9	1.4	2.3	2.0	1.8	3.7	3.1	—	2.5
PL	1.5	1.5	0.9	0.8	2.2	21.9	1.7	1.8	2.5	—

Momentum (c)

	Tide	Surf	Oxy	Cheer	Bold	All	Purex	Dash	Ntl(a)	PL(a)
	0.294	0.144	0.069	0.208	0.017	0.035	0.055	0.027	0.123	0.029

a Composite categories were constructed to represent small-share national brands (Ntl) and private label brands (PL).

b The percentage change in the share of Tide with respect to a one percent change in the price of Surf.

c Scaled so that momentum statistics sum to one. Cross elasticities are equal to momentum times the substitution index. For example, the cross elasticity of Bold with Tide is 0.294 × 3.1 = 0.9.

Source: Russell and Kamakura (1994, pp. 295, 297).

Underlying the use of cross-elasticity is an implicit assumption that customers react to percentage changes in price. The same percentage price change will, however, yield a larger absolute price change for a more expensive brand. If customers react to absolute price changes, the more expensive brand will have a larger elasticity. On the flip side, the same absolute change in sales translates into a higher elasticity for the smaller brand. Thus, one would expect a larger cross-elasticity for the effect of a change of a national brand (larger market share, higher price) on a store brand sales than the reverse. This phenomenon has been termed "scaling bias." One way to address scaling bias would be to use response sensitivity [Equation (3.2)] instead of elasticity. The problem with using response sensitivity is that its value depends on the units of measurement, making it unsuitable for meta-analyses. An alternative measure of cross-effects has been proposed (Sethuraman, Srinivasan, and Kim 1999, p. 26). We rename this absolute measure of cross-effects, *category-adjusted [price] cross-effects response sensitivity*:

$$\gamma_{ij} \equiv \frac{\partial MS_i}{\partial P_j} \times (0.01 P_C) = \eta_{MS,ij} \times \frac{MS_i}{P_j} \times (0.01 P_C), \tag{8.16}$$

where P_C is the market-share weighted average brand price in the category. By using market share and expressing price changes as one-percent of the product category price, the units of measurement problem with response sensitivity is addressed. Use of the measure when sales cross-elasticities are reported requires making the assumption that the category expansion cross-elasticity is zero so that the sales cross-elasticity equals the market share cross-elasticity.

A meta-analysis of 1,060 price cross-elasticities found in studies covering 280 brands in 19 different grocery categories found a strong and significant asymmetric price effect when cross-elasticities were examined (Sethuraman, Srinivasan, and Kim 1999, p. 32). The asymmetric effect, however, tended to disappear when category-adjusted price cross-effects response sensitivity was examined. Sethuraman, Srinivasan, and Kim, hereafter SSK, developed some additional empirical generalizations.

Brands that are closer to each other in price have larger cross-price effects than brands that are priced further apart. [SSK]

A brand is affected the most by discounts of its closest higher-priced brand, followed closely by discounts of its closest lower-priced brand. [SSK]

Support. The meta-analysis above found a strong and significant neighborhood price effects with both price cross-elasticities and category-adjusted price cross-effects response sensitivities (Sethuraman, Srinivasan, and Kim 1999, p. 32). The neighborhood price effect was stronger than the asymmetric price effect.

Brand-level and category-level price elasticities first decrease in absolute value then ultimately increase in absolute value as the product life cycle enters the decline phase.

Support. A study of 17 the first purchases of consumer durable goods found that elasticities in the majority of categories were dynamic over the product life cycle and that elasticity dynamics fell into two broad categories (Parker 1992, p. 365):

1. For (A) necessities or categories having reached and maintained penetration levels exceeding 90 percent and (B) categories with increasing penetration levels, elasticities are either constant, not statistically different from zero, or decline in absolute value toward the later stages of the adoption life cycle.

2. For (A) non-necessities facing penetration decline or disadoption or (B) non-necessities that have reached a stable penetration plateau, elasticities increase in absolute value during one or all stages of the adoption life cycle.

Remember that the decline phase of the product life cycle is due to competitive substitutes and changes in taste. This work was extended to total category sales, which incorporated both first and repeat purchases, in Parker and Neelamegham (1997). They noted that the elasticities were of plausible magnitudes and comparable to an estimate of –2.0 reported for all durables in Tellis (1988). A similar pattern was reported for brand-level sales in Simon (1979). Also see Jain and Rao (1990) and Andrews and Franke (1996).

Advertising's Impact on Price Sensitivity

An increase in price advertising leads to higher price sensitivity among consumers. [KW]

Support. For four product categories (frozen waffles, liquid bleach, bathroom tissue, and ketchup), price elasticities were estimated across markets and their relationship to market characteristics was examined. Higher retailer price advertising was found to lead to higher price elasticity (Bolton 1989a). For a consumer nondurable product, similar results were found for local price advertising (Popkowski-Lesczyck and Rao 1989). Additional support is provided by an experimental study on regular ground coffee, liquid cleaner, disposable diapers, cat litter, hair spray, and sparkling wine (Bemmaor and Mouchoux 1991).

An increase in feature advertising leads to higher price sensitivity among consumers. [KW]

Support. Feature advertising is local, usually newspaper, advertising by a retailer highlighting a reduced-price promotion. Thus, feature advertising is a special case of price advertising and has a similar effect. An experimental study found a substantial negative interaction between feature advertising and retail price for a durable good (Moriarty 1983).

An increase in non-price advertising leads to lower price sensitivity among consumers. [KW]

Support. Prior to 1990, TV advertising was not allowed in the UK's sanitary protection market. Measurements were made that showed that, within 12 months of TV advertising starting, price elasticities had changed from –2.5 pre-1990 to –2.0 post-1990. The markets were still competitive but the brands were stronger (Baker 1999, p. 23).

An examination of 22 heavily advertised brands in Western Europe revealed that the absolute values of price elasticities were related to a measure of advertising intensity (Lambin 1976). In an analysis of diary panel data, sales of heavily advertised brands tended to be less price elastic than sales of less advertised brands (Ghosh, Neslin, and Shoemaker 1983). Using bimonthly data on a consumer packaged good, higher nonprice (national) advertising was associated with lower price sensitivity (Popkowski-Leszczyc and Rao 1989). Another study found that, as the advertising share of a brand increased beyond 40 percent, its price sensitivity decreased (Vanhonacker 1989b). Additional support is found in the split-cable experiments of Prasad and Ring (1976), Staelin and Winer (1976), and Krishnamurthi and Raj (1985).

Implications. Given the empirical evidence of differential effects of price and non-price advertising on consumers' price sensitivity, managers should analyze these tradeoffs when making decisions about advertising and price. Coordination between advertising and pricing decisions is essential (Kaul and Wittink 1995, p. G158).

Blattberg, Briesch, and Fox (1995), hereafter BBF, building on Blattberg and Neslin (1989), designated as BN, proposed some generalizations about sales promotions.

Manufacturer Consumer Promotions

Elasticity of coupon spending on own brand sales is positive but very low. [BG]

Support. Consultants at the Hudson River Group, doing regression analyses of aggregate level data, found an average elasticity of coupon spending of 0.07 (Bucklin and Gupta 1999, p. 259).

When this generalization is coupled with the main advertising generalization, following corollary follows:

Coupon response is less than media response. [BG]

Support. Studies of marketing mix effectiveness done by ACNielsen for products of The Quaker Oats Company revealed that coupons had the lowest impact of any marketing mix element. The reason was unsurprising. The heaviest redeemers of coupons for Quaker brands were their own heaviest users (Bucklin and Gupta 1999, p. 259).

Implications. Packaged goods manufacturers should reduce their spending on coupons—and they have begun to do so. Procter and Gamble has conducted tests in upstate New York where they eliminated the use of coupons. Nestle U.S.A. now uses coupons primarily in conjunction with new product launches. Other companies are stressing more targeted use of coupons, which has been made possible by check-out couponing systems such the one as that from Catalina Marketing, Inc. (Bucklin and Gupta 1999, p. 260).

Manufacturer Trade Promotions

Manufacturers, wholesalers, and retailers are independent economic agents, each with different goals, yet sharing certain common goals. Unfortunately, in many companies, there are often no systems in place for adequately measuring and monitoring of trade promotion expenditures. But when there are, certain interesting findings emerge.

Retailers pass-through is generally less than 100 percent of trade deals. [BBF]

Support. This finding has been reported by Chevalier and Curhan (1976), Walters (1989), and Blattberg and Neslin (1990). *Pass-through* is the percentage of a trade deal that is given to consumers. Be aware that, theoretically, there are classes of important sales response functions for which the optimal retailer pass-through is greater than as well as less than 100 percent (Tyagi 1999).

Manufacturer trade promotions often fund retailer sales promotions and such retailer sales promotions are also referred to as "trade promotions." We discuss these as part of the next section.

Retailer Sales Promotions

Retailer sales promotions are geared toward increasing store sales. However, as just noted, many of the retailer sales promotions are funded by manufacturer trade promotions. Thus, one finds analyses being conducted from the point of view of the manufacturer as well as the retailer. The effects of retail promotions on brand sales have been commonly analyzed at the store or market levels. Additional insights on the differential effects of a brand's promotion on brand- loyal and brand-switching segments have been found by conducting analyses at the individual-household level.[13]

Elasticities for price-cut promotions are higher for categories with relatively less number of brands, higher category penetration, shorter interpurchase times, and higher consumer propensity to stockpile.

Support. A study of 108 product categories with data compiled from weekly scanner data, scanner panel data, and survey data ran three separate regressions with feature, display, and pure price cut elasticities as the dependent variables with category characteristics as the explanatory variables (Narasimhan, Neslin, and Sen 1996). Expected support for a relationship between promotional response and propensity to purchase a category on impulse was not there.

Implications. Managers should take into account the nature of their category, using this finding as a benchmark, in assessing the performance of their promotions. Higher sales response should be expected in categories such as paper products [towels and toilet tissue], canned products [seafood, tomatoes, and vegetables], and pasta. Lower sales response should be expected in categories such as health and beauty aids [cotton balls, first-aid treatment, deodorant, razors, shaving cream, bath products, and suntan lotion] and miscellaneous products [spices, condensed milk, floor cleaners, foil pans, bottled water] (Narasimhan, Neslin, and Sen 1996).

Temporary price reductions (TPRs) substantially increase sales. [BBF]

Support. Sales promotions have a dramatic immediate impact on brand sales. This generalization is supported by the findings of Woodside and Waddle (1975), Moriarty (1985, p. 42), and Blattberg and Wisniewski (1987).

Promotional price elasticities exceed nonpromtional price elasticities. [BBF]

Support. In a model of brand choice using IRI scanner panel data, the promotional price elasticity was higher than the nonpromotional price elasticity for premium-priced ground coffee brands (Lattin and Bucklin 1989). See also Mulhern and Leone (1991). See Table 8-8.

Table 8-8. Price versus Deal Elasticity

Industry	Price Elasticity	Deal Discount Elasticity
Flour, 5-lb. all-purpose		
Pillsbury (0.37, P) *a*	−1.32	5.79
Gold Medal (0.09, P)	−2.59	10.08
Ceresota (0.11, P)	−1.85	5.34
Jewel Maid (0.08, M)	−2.47	14.34
Generic (0.34, G)	*b*	—
Tuna Fish, 6.5 oz. chunk light in oil *c*		
Bumble Bee (0.25, P)	−4.99	10.28
Chicken of the Sea (0.21, P)	−0.72	8.04
Starkist (0.16, P)	−3.08	8.50
Blue Brook (0.07, M)	−2.56	8.10
Generic (0.31, G)	*b*	—
Bathroom Tissue *d*		
Charmin (0.15, P)	−1.21	10.32
Northern (0.10, P)	−3.17	9.03
White Cloud (0.07, P)	−1.69	10.35
Soft 'N Pretty (0.05, P)	−6.53	11.63
Scottissue (0.12, M)	*b*	7.72
Coronet (0.03, M)	−2.02	4.66
Jewel (0.03, M)	*b*	11.26
Sable Soft (0.03, M)		
Generic (0.42, G)	−3.59	—
Margarine, 1 lb. regular stick		
Imperial (0.17, P)	*b*	5.05
Land O'Lakes (0.14, P)	−2.34	4.84
Parkay (0.12, P)	−3.88.	8.65
Bluebonnet (0.06, P)	*b*	0.49
Chiffon (0.04, P)	−2 86	6.42
BlueBrook (0.32, M)	−2.23	2.23
Sunnyland (0.08, M)	—	9.56
Generic (0.07, G)	*b*	—

a (market share, price tier: P = premium, M = moderate, G = generic)
b No regular price variation in the data series used to estimate the model.
c Compare results with Kadiyali, Chintagunta, and Vilcassim (2000, p. 144)
d Compare results with Allenby (1989).

Source: Blattberg and Wisniewski (1987) as reported in Blattberg and Neslin (1990), p. 356.
Market share data from Blattberg and Wisniewski (1989), p. 301.

Display and feature advertising have strong effects on sale items. [BBF]

Support. The mean display multiplier for liquid dishwasher detergent was found to be 1.69, which is greater than one as expected, i.e., increases sales. The display multipliers for individual brands were 1.5 for Crystal White Octagon, 2.6 for Dove, 1.5 for Dawn, 1.4 for Ivory, 1.6 for Palmolive, and 1.8 for Sunlight (Kopalle, Mela, and Marsh 1999, p. 325). The mean competitive display multiplier was found to be

Table 8-9. Price Elasticity versus Multipliers

Industry	Price Elasticity	Feature Multiplier	Display Multiplier	Feature + Display
Powdered Detergent				
Tide 72	−1.97	2.41	2.32	4.22
Tide 147	−1.78	2.44	2.44	4.99
Cheer 147	−1.99	6.55	4.53	12.68
Oxydol 72	−1.95	3.78	2.77	5.26
Oxydol 147	−1.40	3.49	3.39	4.44

Source: Christen et al. (1997, p. 332).

0.88, which is less than one as expected i.e., decrease sales. The mean feature multiplier for liquid dishwasher detergent was found to be 1.65. The feature multipliers for individual brands were 1.4 for Crystal White Octagon, 1.9 for Dove, 1.3 for Dawn, 1.3 for Ivory, 1.6 for Palmolive, and 2.8 for Sunlight. The mean competitive feature multiplier was also 0.88. See Table 8-9 for multipliers for powdered detergents. See Woodside and Waddle (1975), Blattberg and Wisnieski (1987), and Kumar and Leone (1988). Also see Bolton (1989) and Bemmaor and Mouchoux (1991).

Advertised promotions can result in increased traffic. [BBF]

Support. See Walters and Rinne (1986), Gupta (1988), Kumar and Leone (1988), and Walters and MacKenzie (1988). Pauwels, Hanssens and Siddarth (1999) find that the short-term promotion effect on traffic generally dissipates in the long run.

The greater the frequency of deals, the lower the height of the deal spike. [BBF]

Support. Raju (1992) shows that consumers stockpile less as promotional frequency increases. See also Assuncao and Meyer (1993).

Promotions affect sales in complementary and competitive categories. [BBF]

Support. See Walters and Rinne (1986), Walters and Mackenzie (1988), Mulhern and Leone (1991), and Walters (1991).

Higher market-share brands are less deal elastic. [BBF]

Support. See Bolton (1989a), Bemmaor and Mouchon (1991), and Vilcassim and Jain (1991).

Cross-promotional effects are asymmetric, and promoting higher quality brands has a disproportionate effect on weaker brands and private label products. [BBF]

The effect of Brand B's promotion on Brand A's sales. The argument is that higher-price, higher quality brands steal share from brands in the tier below as well as from other brands in the same price-quality tier. However, lower-tier brands do not steal significant share from the tiers above (Blattberg and Wisniewski 1989). Cross-elasticities for actual prices in four product categories are shown in Table 8-10. See Krishnamurthi and Raj (1988 and 1991), Cooper (1988), and Walters (1991). See also Allenby and Rossi (1991), Bemmaor and Mouchoux (1991), Grover and Srinivasan (1992), Kamakura and Russell (1989), Mulhern and Leone (1991), and Vilcassim and Jain (1991).

Support. The effect of Brand A's promotion on Brand B's sales is not the same as

Implications. A brand can use promotions to gain an advantage if effects are asymmetric. If Brand A can attract more of Brand B's customers than Brand B can attract of Brand A's customers, then Brand A will hold the upper hand in a promotional war. Brand B will have difficulty retaliating effectively (Blattberg, Briesch, and Fox 1995, p. G129).

Price versus Promotion

The frequency of deals changes the consumer's reference price. [BBF]

Support. A household-level analysis of scanner panel data from the liquid detergent category found that increased purchases using coupons eroded brand loyalty and increased price sensitivity (Paptla and Krishnamurthi 1996). Frequent dealing makes both loyal and non-loyal segments increasingly price sensitive over time (Mela, Gupta and Lehmann 1997, pp. 255-56). Also see Lattin and Bucklin (1989), Kalwani and Yim (1992), and Mayhew and Winer (1992).

An analysis of the dynamic effect of discounting on sales found that promotions have positive contemporaneous effects on sales accompanied by negative future effects on baseline sales. Empirical results suggested that promotions could lead to *triple jeopardy*: (1) As discounts become more endemic, baseline sales decrease. (2) Temporary price reductions can increase price sensitivity, putting downward pressure on margins. (3) Frequent use of deals makes them a less effective tool for stealing share from competing brands (Kopalle, Mela, and Marsh 1999, p. 330).

Implication. If a product is heavily discounted through frequent and deep discounts, consumers' reference prices fall. Consequently, the product's regular price will look

Table 8-10. Price Cross-Elasticities

Bathroom Tissue a	CHM	NTH	WTC	SNP	SCT	COR	JWL	SBL	GNC
Charmin	—	0.80b	1.14	0.74	NSc	0.24	0.19	NDd	NS
Northern	1.31	—	0.90	0.89	NS	NS	NS	ND	NS
White Cloud	1.47	0.72	—	0.56	NS	NS	NS	ND	NS
Soft 'N Pretty	1.83	1.58	1.69	—	1.37	NS	0.96	ND	NS
Scottissue	NS	NS	NS	1.25	—	0.34	NS	ND	NS
Coronet	NS	NS	NS	NS	1.50	—	1.92	ND	NS
Jewel	NS	0.80	NS	0.71	1.99	1.04	—	ND	0.15
Sable Soft	1.33	1.56	0.98	1.75	1.30	0.39	0.17	ND	NS
Generic	NS	NS	NS	NS	0.92	0.64	0.18	ND	—

Flour	PIL	GMD	CER	JM	GNC
Pillsbury	—	0.99	DRe	0.19	DR
Gold Medal	1.15	—	DR	1.74	DR
Ceresota	0.67	1.21	DR	0.08	DR
Jewel Maid	2.44	1.18	DR	—	DR
Generic	0.65	0.01	DR	0.43	DR

Margarine	IMP	LOL	PKY	BBT	CHF	BBK	SNY	GNC
Imperial	—	NS	NS	0.49	NS	NS	NS	NS
Land O'Lakes	0.84	—	0.34	0.23	NS	NS	0.21	NS
Parkay	0.71	0.63	—	0.25	NS	NS	NS	NS
Bluebonnet	0.27	0.50	0.32	—	NS	NS	0.27	NS
Chiffon	NS	0.44	0.23	0.43	—	NS	NS	NS
BlueBrook	NS	NS	0.15	NS	NS	—	0.25	NS
Sunnyland	0.64	0.75	0.20	NS	0.85	0.30	—	NS
Generic	NS	NS	NS	NS	NS	0.19	0.13	—

Tuna Fish f	BBB	CKN	STK	BBK	GNC
Bumble Bee	—	1.05	0.85	NS	
Chicken of the Sea	0.64	—	0.09	NS	
Starkist	NS	1.26	—	NS	
Blue Brook	1.55	NS	0.54	—	
Generic	NS	NS	NS	NS	

a Compare results with Allenby (1989).
b The percentage change in *unit sales* of Charmin with respect to a one percent change in the *actual price* of Northern.
c NS = not significant. See source for complete results.
d ND = no deals of any type for this brand.
e DR = dealing very rare for this brand.
f Compare results with Kadiyali, Chintagunta, and Vilcassim (2000, p. 144)

Source: Blattberg and Wisniewski (1989, p. 301).

less appealing and regular price sales will decline. In sum, a product can be over-promoted (Blattberg, Briesch, and Fox 1995, p. G128). Excessive discounting could even compromise a brand's asymmetric price advantage (Kopalle, Mela, and Marsh 1999, p. 330).

Distribution Effects

There is a bi-directional relation between distribution and sales.

Increasing distribution (availability) increases sales/market share.

Support. This finding has been established for some time. See Nuttall (1965), Farley and Leavitt (1968), Parsons (1974), Leone and Schultz (1980), and Reibstein and Farris (1995). Distribution is one of the most potent marketing contributors to sales and market share and its elasticity can be substantially greater than one.

Increasing store shelf (display) space has a positive impact on sales of nonstaple grocery items. [SL]

Support. An early review of 20 studies found a mean shelf-space elasticity of 0.15 (1977 study by Heinsbroek reported in Bultez and Naert 1988a, p. 213). Early studies include Pauli and Hoecker [1952], Mueller, Kline, and Trout [1953], *Progressive Grocer* [1963-1964], Cox [1964], Kotzan and Evanson [1969], Cox [1970], Frank and Massy [1970], Kennedy [1970], and Curhan [1972, 1974a,b].[14] In addition, see Walkers Crisps (potato chips) example in Duckworth (1997).

Moreover, higher product sales increase the attractiveness of a product to the channel, thereby further increasing distribution (Reibstein and Farris 1995).

Increasing sales/market share increases distribution (availability, front stocks).

Support. Econometric modeling of Walkers Crisps (potato chips) in the UK found a feedback between volume share and front stock share. The bi-directional sales-distribution relationship creates a momentum for new products that explains their long-term position in the market (Bronnenberg, Mahajan, and Vanhonacker 2000).

High-share brands have more share points per point of distribution. [RF]

Support. The proposition is that the cross-sectional relationships between brand retail distribution show a convex pattern. See Nuttal (1965), Farris, Olver, and de Kluyver (1989), Borin, Van Vranken, and Farris (1991), Mercer (1991), and Verbeke, Clement, and Farris (1994).

Implication. The convex market-share/distribution relationship implies that, when it comes to distribution, the "rich get richer". For example, in most categories, larger stores distribute most brands, so each brand competes with all others. As distribution intensifies, smaller and more specialized stores are tapped. Since these stores typically carry a narrower range of products, the competition facing one of the better-distributed brands lessens; and thus the marginal effect of distribution on sales increases. This effect is amplified by the reverse causal link.

Personal Selling Effects

Sales calls have positive effects on sales, usually with decreasing returns to scale.

Support. Various studies on the effects of military recruiters on youth enlistment in the military have quantified the sales calling effect. The reported elasticities range from 0.26 to 0.98, with most around 0.5. See Morey and McCann (1980), Goldberg (1982), Hanssens and Levien (1983), and Carroll et al. (1985). An analysis of strategic business units (SBUs) using PIMS data found disaggregate elasticity estimates for salesforce expenditures to be 0.006 for "price sensitive" SBUs, 0.075 for "industry standard" SBUs, 0.556 for "salesforce sensitive" SBUs, and 0.568 for quality/salesforce sensitive" SBUs (Ramaswamy et al. 1993, p. 114). The salesforce sensitive SBUs thus also have an elasticity around 0.5.

Implications. Personal communication, or sales calling, is much more sales effective than advertising; it is, however, also more expensive. Managers are well advised to study sales-call elasticities and make sales force allocation decisions accordingly. If the sales-call elasticity show increasing returns to scale, then an expansion of the sales force would seem desirable.

Product Quality Effects

Quantification of product value or quality is difficult, so the empirical evidence is thin.

Product quality increases sales, however, with decreasing returns to quality.

Support. A massive early study of market response incorporated proxy measures of product quality where it could (Lambin 1976, pp. 103-5). Statistically-significant (at the 10 percent level) quality elasticities with the expected sign were found for a soft drink brand (Belgium), two yogurt brands (Belgium), an autotrain (Belgium), and three brands of electric shavers (Germany/ Scandinavia). The average quality elasticity for sales was 0.385. The average quality elasticity for market share was 0.630. The overall quality elasticity was 0.521 (p. 104). The analysis of strategic SBUs mentioned in the last section found disaggregate elasticity estimates for relative quality to be 0.098 for "salesforce sensitive" SBUs, 0.156 for "industry standard" SBUs, 0.249 for "price sensitive" SBUs and 0.611 for quality/salesforce sensitive" SBUs (Ramaswamy et al. 1993, p. 114). The weighted average was 0.194, which is higher than the corresponding advertising elasticity. In another study, a product-value elasticity of 0.4 was found using a longitudinal database of conjoint-inferred product value (Hanssens 1998).

The effectiveness of perceived product quality is a function of order of entry.

Support. The elasticity for product quality decreased 24 percent from the first to the twelfth entrant in the minivan category and decreased 90 percent in the sports utility market (Bowman and Gatignon 1996, p. 238). A study of the U.S. ethical drug industry found higher response for growth-stage entrants compared with pioneers and mature-stage entrants (Shankar, Carpenter, and Krishnamurthi 1999, p. 274).

On average, increased market share has a negative effect on product quality perceptions.

Support. Research using data on 85 brands across 28 product categories yielded this finding (Hellofs and Jacobson 1999). Exclusivity and premium pricing were found to act as moderators. As concerns for exclusivity become greater, the negative impact of market share on perceived quality become greater. The brand characteristic of premium pricing, however, lessens the negative effect of market share gains.

Implication. Managers should realize that quality increases are generally not matched by proportional sales increases, so quality strategies can be costly. Moreover, they need to be concerned that market share expansion may well have a negative impact on customers' perceptions of product quality.

Competitive Reaction Effects

The simple competitive reaction is nonnegative.

Support. If a competitor reacts a firm's action, the direction of change should be the same. Most of the early empirical evidence on reaction elasticities concerned advertising and was due to Lambin (1976) and Metwally (1978).[15] The mean simple advertising reaction elasticity in five product categories studied by Lambin was 0.471. An examination of four brands in a mature nonfood product category found a positive advertising reaction between specific pairs of brands (Jedidi, Mela, and Gupta 1999, p. 12).

Having seen some of what is known about brand sales, we now turn to industry sales.

Industry-Level Findings and Generalizations

Models of industry demand have also been constructed to assess the impact of industry, trade association, or government efforts and to address public policy questions. We have already discussed the increase in primary demand that can occur with advertising by competing brands within an industry. In addition, there may be cooperative *generic advertising*, which emphasizes the product category and not a specific brand. For example, wool producers might want to determine the effectiveness of advertising the "Wool Mark." In the same vein, public health officials might want to evaluate the relationship between cigarette advertising and children's cigarette consumption. These would be examples of "primary" advertising.

Generic Advertising Effects

Generic advertising has a direct and positive influence on total industry (market) sales. [LS]

Suppport. A number of studies have examined industry or generic advertising effects. Some of the findings are as follows. Advertising and promotion expenditures of the two largest organized groups of growers, the Florida Citrus Commission and Sunkist Growers, had a marked impact on the sales of oranges in the United States (Nerlove and Waugh 1961). Generic advertising for tea in the United Kingdom slowed a downward sales trend but could not reverse the slide (Ball and Agarwala 1969). In only four out of ten European product markets did industry advertising increase industry sales (Lambin 1976). A meta-analysis of cigarette consumption studies from eight countries found a positive impact of advertising on sales (Andrews and Franke 1991).[16] Advertising by the Australian Meat and Livestock Corporation for beef and lamb had a positive effect on the demand for beef and a negative effect on the demand for chicken whereas advertising by the Australian Pork Corporation did not have statistically significant effects (Piggott et al 1996).

Various long-run elasticities for generic advertising for fluid milk have been reported. These include 0.0212 (Thompson and Eiler 1977, p. 332) or, more recently, 0.00172 (Liu and Forker 1988, p. 232) in New York City and 0.1214 in Buffalo, New York (Kinnucan 1987, p. 190), which was considered an unusually high value.

As with brand advertising, the influence of generic advertising will vary by media. A study of monthly fluid milk sales in Texas found inverted v-lag patterns for both television advertising and radio advertising (Capps and Schmitz 1991, p. 138).[17] The long-run elasticities (evaluated at the sample means) were 0.0021 for television and 0.0071 for radio. The mean lag was 4.6818 months for television and 6.4923 for radio. Thus, television would be the appropriate medium to bring about changes in fluid milk consumption more quickly but radio would be more appropriate to bring about changes over the long run.

Both generic and brand advertising are seen to have a positive impact on primary demand. For frozen potatoes, mainly frozen french fries, the long-run elasticity of brand advertising was estimated as 0.0742 and the elasticity of generic advertising as 0.054 (Jones and Ward 1989, p. 531).[18] For yogurt (in California)), the long-run elasticity of brand advertising was estimated as 0.11 and the elasticity of generic advertising as 0.03 (Hall and Foik 1983, p. 22). The mean lag was 2.7 months for brand advertising and 2.1 months for generic advertising. One would expect significant complementarity between generic and brand advertising when both are used in a market.

When brand advertising expenditures are markedly larger than generic advertising expenditures, brand advertising has a significant reinforcement effect on generic advertising programs.

Support. One study found that found that a given expenditure on generic cheese advertising produced a greater sales increase when brand advertising expenditures were high than when they are low (Kinnucan and Fearon 1986, p. 100).

When brand advertising expenditures are markedly larger than generic advertising expenditures, the ability of generic advertising to reinforce brand advertising is limited—and marginal gains decline rapidly as the level of generic expenditure increases.

Support. Brand advertising complements generic advertising more so than vice versa. See Kinnucan and Fearon (1986, pp. 100-101).

The influence of primary advertising on total industry sales declines as an industry matures.

Support. Using a model with systematic parameter variation, advertising was shown to influence the diffusion of new telephones in West Germany (Simon and Sebastian 1987). The advertising (goodwill) elasticity attained a maximum of 2.14 percent, then declined nonmonotonically to 0.89 percent within five years. In the meta-analysis of cigarette consumption studies, the impact of advertising on sales declined over time (Andrews and Franke 1991).

Primary Price Effects

Price has a direct and negative influence on total industry (market) sales.

Support. An analysis of mostly 4-digit S.I.C. U.S. food and manufacturing industries revealed that the mean price elasticity estimates uniformly were between zero and minus one (Pagoulatos and Sorensen 1986). Values ranged from –0.008 for flavoring extracts and syrups to –0.756 for cigars. Values for other products are given in Table 8-11. Similarly, the price elasticities for various types of American wines were found to fall between zero and minus one as shown in Table 8-12 (Shapouri, Folwell, and Baritelle 1981). In a meta-analysis of cigarette consumption studies, consumption was inelastic (Andrews and Franke 1991). For example, a study of cigarette consumption in the United Kingdom reported that price elasticities in previous studies tended to cluster in the –0.2 to –0.6 range, which confirmed the reasonableness of its price elasticity estimate of –0.23 (Radfar 1985, p. 228). A survey of gasoline price elasticities found that the estimated values were in the range of –0.60 for long time series and –1.02 for cross-sectional data (Dahl 1986). Two more recent studies (Gately 1992; Hausman and Newey 1995, p. 1461, respectively) put the long run estimate at –0.75 and –0.81. Shrinkage estimates for short-run and long-run elasticities for energy were –0.16 and –0.26 for electricity and –0.10 and –0.28 for natural gas (Maddala et al. 1997, pp. 96-97). The price elasticity for steel in the United Kingdom was –0.62 (Abbott, Lawler and Armistad 1999, p. 1300).

Industry sales are less price elastic than individual brand sales.

Support. Industry price elasticities are typically less than one in absolute magnitude (inelastic) whereas brand price elasticities are typically larger than one in absolute magnitude (elastic). Compare results in this section to those in the *Price Effects* section. Note also that the presweetened segment of the ready-to-eat cereal market in the United States was discovered to be much more price sensitive than the market as a whole (Neslin and Shoemaker 1983). A store-level analysis found that the category elasticity was smaller than the item or brand elasticity in 13 out of 18 categories as shown in Table 8-13 (Hoch et al. 1995, p. 22).

Implications. If industry elasticities are less than one (inelastic), then why do firms not raise price? The answer is, they do when they can—such as in the case of oligopolies with a leader. On the other hand, a government wanting to curtail smoking or gasoline consumption through tax increases may be disappointed.

Industries with higher advertising intensities are less price elastic.
Industries with higher research and development intensities are less price elastic.

Table 8-11. Industry Price Elasticity Estimates

Industry	Mean Elasticity	Standard Error
Meatpacking plants	−0.703	0.0898
Meat processing plants	−0.648	0.1364
Poultry dressing plants	−0.521	0.0706
Creamery butter	−0.418	0.2116
Cheese, natural and processed	−0.585	0.2850
Condensed and evaporated milk	−0.262	0.0554
Ice cream and frozen deserts	−0.349	0.1361
Fluid milk	−0.172	0.0507
Canned specialties	−0.064	0.0360
Canned fruits and vegetables	−0.229	0.1222
Dehydrated fruits and vegetables	−0.207	0.1106
Pickles, sauces, and salad dressings	−0.232	0.0986
Frozen fruits and vegetables	−0.247	0.0828
Flour and grain mill products	−0.082	0.0372
Cereal breakfast foods	−0.031	0.0959
Milled rice	−0.251	0.1059
Blended and prepared flour	−0.035	0.0173
Wet corn milling	−0.054	0.0257
Pet food	−0.061	0.0400
Prepared feeds	−0.102	0.0622
Bread and bakery products	−0.220	0.0751
Cookie and crackers	−0.188	0.1135
Raw cane sugar	−0.019	0.0242
Cane and beet refining	−0.131	0.0273
Confectionery products	−0.074	0.0260
Chocolate and cocoa products	−0.304	0.0440
Chewing gum	−0.187	0.0454
Cottonseed oil mills	−0.009	0.1780
Soybean oil mills	−0.275	0.0830
Vegetable oil mills	−0.222	0.3200
Animal and marine fats and oils	−0.067	0.0285
Shortening, cooking oil and margarine	−0.250	0.0570
Malt beverages	−0.283	0.1781
Malt	−0.222	0.1012
Wines, brandy, and brandy spirits	−0.198	0.5421
Distilled liquor	−0.033	0.0785
Soft drinks	−0.052	0.1180
Flavoring extracts and syrups	−0.008	0.0256
Canned and cured seafood	−0.736	0.2729
Fresh and frozen packaged fish	−0.695	0.2795
Roasted coffee	−0.120	0.0429
Macaroni, Spaghetti, and noodles	−0.102	0.0689
Cigarettes	−0.107	0.2673
Cigars	−0.756	0.5497
Chewing and smoking tobacco	−0.105	0.0905
Stemmed and redried tobacco	−0.306	0.2786

Source: Pagoulatos and Sorensen (1986, p. 240).

Support. See Pagoulatos and Sorensen (1986).

Table 8-12. Price Elasticity Estimates for Wine

Type	Elasticity	Standard Error
Varietal table wines		
Red	−0.77	0.045
White	−0.64	0.062
Pink	−0.93	0.073
Concord	−0.86	0.069
Nonvarietal table wines		
Red	−0.94	0.021
White	−0.89	0.023
Pink	−0.99	0.021
Dessert wines		
Sherry	−0.51	0.038
Port	−0.90	0.053
Sparkling wines		
Champagne	−0.43	0.078
Cold Duck	−0.24	0.067
Sparkling burgundy	−0.41	0.152
Flavored wines		
Apple	−0.35	0.064
Berry	−0.36	0.055
Citrus	−0.87	0.055
Vermouth	−0.74	0.080
Brandy		
Flavored	−0.66	0.088
Natural	−0.31	0.103

Source: Shapouri, Folwell, and Baritelle (1981, p. 21).

Implications. In industry price elasticity is not simply an exogenous element of market structure. It is, at least in part, determined by the strategic behavior of firms within an industry.

Industries producing for derived or intermediate demand are less price elastic than those producing for final demand are.

Support. See Pagoulatos and Sorensen (1986).

Implications. Unlike goods produced for final demand, intermediate goods are used in a complementary fashion with other inputs. Consequently, producer goods are less price elastic.

Primary Promotion Effects

Primary demand is elastic vis-a-vis price promotions in the short run.

Table 8-13. Store-Level Price Elasticities

Category	Category Elasticity	Standard Error	Own Elasticity
Food Items			
Soft dinks	−3.18	0.39	−2.59
Canned seafood	−1.79	0.47	−0.96
Canned soup	−1.62	0.22	−1.66
Cookies	−1.60	0.25	−0.90
Grahams/saltines	−1.01	0.57	−1.46
Snack crackers	−0.86	0.36	−0.79
Frozen entries	−0.77	0.46	−1.65
Refrigerated juice	−0.74	0.51	−2.24
Dairy cheese	−0.72	0.35	−1.44
Frozen juice	−0.55	0.32	−1.95
Cereal	−0.20	0.22	−1.14
Bottled juice	−0.09	0.26	−1.49
Nonfood items			
Bathroom tissue	−2.42	0.19	−2.28
Laundry detergent	−1.58	0.21	−1.99
Fabric softener	−0.79	0.06	−1.77
Liquid dish detergent	−0.74	0.29	−1.64
Toothpaste	−0.45	0.37	−2.00
Paper towels	0.05	0.52	−1.21

Source: Hoch et al. (1981, p. 20).

Support. A major empirical study of the primary demand effects of price promotions in 560 product categories estimated the average short-run promotion elasticity at 2.21 (Nijs et al. 2001).

The predominant long-run promotion elasticity of primary demand is zero.

Support. The same study of 560 product categories showed that, over a four-year period, the promotion elasticities of primary demand gradually decline and become zero in the long run, in all but a few cases (Nijs et al. 2001).

Implications. Promotion is an effective tool for shaping demand patterns in the short run, but rarely defines long-run trends in consumption. As such, the intensive use of price promotions at the expense of other forms of marketing can contribute to the preservation of the status quo in an industry.

The relation between market response and marketing variables is the core of the theory and practice of marketing management. The links between marketing mix variables and their effects on sales are being mapped out through the ongoing search for marketing generalizations.

Notes

[1] The distinction is between a brand's sales (or market share) and any aggregation of sales that includes the brand such as an industry, market, product class, or category.

[2] Some estimated own-elasticities and cross-elasticities of market drivers for various products are shown in Tables 6-7 and 6-8 of our first edition, with sales and market share respectively. For comparison, the own elasticities of some additional products were given in Table 6-5.

[3] Modeling relative price by sinh was also done by Albach (1979). Albach displayed figures showing the change in own and cross-elasticities over time.

[4] The empirical evidence on reaction elasticities is given in Tables 6-9 to 6-11 of our first edition.

[5] Lancaster misclassified deodorants as primary demand only.

[6] The finding that advertising for brand X affects its own sales is too narrow to be an empirical generalization and the statement that some advertising affects some sales is too broad.

[7] An argument has been made that the statistically significant effects of advertising found in studies using market response models may be spurious results reached by the aggregation of the data over time and households (Tellis and Weiss 1995, p. 12).

[8] Some argue that this own-price elasticity appears too low. An elasticity of -2.5 would imply an optimal markup (see Equation 9.3) of $MUC^* = -\dfrac{1}{(\varepsilon_P + 1)} = -\dfrac{1}{(-2.5 + 1)} = 0.67$ or 67%. One seldom sees markup this large for fast moving consumer goods. One reason is that the retailer worries about lost customers.

[9] These elasticities were based on a nested logit model. The consumer was assumed to first choose package size, then if a 32 ounce package was desired, to choose between Heinz and Hunts. Elasticities from a simple logit model (not shown here) had the desirable feature of all being more negative than minus one.

[10] This implies that primary demand for the products studied has not been affected by changes in the absolute price levels. Simon (1979) reports a similar result.

[11] We must note that Moran was working with data that have been made obsolete by scanner data and that price promotion and price effects are different.

[12] Building on the theoretical correspondence between brand switching probabilities and elasticities, price competition among liquid laundry detergents has been estimated using a multinomial logit model (Bucklin, Russell, and Srinivasan 1998).

[13] The identification of market segments is discussed in Grover and Srinivasan (1987).

[14] Criticisms of these studies have been made by Peterson and Cagley (1973) and Lynch (1974). They raise the possibility that the relationship between sales and shelf space should be expressed in terms of a simultaneous system of (nonlinear) equations.

[15] See Tables 6-9 to 6-11 in the first edition of this book.

[16] Media and government publicity about the health effects of smoking reduce the sales impact of advertising. See, for example, McGuinness and Cowling (1975) and Radfar (1985).

[17] Empirical results broken down by whole and lowfat milk are presented in Capps and Moen (1992).

[18] The elasticity of brand advertising is lower for frozen potatoes than for potato chips (*Frito-Lay Industry Perspective*) because most frozen potatoes are purchased in nonretail markets where advertising is less effective.

9   MAKING MARKETING PLANS AND SALES FORECASTS

Our discussion of market response models so far has focused on model development, on the interpretation of response parameters and on empirical findings. Of more importance, however, is the use of such models to make marketing plans and budgets and then to make projections about future market outcomes. This may involve estimating optimal levels of prices and marketing spending or simulating the likely effects of different marketing scenarios.

We first review the theory of optimal marketing resource allocation and review empirical decision models that help diagnose companies' actual pricing and marketing spending decisions. We introduce competition in sales response modeling and review how optimal marketing decisions critically depend on observed and anticipated competitive behavior.

We examine the importance of forecasting to business success, paying particular attention to the role of judgmental and quantitative forecasts. Next we review various measures of forecast accuracy and we look at the recent development of automatic forecasting software that permits companies to implement many of the basic techniques. Finally, we contrast extrapolative and explanatory forecasts and show how the combination of forecasting methods reduces forecast error.

When forecasts are based on explanatory models, they can be used to simulate market outcomes of different resource allocation scenarios. We briefly discuss the state of the art of such market response engines, citing various existing applications. Simulating various scenarios naturally leads to the question of optimal marketing decisions, which returns us to where we start the chapter.

Optimal Marketing Decisions

Sales forecasts and what-if scenarios are practical tools for assessing likely market outcomes to different marketing resource allocations, but they are cumbersome for deriving optimal strategies. If a company or decision maker can specify a policy preference function, then we can resort to mathematical optimization methods for deriving optimal marketing behavior.

An extensive literature exists on optimal marketing mix resource allocation rules. These range from simple profit maximization to complex dynamic programming algorithms, with or without competitive considerations. A detailed discussion of these theoretical market response functions and their optimality consequences is beyond the scope of this book. Instead, we will focus on the basic insights on optimal resource allocation, with a focus on those that are based on *estimated* market response functions. We refer the reader interested in theoretical market response functions and their optimality implications for a variety of marketing mix decisions to Moorthy (1993) and Nguyen (1997).

The determination of the optimal marketing mix begins with the specification of a *policy preference function*, which describes the trade off among various goals—say between larger market share and fatter margins per unit. Often a manufacturer simply focuses on short-run contribution to profit and overhead:

$$\text{profit} - \text{fixed costs} = \text{revenue} - \text{production costs} - \text{marketing costs}$$
$$= PQ - C_1 Q - C_2, \tag{9.1}$$

where

X = marketing control variables other than price P,
$Q = f(P, X, EV)$, in which EV = environmental variables,
$C_1 = g(Q, E, X)$, in which E = accumulated experience (volume), and
$C_2 = h(X)$.

When applied to a retailer, cost is a manufacturer's price less trade promotions.

If the planning horizon is more than one period, attention turns to the long-run contribution, which is usually discounted to yield a present value. Although we focus on maximizing one of these contribution functions, we recognize that some firms have other objectives. Japanese firms often seek to maximize the present value of sales subject to a minimum level of the present valued profit (Tsurumi and Tsurumi 1971). Firms launching new products usually price for profit maximization subject to distribution, sales, or market share targets (Parsons 1974; Saghafi 1988). Established brands often seek to maintain stable sales or market share levels. Theoretical decision models were first developed for pricing.

Theory of the Optimal Marketing Mix

Given the policy preference function above, mathematical optimization techniques can be used to derive optimal prices and marketing spending levels. We begin with the derivation of optimal prices and the optimal marketing mix in the simplest case, which ignores competitive and dynamic effects.

Pricing. When the brand's price is the only factor affecting unit sales, and it only affects current unit sales, then the only other phenomenon influencing performance is the nature of the production unit cost function. If unit production costs are fixed, only the current information is relevant and a static pricing policy can be adopted. The optimal price, expressed in terms of the price elasticity, is

$$P* = \frac{\varepsilon_P}{(\varepsilon_P + 1)} C. \tag{9.2}$$

This is relation is only valid if $\varepsilon_P < -1$, which is almost always the case for individual brands; i.e., for selective demand, as we discussed in the last chapter.[1] The firm combines information on its price elasticity obtained from estimating the sales response function with information on its costs obtained from accounting to determine the most profitable price for its product.[2] Caution in implementing this optimal price must be exercised if a large price change is required. This is because the underlying elasticity estimate only specifies the change in sales for an infinitesimal price change.

It follows (Stigler 1952, p. 38) that the optimal markup on cost is

$$MUC* = -\frac{1}{(\varepsilon_P + 1)}, \tag{9.3}$$

and the optimal markup on selling price is

$$MUSP* = -\frac{1}{\varepsilon_P}. \tag{9.4}$$

An optimal markup is an administratively convenient way for a retailer to delegate future pricing decisions to its various outlets.

However, if experience results in unit production costs declining with accumulated volume or if market demand is time dependent, then a dynamic pricing policy is needed to obtain strategic implications. Price differs from other marketing variables in that the cost of a price reduction manifests itself through a reduction in gross margin. The resulting dynamic pricing policy is derived from optimal control theory (Kamien and Schwartz 1991).

Marketing Spending. Treating the selection of the levels for various marketing instruments as independent decisions, the condition for the optimal marketing mix of price, advertising expenditures, distribution expenditures, and product quality expenditures can be found (Dorfman and Steiner 1954). The Dorfman-Steiner condition is that the negative of the price elasticity equals the marginal revenue product of advertising equals the marginal product revenue of distribution equals the product quality (Q') elasticity times the ratio of price to unit cost, viz.,

$$-\varepsilon_P = P\frac{\partial Q}{\partial A} = P\frac{\partial Q}{\partial D} = \varepsilon_{Q'}\frac{P}{C}. \tag{9.5}$$

While this relation does not directly specify the optimal marketing mix, it can be used to evaluate whether or not a brand is operating efficiently. This assessment may be easier to make if we rearrange the first part of (9.5) as

$$\frac{A^*}{R} = -\frac{\varepsilon_A}{\varepsilon_P}, \tag{9.6}$$

where A/R *is* the ratio of advertising to sales revenue. Of course, the precise values of the elasticities are unknown and a manager must use estimates of the elasticities in allocating resources. Since these estimates are known only with uncertainty, an appropriate method for incorporating this uncertainty must be used to yield rigorous confidence intervals applicable to the ratio of elasticities. See Morey and McCann (1983) for such a method. We make use of (9.6) later in our review of empirical evidence, to wit, in Table 9-1. The optimal advertising-revenue ratio is a constant in a specific situation. However, it will vary across brands, product-market categories, firms, and industries as well as over the product life cycle. Variables that explain variations in the ratio will generally depend on the level of entity aggregation.[3]

In the special case where the sales response function is the multiplicative model (see Equation 3.16) and unit costs are constant, the optimum price is independent of the level of advertising and is simply (9.2).[4] The optimal level of advertising is

$$A^* = \varepsilon_A(P^*-C)Q^*. \tag{9.7}$$

If price is the only other marketing instrument, this becomes

$$A^* = [\varepsilon_A(P^*-C)K(P^*)^{\varepsilon_P}]^{1/(1-\varepsilon_A)}, \tag{9.8}$$

where K is the scaling constant in the sales response function. The Dorfman-Steiner condition has also been applied to other functional forms, for example, a linear sales response function with advertising expressed in logarithms (Naert 1972). A spreadsheet (Microsoft Excel) application of the D-S condition can be found in Hegji (1998).

The Dorfman-Steiner theorem can be applied to a multimedia situation (Bultez and Schultz 1979). In practice, advertising budgets and media plans are usually determined sequentially: first, an advertising budget is specified based on some sales response function; then a media schedule is selected that maximizes some measure of advertising effectiveness within this budget constraint.

A caution about the use of the Dorfman-Steiner framework has been issued by Zenor, Bronnenberg, and McAlister (1998, p. 31). As we noted in the last chapter, promotional elasticities are typically larger in absolute value than the elasticities for other sales drivers. Consequently, application of Dorfman-Steiner would result in a brand allocating a disproportionate percentage of its marketing budget to promotional price cuts. The problem is that the traditional economic analysis of Dorfman and Steiner does not consider baseline sales. The Zenor, Bronnenberg, and McAlister framework says that a brand's baseline sales is smaller in the face of a marketing policy that allocates large percentages of the budget to promotional activity. Their conclusion is that "the traditional allocation rule's blindness to the impact of the allocation rule on future response can lead to a policy that drives out high margin, unpromoted sales."

Empirical Decision Models

Rather than using some abstract sales response function, an empirical decision model uses an estimated sales response function. These empirical studies permit consideration of questions such as, is your marketing mix optimal? Are you overspending on advertising? Do departures from optimal marketing levels really matter?

Is Your Marketing Mix Optimal? The Dorfman-Steiner theorem [(9.5), especially as (9.6)] is often used to evaluate whether a brand is operating efficiently. For example, in the processed grapefruit industry, pricing and advertising are initially set at the processor level. Large processors exercise price leadership. The processors support generic advertising through the Florida Citrus Commission. Although advertising goes directly to consumers, factory prices are converted by the channels of distribution into retail prices. Consumer sales is a function of advertising and retail price. Factory sales are then some function of consumer sales. Ward (1975) specified these relations as

$$Q_c = \beta_0 + \beta_1 P_c + \beta_2 A^{-1}, \tag{9.9}$$

$$P_c = \alpha_0 + \alpha_1 P_f, \tag{9.10}$$

$$Q_f = \gamma_0 + \gamma_1 Q_c, \tag{9.11}$$

where advertising and sales were expressed in millions of dollars and millions of gallons, respectively. From the Dorfman-Steiner theorem, if the marketing mix for the processors is optimal, the negative of the price elasticity should equal the marginal revenue product of advertising. Expressions for these variables can be derived from (9.9), (9.10), and (9.11) using the chain rule:

$$-\varepsilon_P = -\gamma_1 \beta_1 \alpha_1 \frac{P_f}{Q_f}, \tag{9.12}$$

$$P_f \frac{\partial Q_f}{\partial A} = P_f \gamma_1 \frac{-\beta_2}{A^2}. \tag{9.13}$$

Ward's estimated model of the market mechanism was

$$Q_c = 69.82 - 10.15 P_c - 5.34 A^{-1}, \tag{9.14}$$

$$P_c = 0.648 + 0.671 P_f, \tag{9.15}$$

$$Q_f = 1.25 Q_c. \tag{9.16}$$

In the most recent year available to Ward, the factory price was \$0.953/gallon, factory sales were 66.68 million gallons, and advertising was \$1.837 million. The negative of the price elasticity was then

$$-\varepsilon_P = -(1.25)(-10.15)(0.671)\left(-\frac{0.953}{66.68}\right) = 0.128 \tag{9.17}$$

and the marginal revenue product of advertising was

$$P_f \frac{\partial Q_f}{\partial A} = (0.953)(1.25)\left[-\left(\frac{-5.34}{1.837^2}\right)\right] = 1.885. \tag{9.18}$$

These values were not anywhere near being equal. Ward attributed this to the grapefruit industry's desire for manageable inventories. Consequently, the industry selected the price that could achieve a target level of sales, a phenomenon also reported by Kohn and Plessner (1973).

Table 9-1. Application of the Dorfman-Steiner Theorem

Product Class	Study	$\dfrac{-\varepsilon_A}{\varepsilon_P}$	$\dfrac{A}{R}$	Performance[a] Index	Conclusion[b]
Apples	Lambin (1976)	.077	.012	0.156	Underspending
Automobiles	Cowling (1972)	.161	.007	0.043	Underspending
Coffee	Cowling (1972)	.678	.162	0.239	Underspending
	Lambin (1976)	.012	.034	2.833	Overspending
Grapefruit Juice	Ward (1975)	.442	.029	0.066	Underspending
Hair spray	Lambin (1976)	.021	.013	0.619	Near optimal
Margarine	Cowling (1972)	.138	.098	0.710	Near optimal
Soft drinks	Lambin (1976)	.033	.092	2.788	Overspending
Toothpaste	Cowling (1972)	.120	.153	1.275	Near optimal
Tractors	Cowling (1972)	.148	.014	0.095	Underspending
Yogurt	Lambin (1976)	.027	.031	1.148	Near optimal

a. A/R divided by $-\varepsilon_A / \varepsilon_P$.

b. Under the assumption that price is optimal, i.e., Equation (9.2) is satisfied.

Other applications of the Dorfman-Steiner theorem have shown wide variations around optimal spending levels. Some representative results are shown in Table 9-1. If the optimality ratio is not optimal, nothing can be said about the optimality of advertising without first being sure that the value of price is either optimal or unchangeable (Naert 1971, p. 64).

Are You Overspending? There are at least two reasons why a branded consumer good might be overadvertised (Aaker and Carman 1982). First, organizational considerations favor overspending. Most managers are risk adverse. They are reluctant to reduce advertising because of the potential adverse effects for sales and market share. Moreover, they are aware that once a budget has been cut, it is hard to get it restored. On the other hand, managers often respond to competitive pressure as well as other market factors by increasing advertising. These actions are encouraged by agency personnel, who have a vested interest in increasing advertising billings. Managers often overestimate the extent to which customers compare alternative brands. Managers tend to overreact to competitors (Brodie and Bonfrer 1995; Leeflang and Wittink 1996). Overall, there is a tendency for escalation in advertising. Second, the exact nature of sales response to advertising may, in fact, be unknown. Managers may not have the scientific evidence necessary to determine optimal advertising policy. The thrust of this book has been to encourage managers to adopt the ETS analysis so that they will have the scientific information necessary to offset organizational and personal biases.

Declines in advertising effectiveness over the product life cycle may lead to overspending if a firm unthinkingly maintains original sales goals or spending levels. For example, one study of tea calculated that, in the face of a general shift in tastes, generic advertising would have to double over five-year period in order to maintain per capita sales (Ball and Agarwala 1969). Another study found that firms in the ready-to-eat cereal market were overspending on established brands and underspending on new brands (Parsons and Bass 1971).

Does It Matter? Sensitivity analyses, e.g., Naert (1972), have frequently shown that large percentage changes in advertising expenditures result in only small percentage changes in profit over a wide range of expenditure levels. This has come to be known as the *flat maximum principle*. Profit seems to be somewhat more sensitive to departures of price from its optimal level than it is to departures in advertising expenditures.

Tull et al. (1986) were concerned with the misspecification of the function describing sales response to advertising. After examining models that they believed represented three broad classes of sales response functions (diminishing returns, saturation, and supersaturation), they concluded:

> For a set of function parameters that appear plausible and within the domain of those found in the empirical literature, . . . overspending on advertising in our situation by as much as 25%—may cost very little in terms of profit and may even produce long-term benefits in the form of increased market share.

Thus, there is some indication that overadvertising could cost very little in forgone profit and might lead to appreciable sales gains.

In a similar vein, Bultez and Naert (1979; 1985; 1988b) and Magat, McCann, and Morey (1986; 1988) have explored the issue of whether lag structure matters in optimizing advertising expenditures, and if so, when. Bultez and Naert (1979) found that while misspecifications in the lag structure impacted the optimal advertising budget, profits were not very sensitive to such errors. As a consequence, they asserted that it was sufficient to use a flexible lag structure, the Pascal in their case, and that "the current tendency to build and estimate increasingly sophisticated distributed lag models does not seem totally justified."

Magat, McCann, and Morey (1986) investigated whether Naert and Bultez's result was universally true or whether it depended on the characteristics of the product and market analyzed. In their analysis of a constant elasticity sales response function, they determined that for any given error in "optimal" advertising, profits were less sensitive to misspecification (1) the shorter the duration of advertising effect, (2) the greater the advertising elasticity, (3) the less price-elastic the demand, (4) the lower the unit cost of the product, and (5) the lower the firm's discount rate. They were basically assessing the conditions when the profit function is flat relative to advertising. Bultez and Naert (1988b) showed that higher values of the advertising elasticity caused greater errors in "optimal" advertising and that this could outweigh the effect of the flatter profit function. They also noted that the pattern of prior advertising used to estimate the parameters of the sales response function could affect the sensitivity of profit to lag structure misspecification.

Perishable-Asset Revenue Management. Capacity-constrained service firms seek to maximize revenue or yield of the firm. They must decide how much of each type of capacity (inventory) to allocate to different potential demand segments. This inventory could be seats in on an airplane, rooms in a hotel, or cars in a car rental fleet. See *UTA Industry Perspective.*

Market Response Functions and Optimal Marketing Resource Allocation. Last, but not least, we discuss the assumption—commonly used in empirical decision models—that there is no interaction between an observed market response mechanism and the marketing resource allocation decisions used by managers. This assumption has been challenged by examining optimal marketing investment levels under different allocation rules (Mantrala, Sinha & Zoltners 1992). For example, should a senior manager ("investor") spend more or less on advertising as a whole if her advertising managers ("allocators") spend their budget across products using a profit maximization rule, or some simplifying proportional rule (e.g. allocate in proportion to each product's sales potential)?

While the answers are complex and contingent on the shape of the response function, a useful general rule was derived: *marketing allocation decisions do influence aggregate sales response functions.* In the example above, if the response function is concave, and managers use proportional allocation rules, then the senior marketing manager will likely end up *overspending* on advertising as a whole. Consequently, even senior managers should pay close attention to the sub-market level resource allocations, i.e., the budgets across geographical markets, products, or

Product-Line Pricing at UTA

Union des Transports Ariens (UTA) was a French airline. It faced the same forecasting and pricing problems that other airlines face. Airfares differ dramatically. Travelers are a diverse lot—differing in price sensitivity with respect to the decision to travel and willingness to trade off lower prices for travel restrictions. Recognition of segment differences produces a large and growing number of fares.

In this context a market response study was done of its Paris-Abidjan, Ivory Coast route. Competition was limited to one other airline, Air Afrique; and the two airlines jointly set prices and flight schedules. While 20 fares existed, these were combined into three major categories for analysis: full, discount, and deep-discount. Response models were constructed for total volume and for fare class share:

$$Q_t / Q_{t-12} = exp\left[\alpha_0 + \sum_{j=1}^{3} \alpha_j \left(p_{jt} - p_{j,t-12}\right)\right]$$

$$FCS_{it} / FCS_{i,t-12} = exp\left[\beta_{i0} + \sum_{j=1}^{3} \beta_{ij} \left(p_{jt} - p_{j,t-12}\right)\right]$$

Based on this system of response models, optimal fares were calculated and response to those optimal fares forecast. The approach took into account prevailing constraints on fare availability and fleet size.

The empirical results showed an interesting but complex pattern of price effects. High full fares can drive travelers to deep discount fares, indicating that while travelers may not be price sensitive with respect to whether or not to travel, they are price sensitive with respect to what fare class they select. Low discount fares can draw full-fare customers, cannibalizing revenue, without increasing the market. Deep-discount fares principally affect total volume, and have little effect on shares of other class fares.

Presentation of the empirical results to UTA's top managers was well received. Management was, nonetheless, surprised by the size of cannibalization effects. The technical staff was instructed to conduct further analysis using new data, which produced similar qualitative results.

Subsequently, management reviewed the optimal pricing findings. These findings showed while average fares (and consequently fare class shares) were quite close to their optimal values, optimal price profits exceeded actual profits by eight percent. Thus, small deviations from optimal prices can lead to substantial losses in profit.

The current pricing structure proved not well suited to either managing cannibalization or managing optimally. UTA restructured fares by classifying flights as peak business travel flights, near-peak flights, and off-peak flights. For peak flights, reservations are accepted only at full fare. Discount and deep-discount fares are accepted but on an essentially standby basis. Limited seats are available for travelers flying at lower fares on near-peak flights. Discount and deep-discount fares are given full access with reservations for off-peak flights. This policy enabled UTA to reduce cannibalization significantly by effectively limiting the cross-price elasticities without significantly reducing the overall volume.

Drawn from Gregory S. Carpenter and Dominique M. Hanssens, "Market Expansion, Cannibalization, and International Airline Pricing Strategy," International Journal of Forecasting, 10:2 (September 1994), 313-26. Editors' note: UTA merged with Air France.

marketing mix. Company profitability is more sensitive to suboptimal allocations of a given marketing budget than it is to changes in the marketing budget itself. These findings provide strong analytical evidence for our proposition that companies should invest in high-quality marketing databases, estimate market response models, and use them rather than simplifying rules of thumb to make marketing resource allocation decisions.

Embedded Competition

In competitive markets, optimal marketing decision making is influenced, not only by the company's own sales response function, but also by the behavior of competitors. For example, if a brand's price elasticity is estimated at -2.5, and competitors tend to react quickly to price changes, then the optimal price level for the brand may be far removed from the value implied by Equation (9.2).

Insights into the competitive interplay among the marketing decision variables of several firms might be obtained from game theory. Game theory is a collection of mathematical models for the description of conscious, goal oriented, decision-making processes involving more than one brand (Shubik 1975, p. 9). Game-theoretic models may be either descriptive or normative. Marketing review articles include those by Chatterjee and Lilien (1986) and Moorthy (1993). An excellent managerial treatment of game theoretic principles can be found in Brandenburger and Nalebuff (1996).

The play of the game may be collusive, or Pareto-optimal, or a Cournot-Nash equilibrium, or a Stackelberg leader-follower system. Collusive games, which are illegal in many markets, imply cooperative behavior that maximizes a weighted average of all firm's profits. A set of actions by the brands in a game is called *Pareto-optimal* if there does not exist another set of actions that rewards each brand as well and at least one of them better. A *Cournot-Nash strategy* is one in which no competitor, believing that its competitors are committed to their respective strategies, can improve its own performance. In a Stackelberg leader-follower game, one competitor's actions are set independently of the other, but these actions are considered in the decision making of the other. Note that a Cournot-Nash equilibrium solution may or may not be Pareto-optimal.

The marketing science literature does not contain many examples of the combined use of game theory and empirical market response models. The mathematical difficulty of obtaining closed form solutions to game theoretic problems is often prohibitive in all but the most stylized cases. Market response models, on the other hand, often need to be estimated in complex environments using many different variables. Consequently, it is difficult to create marketing insights from the combined use of game theory ("complex analytics/ simple empirics") and market response modeling ("simple analytics/ complex empirics").

One exception is a study of leader-follower pricing behavior in a segment of the American automobile market (Roy, Hanssens, and Raju 1994). This work focused on the optimal pricing rules for price leaders who set prices in order to achieve given sales targets, a practice often encountered in durable goods marketing. Using sales and price data for the Chrysler New Yorker and the Ford Thunderbird, the time-series techniques discussed in Chapter 7 established empirically that the Ford Thunderbird was the price leader. Then multiple-equation econometric estimation and dynamic optimization (Gasmi and Vuong 1988) found that the optimal prices for the Thunderbird were generally higher than the observed price paths. Even this relatively simple market with two competitors and one decision variable necessitated several assumptions in order to reach a closed form pricing solution. Another form of competitive behavior, collusion, has been tested empirically in vertical markets by Leeflang (1997) and in cellular telephone markets by Parker and Roller (1997).

One published market response model that compared actual, myopic profit maximizing and Cournot-Nash prices and marketing is in a simultaneous optimization study of price and advertising for a household product (Carpenter, Cooper, Hanssens, and Midgley 1988). This work demonstrates how the analytical material in this book can be integrated. It used time-series analysis to assess the nature of competition in the market, market response models to estimate response parameters, and multi-brand optimization to derive optimal pricing and marketing spending in a competitive setting. We will now review this approach and findings as a separate illustration.

Empirical Illustration of Cournot-Nash Optimal Marketing Mix

The marketing effectiveness of several competitors in a stable market of eleven brands of an Australian laundry detergent was investigated (Carpenter, Cooper, Hanssens, and Midgley 1988). The market consisted of eight major brands belonging to two conglomerates (1 and 2) and one independent producer (3). For completeness, three "all other" (A) or catchall brands, mainly of the regional and store variety, were considered. Competition in this market occurred mainly on the basis of price, advertising, and product forms, dry (D) and wet (W). Some brands had physical characteristics that offered tangible (T) benefits to the consumer (brands TD1, TD2, and TW2), others position themselves as premium image (I) brands (ID1 and ID2), and still others offer lower prices, which qualifies them as economy (E) brands (ED1, ED2, and ED3). An overview of the brands and their average performance levels for a 26-month time sample is given in Table 9-2. The market share and price data were collected from a national panel of several thousand consumers and the advertising data (mainly television) came from a separate agency.

Since industry demand was stable over the sample period, market share was used as the criterion variable for marketing effectiveness. A differential-effects MCI model was specified (as a result of first not finding stable cross-competitive effects). Next, time-series lag specification techniques, described in Chapter 6, revealed zero-order price response and first-order effects of advertising. To simplify the subsequent optimization, the advertising response parameters reported in Table 9-3 are based on weighted advertising spending levels, with weights equal to the respective importance of lags zero and one. All parameter estimates were obtained with generalized least squares along with the implied elasticities of these parameters for an average scenario. In particular, the implied elasticities in Table 9-3 are based on the average market share for each brand.

We may draw the following marketing inferences from these results:

1. The economy brands (ED1, ED2, and ED3) have the highest price sensitivity, followed by the premium image brands (ID1 and ID2) and the premium tangible brands (TD1, TD2, and TW2). This is an intuitively appealing and managerially very important result. Offering tangible benefits in the product lowers price elasticity more than merely positioning a brand as premium. Offering bargains attracts the price-sensitive customer but makes the brand more vulnerable to price changes.

2. The advertising effectiveness varies significantly across the brands, with the two advertising economy brands having the highest parameters. Interestingly, there is a virtually perfect match between the rank orders of advertising effectiveness and the coefficients of variation in advertising. This finding supports the notion that

Table 9-2. Average Market Shares, Advertising, and Prices*

Brand	Description	Average Market Share	Average Price	Average Advertising
ED1	Economy Dry	5.4	$1.48	$ 8,100
ED2	Economy Dry	2.6	1.51	0
ED3	Economy Dry	7.1	1.59	14,300
ID1	Image Dry	10.0	1.79	34,800
ID2	Image Dry	4.9	1.87	42,400
TD1	Tangible Dry	4.5	2.14	25,600
TD2	Tangible Dry	4.5	1.87	29,400
TW2	Tangible Wet	7.8	1.81	50,000
AO1	All Other Co.1	9.5	1.82	37,000
AD4	All Other Dry	26.2	1.34	2,300
AW4	All Other Wet	17.5	1.00	39,500

* Reprinted by permission. Gregory S. Carpenter, Lee G. Cooper, Dominique M. Hanssens, and David F. Midgley (1988), "Modeling Asymmetric Competition," *Marketing Science,* 7:4, (Fall), p. 398. © 1988, The Institute of Management Sciences and the Operations Research Society of America.

high-variance advertising allocation schemes such as pulsing may be more effective than low variance allocations.

The insights provided by the MCI model so far contain valuable diagnostic information about the market and may be used to make certain strategic recommendations about pricing or advertising for each brand. For example, some brands could be advised that their advertising is ineffective in generating market share, while others might be made aware of unusually high or low consumer sensitivity to their retail prices. Although many ETS projects might be concluded right here, it would also be possible to investigate important issues beyond descriptive market response, in particular the behavior of competitors in the market, and the implications of both for optimal pricing and advertising allocations.

Making Inferences about Optimal Marketing Behavior

The nature of competitive behavior is tested, first, by performing cross-correlations among prices and advertising spending levels to assess leader/follower patterns. Taken as a whole, the results suggest that managers allocate advertising dollars and set price levels without much regard for the actions of other managers within their firm or for the actions of their counterparts in other firms. Competitive reaction is the exception, not the rule. It may be that the delay with which marketing managers receive marketing information updates makes competitive reaction difficult or that

Table 9-3. Attraction Parameters and Implied Elasticities

Brand	Advertising Parameter	Price Parameter	Advertising Elasticity[a]	Price Elasticity[a]
ED1	0.22 (0.04)[b]	−2.70 (0.58)[b]	0.21	−2.55
ED2		−3.60 (0.48)[b]		−3.51
ED3	0.07 (0.02)[b]	−2.59 (0.46)[b]	0.07	−2.41
ID1	0.07 (0.03)[c]	−1.49 (0.50)[b]	0.06	−1.34
ID2	0.02 (0.03)	−2.21 (0.64)[b]	0.02	−2.10
TD1	0.07 (0.04)	−1.35 (0.74)[c]	0.07	−1.29
TD2	0.11 (0.06)[c]	−1.08 (0.57)[c]	0.11	−1.03
TW2	0.00 (0.04)	−1.43 (0.32)[b]	0.00	−1.39
AO1	0.06 (0.03)[c]	−1.31 (0.51)[b]	0.05	−1.19
AD4	0.03 (0.06)	−0.74 (0.44)[c]	0.02	−0.55
AW4	−0.12 (0.07)	−0.22 (0.56)	−0.10	−0.18

a At the mean market share for each brand.

b Significant at $p < .01$.

c Significant at $p < .05$.

monitoring as many as ten competitors is in itself too time-consuming. However, regardless of patterns in competitive marketing, the fact remains that all brands are affected by all competitors' actions.

In the absence of systematic competitive reactions it may prove useful to investigate how individual brands are priced and how their advertising outlays compare to optimal prices and advertising levels derived from the MCI response model. Making inferences about optimal marketing behavior depends on the competitive context. For example, the optimal price rule for a brand may be quite sensitive to the assumption that a key competitor would or would not match a price cut. The pricing and advertising rules derived here use two extremes of competitive scenarios:

1. *Myopic profit maximization.* Each brand maximizes its profit function independently of competitive considerations. In other words, each brand solves its profit function with respect to advertising and price:

$$\max_i \pi = QMS_i(P_i - VC_i) - FC_i - A_i, \tag{9.19}$$

where Q is industry demand, VC is variable cost and FC is fixed cost. The solution is found by setting the first derivatives with respect to advertising and price to zero for each brand separately. It results in the typical marginal-cost-equals-marginal-revenue condition. Competitive behavior does not explicitly enter into these optimal values.

2. *Nash profit maximization.* Each brand maximizes profits under the condition that all other brands do the same. This is an application of a noncooperative solution to a game in prices and advertising. The mathematical solution is again based on the maximization of (9.19), except here it is done simultaneously for all brands' prices and advertising. It is considerably more difficult to find the optimum in this case because it involves solving a set of 22 nonlinear equations. A solution is guaranteed only if the profit functions for brands are strictly quasiconcave in prices and advertising. Fortunately, this quasiconcavity holds under a fairly general set of conditions.

In the absence of any prior information on how prices and advertising levels are set, these two scenarios should be interpreted as extreme. Myopic profit maximization is a best-case scenario for each firm in that it assumes that the firm could pursue its profit goals without competitive retaliation. The Nash solution is a worst-case scenario because we assume that each competitor acts optimally and so the firm cannot enjoy a free ride owing to competitive inertia. Though these extremes may be unrealistic, they provide an interesting optimal range of prices and advertising outlays against which the brand can gauge its current or planned marketing activity.

The two different solutions to (9.19) are cast in terms of price and advertising elasticities, which are not constant in the MCI model. We must therefore fix the elasticities derived from the response model at some reasonable level. Since we are working in a single-period framework, we choose the levels of market shares, prices, and advertising that come closest to an average period.

Table 9-4 shows the results in terms of the following:

1. The optimal single-period prices and advertising under the myopic condition. For brands for which no meaningful optimum can be calculated (e.g., the catchall brands), the actual average values are substituted and held constant in optimization.

2. The optimal single-period prices and advertising under the Nash condition, using the same restriction as in (1).

3. A comparison of the market shares and profits that would result from (1) and (2).

Table 9-4. Current and Optimal Prices, Advertising Expenditures, Market Shares, and Profits By Brand

Brand	Prices[a]			Advertising[b]		
	Actual	Optimal Response	Nash Equilibrium	Actual	Optimal Response	Nash Equilibrium
ED1	$1.53	$1.47	$1.47	$0.00	$35.70	$35.60
ID1	1.89	2.73	2.71	0.00	19.80	18.06
TD1	2.22	3.20	3.17	41.20	14.10	12.40
AO1	1.88	4.83	1.88^c	50.90	70.84	50.90^c
ID2	2.02	1.65	1.64	55.40	2.80	2.66
ED2	1.65	1.19	1.20	0.00	0.00^c	0.00^c
TD2	1.90	4.62	4.58	21.20	19.80	17.00
TW2	1.98	3.03	2.81	67.70	67.70^c	67.70
ED3	1.67	1.70	1.70	0.10	9.30	8.50
AD4	1.38	1.38^c	1.38^c	1.90	1.90^c	1.90^c
AW4	1.02	1.02^c	1.02^c	29.80	29.80^c	29.80^c

Brand	Market Share			Profits[b]		
	Actual	Optimal Response	Nash Equilibrium	Actual	Optimal Response	Nash Equilibrium
ED1	1.0	10.3	10.2	$82.85	$146.00	$146.00
ID1	5.2	5.7	5.2	203.00	268.00	242.00
TD1	5.4	2.9	2.5	143.93	167.00	145.00
AO1	10.9		9.7	220.51	1,019.05	220.51^c
ID2	4.7	7.3	6.8	87.16	151.00	140.00
ED2	1.9		5.8	41.58	16.58	57.35
TD2	5.1	1.6	1.4	125.49	157.00	135.00
TW2	7.8		4.1	230.88	426.65	162.00
ED3	5.4	7.0	6.5	94.76	129.00	118.05
AD4	31.3		28.5	516.50	516.50^c	455.30^d
AW4	21.3		19.3	234.80	234.80^c	206.45^d

[a] Prices in dollars (Australian)
[b] In thousands of dollars (Australian)
[c] Constrained to be the same as the actual value
[d] Estimated using actual prices and advertising expenditures and competitive market shares

The results are revealing from several perspectives. Looking at the market in the aggregate, we would conclude that current prices and advertising levels approximate the optimal competitive levels on average. These prices and advertising levels are well below the myopic levels, suggesting that competitive considerations are not totally absent from marketing decision making in this industry. However, individual brands are not necessarily operating at a competitive optimum in the selected period. There is ample evidence of over- or under-pricing as well as over- or under-advertising. Using the Nash or worst case competitive scenario as a benchmark, we may distinguish two groups of brands:

1. Suboptimal competitors, or those who are currently making less profit than they could with different price-advertising combinations. This group includes brands ED1, IDA, ID2, ED2, and ED3.

2. Supraoptimal competitors, or those who are deriving extra profits from the fact that others are pricing or advertising at suboptimal levels. This group includes brands TD1, TD2, and TW2.

It may not be coincidental that the economy and premium image brands are all suboptimal and that the tangible benefit brands are supraoptimal. For example, there is substantial price pressure on the economy brands because of their high price sensitivities. Even slight deviations from the optimal price level (as with ED1 and ED2) are very costly to an economy brand in terms of profits. On the other hand, the fact that the tangible-benefit brands are either overpriced (TD1) or underpriced (TD2 and TW2) in this period hurts them significantly less under the Nash scenario. Similar conclusions may be drawn for advertising on a brand-by-brand basis.

These conclusions are only illustrative of the power of ETS modeling in diagnosing markets and offering guidelines for improved brand performance. We have chosen one typical period, we have drawn inferences from static as opposed to dynamic optimization, and we have used as benchmarks two rather extreme scenarios of assumed competitive behavior. Other assumptions and scenarios may be introduced depending on the needs of the researcher or the marketing planner.

Forecasting

From the entrepreneur to the mature business, forecasting binds decisions with results. A new business makes decisions on products to offer, markets to serve, production technology, human resources, capitalization, and many other things. Each decision affects operating and sales results in some way. The decision to stock inventory, for example, makes the product available for sale, but *how much* inventory to have on hand requires a forecast of sales. Marketing decisions involving the marketing mix—price, advertising, distribution, selling effort, and other variables—clearly affect sales, but their *values* require a forecast of their impact *on* sales. Market forecasts are central to business firms precisely because businesses exist to produce sales. Few activities of business firms are as strategically important as forecasting.

Another way to look at the importance of market forecasting is to consider the effects of forecast errors. A company that makes a mistake forecasting whether a new product meets consumer needs sets the stage for product failure. For products that do meet needs, companies can (and do) make forecast errors regarding consumer perceptions—as in positioning—and competitive response to marketing actions. Our special interest is *market* forecasting, i.e., estimating sales potential and sales results. The fact that forecast errors necessarily lead to increased costs makes the case for improving the process of market forecasting. Indeed, the opportunity cost of lost sales due to poor forecasting is all too common.

Issues in Forecasting

The forecaster must decide whether a short-term or long-term forecast is needed and whether a judgmental forecast will suffice or a quantitative forecast is required. If a quantitative approach is taken, should it be extrapolative or explanantory.

Short-Run vs. Long-Run Forecasts. The distinction between short- and long-run forecasts used to be clear: the short run was a period of time *within* a planning period and the long run was time *outside* the planning period. Since most companies used (and still use) annual planning periods, the long run was often thought of as just longer than a year. The short run was also defined by data availability. For example, there was little point in talking about quantitative monthly forecasts if only bimonthly data were available. Two recent developments have changed this situation. First, data for many product categories are collected on a more frequent basis. For consumer packaged goods, the availability of scanner data has changed the way business firms think about the short run. While the annual planning period for a brand may have not changed, the fact that the brand's performance can be tracked in real time has made the short run as short as a day.[5]

The second major change is the shortening of the product life cycle. What good is it to talk about annual sales when the product you may be selling a quarter hence is obsolete? High-technology products illustrate this best, but many others do as well. Efficient consumer response, for example, was designed for lower technology products where rapidly changing consumer tastes and buying behavior dictate quick action on the part of manufacturers and retailers. In this world, the short run is as short as the consumer says it is.

Because market response models are built on short-run sales movements, we do not need to delve too deeply into long-run forecasting. In fact, if we think of the long run as outside the company's planning period, market response models are not relevant since, by definition, they include plans. Although surveys and reviews of sales forecasting practices (e.g., Dalrymple, 1987; Winklhofer, Diamantopoulos, and Witt, 1996) report some use of ETS for forecasts longer than one year, they do not examine whether these quantitative sales forecasts are based on models that include marketing mix variables. Odds are that they do not. Most long run sales forecasting continues to be based on subjective techniques such as juries of executive opinion or industry surveys, and on life-cycle modeling techniques such as diffusion of innovation. The long-run time series techniques discussed in Chapters 6 and 7 offer new avenues for data based long-run forecasting and await more empirical applications to assess their contribution.

Judgmental vs. Quantitative Forecasts. By far the favorite market forecasting method is the judgmental forecast. One frequently cited study reported 44.8% use of sales force composite forecasting and 37.3% use of jury of executive opinion in contrast to only about 12% for either multiple regression analysis or econometric models (Dalrymple, 1987). Other studies also report that the use of quantitative sales forecasts hovers at about 10% (e.g., Sanders and Manrodt, 1994). However, the conditions surrounding the use of judgmental forecasts are changing. On the one hand, the market response "industry" has developed, and thus quantitative market forecasts have become more prominent if not more popular. On the other hand, research on judgmental forecasting has progressed to the point where "judgment" means capturing knowledge, not throwing darts.[6]

Although research has been conducted on the use of contextual data (causal data in addition to the time series), the results have been mixed as to whether a manager's insight into the forecasting situation helps reduce forecast error (Sanders and Ritzman, 1992; Goodwin and Wright, 1993). A review of the empirical research was unable to come to a definitive conclusion about when the use of contextual information supersedes judgment or quantitative techniques (Wright, Lawrence, and Collopy 1996). However, domain or contextual knowledge stemming from general forecasting experience or specific product knowledge has been shown to have a much greater effect on forecast error than technical knowledge (Sanders and Ritzman, 1992). This means that any forecasting system that taps such knowledge can improve upon judgmental forecasts.

In addition, experimental evidence has been found "to have clearly shown that forecasting using both statistical forecasts and causal information is best done by statistical methods" (Lim and O'Connor, 1996, p. 150). In particular, regression analysis was found to provide a better way to estimate the effect of a causal variable than judgment. This research, and other research like it, uses contextual variables that are what we call environmental, e.g., daily temperature and number of tourists as causal factors influencing the sales of soft drinks at a famous surfing beach in Australia. None of the extant contextual studies use decision variables.[7]

Despite the current lack of research evidence, we believe that well-calibrated market response models dominate judgment in stable environments, and even more so in turbulent environments (Glazer and Weiss 1993). Market response models are being used in practice as replacements for other forecasting methods—especially judgment—and in combination with other quantitative techniques to manage large forecasting tasks. Many companies rely on market response models in making decisions at the brand and product level. Some decision support systems are *based* on market response models. A seamless integration of data and decisions describes the principal advantage of such an approach and consequently its economic value.

As we saw in Chapter 1, model-based planning and forecasting provides a platform for integrating judgment with statistical inference from data. The approach's special connection with forecasting was discussed by Parsons and Schultz (1994). It is a quantitative approach to market forecasting that goes beyond judgment or judgmental extrapolation to integrate the decision-related contextual variables into the forecasting task.

Largely due to the academic enterprise, aggressive research efforts have been made to expand and perfect the quantitative methods on which quantitative forecasting is based. Much of this book is devoted to reporting on these developments as they relate to market response. We do not repeat these conclusions in this chapter, nor do we attempt to review all of the developments in quantitative forecasting. Many of these conclusions are summarized in Armstrong (1986) and Fildes (1985). For marketing, two special issues of the *International Journal of Forecasting* in 1987 (Volume 3, Number 3/4) and in 1994 (Volume 10, Number 2), and a special issue of the *Journal of Forecasting* in 1998 (Volume 17, Number 3/4) include many of the important papers. The overall organizational setting for market forecasts—including quantitative forecasts—is discussed by Fildes and Hastings (1994).

Extrapolative vs. Explanatory Forecasts. Quantitative forecasts are so entrenched in many areas of business and economics that it is somewhat surprising that marketing continues to hold out to the extent that it has. Companies regularly use quantitative methods for production scheduling and governments regularly use quantitative methods for economic forecasts. These methods include *extrapolative techniques* such as moving averages, exponential smoothing, and univariate time series analysis and *explanatory techniques* such as multiple regression analysis and transfer function analysis. The common denominator of these methods is that they are regarded as "objective" because they rely on data and statistical inference.

Market response models are by definition explanatory or causal in nature. However, if forecasting is the only intended use of the model builder, simple time-series models (reviewed in Chapter 6) that are not causal in nature may suffice and, in some case, produce adequate forecasts.

Extrapolative forecasts. Extrapolative forecasts use only the time series of the dependent variable. Thus, a sales forecast is made only on the basis of the past history of the sales series. Armstrong, Brodie, and McIntyre (1987) summarize research findings on extrapolation as they relate to marketing. It seems as if simple exponential smoothing models perform better than more complicated ones, that seasonal adjustments are necessary, that trends should be dampened, and that forecasts from different extrapolation methods should be combined. It has been found that extrapolative forecasts can be improved through judgmental adjustment, particularly when domain knowledge is employed to select forecasts for revision (Mathews and Diamantopoulous, 1990).

There is also some evidence that extrapolative forecasts can be improved by using interactive graphical tools based on decomposition of the extrapolation task into trend and seasonality (Edmunson, 1990). While not directly related to features of automatic forecasting systems, this latter finding suggests that such systems can benefit from research on methods of presentation as well as methods of analysis.

The main use of extrapolative models in marketing is for baseline sales and price forecasting, i.e. under the assumption that the sales data generation process will not change in the future. In some cases of limited data availability to the firm, sales extrapolation is the only quantitative forecasting method available to management.

Explanatory Forecasts. Explanatory forecasts go beyond extrapolation by including causal factors thought to influence the dependent variable of interest. Hence, a sales forecast becomes the outcome of a model explaining how sales are determined. Of course, forecasts based on market response models are explanatory forecasts. Research findings on explanatory models as they relate to marketing have also been summarized (Armstrong, Brodie, and McIntyre 1987). At the time of that writing, it appeared that simple models were usually to be preferred to more complex models, particularly for predicting market share because model misspecification and aggregation bias often led to empirical results where naïve models outperformed more complicated rivals.

Unconditional vs. Conditional Forecasts. All the explanatory variables in an unconditional forecast are known with certainty. This would be the case when only the firm's own decision variables or lagged environmental variables are used. Since the firm knows what it intends to do, its actions are considered known for forecasting purposes. This does not mean, however, that the firm will do what it intends to do.

The values of one or more variables are not known in a conditional forecast. This is the case for current environmental variables. The firm does not know what actions its competitors are going to take. Similarly, the firm does not know the state of the economy and other autonomous variables. The firm must use forecasts, which introduce errors. The firm may use extrapolative or explanatory forecasts. The explanatory model for competitive variables would be based on reaction functions. The explanatory model for economic variables would be based on a simultaneous equations macroeconomic model. The firm would typically purchase the forecast of economic variables from an outside supplier.

In a sense, all forecasts are "conditional" on the levels of variables used. We will use "scenario" to describe a particular set of values of the variables.

Ex Post vs. Ex Ante Forecasts. An ex post forecast is an unconditional forecast for a period in which the actual value being forecasted is already known. If the actual value were already known, why would a forecast be of interest? The purpose would be to evaluate a forecasting method. Thus, an historical set of observations is partitioned into an estimation sample, which is used to calibrate a model, and a holdout sample, which is used to compare with ex post forecasts generated by the calibrated model. See Figure 9-1.

An ex ante forecast may be unconditional or conditional but applies to a period in which the actual values being forecasted are not yet known. If the historical sample was partitioned into a calibration sample and a holdout sample, it is reconstituted as a single sample and the model recalibrated to obtain more precise estimates of model parameters before making the ex ante forecast. See Figure 9-1 again.

Point vs. Interval Forecasts. Point forecasts yield a single number for each period in the planning horizon. Most planning is based on these numbers. Nonetheless, the manager might well want to know what the margin of error is around a point forecast. Interval forecasts give the θ percent confidence bands around point forecasts. Often θ is chosen to be 95.

Structural Stability of Parameters

A forecast or simulation generated from a market response model rests on the assumption that the estimated response parameters do not change in the future. While we can never be sure that the assumption will hold, we can at least observe some rules that lessen the odds of structural change in the parameters. These include

1. Conduct tests of parameter stability on the available data. In addition to the formal tests described in Chapters 4 and 5, we can trace the time path of market response parameters by estimating a model for the first 30 observations and then successively adding one observation and re-estimating. Modern software packages include parameter stability modules for easy implementation.

2. As discussed in Chapter 6, conduct tests of data stationarity. If the data are non-stationary, then first-order regular or seasonal differencing is usually sufficient to obtain stationarity. Forecasting models based on differences are more likely to capture evolving sales patterns over time than those based on levels.

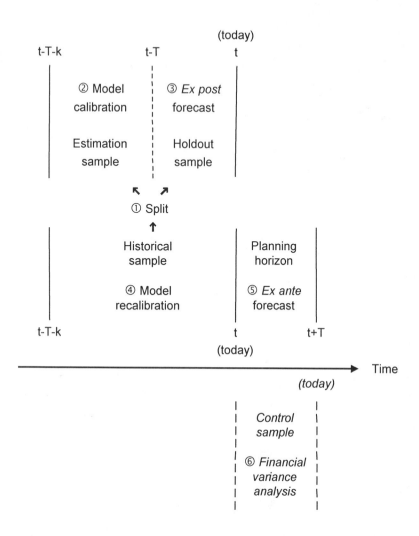

Figure 9-1. Types of Samples and Their Uses

3. Be careful when simulating scenarios that fall outside the observed range of the data. For example, a major price change that has never before been observed, may trigger a chain reaction of consumer and competitor response that is unaccounted for by the market response model. Market simulations based on such scenarios should be interpreted with much caution.

Measures of Forecasting Accuracy

While our primary interest is the selection of an error measure for a single time series, we also want to be able draw conclusions about the choice of error measures for generalizing across multiple time series. Difficulties in making comparisons across series include differences in scale, the amount of change that occurs over the forecast horizon, and the presence of extreme forecast errors. If the scale of the data varies considerably among the series, series with large numbers might dominate comparisons. Forecasts are more difficult for series where large changes occur over the forecast horizon. Outliers may cause a single series to dominate an analysis.

Criteria used to compare error measures include reliability, construct validity, protection against outliers, sensitivity, and relationship to decision-making as well as expense and ease of understanding. Reliability means that repeated applications of a procedure will produce similar results. Construct validity means that a measure does measure what it purports to measure.

Error measures are calculated on a *holdout sample*. For example, in a comparison of the SCAN*PRO model of retail promotion effects at different levels of aggregation: store, chain, and market, 104 weeks of store-level scanner data were available (Foekens, Leeflang, and Wittink 1994, p. 253). The first 52 weeks were used for estimating the model and the last 52 weeks were used for validation. The forecasting accuracy results of four-ahead, 12-ahead, and 52-ahead weekly predictions were found. The findings were consistent across time horizons and only the 52-ahead prediction results were reported. In a second example, an examination of the forecasting performance of market share models was performed on 52 weeks of Infoscan store-level data for diapers, baking chips, and saltine crackers and 44 weeks of data for toilet tissue (Kumar 1994, p. 302). The hold out sample was 8 weeks for diapers and tissue and 16 weeks for baking chips and crackers. One-ahead and six-ahead forecasts were made. The number of observations in the holdout sample did not affect the relative performance of the models. This led the author to recommend that "it is better to have a smaller holdout sample, thus increasing the estimation sample size, which in turn will yield better parameter estimates" (p. 311). The author also concluded,

> Econometric models can be used for scanner data irrespective of the forecasting horizon.

Rather than calculating error measures on the periods after the end of the model estimation period, error measures could be calculated on observations with significantly different policies than those used to estimate the model. The former is called a *time-based holdout* and the latter a *policy-based holdout*.

The most important criterion for choosing a forecast method is its accuracy; that is, how closely the forecast predicts the actual event. If both negative (overprediction) and positive errors (underprediction) forecast errors are equally undesirable, then either Average Absolute Error (AAE), also know as the Mean

Absolute Error (MAE), or the Root Mean Square Error (RMSE) would be a natural choice for the error measure (Abraham and Ledolter 1983, p. 5). The AAE for a particular forecasting method m (of M) for a given horizon h (of H) of a particular series s (of S) is

$$\text{AAE}_{m,h} = \frac{\left| F_{m,h,s} - A_{h,s} \right|}{S},$$

(9.20)

where F is the forecast and A is the actual value. The Average Absolute Error was used in a series of studies of the conditions when market share models are useful in forecasting (Brodie and de Kluyver 1987, Brodie and Bonfrer 1994). The employment of absolute values is to avoid positive and negative errors offsetting each other when summarizing errors using the arithmetic mean. One can accomplish the same thing by taking squaring the errors, yielding the Mean Squared Error (MSE) or the Root Mean Squared Error (RMSE):

$$\text{RMSE}_{m,h} = \left(\frac{\sum_{s=1}^{S} \left(F_{m,h,s} - A_{h,s} \right)^2}{S} \right)^{1/2}.$$

(9.21)

The [Root] Mean Squared Error is generally preferred to the Average Absolute Error because it leads to simpler mathematical solutions. In addition, the MSE is often highly correlated with the AAE (Brodie and de Kluyver 1987, p. 429). Historically, [R]MSE has also been the preferred error measure for generalizing about the accuracy of different forecasting methods, as in Danaher (1994). The problem with [R]MSE in this context is that this is not a unit-free measure and scale variations among series can distort the rankings of forecasting methods. In sum, [R]MSE is poor on reliability, fair on construct validity, poor on outlier protection, good on sensitivity, and good on relationship to decisions (Armstrong and Collopy 1992, p. 77). The Root Median Squared Error (RMdSE) would avoid the outlier problem.

One way to control for scale is to use a relative measure such as percentage errors. The Percentage Error (PE) calculates the error as a percentage of the actual value.

$$\text{PE}_{m,h,s} \equiv \left[\frac{F_{m,h,s} - A_{h,s}}{A_{h,s}} \right] \times 100 = \left[\frac{F_{m,h,s}}{A_{h,s}} - 1 \right] \times 100.$$

(9.22)

There are three limitations of Percentage Error and other relative measures (Armstrong and Collopy 1992). First, they are bounded on the low side by an error of

100% but they have no bound on the high side. Second, they are not highly related to the economic benefits associated with the use of a particular forecasting method. A reduction in errors from 100% to 50% is treated the same as a reduction from 10% to 5%. This last limitation makes relative error measure unattractive for managerial decision-making. Third, they are only suitable for series that are ratio-scaled. Percentage Error was used in a study of how intentions surveys can be used to estimate the impact of a possible new entrant on an industrial market (Alsem and Leeflang 1994). The Absolute Percentage Error (APE) is:

$$\text{APE}_{m,h,s} \equiv \left| \text{PE}_{m,h,s} \right|. \tag{9.23}$$

This leads to the most widely used unit-free measure, the Mean Absolute Percentage Error (MAPE):

$$\text{MAPE}_{m,h} \equiv \frac{\sum_{s=1}^{S} \text{APE}_{m,h,s}}{S} \times 100. \tag{9.24}$$

In market response modeling, this summation may be over stores as well as the number of observations in the holdout sample; see, for example, Kumar (1994. p. 305). MAPE has been used in studies comparing different models for forecasting market share. These studies have looked at three Dutch markets for frequently purchased low-priced consumer goods (Alsem, Leeflang, and Reuyl 1989), the New Zealand cookie market (Lawrence, Guerts, and Parket 1990; Geurts and Whitlark 1992/93), the American markets for disposable diapers, baking chips, saltine crackers, and toilet tissue (Kumar and Heath 1990; Kumar 1994), and the German markets for two food product categories and a personal hygiene product category (Klapper and Herwartz 2000). MAPE has the limitations of a relative measure. In sum, MAPE is fair on reliability, good on construct validity, poor on outlier protection, good on sensitivity, and fair on relationship to decisions (Armstrong and Collopy 1992, p. 77). A related measure, adjusted MAPE (known as MAPE-A), compensates for MAPE's "favorable" treatment of forecasts that are too low by dividing the absolute error by the average of actual and predicted.

An extreme way to address the outlier problem is to use medians; for example, the Median Absolute Percentage Error (MdAPE):

$$\text{MdAPE}_{m,h} \equiv \begin{cases} \text{observation } \dfrac{S+1}{2} & \text{if } S \text{ is odd} \\ \text{average of observations } \dfrac{S}{2} \text{ and } \dfrac{S}{2}+1 & \text{if } S \text{ is even} \end{cases}. \tag{9.25}$$

MdAPE reduces the bias in favor of low forecasts. In sum, MdAPE is fair on reliability, good on construct validity, good on outlier protection, poor on sensitivity, and fair on relationship to decisions (Armstrong and Collopy 1992, p. 77).

One way to address the problem of large changes occurring over the forecast horizon is to employ relative errors and compare forecast errors from a given model against those from another model. The most commonly used alternative model is the random walk (rw). An example is Theil's U2:

$$U2_{m,h,s} \equiv \frac{\left(\dfrac{1}{h} \sum\limits_{h=1}^{H} \left(F_{m,h,s} - A_{h,s} \right)^2 \right)^{1/2}}{\left(\dfrac{1}{h} \sum\limits_{h=1}^{H} \left(F_{rw,h,s} - A_{h,s} \right)^2 \right)^{1/2}} . \tag{9.26}$$

Theil's U2 is rarely used in marketing.

A simple alternative to Theil's U2 is the Relative Absolute Error (RAE):

$$RAE_{m,h,s} \equiv \left| \frac{F_{m,h,s} - A_{h,s}}{F_{rw,h,s} - A_{h,s}} \right|. \tag{9.27}$$

RAE and Theil's U2 will be equivalent for a single horizon, but not for cumulated forecasts over a forecast horizon. These measures tend not to be affected so much by outliers. They should be used with caution if the error from the random walk is very small; i.e., the "division by zero" problem. The replacement of extreme values of the RAE with certain limits, a procedure called Winsoring, is recommended (Armstrong and Collopy 1992, p. 79)

$$[W]RAE_{m,h,s} \equiv \begin{cases} 0.01 & \text{if } RAE_{m,h,s} < 0.01 \\ RAE_{m,h,s} & \text{if } 0.01 \le RAE_{m,h,s} \le 10 \\ 10 & \text{if } RAE_{m,h,s} > 10 \end{cases} . \tag{9.28}$$

Winsoring can also be used to temper the impact of outliers. One problem with Winsoring is how to set the proper limits.

Geometric means can be used to summarize relative error measures. The Geometric Mean of the RAE (GMRAE) is

$$GMRAE_{m,h} = \left(\prod_{s=1}^{S} RAE_{m,h,s} \right)^{1/S} . \tag{9.29}$$

Extreme outliers affect the GMRAE so Winsorized RAEs are always used in the above formula. In sum, GMRAE is fair on reliability, good on construct validity, fair on outlier protection, good on sensitivity, and poor on relationship to decisions (Armstrong and Collopy 1992, p. 77). $MdRAE_{m,h}$ can be found in a similar fashion to $MdRAE_{m,h}$; only now the observations are rank ordered by $RAE_{m,h,s}$. In sum, MdRAE is fair on reliability, good on construct validity, good on outlier protection, poor on sensitivity, and poor on relationship to decisions (Armstrong and Collopy 1992, p. 77). In a comparison of the forecasting accuracy of the SCAN*PRO model of retail promotion effects at different levels of aggregation, MdRAE was used because of the small number of series (Foekens, Leeflang, and Wittink 1994, p. 255). For chain-level forecasts, only 3 brands × 3 chains = 9 series were available. For market-level forecasts, only the 3 brand series were available. MAPE was also used and its results were found to be quite consistent with those from MdRAE. MdRAE was also used for a comparison of attraction models for forecasting market shares because only 6 brands were available (Chen, Kanetkar, and Weiss 1994). This study also calculated RMSE and AAE.

For a particular method, the RAEs are summarized across all of the H horizons for a specific series by

$$CumRAE_{m,s} = \frac{\sum\limits_{h=1}^{H} |F_{m,h,s} - A_{h,s}|}{\sum\limits_{h=1}^{H} |F_{rw,h,s} - A_{h,s}|}. \tag{9.30}$$

Another way to control for scale is to calculate the percentage of forecasts for which a given method is more accurate than the random walk—the Percent Better:

$$Percent\ Better_{m,h} = \frac{\sum\limits_{s=1}^{S} j_s}{S} \times 100, \tag{9.31}$$

where $j_s = \begin{cases} 1 & \text{if } |F_{m,h,s} - A_{h,s}| < |F_{rw,h,s} - A_{h,s}| \\ 0 & \text{otherwise} \end{cases}$.

Percent Better is immune to the outlier problem. Percent Better also shows another way to avoid the amount of change problem. Simply discard information about the amount of change! However, this also means that the amount of improvement cannot be recognized; making Percent Better useless for decision making. In sum, Percent Better is good on reliability, fair on construct validity, good on outlier protection, poor on sensitivity, and poor on relationship to decisions (Armstrong and Collopy 1992, p. 77).

When multiple error measures are used in a particular study, one can calculate a Consensus Rank:

$$\text{Consensus Rank} = \frac{\sum_{e=1}^{E} R_{e,m}}{E}, \qquad (9.32)$$

where $R_{e,m}$ the ranking given by measure e to method i.

For selecting the most accurate forecasting method, the Median RAE (MdRAE) is recommended when using a small number of series and Median Absolute Percentage Error (MdAPE) when many series are available (Amstrong and Collopy, p. 78).

Model Validation Revisited

Marketing Analytics (Ross 1995a) notes that market response models are becoming the key drivers of marketing spending decisions. Model validation techniques separate right model from wrong models. As we discussed in Chapter 5, a number of model validation techniques exist. The best method for a particular situation depends on the purpose of the model. The purpose of market response models is to identify managerially important marketing strategies and policies. Thus, the best validation methods uncover a models ability to *forecast* significant policy changes.

Marketing Analytics reminds us that a good fit does not guarantee a good model. It argues, therefore, that it is best to do several tests and include policy-based holdouts if you are testing policy-driving models. A summary of the strengths and weaknesses of model validation methods is given in Table 9-5.

We turn now to the methods of market forecasting (other than market response per se) that are typically part of automatic forecasting systems (AFS), reasoning that *these* are the techniques that can be easily used to complement model-based planning and forecasting. Together, they provide a comprehensive basis for company planning and forecasting that is both up-to-date and readily accessible.[8]

Forecasting without Market Response Models:
Automatic Forecasting Systems

Automatic forecasting systems have developed in response to a market need for software that allows managers as well as analysts to produce forecasts. One review found 103 programs that can automate forecasting, although a much smaller number are *only* forecasting programs (Rycroft 1993). This smaller set includes commercial successes such as Smart Forecasts, SIBYL/Runner, 4CAST/2, and Forecast Pro. The

Table 9-5 Model Validation Methods

		Validation Method	Pros	Cons
D e c r e a s i n g	o f	Fit error $\left(\text{MAPE, MSE, } R^2, \overline{R}^2\right)$	Shows explanatory power Necessary (for a good model)	Deceptively good if too many variables $\left(\overline{R}^2 \text{ can help}\right)$ Not sufficient (for a good model)
		Standard model diagnostics (significance tests, collinearity assess-ment, residual analysis)	Generally necessary	Significance tests deceptively good with (many) correlated observations Not sufficient
		Coefficient "reasonableness"	Can easily reject some models Necessary	Not sufficient
F r e q u e n c y	U s e	Time-based holdout error (MAPE, MSE) and holdout bias	Shows coefficient accuracy Shows predictive power Necessary	Difficult to read with collinearity—many combinations of incorrect coefficients can do well Not sufficient
		Recovery of coefficients in simulations	Shows coefficient accuracy Shows predictive power under policy changes Necessary if assumptions right	Results dependent on assumed "true" model Not sufficient
		Policy-based holdout error (MAPE or MSE)	Shows predictive power under policy changes Necessary	Not sufficient

Source: Ross (1995a)

last program, for example, offers three univariate methods based on extrapolation—moving averages, exponential smoothing, and Box-Jenkins—and one multivariate method, "dynamic" or multiple regression (Stellwagen and Goodrich, 1994). More elaborate programs combine forecasting with general statistical analysis and/or econometric capabilities. These programs include the PC versions of SAS, SPSS and SCA, as well as dedicated PC packages such as EViews and Statistica.

Although some of the automatic forecasting programs include the simple moving average method, this technique is dominated by methods that assign different weights to different time periods. For example, when the more recent past is a stronger indicator of the future than the more distant past, and when seasonal patterns are present in the data, moving-average forecasts are readily outperformed by exponential smoothing and Box-Jenkins models. For this reason, we restrict our discussion to these two methods.

Exponential Smoothing

The simple exponential smoothing model reflects exponentially declining weights of the past on the present in a simple form:

$$\hat{Q}_t = \alpha\, Q_{t-1} + (1-\alpha)\hat{Q}_{t-1} \tag{9.33}$$

where α is the exponential smoothing weight and hats indicate forecasted values. The higher α, the more the forecasts are sensitive to current events. The lower α, the stronger the smoothing influence of the historical forecast. The value α is typically obtained by searching over the relevant range $[0,1]$ for the value that minimizes squared error.

More complex exponential smoothing models add linear or multiplicative trend, and linear or multiplicative seasonality to the base model. Forecast Pro, for example, uses the Kalman filter to automatically derive simple, Holt, and Winters (multiplicative and additive) models, and selects the best model using the Bayesian Information Criterion.

The main advantage of exponential smoothing is its simplicity of use. Indeed, for the simple model, only two numbers need to be stored for forecast updating, the current forecast and the current sales level. While exponential smoothing forecasts tend to lag the actual values by one period, they track the evolution of sales well. For these reasons the method is most useful in *batch forecasting*, i.e. the routine, automated forecasting of hundreds of even thousands of time series, for example at the SKU level.

Box-Jenkins

As we discussed in Chapter 6, the Box-Jenkins method is the most complete univariate time-series model, as it combines trend, seasonality, smooth autoregressive and spiked forecast-error terms. Recall the overall ARIMA (p,d,q) model

$$\Phi(L)\Delta Q_t = \Theta(L)w_t. \tag{9.34}$$

Despite its apparent complexity, applications of Box-Jenkins forecasting are on the rise, spurred by developments in automated model specification methods (e.g. Forecast Pro and SCA). Box-Jenkins forecasts are also easy to interpret conceptually, even if the underlying model is complex, because they are composites of

- previous levels and same-time-last-year levels, and

- previous forecast errors .

For example, the airline model discussed in Chapter 6 shows the dependence of current forecasts on previous levels and forecast errors.

In terms of forecasting properties, the Box-Jenkins method shares the advantages of exponential smoothing, though in most cases it requires more data storage for forecast updating. Simple exponential smoothing is, in fact, a special case of Box-Jenkins, namely the ARIMA $(0,1,1)$ model. As data storage and automated forecast software capabilities continue to expand, we expect this method to become the forerunner of extrapolative methods.

Programs like Forecast Pro also allow some flexibility in modeling causal factors and events, but fall short of the technology reported in this book to produce comprehensive models of market mechanisms.[9] An automatic forecasting system for market share with logical consistency has been proposed (Terui 2000). It is based on the Bayesian VAR model. One application has been to the daily market shares of butter manufacturers in Japan.

Event Modeling

As discussed in Chapter 7, event modeling or intervention analysis adds isolated events, such as promotions, strikes, or regime shifts, to the extrapolative power of an ARIMA(p,d,q) model. The general model is

$$Q_t = \beta_0 + \frac{\omega(L)}{\delta(L)} L^b P_t + \frac{\Theta(L)}{\Phi(L)} w_t . \tag{9.35}$$

Some automatic forecasting software allows event modeling, for example Forecast Pro XE. A good example of the use of intervention models in marketing is given in Leone (1987).

Forecasting with Market Response Models

In market response forecasting, the principles of evolutionary model building (Urban and Karash 1971) apply. Simple market response models may be sufficient to project demand in function of the planned marketing mix and to help determine the relative sales effectiveness of various communications media. But whether or not the company is able to act on the results and, for example, expand production capacity or reallocate its marketing mix, is a different question. In other words, the successful use of even simple market response forecasts requires an organizational savvy that goes beyond the ability to build accurate forecasting models.

Suppose the company is able to successfully respond to the information in a simple market response forecast. It has then obtained a good answer to one or more important questions, and has improved its own 'best practice'. Very quickly, though, the quest for continued improvement and competitive pressures create new questions that require perhaps more data, better software and more resources to answer. For example, if the company's planned marketing mix and predicted sales materialize, is there likely to be a competitive reaction to the company's improved practice and results? This question may prompt research into the determinants of competitive price response for which new data need to be tapped and multiple-equation models need to be estimated.

While we have shown that there is considerable evidence to support managerial use of response models to describe a marketplace and to provide diagnostic information, the use of market response models, especially market share models, in forecasting has been more controversial. The forecasting ability of a market response model is typically benchmarked against a "naïve" time series model. The naive model does not contain any marketing mix data but does contain the lagged dependent variable, which may capture major *causal* effects because it reflects the carryover effects of marketing effort and/or consumer inertia (see Aaker and Jacobson 1987). Thus, for a market response model to be superior in forecasting, there must be strong current effects from the marketing mix (Brodie and Bonfrer 1994, p. 278). Other conditions, such as data quality, may blur the advantages of market response models over naïve models and we will address them in the following discussions on prediction with linear models, forecasting with nonlinear models, forecasting market share, forecasting competitive actions, and incorporating competition.

Prediction with Linear Models

An example of forecasting using a linear model is given in the *Polaroid Industry Perspective*. If the values of the explanatory variables are known for a new observation, that is, an unconditional forecast is being made, and the least squares

Integrating Market Response Models in Sales Forecasting at Polaroid

Polaroid Corporation is a *Fortune* 500 company with subsidiaries worldwide. Founded in 1937 in Cambridge Massachusetts by Dr. Edwin Land, Polaroid offers a variety of products in the photographic imaging industry. World renown for being the leader in the manufacturing of instant photographic imaging products Polaroid has recently expanded its presence in the electronic and digital imaging categories. In 1996 Polaroid began a sweeping restructuring of all its business activities with emphasis on a market orientation. One of those changes has been a more focused global marketing services group that includes global sales forecasting and marketing analysis. As a result, Polaroid is planning to position itself for growth in the next decade and beyond.

The Global Sales Forecasting and Marketing Analysis department at Polaroid is concerned primarily with providing senior management with actionable decision support analysis. Accurate point estimates are the result of in-depth causal analysis that measure the effects of the marketing mix on retail take-away and the resulting impact on trade shipments. Using ACNielsen scanner data, internal marketing expense data, advertising spending information (e.g., TV media, cable, and print dollars), and external market information we develop market response models that determine the push/pull relationship associated with our business activities. The underlying premise is that if we can better understand what drives our business at retail we can link that to what needs to be shipped to our customers (i.e., Wal-Mart, K-mart, Walgreens, etc.) who distribute Polaroid products through the various channels of distribution (i.e., Food, Drug, Mass Merchandising, and Specialty Camera stores).

Using classical Ordinary Least Squares multiple regression techniques, we build a model that reflects current marketing activities using retail price, sales promotion, advertising, merchandising (%ACV features and displays), store distribution, free-standing inserts (FSIs) for couponing, product rebates and seasonality to predict retail take-away. Then we link retail take-away to trade shipments by building a second model that uses consumer demand (retail) as the primary driver along with trade promotions, gross dealer price, factory dealer rebates, cash discounts (or off-invoice allowances) and seasonality. The basic equations can be written as

Editors' Note: A marketing mix econometric model for Polaroid in the United Kingdom, which was developed by the Hudson River Group, is discussed in "Polaroid" in Kendall (1999), pp. 439-71.

1) Instant Film Retail Take-Away

$$RQ_i = \beta_0 + \beta_1 Price + \beta_2 Cameras + \beta_3 Advertising$$
$$+ \beta_4 Sales\ Promotion + \beta_5 \%ACV\ Features + \beta_6 FSI$$
$$+ \beta_7 Store\ Distribution + \beta_8 Seasonality$$

and

2) Instant Film Factory Shipments

$$FQ_i = \beta_0 + \beta_1 Price + \beta_2 Rebates + \beta_3 Cash\ Discounts$$
$$+ \beta_4 Trade\ Promotions + \beta_5 Seaonality$$

We use dummy variables to measure the unit lift associated with qualitative drivers such as FSIs and factory trade promotions. For example, in the case of FSIs we use the circulation quantity instead of a dummy variable equal to one in the periods that they are dropped, and zeros in the periods where there are no FSIs dropped. This not only allows us to measure the average lift but also the magnitude associated with each million dropped (or circulation). In the case of factory trade promotions we use the traditional method of ones (turned on) and zeros (turned off). However, we create three separate independent variables for each promotion to indicate forward buy, sell through, and post shipments, which reflect the true buying patterns of our customers.

Most recently, we began using polynomial distributed lags to model the cumulative affects of advertising at retail over time t. The general notion of a distributed lag model is that the dependent variable, Y_t, responds not only to changes in an input variable X at time t, but also on the past history of the X_t series. If, for example, we stopped all advertising on Instant film product line Y, its share of the market would not drop to its ultimate point overnight. Rather, we would expect gradual erosion of its market share as consumer's perception of the product dims as memory fades. We found this technique to be extremely effective in helping us better understand the dynamics of advertising awareness which has helped us maximize our advertising spend. The method of regression know as ordinary least squares has some very attractive statistical properties that have made it one of the most popular methods of regression analysis. Ordinary least squares regression may be a linear modeling approach, but many times it works in situations that you would think it normally would not. We have found that sales forecasts using regression models are generally superior to those based on simple extrapolation techniques. They provide a useful starting place for formulating the sales forecast; identifying factors for which judgmental decisions can be made; and providing a framework to insure consistency of the sales forecast process. We have also found that sales forecasts with subjective adjustments generally are more accurate than those obtained from the "purely" mechanical application of the regression model. In other words, a combination of model building and subjective market expertise are required for the successful prediction of the future.

Prepared by Charles W. Chase Jr., Director, Global Sales Forecasting and Marketing Analysis, Polaroid Corporation. He has about 20 years experience in the consumer package goods industry building micro-econometric models to analyze marketing strategies and to forecast sales. Editors' Note: Mr. Chase left Polaroid to join the Coca-Cola Company, then moved on to Wyeth-Ayerst.

estimates of the parameters are available, then the value of the dependent variable, here volume, can be predicted:

$$\hat{Q}_i = \hat{\beta}_0 + \hat{\beta}_1 X_{i1} + \cdots + \hat{\beta}_p X_{ip} = \mathbf{x}_i' \hat{\beta}. \tag{9.36}$$

Assuming the model is correct, this forecast is an unbiased predictor of the actual observation since the expected value of a future forecast error is zero:

$$E\left(Q_i - \hat{Q}_i\right) = E\left(\mathbf{x}_i'\beta + \varepsilon_i - \mathbf{x}_i'\hat{\beta}\right) = \mathbf{x}_i'\beta - \mathbf{x}_i'\beta = 0. \tag{9.37}$$

Moreover, this forecast is the *minimum mean square error forecast* among all linear unbiased forecasts (Pindyck and Rubinfeld 1998, p. 205). The variance of the forecast error is

$$
\begin{aligned}
V\left(Q_i - \hat{Q}_i\right) &= V\left[\varepsilon_i + \mathbf{x}_i'\left(\beta - \hat{\beta}\right)\right] \\
&= \sigma^2 + V\left[\mathbf{x}_i'\left(\beta - \hat{\beta}\right)\right] \\
&= \sigma^2 + \sigma^2 \mathbf{x}_i'\left(\mathbf{X}'\mathbf{X}\right)^{-1}\mathbf{x}_i
\end{aligned}
\tag{9.38}
$$

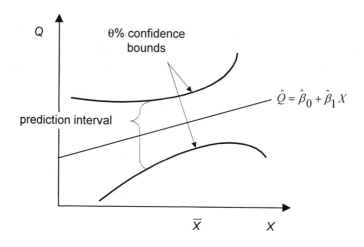

Figure 9-2. Unconditional Forecast Confidence Intervals

$$V\left(Q_i - \hat{Q}_i\right) = \sigma^2\left[1 + \mathbf{x}_i'(\mathbf{X}'\mathbf{X})^{-1}\mathbf{x}_i\right].$$

The estimated variance is found by replacing σ^2 with s^2, the mean square error. The $\theta = 1 - \alpha$ prediction interval for the future Q_i is

$$\hat{Q}_i \pm t_{\alpha/2, n-p-1} s\left[1 + \mathbf{x}_i'(\mathbf{X}'\mathbf{X})^{-1}\mathbf{x}_i\right]^{1/2}. \tag{9.39}$$

This interval is illustrated in Figure 9-2. The message here is that the error of the forecast is smallest when explanatory values are near their mean values (Pindyck and Rubinfeld 1998, p. 205).

When making an ex ante forecast with a model containing environmental variables, the values of these variables are often not known, that is, a conditional forecast is being made. The values of these variables must be forecast and this process introduces additional forecast error. Thus, the θ percent confidence intervals for the error of forecast will be larger for the conditional forecast than the corresponding unconditional forecast (Pindyck and Rubinfeld 1998, p. 205).[10]

Forecasting with Nonlinear Models

Just as with a linear model, once the parameters of a general nonlinear model have been estimated, values of the explanatory variables can be plugged in to yield a forecast:

$$\hat{Q}_i = f\left(1, X_{i1}, \cdots, X_{ip}; \hat{\beta}_0, \hat{\beta}_1, \cdots, \hat{\beta}_p\right). \tag{9.40}$$

The problem is that one cannot say much about the properties of this forecast nor can one compute the associated confidence intervals.[11] In particular, the forecast cannot be said to be unbiased or as having the minimum mean square error. The reason is the forecast errors will not be normally distributed with zero mean (Pindyck and Rubinfield 1998, p. 270).

Linear-in-the-Logs Models. When the nonlinear model is log-log or log-linear, as is often the case in market response modeling, it is relatively easy to make an adjustment to the forecasts of Q so that they remain unbiased (e.g., Kennedy 1983, Miller 1984). Consider, for example the typical multiplicative specification

$$Q = \beta_0 X^{\beta_1} e^u, \tag{9.41}$$

in which $\underline{u}$ is $N(0, \sigma)$. Then it can be shown that

$$E(Q) = \beta_0 X^{\beta_1} e^{1/2\sigma^2}. \tag{9.42}$$

So, taking the logarithms in order to estimate the response function with OLS and make forecasts of Q in logarithms, one has to be careful when retransforming the results back to levels of Q. A direct retransformation will produce a downward bias in the forecast. Instead, the modeler should calculate the forecasts from the expression

$$\hat{Q} = \hat{\beta}_0 X^{\hat{\beta}_1} e^{1/2\hat{\sigma}^2} \tag{9.43}$$

where the OLS estimates are denoted by ^s. This correction is used in the promotion planning model, PromoCast™ (Cooper et al. 1999, p. 308).

One study compared different levels of entity aggregation in a specific double-log model designed to capture retail promotion effects, the SCAN*PRO model (Foekens, Leeflang and Wittink 1994). [Recall that ACNielsen's SCAN*PRO model was described in a boxed insert in Chapter 3.] The alternative model specifications were: store-level models with homogeneous or heterogeneous response parameters across retail chains, with or without weekly indicator variables, (2) chain-level models with homogeneous or heterogeneous response parameters across retail chains, and (3) a market-level model. The empirical analysis using store scanner data showed that

"the statistical significance results favor the homogeneous store models. ... On the other hand, heterogeneous store models provide the best forecasting accuracy results. Either way, disaggregate (store-level) models are favored over aggregate (chain- or market-level) models.

These results apply to a specific model but are likely to be representative of static market response models looking at store promotions. However, they might not apply to dynamic models or ones that include manufacturer advertising.

Forecasting Market Share

Researchers have been interested in the conditions under which market response models do better than naïve models in forecasting market share. Their interest has been peaked by empirical studies, such as Brodie and deKluyver (1987), that indicated that market response models might well do worse than naïve models in forecasting market share. A theoretical analysis has shown that this result is not surprising (Hagerty 1987). This theoretical analysis has been extended by Danaher and Brodie (1992). These analyses use the mean squared error (MSE) to compare the forecasting ability of a linear market response model with a linear naïve model. The naïve model contains only lagged market share. Both models assume that the explanatory variables are known; that is, unconditional forecasting is being done. The linear market response model will be preferred to the naïve linear model for brand i (i.e., have lower estimated MSE) if

$$
\left(1 - R_{ir}^2\right)^2 + \frac{4\left(1 - R_{ik}^2\right)\left(1 - R_{ir}^2\right)}{n - k}\left(r - 1 + \frac{n}{n^*}\right)
$$

$$
+ \frac{\left(1 - R_{ik}^2\right)^2}{(n - k)(n - k + 2)}\left(\begin{array}{l} m^2 - k^2 + 2(r - k)(n + 1) - (n - r + 2)(n + 3r - 4) \\ + \dfrac{4n(2r - n - 2 - k)}{n^*} \end{array} \right) > 0, \qquad (9.44)
$$

where R_{ik}^2 is the R^2 for the market response model for just brand i with k parameters, R_{ir}^2 is the R^2 for the corresponding naïve linear model with r (= 2) parameters, n is the number of estimation data points, and n^* is the number of validation points. An exploration of (9.44) found that the number of validation points are not very important in deciding between the market response model and the naïve model, but that the number of estimation points and the number of parameters are very important (Danaher and Brodie 1992, p. 623). In particular as the number of observations becomes large, the market response model does better than the naïve model.

The following guidelines regarding the forecasting performance of market share models have been developed (Kumar 1994, p. 311):

1. It is important to address the issue of parameter homogeneity on a per product, per market basis.

2. The models need to be fully specified for econometric models to perform better than naïve models.

3. The models need to be fully specified for attraction specification to perform better than the naïve model.

4. The use of econometric models is encouraged at the brand level since their performance is superior to the naïve model.

5. Since the performance of models is not market related, econometric models should be preferred as long as there is sufficient variability in the data.

Forecasting Competitor's Actions

Competitors' actions and other environmental variables must be forecast before a market response model can be used to provide forecasts. The econometric approach is to use competitive reaction functions. For example, an extensive study was conducted on competitive reactions for seven large brands of a frequently purchased nondurable, nonfood consumer product sold in the Netherlands. The results of this study suggest that scanner data can be a useful basis for understanding the nature of competitive reactions implemented at the level of the retailer (Leeflang and Wittink 1992, p. 55).

Incorporating Competition in Forecasts

Market response model forecasts are contingent on estimates of competitive marketing mix decisions. The mean squared error forecasting ability of a multiplicative model and its reduced form, a multiplicative naïve model, can be compared (Danaher 1994). For estimation purposes, the models are expressed in ln-ln form, with each variable divided by the geometric mean of that variable across all brands to ensure logical consistency. Then the multiplicative model will be preferred to the naïve model for brand i (have lower estimated MSE) if

$$\left(1-R_{ir}^2\right)+\frac{2r-n-k}{n-k}\left(1-R_{ik}^2\right)-\sum_{j\neq i}^{B}\left(1-R_{jk}^2\right)\frac{(n+1)(n-2)}{(n-k)(n-k-1)}>0 \qquad (9.45)$$

where R_{ik}^2 is the R^2 for the multiplicative model for just brand i with k parameters and R_{ir}^2 is the R^2 for the corresponding naive multiplicative model with r $(= 2)$ parameters and n is the number of estimation data points.

This is a generalization of the theoretical criteria by Hagerty (1987) and Danaher and Brodie (1992) for the case where there is perfect knowledge of competitors' actions when making forecasts. Note the more brands B to be forecasted, the less likely the market response model will outperform the naive model. To do well, market response models must fit the data well for all brands in the market (Danaher 1994, pp. 292, 294).

1. When competitors' actions are predicted, a better forecasting model should be used to obtain better market share predictions using econometric models.

2. If large errors are incurred in predicting the competitors' actions, then it is better to use a naïve model than an econometric model.

The key conditions when market share models are likely to outperform the forecasts of naïve models are summarized in Brodie et al. (1998). In conclusion, some remarks by Pindyck and Rubinfeld (1998, p. 224) are germane:

> Even if the regression model has a good fit with statistically significant parameters, unconditional forecasts may not be very accurate. A good regression model in terms of unconditional forecasting may perform quite badly when conditional forecasting is attempted. Thus, one should not reject a model with high forecast error if the primary component of that error is due to an error in prediction involved with the explanatory variables.

Simulation with Market Response Models

Market response models deliver not only forecasts of market outcomes but, by changing scenarios, they can easily be extended into *market simulators*—answering a variety of what-if scenario questions that are of interest to managers. A good example is given in the account of Compaq's use of market response models to monitor the evolution of the personal computer market and time Compaq's new-product, price and communications interventions (McWilliams 1995). Compaq models not only the end-user sales response to its marketing mix, but also the price response of key competitors to changing market conditions, and the behavior of retailers in view of these changes. In this case, market response modeling and forecasting becomes a sophisticated scenario analysis in which Compaq's actions trigger consumer response, competitor response and retailer response, each with their own unique response parameters. At the methodological level, such models require simultaneous

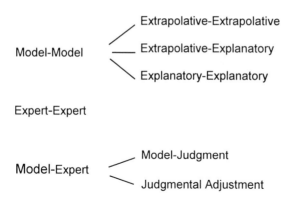

Figure 9-3. Combining Forecasts

structural equations models discussed in Chapter 5 or vector-autoregressive models discussed in Chapter 7.

Market simulations may or may not require specialized statistical software depending on whether the models are built in-house or are deliverables from an outside source.[12] In addition to automatic forecasting software (which we have argued is a complement to model-based planning and forecasting, not a substitute), a company may require programs that allow more sophisticated modeling. This means that the actual models may be built using software such as SAS, SPSS, Statistica or E-views, which are just examples of the many general-purpose programs available in the marketplace.

Consultants often develop their own proprietary estimation software such as Coefficient Generator™ from Marketing Analytics or PromoCast™ from Efficient Market Services (Cooper et al. 1999). Research suppliers such as ACNielsen and IRI have developed various market response simulators that address specific marketing problems such as price setting, product variety planning, account promotion management and overall marketing mix allocation.

Combining Forecasting Methods and Models

Two of the major generalizations of forecasting research are that combined forecasts are more accurate than single forecasts and that simple combining schemes, e.g., averaging, are best (Armstrong, 1986; Clemen, 1989). These generalizations are well supported by empirical research and have found their way into practice. Since model-based planning and forecasting provides a mechanism for integrating models and judgment, we need to understand exactly how this can be done. The different possibilities for combining are shown in Figure 9-3. The three basic ways are model-model, expert-expert, and model-expert. As pure judgmental forecasting is largely irrelevant to market response models, we discuss only the first and third ways.

Model-Model Combination

Combining forecast models makes sense only if the models are extrapolative. With such models there may be no meaningful "true" model (since the models are not designed to explain) and different extrapolation techniques may be equally plausible. In this case, two or more extrapolative models could be combined to reduce forecast error.[13] In model-based planning and forecasting, extrapolation may be used to forecast total market demand, to forecast competitive reactions, to forecast costs, etc. Such situations would benefit greatly from improved accuracy.

Combining extrapolative and explanatory market response models or more than one explanatory model does not make sense. By definition, market response models are designed to explain, so some alternative that doesn't do that isn't much of an alternative. It certainly can't be used for planning. Combining explanatory models would be worse. Although some would argue that "true" models cannot be found, our position has been that that is the *purpose* of market response research.[14]

The Evidence for "True" Models. Twenty-five years ago Parsons and Schultz (1976) argued that there were certain features of marketing that made it a science—among these was the notion that sales are determined by processes discoverable by statistical methods, in particular econometric methods. The first evidence of this was the demonstration that sales response models could be estimated with reasonable statistical accuracy. Since many of the early models were structural models taking observational equivalence and identification into account, the case could be made for the *representativeness* of these models: they represented, adequately enough, the process generating sales, and ruled out, as it were, alternative models and even decision rules. Shortly thereafter, Leone and Schultz (1980) demonstrated that sales response models could be used to uncover generalizations about the effects of the marketing mix variables on sales, generalizations that were virtually *laws* of marketing.

By the time the first edition of this book was published in 1990, market response models were being used not only to represent sales generation and substantiate generalizations, but also to provide a logical basis for marketing *decision making*. Today this is even more the case; an entire industry has developed to support the development of such models for practical application. So, regardless of the philosophical debate, market response models are being treated by researchers and managers *as if they were true*. Model-based planning and forecasting is a means for integrating management judgment (and uncertainty) in a way that does not compromise the possibility of a true, working model of sales.

The Priority of Planning. The main reason for not combining models of sales is that marketing managers need to plan. To compute sales forecasts based on an explanatory market response model and, say, an extrapolative smoothing model, and then average the results would defeat the purpose of marketing decision making. Marketing managers are paid to do something more than make guesses, educated guesses, or even expert guesses—they are compensated for making decisions. Explanatory models presuppose control while extrapolative models merely indicate expectation.

Market response *begins* with decision making. Market forecasts are a byproduct of marketing planning. The combination of forecasting techniques that we recommend is not one of different views of the sales generation process, but one of different techniques for different parts of the overall modeling task. As we have demonstrated in other chapters, times series and other methods have their place in forecasting economic trends, industry sales growth, competitive actions, and so on, and we would expect that any company using market response models would be one to also use complementary techniques, perhaps some of those as combined forecasts. For a particular product or brand, however, forecasting based on market response means forecasting based on a representative model of sales.

We discussed the relationship of market response research to science in the first edition of this book.[15] Our view was—and is—that scientific progress in marketing proceeds pretty much as it does in other sciences: a search for truth. If market response was *only* about forecasting (and sales were *not* influenced by plans), then the major findings of forecasting research on simple models and combined forecasts would probably be adequate. In the real world of marketing decision making, however, market forecasting carries more baggage. It is about plans and decisions, goals and targets, profits and losses. Thus it cannot be simply about the best forecast.

Model-Expert Combination

Model-based planning and forecasting assumes managerial input in many ways. Managers set goals, design the planning process, help to specify market response models, provide estimates of competitive behavior, and evaluate the overall effectiveness of marketing plans. They do not directly forecast sales or provide subjective estimates of decision parameters. Forecasting research has mainly focused on two aspects of judgment: judgmental adjustments of model forecasts and combining models with judgment. Recently, a new approach called rule-based forecasting has introduced the use of expert systems into forecasting practice. Each of these complements model-based planning and forecasting.

The conditions under which judgment improves forecasting with statistical models are summarized in Bunn and Wright (1991). For either combined model-judgment forecasts or simply judgmental adjustment of model forecasts, the value in using experts comes when they are used in their real world roles (exploiting their domain knowledge) and when some form of decomposition or audit trail is employed. Without decomposition methods such as the Analytic Hierarchy Procedure or causal maps—we could add market response models!—or audit trails to explain the reasoning behind, say, adjustments to statistical forecasts, judgmental input may be too capricious. Blattberg and Hoch (1990) have attempted to define the balance of expert and model, coming to the conclusion that equal weighting may be best.

With respect to decision making (and forecasting) Blattberg and Hoch argue that "...both statistical and human inputs should guide final decisions, *at least given the current state of model building and the difficulty in quantifying expert intuition*" (italics ours) (p. 887). They feel that market response models, like the ones in their experiments, can only be used effectively if they have a built-in adjustment mechanism to capture the changing environment. When the environment is changing, Blattberg and Hoch would look to experts to do what they do best: bring diagnosis, attribute evaluation, flexibility, and domain-specific knowledge to the forecasting task. Models would make up for the bias, overconfidence, politics, emotions, and inconsistency that characterize any human endeavor, especially decision making. In their experiments, including more recent studies (Hoch and Schkade, 1996), they found that the best forecasts were those that combined expert and model with 50% weighting for each.

This book testifies to the changing state of model building. It also points out that certain environments do not seem to change very much over reasonable planning (and forecasting) horizons. For many consumer packaged goods markets, products and brands may change but the fundamental way the brands compete does not.[16] Market forecasts for automobiles that first ignored the effects of rebates and then leasing would be seriously off the mark. But once these two variables are known to have a potential impact on sales, their inclusion in market response models reduces the effect of such "environmental change." Model-based planning and forecasting, as we have noted, combines model output with managerial input. Some industry cases document the models' contribution at much greater than 50%. In an efficient world for resource allocation, it would seem that at least some companies have found that the models' contribution can exceed the managers.

Another way to combine model and expert judgment is through rule-based forecasting. Based on a protocol analysis of five forecasting experts, Collopy and Armstrong (1992) identified 99 rules for combining four extrapolation methods (random walk, regression on time, Brown's linear exponential smoothing, and Holt's exponential smoothing) that outperformed equally-weighted combined forecasts by 13 percent for one-year ahead forecasts and 42 percent for six-year ahead forecasts.

They judged the expert system better in situations involving significant trends, low uncertainty, stability, and good domain expertise. With rule-based forecasting the expert's judgment is organized in a model that goes far beyond the ex post justification of audit trails.

It is not difficult to imagine expert systems that incorporate domain knowledge for explanatory models. Substantial similarities among markets and managers lend themselves to this kind of "automation." In such an environment, model-based planning and forecasting could evolve into an expert system that incorporates the skills of both the manager and the analyst. From this, market forecasts would be an output that made the most of the data and the processing capabilities of managers and models.

Notes

[1]   The price elasticity at the category (primary demand) level for mature products often lies between –1 and 0. This suggests that firms signal to raise prices.

[2]   Use in a system involving both a manufacturer and retailer is discussed in Tyagi (1999).

[3]   For insight into the difficulties of modeling the determinants of the advertising/revenue ratio, see Ailawadi, Farris, and Parry (1994, 1997) and Balasubramanian and Kumar (1990, 1997a,b).

[4]   Longman and Pauwels (1998) show the general conditions for price separability, i.e., when the optimal price is not affected by advertising expenditures.

[5]   Strictly speaking, "real time" implies continuous minute-by-minute data, but there are practical reasons for not considering minutes as an appropriate short run for most products. The real issue is how soon could a company respond to a change in sales with new actions.

[6]   A good general review of this literature can be found in Goodwin and Wright (1993).

[7]   Variables such as "promotion" are sometimes used as examples, but have not been used as treatments.

[8]   Since model-based planning and forecasting—as it is presented in this book—includes the major statistical techniques of econometrics and time series analysis (ETS), there is little need to create a third alternative to ETS and AFS.

[9]   Automatic forecasting software offers multiple regression analysis as a way to incorporate explanatory variables or leading indicators into their forecasting models. In Forecast Pro, for example, both the standard multiple regression model and an extension of the Cochrane-Orcott procedure are supported. Diagnostic tests offered by this program include the Bayesian Information Criterion, Durbin-Watson d-statistic, and the Ljung-Box test. In addition, Box-Cox power transforms are available to the user. Since all "dynamic" regression is custom, automatic forecasting in Forecast Pro and other programs means automatic estimation more than automatic selection.

[10]   Prediction intervals for conditional forecasts cannot be derived analytically but must be approximated. See Pindyck and Rubinfeld (1998, pp. 223-24) for an approximation method.

[11]   An ad hoc procedure for calculating confidence intervals can be found in Pindyck and Rubinfield (1998, p. 271).

[12]   This point is elaborated upon in Chapter 10.

[13]   There are many explanations of why combining reduces forecast error, the leading one being that it cancels random error.

[14]   These opposing views are seen in Winkler (1989) and Diebold (1989).

[15]   See pages 317-23.

[16]   Nothing is static, but brand competition is often remarkably similar over time in the number and type of variables that account for sales.

Appendix 9 *Comparative Studies of Forecasting for Market Share Models*

Study	Comparison	Conclusion
Alsem, Leeflang, and Reuyl (1989)	Competitive behavior: known, predicted using sophisticated model, predicted using a naïve model, or ignored.	Market share forecasts are not very sensitive to assumptions made about future competitive behavior. Sophisticated forecasts of competitive marketing behavior are not consistently better than naïve ones. Using predicted values of competitive behavior may provide better market share predictions than observed values of competitive behavior. Using bimonthly data, sophisticated predictions of market share are not systematically better than naïve ones.
Kumar and Heath (1990)	Linear, multiplicative, and attraction models	Using disaggregate (weekly) data, econometric models outperform naïve models.
Chen, Kanetkar, and Weiss (1994)	Aggregate, disaggregate, and pooled weekly data	Data aggregated across stores (chain level) provide better forecasts although pooled data provide better (more consistent in expected sign and reasonable in magnitude) estimates of parameters.
Kumar (1994)	Linear, multiplicative, and attraction models	Attraction models produce best forecasts even (1) at the brand level, and (2) when competitors' actions are predicted. However, if large errors are incurred in predicting the competitor's actions, among the econometric models it is better to use a linear model than an attraction model because the errors are added in the former while they are multiplied in the latter.
Klapper and Herwartz (2000)	Competitive behavior: known, predicted using sophisticated model, or predicted using a naïve model.	Market share predictions of response models outperform those of the naïve model, irrespective of whether competitors' actions are known a priori or if they are forecast.

V CONCLUSION

10   IMPLEMENTATION

The objective of all applied modeling is to influence management decisions. Market response models have great potential in influencing management decisions because they incorporate the basic premise of marketing. If a company can predict the effect of its actions on sales, then it can do a better job of planning and forecasting. Better plans and forecasts imply better decisions and thus improved performance.

The key to influence, however, is use. We need to understand the factors that explain model use in the same way that we come to understand the factors that explain company sales. Fortunately, there are generalizations about model use that have accumulated over the past 30 years. These findings are collectively known as implementation research and are reported in Schultz and Slevin (1975), Doktor, Schultz, and Slevin (1979), Schultz and Ginzberg (1984), the special issue of *Interfaces* edited by Schultz and Ginzberg in 1987, and Lucas, Ginzberg, and Schultz (1990). Specific discussions of the implementation of model-based planning and forecasting have been limited to Parsons and Schultz (1976), Schultz (1984), and the first edition of this book.

In this chapter, we first review the nature of implementation and show how the objects of implementation have changed over time. We next discuss the factors and processes affecting implementation of model-based planning and forecasting. The chapter—and the book—concludes by relating market response analysis to the most important role any product can play in a company: contributing to corporate success.

Nature of Implementation

It seems clear that models are built to be used, but the actual circumstances of use are subtle. Some models can have an impact on decisions without much if any direct use and some models perhaps shouldn't be used. For models that *are* used, it may be difficult to measure their influence on decisions. For these reasons, a definition of implementation based on organizational change has proven to be important to the understanding of implementation:

> *Implementation is defined as changed decision making and successful implementation as improved decision making.*[1]

Implementation Objects

The objects of implementation range from models of the type that we have been discussing in this book to virtually any project or policy. Most of the factors influencing implementation are the same regardless of object since any object can be regarded as the outcome of a project and the factors influencing projects are very general (Schultz, Slevin, and Pinto, 1987). The development of implementation objects over time is shown in Table 10-1.[2]

The first application of science to decision making was the development of operations research (OR) during World War II (Morse and Kimball, 1951). Scientists and engineers were asked to apply their expertise to certain operational problems and the solutions they came up with were "sold" to military commands, often with spectacular results. Thus, from its inception, OR followed a "push" implementation strategy. In the 50's operations research projects were marketed as OR models to help business firms improve their decision making and these also met with considerable success, in part because the problems tackled were quite structured—applications to process industries and logistics were particularly successful. During the decade of the 60's, however, the push strategy became less viable because the problems that management science (MS was the newer name for OR) sought out were less structured and thus more difficult to solve. This is what led to implementation problems and implementation research.

The 70's saw the advent of information systems (MIS) but a continuation of the push strategy. After all, information systems were proprietary solutions to corporate needs designed by specialists. MIS systems often met resistance from users who raised legitimate questions about such factors as management support, user involvement, and costs vs. benefits that were simultaneously emerging in the implementation research literature as factors determining implementation success. As an outgrowth of information systems, if not OR/MS, the decision support systems of the 80's again seem to follow a *Field of Dreams* push strategy. (If you build it, they

Table 10-1. Implementation Objects

Time	Type of Object	Implementation Strategy
1940	Operations Research projects (OR)	Push
1950	Operations Research models (OR)	Push
1960	Management Science models (MS)	Push
1970	Management Information Systems (MIS)	Push
1980	Decision Support Systems (DSS)	Push
1990	Decision Support Products	
	Marketing Decision Support Systems	Push/Pull
	Geodemographic Systems	Pull
	Automatic Forecasting Systems	Pull
2000	Decision Support Utilities	Pull

will use it.) To be sure, the sophistication of implementation continued to rise and few systems were designed without users in mind, but, nevertheless, implementation remained a substantial problem.

A student of marketing would not be surprised by this history because it is the history of marketing. The production orientation of OR only worked if the OR specialists adopted a sales strategy. This "solution" to implementation was perpetuated through MS, MIS, and DSS objects. But finally, as it was with marketing, decision support *products* started to appear that were designed to survive in a *marketplace*. This, of course, required a consumer orientation and the pull strategies that typically go with it. Whether this took place because system development was moving from a proprietary to a commercialized enterprise—or simply as a result of the customer orientation of modern marketing finally breaking through—today there is an environment of implementation where many products are literally on shelves waiting for purchase. No marketing expert can miss the importance of meeting consumer needs in such a case.

The marketing decision support systems, geodemographic systems, and automatic forecasting systems of today (as well as other software) are evolving themselves into decision support utilities in the future. There is already evidence of networks becoming a distribution vehicle for software.[3] Packaged data marts (such as Information Builder's SmartMart or SAS Institute's SAS Warehouse Administrator) are selling as independent products, thus proving the point that, even in the area of data warehousing, products are succeeding or failing *as products*. When software is purchased and used in real time, *only* pull strategies can be effective.

Implementation Scenarios

Marketing planning and forecasting models are implementation objects that can be developed as proprietary, partially commercialized, or fully commercialized systems. Depending on which method is used, implementation factors are more or less important. Since so many marketing models are proprietary (and for good reasons likely to remain so), we take an especially close look at their development. It turns out that most of the findings of implementation research were obtained in situations involving managers who initiate model building and then seek implementation among themselves or other users. Thus, the number of "stages" in the implementation process as well as the use of in-house or outside talent defines the scenarios of implementation.

Proprietary. Because marketing data are private—not public like most financial data—most marketing models are proprietary. As noted in Chapter 1, companies develop models for themselves using their own research departments or the services of consultants. Besides the source of modeling work, the other key dimension of the implementation scenario for proprietary models is the number of stages in the implementation process. The distinction between one- and two-stage implementations was introduced by Schultz, Ginzberg, and Lucas (1984) to explain how the main factors of implementation differed between stages but not within.

One Stage. A one-stage implementation is characterized by direct interaction between the system developers and the person or group of people who will be using the system. The ultimate user commissions system development and also is part of system development, at least in theory.

By far the most common form of market response model building in companies is modeling that is one stage and proprietary. Consumer packaged goods companies, for example, often commission work for individual brands or, if for a set of brands, for the set of individual brand managers. This latter arrangement preserves the form; it is like a series of individually-commissioned models. In this form, support and interaction are crucial. It is the manager's direct involvement in the process that usually assures success.

Two Stage. A two-stage implementation is one where a manager commissions the development of a system for use by subordinates. The ultimate user may or may not participate in system development. The system is designed for multiple users performing similar tasks. Procter & Gamble and other leading companies are developing decision support systems for salespeople and brand managers. One P&G system, for example, is designed to aid salespeople with category management in retail settings by providing data on the impact of brand sales on category and even store sales.

The two-stage, proprietary form of model building is increasingly popular for applications to market response. In this form, a manager (or more typically a management group, often top management) decides that others should make decisions based on decision support software developed with some or considerable independence from users. Many times these decisions are "handed down" to subordinates with little further management of the implementation process. There is considerable evidence that such tactics often fail. Yet many companies see the two-stage implementation as ideal: developing a proprietary solution for uniform planning and forecasting across brands and divisions. What could be more efficient and cutting-edge? Fortunately, research findings from the implementation literature can help increase the chance of implementation success.

Either one- or two-stage models could be developed in-house or by outside consultants.[4] The outside consultants can be individuals, consulting companies (general or specialized), or marketing information vendors. John Totten, formerly of ACNielsen and now with Spectra Marketing, has noted that:

> In the 1960's and early 1970's, many manufacturers retained central staff with modeling expertise, and generated in-house models based on manufacturing data. With the advent of syndicated scanner data, which is generally not available at store level to the manufacturer, the commercial suppliers had a better database for modeling. This occurred at the same time most manufacturers were suffering a cost squeeze. The result was a reduction of corporate staff, and the transfer of model-building to the suppliers. A second argument was that the suppliers could build knowledge over many different product categories, assuring robustness of the models and results. However, most suppliers today work on samples of stores. The new emerging trend is for the retailer to build large data warehouses of their data, or to have a 3rd party manage their data. I expect a lot of work to be done in building retailer-level response models in the next few years. These will be used in supply chain management and shelf pricing decision.[5]

Partially Commercialized. The ascent of information vendors collecting and processing scanner data has led to partially-commercialized models that are delivered to clients as part of a service or service contract. These models are proprietary to the builder and to the client, but they are similar enough in form that they are also commercialized. Furthermore, the models often are branded and thus well known in the industry as archetypes. For example, there are tracking systems such as ACNielsen's SCAN*PRO, SCANTRACK, and HOME*SCAN and Information Resources' InfoScan and Assessor. There are market exception reporting systems such as ACNielsen's Insight and IRI's CoverStory.

Many of the products are dedicated to specific marketing decisions such as ACNielsen's SPACEMAN for merchandising, PROMOTION MANAGER for promotion planning, PRICEMAN for pricing strategies, CATEGORY MANAGER

Table 10-2. Relative Importance of Factors Affecting Implementation

Software Status	Management Support	User Involvement	Personal Stakes	System Characteristics	Implementation Strategy
Proprietary	High	High	High	High	High
Partially Commercialized	Medium	Medium	High	High	Medium
Commercialized	Low/None	Low/None	High	High	Low/None

for category management, and ENTERPRISE for floorspace analysis. Similar dedicated systems developed by IRI include Apollo Briefcase for in-store modification of shelf planograms and Data Server Analyzer for brand management.

Although the partially-commercialized model can be one stage, it is almost always two stage. Upper-level management makes such commitments and brand managers, say, are expected to use the models to improve the quality of decision making. Again, this requires quite a few implementation factors to be in place.

Commercialized. The latest development in marketing modeling is the fully-commercialized marketing model. These are models that are developed as sold as products. We see marketing decision support software, geodemographic software, automatic forecasting software, and so forth. In this form, implementation issues and consumer decision making merge. Implementation factors become product attributes, and leading implementation factors such as personal stake in the model need to be reinterpreted as consumer benefits. For marketing people, this is the easiest form to understand since it is nothing more or less than a product meeting a consumer or buying unit's needs.

Factors Affecting Implementation

Over 30 years of research on implementation has produced a remarkably stable set of generalizations that relate to implementation objects in general and marketing planning and forecasting models in particular. The key factors are management support, user involvement, personal stake, system characteristics, and implementation strategy.[6] In addition, models of the behavioral process of implementation have been created that integrate most of these findings with basic research on organizational change.

The relative importance of these five leading factors varies by software status, as can be seen in Table 10-2. For proprietary software—the focus of all early research—each of the factors has been shown to have high importance. For partially commercialized software, management support, user involvement, and implementation strategy are expected to be as of medium importance, with personal stake and system characteristics remaining high.[7] For example, this would describe a situation where proprietary planning and forecasting models were developed by marketing research vendors and then made available to clients. Finally, for fully commercialized software, we would expect only personal stake and system characteristics to be highly important. For individual users, the other factors would be nonexistent. Even for group use (on networks, for example), the relevance of management support, user involvement, and implementation strategy would be expected to be low relative to the other categories of software.

Management Support

Management support refers to top or divisional management support, or lack of resistance, for the system. Such support is required before, during, and after system development. In a one-stage implementation, where the manager who commissions the system is also the user (as would be the case in most corporate planning and forecasting systems), the support must come from above the manager-user. In a two-stage implementation, where a manager commissions a system for other users, the manager's own acceptance of the system becomes the perceived management support for the set of users. Support can also be interpreted as lack of resistance to change in general and to a system in particular. The evidence for the need for management support is so strong that any attempt to implement a system without it, and without the related conditions of commitment and authority to implement, will probably result in failure.

Three additional variables that may affect implementation through management support are belief in system concept, power, and leadership. Belief in system concept refers to the extent to which a manager believes in the underlying concept or approach behind a system. Planning and forecasting systems based on ETS, for example, require that managers believe in the concept of measuring response with statistical models and historical data. This implies that a manager will have more involvement in system development and more understanding of the system if the concept on which it is based is accepted first. Power and leadership have to do with achieving support from the "right" top managers and applying the support in the "right" way. There is little doubt in the minds of those with experience in implementing systems of the importance of a "champion" for the system.

Management support is typically thought of as upper-level management support and measured by attitudes. In recent thinking, executive support shades into executive *involvement* because the psychological commitment of managers to systems is more strongly associated with the use of information technology than mere executive participation in system planning and/or development (Jarvenpaa and Ives,

1991). But involvement itself has meant the involvement of potential users, not managers.

User Involvement

User involvement indicates the degree of interaction between a manager (user) and a system designer. On one side of the system development process is the system designer or researcher, and on the other side is the user or client. The more involvement between the two sides in terms of quantity and quality of interaction, the more likely it will be that there is mutual confidence. This mutual trust, in turn, may lead to acceptance and use of the system. Involvement also includes communication between the system designer and user, in particular, communication to ensure that the designer understands the user's needs so as to avoid a Type III error—solving the wrong problem—and communication to verify that the user understands the designer's approach.

Other variables that may be related to user involvement are knowledge of the system, assessment of the system and support, and conflict between participants in system development. Knowledge of the system means how well a manager understands a particular system. For an ETS model, such knowledge has more to do with how plans and forecasts are integrated into the system than it does with details of estimation or testing. Assessment of the system and support refers to a user's evaluation of the quality of a system and its supporting mechanisms (e.g., people, hardware, data). Both knowledge and assessment would be expected to directly affect acceptance of the system. Finally, since systems are implemented in organizations made up of different departments and divisions, conflicts will arise, and so techniques of conflict resolution involving negotiation or influence can be important in managing user involvement.

New research provides better insight into different types of involvement. Alvi and Joachimsthaler (1992) find evidence for the original notion of support as "participation in the system development process" in their meta-analysis of many early studies. At the same time, Barki and Hartwick (1989) refer to this as user participation, reserving the term "user involvement" for the psychological state reflecting a system regarded (by the potential user) as both important and personally relevant. By developing separate measures for user participation and user involvement and then testing these in a structural equation analysis, they find that involvement and user attitudes toward the system mediate the relationship between participation and both intended and actual use (Barki and Hartwick 1994). Interestingly, the psychological-state version of involvement resembles *personal stake*, long considered the most important of the implementation factors.

Personal Stake

Personal stake is the extent to which a system user's future performance depends on the system and its use. There is a great deal of evidence showing that the impact of a system on a user's job performance overshadows all other variables in predicting system success. If a planning and forecasting system can improve the quality of a manager's decisions and if improved decision making leads to better performance and more rewards, then the manager is likely to use the system. Two other aspects of personal stake are goal congruence and problem urgency. Goal congruence refers to the fit between the user's goals and those of the organization; a system that makes them more similar will be one that increases acceptance. Problem urgency reflects the urgency of the problems to which a particular system is addressed. A system that deals with an urgent forecasting need, for example, will increase the stake of the manager with that need.

Although not defined as "personal stake," there are other personal variables that affect implementation success. Individual differences such as age, time with company and in job, and educational background affect an individual's willingness to accept a system. In addition to demographics, an individual's attitudes are important to the implementation process; in fact, many of the variables that we have been discussing are measured as attitudes. Decision style, i.e., an individual's characteristic way of solving a problem or making a decision, can also be a factor in implementation. An analytic decision maker with a fondness for data and analysis should be more predisposed to use ETS in planning and forecasting than a heuristic decision maker who places more value on intuition and experience. Finally, interpersonal relations have been shown to be important to implementation. Individuals will resist changes in interpersonal relations and communication patterns that may be brought about by a new system; such changes may affect their personal stake in the system and consequently acceptance and use.

The original finding by Schultz and Slevin (1975b) that effect of a model on job performance is the primary factor in implementation success continues to find corroboration in new research. Whether the focus is on user expectations concerning the system's benefit (Lawrence and Low 1993) or perceived usefulness (Davis 1989), studies find that personal stake is related to use. Todd and Benbasat (1992) refine the performance variable to include effort saving and/or increased decision performance, which makes the concept even more relevant for planning and forecasting systems. The Davis' study also measures the variable perceived ease of use, which takes us back to the long line of research on system characteristics.

System Characteristics

System characteristics include the features and capabilities of a system. The leading variables that make up this factor are system format, system quality, accuracy, and organization support. System format refers to the extent to which a system can be easily understood and used, i.e., the user friendliness of the system. The use of certain optimization procedures in conjunction with model-based planning and forecasting, for example, results in optimal decision rules that very much resemble in form a company's existing decision rules; such a situation greatly facilitates implementation (Bultez and Schultz, 1979). System quality refers to the extent to which a system solves the user's problem. An important aspect of system quality for forecasting models is accuracy. Implementation success, defined as improved decision making, requires system quality (accuracy) and an appropriate format. We shall have more to say about what this format should be for model-based planning and forecasting in the final part of this chapter.

Organizational support, although not strictly a characteristic of the system, also provides a measure of ease of use. A planning and forecasting system does not stand alone; it requires computer access, software availability, data base maintenance, and budgetary support to update the model over time. System characteristics are not motivating factors like management support, user involvement, and personal stake, but research has shown conclusively that they cannot be ignored.

Since Davis (1989) finds that ease of use influences usage indirectly through its effect on usefulness, it seems that anyone attempting to *manage* the implementation process must be aware of how such factors interact, which is why much research has been devoted to the *process* of implementation.

Implementation Strategy and Process

A final set of variables that influences implementation can be categorized as implementation strategy. This factor incorporates the ideas that implementation is a time-dependent process, that implementation can be managed with an appropriate strategy and adequate resources, and that environmental events can and will affect implementation results. First, by recognizing that implementation involves stages from initial need assessment to final behavior change the groundwork is laid for considering what implementation strategy should be employed over the stages. The amount of user education and persuasion needed varies for different types of systems and different organizations. As a general principle, however, there is much to be said for a policy of phased implementation, say from simple models to complex, and virtually nothing good about a rushed installation. In fact, time has been shown to be one of the more important resources necessary to achieve implementation, along with funds and the quantity and quality of human resources. Overall, success depends on the availability of resources to get the implementation job done.

Even the best strategy can fail because of environmental events. The most common event that threatens the implementation of a new system is probably a decline in company sales or earnings. If advertising and promotion are the first things to be cut in a budget crisis, research is usually next, particularly research not directly tied to product development. Planning and forecasting systems are particularly vulnerable—today's problems always come before tomorrow's. Other threats to implementation include personnel changes, departmental reorganizations personal clashes, turbulent environments, even sabotage. The best way to cope with such events seems to be to *anticipate* them, in the sense of planning for the worst and then getting on with the implementation. Many times, however, this simply does not work.

Other variables that may be related to implementation strategy are binding, technology, and structure. Binding, a term borrowed from pharmacokinetics, concerns the process by which new technology replaces existing technology in an organization. A better understanding of the *rate* of implementation and the *potential* for change would help in the management of implementation. Finally, implementation takes place in organizations characterized by certain technologies and certain structures. As technology changes for example, information technology, an organization's structure changes. The relations among strategy, technology, and structure will be an important area for future implementation research.

Since there are now so many ways that decision support systems can be developed, research is beginning to focus on how the process of implementation differs by approach. Lawrence and Low (1993) investigated the situation of user-led development where a small group of users is chosen to represent the user community. In this case, user perception of representation is found to be the most significant determinant of user satisfaction. Where software-buying decisions are made centrally—networks, for example—the perception of representation would seem to be most important. The user wants to know whose preferences are being met.

Thus, research continues to reaffirm the generalizations about the important factors and processes of implementation reported in the first edition of this book. Yoon, Guimares, and O'Neil (1995), for example, find that implementation success for expert systems (another implementation object) is related to several factors including management support, user involvement, impact on job, and system characteristics, factors virtually identical to those reported above. Szajna (1996) confirms linkages found by Davis (1989) using actual use rather than self-reported usage: perceived usefulness and perceived ease of use leads to intention to use which in turn leads to actual use. These factors are also found to affect software use (Szajna 1994).

Implementation Outcomes

The key indicators of success for a planning and forecasting system are acceptance, use, performance, and satisfaction. Acceptance and use are measures of change in decision making (implementation), and performance and satisfaction are measures of improvement in decision making. In other words, they are ways of operationalizing our definition of implementation. They also represent the notions of adoption of an innovation and the postadoption evaluation of its impact. This conceptualization has antecedents in the work of Schultz and Slevin (1975) and Schultz, Lucas, and Ginzberg (1984). The causal relationships were explored by Lucas, Ginzberg, and Schultz (1990). The clean distinction between implementation and successful implementation prevents ambiguity about the subtleties of use, satisfaction, and performance.[8]

Acceptance. Acceptance is a predisposition to use a system. For a planning and fore-casting system, it would be an intention to incorporate the system into a manager's repertoire of behavior. Thus, acceptance signals that implementation is likely. Other things being equal, the manager intends to adopt the system, replacing the existing planning and forecasting process with the new one that results from using the new decision-making technology. Recall that it would be possible for implementation, or change, to take place without use, although in such a case the system qua system might be termed a failure.

Acceptance is usually measured by an attitude scale not unlike the scales used to measure consumer preference or intention. In terms of managing the implementation of a system, there is much to be learned from knowing the level of acceptance of a potential user or group of users.

Use. Use is the actual experience of applying a system and implies that a change has taken place. It represents experience over a period of time, i.e., repeat use. Although use is a sufficient condition for identifying change, it is not a necessary condition. Still, when most people think of the implementation of a system, they think of actual use in a specific task environment.

Use can be measured directly or from self-reports of actual experience. Direct measures of the use of a computer-based forecasting system, for example, could include number of times used, time per use session, type of use, balance of use across time or type, and so forth. Since we separate performance from use, such direct measures will almost always be preferred. With personal computers, however, there may be more need to rely on reports of use, since there is usually no record of system access, although there can be for networks.

Performance. Performance is the quality of decision making, e.g., planning and forecasting, resulting from the use of a system. It is an objective outcome of system use independent from the user's evaluation of the system. It also captures the idea of successful implementation as improved decision making and, together with other management actions and interventions, can lead to improved organizational performance. For many types of systems, performance is difficult to measure, particularly performance of an individual manager. Planning and forecasting systems, however, are typically used for corporate, divisional, or product planning where the focus is on specific operating results. This permits performance to be measured in terms of profit, cost, and forecast accuracy. Thus, improvements in decision making can be tied to the use of a new model or system.

Satisfaction. Satisfaction is the user's overall attitude toward the system, its use, and its impact on performance. If performance is the objective postadoption evaluation of a new system, satisfaction is the subjective evaluation by the managers who use it. Since use and satisfaction are interdependent, continued satisfaction with a system should lead to continued use of the system.

Satisfaction, like acceptance, is usually measured with an attitude scale. Although the problems associated with attitude-intention-behavior sequences are well known to marketing researchers, the practical advantages to system developers of understanding the factors that determine implementation outcomes cannot be overstated.

A system that is developed without recognition of the behavioral and political milieu in which it is to be used will probably fail to accomplish its purpose. The findings of implementation research provide model builders and managers with insight that helps them to avoid such failure and, indeed, to achieve success.

Organizational Validity

The concept of organizational validity, introduced by Schultz and Slevin (1975), has been expanded upon by numerous writers and applied to implementation problems in information systems (e.g., Markus and Robey 1983), public policy (e.g., Wernham 1984, 1985, and Mushkat 1987) and marketing (Lilien, Kotler, and Moorthy 1992), among others. It remains a useful way of summing up the implementation literature, particularly for model-based planning and forecasting.

Organizational validity is the compatibility of an implementation object with the user organization and, as such, suggests the amount of change required to implement any model or system. Models with low organizational validity have poor fits with their organizational environments while those with high organizational validity have good fits. Since there are two ways to achieve fit—by changing the object or the organization—the question arises which way is best.

When this concept was first developed, decision models were in their infancy, and it was thought that significant tradeoffs needed to be made between optimal models and models that would be used because they more closely fit standard management attitudes and practices.[9] Today, however, decision and information technology is seen as a clear path to improved decisions. In many cases, information and information systems have become part of a company's *product*, thus providing a seamless integration of value-added technology and value-added customer benefits. From American Airlines to Federal Express to Wal-Mart, companies have put the result of information and decision technology into their products and services. So, rather than diminishing the quality of the models or information (to achieve fit with more slowly changing human organizations), companies are urging managers to adopt and use such technology before their competitors do.

Model-based planning and forecasting technology is also on the verge of becoming mainstream. But, as we have seen, successful implementation is not a given, especially the further a technology is from being a direct customer benefit. Market response models used for marketing mix optimization, for example, would seem to help the company more than they help the consumer.[10] So organizational validity remains a sine qua non for implementation. Management support, user involvement, personal stake, system characteristics, and implementation strategy must be managed to achieve implementation success.

The Demand for Market Response Models

We have seen that the *idea* of market response models reflects the basic premise of marketing, that the *technology* behind the models (ETS) is well developed, that their *usefulness* in planning and forecasting has been proven, and that their *implementation* follows from their ability to satisfy a need. It is the latter that is most crucial to understanding the future of market response. Market response models have been and will be used for one simple fact: they directly contribute to corporate success.

Market response information is both a strategic and tactical asset. As we stated in Chapter 1, this information is not about customer needs and wants per se, but about how customers and competitors respond to the marketing actions taken to meet those needs and wants. Thus, market response analysis completes the circle of information from firm to market. A successful company develops products that meet needs, adjusts the marketing mix to maximize sales and profit, and institutes planning, budgeting, and forecasting procedures that utilize information from the market so that the company can direct actions to the market. Market response is what makes this process work. See the *Kraft Industry Perspective*.

Price Promotion Models of Scanner Data at Kraft

At Kraft Foods, technological advancements have made it possible to easily and rapidly estimate price-promotion models across a wide portfolio of products and categories. The results of these models can be used by each product team for price and promotion planning. This "mass application" of standard price and promotion models enables Kraft to have ready information at the point of decision making about the implications of marketing actions. There have been two keys to the positive impact of market response modeling on promotion planning at Kraft.

Planners not Analysts. The key organizational decision made at Kraft has been to hire and develop skilled analysts, and then use them in the role of planning rather than as analysts only. While their analytical skills are critical, just as critical is their ability to sit at the small table where decisions are really made. There they are advocates for what the scanner data and other information sources are saying would happen as a result of marketing actions by Kraft or its competitors.

Category Business Teams bring small group, fast, cross-functional management to a wide range of categories and products by including representatives from Operations, Advertising, Sales, Marketing, Finance, Product Development and Marketing Information. The Category Business Teams depend on the Marketing Information group to provide knowledge and insight based on market data. The models and forecasting tools Marketing Information uses enable them to have a data-driven-voice in the decision making.

Standardized and Automated Modeling. Kraft has invested in software to provide automated and standard modeling results and on the information infrastructure to rapidly feed data into this software. This investment has made possible the "mass production" of standard econometric models of price and sales promotion across hundreds of product groupings in dozens of product categories. With a strong partnership with ACNielsen to provide the data and modeling software from Marketing Analytics Inc., Kraft has been able to implement consistent models across all categories. While a standard model does not meet all the needs of each brand (each one has different issues to study), it does provide a common basis and methodology from which the company can address the special concerns of each business. This also enables Kraft to provide a common benchmark with which to compare products across categories and divisions of the company.

One additional benefit of this process of automated modeling is a cross-sectional database of model results that can be further analyzed to produce company-wide insight into the effect of key measures, such as price elasticity and trade merchandising effectiveness, on brand performance. As Kraft continues to build its information base of model results, these "meta-analyses" of lessons learned will be more and more important in establishing norms and expectations for the businesses of the company.

Prepared by L. James Savage, Director, Analytical Development, Kraft Foods.

Strategic Value of Market Response

Consider two companies. One collects market information, analyzes the effect of its plans on sales, and makes new plans based on actual market feedback. The other company collects market information and makes plans on the basis of market position. Which company has more *strategic* information?

Although market response analysis deals with the impact of tactical marketing decisions on sales—and hence is very much a tactical management activity—it also results in information with strategic value. The company with market response information knows which products to promote, which products to maintain, and which products to replace. Products with higher elasticities (which themselves imply better positioning) can be promoted successfully against their competitors. Products with lower elasticities but good market positions can be maintained without promotional changes. Products with weak market positions and lower response to marketing mix changes probably should be replaced. And, of course, market response information is not just limited to promotion, but includes information on the impact of price changes, distribution changes, sales force changes, etc.

The company without market response information only knows market position. Its products are either strong or weak but it doesn't know how they got that way (other than product positioning) or how their market positions can be influenced through marketing mix actions. Clearly, companies using market response have a competitive advantage. Just as clearly, this information has strategic value.

Tactical Value of Market Response

In Chapter 1 we reviewed the main uses of market response models for brand, category, and marketing management. They are the mechanisms for making tactical decisions based on real data. Price, margin, promotion, advertising copy, weight, media selection, and timing, and other brand-specific marketing decisions are implemented through market response models not ad hoc decision rules that often reverse the logic of planning then forecasting. The impact of similar variables on category sales, the effectiveness of company-wide marketing budgets, and such factors as economic cycles and technological change can be studied with market response analysis. Indeed, this book documents these tactical applications.

Thus, market response information has tactical value. This tactical value is created *within* the context of proper product positioning and appropriate product line decisions, although, as we have just seen, even these important marketing decisions are beginning to be influenced by market response analysis. The contemporary marketing manager seeking better decisions can turn to market response analysis with a confidence borne by decades of research and years of practical success.

Information Systems

Companies that want to implement model-based planning and forecasting as a real-time decision tool need access to data organized by the way sales occur, i.e., by the interaction of vendors and customers through marketing activities and product purchases. In a market response analyses, it is far more useful to have data organized by subject matter (customers, say) than by processes or functions (say accounts receivable). Although important, customer billing is not as important as sales. To understand sales *generation*, an information system supporting market response must be based on data that capture the essence of the business enterprise. In addition, market response studies often require data that are specific to market segments or customers. Many companies have implemented data warehouses or data marts to provide access to this type of information.

In addition to subject-oriented data, a data warehouse includes data integrated across information systems that are time-invariant and nonvolatile (Hackathorn, 1995). By making all data time specific and by allowing data to be continuously added, the data warehouse includes the set of data that makes data-based decision making possible.[11] Due to problems of scale and implementation, data marts sometimes are used to support decisions. Data marts provide a source of department-specific data, e.g. data on product sales by time and region for marketing. Completing the database picture, operational data stores can be used to supply on-line, integrated data for clerical needs, e.g., billing (Inmon, Zachman, and Geiger 1997). Architectures such as these imply that model-based decision making will not fail for lack of relevant data.

Regardless of the technological sophistication of the data warehouse, it ultimately represents an attempt to allow a "user view" of data. This idea is consistent with the notion that brand, category, and marketing managers are the users of market response information and market simulators. Rather than asking analysts for reports, managers can directly query the data through the data warehouse/market response/market simulator model. While some software configurations designed (and marketed) to do this might be termed decision support systems (DSS) or executive information systems (EIS), most companies end up with information systems that fit their particular style of decision making—as we have seen, a very important point for implementation.

Data warehouses have a mixed record of implementation success. Even so, the concept of a data warehouse spanning the business chain from suppliers to customers fits well with the notion of models of market mechanisms that describe the sales generation process for a company's products. Such "extreme integration" promises to make both marketing and competition more efficient.[12]

The Elasticity of Market Response

No concept in this book is more fundamental than the concept of elasticity. We have argued that companies possessing knowledge of product elasticities can outperform their competitors in the marketplace. This book demonstrates how to estimate elasticities, how to use them in decision making, and how to incorporate them into optimal decision rules. Yet there is one more elasticity to discuss—the responsiveness of market response use to market response research. This elasticity accounts for the growth of market response applications.

The information return on an investment in market response analysis is high. Companies have improved their sales forecasting, made better marketing decisions, and, consequently, achieved superior performance *because* they used market response. Nothing attracts the attention of management more than a concept that works—and market response works. The evidence is clear: market response is now an important sector of the marketing research industry; the roster of leading corporate users, as the *Industry Perspectives* show, reads like a who's who of top firms; the pace of market response research shows little sign of diminishing. The elasticity of market response is high indeed.

It is fitting that we end this book where it began, with the point that for every brand and product category there exists a process generating its sales. We have seen that market response makes this process known, and, because it is known, manageable. In a world of intense competition, what better thing is there for a company to know and to be able to do?

Notes

[1] This follows from an idea of Schultz and Slevin (1975b) that *influence* on decision processes was the key to understanding implementation. It was first used by Schultz and Henry (1981).

[2] This sequence focuses on the way models are *delivered* to customers; for a view of the evolution of model *characteristics* in marketing see Wierenga and van Bruggen (1997).

[3] The emergence of the Internet as a delivery system for software through Application Service Providers also supports this point.

[4] A study of marketing decision support systems found that 31% were purchased as products and the rest developed in-house (Wierenga and Ophuis, 1997).

[5] Personal correspondence.

[6] The first edition of this book includes tables documenting the earlier research on which these findings are based.

[7] This table reflects our judgment on importance since definitive research has yet to be done on the newer types of software.

[8] For example, Wierenga and Ophuis (1997) consider use a measure of success after a model is "adopted" even though their definition of adoption is in part "a system that is used." (This study also omits what we consider to be the most important aspect of success—performance—despite a previous study demonstrating the importance of performance to success (van Bruggen, Smidts and Wierenga, 1996).

[9] Wierenga and van Bruggen (1997) use a related concept of "fit" in their argument that managers will only use models (or decision support systems) that match their problem solving modes. In our view, the *demand* for market response modeling demonstrates that this fit exists.

[10] To the extent that companies can lower costs and improve products and services through optimal internal decision making, the customer would benefit.

[11] Thus data warehouses support the need for time-sensitive information (Glazer and Weiss 1993).

[12] The model for extreme integration is Wal-Mart. See Darling and Semich (1996).

BIBLIOGRAPHY

Aaker, David A. and James M. Carman (1982), "Are You Overadvertising?" *Journal of Advertising Research,* 22 (August/September), 57-70.

———— and George S. Day (1971), "A Recursive Model of Communication Processes," in *Multivariate Analysis in Marketing: Theory and Application.* Belmont, CA: Wadsworth, 101-14.

————, James M. Carman, and Robert Jacobson (1982), "Modeling Advertising-Sales Relationships Involving Feedback: A Time Series Analysis of Six Cereal Brands," *Journal of Marketing Research,* 19 (February), 116-25.

———— and Robert Jacobson (1987), "The Sophistication of 'Naïve' Modeling," *International Journal of Forecasting,* 3:3/4, 449-51.

Abbott, A. J., K. A. Lawler, and C. Armistead (1999), "The UK Demand for Steel," *Applied Economics,* 31:11 (November), 1299-1302.

Abe, Makato (1995), "Nonparametric Density Estimation Method for Brand Choice Using Scanner Data," *Marketing Science,* 14:3 (Part 1 of 2), 300-325.

Abraham, Bovas and Johannes Ledolter (1983), *Statistical Methods for Forecasting.* New York: Wiley.

Abraham, Magid M. and Leonard M. Lodish (1987), "PROMOTER: An Automated Promotion Evaluation System," *Marketing Science,* 6 (Spring), 101-23.

———— and ———— (1990), "Getting the Most Out of Advertising and Promotion," *Harvard Business Review,* 68:3 (May-June), 50-60.

———— and ———— (1993), "An Implemented System for Improving Promotion Productivity Using Store Scanner Data," *Marketing Science,* 12:3 (Summer 1993), 248-269.

Ackoff, Russell L. and James R. Emshoff (1975), "Advertising Research at AnheuserBusch, Inc. (1963-68)," *Sloan Management Review,* 16 (Winter), 1-15.

Adams, Arthur J. and Mark M. Moriarty (1981), "The Advertising-Sales Relationship: Insights from Transfer-Function Modeling," *Journal of Advertising Research,* 21 (June), 41-46.

Adams, Dennis A., R. Ryan Nelson, and Peter A. Todd (1992), "Perceived Usefulness, Ease of Use, and Usage Information Technology: A Replication," *MIS Quarterly,* 16 (June), 227-47.

Agarwal, Deepak (1996), "Effect of Brand Loyalty on Advertising and Trade Promotions: a Game Theoretic Analysis with Empirical Evidence," *Marketing Science,* 15:1, 86-108.

———— and Christopher Schorling (1996), "Market Share Forecasting: An Empirical Comparison of Artificial Neural Networks and Multinomial Logit Model," *Journal of Retailing,* 72:4 (Winter), 383-402.

Ailawadi, Kusum L., Paul W. Farris, and Mark E. Parry (1994), "Share and Growth Are Not Good Predictors of the Advertising and Promotion/Sales Ratio," *Journal of Marketing,* 58 (January), 86-98.

————, ————, and ———— (1997), "Explaining Variations in the Advertising and Promotional Cost/Sales Ratio: A Rejoinder," *Journal of Marketing,* 61:1 (January), 93-96.

Alavi, Maryam and Erich A. Joachimsthaler (1992), "Revisiting DSS Implementation Research: A Meta-Analysis of the Literature and Suggestions for Researchers," *MIS Quarterly,* 16 (March), 95-116.

Albach, Horst (1979), "Market Organization and Pricing Behavior of Oligopolistic Firms in the Ethical Drugs Industry," *KYKLOS,* 32 (3), 523-40.

Albers, Sönke (1996), "CAPPLAN: A Decision Support System for Planning the Pricing and Sales Effort Policy of a Salesforce," *European Journal of Marketing,* 30:7, 68-82.

―――― (1998), "A Framework for Analysis of Sources of Profit Contribution Variance Between Actual and Plan," *International Journal of Research in Marketing,* 15:2 (May), 109-22.

Alemson, M. A. (1970), "Advertising and the Nature of Competition in Oligopoly over Time: A Case Study," *Economic Journal,* 80 (June), 282-306.

Allenby, Greg M. (1989), "A Unified Approach to Identifying, Estimating, and Testing Demand Structures with Aggregate Scanner Data," *Marketing Science,* 8:3 (Summer), 265-80.

―――― (1990), "Hypothesis Testing with Scanner Data: The Advantage of Bayesian Methods," *Journal of Marketing Research,* 27:4 (November), 379-89.

―――― and Peter E. Rossi (1991), "There Is No Aggregation Bias: Why Macro Logit Models Work," *Journal of Business & Economic Statistics,* 9:1 (January), 1-14.

Alsem, Karel Jan. and Peter S. H. Leeflang (1994), "Predicting Advertising Expenditures Using Intention Surveys," *International Journal of Forecasting,* 10:2 (September), 327-33.

―――― , ―――― , and Jan C. Reuyl (1989) "The Forecasting Accuracy of Market Share Models Using Predicted Values of Competitive Marketing Behavior," *International Journal of Research in Marketing,* 6, 183-198.

Amemiya, Takeshi (1974), "Multivariate Regression and Simultaneous Equation Models When the Dependent Variables Are Truncated Normal," *Econometrica,* 42 (November), 999-1012.

―――― (1979), "The Estimation of a Simultaneous-Equation Tobit Model," *International Economic Review,* 20 (February), 169-81.

―――― (1985), *Advanced Econometrics.* Cambridge, MA: Harvard University Press.

Amoroso, Luigi (1954), "The Static Supply Curve," *International Economic Papers,* 4, 39-65.

Andrews, Donald W. K. and Ray C. Fair (1988), "Inference in Nonlinear Econometric Models with Structural Change," *Review of Economic Studies,* 55 (October), 615-639.

Andrews, Rick L. and George R. Franke (1991), "The Determination of Cigarette Consumption: A Meta Analysis," *Journal of Public Policy & Marketing,* 10:1, 81-100.

Aneuryn-Evans, Gwyn and Angus Deaton (1980), "Testing Linear Versus Logarithmic Regression Models," *Review of Economic Studies,* 48, 275-91.

Arabmazar, Abbas and Peter Schmidt (1981), "Further Evidence on the Robustness of the Tobit Estimator to Heteroscedasticity," *Journal of Econometrics,* 17 (November), 253-58.

―――― and Peter Schmidt (1982), "An Investigation of the Robustness of the Tobit Estimator to Non-Normality," *Econometrica,* 50 (July), 1055-63.

Armstrong, J. Scott (1985), *Long-Range Forecasting: From Crystal Ball to Computer, 2nd Edition.* New York: John Wiley.

―――― (1986), "The Ombudsman: Research on Forecasting: A Quarter Century Review, 1960-1984," *Interfaces,* 16 (January-February), 89-109.

―――― , Roderick J. Brodie, and Shelby H. McIntyre (1987), "Forecasting Methods for Marketing: Review of Empirical Research," *International Journal of Forecasting,* 3:3/4, 355-76.

―――― and Randall L. Schultz (1994), "Principles Involving Marketing Policies: An Empirical Assessment," *Marketing Letters,* 4 (July), 253-65.

Arnold, Stephen J., Tae H. Oum, Bohumir Pazderka, and Douglas J. Snetsinger (1987), "Advertising Quality in Sales Response Models," *Journal of Marketing Research,* 24 (February), 106-113.

Arora, Rajinder (1979), "How Promotion Elasticities Change," *Journal of Advertising Research*, 19 (June), 57-62.

Ashley, R., C.W.J. Granger, and Richard Schmalensee (1980), "Advertising and Aggregate Consumption: An Analysis of Causality," *Econometrica*, 48 (July), 1149-67.

Assmus, Gert (1981), "New Product Models," in *Marketing Decision Models*, Randall L. Schultz and Andris A. Zoltners, eds. New York: Elsevier North-Holland, 125-43.

———, John U. Farley, and Donald R. Lehmann (1984), "How Advertising Affects Sales: A Meta Analysis of Econometric Results," *Journal of Marketing Research*, 21 (February), 65-74.

Assuncao, Joao and Robert J. Meyer (1993), "The Rational Effect of Price Promotions on Sales and Consumption," *Management Science*, 39:5 (May), 517-35.

Atkinson, Anthony C. (1978), "Posterior Probabilities for Choosing a Regression Model," *Biometrika*, 65:1, 39-48.

Aykac, Ahmet, Marcel Corstjens, and David Gautschi (1984), "Is There a Kink in Your Advertising?" *Journal of Advertising Research*, 24 (June-July), 27-36.

———, ———, ———, and Ira Horowitz (1989), "Estimation Uncertainty and Optimal Advertising Decisions" *Management Science*, 35 (January), 42-50.

Baghestani, H. (1991), "Cointegration Analysis of the Advertising-Sales Relationship," *Journal of Industrial Economics*, 34, 671-81.

Baker, Chris, ed. (1993), *Advertising Works 7*, Henley-on-Thames, United Kingdom: NTC Publications.

———, ed. (1995), *Advertising Works 8*, Henley-on-Thames, United Kingdom: NTC Publications.

Baker, Ken (1996), "Data Fusion," *Admap*, 31:7 (April), 20-21.

Baker, Paul (1987), "Econometrics for Pricing Research," *Journal of the Market Research Society*, 29:2, 123-31.

——— (1999), "Surely There Are Lasting Effects of Advertising?" *Admap*, 34:7 (July/August), 21-23.

Balasubramanian, Siva K. and Dipak C. Jain (1994), "Simple Approaches to Evaluate Competing Non-Nested Models in Marketing," *International Journal of Research in Marketing*, 11 (January), 53-72.

——— and V. Kumar, (1990), "Analyzing Variations in the Advertising and Promotional Expenditures: Key Correlates in Consumer, Industrial, and Service Markets," *Journal of Marketing*, 54:2 (April), 57-68.

——— and ——— (1997a), "Explaining Variations in the Advertising and Promotional Cost/Sales Ratio: A Reanalysis," *Journal of Marketing*, 61:1 (January), 85-92.

——— and ——— (1997b), "Explaining Variations in the Advertising and Promotional Cost/Sales Ratio: A Response, Research Criteria, and Guidelines," *Journal of Marketing*, 61:1 (January), 97-98.

Ball, R. J. and R. Agarwala (1969), "An Econometric Analysis of the Effects of Generic Advertising on the Demand for Tea in the U.K.," *British Journal of Marketing*, 4 (Winter), 202-17.

Banks, Seymour (1961), "Some Correlates of Coffee and Cleanser Brand Share," *Journal of Advertising Research*, 1 (June), 22-28.

Barki, Henri and Jon Hartwick (1989), "Rethinking the Concept of User Involvement," *MIS Quarterly*, 13 (March), 53-63.

——— and ——— (1994), "Measuring User Participation, User Involvement, and User Attitude," *MIS Quarterly*, 18 (March), 59-79.

Barnard, Neil (1978), "On Advertising Effectiveness Measurement: An Idiosyncratic View," *ADMAP*, (July), 361-69.

――――― and Gerald Smith (1990), "'Professional and Amateur Econometrics: A Reply to Stewart," *Journal of the Market Research Society*, 32:4 (October), 583-84.

Baron, Steve and Andrew Lock (1995), "The Challanges of Scanner Data," *Journal of the Operational Research Society*, 46:1 (January), 50-61.

Barten, Anton P. (1964), "Consumer Demand Functions Under Conditions of Almost Additive Preferences," *Econometrica*, 32, 1-38.

――――― (1968), "Estimating Demand Equations," *Econometrica*, 36, 213-51.

――――― (1969), "Maximum Likelihood Estimation of a Complete System of Demand Equations," *European Economic Review*, 1 (Fall), 7-73.

Bartlett, M. S. (1946), "On the Theoretical Specification and Sampling Properties of Autocorrelated Time-Series," *Journal of the Royal Statistical Society*, Series B. 8 (April), 27-41, 85-97.

Barwise, Patrick (1995), "Good Empirical Generalizations," *Marketing Science*, 14:3 (Part 2 of 2), G29-35.

Basmann, Robert L. (1964), "On Predictive Testing a Simultaneous Equation Regression Model: The Retail Market for Food in the U.S." Institute Paper No. 78, Krannert Graduate School of Industrial Administration, Purdue University.

――――― (1965) "On the Application of Identifiability Test Statistic in Predictive Testing of Explanatory Economic Models," *Indian Economic Journal*, 13, 387-423.

――――― (1968), "Hypothesis Formulation in Quantitative Economics: A Contribution to Demand Analysis," in *Papers in Quantitative Economics*, James P. Quirk and Arvid M. Zarley, eds. Lawrence, Kansas: University Press of Kansas, 143-98.

――――― (1988), "Causality Tests and Observationally Equivalent Representations of Econometric Models," *Journal of Econometrics*, 39 (September/October), 69-104.

Bass, Frank M. (1969a), "A New Product Growth Model for Consumer Durables," *Management Science*, 15 (January), 215-27.

――――― (1969b), "A Simultaneous Equation Regression Study of Advertising and Sales of Cigarettes," *Journal of Marketing Research*, 6 (August), 291-300.

――――― (1971), "Decomposition Regression Models in Analysis of Market Potentials," *Management Science*, 17 (April), 485-94.

――――― (1980a), "Some Case Histories of Econometric Modeling in Marketing: What Really Happened," *Interfaces*, 10:1 (February), 86-90.

――――― (1980b), "The Relationship Between Diffusion Rates, Experience Curves, and Demand Elasticities for Consumer Durable Technological Innovations," *Journal of Business*, 53 (July), S51-67.

――――― (1995), "Empirical Generalizations and Marketing Science," *Marketing Science*, 14:3 (Part 2 of 2), G6-19.

――――― and Alain V. Bultez (1982), "A Note on Optimal Strategic Pricing of Technological Innovations," *Marketing Science*, 1 (Fall), 371-78.

――――― and Darral G. Clarke (1972), "Testing Distributed Lag Models of Advertising Effect," *Journal of Marketing Research*, 9 (August), 298-308.

――――― and Robert P. Leone (1983), "Estimation of Bimonthly Relations from Annual Data," *Management Science*, 29 (January), 1- 11.

――――― and ――――― (1986), "Estimating Micro Relationships from Macro Data: A Comparative Study of Two Approximations of the Brand Loyal Model under Temporal Aggregation," *Journal of Marketing Research*, 23 (August), 291-79.

――――― and Leonard J. Parsons (1969), "A Simultaneous Equation Regression Analysis of Sales and Advertising," *Applied Economics*, 1 (May), 103-24.

――――― and Thomas L. Pilon (1980), "A Stochastic Brand Choice Framework for Econometric Modeling of Time Series Market Share Behavior," *Journal of Marketing Research*, 17 (November), 486-97.

—— and Jerry Wind (1995), "Introduction to the Special Issue: Empirical Generalizations in Marketing," *Marketing Science*, 14, G1-G5.

—— and Dick R. Wittink (1975), "Pooling Issues and Methods in Regression Analysis with Examples in Marketing Research," *Journal of Marketing Research*, 12 (November), 414-25.

—— and —— (1978), "Pooling Issues and Methods in Regression Analysis: Some Further Reflections," *Journal of Marketing Research*, 15 (May), 277-79.

Basu, Amiya.K. and Rajeev Batra (1988), "ADSPLIT: A Multi-Brand Advertising Budget Allocation Model," *Journal of Advertising Research*, 30:7, 68-82.

——, Atasi Basu, and Rajeev Batra (1995), "Modeling the Response Pattern to Direct Marketing Campaigns," *Journal of Marketing Research*, 32:2 (May), 204-12.

Batra, Rajeev and Wilfried R. Vanhonacker (1988), "Falsifying Laboratory Results Through Field Tests: A Time-Series Methodology and Some Results," *Journal of Business Research*, 16 (June), 281-300.

Battese, George E. (1997), "A Note on the Estimation of Cobb-Douglas Production Functions When Some of Explanatory Variables Have Zero Values," *Journal of Agricultural Economics*, 48:2, 250-52.

Baye, Michael R., Dennis W. Jansen, and Jae-Woo Lee (1992), "Advertising Effects in Complete Demand Systems," *Applied Economics*, 24 (October), 1087-96.

Beckwith, Neil E. (1972), "Multivariate Analysis of Sales Responses of Competing Brands to Advertising," *Journal of Marketing Research*, 9 (May), 168-76.

—— (1973), "Concerning Logical Consistency of Multivariate Market Share Models," *Journal of Marketing Research*, 10 (August), 341-44.

Beggs, John J. (1988), "Diagnostic Testing in Applied Econometrics," *Economic Record*, 64 (June), 81-101.

Beguin, Jean-Mare, Christian Gourieroux, and Alain Monfort (1980), Identification of a Mixed Autoregressive-Moving Average Process: The Corner Method," in *Time Series*, O. D. Anderson, ed. Amsterdam: North-Holland, 423-36.

Bell, David E., Ralph E. Keeney, and John D. C. Little (1975), "A Market Share Theorem," *Journal of Marketing Research*, 12 (May), 136-41.

Bell, David R., Jeongwen Chiang, and V. Padmanabhan (1999), "The Decomposition of Promotional Response: An Empirical Generalization," *Marketing Science*, 18:4, 504-26.

Belsley, David A. (1988), "Conditioning in Models with Logs," *Journal of Econometrics*, 38 (May-June), 127-43.

——, (1991), *Conditioning Diagnostics: Collinearity and Weak Data in Regression.* New York: John Wiley.

Bemmaor, Albert C. (1984), "Testing Alternative Econometric Models on the Existence of Advertising Threshold Effect," *Journal of Marketing Research* 21 (August), 298-308.

—— and Dominique Mouchoux (1991), "Measuring the Short-term Effect of In-store Promotion and Retail Advertising on Brand Sales: A Factorial Experiment," *Journal of Marketing Research*, 28:2 (May), 202-14.

Bender, J. Dennis and Ross Link (1994), "Measuring Marketing-Mix Sales Effectiveness Using Continuous Ad-Awareness Data and Automated Scanner-Data Modeling Software, Marketing Science Conference, Tucson, AZ, March 19.

Bernard John C. and Lois Shertz Willett (1996), "Asymmetric Price Relationships in the U.S. Boiler Industry," *Journal of Agricultural and Applied Economics*, 28:2 (December), 279-89.

Berndt, Ernst R, Linda Bui, David R. Reiley, and Glen L. Urban (1995), "Information, Marketing, and Pricing in the U.S. Antiulcer Drug Market," *American Economic Review*, 85:2 (May), 100-105.

Berry, Michael, and Gordon Linoff (1997). *Data Mining Techniques for Marketing, Sales, and Customer Support*. New York: John Wiley.

Bertrand, Joseph (1883), "Review of Cournot's Recherches sur les Principes Mathematiques de la Theorie des Richesses," *Journal des Savants*, 499-508.

Besanko, David, Sachin Gupta, and Dipak C. Jain (1998), "Logit Demand Estimation Under Competitive Pricing Behavior: An Equilibrium Framework," *Management Science*, 44:11 (November, Part 1), 1533-47.

Bewley, Ronald (1986), *Allocation Models: Specification, Estimation, and Applications*. Cambridge: Ballinger.

———— and Tran Van Hoa, eds. (1992), *Contributions to Consumer Demand and Econometrics*. New York: St. Martins Press.

Bharadwaj, S. and C. B. Bhattacharya (1996), "The Role of the Marketing Mix in Determining Persistence in Marketing Performance," paper presented at the Marketing Science Conference, Gainesville.

Bhattacharya, Chitrabhanu and Leonard M. Lodish (1994), "An Advertising Evaluation System for Retailers," *Journal of Retailing and Consumer Services*, 1:2, 90-100.

Bjørndal, Trond, Kjell G. Salvanes, and Jorun H. Andressen (1992), "The Demand for Salmon in France: The Effects of Marketing and Structural Change," *Applied Economics*, 24, 1027-34.

Blattberg, Robert C., Richard Briesch, and Edward J. Fox (1995), "How Promotions Work," *Marketing Science*, 14:3 (Part 2 of 2), G122-32.

———— and John Deighton (1996), "Manage Marketing by the Customer Equity Test," *Harvard Business Review*, (July-August), 136-44.

———— and E. I. George (1991), "Shrinkage Estimation of Price and Promotion Elasticities: Seemingly Unrelated Equations," *Journal of the American Statistical Association*, 86:414 (May), 304-15.

————, Rashi Glazer, and John D. C. Little, eds. (1994), *The Marketing Information Revolution*. Boston: Harvard Business School Press.

———— and Steven Hoch (1990), "Database Models and Managerial Intuition: 50 % Model and 50% Managers," *Management Science*, 36:8 (August), 887-99.

———— and Abel Jeuland (1981a), "An Assessment of the Contribution of Log-Linear Models to Marketing Research," *Journal of Marketing*, 45 (Spring), 89-97.

———— and ———— (1981b), "A Micromodeling Approach to Investigate the Advertising-Sales Relationship," *Management Science*, 9 (September), 988-1005.

————, Byung-Do Kim, and Jianming Ye (1994), "Large-Scale Databases: The New Marketing Challenge" in *The Marketing Information Revolution*. Robert C. Blattberg, Rashi Glazer, and John D. C. Little, eds. Boston: Harvard Business School Press, 173-203.

———— and Alan Levin (1987), "Modeling the Effectiveness and Profitability of Trade Promotions," *Marketing Science*, 6 (Spring), 124-46.

———— and Scott A. Neslin (1989), "Sales Promotion: The Long and Short of It," *Marketing Letters*, 1:1 (December), 81-97.

———— and ———— (1990), *Sales Promotion: Concepts, Methods, and Strategies*. Engelwood Cliffs, NJ: Prentice-Hall.

———— and ———— (1993), "Sales Promotion Models," in *Handbooks in Operations Research and Management Science: Volume 5: Marketing*, Joshua Eliashberg and Gary Lilien, eds. New York: Elsevier, 553-609.

———— and Kenneth J. Wisniewski (1989), "Price-Induced Patterns of Competition," *Marketing Science*, 8:4 (Fall), 291-309.

Blizzard, Noel and James R. Blaylock (1992), "A Double-Hurdle Approach to Advertising: The Case of Cheese," *Agribusiness*, 8:2, 109-120.

Bloom, Derek (1990), "'Modelling Beyond the Blip'—Rejoinder," *Journal of the Market Research Society*, 32:3 (July), 465-67.

——— (1991), "Beyond the Blip: Comment," *Journal of the Market Research Society*, 33:1 (January), 59-60.

Bolton, Ruth N. (1989a), "The Relationship Between Market Characteristics and Promotional Price Elasticities," *Marketing Science*, 8:2 (Spring), 153-69.

——— (1989b), "The Robustness of Retail-Level Price Elasticity Estimates," *Journal of Retailing*, 65:2 (Summer), 193-219.

——— (1989c), "Sales Response Modeling: Gains in Efficiency from System Estimation," *Journal of Business Research*, 18:2 (March), 107-25.

Bond, Ronald S. and David F. Lean (1977), "Sales Promotion and Product Differentiation in Two Prescription Drug Markets," Federal Trade Commission—Staff Report, Washington, DC: U.S. Government Printing Office.

Bordley, Robert F. (1985), "Relating Elasticites to Changes in Demand," *Journal of Business & Economic Statistics*, 3:2 (April), 156-58.

Borin, Norm, Cynthia Van Vranken and Paul W. Farris (1991), "A Pilot Test of Discrimination in the Japanese Distribution System," *Journal of Retailing*, 67:1 (Spring), 93-106.

Boswijk, H. P. (1994), "Testing for an Unstable Root in Conditional and Structural Error Correction Models," *Journal of Econometrics*, 63, 37-60.

Bowley, A. L. (1924), *The Mathematical Groundwork of Economics.* Oxford: Oxford University Press.

Bowman, Douglas and Hubert Gatignon (1996), "Order of Entry as a Moderator of the Effect of the Marketing Mix on Market Share," *Marketing Science*, 15:3, 222-42.

Bowman, Russell (1980), *Couponing and Rebates: Profit on the Dotted Line.* New York: Lebhar-Freeman Books.

Box, George E. P. and D. R. Cox (1964), "An Analysis of Transformations," *Journal of the Royal Statistical Society, Series B.* 26:2, 211-52.

——— and G. M. Jenkins (1976), *Time Series Analysis: Forecasting and Control,* second edition. San Francisco: Holden-Day.

——— and D. A. Pierce (1970), "Distribution of Residual Autocorrelations in Autoregressive-Integrated Moving Average Time Series Models," *Journal of the American Statistical Association,* 65 (December), 1509-26.

——— and George C. Tiao (1975), "Intervention Analysis with Applications to Economic and Enviromental Problems," *Journal of the American Statistical Association,* 70 (March), 70-79.

——— and George C. Tiao (1976), "Comparison of Forecast and Actuality," *Applied Statistics,* 25:3, 195-200.

Boyer, Kenneth D. and Kent M. Lancaster (1986), "Are There Scale Economies in Advertising?" *Journal of Business*, 59 (July) 509-526.

Brandenburger, Adam M. and Barry J. Nalebuff (1996), *Co-opetition.* New York: Double-Day.

Brester, Gary W. and Ted C. Schroeder (1995), "The Impacts of Brand and Generic Advertising on Meat Demand," *American Journal of Agricultural Economics*, 77 (November), 969-79.

Brewer, K.R.W. (1973), "Some Consequences of Temporal Aggregation and Systematic Sampling for ARMA and ARMAX Models," *Journal of Econometrics*, 1, 133-54.

Briesch, Richard A. (1997), "Does It Matter How Price Promotions Are Operationalized?" *Marketing Letters*, 8:2 (April), 167-181.

Broadbent, Simon (1979), "One-Way TV Advertisements Work," *Journal of the Market Research Society,* 21:3, 139-65.

——— (1980), "Price and Advertising: Volume and Profit," *ADMAP,* 16:11, 532-40.

———, ed. (1981), *Advertising Works,* London: Holt, Rinehart, and Winston.

———, ed. (1983), *Advertising Works 2,* London: Holt, Rinehart, and Winston.

——— (1984), "Modeling with Adstock," *Journal of the Market Research Society,* 26 (October), 295-312.

——— (1986), "Two OTS in a Purchase Interval," *Admap,* (November), 12-16.

——— (1988), "Advertising Effects: More Methodological Issues," *Journal of the Market Research Society,* 30:2 (April), 225-27.

——— (1989), "What is a 'Small' Advertising Elasticity?" *Journal of Advertising Research,* 29:4 (August/September), 37-39, 44.

——— (1990a), "Modelling Beyond the Blip," *Journal of the Market Research Society,* 32:1 (January), 61-102.

——— (1990b), "Reply," *Journal of the Market Research Society,* 32:3 (July), 462-65.

——— (1992), "Using Data Better," *Admap,* (January), 48-54.

——— (1997a), *Accountable Advertising: A Handbook for Managers and Analysts.* Henley-on-Thames, UK: NTC Publications.

——— (1997b), "Single Source—New Analyses," *Journal of the Market Research Society,* 39:2 (April), 363-79.

——— (1999), *When to Advertise.* Henley-on-Thames, UK: Admap Publications.

——— and Stephen Colman (1986), "Advertising Effectiveness: Across Brands," *Journal of the Market Research Society,* 28 (January), 15-24.

——— and T. Fry (1995), "Adstock Modelling for the Longer Term," *Journal of the Market Research Society,* 37:4, 385-403.

Brobst, Robert and Roger Gates (1977), "Comments on Pooling Issues and Methods in Regression Analysis," *Journal of Marketing Research,* 14 (November), 598-600.

Brodie, Roderick J. and Andre Bonfrer (1994), "Conditions When Market Share Models are Useful for Forecasting: Further Empirical Results," *International Journal of Forecasting,* 10:2 (September), 277-85.

——— and ——— (1995), "Do Marketing Managers Focus Too Much on Competition," in *Proceedings of the 24th Annual Conference of the European Marketing Academy,* Michelle Bergadaà, Cergy-Pontoise, France: ESSEC (Ecole Supérieure des Sciences Economiques et Commerciales), 197-207.

——— and ——— (1996), "Do Managers Overreact to Each Other's Promotional Activity," *International Journal of Research in Marketing,* 13:4 (October), 379-87.

———, Peter J. Danaher, V. Kumar, and Peter S. H. Leeflang (2000), "Econometric Models for Forecasting Market Share," in *Principles of Forecasting,* J. S. Armstrong, ed. Norwell, MA: Kluwer.

——— and Cornelius A. de Kluyver (1984), "Attraction Versus Linear and Multiplicative Market Share Models: A Empirical Evaluation," *Journal of Marketing Research,* 21 (May), 194-201.

——— and ——— (1987), "A Comparison of the Short-Term Forecasting Accuracy of Econometric and Naive Extrapolation Models of Market Share," *International Journal of Forecasting,* 3:3/4, 423-37.

Bronnenberg, Bart J., Vijay Mahajan, and Wilfried R. Vanhonacker (2000), "The Emergence of Market Structure in New Repeat-Purchase Categories: A Dynamic Approach and an Empirical Application," *Journal of Marketing Research,* 37:1 (February) 16-31.

Brown, Gordon (1986), "The Link Between Ad Content and Sales Effects," *ADMAP,* March, 151-53.

Brown, Mark G. (1994), "Levels Versions of the Rotterdam Demand Model and Incorporation of Demographic, Stock, and Other Nonprice, Nonincome Variables," *Canadian Journal of Agricultural Economics,* 42:3, 355-66.

————, Jonq-Ying Lee, and James L. Seale, Jr. (1994), "Demand Relationships Among Juice Beverages: A Differential Demand System Approach," *Journal of Agricultural and Applied Economics*, 26:2 (December), 417-29.

Brown, R. J., J. Durbin, and J. Evans (1975), "Techniques for Estimating the Constancy of Regression Relationships over Time," *Journal of the Royal Statistical Society*, Series B, 37, 149-63.

Brown, Randall S. (1978), "Estimating Advantages to Large-Scale Advertising," *Review of Economics and Statistics*, 60, 428-37.

Brunner, Karl (1973), "Review of *Econometric Models of Cyclical Behavior*," *Journal of Economic Literature*, 11 (September), 926-33.

Bucklin, Randolph E. and Sunil Gupta (1999), "Brand Choice, Purchase Incidence, and Segmentation: An Integrated Modeling Approach," *Journal of Marketing Research*, 29, 201-15.

———— and ———— (1999), "Commercial Use of UPC Scanner Data: Industry and Academic Perspectives," *Marketing Science*, 18:3, 247-73.

————, Donald R. Lehmann, and John D.C. Little (1998), "From Decision Support to Decision Automation: A 2020 Vision," *Marketing Letters*, 9:3, 235-46.

————, Gary J. Russell, and V. Srinivasan (1998), "A Relationship Between Price Elasticities and Brand Switching Probabilities in Heterogeneous Markets," *Journal of Marketing Research*, 35:1 (February), 99-113.

Bultez, Alain V. (1978), "Econometric Specification and Estimation of Market Share Models: The State of the Art," in *Marketing: Neue Ergebnisse Ausforschung Und Praxis*, E. Topritzhofer, ed. Weisbaden: Betriebswirschaftlicher Verlag Dr. Th. Gaber K. G., 239-63.

———— (1996), "Mode de Diagnostic de Marchés Concurrentiels," *Recherche et Applications en Marketing*, 11:4, 3-34.

———— (1997), "Econométrie de la Compétitivité: Modèles et Contre-Exemples," *Recherche et Applications en Marketing*, 12:1, 21-44.

————, Els Gijsbrechts, Philippe Naert, and Piet Vanden Abeele (1989), "Asymmetric Cannibalism in Retail Assortments," *Journal of Retailing*, 65:2 (Summer), 153-92.

———— and Philippe A. Naert (1975), "Consistent Sum-Constrained Models," *Journal of the American Statistical Association*, 70 (September), 529-35.

———— and ———— (1979), "Does Lag Structure Really Matter in Optimizing Advertising Expenditures?" *Management Science*, 25 (May), 454-65.

———— and ———— (1985), "Control of Advertising Expenditures Based on Aggregate Models of Carryover Effects," in *New Challenges for Management Research*, A. H. G. Rinnooy Kan, ed. New York: Elsevier Science, 31-43.

———— and ———— (1988a), "S.H.A.R.P.: Shelf Allocation for Retailers' Profit," *Marketing Science*, 7 (Summer), 211-31.

———— and ———— (1988b), "When Does Lag Structure Really Matter ... Indeed?" *Management Science*, 34 (July), 909-16.

———— and Randall L. Schultz (1979), "Decision Rules for Advertising Budgeting and Media Allocation," Krannert Graduate School of Management, Purdue University, Institute Paper No. 694, May.

Bunn, Derek and George Wright (1991), "Interaction of Judgmental and Statistical Methods: Issues and Analysis," *Management Science*, 37 (May), 501-18.

Bureau of the Census (1969), *X-11 Information for the User*. U.S. Department of Commerce. Washington, DC: U.S. Government Printing Office.

Buse, Adolf (1994), "Evaluating the Linearized Almost Ideal Demand System," *American Journal of Agricultural Economics*, 76 (November), 781-93.

Bustos, Oscar H. and Victor J. Yohai (1986), "Robust Estimates for ARMA Models," *Journal of the American Statistical Association*, 81 (March), 155-68.

Buzzell, Robert D. (1964a), *Mathematical Models and Marketing Management*. Boston: Harvard University, Division of Research, 136-56.

———— (1964b), "Predicting Short-Term Changes in Market Share as a Function of Advertising Strategy," *Journal of Marketing Research*, 1 (August), 27-31.

————, Marshall Kolin, and Malcolm P. Murphy (1965), "Television Commercial Test Scores and Short-Term Changes in Market Shares," *Journal of Marketing Research*, 2 (August), 307-3.

Caines, P. E., S. P. Sethi, and T. W. Brotherton (1977), "Impulse Response Identification and Causality Detection For the Lied-Pinkham Data," *Annals of Economic and Social Measurement*, 6:2, 147-63.

Campbell, J. Y. and N. G. Mankiw (1987), "Are Output Fluctuations Transitory," *Quarterly Journal of Economics*, 102, 857-80.

Campbell, Mike and Bruce Dove (1998), "Evaluating the Impact of Advertising on Sales," *Admap*, 33:2 (February), 14-16.

Capps, Oral, Jr. and Daniel S. Moen (1992), "Assessing the Impact of Generic Advertising of Fluid Milk Products in Texas" in *Commodity Advertising and Promotion*, Henry Kinnucan, Stanley R. Thompson, and Hui-Shung Chang, eds. Ames, IA: Iowa State University Press, 24-39.

———— and John D. Schmitz (1991), "Effect of Generic Advertising on the Demand for Fluid Milk: The Case of the Texas Market Order," *Southern Journal of Agricultural Economics*, 23:2 (December), 131-40.

Cardwell, John J. (1968), "Marketing and Management Science A Marriage on the Rocks?" *California Management Review*, 10 (Summer), 3-12.

Carlin, Bradley P. and Thomas A. Louis (1996), *Bayes and Empirical Bayes Methods for Data Analysis*. London: Chapman & Hall.

Carlson, Rodney L. (1978), "Seemingly Unrelated Regression and the Demand for Automobiles of Different Sizes, 1965-75: A Disaggregate Approach," *Journal of Business*, 51:2, 343-62.

Carpenter, Gregory S. (1987), "Modeling Competitive Marketing Strategies: The Impact of Marketing-Mix Relationships and Industry Structure," *Marketing Science*, 6 (Spring), 208-21.

————, Lee G. Cooper, Dominique M. Hanssens, and David F. Midgley (1988), "Modeling Asymmetric Competition," *Marketing Science*, 7 (Fall), 393-412.

———— and Dominique M. Hanssens (1994), "Market Expansion, Cannibalization, and International Airline Pricing Strategy," *International Journal of Forecasting*, 10:2 (September), 313-26.

Carroll, Vincent P., Ambar G. Rao, Hau L. Lee, Arthur Shapiro and Barry L. Bayus (1985), "The Navy Enlistment Marketing Experiment," *Marketing Science*, 4:4, 352-374.

Case, James H. (1974), "On the Form of Market Demand Models," *Econometrica*, 42 (January), 207-13.

Case, Kenneth E. and James E. Shamblin (1972), "The Effects of Advertising Carryover," *Journal of Advertising Research*, 12 (June), 37-44.

Casella, George and Edward I. George (1992), "Explaining the Gibbs Sampler," *American Statistician*, 46, 167-74.

Cashin, Paul (1991), "A Model of the Disaggregated Demand for Meat in Australia," *Australian Journal of Agricultural Economics*, 35:3 (December), 263-83.

Chakravarti, Dipankar, Andrew Mitchell, and Richard Staelin (1979), "Judgment Based Marketing Decision Models: An Experimental Investigation of the Decision Calculus Approach," *Management Science*, 25 (March), 251-63.

Chandrashekaran, Murali and Beth Walker (1993), "Meta-Analysis with Heteroscedastic Effects," *Journal of Marketing Research*, 30:2 (May), 246-55.

Channon, Charles, ed. (1985), *Advertising Works 3*. London: Holt, Rinehart, and Winston.

———, ed. (1987), *Advertising Works 4*. London: Cassell Educational Limited.

Chapman, Simon (1989), "The Limitations of Econometric Analyses in Cigarette Advertising Studies," *British Journal of Addiction*, 84:11, 1267-74.

Chatfield, Christopher (1974), "Some Comments on Spectral Analysis in Marketing," *Journal of Marketing Research*, 11, 97-101.

——— (1979), "Inverse Autocorrelations," *Journal of the Royal Statistical Society, Series A*, 142 (3), 363-77.

——— and D. L. Prothero (1973), Pox-Jenkins Seasonal Forecasting: Problems and a Case Study," *Journal of the Royal Statistical Society, Series A*, 136 (3), 295-352.

Chatterjee, Kalyan and Gary L. Lilien (1986), "Game Theory in Marketing Science: Uses and Limitations," *International Journal of Research in Marketing*, 3 (2), 79-93.

Chen, Youhua, Vinay Kanetkar, and Doyle L. Weiss (1994), "A Forecasting Market Shares with Disaggregate or Pooled Data," *International Journal of Forecasting*, 10:2 (September), 263-76.

Chevalier, Michel (1975), "Increase in Sales Due to In-Store Display," *Journal of Marketing Research*, 12 (November), 426-31.

——— and Ronald Curhan (1976), "Retailer Promotions as a Function of Trade Promotions: A Descriptive Analysis," *Sloan Management Review*, 18 (Fall), 19-32.

Chintagunta, Pradeep K. (1993a), "Investigating Purchase Incidence, Brand Choice and Purchase Quantity Decisions of Households," *Marketing Science*, 12, 184-208.

——— (1993b), "Investigating the Sensitivity of Equilibrium Profits to Advertising Dynamics and Competitive Effects," *Management Science*, 39, 1146-62.

——— and Naufel J. Vilcassim (1992), "An Empirical Investigation of Advertising Strategies in a Dynamic Duopoly," *Management Science*, 38 (September), 1230-44.

Chow, Gregory C. and A. Lin (1971), "Best Linear Unbiased Interpolation, Distribution, Extrapolation of Time Series By Related Series," *Review of Economics and Statistics*, 53, 372-75.

Chowdhury, A.R. (1994), "Advertising Expenditures and the Macro-Economy: Some New Evidence," *International Journal of Advertising*, 13, 1-14.

Christen, Markus, Sachin Gupta, John C. Porter, Richard Staelin, and Dick R. Wittink (1997), "Using Market Level Data to Understand Promotional Effects in a Nonlinear Model," *Journal of Marketing Research*, 34:3 (August), 322-34.

Chu, Chia-Shang James, Maxwell Stinchcombe, and Halbert White (1996), "Monitoring Structural Change," *Econometrica*, 64:5 (September), 1045-65.

Churchill, Gilbert A., Jr., Niel M. Ford, Steven W. Hartley, and Orville C. Walker (1985), "The Determinants of Salesforce Performance: A Meta-Analysis," *Journal of Marketing Research*, 22 (May), 103-18.

Clarke, Darral G. (1973), "Sales-Advertising Cross-Elasticities and Advertising Competition," *Journal of Marketing Research*, 10 (August), 250-61.

——— (1976), "Econometric Measurement of the Duration of Advertising Effect on Sales," *Journal of Marketing Research*, 13 (November), 345-57.

——— (1979), "Measuring the Cumulative Effects of Advertising on Sales: A Response to Peles," *Journal of Marketing Research*, 16 (May), 286-89.

——— and John M. McCann (1977), "Cumulative Advertising Effects: The Role of Serial Correlation: A Reply," *Decision Sciences*, 8, 336-43.

Claycamp, Henry J. (1966), "Dynamic Effects of Short Duration Price Differentials on Retail Gasoline Sales," *Journal of Marketing Research*, 3 (May), 175-78.

Clemen, Robert T. (1989), "Combining Forecasts: A Review and Annotated Bibliography," *International Journal of Forecasting*, 5:4, 559-83.

Clements, Kenneth W. and E. Antony Selvanathan (1988), "The Rotterdam Demand Model and Its Application in Marketing," *Marketing Science*, 7 (Winter), 60-75.

Cleveland, William S. (1972), "The Inverse Autocorrelations of a Time Series and Their Applications," *Technometrics*, 14, 277-93.

Cochrane, J.H. (1988), "How Big is the Random Walk Component in GNP?" *Journal of Political Economy*, 96, 893-920.

Coleman, Stephen and Gordon Brown (1983), "Advertising Tracking Studies and Sales Effects," *Journal of the Market Research Society*, 25:2, 165-83.

Collopy, Fred and J. Scott Armstrong (1992), "Rule-based Forecasting: Development and Validation of an Expert System," *Management Science*, 38 (October), 1394-414.

Cooil, Bruce and Timothy M. Devinney (1992), "The Return to Advertising Expenditure," *Marketing Letters*, 3:2 (April), 137-45.

Cook, R. Dennis and Sanford Weisberg (1999), *Applied Regression Including Computing and Graphics*. New York: John Wiley.

Cook, Thomas D. and Donald T. Campbell (1979), *Quasi-Experimentation: Design and Analysis Issues for Field Settings*. Boston: Houghton Mifflin.

Cooley, Thomas F. and Edward C. Prescott (1973), "Varying Parameter Regression: A Theory and Some Applications," *Annals of Economic and Social Measurement*, 2 (October), 463-73.

Cooper, Lee G. (1988), "Competitive Maps: The Structure Underlying Asymmetric Cross Elasticities," *Management Science,* 34:6 (June), 707-23.

——— (1993), "Market-Share Models," in *Handbooks in Operations Research and Management Science: Volume 5: Marketing*, Joshua Eliashberg and Gary Lilien, eds. New York: Elsevier, 259-314.

———, Penny Baron, Wayne Levy, Michael Swisher, and Paris Gogos (1999), "PromoCast: A New Forecasting Method for Promotion Planning," *Marketing Science*, 18:3, 301-16.

——— and Giovanni Giuffrida (2000), "Turning Data Mining into a Management Science Tool: New Algorithms and Empirical Results," *Management Science*, 46:2 (February), 249-64.

———, Lee G., Jan de Leeuw, and Aram G. Sogomonian (1991), "In Imputation Method for Dealing with Missing Data in Regression," *Applied Stochastic Models and Data Analysis*, 7:3, 213-35.

———, Daniel Klapper, and Akihiro Inoue (1996), "Competitive-Component Analysis: A New Approach to Calibrating Asymmetric Market-Share Models, *Journal of Marketing Research*, 33:2 (May), 224-38.

——— and Masao Nakanishi (1988), *Market Share Analysis: Evaluating Competitive Marketing Effectiveness*. Boston: Kluwer Academic Publishers.

Corkindale, David (1984), "Measuring the Sales Effectiveness of Advertising: The Role for an ADLAB in the UK," *Journal of the Market Research Society*, 26 (January), 29-49.

——— and John Newall (1978), "Advertising Thresholds and Wearout," *European Journal of Marketing*, 12 (5), 328-78.

Cournot, Augustin A. (1838), *Recherches sur les Principes Mathematiques de la Theorie des Richesses*. Paris: Hachette.

Cowling, Keith (1972), "Optimality in Firms' Advertising Policies: An Empirical Analysis," in *Market Structure and Corporate Behavior: Theory and Empirical Analysis of the Firm*, Keith Cowling, ed. London: Gray-Mills Publishing, 85-103.

——— and John Cubbin (1971), "Price, Quality and Advertising Competition: An Econometric Investigation of the United Kingdom Car Market," *Economica*, 38 (November), 378-94.

——— and A. J. Rayner (1970), "Price, Quality, and Market Share," *Journal of Political Economy*, 78 (November/December), 1292-309.

Cox, Keith K. (1964), "The Responsiveness of Food Sales to Shelf Space Changes in Supermarkets," *Journal of Marketing Research,* 1 (May), 63-67.

——— (1970), "The Effect of Shelf Space Upon Sales of Branded Products," *Journal of Marketing Research,* 7 (February), 55-58.

Curhan, Ronald C. (1972), "The Relationship Between Shelf Space and Unit Sales in Supermarkets," *Journal of Marketing Research,* 9 (November), 406-12.

——— (1974a), "Shelf Space Elasticity: Reply," *Journal of Marketing Research,* 11 (May), 221-22.

——— (1974b), "The Effects of Merchandising and Temporary Promotional Activities on the Sales of Fresh Fruits and Vegetables in Supermarkets," *Journal of Marketing Research,* 11 (August), 286-94.

Dahl, C. (1986), "Gasoline Demand Survey," *Energy Journal,* 7, 67-82.

Dalrymple, Douglas J. (1978), "Using Box-Jenkins Techniques in Sales Forecasting," *Journal of Business Research,* 6, 133-145.

——— (1987), "Sales Forecasting Practices: Results from a United States Survey," *International Journal of Forecasting,* 3:3/4, 379-91.

——— and George H. Haines, Jr. (1970), "A Study of the Predictive Ability of Market Period Demand Supply Relations for a Firm Selling Fashion Products," *Applied Economics,* 1 (January), 277-85.

Danaher, Peter J. (1994), "Comparing Naive with Econometric Market Share Models When Competitors' Actions Are Forecast," *International Journal of Forecasting,* 10:2 (September), 287-94.

——— and Roderick J. Brodie (1992), "Predictive Accuracy of Simple Complex Econometric Market Share Models: Theoretical and Empirical Results," *International Journal of Forecasting,* 8, 613-26.

——— and Roland T. Rust (1994), "Determining the Optimal Levels of Media Spending," *Journal of Advertising Research,* 34:1 (January-February), 28-34.

——— and ——— (1996), "Determining the Optimal Return on Investment for an Advertising Campaign," *European Journal of Operational Research,* 95:3 (December 20), 511-21.

Darling, Charles B. and J. William Semich (1996), "Wal-Mart's IT Secret: Extreme Integration," *Datamation,* 42 (November), 48-50

Darmon, René Y. (1987), "A Normative Model of Market Response to Sales Force Activities," *European Journal of Operational Research,* 32 (December), 415-25.

——— (1992), *Effective Human Resource Management in the Sales Force.* Westport, CT: Quorum Books.

Davidson, Russell and James G. MacKinnon (1993), *Estimation and Inference in Econometrics.* Oxford: Oxford University Press.

Davis, Fred D. (1989), "Perceived Usefulness, Perceived Ease of Use, and User Acceptance of Information Technology, *MIS Quarterly,* 13 (September), 319-39.

Deaton, Anton S. (1978), "Specification and Testing in Applied Demand Analysis," *The Economic Journal,* 88, 524-36.

——— and John Muellbauer (1980), "An Almost Ideal Demand System," *American Economic Review,* 70:3 (June), 312-26.

Deb, P. and M. Sefton (1996), "The Distribution of a Lagrange Multiplier Test of Normality," *Economic Letters,* 51, 123-30.

Debertin, David L. and Angelos Pagoulatos (1992), "Research in Agricultural Economics 1919-1990: Seventy-Two Years of Change," *Review of Agricultural Economics,* 14:1 (January), 1-22.

Dekimpe, Marnik G. (1992), "Long-run Modeling in Marketing," unpublished Ph.D. dissertation, Los Angeles, CA: UCLA.

————, Pierre Francois, Srinath Gopalakrishna, Gary L. Lilien, and Christophe Van den Bulte (1997), "Generalizing about Trade Show Effectiveness: A Cross-National Comparison," *Journal of Marketing*, 61:4 (October), 55-64.

———— and Dominique M. Hanssens (1991), "Assessing the Evolution of Competitive Relationships: Do Long-run Market Equilibrium Really Exist?" working paper, Anderson Graduate School of Management, UCLA.

———— and ———— (1995a), "Empirical Generalizations About Market Evolution and Stationarity," *Marketing Science*, 14:3 (Part 2 of 2), G109-21.

———— and ———— (1995b), "The Persistence of Marketing Effects on Sales," *Marketing Science*, 14:1 (Winter), 1-21.

———— and ———— (1999), "Sustained Spending and Persistent Response: A New Look at Long-Term Marketing Profitability," *Journal of Marketing Research*, 36:4 (November), 1-31.

———— and ———— (2000), "Time-Series Models in Marketing: Past, Present and Future," *International Journal of Research in Marketing*, 17, forthcoming.

————, ————, and Jorge Silva-Risso (1999), "Long-Run Effects of Price Promotions in Scanner Markets," *Journal of Econometrics*, 89, 269-91.

————, Martin Mellens, Jan-Benedict E.M. Steenkamp and Pierre Vanden Abeele (1997), "Decline and Variability in Brand Loyalty," *International Journal of Research in Marketing*, 14, 405-20. .

————, Linda van de Gucht, Dominique M. Hanssens, and Keiko Powers (1998), "Long-Run Abstinence after Narcotics Abuse: What Are the Odds?" *Management Science*, 44:11 (November), 1478-92.

de Kluyver, Cornelius A. and Roderick J. Brodie (1987), "Advertising-Versus-Marketing Mix Carryover Effects: An Empirical Evaluation," *Journal of Business Research,* 15 (June), 269-87.

———— and Edgar A. Pessemier (1986), "Benefits of a Marketing Budgeting Model: Two Case Studies," *Sloan Management Review*, 28:1 (Fall), 27-38.

Denton, James W. (1995), "How Good Are Neural Networks for Causal Forecasting?" *Journal of Business Forecasting*, 14 (Summer), 337-46.

Desmet, Pierre and Valerie Renaudin (1996), "Estimating Shelf-Space Elasticity for Product Categories," paper presented at the European Institute for Advanced Studies in Managment/Centre for Research on the Economic Efficiency of Retailing Workshop on Channel Productivity, Mons, Begium, October.

DeSarbo, Wayne S., Vithala R. Rao, Joel H. Steckel, Jerry Wind, and Richard Colombo (1987), "A Friction Model for Describing and Forecasting Price Changes," *Marketing Science,* 6 (Fall), 299-319.

Devinney, Timothy M. (1987), "Entry and Learning," *Management Science, 33* (June), 706-24.

Diamantos, A. and Brian P. Mathews (1993), "Managerial Perceptions of the Demand Curve: Evidence from a Multiproduct Firm," *European Journal of Marketing*, 27:9, 5-18.

di Benedetto, C. Anthony (1985), "A Multiplicative Dynamic-Adjustment Model of Sales Response to Marketing Mix Variables," *Modeling, Simulation, and Control C: Environmental, Biomedical, Human & Social Systems*, 4 (Autumn), 7-18.

Dickey, David A., David P. Hasza and Wayne A. Fuller (1984), "Testing for Unit Roots in Seasonal Time Series," *Journal of the American Statistical Association*, 79, 355-67.

————, William R. Bell, and Robert B. Miller (1986), "Unit Roots in Time Series Models: Tests and Implications," *The American Statistician,* 40 (February), 12-26.

Dickson, Peter R. and J. E. Urbany (1994), "Retailer Reactions to Competitive Price Changes," *Journal of Retailing*, 70, 1-22.

Didow, Nicholas and George Franke (1984), "Measurement Issues in Time-Series Research: Reliability and Validity Assessment in Modeling the Macroeconomic Effects of Advertising," *Journal of Marketing Research*, 21, 12-19.

Diebold, Francis X. (1989), "Forecast Combination and Encompassing: Reconciling Two Divergent Literatures, *International Journal of Forecasting*, 5 (4), 589-92.

Dijkstra, Theo K. and Frans W. Platt (1986), "On the Use of Audit Data in Marketing Models," paper presented at the Annual EMACS Conference, Helsinki, Finland, June.

Dodson, Jr., Joe A. and Eitan Muller (1978), "Models of New Product Diffusion Through Advertising and Word of Mouth," *Management Science*, 24 (November), 1568-78.

Doktor, Robert H. and W. F. Hamilton (1973), "Cognitive Style and the Acceptance of Management Science Recommendations," *Management Science*, 19, 884-94.

――――, Randall L. Schultz, and Dennis P. Slevin, eds. (1979), *The Implementation of Management Science*. New York: North-Holland.

Donatos, G.S. and K.E. Kioulafas (1990), "A Quantitative Analysis of New Car Sales and Advertising in Greece," *European Journal of Operational Research*, 48:3 (October), 311-17.

Doran, Howard E. (1989), *Applied Regression Analysis in Econometrics*. New York: Marcel Dekker.

―――― and J. J. Quilkey (1972), "Harmonic Analysis of Seasonal Data: Some Important Properties," *American Journal of Agricultural Ecnomics*, 54 (1972), 346-51.

Dorfman, R. and P. O. Steiner (1954), "Optimal Advertising and Optimal Quality," *American Economic Review*, 44 (December), 826-36.

Doyle, Peter and John Saunders (1985), "The Lead Effect in Marketing," *Journal of Marketing Research*, 22 (February), 54-65.

―――― and ―――― (1990), "Multiproduct Advertising Budgeting," *Marketing Science*, 9:2 (Spring), 97-113.

Drèze, Xavier, Stephen J. Hoch, and Mary E. Purk (1994), "Shelf Management and Space Elasticity," *Journal of Retailing*, 70:4 (Winter), 301-26.

D'Souza, D. and Arthur Allaway (1995), "An Empirical Examination of the Advertising Spending Decisions of a Multiproduct Retailer," *Journal of Retailing*, 71, 279-96.

Dubin, Jeffrey A. (1998), *Studies in Consumer Demand—Econometric Methods Applied to Market Data*. Norwell, MA: Kluwer Academic Publishers.

――――, Michael J. Grantz, Michael A. Udell, and Louis L. Wilde (1992), "The Demand for Tax Return Preparation Services," *The Review of Economics and Statistics*, 75-82.

Dubin, Robin A. (1988), "Estimation of Regression Coefficients in the Presence of Spatially Autocorrelated Error Terms," *Review of Economics and Statistics*, 70 (August), 466-74.

Duckworth, Gary, ed. (1997), *Advertising Works 9*. Henley-on-Thames, UK: NTC Publications.

Duffy, Martyn H. (1987), "Advertising and the Inter-Product Distribution of Demand: A Rotterdam Model Approach," *European Economic Review*, 31 (July), 1051-70.

East, Robert (1991), "Beyond the Blip: The 15 Brand Experiment," *Journal of the Market Research Society*, 33:1 (January), 57-59.

Eastlack, Jr., Joseph O. and Ambar G. Rao (1986), "Modeling Response to Advertising and Pricing Changes for 'V-8' Cocktail Vegetable Juice," *Marketing Science*, 5 (Summer), 245-59.

Ebbeler, Donald H. (1974), "On the Maximum R^2 Choice Criterion," Claremont Economic Paper Number 113, The Claremont Colleges, August.

Edlund, Per-Olov (1984), "Identification of the Multiple-Input Box-Jenkins Transfer Function Model," *Journal of Forecasting*, 3, 297-308.

Edmunson, Robert H. (1990), "Decomposition: A Strategy for Judgmental Forecasting," *Journal of Forecasting*, 9 (July-September), 305-14.

Ehrenberg, Andrew S. C. (1969a), "The Discovery and Use of Laws of Marketing," *Journal of Advertising Research*, 9:2, 11-17.

——— (1969b), "Laws in Marketing," in *Current Controversies in Marketing Research*, Leo Bogart, ed. Chicago: Markham, 141-52.

——— (1982). *A Primer in Data Reduction*. New York: John Wiley.

——— (1988), *Repeat-Buying: Facts, Theory, and Applications*, London: Charles Griffin.

——— (1994) "Theory or Well-Based Results: Which Comes First?" in *Research Traditions in Marketing*, Gilles Laurent, Gary L. Lilien, and Bernard Pras, eds. Boston: Kluwer Academic Publishers, 79-105.

——— (1995), "Empirical Generalizations, Theory, and Method," *Marketing Science*, 14:3 (Part 2 of 2), G20-35.

——— and J. A. Bound (1993), "Predictability and Prediction," *Journal of the Royal Statistical Society*, 156, 167-206.

——— and L. R. England (1990), "Generalizing a Pricing Effect," *The Journal of Industrial Economics*, 39:1 (September), 47-68.

———, Kathy Hammond, and G. J. Goodhardt (1994), "The After-Effects of Price-Related Consumer Promotions," *Journal of Advertiising Research*, 34 (July/August), 11-21.

Eliashberg, Jehoshua and Gary L. Lilien (1993), *Marketing*. Handbooks in Operations Research and Management Science. 5. Amsterdam: North-Holland.

Elms, Sue (1997), "Linking Sales Tracking Data to Television Viewing," *Admap*, 32:4 (April), 62-65.

Elrod, Terry and Russell L. Winer (1979), "Estimating the Effects of Advertising on Individual Household Purchasing Behavior," in *Proceedings*, Neil Beckwith et al., eds. Chicago: American Marketing Association, 83-89.

Emshoff, J. R. and Alan Mercer (1970), "Aggregated Models of Consumer Purchases," *Journal of the Royal Statistical Society, Series A*, 133:1, 14-32.

Enders, Walter (1995), *Applied Econometric Time Series*. New York: Wiley.

Engle, Robert F. and C. W. J. Granger (1987), "Co-integration and Error Correction: Representation, Estimation, and Testing," *Econometrica*, 55:2 (March), 251-76.

——— and B.S. Yoo (1987), "Forecasting and Testing in Cointegrated Systems," *Journal of Econometrics*, 35, 143-59.

Enis, Ben M. and Michael P. Mokwa (1979), "The Marketing Management Matrix: A Taxonomy for Strategy Comprehension," in *Conceptual and Theoretical Developments in Marketing*, O. C. Ferrell, Stephen W. Brown, and Charles W. Lamb, eds. Chicago: American Marketing Association, 485-500.

Ephron, Erwin and Simon Broadbent (1999), "Two Views of TV Scheduling—How Far Apart?" *Admap*, 34:1 (January), 22-25.

Erickson, Gary M. (1981a), "Time-Varying Parameter Estimation as Exploration," *Decision Sciences*, 12 (July), 428-38.

——— (1981b), "Using Ridge Regression to Estimate Directly Lagged Effects in Marketing," *Journal of the American Statistical Association*, 76 (December), 766-73.

——— (1985), "A Model of Advertising Competition," *Journal of Marketing Research*, 22 (August), 297-304.

——— (1987), "Marketing Managers Need More Than Forecasting Accuracy," *International Journal of Forecasting*, 3:3/4, 453-55.

——— (1990), "Assessing Response Model Approaches to Marketing Strategy Decisions," in *The Interface of Marketing and Strategy*, George Day, Barton Weitz, and Robin Wensley, eds. Greenwich, CT: JAI Press, 353-85.

——— (1991), *Dynamic Models of Advertising Competition*. Boston: Kluwer.

——— (1992), "Empirical Analysis of Closed Loop Duopoly Advertising Strartegies," *Management Science*, 38 (December), 1732-49.

—————— (1995), "Advertising Strategies in a Dynamic Oligopoly," *Journal of Marketing Research*, 32:2 (May), 233-37.

Eskin, Gerald J. (1975), "A Case for Test Market Experiments," *Journal of Advertising Research,* 15 (April), 27-33.

—————— and Penny H. Baron (1977), "Effect of Price and Advertising in Test-Market Experiments," *Journal of Marketing Research,* 14 (November), 499-508.

Evans, G. W. (1989), "Output and Unemployment Dynamics in the United States," *Journal of Applied Econometrics*, 4, 213-37.

—————— and G. Wells (1983), "An Alternative Approach to Simulating VAR Models," *Economic Letters*, 12, 23-29.

Fader, Peter S., James M. Lattin, and John D. C. Little (1992), "Estimating Nonlinear Parameters in the Multinomial Logit Model," *Marketing Science*, 11:4 (Fall), 372-385.

Farley, John U. and Melvin J. Hinich (1970), "A Test for a Shifting Slope Coefficient in a Linear Model," *Journal of the American Statistical Association,* 65 (September), 1320-29.

——————, ——————, and Timothy W. McGuire (1975), "Some Comparisons of Tests for a Shift in the Slopes of a Multivariate Linear Time Series Model." *Journal of Econometrics,* 3 (August), 297-318.

—————— and H. J. Leavitt (1968), "A Model of the Distribution of Branded Products in Jamaica," *Journal of Marketing Research*, 5 (November), 362-69.

—————— and Donald R. Lehmann (1986), *Meta-Analysis in Marketing: Generalization of Response Models.* Lexington, MA: D. C. Heath.

—————— and —————— (1994), "Cross National 'Laws' and Differences in Market Response," *Management Science*, 40 (January), 111-22.

——————, ——————, and Michael J. Ryan (1981), "Generalizing from Imperfect Replication," *Journal of Business,* 54 (October), 597-610.

——————, ——————, and Alan Sawyer (1995), "Empirical Marketing Generalization Using Meta-Analysis," *Marketing Science*, 14:3 (Part 2 of 2), G36-46.

Farris, Paul W. and Mark S. Albion (1980), "The Impact of Advertising on the Price of Consumer Products," *Journal of Advertising Research,* 44 (Summer), 17-35.

——————, James Olver, and Cornelis de Kluyver (1989), "The Relationship Between Distribution and Market Share," *Marketing Science*, 8:2 (Spring), 107-28.

——————, Mark E. Parry, and Kusum L. Ailawadi (1992), "Structural Analysis of Models with Composite Dependent Variables," *Marketing Science*, 11:2 (Winter), 76-94.

—————— and David J. Reibstein (1984), "Over Control in Advertising Experiments?" *Journal of Advertising Research*, 24:3, 37-42.

Feinberg, Fred M. (1992), "Pulsing Policies for Aggregate Advertising Models," *Marketing Science*, 11:3 (Summer), 221-34.

Feldwick, Paul, ed. (1990), *Advertising Works 5*, London: Cassell Educational Limited.

——————, ed. (1991), *Advertising Works 6*, Henley-on-Thames, United Kingdom: NTC Publications.

Fellner, William (1949), *Competition Among the Few.* New York: Alfred Knopf.

Fildes, Robert (1985), "Quantitative Forecasting The State of Art: Econometric Models," *Journal of the Operational Research Society,* 36 (July), 549-80.

—————— and Robert Hastings (1994), "The Organization and Improvement of Market Forecasting," *Journal of the Operational Research Society*, 45 (1), 1-16.

Findley, James J. and J. D. C. Little (1980), "Experiences with Market Response Analysis," working paper, March.

Foekens, Eijte W. (1995), *Scanner Data Based Marketing Modeling: Empirical Applications.* Ph.D.Thesis, University of Groningen, Faculty of Economics, The Netherlands.

———, Wim P. Krijnen, and Tom J. Wansbeek (1994), "Efficient Computation for the Estimation of the Sales Response Model," *Research Memorandum* 561, Institute for Economic Research, University of Groningen, January.

——— and Peter S.H. Leeflang (1992), "Comparing Scanner Data with Traditional Store Audit Data," *Scandinavian Business Review*, 1:1, 71-85.

———, ———, and Dick R. Wittink (1994), "A Comparison and Exploration of the Forecasting Accuracy of a Loglinear Model at Different Levels of Aggregation," *International Journal of Forecasting*, 10:2 (September), 245-61.

———, ———, and ——— (1997), "Hierarchical Versus Other Market Share Models for Markets with Many Items," *International Journal of Research in Marketing*, 14:4 (October), 359-78.

———, ———, and ——— (1999), "Varying Parameter Models to Accommodate Dynamic Promotion Effects," *Journal of Econometrics*, 89:1-2, 249-68.

Forker, Olan D. and Ronald W. Ward (1993), *Commodity Advertising*. New York: Lexington Books.

Fornell, Claes, William T. Robinson, and Birger Wernerfelt (1985), "Consumption Experience and Sales Promotion Expenditure," *Management Science,* 31 (September), 1084-1105.

Frank, Ronald E. and William F. Massy (1967), "Effects of Short-Term Promotional Strategy in Selected Market Segments," in *Promotional Decisions Using Mathematical Models,* Patrick J. Robinson, ed. Boston: Allyn and Bacon, 147-99.

——— and ——— (1970), "Shelf Position and Space Effects on Sales," *Journal of Marketing Research,* 7 (February), 59-66.

——— and ——— (1971), *An Econometric Approach to a Marketing Decision Model.* Cambridge, MA: MIT Press.

Franke, George R. (1994), "U.S. Cigarette Demand, 1961-1990: Econometric Issues, Evidence, and Implications," *Journal of Business Research*, 30:1, 33-41.

——— and Gary Wilcox (1987), "Alcoholic Beverage Advertising and Consumption in the United States, 1964-1984," *Journal of Advertising,* 16:3, 22-30.

Franses, Philip H. (1991), "Primary Demand for Beer in the Netherlands: An Application of ARMAX Model Specification," *Journal of Marketing Research*, 28:2 (May), 240-45.

——— (1994), "Modeling New Product Sales: An Application of Cointegration Analysis", *International Journal of Research in Marketing*, 11, 491-502.

——— and N. Haldrup (1994), "The Effects of Additive Outliers on Tests for Unit Roots and Cointegration," *Journal of Business and Economic Statistics*, 12, 471-78.

Fraser, Cynthia and Robert E. Hite (1988), "An Adaptive Utility Approach for Improved Use of Marketing Models," *Journal of Marketing,* 52 (October), 96-103.

Freeland, James R. and Charles B. Weinberg (1980), "*S*-Shaped Response Functions: Implications for Decision Models," *Journal of the Operational Research Society,* 31:11, 1001-7.

Freeman, Paul (1996), "Defending Advertising Through Market Modeling," *Admap*, 31:8 (September), 27-29.

Friedman, James W. (1977a), "Cournot, Bowley, Stackelberg and Fellner, and the Evolution of the Reaction Function," in *Economic Progress, Private Values, and Public Policy,* Bela Balassa and Richard Nelson, eds. New York: North-Holland, 139-60.

——— (1977b), *Oligopoly and the Theory of Games.* Amsterdam: North-Holland.

——— (1983), "Advertising and Oligopolistic Equilibrium," *Bell Journal of Economics,* 14 (Fall), 464-73.

Fujii, Edwin T. (1980), "The Demand for Cigarettes: Further Empirical Evidence and Its Implications for Public Policy," *Applied Economics,* 12 (December), 479-89.

Fuller, Wayne A. (1976), *Introduction to Statistical Time Series*, New York: Wiley.

Garland, Ron (1992), "Pricing Errors in Supermarkets: Who Pays?" *International Journal of Retail and Distribution Management*, 20:1, 25-30.

Garry, Steve (2000), "RE: Advertising Effects," E-mail to AMODLMKT list, January 27.

Gasmi, Farid and Quang H. Vuong (1988), "An Econometric Analysis of Some Duopolistic Games in Prices and Advertising," working paper, Bell Communications Research/ University of Southern California, May.

Gasmi, Farid, J.J. Laffont, and Quang H. Voung (1992), "Econometric Analysis of Collusive Behavior in a Soft-Drink Market," *Journal of Economics and Management Strategy*, 1:2, 277-311.

Gately, D. (1992), "Imperfect Price-Reversibility of U.S. Gasoline Demand," *Energy Journal*, 13, 179-207.

Gatignon, Hubert (1984), "Competition as a Moderator of the Effect of Advertising on Sales," *Journal of Marketing Research*, 21 (November), 387-98.

———— and Dominique M. Hanssens (1987), "Modeling Marketing Interactions with Application to Salesforce Effectiveness," *Journal of Marketing Research*, 24 (August), 247-57.

Gaver, Kenneth M., Dan Horsky, and Chakravarti Narasimhan (1988), "Invariant Estimators for Market Share Systems and Their Finite Sample Behavior," *Marketing Science*, 7 (Spring), 169-86.

Gensch, Dennis H. and Ulf Peter Welam (1973), "An Optimal Budget Allocation Model in Dynamic, Interacting Market Segments," *Management Science*, 20 (October), 179-90.

George, Jennifer, Alan Mercer, and Helen Wilson (1996), "Variations in Price Elasticities," *European Journal of Operational Research*, 88:1 (January), 13-22.

Geurts, Michael D. and I.B. Ibrahim (1975), "Comparing the Box-Jenkins Approach with the Exponentially Smoothed Forecasting Model: Application to Hawaii Tourists," *Journal of Marketing Research*, 12, 182-88.

Geweke, John, Richard Meese, and Warren Dent (1983), "Comparing Alternative Tests of Causality in Temporal Systems," *Journal of Econometrics*, 21, 161-94.

Ghosh, Avijit, Scott A. Neslin, and Robert W. Shoemaker (1983), "Are There Associations Between Price Elasticity and Brand Characteristics?" in *1983 Educators' Conference Proceedings*, Patrick Murphy et al., eds. Chicago: American Marketing Association, 226-30.

————, ————, and ———— (1984), " A Comparison of Market Share Models and Estimation Procedures,' *Journal of Marketing Research*, 21 (May), 202-10.

Gijsbrechts, Els (1993), "Prices and Pricing Research in Consumer Marketing: Some Recent Developments," *International Journal of research in Marketing*, 10:2 (June), 115-52.

———— and Philippe Naert (1984), "Towards Hierarchical Linking of Marketing Resource Allocation to Market Areas and Product Groups," *International Journal of Research in Marketing*, 1:2, 97-116.

Ginsberg, William (1974), "The Multiplant Firm with Increasing Returns to Scale," *Journal of Economic Theory*, 9 (November), 283-92.

Ginzberg, Michael J. (1979a), "Improving MIS Project Selection," *Omega*, 7:6, 527-37.

———— (1979b), "A Study of the Implementation Process," in *The Implementation of Management Science*, R. Doktor, R. L. Slevin, and D. P. Slevin, eds. New York: North-Holland, 85-102.

———— (1980), "An Organizational Contingencies View of Accounting and Information Systems Implementation," *Accounting, Organizations and Society*, 5:4, 369-82.

———— (1981a), "Early Diagnosis of MIS Implementation Failure: Promising Results and Unanswered Questions," *Management Science*, 27 (April), 459-78.

———— (1981b), "Key Recurrent Issues in the Implementation Process," *MIS Quarterly*, 5 (June), 47-59.

———— (1983), "DSS Success: Measurement and Facilitation," in *Data-Base Management: Theory and Applications*, C. W. Holsapple and A. B. Whinston, eds. Dordrecht, Holland: D. Ridel, 367-87.

————, Henry C. Lucas, Jr., and Randall L. Schultz (1986), "Testing an Integrated Implementation Model with Data from a Generalized DSS," working paper, Case Western Reserve University, March.

Giuffrida, Giovanni, Lee G.Cooper, and W.W. Chu (1998), "A Scalable Bottom-Up Data Mining Algorithm for Relational Databases", paper presented at the 10th International. Conference on Scientific and Statistical Database Management, IEEE, Capri, Italy.

Gius, Mark Paul (1996), "Using Panel Data to Determine the Effect of Advertising on Brand-Level Distilled Spirits Sales," *Journal of Studies on Alcohol*, (January), 57:1, 73-76.

Givon, Moshe (1993), "Partial Carryover of Advertising," *Marketing Letters*, 4:2 (April), 165-73.

———— and Dan Horsky (1990), "Untangling the Effects of Purchase Reinforcement and Advertising Carryover," *Marketing Science*, 9:2 (Spring), 171-87.

———— and ———— (1994), "Intertemporal Aggregation of Heterogeneous Consumers," *European Journal of Operational Research*, 76:2 (July 28), 273-82.

Glaister, Stephen (1974), "Advertising Policy and Returns to Scale in Markets Where Information Is Passed Between Individuals," *Economica*, 41 (May), 138-56.

Glazer, Rashi (1991), "Marketing in an Information-Intensive Environment: Strategic Implications of Knowledge as an Asset," *Journal of Marketing*, 55 (October), 1-19.

———— and Allen M. Weiss (1993), "Marketing in Turbulent Environments: Decision Processes and the Time-Sensitivity of Information," *Journal of Marketing Research*, 30 (November), 509-21.

Goddard, Ellen W. and Alex K. Amuah (1989), "Demand for Canadian Fats and Oils: A Case Study of Advertising Effectiveness," *American Journal of Agricultural Economics*, 71:3, 741-49.

Gold, Laurence N. (1992), "Let's heavy Up in St. Louis and See What Happens," *Journal of Advertising Research*, 32:6 (November/December), 31-38.

Goldberg, L. (1982), "Recruiters, Advertising, and Navy Enlistments," *Naval Research Logistics Quarterly*, 29 (June), 385-98.

Goodstein, Ronald C. (1994), "UPC Scanner Pricing Systems: Are They Accurate?" *Journal of Marketing*, 58:2 (April), 20-30.

Goodwin, P. and G. Wright (1993), "Improving Judgmental Time Series Forecasting: A Review of the Guidance Provided by Research," *International Journal of Forecasting*, 9 (August), 147-61.

Gopalakrishna, Srinath and Rabikar Chatterjee (1992), "A Communications Response Model for a Mature Industrial Product: Application and Implications," *Journal of Marketing Research*, 29:2 (May), 189-200.

———— and Gary L. Lilien (1995), "A Three-Stage Model of Trade Show Performance," *Marketing Science*, (Winter), 22-42.

———— and Jerome D. Williams (1992), "Planning and Performance Assessment of Industrial Trade Shows: An Exploratory Study," *International Journal of Research in Marketing*, 9:3 (August), 207-24.

Granger, C. W. J. (1969), "Investigating Causal Relations by Econometric Models and Cross-Spectral Methods," *Econometrica*, 37, 424-38.

———— (1980), "Long Memory Relationships and the Aggregation of Dynamic Models," *Journal of Econometrics*, 14, 227-38.

———— (1981), "Some Properties of Time Series Data and their Use in Econometric Model Specification," *Journal of Econometrics*, 16, 121-30.

———— (1988), "Some Recent Developments in a Concept of Causality," *Journal of Econometrics,* 39 (September-October), 199-212.

———— and J. Hallman (1991), "Nonlinear Transformations of Integrated Time Series," *Journal of Time Series Analysis,* 12, 207-24.

———— and Paul Newbold (1974), "Spurious Regressions in Econometrics," *Journal of Econometrics,* 2, 111-20.

———— and ———— (1986), *Forecasting Economic Time Series* (Second Edition). New York: Academic Press.

Grapentine, Terry (1997), "Managing Multicollinearity," *Market Research,* (Fall), 11-21.

Grass, Robert G. and Wallace H. Wallace (1969), "Satiation Effects of TV Commercials," *Journal of Advertising Research,* 9 (September), 3-8.

Gray, H. L., G. D. Kelly, and D. D. McIntire (1978), "A New Approach to ARMA Modeling," *Communication in Statistics,* B7, 1-77.

Green, Richard D., Hoy F. Carmen, and Kathleen McManus (1991), "Some Empirical Methods for Estimating Advertising Effects in Demand Systems: An Application to Dried Fruit," *Journal of the Western Agricultural Economics Association,* 16:1, 63-71.

Greenberg, E., W. A. Pollard, and W.T. Alpert (1989), "Statistical Properties of Data Stretching," *Journal of Applied Econometrics,* 4 (October-December), 383-91.

Greene, William H. (1997), *Econometric Analysis,* 3rd Edition. Englewood Cliffs, NJ: Prentice-Hall.

Griliches, Zvi (1967), "Distributed Lags: A Survey," *Econometrica,* 35 (January), 16-49.

Grover, Rajiv and V. Srinivasan (1987), "A Simultaneous Approach to Market Segmentation and Market Structuring," *Journal of Marketing Research,* 24:2 (May), 139-53.

———— and ———— (1992), "Evaluating the Muliple Effects of Retail Promotions on Brand Loyal and Brand Switching Segments," *Journal of Marketing Research,* 29:1 (February), 76-89.

Gruca, Thomas S. and Bruce R. Klemz (1998), "Using Neural Networks to Identify Competitive Market Structures from Aggregate Market Response Data," *Omega,* 26:1 (February), 49-62.

———— and D. Sudharshan (1991), "Equilibrium Characteristics of Multinomial Logit Market Share Models," *Journal of Marketing Research,* 28:4 (November), 480-82.

Guadagni, Peter M. and John D.C. Little (1983), "A Logit Model of Brand Choice Calibrated on Scanner Data," *Marketing Science,* 2 (Summer), 203-38.

Guerts, Michael D. and David Whitlark (1992/93), "Forecasting Market Share," *Journal of Business Forecasting,* 11 (Winter), 17-32.

Guilkey, David K. and Michael K. Salemi (1982), "Small Sample Properties of Three Tests for Granger-Causal Ordering in a Bivariate Stochastic System," *Review of Economics and Statistics,* 64 (November), 668-80.

Gupta, Sachin, Pradeep Chintagunta, Anil Kaul, and Dirk R. Wittink (1996), "Do Household Scanner Data Provide Representative Inferences from Brand Choices: A Comparison With Store Data," *Journal of Marketing Research,* 33:4 (November), 383-98.

Gupta, Sunil (1988), "Impact of Sales Promotions on When, What, and How Much to Buy," *Journal of Marketing Research,* 25 (November), 342-55.

Hackathorn, Richard (1995), "Data Warehouse Energizes Your Enterprise," *Datamation,* 41 (February), 38-45.

Hagerty, Michael R. (1987), "Conditions Under Which Econometric Models will Outperform Naïve Models," *International Journal of Forecasting,* 3:3/4, 457-60.

————, James M. Carman, and Gary Russell (1988), "Estimating Elasticities with PIMS Data: Methodological Issues and Substantive Implications," *Journal of Marketing Research,* 25 (February), 1-9.

Hakkio, C.S. and M. Rush (1991), "Cointegration: How Short is the Long Run," *Journal of International Money and Finance*, 10, 571-81.

Haley, Russell I. (1978), "Sales Effects of Media Weight," *Journal of Advertising Research*, 18 (June), 9-18.

Hall, Graham and Sidney Howell (1985), "The Experience Curve from the Economist's Perspective," *Strategic Management Journal*, 6, 197-212.

Hall, Lana and Ingrid Foik (1983), "Generic versus Brand Advertising for Manufactured Milk Products: The Case of Yogurt," *North Central Journal of Agricultural Economics*, 5:1 (January), 19-24.

Hamilton, Will, Robert East, and Stavos Kalfatis (1997), "The Measurement of Brand Price Elasticities," *Journal of Marketing Management*, 13:4 (May), 285-98.

Hanssens, Dominique M. (1977), "An Empirical Study of Time-Series Analysis in Marketing Model Building," Unpublished Ph.D. Dissertation, Purdue University, Krannert Graduate School of Management.

——— (1980a), "Bivariate Time Series Analysis of the Relationship Between Advertising and Sales," *Applied Economics*, 12 (September), 329-40.

——— (1980b), "Market Response, Competitive Behavior, and Time Series Analysis," *Journal of Marketing Research*, 17 (November), 470-85.

——— (1982), "Expectations and Shocks in Market Response," working paper, Center for Marketing Studies, University of California, Los Angeles, Paper No. 123.

——— (1988), "Marketing and the Long Run," working paper, Center for Marketing Studies, University of California, Los Angeles, Paper No. 164 (Revised), June.

——— (1996), "Customer Information: The New Strategic Asset," *Chief Executive*, (May), 66-68.

——— (1998). "Order Forecasts, Retail Sales and the Marketing Mix for Consumer Durables," *Journal of Forecasting*, 17:3/4 (June-July), 327-46.

——— and Johny K. Johansson (1991), "Synergy or Rivalry? The Japanese Automobile Companies' Export Expansion," *Journal of International Business Studies*, 22:3, 503-26.

——— and Henry A. Levien (1983), "An Econometric Study of Recruitment Marketing in the U.S. Navy," *Management Science*, 29 (October), 1167-84.

——— and Lon-Mu Liu (1983), "Lag Specification in Rational Distributed Lag Structural Models," *Journal of Business and Economic Statistics*, 1 (October),316-25.

——— and Ming Ouyang (2000), "Modeling Marketing Hysteresis," Working Paper, University of California, Los Angeles.

——— and Leonard J. Parsons (1993), "Econometric and Time Series Market Response Models," in *Handbooks in Operations Research and Management Science: Volume 5: Marketing*, Joshua Eliashberg and Gary Lilien, eds. New York: Elsevier, 409-64.

——— and Pierre Vanden Abeele (1987), "A Time-Series Study of the Formation and Predictive Performance of EEC Production Survey Expectations," *Journal of Business and Economic Statistics*, 5:4, 507-19.

Harter, Rachel M. and David F. Cameron (1995), "The Nielsen Survey of Supermarkets," *Amstat News*, (October), 19.

Hartwick, Jon and Henri Barki (1994), "Explaining the Role of User Participation in Information System Use," *Management Science*, 40 (April), 440-65.

Hasza, David P. and Wayne A. Fuller (1982), "Testing for Nonstationary Parameter Specifications in Seasonal Time Series Models," *The Annals of Statistics*, 10, 1209-16.

Haugh, Larry D. (1976), "Checking the Independence of Two Covariance-Stationary Time Series: A Univariate Residual Cross-Correlation Approach," *Journal of the American Statistical Association*, 71 (June), 378-85.

——— and George E. P. Box (1977), "Identification of Dynamic Regression (Distributed Lag) Models Connecting Two Time Series," *Journal of the American Statistical Association*, 72 (March), 121-29.

Hausman, Jerry A. (1978*),* "Specification Tests in Econometrics," *Econometrica,* 46 (November), 1251-72.

——— and Whitney K. Newey (1995), "Nonparametic Estimation of Exact Consumers Surplus and Deadweight Loss," *Econometrica*, 63:6 (November), 1445-76.

——— and W. E. Taylor (1981), "A Generalized Specification Test," *Economic Letters*, 8, 239-47.

Heath, Rebecca Piirto (1996), "Wake of the Flood," *Marketing Tools*, (November/ December). 58-63.

Heckman, James J. (1976), "The Common Structure of Statistical Models of Truncation, Sample Selection, and Limited Dependent Variables and a Simple Estimator for Such Models," *Annals of Economic and Social Measurement,* 5 (Fall), 475-92.

Hegji, Charles E. (1998), "A Spreadsheet Application of Dorfman and Steiner's Rule for Optimal Advertising," *Managerial and Decision Economics*, 19:1 (February), 59-62.

Hellofs, Linda L., and Robert Jacobson (1999), "Market Share and Customers' Perceptions of Quality," *Journal of Marketing*, Vol. 63:1 (January), 16-25.

Helmer, Richard M. and Johny K. Johansson (1977), "An Exposition of the Box-Jenkins Transfer Function Analysis with Application to the Advertising-Sales Relationship," *Journal of Marketing Research,* 14 (May), 227-39.

Helmuth, John A. (1987), "Dealership Automobile Demand: Advertising Elasticity and Optimality," *Akron Business and Economic Review*, 18:1 (Spring), 37-44.

Hendon, Donald W. (1981), "The Advertising-Sales Relationship in Australia," *Journal of Advertising Research,* 21 (February), 37-47.

Hendry, David, ed. (1986), "Economic Modeling with Cointegrated Variables (Special Issue)," *Oxford Bulletin of Economics and Statistics,* 48 (3).

Heuts, R. M. J. and J. H. J. M. Bronckers (1988), "Forecasting the Dutch Heavy Truck Market: A Multivariate Approach," *International Journal of Forecasting*, 4, 47-79.

Hill, R. Carter and Phillip A. Cartwright (1994), "The Statistical Properties of the Equity Estimator," *Journal of Busieness & Economic Statistics*, 12, 141-7.

———, ———, and Julia F. Arbaugh (1990), "Using Aggregate Data to Estimate Micro-Level Parameters with Shrinkage Rules," *Proceedings of the Business and Economic Statististics Section.* American Statististical Association, Washington, DC, 339-44.

———, ———, and ——— (1991), "Using Aggregate Data to Estimate Micro-Level Parameters with Shrinkage Rules: More Results," *Proceedings of the Business and Economic Statististics Section.* American Statistical Association, Washington, DC.

Hoch, Stephen J. (1994), "Experts and Models in Combination" in *The Marketing Information Revolution.* Robert C. Blattberg, Rashi Glazer, and John D. C. Little, eds. Boston: Harvard Business School Press, 253-69.

——— and Shumeet Banerji (1993), "When Do Private Labels Succeed?" *Sloan Management Review*, 54 (Summer), 57-67.

———, Byuong-Do Kim, Alan J. Montgomery, and Peter E. Rossi (1995), "Determinants of Store-Level Price Elasticity," *Journal of Marketing Research*, 32 (February), 17-29.

——— and David A. Schkade (1996), "A Psychological Approach to Decision Support Systems," *Management Science*, 42 (January), 51-64.

Hogarty, Thomas F. and Kenneth G. Elzinga (1972), "The Demand for Beer," *Review of Economics and Statistics,* 54 (May), 195-98.

Hollis, Nigel S. (1990), "Separating Advertising From Promotional Effects with Econometric Modeling," *Journal of Advertising Research*, 30:3 (June/July 1990), RC6-RC12.

Holmes, Mike (1990), "'Modelling Beyond the Blip'—Some Thoughts and Comments," *Journal of the Market Research Society*, 32:3 (July), 467-89.

Holthausen, Duncan M., Jr. and Gert Assmus (1982), "Advertising Budget Allocation under Uncertainty," *Management Science*, 28 (May), 487-99.

Hooley, Graham J. and Nick Wilson (1988), "Advertising Effects: More Methodological Issues—A Reply," *Journal of the Market Research Society*, 30:2 (April), 231-34.

——, ——, and P. Wigodsky (1988), "Modeling the Effects of Advertising: Some Methodological Issues," *Journal of the Market Research Society*, 30:1 (January), 45-58.

Horowitz, Joel L. (1998) *Semiparametric Methods in Econometrics*. New York: Springer-Verlag.

Horsky, Dan (1977a), "Market Share Response to Advertising: An Example of Theory Testing," *Journal of Marketing Research*, 14 (February), 10-21.

—— (1977b), "An Empirical Analysis of the Optimal Advertising Policy," *Management Science*, 23 (June), 1037-49.

—— and Leonard S. Simon (1983), "Advertising and the Diffusion of New Products," *Marketing Science*, 2 (Winter), 1-17.

—— and Karl Mate (1988), "Dynamic Advertising Strategies of Competing Durable Goods Producers," *Marketing Science*, 7 (Fall), 356-67.

Houston, Franklin S. (1977a), "Aggregated and Disaggregated Cumulative Advertising Models," in *Proceedings*, B. A. Bellenger and D. N. Bellenger, eds. Chicago: American Marketing Association.

—— (1977b), "An Econometric Analysis of Positioning," *Journal of Business Administration*, 9 (Fall), 1-12.

—— and Leonard J. Parsons (1986), "Modeling Cumulative Advertising as a Continuous Function," TIMS/ORSA Marketing Science Conference, University of Texas, Dallas.

——, Vinay Kanetkar, and Doyle L. Weiss (1991), "Simplified Estimation Procedures for MCI and MNL Models: A Comment," working paper, University of Toronto.

——, Vinay Kanetkar, and Doyle L. Weiss (1992), "Estimation Procedures for MCI and MNL Models: A Comparison of Reduced Forms," working paper, University of Toronto.

—— and Doyle L. Weiss (1974), "An Analysis of Competitive Market Behavior," *Journal of Marketing Research*, 11 (May), 151-55.

—— and —— (1977), "Cumulative Advertising Effects: The Role of Serial Correlation," *Decision Sciences*, 6, 471-81.

Hruschka, Harald (1993), "Determining Market Response Functions by Neural Network Modeling: A Comparison of Econometric Techniques," *European Journal of Operational Research*, 66, 27-35.

—— and Martin Natter (1996), "Specification and Estimation of Nonlinear Models with Dynamic Reference Prices," in S. Jorgensen & G. Zaccour, eds., *Proceedings of the International Workshop on Dynamic Competitive Analysis in Marketing*. Berlin: Springer.

Hunter, John E. and Frank L. Schmidt (1990), *Methods of Meta Analysis*. Newbury Park, CA: Sage.

Hylleberg, Svend (1986), *Seasonality in Regression*. Orlando, FL: Academic Press.

Imhof, J. P. (1961), "Computing the Distribution of Quadratic Forms in Normal Variables," *Biometrika*, 48, 419-26.

Ingene, Charles A. and Mark E. Perry (1995), "A Note on Multi-regional Marketing," *Management Science*, 41 (July), 1194-201.

Inman, J. Jeffrey and Lee McAlister (1994), "Do Coupon Expiration Dates Affect Consumer Behavior?" *Journal of Marketing Research*, 31:3 (August), 423-28.

Inmon, W. H., John A. Zachman and Jonathon G. Geiger (1997), *Data Stores, Data Warehousing and the Zachman Framework: Managing Enterprise Knowledge*. New York: McGraw-Hill.

Jacobson, Robert and David Aaker (1993), "Composite Dependent Variables and the Market Share Effect," *Marketing Science*, 12:2 (Spring), 209-12.

———— and Franco M. Nicosia (1981), "Advertising and Public Policy: The Macroeconomic Effects of Advertising," *Journal of Marketing Research*, 18 (February), 29-38.

Jagpal, Harsharanjeet S. (1981), "Measuring Joint Advertising Effects in Multiproduct Firms," *Journal of Advertising Research*, 21:1, 65-69.

———— (1982), "Multicollinearity in Structural Equation Models with Unobservable Variables," *Journal of Marketing Research*, 19 (November), 431-39.

———— and Balwin S. Hui (1980), "Measuring the Advertising-Sales Relationship: A Multivariate Time-Series Approach," in *Current Issues and Research in Advertising.* Ann Arbor, MI: Division of Research, Graduate School of Business, 211-28.

————, Ephraim F. Sudit, and Hrishikesh D. Vinod (1979), "A Model of Sales Response to Advertising Interactions," *Journal of Advertising Research*, 19 (June), 41-47.

————, ————, and ———— (1982), "Measuring Dynamic Maketing Mix Interactions Using Translog Functions," *Journal of Business*, 55 (July), 401-15.

Jain, Arun K. and Vijay Mahajan (1979), "Evaluating the Competitive Environment in Retailing Using Multiplicative Competitive Interactive Model," in *Research in Marketing*, 2, Jagdish N. Sheth, ed. Greenwich, CT: JAI Press, 217-57.

Jain, Dipak C. and Ram C. Rao (1990), "Effect of Price on the Demand for Durables: Modeling, Estimation and Findings," *Journal of Business & Economic Statistics*, 8:2 (April), 163-70.

———— and Naufel J. Vilcassim (1991), "Investigating Household Purchase Timing Decisions: A Conditional Hazard Function Approach," *Marketing Science*, 10, 1-23.

————, ————, and Pradeep K. Chintagunta (1994), "A Random-Coefficient Logit Brand Choice Model Applied to Panel Data," *Journal of Business & Economic Statistics*, 12:3 (July), 317-28.

Jarvenpaa, Sirkka and Blake Ives (1991), "Executive Involvement and Participation in the Management of Information Technology," *MIS Quarterly*, 15 (June), 205-227.

Jastram, Roy W. (1955), "A Treatment of Distributed Lags in the Theory of Advertising Expenditures," *Journal of Marketing*, 20 (July), 36-46.

Jedidi, Kamel, Jehoshua Eliashberg, and Wayne DeSarbo (1989), "Optimal Advertising and Pricing for a Three-Stage Time-Lagged Monopolistic Diffusion Model Incorporating Income," *Optimal Control Applications & Methods*, 10 (October-December), 313-31.

————, Carl F. Mela, and Sunil Gupta (1999), "Managing Advertising and Promotion for Long-Run Productivity," *Marketing Science*, 18:1, 1-22.

Jeuland, Abel P. and Robert J. Dolan (1982), "An Aspect of New Product Planning: Dynamic Pricing," in *Marketing Planning Models,* Adris A. Zoltners, ed. Amsterdam: North-Holland, 1-21.

Jex, Colin F. (1985), "Short Term Modelling of Advertising Effectiveness: A Confirmation of Broadbent's Model," *Journal of the Market Research Society*, 27:4 (October), 293-97.

———— (1990), "Sequential Estimation of a Time Dependent Advertising Effectiveness Model," *European Journal of Operational Research*, 48:3 (October), 318-331.

———— (1994), "Recursive Estimation as an Aid to Exploratory Data Analysis: An Application to Market Share Models," *International Journal of Forecasting*, 10:3 (November), 445-53.

Johansen, Soren. (1988), "Statistical Analysis of Cointegration Vectors," *Journal of Economic Dynamics and Control*, 12, 231-254.

———— and Katarina Juselius (1990), "Maximum Likelihood Estimation and Inference on Cointegration—With Applications to the Demand for Money," *Oxford Bulletin of Economics and Statistics*, 52:2, 169-210.

Johansson, Johny K. (1973), "A Generalized Logistic Function with an Application to the Effect of Advertising," *Journal of the American Statistical Association,* 68 (December), 824-27.

———— (1974), "Price-Quantity Relationships Varying across Brands and over Time," paper presented at the ORSA/TIMS National Meeting, San Juan, Puerto Rico, October.

———— (1979), "Advertising and the *S*-Curve: A New Approach," *Journal of Marketing Research,* 16 (August), 346-54.

Johnson, J.A., E.H. Oksanen, M.R. Veall and D.Fretz (1992), "Short-Run and Long-Run Elasticities for Canadian Consumption of Alcoholic Beverages: An Error-Correction Mechanism/Cointegration Approach," *The Review of Economics and Statistics,* 74, 64-74.

Johnson, L.W. (1985), "Alternative Econometric Estimates of the Effect of Advertising on the Demand For Alcohol in the U.K.," *International Journal of Advertising,* 4, 19-25.

Johnston, Jack and John DiNardo (1997), *Econometric Methods,* 4th Edition. New York: McGraw-Hill.

Jonas, Kerry (1997), "European Advertising Monitors," *Admap,* 32:2 (February), 10-11.

Jones, Eugene and Ronald W, Ward (1989), "Effectiveness of Generic and Brand Advertising on Fresh and Processed Potato Products," *Agribusiness,* 5:5, 523-36.

Jones, John P. (1984), "Universal Diminishing Returns: True or False? *International Journal of Advertising,* 3 (1), 27-41.

———— (1989), *Does It Pay to Advertise? Cases Illustrating Successful Brand Advertising.* New York: Lexington Books.

———— (1990), "Ad Spending: Maintaining Market Share," *Harvard Business Review,* (January-February), 38-42.

———— (1992), *How Much is Enough? Getting the Most for Your Advertising Dollar.* New York: Lexington Books.

———— (1995a), "Single-Source Research Begins to Fulfill Its Promise," *Journal of Advertising Research,* 35 (May/June), 9-16.

———— (1995b), *When Ads Work: New Proof that Advertising Triggers Sales.* New York: Lexington Books.

Judge, George G., William E. Griffiths, R. Carter Hill, Helmut Lutkepohl, and Tsoung Chao Lee (1985), *The Theory and Practice of Econometrics,* 2nd Edition. New York: John Wiley.

Jung, C. and B. Seldon (1995), "The Macroeconomic Relationship between Advertising and Consumption," *Southern Economic Journal,* 61, 577-87.

Kadiyali, Vrinda, Naufel J. Vilcassim, and Pradeep K. Chintagunta (1996), "Empirical Analysis of Competitive Product Line Pricing Decisions," *Journal of Business,* 69:4 (October), 459-87.

Kaiser, Henry M., Donald J. Liu, Timothy D. Mount, and Olan D. Forker (1992*),* "Impacts of Dairy Promotion from Consumer Demand to Farm Supply" in *Commodity Advertising and Promotion,* Henry Kinnucan, Stanley R. Thompson, and Hui-Shung Chang, eds. Ames, IA: Iowa State University Press, 40-57.

Kalwani, Manohar U. and Chi Kin Yim (1992), "Consumer Price and Promotion Expectations: An Experimental Study," *Journal of Marketing Research,* 29:1 (February), 90-100.

————, ————, Heikki J.Rinne, and Yoshi Sugita (1990), "A Price Expectations Model of Customer Brand Choice," *Journal of Marketing Research,* 27:3 (August), 251-62.

Kalyanam, Kirthi (1996), "Pricing Decisions Under Demand Uncertainty: A Bayesian Mixture Model Approach," *Marketing Science,* 15:3, 207-21.

———— and Thomas S. Shively (1998), "Estimating Irregular Price Effects: A Stochastic Spline Regression Approach," *Journal of Marketing Research,* 35:1 (February), 16-29.

Kalyanaram, G. and Rusell S. Winer (1995), "Empirical Generalizations from Reference Price Research," *Marketing Science,* 14:3, G161-69.

Kamakura, Wagner A. and Gary J. Russell (1989), "A Probabilistic Choice Model for Market Segmentation and Elasticity Structure," *Journal of Marketing Research*, 26:4 (November), 379-90.

Kamien, Morton I. and Nancy L. Schwartz (1991), *Dynamic Optimization: The Calculus of Variations and Optimal Control in Economics and Management*. Advanced Textbooks in Economics. 31. Amsterdam: North-Holland.

Kanetkar, Vinay, Charles B. Weinberg, and Doyle L. Weiss (1986a), "Recovering Microparameters from Aggregate Data for the Koyck and Brand Loyal Models," *Journal of Marketing Research*, 23 (August), 298-304.

———, ———, and ——— (1986b), "Estimating Parameters of the Autocorrelated Current Effects Model from Temporally Aggregated Data," *Journal of Marketing Research*, 23 (November), 379-86.

———, ———, and ——— (1992), "Price Sensitivity and Television Advertising Exposures: Some Empirical Findings," *Marketing Science*, 11:4 (Fall), 359-371.

Kapoor, S. G., P. Madhok and A. M. Wu (1981), "Modeling and Forecasting Sales Data by Time Series Analysis," *Journal of Marketing Research*, 18, 94-100.

Karnani, Aneel (1985), "Strategic Implications of Market Share Attraction Models," *Management Science*, 31 (May), 536-47.

Katahira, Hotaka and Shigeru Yagi (1994), "Marketing Information Technologies in Japan" in *The Marketing Information Revolution*. Robert C. Blattberg, Rashi Glazer, and John D. C. Little, eds. Boston: Harvard Business School Press, 306-27.

Kaul, Anil and Dick R. Wittink (1995), "Empirical Generalizations About the Impact of Advertising on Price Sensitivity and Price," *Marketing Science*, 14:3 (Part 2 of 2), G151-60.

Kendall, Maurice and Alan Stuart (1973), *The Advanced Theory of Statistics*. New York: Hafner.

Kendall, Nick, ed. (1999), *Advertising Works 10*, Henley-on-Thames, United Kingdom: NTC Publications.

Kennedy, John R. (1970), "The Effect of Display Location on the Sales and Pilferage of Cigarettes," *Journal of Marketing Research*, 7 (May), 210-15.

Kennedy, Peter (1983), "Logarithmic Dependent Variables and Prediction Bias," *Oxford Bulletin of Economics & Statistics*, 45, 4 (November), 384-92.

——— (1998), *A Guide to Econometrics*, 4th Edition. Cambridge, MA: The MIT Press.

Kim, Byung-Do (1995), "Incorporating Heterogeneity with Store-Level Aggregate Data," *Marketing Letters*, 6:2 (April), 158-69.

Kimball, George E. (1957), "Some Industrial Applications of Military Operations Research Methods," *Operations Research*, 5 (April), 201-4.

Kinnucan, Henry (1987), "Effect of Canadian Advertising on Milk Demand: The Case of the Buffalo, New York Market," *Canadian Journal of Agricultural Economics*, 35 (March), 181-96.

——— and Deborah Fearon (1986), "Effects of Generic and Brand Advertising of Cheese in New York City with Implications for Allocation of Funds," *North Central Journal of Agricultural Economics*, 8:1 (January), 93-107.

——— and Olan D. Forker (1986), "Seasonality in Consumer Response to Milk Advertising with Implications for Milk Promotion Policy," *American Journal of Agricultural Economics*, 68:3 (August), 563-71.

——— and ——— (1988), "Allocation of Generic Advertising Funds Among Products: A Sales Maximization Approach," *Northeastern Journal of Agricultural and Resource Economics*, 17:1, 64-71.

———, Stanley R. Thompson, and Hui-Shung Chang, eds. (1992), *Commodity Advertising and Promotion*. Ames, IA: Iowa State University Press.

———— and Meenakshi Venkateswaran (1990), "Effects of Generic Advertising on Perceptions and Behavior: The Case of Catfish," *Southern Journal of Agricultural Economics*, (December), 137-51.

———— and ———— (1994), "Generic Advertising and Structural Heterogeneity Hypothesis," *Canadian Journal of Agricultural Economics*, 42:3, 381-96.

Klapper, Daniel and Helmut Herwartz (2000), "Forecasting Market Share Using Predicted Values of Competitive Behavior," *International Journal of Forecasting*, 16:3 (July-September), 399-421.

Kleinbaum, Robert M. (1988), *Multivariate Time Series Forecasts of Market Share*, Marketing Science Institute Report No. 88-102, April.

Koehler, Gary J. and Albert R. Wildt (1981), "Specification and Estimation of Logically Consistent Linear Models," *Decision Sciences*, 12, 1-31.

Koerts, J. and A.P.J. Abrahamse (1969), *On the Theory and Application of the General Linear Model*. Rotterdam: Rotterdam University Press.

Kohn, Meir G. and Yakir Plessner (1973), "An Applicable Model of Optimal Marketing Policy," *Operations Research*, 21 (March-April), 401-12.

Kondo, Fumiyo N. and Genshiro Kitagawa (2000), "Time Series Analysis of Daily Scanner Sales: Extraction of Trend, Day-of-Week Effect, and Price Promotion Effect," *Marketing Intelligence & Planning*, 18:2, 53-66.

Kopalle, Praveen K., Carl F. Mela, and Lawrence Marsh (1999), "The Dynamic Effects of Discounting on Sales: Empirical Analysis and Normative Pricing Implications," *Marketing Science*, 18:3, 317-32.

Kotler, Philip (1971), *Marketing Decision Making: A Model-Building Approach*. New York: Holt, Rinehart, and Winston.

———— and Randall L. Schultz (1970), "Marketing Simulations: Review and Prospects," *Journal of Business*, 43 (July), 237-95.

Kotzan, Jeffrey A. and Robert V. Evanson (1969), "Responsiveness of Drug Store Sales to Shelf Space Allocation, *Journal of Marketing Research*, 6 (November), 465-69.

Koyck, L. M. (1954), *Distributed Lags and Investment Analysis*. Amsterdam: North-Holland.

Krishna, Aradhna and Z. John Zhang (1999), "Short- or Long Duration Coupons: The Effect of Expiration Date on the Profitability of Coupon Promotions," *Management Science*, 45:8 (August), 1041-56.

Krishnamurthi, Lakshman, Jack Narayan, and S. P. Raj (1986), "Intervention Analysis of a Field Experiment to Assess the Buildup Effect of Advertising," *Journal of Marketing Research*, 23 (November), 337-45.

———— and S. P. Raj (1985), "The Effect of Advertising on Consumer Price Sensitivity," *Journal of Marketing Research*, 22 (May), 119-29.

———— and Arvind Rangaswamy (1987), "The Equity Estimator for Marketing Research," *Marketing Science*, 6 (Fall), 336-57.

———— and ———— (1994), "Statistical Properties of the Equity Estimator," *Journal of Business & Economic Statistics*, 12:2 (April), 149-53.

————, S. P. Raj, and Raja Selvam (1988), "Statistical and Managerial Issues in Cross-Sectional Aggregation," working paper, J. L. Kellogg Graduate School of Management, Northwestern University, August.

Kristensen, Kai (1984), "Hedonic Theory, Marketing Research, and the Analysis of Complex Goods," *International Journal of Research in Marketing*, 1:1, 17-36.

Kuehn, Alfred A. (1961), "A Model for Budgeting Advertising," in *Mathematical Models and Methods in Marketing*, Frank M. Bass et al., eds. Homewood, IL: Richard D. Irwin, 315-48.

———— (1962), "How Advertising Performance Depends on Other Marketing Factors," *Journal of Advertising Research*, (March), 2-10.

————, Timothy W. McGuire, and Doyle L. Weiss (1966), "Measuring the Effectiveness of Advertising," in *Proceedings*, R. M. Haas, ed. Chicago: American Marketing Association, 185-94.

———— and Doyle L. Weiss (1965), "Marketing Analysis Training Exercise," *Behavioral Science*, 10 (January), 51-67.

Kumar, V. (1994), "Forecasting of Market Share Models: An Assessment, Additional Insights, and Guidelines," *International Journal of Forecasting*, 10:2 (September), 294-312.

———— and T.B. Heath (1990), "A Comparative Study of Market Share Models Using Disaggregate Data," *International Journal of Forecasting*, 6, 163-74.

———— and Robert P. Leone (1988), "Measuring the Effect of Retail Store Promotions on Brand and Store Substitution," *Journal of Marketing Research*, 25:2 (May), 178-185.

Kvålseth, Tarald O. (1985), "Cautionary Note about R^2," *The American Statistician*, 39 (November), 279-85.

Kwiatkowski, D., P. Phillips, P. Schmidt and Y. Shin (1992), "Testing the Null Hypothesis of Stationarity against the Alternative of a Unit Root," *Journal of Econometrics*, 54, 159-78.

Lal, Rajiv and V. Padmanabhan (1995), "Competitive Response and Equilibria," *Marketing Science*, 14:3 (Part 2 of 2), G101-08.

———— and Richard Staelin (1986), "Salesforce Compensation Plans in Environments with Asymmetric Information," *Marketing Science*, 5 (Summer), 179-98.

Lam, Shunyin, Mark Vandenbosch, and Michael Pierce (1998), "Retail Sales Force Scheduling Based on Store Traffic Forecasting," *Journal or Retailing*, 74:1 (Spring), 61-88.

Lambert, Zarrel V. (1968), *Setting the Size of the Sales Force*. State College, PA: Pennsylvania State University Press.

Lambin, Jean-Jacques (1969), "Measuring the Profitability of Advertising: An Empirical Study," *Journal of Industrial Economics*, 17 (April), 86-103.

———— (1970a), "Advertising and Competitive Behavior: A Case Study," *Applied Economics*, 2 (January), 231-51.

———— (1970b), "Optimal Allocation of Competitive Marketing Efforts: An Empirical Study," *Journal of Business*, 17 (October), 468-84.

———— (1972a), "A Computer On-Line Marketing Mix Model," *Journal of Marketing Research*, 9 (May), 119-126.

———— (1972b), "Is Gasoline Advertising Justified?" *Journal of Business*, 45 (October), 585-619.

———— (1976), *Advertising, Competition, and Market Conduct in Oligopoly over Time*. Amsterdam: North-Holland.

————, Philippe A. Naert, and Alain Bultez (1975), "Optimal Marketing Behavior in Oligopoly," *European Economic Review*, 6, 105-28.

———— and Robert Peeters (1982), *Anticipating Dynamic Market Response to Brand Advertising: The Case of Automobile Advertising in Belgium*, CESAM, Louvain-laNeuve, Belgium, December.

Lancaster, Kent M. (1984), "Brand Advertising Competition and Industry Demand," *Journal of Advertising*, 13 (4), 19-24.

Lattin, James M. and Randolph E. Bucklin (1989), "Reference Effects on Price and Promotion on Brand Choice," *Journal of Marketing Research*, 26:3 (August), 299-310.

Lawrence, Kenneth, Michael Guerts, and I. Robert Parket (1990), "Forecasting Market Share Using a Combination of Time Series Data and Explanatory Variables: A Tutorial," *Journal of Statistical Computation and Simulation*, 36, 247-53.

Lawrence, Michael and Graham Low (1993), "Exploring Individual User Satisfaction Within User-Led Development," *MIS Quarterly*, 17 (June), 195-208.

Lee, H. S. (1994), "Maximum-Likelihood Inference on Cointegration and Seasonal Cointegration," *Journal of Econometrics*, 54, 1-47.

Lee, Jonq-Ying (1984), "Demand Interrelationships Among Fruit Beverages," *Southern Journal of Agricultural Economics*, (December), 135-43.

——— and Mark G. Brown (1985), "Coupon Redemption and the Demand for Concentrated Orange Juice: A Switching Regression," *American Journal of Agricultural Economics*, 67, 647-53.

——— and ——— (1992), "Lag Structures in Commodity Advertising Research," *Agribusiness*, 8:2, 143-54.

Leeflang, Peter S. H. (1977), "A Comparison of Alternative Specifications of Market Share Models," in *Modeling for Government and Business*, C. A. van Bochove, ed. Leiden: Martinus Nijhoff, 247-81.

——— (1997), "Vertical Competition," Paper presented at the EMAC Conference, Warwick, May.

———, Karel Jan Alsem, and Jan C. Reuyl (1991), "Diagnosing Competition for Public Policy Purposes," working paper no. 207, Marketing Studies Center, John Anderson Graduate School of Management, UCLA.

——— and Jacob J. van Duyn (1982a), "The Use of Regional Data in Marketing Models: The Demand for Beer in the Netherlands, Part 1: Regional Models," *European Research*, 10, 2-9.

——— and ——— (1982b), "The Use of Regional Data in Marketing Models: The Demand for Beer in the Netherlands, Part 2: Pooling Regional Data," *European Research*, 10, 64-71.

———, Gregory M. Mijatovic, and John Saunders (1992), "Identification and Estimation of Complex Multivariate Lag Structures: A Nesting Approach," *Applied Economics*, 24, 273-83.

——— and Alex J. Olivier (1985), "Bias in Consumer Panel and Store Audit Data," *International Journal of Research in Marketing*, 2:1, 27-41.

——— and F. W. Platt (1984a), "Linear Structural Relation Market Share Models," European Marketing Academy Conference (EMAC), Nijrode, The Netherlands, April.

——— and ——— (1984b), "Consumer Response in an Era of Stagflation: Preliminary Results," in *Advances in Marketing Research in Theory and Practice*. (EMAC/ ESOMAR Symposium, Copenhagen, October), 195-227.

——— and Jan C. Reuyl (1984), "on the Predictive Power of Market Share Attraction Models," *Journal of Marketing Research*, 21 (May), 211-15.

——— and ——— (1985a), "Competitive Analysis Using Market Response Functions," *Proceedings*. Chicago: American Marketing Association, 388-95.

——— and ——— (1985b), "Advertising and Industry Sales: An Empirical Study of the West German Cigarette Market," *Journal of Marketing*, 49 (Fall), 92-98.

——— and ——— (1986), "Estimating the Parameters of Market Share Models at Different Levels of Aggregation with Examples from the West German Cigarette Market," *European Journal of Operational Research*, 23, 14-24.

——— and Dick R. Wittink (1992), "Diagnosing Competitive Reactions Using (Aggregated) Scanner Data," *International Journal of Research in Marketing*, 9:1 (March), 39-57.

——— and ——— (1996a), " Competitive versus Consumer Response: Do Managers Overreact?," *International Journal of Research in Marketing*, 13:2 (April), 103-19.

——— and ——— (1996b), " Explaining Competitive Reaction Effects," working paper, Department of Economics, University of Groningen.

———, ———, Michel Wedel, and Philippe A. Naert (2000), *Building Models for Marketing Decisions*. Boston: Kluwer.

BIBLIOGRAPHY

Lenk, Peter J. and Ambar G. Rao (1990), "New Models from Old: Forecasting Product Adoption by Hierarchical Bayes Procedures," *Marketing Science*, 9:1 (Winter), 42-53.

Leone, Robert P. (1983), "Modeling Sales-Advertising Relationships: An Integrated Time Series-Econometric Approach," *Journal of Marketing Research*, 20 (August), 291-95.

———— (1987), "Forecasting the Effect of an Environmental Change on Market Performance: An Intervention Time-Series Approach," *International Journal of Forecasting*, 3, 463-78.

———— (1995), "Generalizing What Is Known of Temporal Aggregation and Advertising Carryover," *Marketing Science*, 14:3 (Part 2 of 2), G141-50.

———— and Randall L. Schultz (1980), "A Study of Marketing Generalizations," *Journal of Marketing*, 44 (Winter), 101-18.

———— and Srini S. Srinivasan (1996), "Coupon Face Value: Its Impact on Coupon Redemptions, Brand Sales, and Brand Profitability," *Journal of Retailing*, 72:3 (Fall), 273-89.

Lepak, Greg M. and John J. Considine (1994), "Measuring the Effects of Marketing Changes in Transit Systems Using Multiple Time Series Modeling," *Journal of Nonprofit & Public Sector Marketing*, 2:1, 61-73.

Levy, Haim and Julian L. Simon (1989), "A Generalization That Makes Useful the Dorfman-Steiner Theorem with Respect to Advertising," *Managerial and Decision Economics*, 10:1 (March 1989), 85-87.

Lilien, Gary L. (1979), "ADVISOR 2: Modeling Marketing Mix Decisions for Industrial Products," *Management Science*, 25 (February), 191-204.

————, Philip Kotler, and K. Sridhar Moorthy (1992), *Marketing Models*. Englewood Cliffs, NJ: Prentice-Hall.

———— and Arvind Rangaswamy (1998), *Marketing Engineering*. Reading, MA: Addison-Wesley.

———— and Ambar G. Rao (1976), "A Model for Allocating Retail Outlet Building Resources Across Market Areas," *Operations Research*, 24 (January-February), 1-14.

———— and A. Api Ruzdic (1982), "Analyzing Natural Experiments in Industrial Markets," in *Marketing Planning Models*, Andris A. Zoltners, ed. New York: North-Holland, 241-69.

———— and Eunsang Yoon (1988), "An Exploratory Analysis of the Dynamic Behavior of Price Elasticity over the Product Life Cycle: An Empirical Analysis of Industrial Chemical Products," in *Issues in Pricing*, Timothy M. Devinney, ed. Lexington, MA: Lexington Books, 261-87.

Lim, Joa Sang and Marcus O'Connor (1996), "Judgmental Forecasting with Time Series and Causal Information," *International Journal of Forecasting*, 12 (March), 139-53.

Lindley, David V. and Adrian F.M. Smith (1972), "Bayes Estimates for the Linear Model," *Journal of the Royal Statistical Society*, Series B, 34, 1-41.

Link, Ross (1995a), "Marketing Mix Model Validation," American Marketing Association's Behavioral Research Conference, Scottsdale, AZ, January.

———— (1995b), "Are Aggregate Scanner Data Models Biased?" *Journal of Advertising Research*, 35:5 (September/October), RC-8-12.

———— (1996), "Modeling Seasonality," E-mail to AMODLMKT list, February 14.

———— (1999), "RE: Weekly Sales Forecasting and Aggregation," E-mail to AMODLMKT list, August 26.

Litterman, Robert B. (1984), "Forecasting and Policy Analysis with Bayesian Vector Autoregression Models," *Federal Reserve Bank of Minneapolis Quarterly Review*, 8 (Fall), 30-41.

Little, John D. C. (1966), "A Model of Adaptive Control of Promotional Spending," *Operations Research*, 14 (November-December), 1975-97.

———— (1970), "Models and Managers: The Concept of a Decision Calculus," *Management Science*, 16 (April), 466-85.

———— (1975a), "BRANDAID: A Marketing-Mix Model, Part 1: Structure," *Operations Research,* 23 (July-August), 628-55.

———— (1975b),"BRANDAID: A Marketing-Mix Model, Part 2: Implementation, Calibration, and Case Study," *Operations Research,* 23 (July-August), 656-73.

———— (1979a), "Aggregate Advertising Models: The State of the Art," *Operations Research,* 27 (July-August), 629-67.

———— (1979b), "Decision Support Systems for Marketing Managers," *Journal of Marketing,* 43 (Summer), 9-26.

———— (1994), "Modeling Market Response in Large Customer Panels" in *The Marketing Information Revolution.* Robert C. Blattberg, Rashi Glazer, and John D. C. Little, eds. Boston: Harvard Business School Press, 173-203.

———— (1998), "Aggregate Measures for Merchandising and Distribution," *International Journal of Research in Marketing,* 15:5 (December), 473-85.

———— and Leonard M. Lodish (1981), "Commentary on 'Judgment-Based Marketing Decision Models,'" *Journal of Marketing,* 45 (Fall), 24-29.

Little, Roderick J. A. (1992), "Regression with Missing X's: A Review," *Journal of the American Statistical Association,* 87:420 (December), 1227-37.

Liu, Donald J. and Olan D. Forker (1988), "Generic Fluid Milk Advertising, Demand Expansion, and Supply Response: The Case of New York City," *American Journal of Agricultural Economics,* 70:2 (May), 229-36.

———— and ———— (1990), "Optimal Control of Generic Fluid Milk Advertising Expenditures," *American Journal of Agricultural Economics,* 72:4 (November), 1047-55.

————, Harry M. Kaiser, Olan D. Forker, and Timothy D. Mount (1990), "An Economic Analysis of the U.S. Generic Advertising Program Using an Industry Model," *Northeastern Journal of Agricultural and Resource Economiccs,* 19:1 (April), 37-48.

Liu, Lon-Mu and Dominique M. Hanssens (1981), "A Bayesian Approach to Time-Varying Cross-Sectional Models," *Journal of Econometrics,* 15 (April), 341-56.

———— and ———— (1982), ''Identification of Multiple-Input Transfer Function Models," *Communication in Statistics Theory and Methods,* 11:3, 297-314.

Ljung, G. M. and George E. P. Box (1978), "On a Measure of Lack of Fit in Time Series Models," *Biometrika,* 65:2, 297-303.

Lodish, Leonard M. (1976), "Assigning Salesmen to Accounts to Maximize Profits,'' *Journal of Marketing Research,* 13 (November), 440-44.

———— (1981), "Experience with Decision-Calculus Models and Decision Support Systems," in *Marketing Decision Models,* Randall L. Schultz and Andris A. Zoltners, eds. New York: Elsevier North-Holland, 99-122.

————, Magid M. Abraham, Jeanne Livelsberger, Beth Lubetkin, Bruce Richardson, and Mary Ellen Stevens (1995), "A Summary of Fifty-Five In-Market Experimental Estimates of the Long-Term Effect of TV Advertising," *Marketing Science,* 14:3 (Part 2 of 2), G133-40.

Longman, Marc and Wifried Pauwels (1998), "Analysis of Marketing Mix Interaction Effects and Interdepencies: A Normative Approach," *Managerial and Decision Economics,* 19:6 (September), 343-53.

Lucas, Jr., Henry C., Michael J. Ginzberg, and Randall L. Schultz (1990), *Information Systems Implementation: Testing a Structural Model.* Norwood: NJ: Ablex.

Lütkepohl, Helmut (1982), "Non-Causality Due to Omitted Variables," *Journal of Econometrics,* 19, 367-78.

———— and H.-E. Reimers (1992), "Impulse-Response Analysis of Cointegrated Systems," *Journal of Economic Dynamics and Control,* 16, 53-78.

Lynch, J. E. and G. J. Hooley (1990), "Increasing Sophistication in Advertising Budget Setting," *Journal of Advertising Research,* 30 (February), 67-75.

Lynch, Michael (1974), "Comment on Curhan's 'The Relationship Between Shelf Space and Unit Sales in Supermarkets,'" *Journal of Marketing Research*, 11 (May), 218-20.

Lyon, Charles C. and Gary D. Thompson (1993), "Temporal and Spatial Aggregation: Alternative Marketing Margin Models," *American Journal of Aggricultural Economics*, 75:3 (August), 523-36.

Maddala, G. S. (1992), *Introduction to Econometrics*, 2nd Edition. Englewood Cliffs, NJ: Prentice-Hall.

Magat, Wesley A., John M. McCann, and Richard C. Morey (1986), "When Does Lag Structure Really Matter in Ooptimizing Advertising Expenditures?" *Management Science*, 32 (February), 182-93.

———, ———, and ———(1988), "Reply to 'When Does Lag Structure Really Matter ... Indeed?'" *Management Science*, 34 (July), 917-18.

Mahajan, Vijay, Stuart I. Bretsehneider, and John W. Bradford (1980), "Feedback Approaches to Modeling Structural Shifts in Market Response," *Journal of Marketing*, 44 (Winter), 71-80.

———, Arun K. Jain, and Miehel Bergier (1977), "Parameter Estimation in Marketing Models in the Presence of Multicollinearity," *Journal of Marketing Research*, 14 (November), 586-91.

——— and Eitan Muller (1986), "Advertising Pulsing Policies for Generating Awareness for New Products," *Marketing Science*, 5 (Spring), 89-106.

———, Subhash Sharma, and Yoram Wind (1984), "Parameter Estimation in Marketing Models in the Presence of Influential Response Data: Robust Regression and Applications," *Journal of Marketing Research*, 21 (August), 268-77.

Mandese, Joe (1993), "Data from 4A's Reveal 4% Error in TV Ad Counts," *Advertising Age*, (December 13).

Mann, Don H. (1975), "Optimal Advertising Stock Models: A Generalization Incorporating the Effects of Delayed Response to Promotion Expenditures," *Management Science*, 21 (March), 823-32.

Mantrala, Murali K., Prabhakant Sinha, and Andris A. Zoltners (1992), "Impact of Resource Allocation Rules on Marketing Investment-Level Decisions and Profitability," *Journal of Marketing Research*, 29:2 (May), 162-75.

Maravall, Augustin (1981), "A Note on Identification of Multivariate Time-Series Models," *Journal of Econometrics*, 16 (June), 237-47.

Markus, M. Lynne and Daniel Robey (1983), "The Organizational Validity of Information Systems," *Human Relations*, 36:3, 203-26.

Mason, Charlotte H. and William D. Perreault, Jr. (1991), "Collinearity, Power, and Interpretation of Multiple Regression Analysis," *Journal of Marketing Research*, 28 (August), 268-80.

Massy, William F. and Ronald E. Frank (1965), "Short-Term Price and Dealing Effects in Selected Market Segments," *Journal of Marketing Research*, 2 (May), 171-85.

Matthews, Brian P. and A. Diamantopoulas (1990), "Judgmental Revision of Sales Forecasts: Effectiveness of Forecast Selection," *Journal of Forecasting*, 9 (July-September), 407-15.

Mayhew, Glenn E. and Russell S. Winer (1992), "An Empirical Analysis of Internal and External Reference Prices Using Scanner Data," *Journal of Consumer Research*, 19:1 (June), 62-70.

McCann, John M. (1974), "Market Response to the Marketing Decision Variables," *Journal of Marketing Research*, 11 (November), 399-412.

McDonald, Colin (1997), "Short-Term Advertising Effects: How Confident Can We Be?" *Admap*, 32:6 (June), 36-39.

McGuiness, Tony and Keith Cowling (1975), "Advertising and the Aggregate Demand for Cigarettes," *European Economic Review*, 6:3, 311-28.

McGuire, Timothy W., John U. Farley, Robert E. Lucas, and Winston J. Ring (1968), "Estimation and Inferences for Linear Models in Which Subsets of Dependent Variables Are Constrained," *Journal of the American Statistical Association,* 63 (December), 1201-13.

—— and Richard Staelin (1983), "An Industry Equilibrium Analysis of Downstream Vertical Integration," *Marketing Science,* 2 (Spring), 161-90.

—— and Doyle L. Weiss (1976), "Logically Consistent Market Share Models II," *Journal of Marketing Research,* 13 (August), 296-302.

——, ——, and Frank S. Houston (1977), "Consistent Multiplicative Market Share Models," in *Proceedings,* Barnett A. Greenberg and Danny N. Bellinger, eds., Chicago: American Marketing Association, 129-34.

McIntyre, Shelby H. (1982), "The Impact of Judgment-Based Marketing Models," *Management Science,* 28 (January), 17-33.

——, David B. Montgomery, V. Srinivasan, and Barton A. Weitz (1983), "Evaluating the Statistical Significance of Models Developed by Stepwise Regression," *Journal of Marketing Research,* 20 (February), 1-11.

McMaster, Derek (1987), "Own Brands and the Cookware Market," *European Journal of Marketing,* 1:21, 83-84.

McWilliams, G. (1995), "At Compaq, a Desktop Crystal Ball," *Business Week,* 20 (March), 96.

Meade, William K. (1994), "Critical Issues in Baseline Interpretation," Advertising Research Foundation Annual Workshop on Scanner Research, New York: March.

Meissner, F. (1961), "Sales and Advertising of Lettuce," *Journal of Advertising Research,* 1 (March), 1-l0.

Mela, Carl F., Sunil Gupta and Donald R. Lehmann (1997), "The Long-Term Impact of Promotion and Advertising on Consumer Brand Choice," *Journal of Marketing Research,* 34:2 (May), 248-61.

—— and Praveen K. Kopalle (1998), "The Impact of Collinearity on Regression: The Asymmetric Effect of Negative and Positive Correlations," working paper, University of Notre Dame, May.

Mentzer, John T. and Carol C. Bienstock (1998), *Sales Forecasting Management.* Thousand Oaks, CA: Sage Publications.

Mercer, Alan (1991), *Implementable Marketing Research,* Englewood Cliffs, NJ: Prentice Hall.

—— (1996), "Non-linear Price Effects," *Journal of the Market Research Society,* 38:3 (July), 227-34.

Metwally, M. M. (1978), "Escalation Tendencies of Advertising," *Oxford Bulletin of Economics and Statistics,* 40 (May), 153-63.

—— (1980), "Sales Response to Advertising of Eight Australian Products," *Journal of Advertising Research,* 20 (October), 59-64.

Mickwitz, Gosta (1959), *Marketing and Competition.* Helsingfors: Centraltrykeriet, 87-89.

Miller, Don M. (1984), "Reducing Transformation Bias in Curve Fitting," *The American Statistician,* 38, 2 (May), 124-26.

Miller, S. E., O. Capps, Jr., and G. J. Wells (1984), "Confidence Intervals for Elasticities and Flexibilities from Linear Equations," *American Journal Agricultural Economics,* 66, 392-6.

Mills, Harland D. (1961), "A Study in Promotional Competition," in *Mathematical Models and Methods in Marketing,* Frank M. Bass et al., eds. Homewood, IL: Richard D. Irwin, 271-301.

Millward Brown International (1995), "Is There a Relationship between Television Awareness and Sales?" *Broader Perspective.*

Mittelhammer, Ron C., George G. Judge, and Douglas J. Miller (2000), *Econometric Foundations*. Cambridge: Cambridge University Press.

Mohler, R. R., ed. (1988), *Nonlinear Time Series and Signal Processing*. Berlin: Springer-Verlag.

Montgomery, Alan L. (1997a), "Creating Micro-Marketing Pricing Strategies Using Supermarket Scanner Data," *Marketing Science*, 16:4, 315-37.

―――― (1997b), "Improving Price Elasticity Estimates Using Economic Theory and Shrinkage," Marketing Science Conference, Berkeley, CA, March 24.

―――― and Peter E. Rossi (1999), "Estimating Price Elasticities with Theory-Based Priors," *Journal of Marketing Research*, 36:4 (November), 413-23.

Montgomery, David B. and Alvin Silk (1972), "Estimating Dynamic Effects of Market Communications Expenditures," *Management Science*, 18, B485-501.

―――― and Glen L. Urban (1970), "Marketing Decision Information Systems: An Emerging View," *Journal of Marketing Research*, 7 (May), 226-34.

―――― and Charles B. Weinberg (1979), "Strategic Intelligence Systems," *Journal of Marketing*, 43 (Fall), 41-53.

Montgomery, Douglas C. and Ginner Weatherby (1980), "Modeling and Forecasting Time Series Using Transfer Function and Intervention Methods," *AIEE Transactions*, (December), 289-307.

Moore, William L. and Edgar A. Pessemier (1992), *Product Planning and Management: Designing and Delivering Value*. New York: McGraw-Hill.

―――― and Russell S. Winer (1987), "A Panel-Data-Based Method for Merging Joint Space and Market Response Function Estimation," *Marketing Science*, 6 (Winter), 25-42.

Moorthy, K. Sridhar (1993), "Competitive Marketing Strategies: Game-Theoretic Models," in *Handbooks in Operations Research and Management Science: Volume 5: Marketing*, Joshua Eliashberg and Gary Lilien, eds. New York: Elsevier, 409-64.

Moran, William T. (1978), "Insights from Pricing Research," in *Pricing Practices and Strategies*, in Earl L. Bailey, ed. New York: The Conference Board, 7-13.

Morey, Richard C. and John M. McCann (1980), "Evaluating and Improving Resource Allocation for Navy Recruiting," *Management Science*, 26 (December), 1198-1210.

―――― and ―――― (1983), "Estimating the Confidence Interval for the optimal Marketing Mix: An Application of Lead Generation," *Marketing Science*, 2 (Spring), 193-202.

Moriarty, Mark M. (1975), "Cross-Sectional, Time-Series Issues in the Analysis of Marketing Decision Variables," *Journal of Marketing Research*, 12 (May), 142-50.

―――― (1983), "Carryover Effects of Advertising on Sales of Durable Goods," *Journal of Business Research*, 11 (March), 127-37.

―――― (1985a), "Transfer Function Analysis of the Relationship Between Advertising and Sales: A Synthesis of Prior Research," *Journal of Business Research*, 13,247-57.

―――― (1985b), "Design Features of Forecasting Systems Involving Management Judgments," *Journal of Marketing Research*, 22 (November), 353-64.

―――― (1985c), "Retail Promotional Effects on Intra- and Interbrand Sales Performance," *Journal of Retailing*, 61 (Fall), 27-48.

―――― and Arthur Adams (1979), "Issues in Sales Territory Modeling and Forecasting Using Box-Jenkins Analysis," *Journal of Marketing Research*, 16 (May), 221-32.

―――― and G. Salamon (1980), "Estimation and Forecasting Performance of a Multivariate Time Series Model of Sales," *Journal of Marketing Research*, 17, 558-64.

Moriguchi, C. (1970), "Aggregation Over Time in Macroeconomic Relations," *International Economic Review*, 11 (October), 427-40.

Morrison, Donald G. and Jorge Silvo-Risso (1995), "A Latent Look at Empirical Generalizations," *Marketing Science*, 14:3 (Part 2 of 2), G61-70.

Morse, Philip M. and George E. Kimball (1951), *Methods of Operations Research*. New York: John Wiley.

Morwitz, Vicki G. and David C. Schmittlein (1998), "Testing New Direct Marketing Offerings: The Interplay of Management Judgment and Statistical Models," *Management Science*, 44 (May), 610-28.

Moschini, Giancarlo (1995), "Units of Measurement and the Stone Index in Demand System Estimation," *American Journal of Agricultural Economics*, 77 (February), 63-8.

Mulhern, Francis J. and Robert J. Caprara (1994), "A Nearest Neighbor Model for Forecasting Market Response," *International Journal of Forecasting*, 10:2 (September), 191-207.

——— and Robert P. Leone (1990), "Retail Promotional Advertising: Do the Number of Deal Items and Size of Deal Discounts Affect Store Performance?" *Journal of Business Research*, 21, 179-94.

——— and ——— (1991), "Implicit Price Bundling of Retail Products: A Multiproduct Approach to Maximizing Store Profitability," *Journal of Marketing*, 55:4 (October), 63-76.

Muller, Robert W., George E. Kline, and Joseph J. Trout (1953), "Customers Buy 22% More When Shelves Are Well Stocked," *Progressive Grocer*, 32 (June), 40-48.

Mundlak, Y. (1961), "Aggregation Over Time in Distributed Lag Models," *International Economic Review*, 2 (May), 154-63.

Murray, Jane (1984), "Retail Demand for Meat in Australia: A Utility Theory Approach," *Economic Record*, 60 (March), 45-56.

Mushkat, Miron (1987), "Improving the Prospects for Plan Acceptance in Public Organizations," *Long Range Planning*, 20 (February), 52-66.

Naert, Philippe A. (1971), "Optimizing Consumer, Intermediary Advertising, and Markup in a Vertical Market Structure," *Management Science*, 18 (December), 90- 101.

——— (1971), "Observations on Applying Marginal Analysis in Marketing: Part I," *Journal of Business Administration*, 4 (Fall), 49-67.

——— (1972), "Observations on Applying Marginal Analysis in Marketing: Part II," *Journal of Business Administration*, 4 (Spring), 3-14.

——— and Alain V. Bultez (1973), "Logically Consistent Market Share Models," *Journal of Marketing Research*, 10 (August), 334-40.

——— and Peter S. H. Leeflang (1978), *Building Implementable Marketing Models*. Leiden: Martinus Nijhoff.

——— and Marcel Weverbergh (1981a), "On the Predictive Power of Market Share Attraction Models," *Journal of Marketing Research*, 18 (May), 146-53.

——— and ——— (1981b), "Subjective Versus Empirical Decision Models," in *Marketing Decision Models*, Randall L. Schultz and Andris A. Zoltners, eds. New York: Elsevier North-Holland, 99-122.

——— and ——— (1985), "Market Share Specification, Estimation, and Validation: Toward Reconciling Seemingly Divergent Views," *Journal of Marketing Research*, 22 (November), 453-67.

Naik, Prasad A. (1999), "Estimating the Half-Life of Advertisements," *Marketing Letters*, 10:3 (November), 351-62.

——— and Chih-Ling Tsai (2000), "Controlling Measurement Errors in Models of Advertising Competition," *Journal of Marketing Research*, 37:1 (February), 113-124.

Nakanishi, Masao (1973), "Advertising and Promotional Effects on Consumer Response to New Products," *Journal of Marketing Research*, 10 (August), 242-49.

——— and Lee G. Cooper (1974), "Parameter Estimation for a Multiplicative Competitive Interaction Model Least Squares Approach," *Journal of Marketing Research*, 11 (August), 303-11.

——— and ——— (1982), "Simplified Estimation Procedures for MCI Models," *Marketing Science,* 1 (Summer), 314-22.

———, ———, and Hal Kassarjian (1974), "Voting for a Political Candidate Under Conditions of Minimal Information," *Journal of Consumer Research,* 1, 314-22.

Narasimhan, Chakravarti (1984), "A Price Discrimination Theory of Coupons," *Marketing Science,* 3 (Spring), 128-47.

———, Scott A. Neslin, and Subrata Sen (1996), "Promotional Elasticities and Category Characteristics," *Journal of Marketing,* 60:2 (April), 17-30.

Narayan, J. and J. Considine (1989), "Assessing the Impact of Fare Increases in a Transit System by Using Intervention Analysis," *Journal of Business Research,* 19, 245-54.

Nelson, Charles R. (1972), "The Prediction Performance of the FRB-MIT-PENN Model of the U.S. Economy," *American Economic Review,* 62, 902- 17.

——— and G. William Schwert (1979), "Tests for Granger/Weiner Causality: A Monte Carlo Investigation," University of Rochester, Graduate School of Management, working paper no. 7905.

——— and H. Kang (1984), "Pitfalls in the Use of Time as an Explanatory Variable in Regression," *Journal of Business and Economic Statistics,* 2, 73-82.

Nelson, Forrest D. (1976), "On a General Computer Algorithm for the Analysis of Models with Limited Dependent Variables," *Annals of Economic and Social Measurement,* 5 (Fall), 493-509.

——— and L. Olson (1978), ''Specification and Estimation of a Simultaneous Equation Model with Limited Dependent Variables," *International Economic Review,* 19, 695-710.

Nerlove, Marc and F. Waugh (1961), "Advertising Without Supply Control: Some Implications for the Study of the Advertising of Oranges," *Journal of Farm Economics,* 43:4 (Part I), 813-37.

Neslin, Scott A. (1990), "A Market Response Model for Coupon Promotions," *Marketing Science,* 9:2 (Spring), 125-45.

——— and Robert W. Shoemaker (1983a), "Using a Natural Experiment to Estimate Price Elasticity: The 1974 Sugar Shortage and the Ready-to-Eat Cereal Market," *Journal of Marketing,* 47 (Winter), 44-57.

——— and ——— (1983b), "A Model for Evaluating the Profitability of Coupon Promotions," *Marketing Science,* 2 (Fall), 389-405.

Newbold, Paul (1974), "The Exact Likelihood Function for a Mixed Autoregressive-Moving Average Process," *Biometrica,* 61:3, 423-26.

Newell, Allen and Herbert A. Simon (1972), *Human Problem Solving.* Englewood Cliffs, NJ: Prentice-Hall.

Nguyen, Dung (1985), "An Analysis of Optimal Advertising Under Uncertainty," *Management Science,* 31 (May), 622-33.

Nielsen Marketing Research (1992), *Category Management.* Lincolnwood, IL: NTC Business Books.

Nijs, Vincent R., Marnik G. Dekimpe, Jan-Benedict E.M. Steenkamp and Dominique M. Hanssens (2001), "The Category Demand Effects of Price Promotions," *Marketing Science,* forthcoming.

Nissen, David H. and Armando M. Lago (1975), "Price Elasticity of the Demand for Parcel Post Mail," *Journal of Industrial Economics,* 23:4 (June), 281-99.

Nguyen, Dung (1997). *Marketing Decisions Under Uncertainty.* Boston: Kluwer.

Nuttall, C. (1965), "The Relationship Between Sales and Distribution of Certain Confectionery Lines," *Commentary,* 7:4, 272-85.

O'Donnell, Jayne (1998), "Survey Swipes at Scanner Pricing," *USA Today,* (December 17), p. 3B.

Ofir, Chezy and Andre Khuri (1986), "Multicollinearity in Marketing Models: Diagnostics and Remedial Measures," *International Journal of Research in Marketing*, 3:3, 181-205.

Ogawa, Kosuke (1996), "Measuring Brand Power by Pricing Experiment," *Chain Store Age (Japan)*, February 15.

———, Shigeru Kido, and Shhigeru Yagi (1996), "Measuring the Short-Term Efffect of TV Advertising on Consumer Purchase Using Scanner Data," INFORMS Marketing Science Conference, University of Florida (March).

O'Herlihy, Callaghan (1988), "A Commercial Perspective on Advertising Modeling as Presented by Dr. Hooley et al.," *Journal of the Market Research Society*, 30:2 (April), 227-31.

Openshaw, S. and P. J. Taylor (1979), "A Million or So Correlation Coefficients: Three Experiments on the Modified Areal Unit Problem," in *Statistical Applications in the Spatial Sciences*, N. Wrigley, ed. London: Pion, 127-44.

Ornstein, Stanley I. and Dominique M. Hanssens (1987), "Resale Price Maintenance: Output Increasing or Restricting? The Case of Retail Liquor Stores," *Journal of Industrial Economics*, 36, 1, 1-18.

Ottesen, Otto (1981), "A Theory of Short-Run Response to Advertising," in *Research in Marketing*, 4, Jagdish N. Sheth, ed. Greenwich, CT: JAI Press, 181-222.

Pagoulatos, Emilio and Robert Sorensen (1986), "What Determines the Elasticity of Industry Demand?" *International Journal of Industrial Organization*, 4, 237-50.

Palda, Kristian S. (1964), *The Measurement of Cumulative Advertising Effects*. Englewood Cliffs, NJ: Prentice-Hall.

——— (1969), *Economic Analysis for Marketing Decisions*. Englewood Cliffs, NJ: Prentice-Hall.

——— and Larry M. Blair (1970), "A Moving Cross-Section Analysis of the Demand for Toothpaste," *Journal of Marketing Research*, 7 (November), 439-49.

Papadopoloulos, Socrates (1987), "Strategic Marketing Techniques in International Tourism," *International Marketing Review* (Summer), 71-84.

Papatla, Purushhottam and Lakshman Krishnamurthi (1996), "Measuring the Dynamic Effects of Promotions on Brand Choice," *Journal of Marketing Research*, 33:1, 20-35.

Park, Sehoon and Minhi Hahn (1991), "Pulsing in a Discrete Model of Advertising Competition," *Journal of Marketing Research*, 28:4 (November), 397-405.

Parker, Philip M. (1992), "Price Elasticity Dynamics Over the Adoption Life Cycle," *Journal of Marketing Research*, 29:2 (August), 358-67.

——— (1994), "Aggregate Diffusion Forecasting Models in Marketing: A Critical Review," *International Journal of Forecasting*, 10:2 (September), 353-80.

——— and Ramya Neelamegham (1997), "Price Elasticity Dynamics over the Product Life Cycle," *Marketing Letters*, 8:2 (April), 205-16.

——— and Lars-Hendrik Roller (1997), "Collusive Conduct in Duopolies: Multimarket Contact and Cross-Ownership in the Mobile Telephone Industry," *Rand Journal of Economics*, 28:2 (Summer), 304-22.

Parker, Thomas H. and Ira J. Dolich (1986), "Toward Understanding Retail Bank Strategy: Seemingly Unrelated Regression Applied to Cross-Sectional Data," *Journal of Retailing*, 62 (Fall), 298-321.

Parsons, Leonard J. (1968), "Predictive Testing: A Simultaneous Equations Model of Sales and Advertising," Unpublished Ph.D. Dissertation, Purdue University, 1968.

——— (1974), "An Econometric Analysis of Advertising, Retail Availability, and Sales of a New Brand," *Management Science*, 20 (February), 938-47.

——— (1975a), "Econometric Approaches to Integrating Marketing Information from Diverse Sources," in *Proceedings*. Chicago: American Marketing Association, 49-53.

—— (1975b), "The Product Life Cycle and Time-Varying Advertising Elasticities," *Journal of Marketing Research*, 12 (November), 476-80.

—— (1976), "A Rachet Model of Advertising Carryover Effects," *Journal of Marketing Research*, 13 (February), 76-79.

—— (1981), "Models of Market Mechanisms," in *Marketing Decision Models*, Randall L. Schultz and Andris A. Zoltners, eds. New York: North-Holland, 77-98.

—— and Frank M. Bass (1971), "Optimal Advertising Expenditure Implications of a Simultaneous-Equation Regression Analysis," *Operations Research*, 19 (May-June), 822-31.

——, Els Gijsbrechts, Peter S. H. Leeflang, and Dick R. Wittink (1994) "Marketing Science, Econometrics, and Managerial Contributions" in *Research Traditions in Marketing*, Gilles Laurent, Gary L. Lilien, and Bernard Pras, eds. Boston: Kluwer Academic Publishers, 52-78.

—— and Randall L. Schultz (1976), *Marketing Models and Econometric Research*. New York: North-Holland.

—— and —— (1994), "Forecasting Market Response," Introduction to *Forecasting with Market Response Models*, Special Issue of the *International Journal of Forecasting*, 10 (1994), 181-89.

—— and Piet Vanden Abeele (1981), "Analysis of Sales Call Effectiveness," *Journal of Marketing Research*, 18 (February), 107-13.

Pauli, Hans and R. W. Hoecker (1952), *Better Utilization of Selling Space in Food Stores: Part I: Relation of Size of Shelf Display to Sales of Canned Fruits and Vegetables*, Marketing Research Report No. 30, Washington, DC: United States Government Printing office.

Pauwels, Koen, Dominique M. Hanssens and S. Siddarth (1999), "The Long-Term Effects of Pricing and Promotion on Category Traffic, Brand Choice and Purchase Quantity," working paper, University of California, Los Angeles, December.

Pedrick, James H. and Fred S. Zufryden (1993), Measuring Competitive Effects of Advertising," *Journal of Advertising Research*, 33:6 (November-December), 11-20.

Peles, Yoram C. (1971a), "Economies of Scale in Advertising Beer and Cigarettes," *Journal of Business*, 44 (January), 32-37.

—— (1971b), "Rates of Amortization of Advertising Expenditures," *Journal of Political Economy*, 79 (September-October), 1032-58.

—— (1979), "Econometric Measurement of the Duration of Advertising Effect on Sales," *Journal of Marketing Research*, 16 (August), 286-89.

Perron, Pierre and Timothy J. Vogelsang (1992), "Testing for a Unit Root in a Time Series with a Changing Mean: Corrections and Extensions," *Journal of Business and Economic Statistics*, 10, 467-70.

Pesaran, M.H., R.G. Pierse and K.C. Lee (1993), "Persistence, Cointegration and Aggregation: A Disaggregated Analysis of Output Fluctuations in the U.S. Economy," *Journal of Econometrics*, 56, 57-88.

Peterson, Robert A. and James W. Cagley (1973), "The Effect of Shelf Space Upon Sales of Branded Products: An Appraisal," *Journal of Marketing Research*, 10 (February), 103-4.

Phillips, P. C. B. and Pierre Perron (1988), "Testing for Unit Roots in Time Series Regressions," *Biometrica*, 75, 335-46.

Picconi, Mario J. and Charles L. Olson (1978), "Advertising Decision Rules in a Multibrand Environment: Optimal Control Theory and Evidence," *Journal of Marketing Research*, 15 (February), 82-92.

Pierce, David A. (1972), "Residual Correlations and Diagnostic Checking in Dynamic-Disturbance Time Series Models," *Journal of the American Statistical Association*, 67 (September), 636-40.

———— (1977), "Relationships—and the Lack Thereof Between Economic Time Series, with Special Reference to Money and Interest Rates," *Journal of the American Statistical Association*, 72 (March), 11-22.

———— and Larry D. Haugh (1977), "Causality in Temporal Systems," *Journal of Econometrics*, 5, 265-93.

Piggott, Nicholas E., James A. Chatfant, Julian M. Alston, and Garry R. Griffith (1996), "Demand Response to Advertising in the Australian Meat Industry," *American Journal of Agricultural Economics*, 78:3 (May), 268-79.

Piggott, Roley R., Nicholas E. Piggott, and Vic E. Wright (1995), "Approximating Farm-Level Returns to Incremenetal Advertising Expenditure: Methods and Application to Australian Meat Industry," *American Journal of Agricultural Economics*, 77 (August), 497-511.

Pilz, Jurgen (1991), *Bayesian Estimation and Experimental Design in Linear Regression Models*, 2nd Edition. New York: John Wiley.

Pindyck, Robert S. and Daniell L. Rubinfeld (1998), *Econometric Models and Economic Forecasts*, 4th Edition. New York: McGraw-Hill.

Plat, F. W. and Peter S. H. Leeflang (1986a), "Competitive Analysis in Segmented Markets," Research Memorandum, Institute of Economic Research, Faculty of Economics, University of Groningen, The Netherlands.

———— and Peter S. H. Leeflang (1986b), "Decomposing Sales Elasticities in Segmented Markets," Research Memorandum, Institute of Economic Research, Faculty of Economics, University of Groningen, The Netherlands.

Plosser, Charles I. and G. William Schwert (1977), "Estimation of Non-Invertible Moving Average Processes: The Case of Overdifferencing," *Journal of Econometrics*, 6, 199-224.

Poirier, Dale J. (1973), "Piecewise Regression Using Cubic Splines," *Journal of the American Statistical Association*, 68 (September), 515-24.

Pollak, Robert A. and Terence J. Wales (1992), *Demand System Specification and Estimation*. Oxford: Oxford University Press.

Pollard, Lisa (1998), "Measuring the Effectiveness of Magazine Advertising," *Admap*, 33:1 (January), 22-25.

Pollay, Richard W. (1979), "Lydiametrics: Applications of Econometrics to the History of Advertising," *Journal of Advertising History*, 1 (January), 3-18.

————, S, Siddath, Michael Siegel, Anne Haddix, Robert K. Merritt, Gary A. Giovino, and Michael P. Eriksen (1996), "The Last Straw? Cigarette Advertising and Realized Shares Among Youths and Adults, 1979-1993," *Journal of Marketing*, 60:2 (April), 1-16.

Popkowski-Leszczyc, Peter T.L. (1996), "Tests of Stationarity and Equilibrium," paper presented at the Marketing Science Conference, Gainesville.

———— and Ram C. Rao (1990), "An Empirical Analysis of National and Local Advertising Effect on Price Elasticity," *Marketing Letters*, 1:2, 149-60.

Powers, Keiko I. and Dominique M.Hanssens (1997), "Long-Term Time-Series Analysis for Psychological Research," working paper, Anderson School at UCLA, May.

————, ————, Yih-Ing Hser, and M. Douglas Anglin (1991), "Measuring the Long-Term Effects of Public Policy: The Case of Narcotics Use and Property Crime," *Management Science*, 37:6, (June), 627-44.

————, ————, ————, and ———— (1993), "Policy Analysis with a Long-Term Time Series Model: Controlling Narcotics Use and Property Crime," *Mathematical and Computer Modeling*, 17:2, 89-107.

Prasad, V. Kanti and L. Winston Ring (1976), "Measuring Sales Effects of Some Marketing Mix Variables and Their Interactions," *Journal of Marketing Research*, 13 (November), 391-96.

Pratt, John W. and Robert Schlaifer (1988), "On the Interpretation and Observation of Laws," *Journal of Econometrics,* 39 (September-October), 23-54.

Progressive Grocer (1963-1964), "The Colonial Study," 42 (September), 43 (March).

Radfar, Mehran (1985), "The Effect of Advertising on Total Consumption of Cigarettes in the U.K.," *European Economic Review,* 29 (November), 225-31.

Raju, Jagmohan S. (1992), "The Effect of Price Promotions on Variability in Product Category Sales," *Marketing Science,* 11:3 (Summer), 207-220.

———, Raj Sethuraman and Sanjay K. Dhar (1995), "The Introduction and Performance of Store Brands," *Management Science,* 41:6 (June), 957-78.

Ramsey, James B. (1969), "Tests for Specification Errors in Classical Least-Squares Regression Analysis," *Journal of the Royal Statistical Society, Series B.* 21, 350-71.

——— (1972), "Limiting Functional Forms for Market Demand Curves," *Econometrica,* 40 (March), 327-41.

——— (1974), "Classical Model Selection Through Specification Error Tests," in *Frontiers in Econometrics,* Paul Zarembka, ed. New York: Academic Press, 13-48.

Rangan, V. Kasturi (1987), "The Channel Design Decision: A Model and an Application," *Marketing Science,* 6 (Spring), 156-74.

Rangaswamy, Arvind and Lakshman Krisnamurthi (1991), "Response Function Estimation Using the Equity Estimator," *Journal of Marketing Research,* 28 (February), 72-83.

——— and ——— (1995), "Equity Estimation and Assessing Market Response: A Rejoinder," *Journal of Marketing Research,* 32:4 (November), 480-5.

———, Prabhakant Sinha, and Andris Zoltners (1990), An Integrated Model-Based Approach for Sales Force Structuring, *Marketing Science,* 9:4 (Fall), 279-98.

Rao, Ambar G. (1970), *Quantitative Theories in Advertising.* New York: John Wiley.

——— and Peter B. Miller (1975), "Advertising/Sales Response Functions," *Journal of Advertising Research,* 15 (April), 7-15.

Rao, Ram C. (1984), "Advertising Decisions in Oligopoly: An Industry Equilibrium Analysis," *Optimal Control Applications & Methods,* 5 (October-December), 331-44.

——— (1986), "Estimating Continuous Time Advertising-Sales Models," *Marketing Science,* 5 (Spring), 125-42.

——— and Frank M. Bass (1985), "Competition, Strategy, and Price Dynamics: Theoretical and Empirical Investigation," *Journal of Marketing Research,* 22 (August), 283-96.

——— and Ronald E. Turner (1984), "Organization and Effectiveness of the Multiproduct Salesforce," *Journal of Personal Selling and Sales Management,* (May), 24-30.

Rao, Vithala R. (1972), "Alternative Econometric Models of Sales-Advertising Relationships," *Journal of Marketing Research,* 9 (May), 177-81.

———, Jerry Wind, and Wayne S. DeSarbo (1988), "A Customized Market Response Model: Development, Estimation, and Empirical Testing," *Journal of the Academy of Marketing Science,* 16 (Spring), 128-40.

Rasmussen, A. (1952), "The Determination of Advertising Expenditure," *Journal of Marketing,* 16 (April), 439-46.

Reekie, W. Ducan (1994), "Consumers' Surplus and the Demand for Cigarettes," *Managerial and Decision Economics,* 15:3 (May-June), 223-34.

Reibstein, David J. and Paul W. Farris (1995), "Market Share and Distribution: A Generalization, a Speculation, and Some Implications," *Marketing Science,* 14:3 (Part 2 of 2), G190-202.

——— and Hubert Gatignon (1984), "Optimal Product Line Pricing: The Influence of Cross-Elasticities," *Journal of Marketing Research,* 21 (August), 259-67.

Reuijl, Jan C. (1982), *On the Determination of Advertising Effectiveness.* Boston: Kluwer Academic Publishers.

Riddington, G. L. (1993), "Time Varying Coefficient Models and Their Forecasting Performance," *OMEGA*, 21:5 (September), 573-83.

Riskey, Dwight W. (1997), "How Advertising Works: An Industry Response," *Journal of Marketing Research*, 34:2 (May), 292-93.

Roberts, David L. and Stephen Nord (1988), "Causality Tests and Functional Form Sensitivity," *Applied Economics*, 17, 135-41.

Robinson, Bruce and Chet Lakhani (1975), "Dynamic Price Models for New-Product Planning," *Management Science*, 21 (June), 1113-22.

Rosenberg, Barr (1973), "The Analysis of a Cross-Section of Time Series by Stochastically Convergent Regression," *Annals of Economic and Social Measurement*, 2 (October), 399-428.

Rosett, Richard N. (1959), "A Statistical Model of Friction in Economics," *Econometrica*, 27 (April), 263-67.

———— and Forrest D. Nelson (1975), "Estimation of the Two-Limit Regression Model," *Econometrica*, 43 (January), 141-46.

Roy, Abhik, Dominique M. Hanssens and Jagmohan S. Raju (1994), "Competitive Pricing by a Price Leader," *Management Science*, 40:7 (July), 809-23.

Russell, Gary J. (1988), "Recovering Measures of Advertising Carryover from Aggregate Data: The Role of the Firm's Decision Behavior," *Marketing Science*, 7 (Summer), 252-70.

———— (1992), "A Model of Latent Symmetry in Cross Elasticities," *Marketing Letters*, 3:2 (April), 157-69.

———— and Ruth N. Bolton (1988), "Implications of Market Structure for Elasticity Structure," *Journal of Marketing Research*, 25 (August), 229-41.

————, Randoph E. Bucklin, and V. Srinivasan (1993), "Identifying Multiple Preference Segments from Own- and Cross-Price Elasticities," *Marketing Letters*, 4 (January), 5-18.

————, Michael R. Hagerty, and James M. Carman (1991), "Bayesian Estimation of Marketing Mix Elasticities Using PIMS Priors," working paper, March.

———— and Wagner A. Kamakura (1994), "Understanding Brand Competition Using Micro and Macro Scanner Data," *Journal of Marketing Research*, 31:2 (May), 289-303.

Rust, Roland T. (1988), "Flexible Regression," *Journal of Marketing Research*, 25:1 (February), 10-24.

————, Donald R. Lehmann, and John U. Farley, (1990), "Estimating Publication Bias in Meta-Analysis," *Journal of Marketing Research*, 27:2 (May), 220-26.

———— and David C. Schmittlein (1985), "A Bayesian Cross-Validated Likelihood Method for Comparing Alternative Specifications of Quantitative Models," *Marketing Science*, 4 (Winter), 20-40.

Ruud, Paul A. (1984), "Tests of Specification in Econometrics," *Econometric Reviews*, 3 (2), 211-42.

Ryans, Adrian B. and Charles B. Weinberg (1979), "Territory Sales Response," *Journal of Marketing Research*, 16 (November), 453-65.

Rycroft, Robert S. (1993), "Microcomputer Software of Interest to Forecasters in Comparative Review: An Update," *International Journal of Forecasting*, 9 (December), 531-75.

Saghafi, Massoud M. (1988), "Optimal Pricing to Maximize Profits and Achieve Market-Share Targets for Single-Product and Multiproduct Companies," in *Issues in Pricing*, Timothy M. Devinney, ed. Lexington, MA: Lexington Books, 239-53.

Samuels, J. M. (1970/1971), "The Effect of Advertising on Sales and Brand Shares," *European Journal of Marketing*, 4 (Winter), 187-207.

Sanders, N. and K. Manrodt (1994), "Forecasting Practices in US Corporations: Survey Results, *Interfaces*, 24, 92-100.

————— and L. Ritzman (1992), "The Need for Contextual and Technical Knowledge in Judgmental Forecasting," *Journal of Behavioral Decision Making*, 5 (January-March), 39-52.

Sasieni, Maurice W. (1971), "Optimal Advertising Expenditure," *Management Science*, 18 (December), 64-72.

————— (1980), "Testing the Validity of Econometric Analyses of Markets," *Admap*, (May), 212-14.

————— (1982), "The Effects of Combining Observation Periods in Time Series," *Journal of the Operational Research Society*, 33, 647-53.

————— (1989), "Optimal Advertising Strategies," *Marketing Science*, 8:4 (Fall), 358-70.

Saunders, John (1987), "The Specification of Aggregate Market Models," *European Journal of Marketing*, 21:2, 5-47.

Savage, Leonard J. (1954), *The Foundations of Statistics*. New York: John Wiley.

Sawyer, Alan and Scott Ward (1979), "Carryover Effects in Advertising Communication," in Jagdish N. Sheth, ed., *Research in Marketing*, 2, JAI Press, 259-314.

Schmalensee, Richard (1972), *The Economics of Advertising*. New York: North-Holland.

————— (1976), "A Model of Promotional Competition in Oligopoly," *Review of Economic Studies*, 43 (October), 493-507.

————— (1978), "A Model of Advertising and Product Quality," *Journal of Political Economy*, 86 (June), 485-503.

Schmidt, Frank (1994), "Statistical Significance Testing and Cumulative Knowledge in Psychology: Implications for the Training of Researchers," *Psychological Methods*, 1, 115-29.

Schmidt, Peter (1973), "Calculating the Power of the Minimum Standard Error Choice Criterion," *International Economic Review*, 14 (February), 253-55.

Schultz, Don E., William A. Robinson, and Lisa A. Petrison (1998), *Sales Promotion Essentials*, 3rd Edition. Lincolnwood, IL: NTC Business Books.

Schultz, Randall L. (1971a), "Market Measurement and Planning With a Simultaneous-Equation Model," *Journal of Marketing Research*, 8 (May), 153-64.

————— (1971b), "The Measurement of Aggregate Advertising Effects," *Proceedings*. Chicago: American Marketing Association, 220-24.

————— (1984), "The Implementation of Forecasting Models," *Journal of Forecasting*, 3 (January-March), 43-55.

————— and ————— (1978), "An Empirical-Simulation Approach to Competition," *Research in Marketing*, 1, 269-301.

—————, Michael J. Ginzberg, and Henry C. Lucas, Jr. (1984), "A Structural Model of Implementation," in *Management Science Implementation*, Randall L. Schultz and Michael J. Ginzberg, eds. Greenwich, CT: JAI Press, 55-87.

————— and ————— (1975a), "Implementation and Organizational Validity: An Empirical Investigation," in *Implementing Operations Research/Management Science*, Randall L. Schultz and Dennis P. Slevin, eds. New York: American Elsevier, 153-72.

————— and ————— (1975b), *Implementing Operations Research/Management Science*. New York: American Elsevier, 1975.

————— and Wilfried R. Vanhonacker (1978), "A Study of Promotion and Price Elasticity," Institute Paper No. 657, Krannert Graduate School of Management, Purdue University, March.

————— and Dick R. Wittink (1976), "The Measurement of Industry Advertising Effects," *Journal of Marketing Research*, 13 (February), 71-75.

Schwert, G. William (1979), "Tests of Causality: The Message in the Innovations," *Journal of Monetary Economics*, 10, 55-76.

Scitovsky, Tibor (1978), "Asymmetries in Economics," *Scottish Journal of Political Economy,* 25 (November), 227-37.

Seldon, Barry J., Sudip Banerjee, and Roy G. Boyd (1993), "Advertising Conjectures and the Nature of Advertising Competition in an Oligopoly," *Managerial and Decision Economics,* 14:6 (November), 489-98.

Sethuraman, Raj (1995), "A Meta-Analysis of National Brand and Store Brand Cross-Promotional Price Elasticities," *Marketing Letters,* 6:4 (October), 275-86.

———— (1996), "A Model of How Discounting High-Priced Brands Affects Sales of Low-Priced Brands," *Journal of Marketing Research,* 33:4 (November), 399-409.

————, V. Srinivasan, and Dolye Kim (1999), "Asymmetric and Neighborhood Cross-Price Effects: Some Empirical Generalizations," *Marketing Science,* 18:1, 23-41.

———— and Gerald Tellis (1991), "An Analysis of the Tradeoff Between Advertising and Price Discounting," *Journal of Marketing Research,* 28:2 (May), 160-74.

Sexton, Donald E. (1970), "Estimating Marketing Policy Effects on Sales of a Frequently Purchased Branded Product," *Journal of Marketing Research,* 7 (August), 338-47.

———— (1972), "A Microeconomic Model of the Effects of Advertising," *Journal of Business,* 45 (January), 29-41.

Shakun, Melvin F. (1965), "Advertising Expenditures in Coupled Markets A GameTheory Approach," *Management Science,* 11 (February), B42-47.

———— (1966), "A Dynamic Model for Competitive Marketing in Coupled Markets," *Management Science, 12* (August), B525-29.

———— (1968), "Competitive Organizational Structures in Coupled Markets," *Management Science, 14* (August), B663-73.

Shane, H. D. (1977), "Mathematical Models for Economic and Political Advertising Campaigns," *Operations Research, 25,* 1-14.

————, Gregory S. Carpenter, and Lakshman Krishnamurthi (1999), "The Advantage of Entry in the Growth Stage of the Product Life Cycle: An Empirical Analysis," *Journal of Marketing Research,* 36 (May), 269-76.

Shankar, Venkatesh and Lakshman Krishnamurthi (1996), "Relating Price Sensitivity to Retailer Promotional Variables and Pricing Policy: An Empirical Analysis," *Journal of Retailing,* 72:3 (Fall), 249-72.

Shapouri, S., R.J. Folwell, and J.L. Baritelle (1981), "Statistical Estimation of Firm-Level Demand Functions: A Case Study in an Oligopolistic Industry," *Agricultural Economics Research,* 33:2 (April), 18-25.

Sharma, Subhash and William L. James (1981), "Latent Root Regression: An Alternate Procedure for Estimating Parameters in the Presence of Multicollinearity," *Journal of Marketing Research,* 18 (May), 154-61.

Shiller, P.J. and Pierre Perron (1985), "Testing the Random-walk Hypothesis: Power versus Frequency of Observation," *Economics Letters,* 18, 381-86.

Shipchandler, Zoher E. and James S. Moore (1988), "Examining the Effects of Regression Procedures on the Temporal Stability of Parameter Estimates in Marketing Models," *Journal of the Academy of Marketing Science,* 16 (Fall), 79-87.

Shoemaker, Robert W. (1986). "Comment on 'Dynamics of Price Elasticity and Brand Life Cycles: An Empirical Study,'" *Journal of Marketing Research,* 23 (February), 78-82.

———— and Lewis G. Pringle (1980), "Possible Biases in Parameter Estimation with Store Audit Data," *Journal of Marketing Research,* 16 (February), 91-96.

Shubik, Martin (1975), *The Uses and Methods of Gaming.* New York: Elsevier.

Sickles, Robin C. and Peter Schmidt (1978), "Simultaneous Equations Models with Truncated Dependent Variables: A Simultaneous Tobit Model," *Journal of Economics and Business,* 31 (Fall), 11 -21.

————, Peter Schmidt, and Ann D. White (1979), "An Application of the Simultaneous Tobit Model: A Study of the Determinants of Criminal Recidivism," *Journal of Economics and Business,* 31 (Spring), 166-71.

Silk, Alvin J. and Glen L. Urban (1978), "Pre-Test Market Evaluation of New Packaged Goods: A Model and Measurement Methodology," *Journal of Marketing Research,* 15 (May), 171-91.

Silva-Risso, Jorge M., Randolph E. Bucklin, and Donald G. Morrison (1999), "A Decision Support System for Planning Manufacturers' Sales Promotion Calendars," *Marketing Science,* 18:3, 274-300.

Simester, Ducan (1997), "Optimal Promotional Strategies: A Demand-Sided Characterization," *Management Science,* 43:2 (February), 251-56.

Simon, Hermann (1979), "Dynamics of Price Elasticity and Brand Life Cycles: An Empirical Study," *Journal of Marketing Research,* 16 (November), 439-52.

———— (1982), "ADPULS: An Advertising Model with Wearout and Pulsation," *Journal of Marketing Research,* 19 (August), 352-63.

———— (1997), "Hysteresis in Marketing—A New Phenomenon?" *Sloan Management Review,* 38:3 (Spring), 39-49.

———— and Karl-Heinz Sebastian (1987), "Diffusion and Advertising: The German Telephone Campaign," *Management Science,* 33 (April), 451-66.

Simon, Julian L. (1965), "A Simple Model for Determining Advertising Appropriations," *Journal of Marketing Research,* 2 (August), 285-92.

———— (1969a), "The Effect of Advertising on Liquor Brand Sales," *Journal of Marketing Research,* 6 (August), 301-13.

———— (1969b), "A Further Test of the Kinky Oligopoly Demand Curve," *American Economic Review,* 59 (December), 971-75.

———— (1970), *Issues in the Economics of Advertising.* Urbana, IL: University of Illinois Press.

———— and Johan Arndt (1980), "The Shape of the Advertising Function," *Journal of Advertising Research,* 20 (August), 11-28.

Sims, Christopher A. (1972), "Money, Income and Causality," *American Economic Review,* 62 (September), 540-52.

Singer, A. and Roderick J. Brodie (1990), "Forecasting Competitors' Actions: An Evaluation of Alternative Ways of Analyzing Business Competition," *International Journal of Forecasting,* 6, 75-88.

Skiera, Bernd and Sönke Albers (1998), "COSTA: Contribution Optimizing Sales Territory Alignment," *Marketing Science,* 17:3 (May), 196-213.

Slade, Margaret E. (1995), "Product Rivalry with Multiple Strategic Weapons: An Analysis of Price and Advertising Competition," *Journal of Economics & Management Strategy,* 4:3 (Fall), 445-76.

Smith, Adrian F.M. (1973), "A General Bayesian Linear Model," *Journal of the Royal Statistical Society,* Series B, 35, 67-75.

Smith, Stephen A., Shelby H. McIntyre, and Dale D. Achabal (1994), "A Two-Stage Sales Forecasting Procedure Using Discounted Least Squares," *Journal of Marketing Research,* 31:1 (February), 44-56.

Snell, Andy and Ian Tonks (1988), "The Sweet Taste of Information: A Study of the Demand for New Brands in the UK Confectionery Industry," *Applied Economics,* 20:8 (August), 1041-55.

Snetsinger, Douglas W. (1985a), "Multiproduct Firm Competition: The Role of Product and Advertising Policies," AMA Doctoral Dissertation Competition Abstract, April.

———— (1985b), "Reaction to Advertising of New Brands: A Vector ARMA Modeling Approach," working paper no. 9184, Wilfrid Laurier University.

Somers, T.M., Y.P. Gupta and S.C. Herriot (1990), "Analysis of Cooperative Advertising Expenditures: A Transfer Function Modeling Approach," *Journal of Advertising Research*, 30:5 (October/November), 35-49.

Spencer, David E. and Kenneth N. Berk (1981), "A Limited Information Specification Test," *Econometrica*, 49:4 (July), 1079-85.

Spitzer, John J. (1978), "A Monte Carlo Investigation of the Box-Cox Transformations in Small Samples," *Journal of the American Statistical Association*, 73 (September), 488-95.

Srinivasan, Shuba, Peter T. L. Popkowski Leszczyc and Frank M. Bass (1999), "Market Share Equilibrium and Competitive Interaction: The Impact of Temporary, Permanent and Structural Changes in Prices," working paper, University of California, Riverside, August.

Srinivasan, Srini S., Robert P. Leone, and Francis J. Mulhern (1995), "The Advertising Exposure Effect of Free Standing Inserts," *Journal of Advertising*, 24:1 (Spring), 32-40.

Srinivasan, V, (1976), "Decomposition of a Multiperiod Media Scheduling Model," *Management Science*, 23 (December), 349-60.

——— (1981), "An Investigation of the Equal Commission Rate Policy for a Multiproduct Salesforce," *Management Science*, 27 (July), 731-56.

——— and Charlotte Mason (1986), "Nonlinear Least Squares Estimation of New Product Diffusion Models," *Marketing Science*, 5, 169-78.

——— and Helen A. Weir (1988), "A Direct Approach to Inferring Microparameters of the Koyck Advertising-Sales Relationship from Macro Data," *Journal of Marketing Research*, 25 (May), 145-56.

Stackelberg, Heinrich von (1934), *Marktform und Gleichgewicht.* Vienna: Julius Springer.

Staelin, Richard and Russell S. Winer (1976), "An Unobservable Variables Model for Determining the Effect of Advertising on Consumer Purchases," in *1976 Educators' Proceedings*, Kenneth L. Bernhardt, ed., Chicago, American Marketing Association, 671-76.

——— and Ronald E. Turner (1973), "Error in Judgmental Sales Forecasts: Theory and Results," *Journal of Marketing Research*, 10 (February), 10-16.

Steckel, Joel H. and Wilfried R. Vanhonacker (1993), "Cross-Validation Models in Marketing Research," *Marketing Science*, 12:4 (Fall), 415-27.

Steiner, Robert L. (1987), "The Paradox of Increasing Returns to Advertising," *Journal of Advertising Research*, 27 (February-March), 45-53.

Stellwagen, Eric A. and Robert L. Goodrich (1994), *Forecast Pro for Windows* (User's Manual). Belmont, MA.

Stewart, Michael J. (1978), "The Long Term Effects of Econometrics," *ADMAP*, (February), 64-69.

——— (1990), "A Comment on 'Modelling Beyond the Blip'," *Journal of the Market Research Society*, 32:3 (July), 457-62.

Stigler, George J. (1947), "The Kinky Oligopoly Demand Curve and Price," *Journal of Political Economy*, 55, 432-49.

——— (1952), *Theory of Price.* New York: Macmillan.

——— (1961), "Economics of Information," *Journal of Political Economy*, 69 (June), 213-25.

Stock, James H. and Mark Watson (1988), "Testing for Common Trends," *Journal of American Statistical Association*, 83, 1097-1107.

Stowsand, Heino and Wilfried Wenzel (1979), "Market Mechanics: A Study to Measure the Effect of Marketing Instruments on the Market Position of Fast-Moving Consumer Goods," *Journal of Business Research*, 7, 243-57.

Sturgess, Brian and Peter Wheale (1985), "Advertising Interrelations in an Oligopolistic Market: An Analysis of Causality," *International Journal of Advertising* 4:4, 305-18.

Sunoo, Don and Lynn Y. S. Lin (1978), "Sales Effects of Promotion and Advertising" *Journal of Advertising Research*, 18 (October), 37-40.

Swait, Joffre and Jordan Louviere (1993), "The Role of the Scale Parameter in the Estimation and Comparison of Multinomial Logit Models," *Journal of Marketing Research*, 30 (August), 305-14.

Swamy, P.A.V.B. (1971), *Statistical Inference in Random Coefficient Models.* New York: Springer-Verlag.

———— and Peter von zur Muehlen (1988), "Further Thoughts on Testing for Causality with Econometric Models," *Journal of Econometrics*, 39 (September-October), 105-47.

Sweezy, Paul M. (1939), "Demand Under Conditions of Oligopoly," *Journal of Political Economy*, 47, 568-73.

Szajna, Bernadette (1994), "Software Evaluation and Choice: Predictive Validity of the Technology Assessment Instrument," *MIS Quarterly*, 18 (September),

———— (1996), "Empirical Evaluation of the Revised Technology Acceptance Model," *Management Science*, 42 (January), 85-92.

Takada, Hirokazu and Frank M. Bass (1998), "Multiple Time Series Analysis of Competitive Marketing Behavior," *Journal of Business Research*, 44.

Taylor, Lester D. (1993), "The Demand for First-Class Mail: An Econometric Analysis," *Review of Industrial Organization*, 8:5, 523-44.

Tellis, Gerard J. (1988), "The Price Sensitivity of Selective Demand: A Meta-Analysis of Econometric Models of Sales," *Journal of Marketing Research*, 25 (November), 391-404.

———— (1989), "Interpreting Advertising and Price Elasticities," *Journal of Advertising Research*, 29:4 (August/September), 40-43.

————, Rajesh K. Chandy, and Pattana Thaivanich (2000), "Which Ads Work, When, Where, and How Often? Modeling the Effects of Direct Television Advertising," *Journal of Marketing Research*, 37:1 (February), 32-46.

———— and Claus Fornell (1988), "The Relationship Between Advertising and Product Quality over the Product Life Cycle: A Contingency Theory," *Journal of Marketing Research*, 25 (February), 64-71.

———— and Doyle L. Weiss (1995), "Does TV Advertising Really Affect Sales? The Role of Measures, Models, and Data Aggregation," *Journal of Adverttising*, 24:3 (Fall), 1-12.

Telser, Lester G. (1962a), "The Demand for Branded Goods as Estimated from Consumer Panel Data," *Review of Economics and Statistics*, 44 (August), 300-324.

———— (1962b), "Advertising and Cigarettes," *Journal of Political Economy*, 70 (October), 471-99.

Terui, Nobuhiko (2000), "Forecasting Dynamic Market Share Relationships," *Marketing Intelligence & Planning*, 18:2, 67-77.

Theil, Henri (1965), "The Information Approach to Demand Analysis," *Econometrica*, 33 (January), 67-87.

———— (1971), *Principles of Econometrics.* New York: John Wiley.

Thompson, Stanley R., (1974), "Sales Response to Generic Promotion Efforts and Some Implications of Milk Advertising and Economic Surplus," *Journal of the Northeastern Agricultural Economics Council*, 3:2, 78-90.

———— and Doyle A. Eiler (1977), "Determinants of Milk Advertising Effectiveness," *American Journal of Agricultural Economics*, 59 (May), 330-35.

Tiao, George C. and George E. P. Box (1981), "Modeling Multiple Time Series with Applications," *Journal of the American Statistical Association*, 76 (December), 802- 16.

———— and Ruey S. Tsay (1983), "Multiple Time Series Modeling and Extended Sample Cross-Correlations," *Journal of Business and Economic Statistics*, 1 (January), 43-56.

Tobin, James (1958), "Estimation of Relationships for Limited Dependent Variables," *Econometrica*, 26 (January), 24-36.

Todd, Peter and Izak Benbasat (1992), "The Use of Information in Decision Making: An Experimental Investigation of the Impact of Computer-Based Decision Aids," *MIS Quarterly,* 16 (September), 373-93.

Tonks, Ian (1986), "The Demand for Information and the Diffusion of a New Product, *International Journal of Industrial Organization,* 4:4, 397-408.

Totten, John C. (1993), "Baseline Methods Comparison," memorandum.

———— (1995), "Baseline Estimation Fundamentals," Chicago Area Marketing Modeler's Group, March 2.

———— (1997), Letter to Ross Link, November 16.

———— (1999), "Aggregation—The Problem of Price," E-mail to AMODLMKT list, August 22.

———— (2000), "RE: Advertising Effects," E-mail to AMODLMKT list, February 4.

———— and Martin P. Block (1994), *Analyzing Sales Promotion,* 2nd Edition. Chicago: Dartnell.

Tsay, Ruey S. (1985), "Model Identification in Dynamic Regression (Distributed Lag) Models," *Journal of Business and Economic Statistics,* 3 (July), 228-37.

———— and George C. Tiao (1984), "Consistent Estimates of Autoregressive Parameters and Extended Sample Autocorrelation Functions for Stationary and Nonstationary ARMA Models," *Journal of the American Statistical Association,* 79 (March), 84-96.

Tsurumi, Hiroki (1973), "A Comparison of Alternative Optimal Models of Advertising Expenditures: Stock Adjustment Versus Control Theoretic Approaches," *Review of Economics and Statistics,* 55 (May), 156-68.

———— and Yoshi Tsurumi (1971), "Simultaneous Determination of Market Share and Advertising Expenditure under Dynamic Conditions: The Case of a Firm Within the Japanese Pharmaceutical Industry," *Kikan riron-keizaisaku,* 22 (December), 1-23.

Tull, Donald S. (1955), 'A Re-Examination of the Causes of the Decline in Sales of Sapolio," *Journal of Business,* 28 (April), 128-37.

————, Van R. Wood, Dale Duhan, Tom Gillpatriek, Kim R. Robertson, and James G. Helgeson (1986), "'Leveraged' Decision Making in Advertising: The Flat Maximum Principle and Its Implications," *Journal of Marketing Research,* 23 (February), 25-32.

Turner, Ronald E. (1971), "Market Measures from Salesmen: A Multidimensional Scaling Approach," *Journal of Marketing Research,* 8 (May), 165-72.

Tyagi, Rajeev K. (1999), "A Characterization of Retailer Response to Manufacturer Trade Deals," *Journal of Marketing Research,* 36:4 (November), 510-16.

Tybout, Alice M. and John R. Hauser (1981), "A Marketing Audit Using a Conceptual Model of Consumer Behavior: Application and Evaluation," *Journal of Marketing,* 45 (Summer), 82-101.

Umashankar, S. and Johannes Ledolter (1983), "Forecasting with Diagonal Multiple Time Series Models: An Extension of Univariate Models," *Journal of Marketing Research,* 20, 58-63.

Urban, Glen L. (1969), "A Mathematical Modeling Approach to Product Line Decisions," *Journal of Marketing Research,* 6 (February), 40-47.

———— (1975), "PERCEPTOR Model for Product Positioning," *Management Science,* 21 (April), 858-71.

———— and John R. Hauser (1993), *Design and Marketing of New Products* (Second Edition). Englewood Cliffs, NJ: Prentice-Hall.

———— and Richard Karash (1971), "Evolutionary Model Building," *Journal of Marketing Research,* 8:1 (February), 62-70.

Urzua, C.M., (1996), "On the Correct Use of Omnibus Tests for Normality," *Economic Letters,* 53, 247-51.

van Bruggen, Gerrit H., Ale Smidts, and Berend Wierenga (1996), "The Impact of a Marketing Decision Support System: An Experimental Study," *International Journal of Research in Marketing*, 13 (October), 331-43.

——, ——, and —— (1998), "Improving Marketing Decision Making by Means of a Marketing Decision Support System," *Management Science*, 44 (May), 645-58.

Vandaele, Walter (1983), *Applied Time Series and Box-Jenkins Models.* New York: Academic Press.

Vanden Abeele, Piet, Els Gijsbrechts, and Marc Vanhuele (1990), "Specification and Empirical Evaluation of a Cluster-Asymmetry Market Share Model," *International Journal of Research in Marketing*, 7:4, 223-47.

——, ——, and —— (1992), "Specification and Empirical Evaluation of a Cluster-Asymmetry Market Share Model: Erratum," *International Journal of Research in Marketing*, 9:2, 359.

Vandenbosch, Mark B., and Charles B. Weinberg (1993), "Salesforce Operations," in *Marketing.* Handbooks in Operations Research and Management Science. 5. J. Elaishberg and G.L. Lilien, eds. Amsterdam: North-Holland, 653-94.

van Heerde, Harald J., Peter S.H. Leeflang, and Dick R. Wittink (2000), "The Estimation of Pre- and Postpromotion Dips with Store-Level Scanner Data," *Journal of Marketing Research*, 37:3 (August), 383-95.

——, ——, and —— (2001), "Semiparametric Analysis to Estimate the Deal Effect Curve," *Journal of Marketing Research*, forthcoming.

Vanhonacker, Wilfried R. (1983), "Carryover Effects and Temporal Aggregation in a Partial Adjustment Framework," *Marketing Science*, 2 (Summer), 297-317.

—— (1984), "Estimation and Testing of a Dynamic Sales Response Model with Data Aggregated over Time: Some Results for the Autoregressive Current Effects Model," *Journal of Marketing Research*, 21 (November), 445-55.

—— (1987), "Estimating the Duration of Dynamic Effects with Temporally Aggregated Observations,' *Journal of Statistical Computation and Simulation*, 27 (April), 185-209.

—— (1988), "Estimating an Autoregressive Current Effects Model of Sales Response When Observations Are Aggregated over Time: Least Squares Versus Maximum Likelihood," *Journal of Marketing Research*, 25 (August), 301-7.

—— (1989a), "Estimating Dynamic Response Models When Data Are Subject to Different Temporal Aggregation," *Marketing Letters*, 1:2 (June), 125-37.

—— (1989b), "Modeling the Effect of Advertising on Price Response: An Econometric Framework and Some Preliminary Findings," *Journal of Business Research*, 19, 127-49.

—— and Diana Day (1987), "Cross-Sectional Estimation in Marketing: Direct Versus Reverse Regression," *Marketing Science*, 6 (Summer), 254-67.

——, Donald R. Lehmann, and Fareena Sultan (1990), "Combining Related and Sparse Data in Linear Regression Models," *Journal of Business & Economic Statistics*, 8:3, 327-35.

—— and Lydia J. Price (1992), "Using Meta-Analysis in Bayesian Updating: The Empty Cell Problem," *Journal of Business & Economic Statistics*, 10:4 (October), 427-35.

van Wezel, Michiel C. and Walter R. J. Baets (1995), "Predicting Market Responses with a Neural Network: The Case of Fast Moving Consumer Goods," *Marketing Intelligence & Planning*, 13:7 , 23-30.

Van Wormer, Theodore A. and Doyle L. Weiss, (1970), "Fitting Parameters to Complex Models by Direct Search," *Journal of Marketing Research*, 7 (November), 503-12.

Verbeke, W., F. Clement, and P. W. Farris (1994), "Product Availability and Market Share in an Oligopolistic Market: The Dutch Detergent Market," *The International Review of Retail, Distribution and Consumer Research*, 4:3, 277-96.

Verma, Vinod K. (1980), "A Price Theoretic Approach to the Specification and Estimation of the Sales-Advertising Function," *Journal of Business,* 53 (July), S115-37.

Vidale, M. L. and H. B. Wolfe (1957), "An Operations Reseach Study of Sales Response to Advertising," *Operational Research Quarterly,* 5 (June), 370-81.

Vilcassim, Naufel J. and Dipak C. Jain (1991), "Modeling Purchase-Timing and Brand-Switching Behavior Incorporating Explanatory Variables and Unobserved Heterogeneity," *Journal of Marketing Research,* 28:1 (February), 29-41.

―――, Vrinda, Kadiyali, and Pradeep K. Chintagunta (1999), "Investigating Dynamic Multifirm Market Interactions in Price and Advertising," *Management Science,* 45:4 (April), 499-518.

von Gonten, Michael F. (1998), "Tracing Advertising Effects: Footprints in the Figures," *Admap,* 33:9 (October), 43-45.

――― and James F. Donius (1997), "Advertising Exposure and Advertising Effects: New Panel-Based Findings," *Journal of Advertising Research,* 37:4 (July-August), 51-60.

Vuong, Quang H. (1989), "Likelihood Ratio Tests for Model Selection and NonNested Hypotheses," *Econometrica,* 57:2, 307-33.

Waid, Clark, Donald F. Clark, and Russell L. Ackoff (1956), "Allocation of Sales Effort in the Lamp Division of General Electric Company," *Operations Research,* 4 (December), 629-47.

Wallace, T.D. (1972) "Weaker Criteria and Tests for Linear Restrictions in Regression," *Econometrica,* 40 (July), 689-98.

Walters, Rockney G. (1989), "An Empirical Investigation into Retailer Response to Manufacturer Trade Promotions," *Journal of Retailing,* 65:2 (Summer), 253-72.

――― (1991), "Assessing the Impact of Retail Price Promotions on Product Substitution, Complementary Purchase, and Interstore Sales Displacement," *Journal of Marketing,* 55:2 (April), 17-28.

――― and William Bommer (1996), "Measuring the Impact of Product and Promotion-Related Factors on Product Category Price Elasticities," *Journal of Business Research,* 36:3 (July), 203-216.

――― and Scott B. MacKenzie (1988), "A Structural Equations Analysis of the Impact of Price Promotions on Store Performance," *Journal of Marketing Research,* 25:1 (February), 51-63.

――― and Heikki J Rinne (1986), "An Empirical Investigation into the Impact of Price Promotions on Retail Store Performance," *Journal of Retailing,* 62:3 (Fall), 237-66.

Ward, Ronald W. (1975), "Revisiting the Dorfman-Steiner Static Advertising Theorem: An Application to the Processed Grapefruit Industry," *American Journal of Agricultural Economics,* (August), 500-504.

――― and James Davis (1978a), "Coupon Redemption," *Journal of Advertising Research,* 18 (August), 51-58.

――― and ――― (1978b), "A Pooled Cross Sectional Time Series Model of Coupon Promotions," *American Journal of Agricultural Economics,* (November), 393-401.

――― and Bruce L. Dixon (1989), "Effectiveness of Fluid Milk Advertising Since the Dairy and Tobacco Adjustment Act of 1983," *American Journal of Agricultural Economics,* 71:3 (August), 730-39.

――― and Richard L. Kilmer (1989), *The Citrus Industry.* Ames, IA: Iowa State University Press.

――― and C. Lambert (1993), "Generic Promotion of Beef: Measuring the Impact of the U.S. Beef Checkoff," *Journal of Agricultural Economics,* 44 (September), 456-65.

――― and Lester H. Myers (1979), "Advertising Effectiveness and Coefficient Variation Over Time," *Agricultural Economics Research,* 31:1 (January), 1-11.

Wartenberg, F. and R. Decker (1995), "Analysis of Sales Data: A Neural Net Approach," in *From Knowledge to Data*, Wolfgag Gaul and Dietmar Pfeifer, eds. Berlin: Springer-Verlag, 326-33.

Webster, Frederick E., Jr. (1992), "The Changing Role of Marketing in the Corporation," *Journal of Marketing*, 56 (October), 1-17.

Weinberg, Charles B. and Doyle L. Weiss (1982), "On the Econometric Measurement of the Saturation of Advertising Effects on Sales," *Journal of Marketing Research*, 9 (November), 585-91.

—— and —— (1986), "A Simpler Estimation Procedure for a Micromodeling Approach to the Advertising-Sales Relationship," *Marketing Science*, 5 (Summer), 269-72.

Weiss, Doyle L. (1968), "The Determinants of Market Share," *Journal of Marketing Research*, 5 (August), 290-95.

—— (1969), "An Analysis of the Demand Structure for Branded Consumer Products," *Applied Economics*, 1 (January), 37-44.

——, Franklin S. Houston, and Pierre Windal (1978), "The Periodic Pain of Lydia E. Pinkham," *Journal of Business*, 51, 91-101.

——, Charles B. Weinberg, and Pierre M. Windal (1983), "The Effects of Serial Correlation and Data Aggregation on Advertising Measurement," *Journal of Marketing Research* 20, (August), 268-79.

—— and Pierre M. Windal (1980), "Testing Cumulative Advertising Effects: A Comment on Methodology," *Journal of Marketing Research*, 17 (August), 371-78.

Welch, Joe L. and Tom K. Massey, Jr. (1988), "Consumer Cost Implications of Reducing Item Omission Errors in Retail Optical Scanner Environments," *Akron Business and Economic Review*, 19 (Summer), 97-105.

Wernham, Roy (1984), "Bridging the Awful Gap Between Strategy and Action," *Long Range Planning*, 17 (December), 34-42.

—— (1985), "Obstacles to Strategy Implementation in a Nationalized Industry," *Journal of Management Studies*, 22 (November), 632-648.

Wichern, Dean W. and Richard H. Jones (1977), "Assessing the Impact of Market Disturbances Using Intervention Analysis," *Management Science*, 23 (November), 329-37.

Wierenga, Berend (1981), "Modeling the Impact of Advertising and Optimising Advertising Policy," *European Journal of Operational Research*, 8, 235-48.

—— and Jack Kluytmans (1994), "Neural Nets versus Marketing Models in Time Series Analysis: A Simulation Study," in *Proceedings of the 23rd Annual Conference of the European Marketing Academy*, J. Bloemer, Jos Lemmink, and H. Kasper, eds. Maastricht, 1139-53.

—— and Jack Kluytmans (1996), "Predicting Neural Nets in Marketing with Time Series Data," Management Series Report No. 258, Rotterdam School of Management, Eramus University,.March.

—— and Peter A. M. Oude Ophuis (1997), "Marketing Decision Support Systems: Adoption, Use, and Satisfaction, *International Journal of Research in Marketing*, 14 (July), 275-90.

—— and Gerrit H. van Bruggen (1997) "The Integration of Marketing Problem-Solving Modes and Marketing Management Support Systems," *Journal of Marketing*, 51 (July), 21-37.

Wildt, Albert R. (1974), "Multifirm Analysis of Competitive Decision Variables," *Journal of Marketing Research*, 11 (November), 50-62.

—— (1976), "The Empirical Investigation of Time-Dependent Parameter Variation in Marketing Models," *Proceedings*. Chicago: American Marketing Association.

—— (1977), "Estimating Models of Seasonal Market Response Using Dummy Variables," *Journal of Marketing Research*, 14 (February), 34-41.

—————— (1993), "Equity Estimation and Assessing Market Response," *Journal of Marketing Research*, 30:4 (November), 437-51.

——————, James D. Parker, and Clyde E. Harris (1987), "Assessing the Impact of Sales- Force Contests: An Application," *Journal of Business Research*, 15 (April), 145-55.

—————— and Russell S. Winer (1983), "Modeling and Estimation in Changing Market Environments," *Journal of Business*, 56 (July), 365-88.

Wilson, Nick and Graham J. Hooley (1988), "Advertising Effects: More Methodological Issues: A Reply," *Journal of the Market Research Society*, 30 (April), 231-34.

Windal, Pierre M. and Doyle L. Weiss (1980), "An Iterative GLS Procedure for Estimating the Parameters of Models with Autocorrelated Errors Using Data Aggregated over time," *Journal of Business*, 53 (October), 415-24.

Winer, Russell S. (1979), "An Analysis of the Time Varying Effects of Advertising: The Case of Lydia Pinkham," *Journal of Business*, 52 (October), 563-76.

—————— (1983), "Attrition Bias in Econometric Models Estimated by Panel Data," *Journal of Marketing Research*, 20 (May), 177-86.

—————— (1985), "A Price Vector Model of Demand for Consumer Durables: Preliminary Developments," *Marketing Science*, 4 (Winter), 74-90.

—————— (1986), "A Reference Price Model of Brand Choice for Frequently Purchased Products," *Journal of Consumer Research*, 13 (September), 250-56.

—————— (1993), "Using Single-Source Scanner Data as a Natural Experiment for Evaluating Advertising Effects, *Journal of Marketing Science*, 2:12, 15-31.

—————— and William L. Moore (1989), "Evaluating the Effects of Marketing Mix Variables on Brand Positioning," *Journal of Advertising Research*, 29:1 (February-March), 39-45.

Winkelhofer, Heidi, Adamantios Diamantopoulos, and Stephen F. Witt (1996), "Forecasting Practice: A Review of the Empirical Literature and an Agenda for Future Research," *International Journal of Forecasting*, 12 (June), 193-221.

Winkler, Robert L. (1989), "Combining Forecasts: A Philosophical Basis and Some Current Issues," *International Journal of Forecasting*, 5 (4), 605-09.

Wittink, Dick R. (1973), "Partial Pooling: A Heuristic," Institute Paper No. 419, Krannert Graduate School of Industrial Administration, Purdue University, July.

—————— (1977a), "Advertising Increases Sensitivity to Price," *Journal of Advertising Research*, 17 (April), 39-42.

—————— (1977b), "Exploring Territorial Differences in the Relationship Between Marketing Variables," *Journal of Marketing Research*, 14 (May), 145-55.

—————— (1983a), "Standardized Regression Coefficients: Use and Misuse," Graduate School of Management, Cornell University, September.

—————— (1983b), "Autocorrelation and Related Issues in Applications of Regression Analysis," Graduate School of Management, Cornell University, October.

—————— (1987), "Causal Market Share Models in Marketing: Neither Forecasting nor Understanding?" *International Journal of Forecasting*, 3:3/4, 445-48.

—————— (1988), *The Application of Regression Analysis*. Boston, MA: Allyn and Bacon.

——————, Michael Addona, William Hawkes, and John Porter, (1988), "SCAN*PRO: The Estimation, Validation, and Use of Promotional Effects Based on Scanner Data," working paper, Johnson Graduate School of Management, Cornell University, February.

—————— and John C. Porter (1991), "Pooled Store-Level Data versus Market Aggregates: A Comparison of Econometric Models," working paper, Johnson Graduate School of Management, Cornell University.

——————, ——————, and Sachin Gupta (1994), "Biases in Parameter Estimates from Linearly Aggregated Data When the Disaggregate Model is Nonlinear," working paper, Johnson Graduate School of Management, Cornell University, December.

Wolfe, Michael (1996), "RE: Modeling Seasonality," E-mail to AMODLMKT list, February 14.

Wolffram, Rudolf (1971), "Positivistic Measures of Aggregate Supply Elasticities: Some New Approaches Some Critical Notes," *American Journal of Agricultural Economics*, 53, 356-59.

Woodside, Arch G and Gerald L. Waddle (1975), "Sales Effects of In-Store Advertising," *Journal of Advertising Research*, 15:3 (June), 29-33.

Wright, George, Michael J. Lawrence, and Fred Collopy (1996), "The Role and Validity of Judgment in Forecasting," *International Journal of Forecasting*, 12 (March), 1-8.

Yi, Youjae (1988), "Assessing Main Effects in Interactive Regression Models," *Proceedings*. Chicago: American Marketing Association, 298.

Yokum, J. Thomas and Albert R. Wildt (1987), "Forecasting Sales Response for Multiple Time Horizons and Temporally Aggregated Data: A Comparison of Constant and Stochastic Coefficient Models," *International Journal of Forecasting*, 3 (314), 479-88.

Yoon, Youngohc, Tor Guimaraes and Quinton O'Neil (1995), "Exploring Factors Associated With Expert Systems Success," *MIS Quarterly*, 19 (March), 83-106.

Young, Kan H. and Lin Y. Young (1975), "Estimation of Regression Involving Logarithmic Transformation of Zero Values in the Dependent Variable," *The American Statistician*, 29 (August), 118-20.

Young, Trevor (1982), "Addiction Asymmetry and the Demand for Coffee," *Scottish Journal of Political Economy*, 29 (February), 89-98.

———— (1983), "The Demand for Cigarettes: Alternative Specifications of Fujii's Model," *Applied Economics*, 15 (April), 203- 11.

Yule, G. U. (1926), "Why Do We Sometimes Get Nonsense Correlations Between Time Series? A Study in Sampling and the Nature of Time Series," *Journal of the Royal Statistical Society*, 89, 1-64.

Zanias, G.P. (1994), "The Long Run, Causality, and Forecasting in the Advertising-Sales Relationship," *Journal of Forecasting*, 13, 601-10.

Zellner, Arnold (1971), *An Introduction to Bayesian Inference in Econometrics*. New York: John Wiley.

———— (1988a), "Bayesian Analysis in Econometrics," *Journal of Econometrics*, 39 (January), 27-50.

———— (1988b), "Causality and Causal Laws in Econometrics," *Journal of Econometrics*, 39 (September-October), 7-21.

———— and M.S. Geisel (1970), "Analysis of Distributed Lag Models with Application to Consumption Function Estimation," *Econometrica*, 38 (November), 865-88.

————, J. Kmenta, and J. Dreze (1966), "Specification and Estimation of Cobb-Douglas Production Function Models," *Econometrica*, 34 (October), 784-95.

———— and Franz Palm (1974), "Time Series Analysis and Simultaneous Equation Regression Models," *Journal of Econometrics*, 2, 17-54.

Zenor, Micheal J., Bart J. Bronnenberg, and Leigh McAlister (1998), "The Impact of Marketing Policy on Promotional Price Elasticities and Baseline Sales," *Journal of Retailing and Consumer Services*, 5:1 (January), 25-32.

Zentler, A. P. and Dorothy Ryde (1956), "An Optimal Geographic Distribution of Publicity Expenditure in a Private Organization," *Management Science*, 4 (July), 337-52.

Zidack, Walter, Henry Kinnucan, and Upton Hatch (1992), "Wholesale- and Farm-level Impacts of Generic Advertising: The Case of Catfish," *Applied Economics*, 24, 959-68.

Zielske, Hugh A. (1986), "Comments," *Marketing Science*, 5 (Spring), 109.

Zoltners, Andris A. (1981), "Normative Marketing Models," in *Marketing Decision Models*, Randall L. Schultz and Andris A. Zolthers, eds. New York: North-Holland, 55-76.

———— and Prahakant Sinha (1980), "Integer Programming Models for Sales Resource Allocation," *Management Science,* 26 (March), 242-60.

Zufryden, Fred S. and James H. Pedrick (1993), "Measuring the Reach and Frequency Elasticities of Advertising Media," *Marketing Letters*, 4:3, 215-25.

AUTHOR INDEX

COMPANY/BRAND INDEX

INDUSTRY/CATEGORY/ PRODUCT INDEX

SUBJECT INDEX